The American Political Dictionary

Fourth Edition

The American Political Dictionary

Fourth Edition

Jack C. Plano

Milton Greenberg

Holt, Rinehart and Winston
New York

To Ellen and Sonia

Copyright © 1976 by The Dryden Press
A division of Holt, Rinehart and Winston
All rights reserved including the right to reproduce
this book or portions thereof in any form.
Published simultaneously in Canada by
Holt, Rinehart and Winston of Canada, Limited
Library of Congress Catalog Card Number 75-6195
ISBN Trade: 0-03-016736-1
ISBN College: 0-03-089498-0
Fourth Edition
Designer: Stephen Rapley
Printed in the United States of America
10 9 8 7 6 5 4 3 2

Preface to the Fourth Edition

Acceptance of earlier editions of *The American Political Dictionary* has reinforced the authors' belief in the utility of this unique approach to political lexicography. The new edition maintains the format of the first three editions. Materials basic to an understanding of American political events are arranged topically within chapters and discussed in the context of their historical and institutional settings.

The years since publication of the first edition in 1962 have seen substantial changes in what are sometimes thought to be unchanging and timeless institutions. While the meaning of a term may not change, its relevance to contemporary political life may alter with changing political realities. New developments in civil rights, foreign affairs, welfare, poverty, space exploration, criminal rights, education, environment, and national-state relations demanded a revision of most of the entries which this edition incorporates. In addition, numerous new terms have been included to bring the book into focus with the contemporary political scene.

The world of politics is as close to the citizen as his daily newspaper, weekly news magazine, radio, or television set. Confronted with problems ranging from parking places to the question of survival, the American people have turned to government—national, state, and local—for solutions. As a consequence countless numbers of agencies, laws, officials, programs, and politicians surround, and often confuse, the citizen trying to play his political role. While American government has become complex and detailed, it is not beyond the understanding of the interested citizen. Indeed, for the citizen in a democratic republic, understanding is essential if he is to choose his leaders wisely and give direction to their actions.

Politics, like other fields of knowledge, has a technical language. Unlike such fields as medicine, however, the language of politics is not limited to professional journals or to the practitioner. It is broadly and freely used in public and private conversations and by mass media of communication. While this is basically a healthy situation, lack of precision in the use of political terminology serves only to obscure the issues of today. This dictionary is intended to help the citizen who seeks a deeper and more precise understanding of the historical, social, economic, and institutional forces that make up the life blood of the most exciting political system in the world.

The American Political Dictionary consists of 1200 terms, agencies, court cases, and statutes that are most relevant for a basic comprehension of American governmental institutions, practices, and problems. Each item is defined or described; a statement of its significance to American government and to the citizen follows. Terms are discussed within subject matter chapters to place them in their proper frame of reference. Hundreds of additional concepts are defined and discussed within the major entries.

This book can be used in two ways. First, it is a dictionary in which terms are listed alphabetically by subject matter; the reader can find a term by consulting a particular chapter or, when in doubt as to the usage of a term, by consulting the index. Second, the complete reading of a chapter will provide a useful, basic understanding of an entire subject area. State and local governmental issues and procedures are integrated with national governmental practice in most instances, since similar terms are used at all levels of government. A separate chapter on state and local government is included, however; it focuses on terms that have specific application to state and local governmental problems and practices. With the exception of the case of *Eakin v. Raub* in Chapter 10, all cases discussed were decided by the United States Supreme Court.

It has become commonplace to speak of the need for an informed citizenry to maintain a free society. Ignorance and lethargy about our government pose as great a danger to American democracy as do external threats. The authors hope that this book will help to meet the challenge.

Jack C. Plano
Kalamazoo, Michigan

Milton Greenberg
Chicago, Illinois

January 1976

A Note on How to Use This Book

The American Political Dictionary can be used in two ways. It is a *dictionary* in which terms are listed alphabetically by subject matter; the reader can find a term by consulting a particular chapter or, when in doubt as to the usage of a term, by consulting the index. It is also a *guide* to the contemporary political scene; a complete reading of a chapter will provide the reader with basic information in an entire subject area.

The material is divided into eighteen chapters covering major areas of American government. State and local governmental issues and procedures are integrated with national practice in most instances. For example, terms used to describe legislative, executive, or judicial functions are essentially the same at all levels of government. A separate chapter on state and local government focuses on terms that have specific application to state and local governmental problems and practices.

With few exceptions, each chapter has four sections. The first and longest in each case is an alphabetical listing of terms. Each term is defined and then followed by a paragraph on its significance to overall operations, theories, and problems of American government. A few terms are used in more than one chapter because they have more than one meaning or application. In such instances, the definition and significance are related to the subject matter of the particular chapter. When deemed useful, cross-references are provided to similar or closely related terms.

The listing of terms is followed by sections on important agencies, cases, and statutes. Each section contains an alphabetical listing of definitions or descriptions of items and a statement of their significance. Many terms found in the first part of a chapter contain mention of agencies, cases, and statutes, but detailed treatment is given only to a highly select group. United Nations agencies and other international organizations in which the United States plays a role are treated as regular items in Chapter 16.

The index contains a complete listing of all major entries as well as all significant terms discussed within these entries.

Contents

The American Political Dictionary

Fourth Edition

1 Political Ideas

Absolutism Unrestrained powers exercised by government. Absolutism is the opposite of constitutionalism, which provides for government limited by law. Although constitutionalism or limited government may serve as a means for preventing the rise of absolute power, as in the American system, once established, an absolutist regime typically defines and determines the scope of its own powers whether or not a constitution exists. *See also* AUTOCRACY, page 3; CONSTITU-TIONALISM, page 5; DIVINE RIGHT, page 8; FASCISM, page 9; TOTALITARIANISM, page 19.

Significance Prior to the American and French revolutions, absolutism took the form of absolute monarchy based on the theory of the divine right of kings. In modern times, it has taken the form of dictatorship of the right (fascism) or of the left (Stalinist communism). The American Founding Fathers feared absolutism and established a system of separation of powers, with checks and balances to safeguard against it. The historic struggle between absolutism and democratic constitutionalism continues today, both within and between nations. Although no government exercises completely unrestrained powers in all areas, the absolutist model provides a useful concept for political systems where vast powers are exercised by governments free from *legal* restraints.

Accountability The concept, underlying democratic representative government, that elected officials are responsible to the people for their actions. Accountability under law is one of the features distinguishing governments based on the concepts of constitutional democracy from those embracing the principles of absolutism. *See also* DEMOCRACY, page 6; REPRESENTATIVE GOV ERNMENT, page 16.

Significance Accountability implies that citizens in a democracy are familiar with their elected officials and the decisions they make, and have an opportunity to pass judgment on them. This in turn requires short ballots, frequent elections, and an effective opposition. In our national government, the voters can hold the President accountable for all decisions and actions undertaken in the executive branch because under the Constitution he alone is accorded authority and responsibility for them. In Congress, accountability is based on individual performance; frequent roll-call votes on important bills and extensive press, television, and radio coverage of the activities of congressmen enable voters to judge members of the House every two years and senators every six years. When bills are killed through minority blocking tactics, or when parliamentary maneuvers are used to conceal political actions or to confuse voters, accountability is reduced.

Anarchism   The doctrine that government is an unnecessary evil and should be replaced by voluntary cooperation among individuals and groups. Anarchists regard the state as an instrument used by the propertied classes to dominate and exploit the people. Anarchist thinking varies from individualism to collectivism, from pacifism to advocacy of violent revolution. All anarchists, however, hold the state's coercive system responsible for the warping of man's personality and look to the day when every form of government will be abolished *See also* NEW LEFT, page 129.

Significance   In Europe, anarchism has been represented primarily by syndicalist parties; similarly, in the United States, anarchists have worked through the organization of Industrial Workers of the World. Anarchism has never been a successful political ideology, but its advocates terrorized Europe's royal families and political leaders during the nineteenth and early twentieth centuries by the widespread use of assassination as a political weapon. Anarchists have also had considerable influence on other political theorists and movements. Marxian communism, for example, views government as an evil instrument of class exploitation and provides for a "final stage" in which government "withers away" and people in a "stateless, classless society" spontaneously cooperate with one another. The New Left movement during the 1960s produced a renaissance of anarchist belief and action in many countries.

Aristocracy   The exercise of political power by a small ruling clique of a state's "best" citizens. The selection of the aristocrats may be made on the basis of birth, wealth, or ability, or economic, social, or ecclesiastical position. *See also* ELITE, page 120.

Significance   Aristocracies are characterized by limited suffrage and great emphasis on property rights. Postrevolutionary America had characteristics of aristocracy, with property and religious qualifications for voting and holding office. The "Jeffersonian Democracy" of that era emphasized rule by an aristocracy of ability. The democratic reforms ushered in during the age of Jackson provided a leveling influence. In modern America, an "establishment" of WASPs (White Anglo-Saxon Protestants) functioned for many years as an informal aristocracy in government, business, the professions, and the military.

Authoritarianism   Concentration of political authority in one man or a small group. Authoritarian regimes emphasize obedience by the people to their rulers and the absolute power of rulers over their subjects. Individual freedoms and rights are completely subordinated to the power of the state. *See also* AUTOCRACY, page 3; FASCISM, page 9; TOTALITARIANISM, page 19.

Significance   Political history has been characterized by continuing struggles between the rival doctrines of authoritarianism and democracy. Although authoritarianism was set back by the defeat of the Axis powers in World War II, today it threatens again with the spread of communism and military take-overs in the new states of Asia and Africa. In many cases, modern authoritarian regimes operate behind a facade of democratic and constitutional institutions. Fascism is a highly nationalistic form of authoritarianism of the extreme Right that defends the established economic order; communism, conversely, is a doctrine of the extreme Left that fosters revolutionary change. Both forms can be equally ruthless in pursuit of their objectives.

Autocracy Any system of government in which political power and authority are focused in a single individual. *See also* ABSOLUTISM, page 1; AUTHORITARIANISM, page 2; FASCISM, page 9; TOTALITARIANISM, page 19.

Significance Historically, autocrats have maintained their positions of power by such means as Machiavellian intrigues, myth systems, ideological and religious support systems, and the employment of sheer naked power, unrestrained by moral or ethical concerns. Fascist and Stalinist dictatorships are modern adaptations of ancient autocratic systems. Contemporary autocrats not only use whatever levels of coercion are necessary to maintain their rule but also attempt to use the communications media to cultivate mass support.

Capitalism An economic system based on private ownership of the means of production and on a supply-demand market economy. Capitalism is often related to laissez-faire theory, which emphasizes the absence of governmental restraints on ownership, production, and trade. In theory, the natural balancing forces of the marketplace, guided by Adam Smith's "invisible hand," provided stability for the system. Since World War II, the ideas of Keynesianism have replaced laissez-faire theories, providing for a central role for government in guiding and directing the economy. *See also* CONVERGENCE THEORY, page 385; KEYNESIANISM, page 287; LAISSEZ-FAIRE, page 11.

Significance Capitalism as a working economic system developed in Europe and the United States in the late eighteenth and early nineteenth centuries, replacing the state-fostered mercantilist system. Historically, capitalism in its pure state has never been practiced for long, since each major economic group has soon looked to the government of its country to improve its own economic position, and since each government in time has assumed a substantial promotional and regulatory role. Today, all capitalist states have mixed economies in which private ownership and market economies are matched with extensive governmental intervention. Free trade, a hallmark of capitalism, has been replaced by national and regional international trade restrictions, and the concepts of economic freedom that characterize capitalism are being challenged by socialism and communism.

Centrist An individual or political group advocating a moderate or temperate approach to political decision making and to the solution of social problems. Centrists tend generally to uphold the status quo against demands by leftists or rightists for radical change. *See also* LEFTIST, page 11; RIGHTIST, page 17.

Significance In the American political system both major parties and most voters tend to view politics from a centrist perspective. Centrists are sometimes referred to as the "vital majority" that provides substantial support for "the establishment." European center parties, however, have been typically weak in voter appeal because of the tendency toward political polarization and the cultivation of programmatic parties offering change to the voters.

Collectivism A generic term that describes various theories and social movements calling for the ownership and control of all land and means of production by the state or groups rather than by individuals. The term is often used synonymously with the more specific doctrines of socialism and communism, for collectivism rejects the economic freedoms and individual rights of capitalism. *See also* COMMUNISM, page 4; SOCIALISM, page 18.

Significance The major ideological conflicts of modern times have involved clashes between supporters of collectivist doctrines and defenders of the concepts of individualism. The former have emphasized the advantages of cooperation and group effort, the latter the advantages of competition and individual enterprise. Many Communist countries are increasingly substituting profit motivations for collectivistic planning and control in their economies.

Communism
A political, economic, and social theory based on a collectivistic society in which all land and capital are socially owned and political power is exercised by the masses. Modern communism is based on the theories and practices of Karl Marx, V. I. Lenin, Josef Stalin, Nikita Khruschchev, and contemporary Soviet leaders, with variations provided by Mao Tse-tung and the Chinese Communists. Communism in theory espouses the doctrines of historical inevitability, economic determinism, labor value, the "inner contradictions" of capitalism, class conflict, capitalist colonialism and imperialism, world wars resulting from competition for markets, the destruction of the bourgeoisie, the dictatorship of the proletariat, the socialist revolution, and the final "withering away" of the state. Plato and other political theorists have also advocated communism in the form of communal living and various church and social groups have practiced it. *See also* CONVERGENCE THEORY, page 385; ECONOMIC DETERMINISM, page 8.

Significance Since World War II, communism as an ideology has been used by the Communist states, especially the Soviet Union, in a worldwide offensive against capitalism and democracy. Communism in theory is largely destructive, basing its main attack on the evils and weaknesses of nineteenth-century capitalism. In practice, communism has been highly pragmatic: Soviet leaders often supplement their Socialist approaches with capitalistic practices to provide incentives and to secure some degree of political stability and economic viability. During the period of transition from socialism to communism, the "dictatorship of the proletariat" has proved to be a quite permanent dictatorship by one man or by a ruthless oligarchy. Communists have seldom been successful in winning mass support and political elections, but they have been successful in infiltrating and capturing control of several independence movements in Asia and Africa.

Concurrent Majority
The political doctrine, expounded by John C. Calhoun of South Carolina prior to the Civil War, that democratic decisions should be made only with the concurrence of all major segments of society. Without such concurrence, Calhoun argued, a decision should not be binding on those groups whose interests it violates. *See also* CONSENSUS, page 5; MAJORITY RULE, page 12; NULLIFICATION, page 39.

Significance The idea of concurrent majority was central to a systematic effort by Calhoun to justify the secession of southern states from the Union. He held that the decisions made by Congress concerning tariffs and slavery were inimical to the interests of the South. Each southern state, therefore, had to decide whether it would accept these decisions or reject them and withdraw from the Union. Today, some interpreters of democratic theory reject majority rule and argue that only decisions reached by consensus are truly democratic.

Consensus Agreement approaching unanimity, usually without a vote. Consensus may range from the acceptance of a society's basic values to concurrence in a specific decision by members of a group. In a democracy, "government by consensus" sometimes replaces majority rule and reduces the role of the opposition. A working bipartisan foreign policy, for example, might eliminate foreign policy issues from a subsequent election. *See also* CONCURRENT MAJORITY, page 4; MAJORITY RULE, page 12.

Significance Consensus provides the cementing force for a society. When consensual bonds are broken and revolution or civil war results, new ones must evolve if stability is to be restored. The process of building a consensus for a specific decision within a group is usually based on compromise or strong leadership. Some political investigators reject the linkage between consensus and stability, holding that a highly pluralistic society may ultimately be more stable than one in which the government forges an artificially high level of consensus.

Conservatism Defense of the status quo against major changes in the political, economic, or social institutions of a society. The classic statement of the philosophy of conservatism was expounded by the English statesman, Edmund Burke. He held that political stability could be maintained only if the forces of change could be moderated by a slow and careful integration of new elements into time-tested institutions. *See also* LIBERALISM, page 12; REACTIONARY, page 16.

Significance Both major American political parties have conservative wings that frequently unite in opposing liberal legislation. Today, in American politics the term "conservative" has no precise meaning and is often used accusatorially against a rival party or candidate. The general conservative position on issues, however, has been fairly consistently opposed to governmental regulation of the economy and civil rights legislation, and in favor of state over federal action, fiscal responsibility, decreased governmental spending, and lower taxes. Although conservatism received a setback in the 1964 defeat of Republican presidential candidate Barry Goldwater, conservative groups in the United States are well organized and remain powerful in American politics. Conservative strength in the United States is divided between the populist, radical, predominantly blue-collar wing, and the upper- and upper-middle-class liaison between the inheritors of wealth and the nouveaux riches.

Constitutionalism The political principle of limited government under a written or unwritten contract (constitution). Constitutionalism assumes that the sovereign people draw up a constitution, by the terms of which a government is created and given powers. In the American system, the Supreme Court acts as the guardian of the Constitution through its powers to void governmental actions that exceed these limitations (judicial review). The Founding Fathers also incorporated into the system various limitations that restrain the individuals who exercise power. The most significant of these include the separation of powers, checks and balances, federalism, subordination of military to civilian control, and the Bill of Rights. *See also* CONSTITUTION, page 24; CONTRACT THEORY, page 6; DEMOCRACY, page 6; MADISONIANISM, page 12.

Significance The American system of constitutional government has been fairly effective throughout most of its history in maintaining limitations upon government. In recent years, however, public sentiment has favored bigger government with more flexible approaches and expanded powers. The Industrial Revolution, depressions, wars, alien ideologies, and other domestic and foreign threats have overriden the fear of stronger government. Expanding democratic government is viewed by many as a means of achieving better protection for their personal rights, values, and welfare, rather than as a threat. The Nixon Administration sought to reverse this trend toward national centralization through decentralization of domestic programs and a revenue-sharing scheme to help state and local units finance the programs. The problem remains essentially one of maintaining an equilibrium between the needs for liberty and for order, and of enabling government to meet new and challenging responsibilites while still maintaining the restraints of constitutionalism.

Contract Theory   A class of theories that seeks to explain the origin of society and government and to set out the respective authority and responsibility of government and individuals under their contractual obligations. Contract theorists regard man as having lived in a state of nature prior to the organization of civil society. Once a "body politic" has been created through a contract or compact among the people, a government is then founded and empowered through a second contract or constitution concluded between the people and the government. The nature of the relationship established by the governmental contract varies, in these theories, from the individualism of John Locke's popular sovereignty and limited government to the authoritarianism of Thomas Hobbes's *Leviathan. See also* CONSTITUTIONALISM, page 5; DEMOCRACY, page 6; POPULAR SOVEREIGNTY, page 15.

Significance   The contract theory was developed by various political philosophers during the Middle Ages as an intellectual challenge to the existing absolutism based on the theory of the divine rights of kings. Progressively the new doctrine gained adherents and the absolute power of some monarchs was mildly curtailed, but its full flowering and broad democratic implications emerged during the Age of Enlightenment. The advocacy of the doctrine by John Locke, Jean Jacques Rousseau, and James Harrington helped to gain the support of the intellectual classes and laid the foundations for the English, American, and French revolutions. The American Declaration of Independence, described by Thomas Jefferson as "pure Locke," based its justification of revolution on the violation of contract by the English government. Although the theories of a social contract are somewhat out of vogue today, the great ideas they fostered remain part of the concept of democracy based on limited government and individual rights.

Democracy   A system of government in which ultimate political authority is vested in the people. The term is derived from the Greek words "demos" (the people) and "kratos" (authority). Democracy may be direct, as practiced in ancient Athens and in New England town meetings, or indirect and representative. In the modern pluralistic democratic state, power typically is exercised by groups or institutions in a complex system of interactions that involve compromises and bargaining in the decision process. The Democratic Creed includes the following concepts: (1) individualism, which holds that the primary task of government is to enable each individual to achieve the highest potential of development; (2) liberty, which allows each individual the greatest amount of freedom consistent with order; (3) equality, which maintains that all men are created equal and have equal rights and opportunities; and (4) fraternity, which postulates that individuals will not misuse their freedom but will cooperate in creating a wholesome society. As a political system, democracy starts with the assumption of popular sovereignty, vesting ultimate power in the people. It presupposes that man can control his destiny, that he can make moral judgments and practical decisions in his daily life. It implies a continuing search for truth in the sense of man's pursuit of improved ways of building social institutions and ordering human relations. Democracy requires a decision-making system based on majority rule, with minority rights protected. Effective guarantees of freedom of speech, press, religion, assembly, and petition, and equality before the law are indispensable to a democratic system of government. Politics, parties, and politicians are the catalytic agents that make democracy workable. *See also* ACCOUNTABILITY, page 1; CONSTITUTIONALISM, page 5; CONTRACT THEORY, page 6; DIRECT DEMOCRACY, page 8; INDIVIDUALISM, page 10; MAJORITY RULE, page 12; NATURAL LAW, page 13; POPULAR SOVEREIGNTY, page 15; REPRESENTATIVE GOVERNMENT, page 16; RULE OF LAW, page 17.

Significance Most Americans think of their political and social systems as best described by the term "democratic." Yet the term appears neither in the Declaration of Independence nor in the United States Constitution. For many centuries democracy was regarded as a dangerous but unworkable doctrine, but its ideas swept the Western world during the nineteenth and twentieth centuries as one of the forces unleashed by the American and French revolutions. In the twentieth century, democracy has clashed with new authoritarian ideologies, and the struggle continues, particularly in the new nations of Asia and Africa. Democracy is under attack not only from the ideologies of the extreme right and left, but from within as well—by those who oppose it as a mob rule that vulgarizes society and makes a virtue of incompetence and mediocrity and by those who charge that it is a sham, impossible in practice because of an "iron law of oligarchy." Supporters of democracy reject such attacks, pointing to the evidence of the superiority of democracy as practiced in the United States, Britain, and Scandinavia. Yet a facade of democracy exists in many countries where, despite forms and appearances, a small oligarchic group manipulates all power. Workable democracy seems to require a special environment, including an educated and responsible people, some degree of economic stability, and some social cohesion and consensus. Above all, it demands an acceptance of the democratic "rules of the game," namely, that there will be fair and frequent elections, that the losers will accept the verdict of the voters and allow the majority to govern, that the majority will respect the right of the minority to furnish opposition, and that if the minority wins a future election it will then be permitted to take over the reins of government. Although democracy in practice will never achieve the perfection of the Democratic Creed, yet so long as such goals are held worthy and efforts are made to move in their direction, the system may be called democratic. American democracy, like its British counterpart, is an evolutionary and organic system that has pragmatically overcome obstacles and crises.

Democratic Socialism An economic system established by a democratic nation in which the people, through industrial groups or government, take over ownership and direction of basic industry, banking, communication, transportation, and other segments of the economy. The extent of the government's role in the economy is determined by free elections rather than by ideological dogma. Although a private sector of the economy may continue to exist, much effort is expended by government or groups in planning, directing, and regulating it, and in providing welfare services for the needy. *See also* SOCIALISM, page 18; WELFARE STATE, page 19.

Significance Democratic socialism has been partially instituted in several countries, particularly in Britain and the Scandinavian countries. Some observers regard it as the best answer to the economic challenge of communism. Communists are especially hostile toward democratic socialism because they fear it will correct the evils and "inner contradictions" of capitalism upon which they place their hope for economic collapse. American conservatives oppose it as a danger-ous leftward step toward communism.

Direct Democracy A system of government in which political decisions are made by the people directly rather than by their elected representatives. Under direct democracy, the citizens assemble periodically and function as a legislative body, or they vote on public issues to determine government policies. *See also* INITIATIVE, page 172; RECALL, page 140; REFERENDUM, page 182; REPRESENTATIVE GOVERNMENT, page 16.

Significance Direct democracy has been used in ancient Greece and Rome, in some Swiss cantons, in New England town meetings, and in some midwestern township meetings. A modern adaptation of direct democracy is found in fewer than half the American states—those that provide for initiative, referendum, and recall action by the people. Many local units of government also use binding and advisory referendums in reaching decisions on important issues. Direct democracy, however, is not provided for nor recognized by the United States Constitution. Ordinarily, direct democracy is practicable only in small communities and in resolving simple issues.

Divine Right A theory supporting absolutism based on the divinity of a person or his office, or on a right to rule inherited from ancestors believed to have been appointed by a Supreme Being. *See also* ABSOLUTISM, page 1; THEOCRACY, page 18.

Significance The political philosophy of the divine right of kings was accepted in theory and practice throughout most of the Western world from the fifteenth through the eighteenth centu-ries. The system was perpetuated through family inheritance of the ruling power and the intermar-riage of ruling families. Any challenge to or revolt against a king was regarded not only as a treasonable act but as a sin. In time, the divine right of kings was first weakened and then overcome by the new contract theory, which held that a ruler's power was granted to him not by God but by the sovereign people.

Economic Determinism The theory that the methods of production and exchange of goods control the form of a state's political and social organization and shape the intellectual and moral development of its people. Some economic determinists view history in terms of epochs in which the prevailing economic system pits the servile class against the dominant class, a struggle that eventually results in a new alignment. *See also* COMMUNISM, page 2.

Significance Vague beliefs in some aspects of economic determinism are widespread and are held by people of many persuasions. The most celebrated systematic theory was set forth by Marx and Engels, who used it to explain the movement of history in response to changing economic relationships. Economic determinism is the core of such theories as class struggle, the predicted collapse of capitalism, and the eventual victory of communism.

Fascism The political system of the extreme right, which incorporates the principles of the leader (dictator), a one-party state, totalitarian regimentation of economic and social activity, and the arbitrary exercise of absolute power by the regime. After 1922, Benito Mussolini fashioned the fascist prototype in Italy and was emulated in the 1930s by Adolf Hitler in Germany, Francisco Franco in Spain, and Juan Perón in Argentina. Fascism's glorification of the leader makes the system vulnerable and unstable, and poses serious problems of succession. Unlike communism, fascism retains private ownership of land and capital, but most economic activity is controlled and regimented by the state through a system of national socialism. *See also* ABSOLUTISM, page 1; AUTOCRACY, page 3; TOTALITARIANISM, page 19.

Significance Fascism is contemptuous of democratic parliamentarianism and personal liberty but is actively hostile toward communism. Fascists generally have come to power during a crisis in which the landed or industrial leaders of a state have feared the rise of communism. Although fascism was dealt a destructive blow by the defeat of the Axis powers in World War II, neofascism in the form of military dictatorship is on the rise throughout much of the world.

Government The political and administrative hierarchy of an organized state. Governments exercise legislative, executive, and judicial functions; the nature of the governmental system is determined by the distribution of these powers and by the means and extent of control exercised by the people. Government may take many forms, but to rule effectively it must be sufficiently powerful and stable to command obedience and maintain order. A government's position also depends on its acceptance by the community of nations through its diplomatic recognition by other states.

Significance Questions concerning the form of government and who will exercise political power within a state have always been matters of contention. Government has helped to bring peace and order to many states, but it has also been the cause of civil wars, revolutions, ideological struggles, and conflicts between states. As populations grow and technology develops, people become increasingly interdependent and turn to government for help in solving their problems, making government an increasingly significant force for good or evil.

Hamiltonianism The philosophy of Alexander Hamilton, leader of the Federalist party, chief architect of the national monetary system, and promoter of a special government role in support of the nation's economic system. The Hamiltonian model incorporates the idea of a powerful national government with strong executive power providing unity for the nation and a base on which to build a viable national economy. *See also* JEFFERSONIANISM, page 10; MADISONIANISM, page 12; PATERNALISM, page 14.

Significance Under Alexander Hamilton's energetic leadership, the new nation established a national banking system, a standard currency, business subsidies, a tax system, a national debt, a mint, and a protective tariff. The Federalist party generally espoused and supported the philosophy of Hamiltonianism. Many present-day Republicans regard Alexander Hamilton as the ideological godfather of the Republican party.

Ideology The "way of life" of a people reflected in terms of their political system, economic order, social goals, and moral values. Ideology is particularly concerned with the form and role of government and the nature of a state's economic system. Ideology is the means by which the basic values held by a party, class, group, or individual are articulated. *See also* IDEOLOGICAL WARFARE, page 393.

Significance Ideology serves to justify for the individual or for groups an existing social system, or postulates a desirable future social order. Two rival ideologies—communism and capitalism—are dominant today. Other ideologies exist, but they are overshadowed by the size and intensity of this major struggle. Ideology provides the basic propaganda ammunition for psychological warfare. Each side seeks to sell its ideology by emphasizing its own good points and its opponent's weaknesses. An individual tends to derive his attitudes and actions on political, economic, and social issues from the set of primary values that constitute his ideology.

Individualism The political, economic, and social concept that places primary emphasis on the worth, freedom, and well-being of the individual rather than on those of the group, society, or nation. The concept of individualism may be contrasted with that of collectivism, which describes those systems in which primary emphasis is placed on the rights and welfare of the group. *See also* DEMOCRACY, page 6; LAISSEZ-FAIRE, page 11.

Significance Individualism is the central idea in the political doctrine of constitutional democracy and in the economic theory of laissez-faire. The broad guarantees afforded to each person and to his property by the Constitution exemplify the American focus on individual rights. Although the term "individualism" was first used by Alexis de Tocqueville in 1840 in his classic *Democracy in America,* the idea embodied in the concept is several centuries older.

Jacksonian Democracy A political and social equalitarian movement in the United States that rejected political aristocracy and emphasized the "common man." The chief apostle of the new equality and democracy was Andrew Jackson, who brought to the presidency the leveling influences of the frontier. *See also* JEFFERSONIANISM, page 10; LONG BALLOT, page 126; SPOILS SYSTEM, page 231.

Significance The election of Jackson in 1828 ushered in an era of democratic changes on the national, state, and local governmental levels. Jacksonian Democracy emphasized and largely brought about universal manhood suffrage, popular election of officials, short terms of office, and the spoils system. The ideas of Jacksonian Democracy have continued to have an impact on government at all three levels—national, state, and local—especially in expanding the electorate.

Jeffersonianism The philosophy of Thomas Jefferson, espousing a democratic, laissez-faire styled agrarianism. Jeffersonianism rejected the Hamiltonian idea that a strong central government be created to spur the growth of urban industrialism and commercialism. The Jeffersonian model incorporates the ideal of an independent republic, democratically governed by an intellectual aristocracy under a strictly construed constitutional system, with a national government of limited powers and with major emphasis on individual freedom and responsibility and states' rights. *See also* JACKSONIAN DEMOCRACY, page 10; MADISONIANISM, page 12.

Significance The ideal of Jeffersonianism has had an impact on the American political system for two hundred years. Because it represents a relatively simple approach to meeting the needs of society and tends to be negative in relation to governmental powers, it has generally been placed on the defensive in a society that has demanded expanded economic growth and a larger and more powerful role by government. As the small farmer, laboring man, businessman, and artisan began to realize that they could cope with powerful business and industrial interest groups only by gaining political power, the two groups tended to exchange roles. The big businessman in the modern era espouses Jeffersonian laissez-faire freedoms, while the former Jeffersonians demand a more active central government.

Laissez-faire The economic theory, propounded by the French physiocrats and popularized by Adam Smith (*The Wealth of Nations,* 1776), that calls for a "hands-off" policy by government toward the economy. Laissez-faire rejects state control and regulation and emphasizes economic individualism, a market economy, and natural economic laws to guide the production and consumption of goods. Tariffs and other trade restrictions are rejected in favor of a worldwide system of free trade. The economic system becomes self-regulatory in nature, and each individual's pursuit of his own self-interest contributes to the well-being of all. *See also* CAPITALISM, page 3; CAVEAT VENDITOR, page 306; FREE TRADE, page 391; KEYNESIANISM, page 287.

Significance The wide acceptance in practice of the theory of laissez-faire in the Western world during the eighteenth and nineteenth centuries ushered in the new economic era of capitalism. Laissez-faire was largely a reaction to the severe production and trade restrictions imposed by governments under the previous system of mercantilism. The American Revolution was a product of these economic forces of change as well as of new political ideas, all of which were based on individualism. Today, laissez-faire has been modified by the expanding role of government in economic affairs, so that the United States now has a "mixed economy" combining capitalism with governmental promotion and regulation.

Leftist An individual or a political group advocating liberal, radical, or revolutionary political or economic programs, an expanded role by democratic government, or empowering the masses. Leftists include such categories as "welfare-statists," democratic socialists, Marxian socialists, Communists, and anarchists. The use of the term stems from the practice in European parliaments of seating radical parties to the left of the presiding officer. *See also* COMMUNISM, page 4; NEW LEFT, page 129; RADICAL, page 16; SOCIALISM, page 18.

Significance The moderate leftist has played a significant role in advocating governmental action to correct injustices and shortcomings in existing societies. Leftists have been particularly active in calling for changes and modifications in capitalism and political democracy. American leftist movements have included the Progressive, the Socialist, the Socialist Labor, and the Socialist Workers parties. The New Left that functioned as a loose coalition of antiwar groups during the Vietnam War largely shunned political parties in favor of direct action through mass protests. Leftist views on social, economic, and political matters have often been in advance of popularly held beliefs. Extremes of the political left, like those of the right, tend to culminate in dictatorship. Leftist groups and parties have received little public support in American politics.

Liberalism   A political view that seeks to change the political, economic, or social status quo to foster the development and well-being of the individual. Liberals regard man as a rational creature who can use his intelligence to overcome human and natural obstacles to a good life for all without resorting to violence against the established order. Liberalism is more concerned with process, with the method of solving problems, than with a specific program. *See also* CONSERVATISM, page 5.

Significance   Liberalism evolved in the eighteenth and nineteenth centuries as a doctrine emphasizing the full development of the individual, free from the restraints of government. The twentieth-century liberal, conversely, looks to government as a means of correcting the abuses and shortcomings of society through positive programs of action. In civil rights, for example, today's liberal views government as a positive force that can ameliorate wrongs and expand the freedom of the individual, rather than as, in the traditional sense, the major threat to individual freedom. Liberals have fought totalitarianism of the left and right by pursuing policies that seek to reduce economic and social inequalities and to produce political stability.

Madisonianism   The philosophy of James Madison, espousing a political system based on checks and balances, moderation, and the fostering of a harmony of interests. The Madisonian model begins with the assumption that the greatest dangers to republican government are those of the divisive power of faction and the threat of tyranny resulting from too great a concentration of political power. Madison's solution to these problems was to establish a powerful national government that could balance state and local units and maintain its own checks and balances to ensure moderation in the exercise of power. *See also* JACKSONIAN DEMOCRACY, page 10; JEFFERSONIANISM, page 10.

Significance   Madisonianism as a philosophy of government has left a continuing imprint on the nature and functioning of the American system. The Constitution that finally emerged from the Philadelphia Convention of 1787 is often referred to as the "Madisonian system" because it incorporates Madison's basic idea that power must be checked and balanced to avoid tyranny. In his contributions to *The Federalist* papers (particularly No. 10 and No. 51) and during his presidential tenure, Madison did much to gain acceptance for a powerful central government limited by its internal system of power equilibrium. He is often regarded as the leading strategist of the American political system.

Majority Rule   A basic principle of democracy which asserts that the greater number of citizens in any political unit should select officials and determine policies. A majority is normally 50 percent plus one of the total vote cast, or of the total number of potential voters. Special majorities are sometimes needed for decisions, as, for example, in the constitutional requirement that the Senate approve treaties by a two-thirds vote. In 1971, the Supreme Court held (*Gordon v. Lance,* 403 U.S. 1) that the requirement that a bond issue be adopted by a 60 percent extraordinary majority in a state election does not violate the equal protection clause of the Fourteenth Amendment. Majority rule is justified on the grounds that it rests on superior force, is commonly accepted in practice, and is a logical means for reaching decisions, and that, pragmatically, no reasonable democratic alternative exists. *See also* CONCURRENT MAJORITY, page 4; CONSENSUS, page 5; DEMOCRACY, page 6; PLURALITY, page 133.

Significance Political philosophers have long debated whether it is any more justifiable for the majority to impose its will on the minority than for the minority to rule. Some theories reject majority rule in favor of government by consensus or by a concurrent majority. In the United States, majority rule is not rigidly adhered to; for example, in most cases only a plurality is needed to win an election. Other practices that depart from majority rule include the equal representation of the states in the Senate, gerrymandering, the use of the rules and procedures and the committee system of Congress to thwart the majority, and the election of the President by the Electoral College. Also, when an extraordinary majority vote is required, such as a two-thirds vote, then one-third plus one of the minority can determine the outcome.

Monarchy Any form of government in which the supreme powers of the state are exercised, or ceremoniously held, by a king, queen, emperor, or other regal potentate. Monarchs may acquire their position through inheritance or election, although the latter is unusual. Absolute monarchs exercise full ruling powers, whereas constitutional monarchs either share governmental powers with elected parliaments or are mere figureheads. *See also* DIVINE RIGHT, page 8.

Significance Absolute monarchs once ruled nearly all the states of Europe. Today, in the few countries that have retained their monarchs—Britain, Sweden, Norway, the Netherlands, for example—the king or queen is assigned a ceremonial role as chief of state. In several semifeudal states of Asia, Africa, and the Middle East, however, monarchs continue to have absolute power.

Nation Any sizable group of people united by common bonds of geography, religion, language, race, custom, and tradition, and through shared experiences and common aspirations. The term is often used interchangeably with "state," but not all national groups have achieved statehood, although they all aspire to it. Moreover, the nation and the state may be essentially the same, as in the case of a nation-state like Ireland or Israel, or a state may be multinational, as are Switzerland and the Soviet Union. Modern nations began to emerge from feudalism in the ninth century. The community of nation-states was given political and legal recognition by the Peace of Westphalia in 1648. *See also* NATIONALISM, page 399; STATE, page 18.

Significance In the modern era, the nation has provided the unifying concept with which the individual can identify. The results have not always been good, for many national groups have built their unity on a real or imagined fear and a shared hatred of other groups or on a desire to bring others under their dominion. These conflicting national interests, which characterize the world's state system, have contributed to the instability of international relations and to the outbreak of wars.

Natural Law The concept that human relations are governed by an immutable set of laws, similar to the physical laws of the universe and recognizable through human reason. Such laws are regarded as ethically binding in human society. The theory of *jus naturale* was expounded by the Stoics and was highly developed by the eighteenth-century natural-rights philosophers. *See also* DEMOCRACY, page 6; NATURAL RIGHTS, page 75.

Significance The concept of natural law has been influential in the development of legal and political theories and institutions, morals and ethics, and religion. Its main significance historically has been its use as a moral standard for judging individual and governmental conduct. Its ambiguities, however, subject it to conflicting interpretations and challenges. It constitutes the basis for the natural-rights philosophy that underlies democratic systems of government.

Oligarchy Any system of government in which a small elite group holds the ruling power. Oligarchical systems are usually based on wealth, military power, or social position. *See also* ARISTOCRACY, page 2; ELITE, page 120.

Significance Oligarchs traditionally rule with absolute power, unencumbered by democratic restraints. Even in democratic systems, however, oligarchic groups may temporarily hold a decisive influence over the government because of their economic position or social status. Two European philosophers, Robert Michels and Vilfredo Pareto, developed a theory of the "iron law of oligarchy" which propounds the impossibility of democracy in practice because of the tendency of small groups to dominate and control the majority. Local communities are in some cases governed by the leaders of a political machine or by an elite "power structure" or "establishment."

Parliamentary System A system of government, often based on the British prototype, in which governmental authority is vested in the legislative body (parliament) and in a cabinet headed by a prime minister or premier. The cabinet exercises political leadership and directs the administration. Cabinet ministers are entirely or largely selected from the membership of parliament, and the cabinet continues in power so long as it commands the support of a majority of the parliament. Substantial disagreement between the parliament and the cabinet results in either the appointment of a new ministry or the election of a new legislature. *See also* PRESIDENTIAL GOVERNMENT, page 15.

Significance The major advantage of the parliamentary system is that it avoids continuing controversy or deadlocks between the legislative and executive branches and provides for clear accountability to the people. These advantages, however, result in the loss of checks and balances, and the American people have never seriously considered adopting this system. Most of the world's democracies are patterned after the British or continental European parliamentary systems, rather than after the American presidential system with its separation of powers.

Paternalism A philosophy or governmental policy which holds that the state should act as a father-guardian of its citizen-children in looking out for their general welfare. Paternalism holds that it is the responsibility of the state to determine the best interests of its citizens for them and to inaugurate specific policies and programs aimed at achieving paternalistic goals. *See also* WELFARE STATE, page 19.

Significance The ideas embodied in the philosophy of paternalism are more attuned to the welfare-state ideal than to the tenets of socialism. Examples of paternalism in the United States include the Social Security System, Medicare and Medicaid, unemployment insurance, fluoridation of water, and veterans' benefit programs. Paternalism is also used politically as a negative propaganda concept that connotes lack of individual initiative and zeal resulting from governmental handouts.

Political Science　An academic and research discipline that deals with the theory and practice of politics and the description and analysis of political systems and political behavior. Fields and subfields of the political science discipline include political theory and philosophy, national systems, cross-national political analysis, international relations, foreign policy, international law and organization, public administration, administrative behavior, public law, judicial behavior, and politics and public policy. Approaches to the discipline include classical political philosophy, structuralism, and behavioralism. Political science, as one of the social sciences, uses methods and techniques that relate to the kinds of data and the investigatory goals sought: historical documents, newspaper reports, scholarly journal articles, official records, personal observation, laboratory experiments, survey research, statistical analysis, model building, and simulation.

Significance　Political science in its broadest philosophical sense dates back even earlier than Plato and Aristotle. For many centuries, the study of politics was concerned mainly with normative determinations of what ought to be and with deducing the characteristics and functions of the ideal state. In time, usually regarded as starting with Machiavelli, modern political science with its emphasis on direct empirical observation of political institutions and actors began to evolve. In the 1950s and 1960s, a behavioral revolution stressing the systematic and rigorously scientific study of individual and group political behavior swept the discipline. At the same time that political science moved toward greater depth of analysis and more specialization, it also moved toward a closer working relationship with other disciplines, especially sociology, anthropology, psychology, social psychology, biology, ecology, statistics, and communication sciences. Increasingly, students of political behavior have used the scientific method to create an intellectual discipline based on the postulating of hypotheses followed by empirical verification and the ascertainment of probable trends, and of generalizations that explain individual and group political actions. In the 1970s the discipline has placed an increasing emphasis on "relevance" or the use of new approaches and methodologies to solve current political and social problems.

Popular Sovereignty　The natural-rights concept that ultimate political authority rests with the people and can be exercised to create, alter, or abolish government. In practice, popular sovereignty is ordinarily exercised through representative institutions. *See also* DEMOCRACY, page 6; SOVEREIGNTY, page 18.

Significance　Popular sovereignty was enunciated by the natural-rights philosophers in their attack on governmental absolutism based on the theory of divine right. The concept that the people possess supreme political power pervades the Declaration of Independence and is implicit in the United States Constitution. Popular sovereignty is most directly practiced by the American people when engaged in the writing, amending, and revising of federal, state, and local constitutions or charters.

Presidential Government　A system that features separation of powers between the legislative and executive branches and the independent election of an executive serving a fixed term. Presidential government is also used in the United States to describe the trend toward strong executive leadership, often at the expense of the legislative branch. *See also* PARLIAMENTARY SYSTEM, page 14; PRESIDENT, page 206.

Significance The main advantages claimed for the presidential system are the choosing of the executive by the voters rather than by the legislature, the effective use of checks and balances, and the encouragement of strong executive leadership. Critics, however, claim that the system creates a gulf between the legislature and the executive, encourages disagreement and deadlock, and disperses responsibility. In presidential government, the executive tends to emerge as the central figure in the political system.

Radical An advocate of substantial or fundamental political, social, and economic changes. Although no precise use of the term exists, a radical is generally regarded as a leftist or rightist who is extreme in his demands for change. While the term usually refers to extremist individuals and parties of the political left, it can be used to describe anyone who favors drastic political, economic, or social change. The original Greek etymology of "radical" meant going to the root or origin of a matter; hence, a radical is one who asks basic questions or tries to answer them. *See also* LEFTIST, page 11; NEW LEFT, page 129; RIGHTIST, page 17.

Significance The American guarantees of freedom of speech, press, and association have encouraged the expression of radical views. Some radical parties have played a significant role in gaining popular support for some of their proposals, and these have been incorporated into platforms of the major parties. Extreme radical parties of the left are often Marxist-oriented. Ultraconservative groups in contemporary American politics are referred to, however, as the "radical right." The term radical is freely used in political campaigns in attempts to discredit opponents or their proposals.

Reactionary A person who advocates substantial political, social, or economic changes favoring a return to an earlier, more conservative system. Reactionaries believe that most social problems result from democratic excesses favoring the propertyless masses; they usually prefer government by oligarchy. Although the use of the term is not precise, reactionaries are political rightists who are more extreme in their views than are conservatives and who are more likely to adopt militant tactics to achieve their objectives. *See also* RIGHTIST, page 17.

Significance Some of the new nations of Asia and Africa have come under the control of reactionary regimes after early failures of democracy following independence. In American politics, reactionaries have generally favored laissez-faire and have opposed social-welfare legislation. The term is freely used in political campaigns in attempts to discredit opponents or their proposals.

Representative Government Any democratic system of government in which the people elect representatives to act as their agents in making and enforcing laws and decisions. Authoritarian regimes often have a facade of representative institutions, but they lack the vital element of accountability of democratic governments. *See also* DEMOCRACY, page 6; REPUBLIC, page 17.

Significance Any large and populous political unit must resort to some form of representative government, although small units may provide for direct decision making by the people. Representatives may act for a special class or group, as in medieval assemblies; for an occupational or social group, as in a system of functional representation; or for a geographical community, as in most contemporary legislatures. One theory, expounded by the English statesman, Edmund Burke, holds that a representative should exercise his own intelligent discretion in reaching decisions; another views his role to be that of an agent of the people who is expected to vote according to their wishes and interests.

Republic A form of government in which sovereign power resides in the electorate and is exercised by elected representatives who are responsible to the people. Republican government stands in contradistinction to monarchial or oligarchical government, in which the rulers have a vested right to office. It is also to be distinguished from pure democracy, in which the people govern directly. *See also* REPRESENTATIVE GOVERNMENT, page 16.

Significance In the century following the American and French revolutions, republican government emerged in many countries to replace monarchical systems. The Founding Fathers significantly wrote into the Constitution a guarantee by the national government of a republican form of government in every state. In American politics, the distinction between a republic and a democracy is one frequently drawn by conservatives to emphasize the representative character of the American system in contrast to what they consider the "excesses" of democracy.

Rightist An individual or group advocating conservative or reactionary political or economic programs, a restriction on the power of the masses, and oligarchical rule. Rightists tend to favor laissez-faire and strong executive power; the extreme right wing supports Fascist dictatorships. The term is derived from the common practice in European parliaments of seating conservative parties to the right of the presiding officer. *See also* REACTIONARY, page 16.

Significance Rightist parties exercise considerable influence in most democratic states. In the United States, both major parties have conservative members who hold positions of influence in Congress. Prominent American rightist movements include the American Nazi party, the Ku Klux Klan, the Conservative party, the American Independent party, the Minutemen, and the Young Americans for Freedom. Most rightists regard themselves as "moderates" or "middle of the road" in their approach to politics, whereas others in the American body politic may regard them as extremists. Extreme right-wing groups have never found much support in American politics.

Rule of Law An Anglo-American concept that emphasizes the supremacy of the law and restricts the discretionary power of public officials. The rule of law particularly stresses the protection of individual rights from the arbitrary interference of officials. *See also* DEMOCRACY, page 6.

Significance The rule of law provides the foundation for democratic constitutionalism. In the United States, for example, the rule of law requires that each individual accused of crime be treated equally under the law, receive a fair trial with established procedures, and be accorded due process in all official actions undertaken against him. Guarantees provided by the rule of law are in contrast with the operations of a police state. A vital maxim of democratic government is "government of law and not of men." Law Day is celebrated in the United States on May 1 each year in an effort to counter the "May Day" public spectacles of leftist parties.

Socialism   A doctrine that advocates economic collectivism through governmental or industrial group ownership of the means of production and distribution of goods. Its basic aims are to replace competition for profit with cooperation and social responsibility, and to secure a more equitable distribution of income and opportunity. Though these aims are common to all socialists, a wide variety of schools of thought have arisen, distinguished mainly by their approaches to the problem of how best to achieve socialism. These vary from the peaceful and democratic ideas of utopian and Christian socialists to the aggressive, and sometimes violent, approaches of anarchists and Communists. *See also* CONVERGENCE THEORY, page 385; DEMOCRATIC SOCIALISM, page 7.

Significance Socialism has been a significant force, particularly in Europe, since the middle of the nineteenth century. In the United States, Socialist parties have had little success at the ballot box, but their ideas have gained some measure of acceptance through liberal economic and social-welfare programs. The democratic Socialist party of Eugene Debs and Norman Thomas has had great influence on American politics but has waned in recent years. The more radical Trotskyite Socialist Labor party still runs a presidential candidate but has few adherents.

Sovereignty   The supreme power of a state, exercised within its boundaries, free from external interference. The idea behind sovereignty is an ancient one, but it was first developed into an elaborate doctrine by philosophers of the sixteenth and seventeenth centuries. They sought to justify the absolutism of the kings of the new state system by cultivating the myth that the monarch had been accorded supreme power by divine action. *See also* SOVEREIGNTY, page 408.

Significance The early absolutist implications of sovereignty developed by Jean Bodin and Thomas Hobbes gave way in time to the new concept of popular sovereignty developed by Jean Jacques Rousseau and John Locke. The idea of sovereignty remains a significant factor in international relations. The concept of absolute sovereignty, however, has been modified by state consent, as demonstrated in treaties, international law, and international organizations.

State   A political community occupying a definite territory, having an organized government, and possessing internal and external sovereignty. Recognition of a state's claim to independence by other states, enabling it to enter into international engagements, is important to the establishment of its sovereignty. The term is also used to describe territorial divisions within a federal system, such as in the United States, *See also* NATION, page 13.

Significance More than 150 states comprise the community of nations. The state, the basic political unit of the world since the sixteenth century, is slowly giving way to evolutionary internationalism in the form of world and regional organizations. The basic challenge today is whether a stable system of international cooperation can be created before the state system destroys itself in a world war.

Theocracy   Any political system in which political power is exercised directly or indirectly by a clergy, and in which church law is superior to or replaces civil law. The implication is that decisions are made by a Supreme Being and are transmitted to man through agents who rule in a theocracy. *See also* OLIGARCHY, page 14.

Significance Theocracies typically are nondemocratic systems in which political power is exercised by an oligarchic council of priests, ministers, monks, or other church officials, or by a single church leader. Examples of theocracies include Geneva under John Calvin and Tibet prior to the Communist conquest.

Totalitarianism A modern form of authoritarianism in which the state controls nearly every aspect of the individual's life. Totalitarian governments do not tolerate activities by individuals or groups, such as labor unions and youth organizations, that are not directed toward the state's goals. Totalitarian dictators maintain themselves in power by means of a secret police, propaganda disseminated through all of the media of communications, the elimination of free discussion and criticism, and widespread use of terror tactics. Internal scapegoats and foreign military threats are created and used to foster unity through fear. *See also* ABSOLUTISM, page 1; FASCISM, page 9.

Significance Totalitarianism has developed in the twentieth century through new techniques that mobilize entire populations in support of an authoritarian government and a political ideology. The main totalitarian governments have included Nazi Germany, Fascist Italy, the Soviet Union under Josef Stalin, and Communist China. Totalitarian systems, however, may not in fact be as monolithic as they appear to be, since such systems may hide a political process in which several groups—the army, political leaders, industrialists, and others—compete for power and influence.

Utopia An imaginary human paradise created in the mind and writings of Sir Thomas More. More's ideal commonwealth was located on an island untouched by worldly vices and provided a nearly perfect society. The word "utopia" means literally "no place" and is taken from the title of More's book published in 1516.

Significance More's *Utopia* is part of the body of speculative political theory that has fostered the imaginative creation of ideal states and social systems, such as Plato's *Republic* and Tommaso Campanella's *City of the Sun*. The adjective "utopian" is also used to describe the idealistic nineteenth-century socialistic programs offered by Robert Owen, Claude Saint-Simon, and François Fourier. American democracy has been influenced by utopianism and has established ideals of perfect freedom, equality, and brotherhood in the Democratic Creed.

Welfare State A concept that stresses the role of government as the provider and protector of individual security and social good through governmental economic and social programs. This role for government represents a shift from that of a minimal protector of persons and property to that of a positive promoter of human welfare. *See also* PATERNALISM, page 14.

Significance The welfare state is a product of the Industrial Revolution, urbanization, and the social and economic consequences of depressions and wars. Opponents of government's welfare role charge that "cradle to the grave" security destroys the individual's initiative and enterprise and promotes fiscal irresponsibility. Supporters point out that programs involving social security, health, subsidized housing, and the like provide necessary minimum standards of life for all, and that no civilized society can avoid this responsibility. Nearly all modern governments have engaged in some such practices, but the rich, industrialized nations have been able to afford the most extensive welfare programs.

2 The United States Constitution:

Background, Principles, Development

Amendment Changes in, or additions to, a constitution. In the United States Constitution, Article V spells out the methods. Amendments may be proposed by a two-thirds vote of both houses of Congress or by a convention called by Congress at the request of the legislatures of two-thirds of the states. Only the first method has been used. Such proposals must be ratified by either the legislatures of three-fourths of the states or by conventions called for that purpose in three-fourths of the states, as determined by Congress. Only the Twenty-first Amendment (repealing prohibition) was submitted to conventions. The President may not veto an amendment proposal. Congress may stipulate a time limit, usually seven years, within which a proposal must be ratified. A state that has rejected an amendment may change its mind, but once a proposal is ratified by a state legislature, it stands. Ratification by a state may not be accomplished by a referendum of the people, but only by the legislature or convention. Though thousands of proposals have been made in Congress to amend the Constitution, only thirty-four have received endorsement from both houses; of these, twenty-six have been adopted. Amendments are appended to the Constitution and not placed within the article or section that may have been changed, as is done in some state constitutions. *See also* AMENDMENT, page 155; *Coleman v. Miller,* page 30; CONSTITUTIONAL AMENDMENTS, STATE, page 438; CONSTITUTIONAL CONSTRUCTION, page 24; USAGE, page 29. (See also specific amendments.)

Significance A constitution, no matter how well designed, requires adjustment from time to time. A reasonable amendment procedure makes adjustment possible, without resort to force, in basic governmental arrangements. The Founding Fathers considered that proposal of amendments by the national government, with ratification controlled by the states, would safeguard the basic division of powers under the federal system. The executive and judicial branches are excluded from the proposal and ratification process. While most amendments adopted to date have not involved fundamental changes in American government, a few, such as the Fourteenth and Sixteenth, have had profound effects. The present methods of amendment have been criticized largely on the ground that minorities may block the majority will because of the two-thirds- and three-fourths-vote requirements. However, other less formal methods of change, such as judicial interpretation and custom and usage, have made frequent resort to the amendment process unnecessary.

Annapolis Convention   A conference called by the Virginia legislature in 1786, whereby states were invited to send delegates to Annapolis, Maryland, to discuss trade regulations. Only five states were represented. Under the leadership of Alexander Hamilton and James Madison, the group urged Congress and the states to call another convention in Philadelphia in 1787 to consider revision of the Articles of Confederation. *See also* ARTICLES OF CONFEDERATION, page 22.

Significance   The Annapolis Convention was an important prelude to the framing of the Constitution of the United States in Philadelphia the following year. Dissatisfaction with the Articles of Confederation, particularly in the areas of trade and commerce, led to this movement for reform.

Antifederalists   Persons who opposed adoption of the United States Constitution framed in Philadelphia in 1787. They opposed the centralist tendencies of the Constitution and attacked the failure of the framers to include a bill of rights. The group included many who had signed the Declaration of Independence or had strongly supported the Revolution.

Significance   A substantial number of people opposed ratification, but strong opposition to the Constitution rapidly dwindled after its adoption. The Antifederalist group, however, became the supporters of Thomas Jefferson whose views on the nature of the Union, as distinguished from those of Alexander Hamilton and other Federalists, continue to be influential and controversial in American politics today.

Articles of Confederation   The compact made among the thirteen original American states to form the basis of their government. Though prepared in 1776, the Articles were not officially adopted by all states until 1781 and were replaced in 1789 by the United States Constitution. The Confederation was a league of sovereign states. Each state had one vote in a one-house legislature. No provision was made in the Articles for a separate national executive or judiciary. The Congress was assigned a limited number of powers, but the approval of nine states was necessary for effective action. The central government lacked significant powers, including the powers to tax, to regulate commerce or the currency, or to make its laws directly applicable to the people without further state action. In short, the Congress could not force states or individuals to comply with its decisions, resembling, in many respects, an international organization. Any amendments to the Articles required the unanimous approval of the thirteen states. *See also* CONFEDERATION, page 32.

Significance   The Articles, and the lessons learned under their operation, formed the backdrop against which the states could move toward "a more perfect union." The Confederation brought the Revolutionary War to a conclusion, accomplished much toward the development of the American continent through the Northwest Ordinance, and established the principle of interstate cooperation through such means as interstate rendition and full faith and credit. Many of the defects of the Articles were rectified in the United States Constitution.

Charter Colony   One of the three types of colonial governments—charter, proprietary, royal —found in colonial America. Charter colonies, namely Rhode Island and Connecticut, operated under charters agreed to by the colony and the king. The legislature was elected and was allowed much autonomy by England. The governor was chosen by the legislature. *See also* PROPRIETARY COLONY, page 28; ROYAL COLONY, page 28.

Significance Charter colonies enjoyed the greatest degree of independence from the Crown. The charters of Connecticut and Rhode Island proved so satisfactory for local self-government that they served as state constitutions until 1818 and 1842 respectively.

Checks and Balances A major principle of the American governmental system whereby each department of the government exercises a check upon the actions of the others. The principle operates not only among the legislative, executive, and judicial branches but also between the two houses of the legislature and between the states and the national government. Each department has some authority to control the actions of one or more of the others by participation in their functions. Examples include the President's veto power and the congressional power to override the veto, judicial review of legislative and executive actions, presidential appointment of judges with senatorial approval, and the congressional power to impeach. *See also* DISTRIBUTION OF POWERS, page 26; SEPARATION OF POWERS, page 28.

Significance Through the various devices of check and balance, the framers of the Constitution sought to prevent the accumulation of all power in one branch, or in one or several persons, by giving each branch the authority to prevent the encroachment of the others. The check and balance system stresses the interdependence (rather than complete separation) of the various units of government and the need for compromise; it also prevents the usurpation of power. Major defects of this system are its tendencies to create deadlocks and to prevent swift action during crises.

Commerce and Slave Trade Compromise An agreement reached at the Constitutional Convention of 1787, giving the national government power to regulate foreign commerce, requiring the consent of two-thirds of the Senate to treaties, and prohibiting the national government from taxing exports or interfering with the slave trade until 1808.

Significance One of the major purposes for which the convention was called was to strengthen national control over commerce. Southern delegates, however, feared that northern majorities might cut off the slave trade and discriminate against the profitable cotton trade. They agreed to grant the national government control over foreign commerce provided that the South was given a check over treaties and that Congress would not tax exports. It was believed that a sufficient number of slaves would be available by 1808. The treaty and foreign commerce provisions continue to influence the making of American foreign policy.

Connecticut Compromise The agreement reached in the Constitutional Convention of 1787 that resolved the question of representation in the national Congress. Each state is represented in the House of Representatives according to population, and in the Senate each state is represented equally. The Compromise, also called the "Great Compromise," satisfied the small states in particular and made it possible for them to agree to the establishment of a strong central government. *See also* BICAMERALISM, page 157.

Significance While the Connecticut Compromise was the "price of union" in 1787, it has had lasting significance. The equal representation of states in the Senate has resulted in a disproportionate influence of sparsely settled states and regions. Though the states are represented by population in the House, bills must pass both houses to become law. Thus the Compromise of 1787 is felt in the daily workings of Congress. The Connecticut Compromise was the crucial step in the formation of the Constitution.

Constitution A fundamental or "organic" law that establishes the framework of government of a state, assigns the powers and duties of governmental agencies, and establishes the relationship between the people and their government. Constitutions may be written or unwritten. The English operate under an unwritten constitution, that is, one consisting largely of legislative acts, legal decisions, and customs that have never been comprehensively gathered in one document. American constitutions are written, but much fundamental law is unwritten and is in the form of custom and usage. The United States Constitution went into effect on March 4, 1789, and has been amended twenty-six times. The supreme law of the land, its basic principles include limited government, popular sovereignty, separation of powers, checks and balances, and federalism. *See also* CONSTITUTION, STATE, page 437; DISTRIBUTION OF POWERS, page 26.

Significance The United States Constitution, the oldest and most successful written constitution in history, has served the nation with remarkably little formal alteration during periods of rapid social change. This is due to the wisdom of the framers who wrote a brief and flexible instrument, and to the policy of liberal construction that has characterized many important Supreme Court decisions. The Constitution has not only served as an effective instrument of government and a guardian of human rights but has come to be a revered symbol of how people with diverse interests, and geographically spread out, can live together in freedom.

Constitutional Construction The method of interpreting the Constitution. Some favor a "loose" or "liberal" construction of constitutional phrases; others, a "strict" interpretation. The difference is largely expressed in terms of the interpreter's attitude toward broad grants of power to the national government (loose construction) as opposed to the retention of as much power as possible in the states (strict construction). *See also* JURISPRUDENCE, page 253; *McCulloch v. Maryland,* page 45.

Significance The issue of loose versus strict construction arose early in American history and contributed to the emergence of political parties. The Federalist party favored a broad interpretation of national powers, while the Jeffersonian Antifederalists stood for a narrow construction of such powers. The legal issue arose in the famous case of *McCulloch v. Maryland,* 4 Wheaton 316 (1819), which involved the question of whether the national government was limited to those powers *expressly* delegated to it or whether it had *implied* powers. Chief Justice Marshall resolved the issue in favor of the implied-powers doctrine and established the principle of, and necessity for, a loose construction of the Constitution. From time to time, the strict constructionists have had their way, depending largely on the party in power and the attitude of the Supreme Court. Loose construction, however, remains the basis for constitutional interpretation and has facilitated adaptation of the Constitution to the needs of the time.

Constitutional Convention of 1787   The convention held in Philadelphia from May 25 to September 18 that framed the Constitution of the United States. Called by the Confederation Congress to revise the Articles of Confederation, the delegates proceeded to draft an entirely new document. Rhode Island sent no delegates and only fifty-five of the seventy-four men originally appointed as delegates attended. Presided over by George Washington, the deliberations were conducted in secret but have been made known through notes kept by James Madison. The delegates made compromises on various differences between large and small states, North and South, agrarian and commercial interests, and advocates of a strong or a weak central government. They not only ignored their instructions merely to revise the Articles of Confederation, but also ignored the provision of the Articles requiring unanimous consent of the state legislatures for revision by providing that the new constitution would go into effect when nine states ratified it in state conventions. *See also* COMMERCE AND SLAVE TRADE COMPROMISE, page 23; CONNECTI-CUT COMPROMISE, page 23; ECONOMIC INTERPRETATION OF THE CONSTITUTION, page 26; MADI-SION'S JOURNAL, page 27; NEW JERSEY PLAN, page 27; THREE-FIFTHS COMPROMISE, page 29; VIRGINIA PLAN, page 30.

Significance   The convention was a conservative reaction to the excesses of the Revolutionary period and to the commercial disorder under the Articles of Confederation. Its membership was young and well-informed on government and politics, and was representative of propertied and commercial interests. The convention has been the only national constitutional convention in American history, but by law, another can be called by Congress on the request of two-thirds of the states.

Continental Congress   The body of delegates representing the colonies that first met to protest the British treatment of the colonies and eventually became the government of the United States. The First Continental Congress met in 1774 and drafted a Declaration of Rights. The Second Congress, meeting the following year, adopted the Declaration of Independence, conduct-ed the War of Independence, and served as the national government until the Articles of Confeder-ation went into effect in 1781.

Significance   The First Congress met in an atmosphere in which the colonists still considered themselves Englishmen who were being abused. The Second Congress convened after open conflict with England had begun. Though the Second Congress rested on no legal base, it served as a *de facto* government. Delegates were selected by the state legislatures. While the states did not feel bound by decisions of the Continental Congress, it did bring the war to a successful conclusion. It also developed an American consciousness, which led to the adoption of the Articles of Confederation and, eventually, to the Constitution of the United States.

Declaration of Independence   The document adopted by the Second Continental Con-gress on July 4, 1776, declaring the independence of the American colonies from Great Britain and justifying the rebellion. It was drafted by a committee of five men: Thomas Jefferson, John Adams, Benjamin Franklin, Roger Sherman, and Robert Livingston. The draft was largely the work of Jefferson, who drew heavily from the natural-rights doctrine of the English philosopher, John Locke. The Declaration enumerated the grievances against the Crown and eloquently defended the rights of man and the right of self-government.

Significance The Declaration of Independence does not have any legal effect today. Nevertheless, it is recognized throughout the world as a basic statement of the American creed. Its opening passage declares the equality of man, the natural rights of man endowed by God, the principle of limited government, government by consent, and the right of people to rebel against tyrannical government.

Distribution of Powers An underlying principle of the American constitutional system designed to prevent tyranny by assigning powers to different governments and agencies and by checking the exercise of power. The distribution takes the following forms: (1) dividing power between the national and state governments under a federal system; (2) separating power among the three major branches of the government—legislative, executive, and judicial—giving each branch a check upon the operations of the others; (3) selecting the personnel of the three branches by different procedures and electorates, assigning them different terms of office, and making them responsible to different pressures; (4) limiting all governments by specific constitutional restrictions. *See also* FEDERALISM, page 34; SEPARATION OF POWERS, page 28.

Significance The framers sought to prevent all governmental power from falling into the hands of any individual or group. They feared majority tyranny as much as minority or individual tyranny. Hence they provided for a wide distribution of authority, limited in scope, and designed to effect a balancing of interests. The distribution of powers has been modified by the expanding role of the national government, the increasing influence of the President over legislation and foreign affairs, and the development of independent regulatory agencies that exercise some legislative and judicial power in their supervision of the economy.

Economic Interpretation of the Constitution The theory that the framers of the Constitution represented the well-to-do classes and that the Constitution was designed to protect their interests. The theory was developed by the distinguished historian Charles A. Beard in his *An Economic Interpretation of the Constitution of the United States* (1913).

Significance Beard did not attribute any malice to the framers but tried to show that they had much to gain from the creation of a strong and stable national government. He pointed out that the delegates were professional or propertied men with extensive holdings in public securities, land, manufacturing, shipping, and slaves. Although the framers were a conservative-minded group who were affected by their own backgrounds and interests, Beard and other historians have emphasized that economic interest was only *one* of the factors that motivated them.

Federalist Papers A series of eighty-five essays written by Alexander Hamilton, James Madison, and John Jay (all using the name *Publius*), which were published in New York newspapers in 1787 to convince New Yorkers to adopt the newly proposed Constitution drafted in Philadelphia. These essays have been collected and published under the title *The Federalist*. *See also* MADISONIANISM, page 12.

Significance *The Federalist,* although written in haste and for the specific purpose of winning support for the Constitution, is widely regarded as the best single commentary on the Constitution. Governmental officials, especially judges, often rely on *The Federalist* in interpreting the meaning of the Constitution. Moreover, it is considered to be the outstanding American contribution to political theory.

Madison's Journal   Notes kept by James Madison of the proceedings of the Constitutional Convention of 1787. Although an official journal of the convention was kept, it contained only formal motions and votes by states. Madison kept a record of the debates as well. These notes were not published until 1840, four years after Madison's death.

Significance   The proceedings of the convention were conducted in secrecy and Madison's notes are the only reliable source of information. For more than fifty years, the Constitution was interpreted without the benefit of these materials, which cast important light upon the intentions of the framers.

Mayflower Compact   An agreement signed in 1620 by all adult males on board the ship *Mayflower,* prior to landing at Plymouth, to form a civil body politic governed by majority rule. *See also* CONTRACT THEORY, page 6.

Significance   The Mayflower Compact established the first government in New England based on the consent of the governed and remained the basis for government in Plymouth Colony until it joined Massachusetts in 1691. The document also represents an underlying feature of American political theory that government results from a social contract among individuals for their mutual benefit.

New Jersey Plan   A plan submitted by William Paterson of New Jersey to the Constitutional Convention of 1787 representing the views of the small states and states' rights advocates. It was expressly designed as a counterproposal to the strong nationalistic Virginia Plan. The essence of the New Jersey Plan was a single-house Congress, with each state having an equal vote. Moreover, the Plan looked toward a moderate modification of the Articles of Confederation rather than the drafting of a new document. *See also* VIRGINIA PLAN, page 30.

Significance   The New Jersey Plan, along with the Virginia Plan, drew the major battle lines of the convention. Though the basic idea of the New Jersey Plan to retain the Articles of Confederation was defeated by the convention, the demand for equal representation resulted in the Connecticut Compromise. The assurance that the states would receive equal representation in one house of Congress made it possible for the convention to complete its deliberations.

Preamble   The statement affixed at the beginning of the Constitution, stating the source of its authority and the purposes it is to serve. The Preamble to the United States Constitution is of no legal effect but may serve as a guide to the intent of the framers.

Significance   Particular importance is attached to the fact that the Preamble begins with the words "We the people" rather than "The states of New York, . . ." The wording establishes the supremacy of the national Constitution as emanating from all the people rather than as a contract among sovereign states. This was of particular significance in the great debate over the nature of the Union prior to the Civil War. The Preamble is also noted as a concise statement of the enduring principles of a free people.

Proprietary Colony   One of the three types of colonial governments—charter, proprietary, royal—found in colonial America. Proprietary colonies were governed by charters issued by the "proprietor," an individual to whom the king had made a land grant. Pennsylvania was established under such a charter bestowed by William Penn. Other proprietary colonies were Delaware and Maryland. Though the lower house of the legislature was elected, the upper house and the governor were chosen by the proprietor, subject to approval of the Crown. *See also* CHARTER COLONY, page 22; ROYAL COLONY, page 28.

Significance   The proprietor represented the Crown, and the colonies were largely ruled from England. Nevertheless, important lessons in self-government were learned. Increasing efforts by the Crown to control these colonies were contributing factors to the Revolution. The "frame of government" drawn up by William Penn for Pennsylvania was a relatively democratic document.

Royal Colony   One of the three types of colonial governments—charter, proprietary, royal—found in colonial America. Eight colonies were royal colonies. The lower house of the legislature was elected but the upper house and the governor were appointed by the king. Royal governors exercised almost complete authority over the colony through instructions received from England. *See also* CHARTER COLONY, page 22; PROPRIETARY COLONY, page 28.

Significance   It was in the royal colonies that much of the resentment against the king grew, resulting in the Revolution. The royal governor, in particular, was the object of resentment and fear, and the first state constitutions reflected this by giving little authority to state governors. This tradition has lasted until recent times, but the current tendency is to strengthen executive power in the states.

Separation of Powers   A major principle of American government whereby power is distributed among three branches of government—the legislative, the executive, and the judicial. The officials of each branch are selected by different procedures, have different terms of office, and are independent of one another. The separation is not complete, in that each branch participates in the functions of the other through a system of checks and balances. The separation, however, serves to ensure that the same person or group will not make the law, enforce the law, and interpret and apply the law. *See also* CHECKS AND BALANCES, page 23.

Significance   The separation of lawmaking, law enforcement, and law interpretation is designed to prevent tyranny. It also serves to make the three branches responsive to different pressures. At the same time, the system frequently results in lack of unity between the legislative and executive branches, particularly when they are controlled by different parties. This fragmentation of power is a major factor in the operation of the American governmental system. The judiciary plays the critical role in maintaining the branches within their assigned powers.

Shays' Rebellion   An armed revolt by farmers in western Massachusetts in 1786-1787, seeking relief from debts and possible foreclosures of mortgages. Led by Daniel Shays, a Revolutionary War officer, the group prevented judges from hearing mortgage foreclosure cases and attempted to capture an arsenal. They were repelled by the state militia.

Significance   While its seriousness may be questioned, Shays' Rebellion is credited with being a major factor in the demand for a revision of the Articles of Confederation. The event highlighted the economic difficulties facing the states at that time and caused alarm among the creditor and commercial interests.

State Sovereignty   Independence of a state from external control. The concept of state sovereignty was an integral part of government under the Articles of Confederation and was part of the great debate on the Union that took place prior to the Civil War. In effect, state sovereignty is a rejection of the principle of national supremacy under the United States Constitution. *See also* STATES' RIGHTS, page 42.

Significance   The states of the Union were sovereign under the Articles of Confederation. Prior to the Civil War, it was claimed by southern states that the Constitution was a compact among states rather than among the people and that the states were free to secede. State sovereignty as a legal doctrine is rejected, although the states' rights political argument reappears from time to time, invoked by the opponents of expanding federal power.

Three-fifths Compromise   An agreement reached at the Constitutional Convention of 1787 to count only three-fifths of the slave population in determining representation in the House of Representatives and in apportioning direct taxes (Art. I, sec. 2).

Significance   At the Constitutional Convention, the issue of whether to count slaves for representation and tax purposes sharply divided the northern and southern delegates. The issue was essentially that of representation of property interests and the resultant compromise was one of many made at the convention. This provision of the Constitution is no longer pertinent.

Usage   A custom that, because it is well-established, is regarded as a part of the American constitutional system. Though not precisely provided for in the words of the Constitution, such practices form an important element of the actual operations of government. Among these are such vital components as the role of political parties, the operations of the Electoral College, the presidential Cabinet, and the inner organization of Congress.

Significance   Little can be learned about how American government works solely by a reading of the Constitution. Usage is one of the major methods by which the Constitution has been developed to meet practical problems. A full understanding of the American constitutional system requires a knowledge not only of the written document itself, but also of the various usages. A well-established usage becomes part of the "unwritten constitution" and may have the same effect as, or greater than, an actual constitutional amendment.

Virginia Plan A plan, submitted by Edmund Randolph of Virginia to the Constitutional Convention of 1787, that called for scrapping the Articles of Confederation and establishing a new and strong national government. It provided for a two-house legislature based on state population or wealth, a national executive, and a judiciary. Congress would have had power to disallow state legislation and was to be invested with broad power over matters of national concern. *See also* NEW JERSEY PLAN, page 27.

Significance The Virginia Plan served as the major basis for discussion in the convention. Once a compromise over representation (equal representation in one house) that satisfied the small states was reached, the delegates proceeded to draft a constitution as envisaged by the Virginia Plan. A strong central government was established with power to act directly on individuals rather than through the states.

IMPORTANT CASES

Coleman v. Miller, 307 U.S. 433 (1939): A case establishing the principle that the process of amending the Constitution is essentially political in nature and not subject to judicial interference. Specifically, the Supreme Court held that a state legislature may ratify the child labor amendment proposal after once rejecting it, and that whether the pending proposal was still valid after many years is a political question for Congress to determine. *See also* AMENDMENT, page 21.

Significance No case involving the amending clause of the Constitution has come before the Supreme Court since *Coleman v. Miller.* The decision has had the effect of removing the Court from involvement in the amending process, leaving Article V to the political branches of the government.

IMPORTANT STATUTES

Northwest Ordinance An enactment of the Congress under the Articles of Confederation providing for the government of the territory north of the Ohio River and west of New York to the Mississippi River. The Ordinance provided for the eventual statehood of areas of the territory when they acquired 60,000 inhabitants. Liberal provision was made for local self-government, civil and political rights, and education. Slavery was forbidden in the territory. A previous ordinance of 1785, establishing the township system of dividing land and providing for local schools, was reaffirmed in the Ordinance of 1787.

Significance The Northwest Ordinance was the most significant measure passed by the Confederation Congress. It was readopted by Congress under the Constitution and served as the basis for later territorial acts. It established the important policy that territories were not to be kept in subjection but were to be developed for admission to statehood on an equal footing with other states.

3   The Federal Union

Admission of New States   The Constitution empowers Congress to admit new states to the Union (Art. IV, sec. 3). Limitations on this power are that no state may be created within an existing state, nor may any state be formed by the union of two or more states or parts of states without the consent of the states concerned and of Congress. The usual procedure for admission is (1) the people of the territory through their territorial assembly petition Congress; (2) Congress passes an "enabling act" that, when signed by the President, authorizes the territory to frame a constitution; (3) Congress passes an act of admission approved by the President. Though Congress and the President may insist upon certain conditions for admission to the Union, a state, once admitted, is equal with all other states. No state may constitutionally withdraw from the Union. *See also Coyle v. Smith,* page 44; ENABLING ACT, page 34; TERRITORY, page 42

Significance   The Founding Fathers recognized the desirability of expanding the federal Union by giving Congress power to admit new states. Political considerations, such as which political party the people of the area are likely to support, may influence the majority party in Congress. With the exception of the thirteen original states, thirty were elevated from territorial status; five (Vermont, Kentucky, Tennessee, Maine, and West Virginia) were formed by separation from other states; and two, Texas and California, were formed from an independent republic and by acquisition from Mexico, respectively.

Centralization   The tendency for political power and authority to gravitate from state governments to the national government. Though the functions performed by all governments in the United States have increased, the nationwide impact of economic, social, and defense problems has led to an increased assumption of responsibility by the national government.

Significance   The proper division of powers between the national and state governments has been a cause for controversy throughout American history. It is argued that centralization permits more efficient handling of problems that are nationwide in scope. Opponents contend that decentralized activity prevents tyranny, permits experimentation, and encourages local solutions to problems. Various groups tend to support the management of a function by that level of government most responsive to their needs.

Commerce Power   The authority delegated to Congress by the Constitution (Art. 1, sec. 8) to regulate commerce with foreign nations and among the states. The term "commerce" has been interpreted to include the production and buying and selling of goods as well as the transportation of commodities. Any of these functions are subject to national regulation and control if they affect more than one state. *See also* COMMERCE, page 306; *Gibbons v. Ogden,* page 327.

Significance   The commerce power is one of the major constitutional provisions used by Congress to expand national power. A broad interpretation of what constitutes interstate commerce has enabled Congress to regulate such matters as manufacturing, child labor, farm production, wages and hours, labor unions, civil rights, and criminal conduct. Any activity that in any way "affects" interstate commerce is subject to national rather than state control. So many functions are now interstate in character that the role of the states in the federal system has been considerably altered.

Concurrent Powers   Authority possessed by both the national and state governments. Examples include the powers to tax, maintain courts, and charter banks. The states exercise concurrently with the national government any power that is not exclusively conferred on the national government by the Constitution and that does not conflict with national law. *See also* DELEGATED POWERS, page 33; RESERVED POWERS, page 41.

Significance   Under the American federal system, it is essential that both national and state governments possess those powers necessary to enable them to function. The power to tax is a noteworthy example. The fact that this power is delegated to the national government does not mean that the states may not also tax. States frequently legislate in areas in which the national government has not, despite its power to do so, sought to legislate. Should the national government determine to occupy a particular field of activity delegated to it under the Constitution, then the principle of national supremacy prevails. In the regulation of interstate commerce, the national government has frequently allowed state control over some elements of such commerce. The Supreme Court has disallowed state action when it has determined that national uniformity is desirable.

Confederation   A league of independent states. A central government or administrative organ handles those matters of common concern delegated to it by the member states. The central unit may not make laws directly applicable to individuals without further action by its member units. The governments under the Articles of Confederation and the Confederate States of America are two examples from American history. The United Nations is often referred to as a confederation. *See also* ARTICLES OF CONFEDERATION, page 22; FEDERALISM, page 34; UNITARY STATE, page 43.

Significance   A confederation is generally distinguished from a federation in which, as in the United States, the central unit is invested with supreme authority and may act directly upon individuals. American experience under the Articles of Confederation is credited with being an essential step toward the formation of the "more perfect union." A confederated structure enables sovereign states to cooperate in seeking solutions to mutual problems without giving up their autonomy.

Cooperative Federalism A concept that views the states and the national government as cooperating partners in the performance of governmental functions rather than as antagonistic competitors for power. The grant-in-aid programs typify this relationship between the national and state governments. *See also* CREATIVE FEDERALISM, page 33; GRANT-IN-AID, page 35; REGIONAL DEVELOPMENT AGENCIES, page 352.

Significance Many current problems cut across traditional divisions of authority between the national and state governments. Cooperation between these units to meet common problems has enabled American federalism to adjust to new problems and to find some middle ground between extreme centralization of power and unworkable decentralization. For example, a vast interstate highway system would be unlikely without national and state cooperation.

Creative Federalism A term coined by the Johnson Administration during the 1960s emphasizing joint and mutual decision making as the basis for the planning and management of intergovernmental programs. Creative federalism goes beyond cooperative federalism in that in addition to furnishing funds to state and local units, federal officials consult directly with state and local officials in implementing plans and programs. In addition, creative federalism looks toward the reinvigoration of local responsibility by providing block grants or revenue-sharing programs to state and local units with few, if any, strings attached. *See also* GRANT-IN-AID, page 35; REVENUE SHARING, page 293.

Significance The regional and nationwide nature of most economic and social problems facing the United States has threatened the vitality of the federal system. Increased use of conditional grants by the national government has reduced state and local governments to administrative units for major programs. Recent innovations designed to restore local initiative and responsibility include block grants to states for law enforcement and various housing and urban development programs which require extensive local participation. Proposals for broad-scale revenue sharing of federal taxes with state and local governments have received extensive attention in recent years.

Delegated Powers Powers granted to the national government under the Constitution. Generally, the delegated powers are those found enumerated in the first three articles of the Constitution, relative to the legislative, executive, and judicial branches of the national government. Article I, section 8 contains the main compilation of these powers. The terms "delegated," "enumerated," "granted," and "specific" may be used interchangeably. *See also* IMPLIED POWERS, page 36; RESERVED POWERS, page 41.

Significance Under American federalism, the national government is one of delegated powers. With the exception of foreign affairs, it must find justification for its actions in a specifically authorized power, or in one that can be reasonably implied from those specifically authorized. The national government does not possess unlimited or general governmental power but only such power as is given to it in the Constitution.

District of Columbia The seat of the government of the United States of America, commonly called Washington, D.C. It consists of some seventy square miles of land carved out of the state of Maryland. Article I, section 8 of the Constitution grants Congress exclusive control over the nation's capital city. Until 1974, the District was managed by officials appointed by the President with the consent of the Senate, and Congress acted as the city council. In 1974 the voters of the District approved a charter proposed by Congress providing for the election of a mayor and a thirteen-member city council. Congress, however, retains power to rescind council actions. Funds for the District are secured largely through local taxation. The District is a highly urbanized area of about one million inhabitants. Under the Twenty-third Amendment to the Constitution adopted in 1961, residents of the District may vote in presidential elections. Legislation enacted by Congress in 1968 authorized the District's first elected school board. In 1970 Congress granted the District a nonvoting delegate in the House of Representatives and established a local court system.

Significance The modified home rule acquired in 1974 was the culmination of many years of effort to secure self-government for the people of the District of Columbia. Major obstacles included the inability of Congress to agree on a scheme of government and opposition from those concerned that a large portion of the residents are black. Critics, however, pointed to the great amount of time devoted by Congress to affairs of the District. Even with home rule, some measure of congressional control is essential under the Constitution.

Enabling Act An act of Congress authorizing the people of a territory to take the necessary steps to prepare for statehood. This would include calling a convention to frame a constitution. *See also* ADMISSION OF NEW STATES, page 31.

Significance The enabling act constitutes an official indication that Congress and the President look with favor upon a territory's petition for statehood. Congress and the President are vested with considerable authority over what areas and under what conditions statehood will be granted. They must still approve the territory's constitution before officially granting statehood. On occasion, such as in the case of Alaska, a state has bypassed the petition and enabling act steps and has gone directly to Congress with its proposed constitution.

Exclusive Powers Those powers that, under the Constitution, belong exclusively to, and may be exercised only by, either the national government or the governments of the various states. An example of an exclusive national power is that over foreign affairs; an exclusive state power is control over local government. *See also* CONCURRENT POWERS, page 32.

Significance The concept of exclusive power emphasizes the federal nature of the United States—two governments, existing side by side, each supreme within its own sphere of authority. Many problem areas, once considered within the exclusive realm of state power, have, however, under changing social conditions, fallen under national control. Civil rights and welfare programs illustrate how the national government has moved into fields previously under exclusive state control.

Federalism A system of government in which power is divided by a written constitution between a central government and regional or subdivisional governments. Both governments act directly upon the people through their officials and laws. Both are supreme within their proper sphere of authority. Both must consent to constitutional change. By contrast, a "unitary" system of government is one in which the central government is supreme and in which regional and local governments derive their authority from the central government. Federal systems are found in the United States, Canada, Switzerland, Mexico, Australia, India, and West Germany, among others. In the United States, the term "federal government" is used as a synonym for the national government. *See also* CONFEDERATION, page 32; UNITARY STATE, page 43.

Significance Federalism is a compromise between an extreme concentration of power and a loose confederation of independent states for governing a variety of people, usually in a large expanse of territory. At the Constitutional Convention of 1787, this compromise was essential in order to convince the independent states to join together. Federalism has the virtue of retaining local pride, traditions, and power, while making possible a central government that can handle common problems. In the United States, federalism has facilitated growth through the admittance of new states to the Union. The basic principle of American federalism is fixed in the Tenth Amendment to the Constitution, which provides that the national government is to have those powers delegated in the Constitution with all other powers reserved to the states. In some countries using the federal system (for example, in Canada), the pattern is reversed, with the regional governments possessing only delegated authority. Federalism is one of the major principles underlying the American Constitution and has a continuing impact upon American life and politics.

Full Faith and Credit One of the obligations of each state in its relations with other states. Article IV, section 1, of the Constitution provides that "Full faith and credit shall be given in each state to the public acts, records, and judicial proceedings of every other state." The clause applies to civil but not criminal proceedings. It ensures that rights established under wills, contracts, deeds, and other property rights will be honored in all states. A judicial decision in one state will be honored and enforced in all states. One area of difficulty has arisen with regard to divorce decrees. Some states have refused to recognize uncontested divorces granted by sister states because of questions over domicile (*Williams v. North Carolina,* 325 U.S. 226 [1945]). *See also* HORIZONTAL FEDERALISM, page 36.

Significance This clause was originally put into the Articles of Confederation to promote "mutual friendship and intercourse among the people of the different states in this Union." It was carried over to the Constitution and has contributed to the unity of the American people. It protects the legal rights of citizens as they move about the various states and prevents evasion of legal responsibilities. The increasing mobility of the American people and the expanse of business operations have increased the importance of the clause.

Grant-in-Aid Funds made available by Congress to the state and local governments for expenditure in accordance with prescribed standards and conditions. State legislatures also make such grants to local governments. Some measure of supervision over the expenditure of the funds accompanies the grants. In addition, the receiving government is required to match the contribution dollar-for-dollar or in some other ratio. Highways, airports, agriculture, education, welfare, and health are among the major functions financed through the grant-in-aid device. *See also* COOPERATIVE FEDERALISM, page 33; FEDERAL AID HIGHWAY ACT, page 46; *Massachusetts v. Mellon,* page 45; REVENUE SHARING, page 293.

Significance Extensive use is being made of grants-in-aid to make available the superior tax resources of the national government for financing activities administered by the state and local governments. It has enabled the national government to enter fields formerly considered to be within the reserved powers of the states. The states have accepted some national control because they need federal funds. Often, because state governments have been unwilling or unable to deal with pressing problems, people have turned to Washington for help. In recent years this has also been true in local areas. This has enabled all sections of the country to benefit from governmental services that otherwise might be available only in wealthier states. In addition, states have been stimulated to undertake needed activities and improve their administrative and technical standards. The major disadvantage of the grant-in-aid system is that it transfers policy-making authority to the national government in areas formerly handled by state and local governments. The system, however, represents an alternative to extreme centralization of the administration of services.

Horizontal Federalism The relationships among the states of the Union either imposed by the Constitution or undertaken voluntarily. This term is used to distinguish state-state relations from national-state relations (denoted by the term "vertical federalism"). Requirements imposed by the Constitution are that each state afford full faith and credit to the public acts, records, and judicial proceedings of other states, grant the citizens of each state the privileges and immunities of citizens of their own state, and return fugitives from justice. Voluntary arrangements include interstate compacts, uniform laws, reciprocal agreements, and cooperation through consultation. *See also* FULL FAITH AND CREDIT, page 35; INTERSTATE COMPACT, page 38; INTERSTATE RENDITION, page 38; PRIVILEGES AND IMMUNITIES, page 40; UNIFORM STATE LAWS, page 453.

Significance Under federalism, the relationships among the states may be of equal importance to the relationship between the national and state governments. Since each state retains a good deal of authority, certain requirements have been laid down to assure cooperation. The requirement of full faith and credit, for example, helps to guarantee legal rights of citizens throughout the country. The states have sought to forestall national intervention into problem areas that cross state lines by entering into voluntary agreements. States have not, however, shown sufficient initiative in meeting mutual problems, which results in increasing dependence by the people upon the national government.

Implied Powers Authority possessed by the national government by inference from those powers delegated to it in the Constitution. For example, the power to draft men into the armed forces may be deduced from the power delegated to raise armies and navies. The implied power concept derives from the "necessary and proper" clause in Article I, section 8, which empowers the national government to do all things necessary and proper to carry out its delegated powers. This principle was officially enunciated by the Supreme Court in *McCulloch v. Maryland,* 4 Wheaton 316 (1819). *See also* CONSTITUTIONAL CONSTRUCTION, page 24; *McCulloch v. Maryland,* page 45; NECESSARY AND PROPER CLAUSE, page 39.

Significance In the early days of the Union, conflicting opinions arose over whether the national government was limited to exercising only those powers expressly delegated to it in the Constitution. It is unlikely that the national government could have emerged as a powerful force had the more limited view prevailed. Through the use of implied powers, the national government has been able to strengthen and broaden the scope of its authority to meet many problems unforeseen by the framers.

Inherent Powers　Authority vested in the national government, particularly in the area of foreign affairs, that does not depend upon any specific grant of power in the Constitution. Inherent powers derive from the fact that the United States is a sovereign power among nations. The Supreme Court has pointed out that even if the Constitution made no mention of it, the national government could still, for example, make international agreements or acquire territory. Whether or not the President has inherent powers to meet emergencies in internal affairs by virtue of his position as chief executive, is a matter of dispute. *See also* INHERENT POWERS, page 393; *United States v. Curtiss-Wright Export Corp.,* page 414; *Youngstown Sheet and Tube Co. v. Sawyer,* page 217.

Significance　Since the national government is one of delegated powers, justification for its actions must be found either directly or by implication from a specific grant of power. In the field of international affairs, however, the United States must be presumed to have the same power as any other nation in the world. Many Presidents have taken unauthorized action to meet emergency situations, notably Abraham Lincoln during the Civil War. However, in 1952, during the Korean conflict, the Supreme Court ruled that the President could not seize private property (steel mills) without authorization from Congress (*Youngstown Sheet and Tube Co. v. Sawyer,* 343 U.S. 579).

Intergovernmental Tax Immunity　The exemption of state and national governmental agencies and property from taxation by each other. The doctrine of intergovernmental tax immunity had its origin in the case of *McCulloch v. Maryland,* 4 Wheaton 316 (1819), in which the Supreme Court declared that the states may not burden the national government by the taxation of its agents or functions. This doctrine was later extended to national taxation of state agents and functions. For a time, even the salaries of governmental employees and contractors were exempt from taxation; this is no longer the case. National governmental functions and properties are exempt from state taxation, but where hardship may result, because of extensive federal holdings in a state, payments in lieu of taxes may be authorized by Congress. State or local activities may be taxed by the national government if the function is nongovernmental in character. An example of this is national taxation of state-owned liquor stores. *See also* Graves *v. New York,* page 44; *McCulloch v. Maryland,* page 45; PROPRIETARY FUNCTION, page 314; *South Carolina v. United States,* page 301.

Significance　Intergovernmental tax immunity prevents undue interference by one government with the proper exercise of power by another government. This rule is essential to the effective operation of a federal system of government. Without such a rule, one level of government might use its tax power to weaken or destroy operations of the other. National taxation of state nongovernmental functions remains a matter of controversy, since it is questionable whether any state or local activity can be classified as nongovernmental in character. The courts have been reluctant to interfere with congressional judgment on this matter.

Interposition   A concept that holds that a state may place itself between its citizens and the national government so as to prevent the enforcement of national law upon its citizens. According to this doctrine, each state may be the judge of the legality or constitutionality of national action, and may "interpose" its sovereignty to nullify federal action. This theory was propounded by Thomas Jefferson and James Madison in the Kentucky and Virginia resolutions of 1799 protesting the Alien and Sedition Acts, and by the South prior to the Civil War. Southern leaders reactivated the theory in the 1950s in opposition to the desegregation rulings of the Supreme Court. The federal courts, however, have rejected the doctrine as contrary to the national supremacy clause of Article VI. *See also* NULLIFICATION, page 39.

Significance   Interposition represents a challenge to national supremacy in an extreme form. Obviously, fifty different interpretations of the Constitution would dissolve the Union. From time to time, the right to interpose state sovereignty has been claimed by states in all sections of the country. This claim of state sovereignty has generally been made to cover up underlying social and economic interests of particular groups that feel themselves threatened by national policy. When interposition is invoked, it is a sign that the federal principle is under strain.

Interstate Compact   An agreement between two or more states. The Constitution (Art. I, sec. 10) requires such agreements or compacts to have the consent of Congress. Many agreements on minor matters, however, are made without such consent. Generally, any compact that tends to increase the power of the contracting states relative to other states or to the national government requires consent. One of the earliest and best-known compacts was concluded between New York and New Jersey, in 1921, to establish the Port of New York Authority for purposes of regulating the New York harbor and other facilities. A great variety of other compacts are in existence covering a wide range of subjects from flood control to petroleum conservation. Congress has, at times, granted advance blanket approval to certain kinds of compacts, as in civil defense matters and water pollution. *See also* HORIZONTAL FEDERALISM, page 36; *Virginia v. Tennesee,* page 45.

Significance   One intent of the requirement that congressional consent be acquired for interstate compacts was to prevent the states from threatening the Union through alliances among themselves. Today, interstate compacts serve as means for the states to solve regional problems without resort to national aid. In this way the states may avoid the centralizing tendencies of recent years.

Interstate Rendition   The return of a fugitive from justice by a state upon the demand of the executive authority of the state in which the crime was committed. This is one of the obligations imposed upon the states by Article IV, section 2. Though the language of the Constitution is positive on this obligation, the federal courts will not order the governor of one state to deliver a fugitive wanted in another state. Compliance by a governor is viewed as a moral duty. Rendition is routinely followed in most cases but, on occasion, a governor has refused to comply. Refusal may be based on such grounds as the good behavior of the fugitive since his escape, the suspicion that a fair trial will not be granted, or for political or other reasons known only to the governor. Congress has supplemented the requirement by making it a federal crime to flee across state lines to avoid prosecution for certain felonies. When apprehended by federal agents, the fugitive is usually turned over to the state from which he fled. The term "extradition" is used to describe this practice among nations under international law. *See also* EXTRADITION, page 390; HORIZONTAL FEDERALISM, page 36; *Kentucky v. Dennison,* page 44.

Significance The practice of rendition is designed to prevent an accused person from escaping prosecution by leaving a state. Although the governor may refuse to return the fugitive, he may invite retaliation of the other state by such action. Considerable doubt exists as to whether Congress could compel a governor to return a fugitive, despite a Supreme Court decision suggesting that this could not be done (*Kentucky v. Dennison,* 24 Howard 66 [1861]).

National Supremacy A basic constitutional principle of American government that asserts the superiority of national law. This principle is rooted in Article VI, (the "Kingpin Clause"), which provides that the Constitution, laws passed by the national government under its constitutional powers, and all treaties are the supreme laws of the land. The Article requires that all national and state officers and judges be bound by oath to support the Constitution regardless of any state constitutional or legislative provisions. Thus, any legitimate exercise of national power supersedes any conflicting state action. Determination of whether such a conflict exists rests in the hands of the judiciary, with the final decisions made by the Supreme Court. *See also Cohens v. Virginia,* page 268; *McCulloch v. Maryland,* page 45.

Significance National supremacy is crucial to the successful operation of the federal system. The national government is the government of all the people; a state speaks for only some of the people. The application of the principle of national supremacy has been a source of constant conflict, with such extreme results as the Civil War. The major *legal* challenge to national supremacy was expounded by the Supreme Court in the concept of "dual federalism," which held that a grant of authority to the national government does not destroy local power reserved to the states. Since 1937, the Court has rejected this concept and applied a broad construction of national authority.

Necessary and Proper Clause The final paragraph of Article I, section 8, of the Constitution, which delegates legislative powers to Congress. It authorizes all laws "necessary and proper" to carry out the enumerated powers. This clause, sometimes called the "elastic" clause, was used by the Supreme Court in *McCulloch v. Maryland,* 4 Wheaton 316 (1819), to develop the concept of "implied powers." *See also* DELEGATED POWERS, page 33; IMPLIED POWERS, page 36; *McCulloch v. Maryland,* page 45.

Significance Congressional authority is limited to its delegated powers. The necessary and proper clause, however, allows Congress to choose the *means* by which it will execute its authority. Broad construction of this phrase has enabled the national government to adapt its powers to the needs of the times. It has given elasticity to our constitutional system and has reduced the need for frequent constitutional amendment.

Nullification A declaration by a state that a national law is null and void, and therefore not binding upon its citizens. South Carolina, in 1832, attempted to nullify the Tariff Acts of 1828 and 1832. The theory of nullification, a logical extension of the theory of interposition, was formulated by John C. Calhoun. The theory holds that the Union is a compact among sovereign states and that the national government is not the final judge of its own powers; a state may nullify any national law and even secede from the Union. *See also* INTERPOSITION, page 38.

Significance Although nullification is a discredited theory, racial segregation problems gave rise to nullification talk by some southern leaders during the 1950s and 1960s. The Supreme Court nas rejected the theory as contrary to the principle of national supremacy. Nevertheless, some states have continued to thwart the national government's efforts to achieve full desegregation.

Police Power   Authority to promote and safeguard the health, morals, safety, and welfare of the people. In the context of the American federal system, police power is reserved to the states. The national government, exercising only delegated powers, does not possess a general police power. Many national laws enacted under the commerce and postal powers, such as those which prohibit shipment of impure drugs in interstate commerce or mailing of obscene literature, are, however, examples of what may be termed "federal police power." State laws enacted under the police power may legally invade national jurisdiction if such laws are pertinent to the health, safety, or welfare of the people of the state, such as a state law regulating grade crossings for interstate trains. *See also* POLICE POWER, page 76; RESERVED POWERS, page 41.

Significance Police powers, in recognition of the responsibility of state government to safeguard individual well-being, are the most vital powers reserved to the states under the Constitution. The judiciary plays a large role in determining the proper scope for the exercise of police power. The police power enlarges the area of state and local control over the individual.

Privileges and Immunities   Special rights and exemptions provided by law. The Constitution contains two clauses that use the term "privileges and immunities." Article IV, section 2, provides that, "The citizens of each state shall be entitled to all privileges and immunities of citizens in the several states." The Fourteenth Amendment provides that, "No state shall make or enforce any law which shall abridge the privileges or immunities of citizens of the United States." The first provision is considered to be an instrument of federalism, one of the obligations of states in their relations with each other. Basically, it means that a citizen of one state is not to be treated as an alien when in another state; he may not be discriminated against by denial of such privileges and immunities as legal protection, access to courts, travel rights, or property rights. Out-of-state residents, however, may be denied certain political rights, such as voting, or other privileges reserved to that state's residents, such as lower tuition at state universities. The full and precise meaning of the term has never been established by the courts. The Fourteenth Amendment's privileges and immunities clause has, similarly, not received complete definition. It is basically an instrument of civil liberties, placing certain restrictions upon each state in its dealings with United States citizens. The clause has been interpreted to apply only to those privileges that apply to the individual by virtue of his national citizenship (*Slaughterhouse Cases*, 16 Wallace 36 [1873]). These include the rights to travel, to have access to national officials, and to engage in interstate and foreign commerce. As interpreted, the clause confers no new rights upon citizens nor does it affect the citizen in those privileges that he enjoys by virtue of his state citizenship.

Significance Neither of these clauses has proved to be of great importance in American history. The narrow interpretation given by the courts to the Fourteenth Amendment has disappointed those who saw in it a boon to Negro rights after the Civil War. Article IV has served, in part, to strengthen economic and social ties among the people of the various states, but its use has been limited, due to the vagueness of language, and uncertain judicial interpretation.

Regionalism A method of decentralizing power on a geographical basis. In the United States, regionalism is often proposed as an alternative or supplement to the states. For example, the country could be divided into nine or ten regional subdivisions instead of into fifty states. The term is also applied to regional administration of federal projects, such as the Tennessee Valley Authority, and to regional interstate compacts.

Significance Advocates of regionalism argue that since the states do not reflect realistic economic and social patterns, they should be united into regions having genuine unity, such as the Missouri Valley area and New England. People of the United States tend to take a regional or sectional rather than a state outlook on many problems. The strong tradition and constitutional power of the individual states make their elimination unlikely, but states are increasingly acting together to meet common problems.

Republican Form of Government A government that operates through elected representatives of the people. It is generally distinguished from a pure democracy in which the people govern directly. Article IV, section 4 of the Constitution, known as the "guarantee clause," provides that the national government shall guarantee to each state a republican form of government. The precise meaning of the guarantee clause has never been determined; the Supreme Court has held this to be a "political question" to be answered by Congress or the President. *See also Luther v. Borden,* page 44; *Pacific States Telephone and Telegraph Co. v. Oregon,* page 194.

Significance A state government is considered to be republican in form if the houses of Congress accept the elected representatives of the state. In addition, the President could conceivably use the armed forces to dispossess a state government considered by him to be other than republican in form. This guarantee is classified by political scientists as one of the obligations of the national government toward the states in maintaining the federal system. State citizens are thereby protected against arbitrary seizure of power of state government and abuse of state electoral systems.

Reserved Powers Powers of state governments under the American federal system. The states retain all powers not delegated to the national government, or prohibited to them, by the Constitution. These powers are frequently referred to as "residuary." It is not possible to make a definitive list of state powers since, in the very nature of the federal system, the states may exercise any power that is not delegated to the national government. This usually includes authority over internal affairs of the state and general police power over the health, safety, morals, and welfare of the people. State constitutions may place specific restrictions upon state powers. *See also* DELEGATED POWERS, page 33.

Significance The division of authority between national and state governments is a basic principle of American federalism. The concept that certain powers are "reserved" to the states is stated in the Tenth Amendment. Exactly what constitutes a reserved power is often a matter of dispute. With problems continuously changing in scope, a power formerly exercised by a state may fall under national control. This is particularly true in matters of commerce, as these increasingly become interstate in character. The judiciary is frequently called upon to determine the proper division of authority between the nation and the states.

Resulting Powers   Powers of the national government derived from a combination of delegated or implied powers; hence, powers that "result" from a number of powers, rather than inferred from one of the delegated powers. *See also Legal Tender Cases,* page 300.

Significance   Resulting powers are an extension of the implied powers doctrine. They make possible an exercise of national power that logically follows from a series of granted powers. For example, the United States Criminal Code provides that the violation of any national law is subject to punishment. The Constitution does not explicitly delegate this power, nor is it implied by any single grant of power. Rather, it "results" from the aggregate of power delegated to the national government.

States' Rights   A term used to connote opposition to increasing the national government's power at the expense of that of the states. States' rights adherents call for an interpretation of the Constitution that would place limits on the federal assumption of implied powers and give expanded interpretation to the reserved powers of the states. *See also* STATE SOVEREIGNTY, page 29.

Significance   Strong support for states' rights usually comes from those groups who feel that their particular interest will be better served b state than by national action. Though the term is common in American political life, it has rarely been used with consistency. For example, southern politicians who oppose national action in the field of civil rights actively seek federal grants-in-aid for state projects. The proper balance between national and state power is a continuing American problem under the federal system. The balance is usually determined by the strength of political forces rather than by the language of the Constitution.

Tenth Amendment   The final item of the Bill of Rights in the Constitution, which defines the principle of American federalism: "The powers not delegated to the United States by the Constitution, nor prohibited by it to the states, are reserved to the states respectively, or to the people." *See also* FEDERALISM, page 34.

Significance   The Tenth Amendment was added to the Constitution to make clear the position of the states in the Union. Although it was generally understood that the framers intended that the states would retain all powers not prohibited by the Constitution or delegated to the national government, the people insisted upon an express provision to that effect. Exactly what is meant by the phrase "or to the people" has never been determined.

Territory   An area belonging to the United States that is not included within any state of the Union. Though the Constitution does not expressly grant the power to acquire territory, Article IV, section 3, authorizes Congress to make rules respecting the territory of the United States. Power to acquire territory also results from the national government's power to make treaties, admit new states, and make war that might result in conquest. The District of Columbia, though not a part of any state, is not considered a territory. Major territorial possessions of the United States now include Guam, Puerto Rico, the Panama Canal Zone, Samoa, the Virgin Islands, and the Territory of the Pacific Islands. The Department of the Interior supervises the territories except for the Panama Canal Zone, which is presently under the Department of the Army. *See also* ADMISSION OF NEW STATES, page 31; RESIDENT COMMISSIONER, page 183.

Significance Most of the territory acquired by the United States through purchase, conquest, or treaty has eventually become part of the United States. Current possessions are important mainly for strategic reasons. The United States has rarely used its territories as "colonies" to be exploited. Rather, inhabitants have been trained for self-government and given independence (the Philippines) or statehood (Hawaii). Residents of Guam, Puerto Rico, and the Virgin Islands are citizens of the United States. Samoans are nationals of the United States. Puerto Rico holds the status of a free commonwealth associated with the United States, a relationship also offered to the Pacific Islands. Negotiations are underway, which will eventually give Panama control over the Canal Zone.

Twenty-first Amendment An amendment to the Constitution, adopted in 1933, permitting the sale of intoxicating beverages in the United States. The Amendment protects states that retain prohibition, by barring the importation or transportation of liquor into such states. It repealed the Eighteenth Amendment, which had imposed prohibition on the entire country.

Significance The Twenty-first is the only amendment that repeals a prior amendment. It is also the only one to have been ratified by conventions in the states rather than by state legislatures. By prohibiting the transportation of intoxicants into "dry" states, the Amendment lends national support to state laws. In a rare application of the Amendment, the Supreme Court held in 1972 that a state may ban obscene forms of entertainment in bars under the power given to states by the Twenty-first Amendment to regulate the importation and, therefore, the sale of liquor (*California v. LaRue,* 409 U.S. 109).

Unitary State A centralized government in which local or subdivisional governments exercise only those powers given to them by the central government. It differs from a federal system in which power is constitutionally divided between a central and subdivisional government. The United Kingdom and France are examples of the unitary form. In the United States, local governments, such as cities and counties, stand in a unitary relationship to the state governments that assign specific rights and duties to them. An exception to this is found in those states in which cities are given "home rule" by constitutional provision. *See also* FEDERALISM, page 34.

Significance A unitary system provides a unified and consistent administration of policy while at the same time permitting variations to be made by the central authority. It allows more efficient handling of nationwide problems and is more sensitive to national majorities. Opponents of unitary government claim that federalism is superior because it permits more experimentation in local government and greater freedom in meeting local needs.

IMPORTANT CASES

Coyle v. Smith, 221 U.S. 599 (1911): Established the principle that all states are admitted to the Union on an equal footing. Congress may not enforce conditions that would undermine the equality of the states. In this case, the Supreme Court upheld the right of Oklahoma to change its capital city contrary to a requirement in the congressional enabling act that preceded statehood. *See also* ADMISSION OF NEW STATES, page 31.

Significance Congress may stipulate any conditions it chooses for the admission of a state. Once admitted to the Union, a state may not be compelled to abide by any condition that would interfere with its right to manage its internal affairs or that would create different classes of states.

Graves v. New York ex rel. O'Keefe, 306 U.S. 466 (1939): Held that a state may tax the income of a federal employee and that such a tax does not impose an unconstitutional burden upon the national government. *See also* INTERGOVERNMENTAL TAX IMMUNITY, page 37; *McCulloch v. Maryland,* page 45.

Significance This was one of the last in a long line of cases that arose out of the decision in *McCulloch v. Maryland,* that a state may not tax an instrumentality of the federal government, since the power to tax is the power to destroy. This doctrine was carried to the point that neither the state nor the national government could tax each other in any way, including the salaries of their respective employees. In the *Graves* case, the Court reversed its position and sustained congressional authorization of state taxation of federal employees' incomes. Federal taxation of state employees had been upheld the previous year in *Helvering v. Gerhardt,* 304 U.S. 405 (1938).

Kentucky v. Dennison, 24 Howard 66 (1861): Decided that the constitutional duty of a governor to return a fugitive to the state from which he fled is only a moral obligation rather than a mandatory one. The Court found that a national statute of 1793 dealing with the return of fugitives provided no means by which a governor could be compelled to perform his duty and, in any case, that the national government lacked authority to coerce a state officer. *See also* INTERSTATE RENDITION, page 38.

Significance The *Kentucky* case enabled the Court to shun the difficult practical question of how a state governor could actually be compelled to perform his duty. Though the supremacy of the national government is clear in most national-state controversies, this decision has been respected by the national government and all states, thereby keeping interstate rendition a discretionary act for the governors.

Luther v. Borden, 7 Howard 1 (1848): Held that the question of whether a state has a republican form of government is a political and not a judicial question. The Supreme Court refused to define a republican form of government, holding that Congress and the President must decide. The case arose out of Dorr's Rebellion in Rhode Island in 1841, when rival groups claimed to be the true government of the state. *See also* REPUBLICAN FORM OF GOVERNMENT, page 41.

Significance The constitutional requirement that the national government guarantee each state a republican form of government will not be enforced by the courts. Congressional power to accept the state's representatives, and the President's power to use force to quell a rebellion are the means by which the guarantee is honored.

Massachusetts v. Mellon and Frothingham v. Mellon, 262 U.S. 447 (1923): Rejected claims by a state that the federal grant-in-aid program to protect the health of mothers and infants was an unconstitutional invasion of the reserved powers of the states guaranteed by the Tenth Amendment. In a companion case (*Frothingham v. Mellon*), the Court rejected the claim of Mrs. Frothingham that the grant-in-aid program would take her property under the guise of taxation. *See also Frothingham v. Mellon,* page 269.

Significance Three important rules were established by these two cases: (1) a state cannot validly seek to protect its citizens who are also citizens of the United States from the enforcement of federal laws; (2) a grant-in-aid system based on voluntary acceptance of programs by the states is a political and not a judicial question; (3) an individual taxpayer who cannot show suffering and injury different from that of the general taxpaying public has no standing in court to challenge the constitutionality of tax laws (Frothingham rule). Today, under this rule, it continues to be difficult for an individual to test the constitutionality of a tax law in the federal courts, unless he can demonstrate that Congress may have exceeded a specific limitation on its taxing power, such as taxing and spending funds to violate the separation between church and state (*Flast v. Cohen,* 389 U.S. 895 [1968]).

McCulloch v. Maryland, 4 Wheaton 316 (1819): Upheld, in a landmark decision of the Supreme Court, the power of the national government to establish a bank, and denied the state of Maryland the power to tax a branch of the bank. In the opinion by Chief Justice John Marshall, the Court held that it was not necessary for the Constitution expressly to authorize Congress to create a bank. Rather, the power to do so was implied from Congress' power over financial matters and from the "necessary and proper" clause of the Constitution. Maryland could not tax a legitimate instrumentality of the national government, said the Court, since this would be an invasion of national supremacy. "The power to tax involves the power to destroy. . . ." From this was derived the principle of intergovernmental tax immunity. *See also* IMPLIED POWERS, page 36; INTERGOVERNMENTAL TAX IMMUNITY, page 37.

Significance Two important principles of American government were firmly established by this decision: the doctrine of "implied powers," which has given the national government a vast source of power; the principle of "national supremacy," which denies to the states any right to interfere in the constitutional operations of the national government. Had the decision favored Maryland, the national government would not have been able to meet the problems of an expanding nation and the Constitution would not have become a "living" document.

Virginia v. Tennessee, 148 U.S. 503 (1893): Denied a suit brought by Virginia to void the boundary line between it and Tennessee on the ground that the line had been established by agreement between the states without the consent of Congress. The Court held that the agreement did not constitute a compact between the states that required the positive approval of Congress. The only compacts or agreements requiring approval are those that tend to increase state power at the expense of the national government. In other instances, Congress may give its approval by implication. *See also* INTERSTATE COMPACT, page 38.

Significance Although the Constitution prohibits states from entering into agreements or compacts without consent of Congress, this decision made it clear that the restriction did not apply to every agreement between states. This has made it possible for states to solve mutual problems without involving Congress. Yet Congress is always free to intervene if it feels that the agreement threatens the national government in any way.

IMPORTANT STATUTES

Federal Aid Highway Act   A major example of federal grants-in-aid to the states; the first such grant was given in 1916 for the building of highways. From this time, grants have been given for trunk roads, secondary roads, urban extensions of highways, and, since 1956, an extensive interstate highway system. The states must meet national requirements regarding matching funds, maintenance of roads, location, and engineering details. The 1956 Act provided for a thirteen-year program for the building of 41,000 miles of multilane highways connecting all major cities. In 1968 Congress authorized an additional 1500 miles. The national government is financing 90 percent of the cost. The program is administered by the Federal Highway Administration in the Department of Transportation.

Significance The Federal Aid Highway Act is a leading example of a successfully operated grant-in-aid. Through it, the national government has shaped state and local road policy, although it does not actually build the highways. Highway expenditures of state and local governments are exceeded only by expenditures for education. The grant-in-aid program has provided states with substantial revenue, but it has limited the discretion of the state and local authorities over a major function.

4 Immigration and Citizenship

Alien An individual who is neither a citizen nor a national of the state in which he is living. Aliens generally owe allegiance to a foreign power, but may acquire citizenship by following prescribed procedures. *See also* ALIEN REGISTRATION ACT, page 55; *Truax v. Raich,* page 54.

Significance In the United States, aliens enjoy many of the civil rights that the Constitution accords to "persons" as distinguished from citizens. These include most provisions of the Bill of Rights and freedom from arbitrary discrimination. Aliens are subject to the laws of the United States, must pay taxes, and may be drafted. Military service and other duties and rights of aliens are generally in accord with treaties between the United States and other nations. An alien who does not have permanent resident status can refuse to be drafted, but in so doing he forfeits his right ever to become a citizen. Under the laws of most American states, an alien may not engage in certain professions, own firearms, hold government employment, or, in some states, own real estate. However, the Supreme Court has taken a dim view of restrictions which deny aliens economic rights or opportunities. In no case may an alien enjoy such political rights as voting or holding public office. The most serious disability imposed upon an alien is the continuing possibility of deportation. Since an alien has no *right* to live in the United States, he may be deported for moral turpitude or for past or present affiliation with the Communist party. In time of war, aliens who are subjects of enemy states may be severely restricted. Under present law, all aliens must register with the Attorney General every year.

Citizen An individual who is a native or naturalized member of a state, owes allegiance to that state, and is entitled to the protection and privileges of its laws. Citizenship in the United States is defined in the Fourteenth Amendment to the Constitution: "All persons born or naturalized in the United States, and subject to the jurisdiction thereof, are citizens of the United States and of the state wherein they reside." Citizenship is based mainly on one's place of birth (*jus soli*) but may be acquired through naturalization and, under circumstances defined by Congress, through blood relation (*jus sanguinis*). *See also Jus Sanguinis,* page 50; *Jus Soli,* page 50; NATIONAL, page 50; *United States v. Wong Kim Ark,* page 55.

Significance Two basic problems were raised prior to the Civil War: (1) Should Negroes born in the United States be considered citizens? (2) Is state citizenship secondary and incidental to national citizenship? The Fourteenth Amendment provides affirmative answers to both questions.

47

Recent developments include the extension of citizenship by birth to American Indians and to the people of Guam, Puerto Rico, and the Virgin Islands. Prior to 1922, a married woman took the citizenship of her husband, but under the Cable Act of 1922 women are treated the same as men, with the exception that an alien woman marrying an American citizen may be naturalized after a shorter period of residence. Children of foreign diplomatic agents who are born here are not citizens, since they are not "subject to the jurisdiction" of the United States.

Denaturalization   The revoking of citizenship that has been acquired by naturalization. This may be done only by court order in accordance with due process of law.

Significance   The most common ground for denaturalization is fraud or willful misrepresentation when being naturalized. Lengthy residence abroad by a naturalized citizen, once a ground for denaturalization, may no longer, under Supreme Court ruling, result in termination of citizenship (*Schneider v. Rusk*, 377 U.S. 163 [1964]). Recent legislation permits denaturalization of those who affiliate with subversive organizations within five years after naturalization, or those who are convicted of contempt of Congress for refusal to testify in an investigation into subversive activities within ten years after naturalization. Many observers charge that such provisions make "second-class" citizens of naturalized persons, since native-born citizens are not affected by such laws. A commonly held assumption, that one loses his citizenship when convicted of a serious crime, is not true. One may lose certain privileges of citizenship, such as the right to vote or hold certain jobs, but citizenship is retained.

Deportation   Compulsory expulsion of an alien from a state to his country of origin. Deportation is a civil, rather than a criminal, proceeding under American law; hence, various constitutional safeguards do not apply. With the exception of naturalized citizens who lose their citizenship, a citizen may not be deported. *See also Fong Yue Ting v. United States,* page 54.

Significance   Aliens remain in the United States at the sufferance of Congress, which has virtually unlimited power to establish grounds for deportation. Illegal entry is the most common cause of deportation, but in recent years Congress has considerably increased the number of grounds for deportation, particularly for Communists and other political undesirables and for aliens convicted of serious crimes. Constitutional safeguards with regard to bail and ex post facto laws, for example, do not apply to deportation proceedings, and great discretion is vested in the Attorney General. Many public officials and citizens have questioned the fairness of procedures used in deportation cases. The courts have been reluctant to interfere, since the issue involves the plenary powers of the national government in international affairs.

Dual Citizenship   Holding citizenship in two or more countries. This may occur because most countries recognize as citizens those born within their boundaries as well as children of their subjects born abroad. Thus, a person born abroad of American parents is an American citizen (*jus sanguinis*) and he may also be a citizen of the country in which he was born (*jus soli*).

Significance   Dual citizenship has become widespread because of increasing mobility. It may cause hardship when, for example, conflicting claims are made over the right to require military service. Under American law, a person who, after reaching the age of twenty-two, lives for three years in another country that also claims him as a citizen, forfeits his American citizenship unless he takes an oath of allegiance to the United States before a diplomatic official.

Expatriation Voluntary withdrawal of allegiance or residence from the country in which citizenship is held. Since 1865, Congress has expressly recognized the right of expatriation and has set forth specific grounds. Actions that constitute expatriation include: naturalization in a foreign state, taking an oath of allegiance to another state, serving in a foreign army without consent, taking a job open only to citizens of another state, and conviction of treason or attempt to overthrow the government by force. The Supreme Court has taken a dim view of expatriation laws, holding that citizenship is a constitutional right which can be given up only by a truly voluntary act. A citizen living abroad may voluntarily renounce his citizenship before a diplomatic officer but renunciation is permitted within the United States only during wartime with the consent of the Attorney General. *See also Afroyim v. Rusk,* page 53.

Significance Congress recognized the right of expatriation as a "natural and inherent right of all people," essential for the rights to life, liberty, and the pursuit of happiness. The major purpose of this declaration was to justify before the world the great number of people from foreign lands who were emigrating to the United States. The expatriation laws assume that the person committing certain acts, whether or not they intend them to be acts of expatriation, acted voluntarily and with full knowledge of the consequences. Supreme Court decisions, however, have declared unconstitutional several statutory provisions on expatriation, including: (1) leaving the United States to avoid military service (*Rusk v. Cort,* 372 U.S. 144 [1963]); (2) conviction for wartime desertion, a decision based on the ground that expatriation for desertion is cruel and unusual punishment (*Trop v. Dulles,* 356 U.S. 86 [1958]); and (3) voting in a foreign election (*Afroyim v. Rusk,* 387 U.S. 253 [1967]), since such acts do not necessarily indicate an intention to renounce citizenship.

Immigration Admittance of a person to a country of which he is not a native for the purpose of establishing permanent residence. Early attempts by seaboard states to regulate immigration into the United States were invalidated by the Supreme Court, which declared immigration as an exclusive function of the national government, incidental to its power over foreign affairs. Immigration into the United States was unlimited until 1882, when Congress began to impose restrictions on the admission of criminals, mentally ill or diseased persons, paupers, illiterates, the Chinese, anarchists, and advocates of violent governmental change. In 1924, Congress barred Asiatics and established the "national origins quota" system, which limited annual immigration and assigned a quota to each country based on the numerical contribution it had made to the national stock as of 1920. In 1952, Congress erased racial exclusions but retained the quota system and the annual limit. Restrictions against the admission of Communists or other suspected subversives were increased. In 1965, Congress abolished the national origins quota system and established a new annual limit of 170,000, with preference given to relatives of citizens and persons with special skills. Immigration from the Western Hemisphere was restricted (to 120,000) for the first time. Immigration laws are administered by the Departments of State and Justice, which have been given extensive discretion to determine who may enter the United States. *See also* IMMIGRATION ACT OF 1965, page 55; *The Passenger Cases,* page 54.

Significance More than 40 million people have come to the United States from all over the world. From time to time, Congress has relaxed quota restrictions by admitting large numbers of refugees and displaced persons from war-torn and iron curtain countries. Pressures for limiting immigration have come largely from labor organizations, from those who fear the introduction of alien ideologies, and from those who, though immigrants or descendants of immigrants themselves, look down upon new groups seeking admission. Criticisms of the quota system as discriminatory led to passage of the 1965 immigration law, which eliminates race and ancestry as the basis for immigration policy. Many continue to protest the red tape required for admission to the country and the vast discretion vested in immigration officials to deny entrance to aliens. The United States has, however, a proud record of achievement in absorbing millions of immigrants and, in turn, the nation has benefited immeasurably from the contributions of many people of varied backgrounds and talents.

Jus Sanguinis "Law of the blood"—a principle by which citizenship is determined by parentage rather than by place of birth (*jus soli*).

Significance The Fourteenth Amendment recognizes only birth and naturalization as bases for citizenship, but Congress has adopted the rule of *jus sanguinis* to apply in special circumstances. Thus, one may be a citizen of the United States if born abroad, provided that either or both of one's parents are citizens. If only one parent is a citizen, that parent must have lived in the United States or one of its possessions for ten years, five of them after the age of fourteen; and the child, in order to remain a citizen, must live in the United States continuously for five years between the ages of fourteen and twenty-eight. The latter provision was upheld by the Supreme Court as not violating the rights of a person claiming citizenship since the person was not born or naturalized in the United States (*Rogers v. Bellei,* 401 U.S. 815 [1971]).

Jus Soli "Law of the soil"—the basic rule under which American citizenship is determined by place of birth rather than by parentage (*jus sanguinis*). *See also United States v. Wong Kim Ark,* page 55.

Significance The Fourteenth Amendment's provision that all persons born in the United States are citizens (with minor exceptions, as for example, children born to foreign diplomats who are not under American jurisdiction) is far-reaching. Anyone born here is a citizen whether his parents are resident aliens or merely visitors. For purposes of citizenship, Congress has delcared that the soil of the United States includes Puerto Rico, Guam, and the Virgin Islands.

National A person who owes allegiance to a country, though not a citizen thereof. The term is used at times, however, in the same sense as the term "citizen." Under American law, a national is an inhabitant of an outlying possession of the United States to whom Congress has not granted citizenship. Residents of the Philippine Islands were considered nationals until independence was granted, whereas the people of Puerto Rico were granted citizenship in 1917 after a period as nationals. Residents of American Samoa are nationals.

Significance The term "national" is basically a concept of international law. American nationals are accorded most of the protections that citizens have, but the actual distinction is hazy. By granting the status of nationals to a people, Congress identifies them as belonging to and entitled to the protection of the United States, particularly for purposes of international relations.

Natural-born Citizen   A native of the United States. The term is used in Article II, section 1 of the Constitution, which stipulates that "No person except a natural-born citizen" may be President of the United States.

   Significance The language of Article II is the only place in the Constitution where a distinction is drawn between a natural-born and a naturalized citizen. Whether or not a person born abroad of American parents, and, therefore, a citizen under the rule of *jus sanguinis*, is eligible for the presidency has never been resolved. Although the Constitution makes no other distinctions between natural-born and naturalized citizens, the former cannot be denaturalized or deported.

Naturalization   The legal procedure by which an alien is admitted to citizenship. Congress is authorized by Article I, section 8 of the Constitution to establish uniform rules for naturalization. Naturalization may be individual or collective. Collective naturalization confers citizenship upon entire populations by statute or treaty as was done in the cases of Alaska, Hawaii, Texas, Puerto Rico, Guam, and the Virgin Islands. An individual over eighteen years of age may be naturalized after meeting certain qualifications. These include: (1) residence in the United States for five years; (2) ability to read, write, and speak English; (3) proof of good moral character; (4) knowledge of the history and attachment to the principles of American government; (5) neither advocacy of Communist or other subversive doctrine nor membership (unless involuntary) in any subversive or totalitarian organization; and (6) taking of an oath of allegiance to the United States and renunciation of allegiance to his former country. Detailed administration of naturalization is handled by the Immigration and Naturalization Service of the Department of Justice with final examination and administration of the oath by a judge of a federal court or a state court of record. The residence requirement is lowered for spouses of citizens and for aliens who serve in the armed forces. Minors become citizens when their parents are naturalized. *See also Girouard v. United States,* page 54.

   Significance Millions of people have met the requirements established by Congress and have become American citizens. Some critics maintain that efforts to measure moral standards and political views are not always fair, particularly during times of crises, since officials may abuse their discretion. Others, though not critical of the naturalization procedure itself, point out that a naturalized citizen is a "second-class" citizen, since he may lose his citizenship under conditions that would not affect the citizenship status of the native born. The procedure is designed, however, to foster the "Americanization" of the alien, many of whom become more knowledgeable and appreciative citizens than some of the native born. Through collective naturalization, the United States has demonstrated to the world its desire to give equal rights to all people under its control and, in some cases, to prepare them for eventual statehood.

Nonimmigrant   One who comes to the United States on a temporary basis. This includes visitors, seasonal workers, tradesmen, crewmen, students, members of the press, and accredited representatives of foreign nations. Nonimmigrants must meet many of the qualifications imposed upon regular immigrants.

Significance For a time, a good deal of controversy raged over the stringent red tape that visitors, many of whom were distinguished persons, had to face to enter the United States. This included many searching questions, delays in securing visas, and even fingerprinting. Some of these requirements have been relaxed, but rather close inspection continues. In 1974 the Supreme Court upheld the practice under which thousands of daily and seasonal commuters from Canada and Mexico work in the United States under a fictional classification as "immigrants lawfully admitted for permanent residence." (*Saxbe v. Bustos,* 419 U.S. 65).

Passport A certificate, issued by an official governmental agency, that identifies a person as a citizen of a country and authorizes him to travel abroad. Passports are granted to Americans by the Passport Office of the State Department, by territorial governors, and by diplomatic officials abroad.

Significance No American citizen may leave the country without a passport (except for trips to Canada, Mexico, and certain other nearby areas), and few countries will admit a traveler without a valid passport. A passport entitles a person to the privileges accorded travelers by international custom and various treaties. In 1958, the Supreme Court ruled that the Secretary of State could not deny a passport to a citizen because of his political beliefs or associations, without explicit authorization from Congress (*Kent v. Dulles,* 357 U.S. 116). The Court also struck down the section of the Internal Security Act of 1950 that forbids issuance of passports to members of Communist organizations, on the ground that such denial constitutes a violation of the right to travel (*Aptheker v. Secretary of State,* 378 U.S. 500 [1964]). The State Department has refused to issue passports for travel to Cuba, North Korea, and North Vietnam. The Supreme Court has upheld such limits on the right to travel if travel to such countries is likely to prove detrimental to the foreign policy interests of the United States (*Zemel v. Rusk,* 381 U.S. 1 [1965]). However, the Court later ruled that a person holding a valid passport is not guilty of a crime if he travels to a restricted area (*United States v. Laub,* 385 U.S. 475 [1967]).

Visa A permit to enter a country. Persons seeking admission to the United States must get a visa from a United States consul located abroad. Many countries require visas as well as passports. Visas are usually stamps of approval affixed to the passport by an official of the country to be visited or entered permanently.

Significance The visa procedure is an instrument of national policy that enables a country to screen applicants prior to their departure for that country. In the United States, before 1924, screening was done at ports of entry, causing great hardship to those rejected. Consular officers stationed abroad have unlimited discretion to grant or refuse visas, resulting in occasional charges of abuse of power.

IMPORTANT AGENCIES

Board of Immigration Appeals A board appointed by the Attorney General to hear appeals from decisions of the Immigration and Naturalization Service relative to the exclusion or deportation of aliens. *See also* DEPORTATION, page 48.

Significance Only on rare occasions will the courts hear appeals on immigration or deportation matters, since Congress has broad authority in these areas. Hence, for most aliens, the Board is the "court of last resort" on matters of entry or deportation.

Bureau of Security and Consular Affairs The part of the State Department that supervises the issuance of passports and visas. The Bureau was established by the Immigration and Nationality Act of 1952 and, under its supervision, consular agents abroad determine whether foreigners will be permitted to enter the United States. *See also* PASSPORT, page 52; VISA, page 52.

Significance Fear of Communist and other subversive elements has led to the extensive screening of applicants for visas to enter the United States. The decisions of consular officers are final.

Immigration and Naturalization Service The part of the Department of Justice that administers the laws regarding the admission, naturalization, and deportation of aliens. The Service investigates the credentials of immigrants at ports of entry. Immigration and Naturalization Service officers also patrol the Canadian and Mexican borders to prevent the illegal entry of aliens. Aliens seeking to become citizens are investigated by agents of the Service, who recommend to the courts whether or not the alien should be naturalized. *See also* IMMIGRATION, page 49; NATURALIZATION, page 51.

Significance Agents of the Immigration and Naturalization Service exercise considerable discretion in determining whether persons may enter the United States, become citizens, or be subject to deportation. Some critics have charged that the Service does not always follow fair procedures in reaching its decisions, particularly with regard to determining the character and political beliefs of aliens. Decisions of the Service may be appealed to the Board of Immigration Appeals in the Department of Justice.

IMPORTANT CASES

Afroyim v. Rusk, 387 U.S. 253 (1967): Declared unconstitutional a law providing that native-born citizens forfeit their citizenship by voting in a foreign election. The Court stressed that in the United States, where the people are sovereign, the citizen has a constitutional right to remain a citizen unless he voluntarily relinquishes it. *See also* EXPATRIATION, page 49.

Significance The Court had earlier upheld the law regarding voting in a foreign election on the ground that it was a matter of foreign affairs (*Perez v. Brownell,* 356 U.S. 44 [1958]). The *Afroyim* decision calls into question the validity of all laws on expatriation except for actual naturalization in a foreign state. Ordinarily, when a person expatriates himself, he becomes a citizen of another state, but American expatriation laws could leave a person stateless.

Fong Yue Ting v. United States, 149 U.S. 698 (1893): Supported the authority of the national government to deport aliens under its sovereign power in the field of international affairs. The Court upheld a federal law that authorized the deportation of Chinese laborers who had failed to get certificates of residence. Furthermore, the Court held that deportation is not criminal punishment and, therefore, does not require a judicial trial. *See also* DEPORTATION, page 48.

Significance The major points of the case, that Congress has full power to deport aliens and that such action is not considered to be punishment, remain basic to American law. While the Court has, in subsequent cases, demanded that basic elements of fairness or due process be observed in deportation proceedings, it has not insisted that a judicial trial is required.

Girouard v. United States, 328 U.S. 61 (1946): Established that an alien may be admitted to citizenship even if he refuses, on religious grounds, to swear that he will bear arms in defense of the United States. In this case, the Supreme Court reversed its earlier stand on this question and upheld Girouard's right to become a citizen since he was otherwise eligible and was willing to perform noncombatant duties. *See also* CONSCIENTIOUS OBJECTOR, page 63.

Significance In the Immigration and Nationality Act of 1952, Congress voiced its approval of the *Girouard* decision. The Act provides that conscientious objectors may be admitted to citizenship if they are willing to perform noncombatant service. It specifies that the exception applies only to persons who object to bearing arms on religious and not on general philosophical grounds.

The Passenger Cases, 7 Howard 283 (1849): Declared that immigration is the exclusive concern of the national government and not subject to state control. The seaboard states had sought to regulate the heavy flow of immigrants to their shores by levying a tax on ships carrying immigrants. *See also* IMMIGRATION, page 49.

Significance The *Passenger* decision helped to promote a uniform immigration policy prior to the great influx of immigrants in the late nineteenth and early twentieth centuries. It was not, however, until 1882 that the national government assumed the full responsibility of regulating immigration.

Truax v. Raich, 239 U.S. 33 (1915): Declared unconstitutional an Arizona law requiring that at least 80 percent of the employees of any private business must be citizens, as a denial of equal protection of the law. The Court held that a state may not deny a person the right to earn a living, regardless of his race or nationality. *See also* ALIEN, page 47.

Significance The *Truax* case and others that have followed it underscore the fact that an alien is entitled to most of the rights of a citizen, since the Constitution speaks of "persons" rather than citizens, with regard to most rights. Recent examples include the rulings in *Graham v. Richardson,* 403 U.S. 365 (1971), that states may not deny welfare benefits to resident aliens, *Sugarman v. Dougall,* 413 U.S. 634 (1973), that aliens may not be barred from civil service jobs, and *In Re Griffiths,* 413 U.S. 717 (1973), that aliens may not be denied admission to the bar.

United States v. Wong Kim Ark, 169 U.S. 649 (1898): Established that all persons born in the United States are citizens of the United States, even if the parents are aliens ineligible for citizenship. The only major exceptions are children born to foreign diplomats stationed here. The Court held that a Chinese person born in California who went to China for a visit could not be denied readmission to the United States. *See also Jus Soli,* page 50.

Significance The *Wong Kim Ark* case involved a major interpretation of the meaning of the Fourteenth Amendment, which confers citzenship upon "all persons" born in the United States and subject to its jurisdiction. The Court made it clear that citizenship by birth, regardless of parentage, is the basic rule of American citizenship.

IMPORTANT STATUTES

Alien Registration Act of 1940 (Smith Act) An act requiring the annual registration of all aliens over the age of fourteen. Aliens are required to be fingerprinted, to inform the government of their address, occupation, and other data, and to carry registration cards at all times. *See also* ALIEN REGISTRATION ACT, page 103.

Significance The Alien Registration Act is a major sedition law that makes it criminal to teach, advocate, or join an organization advocating violent overthrow of government. The alien registration requirement is designed to make it easier for the government to know the whereabouts of aliens who might prove dangerous in time of war.

Immigration Act of 1965 A major revision of American immigration policy that eliminated the national-origins quota system. Under the quota system, in effect since 1924, American immigration policy discriminated against Asians, Africans, and southern and eastern Europeans. The overall quota was set at less than 157,000 immigrants per year, with nearly 127,000 assigned to northern and western Europe. It was often criticized as racist in philosophy and as detrimental to the American international position. The 1965 law ended the quota system, established an annual limit of 170,000 immigrants (no more than 20,000 from one country), and gave preference to relatives of citizens and persons with special skills. For the first time, a limit (120,000) was placed on immigrants from the Western Hemisphere. *See also* IMMIGRATION, page 49.

Significance The Immigration Act of 1965 climaxed a forty year effort by ethnic groups to eliminate race and ancestry as bases of American immigration policy. The new law's stress on reuniting families and on admitting skilled persons regardless of ancestry reflects growing national concern with domestic racial problems and foreign policy considerations.

Immigration and Nationality Act of 1952 (McCarran-Walter Act)   A major revision and restatement of the immigration and citizenship policies of the United States. The Act maintained the quota system for immigration and placed restrictions upon the immigration and naturalization of Communists and other totalitarians. All racial barriers to immigration were eliminated by the Act, but Asians, Africans, and southern and eastern Europeans were assigned small quotas. (The Immigration Act of 1965, however, eliminated the quota system.) Communists or other persons advocating violent overthrow of the government are denied admission to the United States. Further, such persons residing in this country may not be naturalized, and citizenship may be taken from naturalized persons who join the Communist party or refuse to testify before a congressional committee investigating subversive activities. *See also* DENATURALIZATION, page 48; IMMIGRATION, page 49; NATURALIZATION, page 51.

Significance   The Immigration and Nationality Act of 1952 is a comprehensive collection of the immigration and citizenship laws of the United States. Most opponents of the Act protested its retention of a discriminatory immigration policy and its continuation of the policy of making naturalized citizens subject to loss of citizenship on grounds not applicable to native-born citizens. In 1965, Congress, in response to extensive ethnic group pressures and foreign policy considerations, eliminated the discriminatory national origins quota system. The Supreme Court has moved in the direction of ending the "second-class citizenship" of naturalized citizens.

5　Civil Liberties and Civil Rights

Academic Freedom　The principle that teachers and students have the right and the duty to pursue the search for truth wherever the inquiry may lead, free of political, religious, or other restrictions except those of accepted standards of scholarship. Important corollaries to the principle are that alleged violations of academic freedom will be investigated under procedures consonant with due process, and that the tenure of teachers will not depend upon adherence to any orthodoxy.

Significance　Academic freedom is not a constitutionally enforceable right, although it is commonly recognized as a major element of a free society. Academic freedom is continually under stress, its degree and nature varying with the political, religious, and social values of a community. Major contemporary problems of academic freedom involve the fear of communism and disloyalty, which result in loyalty oaths for teachers, investigations into school and college activities, and attempts to control the civil rights activities of teachers and students. The courts have been protective of the values underlying academic freedom and have resisted imposition of conditions that stifle the freedom to teach and learn.

Acquittal　Formal certification by a court of the innocence of a person charged with a crime. Ordinarily this occurs after a trial and a finding of "not guilty" by a judge or jury. An acquittal may also take place before trial because the charges are improper or the evidence insufficient.

Significance　Once a person is acquitted of a charge, he can never be tried again on that charge. To do so would constitute double jeopardy. An acquittal should not be confused with a pardon since the latter frees one from punishment but is not a declaration of innocence.

Affirmative Action　A plan or program to remedy the effects of past racial or sexual discrimination in employment and to prevent its recurrence. Affirmative action usually involves a workforce utilization analysis, the establishment of goals and timetables to increase use of underrepresented classes of persons, explanation of methods to be used to eliminate discrimination, and establishment of administrative responsibility to implement the program. Good faith and a positive effort to remedy past discrimination must also be shown. Affirmative action is required by law or regulation for all governmental agencies and for recipients of public funds, such as contractors and universities. Affirmative action is to be distinguished from antidiscrimination laws, which forbid unequal treatment rather than requiring positive corrective measures. *See also* EQUAL RIGHTS, page 66; FAIR EMPLOYMENT PRACTICES LAWS, page 67.

Significance Affirmative action is supported by those who argue that some form of preferential treatment is essential to break down long-standing patterns of discrimination against minorities and women so that employment patterns more accurately reflect the pluralistic nature of American society. Such action, it is believed, will strengthen confidence in public and private institutions. Critics of affirmative action claim that it constitutes "reverse discrimination" and whatever the merits of preferential treatment, the result will be to deny equality of opportunity based on merit. Major examples of affirmative action programs are the "Philadelphia Plan" initiated in 1969, which sets quotas for nonwhite workers to be hired in construction projects financed with federal funds, and the settlement reached in 1973 and 1974 between the government and the American Telephone and Telegraph Company involving millions of dollars in back pay and other employment benefits for minority group and female employees of ATT. Unresolved problems likely to arise out of affirmative-action programs are in their application to longstanding practices relating to layoffs, tenure rights, longevity benefits, and retirement plans, since these tend to work to the detriment of former victims of discrimination.

Arraignment A stage in criminal proceedings in which the accused is brought before the court to hear the formal charges against him as prepared by a grand jury or prosecutor. The accused is then asked to plead guilty or not guilty. The Supreme Court has ruled that there must be no unnecessary delay between arrest and arraignment. A confession or other evidence obtained as a result of such delay will be barred as evidence (*Mallory v. United States,* 354 U.S. 449 [1957]). In the Speedy Trial Act of 1974, Congress provided that an accused person must be arraigned within ten days of being charged. *See also McNabb v. United States,* page 95; SPEEDY TRIAL, page 83.

Significance A major factor in fair criminal procedure is that the accused be informed of the charges against him so that he can prepare his defense. Speedy arraignment acts as a safeguard against arbitrary arrest, prolonged detention, and unsavory police tactics. Police officials across the country argue that too stringent application of the *Mallory* rule handicaps law enforcement. The Omnibus Crime Control and Safe Streets Act of 1968 permits a voluntary confession to be used as evidence in a federal court if obtained within six hours of arraignment.

Arrest Warrant An order issued in writing by a court or magistrate authorizing the detainment of a person. The Fourth Amendment to the Constitution specifies that such warrants are to be issued only upon "probable cause," supported by oath, describing the person to be seized. All state constitutions have similar provisions. *See also* SEARCH AND SEIZURE, page 80.

Significance This guarantee has the effect of protecting persons against overzealous officers. Arrests may be made without a warrant if the law officers have "probable cause" for making the arrest. For example, an officer who witnesses a crime need not secure a warrant. Whether an arrest has been properly made is a matter for judicial determination. An arbitrary arrest may void any subsequent conviction.

Attorney General's List A list of organizations, deemed to be subversive, formerly compiled by the Attorney General of the United States. The Attorney General's list was drawn up as part of the loyalty program established by President Truman in 1947. Membership in any listed organization had been taken into account in determining the loyalty of governmental employees. In *Joint Anti-Fascist Refugee Committee v. McGrath,* 341 U.S. 123 (1951), the Supreme Court declared that an organization could not be listed without being given notice and an opportunity to be heard. The Attorney General's list was abolished by executive order in 1974. *See also* LOYALTY-SECURITY PROGRAMS, page 74; SUBVERSIVE ACTIVITIES CONTROL BOARD, page 87.

Significance The Attorney General's list of subversive organizations did not carry any legal weight. The legal determination of what constituted a subversive organization was the responsibility of the Subversive Activities Control Board, established under the Internal Security Act of 1950. The Attorney General's list was used informally in determining the loyalty of particular persons. Some critics of the list pointed out that it did not distinguish between organizations in terms of the date of their inception or the degree of their subversive connections, and that its very existence imputed guilt by association to the members of these groups. Some state and local governments accepted the list at face value in determining the loyalty of employees. The list did put innocent individuals on notice of the possible subversive character of their organizations. When the list was abolished in 1974, all but thirty of three hundred listed organizations had been out of existence for a period of five years or more.

Bad Tendency Rule A test used by the Supreme Court to determine the permissible bounds of free speech. The bad tendency rule holds that speech or other First Amendment freedoms may be curtailed if there is a possibility that they might lead to some evil. Judges who hold this view feel that it is the legislature's duty, not the Court's, to determine what kinds of speeches have a bad tendency. It is to be distinguished from the "clear and present danger" doctrine, which holds that an individual's liberty may not be curtailed unless it presents some imminent danger of illegal action. *See also* CLEAR AND PRESENT DANGER RULE, page 62; *Dennis v. United States,* page 90.

Significance The bad tendency test, like the clear and present danger test, proceeds from the search for some formula to solve the problem of balancing individual freedom against the rights of society. Both tests have been used by the Supreme Court over the years, with results determined by the nature of the times and the ideas of the justices. In the years from 1948 to 1952, known as the "era of McCarthyism," the bad tendency rule prevailed against accused subversives. More liberal majorities on the Court have since rejected the bad tendency rule in favor of the clear and present danger doctrine or other approaches which give special weight to free speech interests.

Balancing Doctrine A concept used by judges to weigh the competing interests or values in a case. Typically this involves striking a balance between the interests that society seeks to preserve and the rights of the individual. For example, balancing the government's interest in national security or merely traffic control on a busy street against the free exercise of speech or assembly are common problems. *See also* POLICE POWER, page 76.

Significance Controversy over the balancing doctrine has emerged on the Supreme Court with some regularity, particularly in civil liberty cases. One viewpoint holds that the limits placed on government by the Bill of Rights should not be "balanced away" with rationalizations based on contemporary problems. Another view holds that constitutional rights are not absolute and may be limited when outweighed by society's needs.

Bill of Attainder   A legislative act that declares the guilt of an individual and metes out punishment without a judicial trial. The state legislatures and Congress are forbidden to pass such acts by Article I, sections 9 and 10 of the Constitution. *See also United States v. Lovett,* page 102.

  Significance A legislative body may not exercise the judicial function of ascertaining guilt and pronouncing sentence. Rather, the legislature is limited to passing general laws, with specific applications left to the courts. This is an important ingredient of the separation of powers and of freedom itself.

Bill of Rights   The first ten amendments to the United States Constitution. Bills of rights, sometimes called declarations of rights, are also found in all state constitutions. They contain a listing of the rights a person enjoys that cannot be infringed upon by the government. Many important rights, such as trial by jury and the guarantee of habeas corpus, are stated in other parts of the United States Constitution. All bills of rights contain provisions designed to protect the freedom of expression, the rights of property, and the rights of persons accused of crime. No rights are absolute, however, and all are subject to reasonable regulation through law. *See also* CIVIL LIBERTIES page 61.

  Significance Bills of rights are restrictions on government rather than on individuals or private groups. History teaches that unchecked governmental powers can lead to the decay of freedom. A bill of rights provides the legal mechanism through which the individual can challenge the oppressive acts of governmental officials in courts of law. Without guarantees for individual freedom, democracy would become meaningless and unworkable. Some state bills of rights antedate the federal Bill of Rights. The federal Bill of Rights was added to the Constitution as a condition for its ratification, on the insistence of people who feared a strong central government. Although these rights were intended to restrain only the national government, since 1925 the Supreme Court has gradually extended them as restraints upon state action through the due process clause of the Fourteenth Amendment.

Censorship   The curbing of ideas either in speech or in writing *before* they are expressed. Accountability *after* expression is provided by laws regulating libel and slander, obscenity, incitement to crime, contempt of court, or seditious utterance. Except in time of war or other national emergency, any prior restraint upon freedom of speech or of the press is forbidden. *See also Freedman v. Maryland,* page 91; FREEDOM OF THE PRESS, page 69; *Miller v. California,* page 96; *Near v. Minnesota,* page 98; *New York Times v. United States,* page 98; *Roth v. United States,* page 100.

  Significance The rights of freedom of speech or of the press would be meaningless if prior censorship could be exercised. While a person must bear the consequences of any expression, no governmental official may determine in advance what may be said or written. The Supreme Court has made an exception in the case of motion pictures, holding that a city may require submission of films to a censor (*Times Film Corporation v. Chicago,* 365 U.S. 43 [1961]), provided prompt judicial review is available (*Freedman v. Maryland,* 380 U.S. 51 [1965]).

Civil Disobedience   Refusal to obey a law, usually on the ground that the law is morally reprehensible. Recent examples of civil disobedience include Negro refusals to obey segregation laws and the actions of anti-Vietnam war groups in refusing to honor draft regulations. Civil disobedience ordinarily takes the form of nonviolent resistance and is aimed at arousing public opinion against the law.

Significance   Civil disobedience is to be distinguished from direct or revolutionary attacks upon constituted authority. An individual or group practicing civil disobedience seeks to call attention to a situation considered unjust and willingly suffers community ostracism and imprisonment for such disobedience.

Civil Liberties   Those liberties usually spelled out in a bill of rights or a constitution that guarantee the protection of persons, opinions, and property from the arbitrary interference of governmental officials. Restraints may be placed upon the exercise of these liberties only when they are abused by individuals or groups and when the public welfare requires them. *See also* BILL OF RIGHTS, page 60.

Significance   Civil liberties are basic to a free society as contrasted with a totalitarian society, which makes no such guarantees. They are a restraint upon the government rather than upon individuals. Civil liberties may be distinguished from "civil rights" in that the latter is generally understood to refer to positive policies of government to protect individuals from arbitrary treatment both by government and by other individuals. However, the terms are often used interchangeably.

Civil Rights   Positive acts of government designed to protect persons against arbitrary or discriminatory treatment by government or individuals. Civil rights guarantees are sometimes written into constitutions, but frequently take the form of statutes. Though the term is often used interchangeably with "civil liberties," the latter generally refers to restraints upon government as found in bills of rights. The term "civil rights" is also to be distinguished from "political rights," which generally refers to the rights to participate in the the management of government through such practices as voting. Civil rights have taken on special importance since the Civil War, as Congress and state and local legislatures have endeavored to secure equal treatment for blacks. *See also* CIVIL RIGHTS ACTS, pages 104–105.

Significance   Since 1940, there have been extensive attempts by government at all levels to secure civil rights for blacks and other minorities in such areas as employment, housing, and public facilities. Traditional constitutional civil liberty provisions have not always proved workable to meet the challenges of private and governmental discrimination against minority groups. The precise role and extent of governmental action to secure civil rights remains a controversial question. Examples of civil rights legislation include the Civil Rights Acts of 1957, 1960, 1964, and 1968 and the civil rights laws enacted in many states and local communities.

Civil Rights Organizations   Groups organized to promote observance of the Bill of Rights and related constitutional provisions. These include organizations concerned with civil rights as well as those with broader interests and goals. The major black civil rights groups include the National Association for the Advancement of Colored People (NAACP), which concerns itself mainly with legislative and legal matters; the National Urban League, which concentrates on economic improvement for blacks; and the Southern Christian Leadership Conference (SCLC), which concentrates on mass demonstrations, boycotts, and sit-ins. Among the leading general civil rights and liberties groups are the American Civil Liberties Union (ACLU), the National Council of Churches of Christ, most labor unions, and ethnically oriented groups such as the American Jewish Congress. *See also* PRESSURE GROUP, page 138.

Significance   Civil rights organizations differ from most American pressure groups in that they are not primarily concerned with promoting the economic interests of their members. While civil rights groups have compelled public attention, organizations like the ACLU support court tests and in other ways protect First Amendment freedoms of expression and the rights of persons accused of crime. Few organizations are blatantly anti-civil rights, although the Ku Klux Klan, black separatist groups, and certain right-wing extremist groups oppose the efforts of civil rights organizations.

Class Action   A lawsuit in which one or more persons sue or are sued as representatives of a larger group similarly situated. The class action makes it possible for persons with small individual claims and inadequate financial resources to represent others so as to make a lawsuit financially viable. The Court's decision in such cases may be more sweeping in application than is usually the case. While class action suits have been possible for many years, their number has increased substantially since the 1940s as vehicles for issues involving civil rights, legislative apportionment, welfare, consumer protection and environmental problems. Two Supreme Court decisions during its 1973–74 term, however, may stem the tide of class action suits. In one case, the Court refused to permit a class action suit brought to a federal court under diversity jurisdiction, against a corporation for pollution damage to property, because each person in the class did not have a claim for the $10,000 or more required for federal Court jurisdiction (*Zahn v. International Paper Co.,* 414 U.S. 291 [1973]). In the other, the Court ruled that persons initiating a class action suit against stock brokerage houses for alleged overcharges of more than two million people, must notify, at their own expense, all other persons in the class (*Eisen v. Carlisle & Jacquelin,* 417 U.S. 156 [1974]). *See also* DIVERSITY OF CITIZENSHIP page 247; JUSTICIABLE QUESTION, page 254.

Significance   Class action suits have made it possible for litigants to overcome the general rule that a plaintiff in a suit must have an interest at stake beyond that of the general public. The courts have thus been able to entertain suits on major social issues in which the plaintiff was not the only person subject to possible injury such as in the case of legislative apportionment. The average citizen lacks the resources to challenge huge corporations or the government and often his claim is small. The Supreme Court's limiting rules may sharply decrease the use of class action suits except by well-organized groups.

Clear and Present Danger Rule   A test used by the Supreme Court to measure the permissible bounds of free speech. The test was formulated by Justice Oliver Wendell Holmes in *Schenck v. United States,* 249 U.S. 47 (1919): "The question in every case is whether the words used are used in such circumstances and are of such a nature as to create a clear and present danger that they will bring about the substantive evils that Congress has a right to prevent. It is a question of proximity and degree." The application of this test has varied a good deal since 1919. *See also* BAD TENDENCY RULE, page 59; *Schenck v. United States,* page 101.

Significance   Freedom of speech is not absolute, particularly when its exercise has a close relationship to some unlawful act, such as the violent overthrow of the government. Yet, the relationship between mere speech or the advocacy of a doctrine and the performance of an illegal act is not easy to determine. As Justice Holmes put it, one could not falsely shout "Fire!" in a crowded theatre and claim one's right to do so as an element of free speech. The clear and present danger rule is one attempt to establish a criterion for the protection of the individual's right to speak in light of society's right to protection.

Confession   An admission of guilt by one accused of a crime. A confession must be voluntary and not induced by force, "third degree" methods, prolonged interrogation, threats, psychological coercion, or promise of leniency. A confession must be corroborated with evidence that a crime has actually been committed. *See also Ashcraft v. Tennessee,* page 88; *McNabb v. United States,* page 95; *Miranda v. Arizona,* page 97; PLEA BARGAINING, page 258.

Significance   A confession exacted by any illegal means is not admissible in a trial and may result in the release of the accused. Corroboration prevents the conviction of deranged persons who confess to crimes they have not committed. The courts have been strict in demanding proof that a confession was made voluntarily and, preferably, in the presence of counsel.

Confrontation Clause   The part of the Sixth Amendment to the Constitution which guarantees that, in criminal prosecutions, the accused shall have the right "to be confronted with the witnesses against him." An important corollary is the right to cross-examine such witnesses. In 1965 the Supreme Court ruled that the right of confrontation of witnesses also applied in state trials under the due process clause of the Fourteenth Amendment (*Pointer v. Texas,* 380 U.S. 400). *See also* WITNESS, page 86.

Significance   The confrontation clause safeguards defendants against faceless and nameless informers, permits the defendant to hear the testimony and to see the evidence, and enables him, through his attorney, to fully challenge the witness by cross-examination. Conversely, those who testify against an accused must be ready to face the defendant in open court and withstand cross-examination. Along with other provisions of the Sixth Amendment, the confrontation clause is vital to a fair trial.

Conscientious Objector   A person who refuses to render military service because of religious training and belief. While the right to religious freedom does not extend to refusal to serve in the military service, Congress has, as an act of grace, authorized noncombatant service or exemption from military service for conscientious objectors. The law does not exempt persons who oppose military service because of "political, sociological, or philosophical views or a merely personal moral code," but the Supreme Court has interpreted this liberally to include nontraditional conscientious objection held with the fervor of religious conviction, *See also Girouard v. United States,* page 54; SELECTIVE SERVICE, page 424.

Significance A person does not have the right to refuse military duty. A high regard for those whose beliefs make them unable to participate in a war effort has led Congress to this policy of leniency. In effect, Congress gives such people preferred treatment when it excuses them from actual combat, instead of penalizing them by requiring them to do other service. Whether a person is a true conscientious objector and not a "draft dodger" is a question to be determined by draft boards and, at times, the courts. In 1965, the Supreme Court held in *United States v. Seeger,* 380 U.S. 128, that persons without formal or traditional religious affiliation or belief could qualify as conscientious objectors if their beliefs occupy "a place parallel to that filled by the God of those admittedly qualifying for the exemption. . . ." The standard was further broadened in 1970 to include one whose beliefs are rooted in moral or ethical grounds if held "with the strength of more traditional religious convictions" (*Welsh v. United States,* 398 U.S. 333). Conscientious objector status for objection to a specific war (for example, Vietnam), however, has been denied (*Gillette v. United States,* 401 U.S. 437 [1971]).

Conspiracy Any agreement between two or more persons to commit an unlawful act. Conspiracy is a crime under numerous criminal statutes; in the realm of business and labor activities the law forbids conspiracies in restraint of trade. The most prominent conspiracy provision in the field of civil liberties is that found in the Smith Act of 1940, which makes it a crime to conspire to teach, advocate, or organize groups that advocate the overthrow of government by force. *See also* GUILT BY ASSOCIATION, page 70.

Significance Conspiracy laws are designed to punish persons who participate in the planning of a criminal act. In the areas of speech, press, and association, conspiracy laws pose the danger that persons who do not have actual plans to do evil may be punished for foolish conjecture.

Cruel and Unusual Punishment Any lingering torture, mutilation, or degrading treatment, or any sentence too severe for the offense committed. The Eighth Amendment to the Constitution forbids such punishment, leaving the scope of the ban to be determined by the courts. *See also* CAPITAL PUNISHMENT, page 239.

Significance The idea of humane treatment for criminals is a relatively modern concept, which holds that even the undesirable elements of the community should have their individual dignity preserved. Whether a particular punishment is cruel depends upon community standards as determined by the courts. Changing attitudes are reflected by Supreme Court decisions holding as cruel and unusual punishment the deprivation of citizenship for wartime desertion (*Trop v. Dulles,* 356 U.S. 86 [1958]) and a state law making it a crime to be addicted to the use of narcotics (*Robinson v. California,* 370 U.S. 660 [1962]). In 1972 the Supreme Court held that the death penalty as then imposed in the United States constituted cruel and unusual punishment (*Furman v. Georgia,* 408 U.S. 238), but the penalty has been restored in numerous jurisdictions.

De Facto Segregation The existence of racially segregated facilities that are, however, not required by law (*de jure*). De facto segregation refers especially to the school system in typical northern communities, in which neighborhood racial patterns lead "in fact" to predominantly black and white schools similar to those in the South that, in the past, were segregated by law. *See also* ELEMENTARY AND SECONDARY EDUCATION ACT, page 375; *Milliken v. Bradley,* page 96; *Swann v. Charlotte,* page 102.

Significance De facto segregation in northern schools has led to mass protest demonstrations and to violence in some large cities. Minority groups have demanded integrated schools, charging that segregation results from housing discrimination and from deliberate policies of school officials. White parents often resist integration efforts, demanding retention of neighborhood schools. Some school districts have tried to integrate schools by "bussing" children to distant schools or by a variety of school mixing plans. Current law does not require elimination of de facto segregation, and Congress has restricted positive action to achieve racial balance in schools. The massive ghettos in major cities may make it virtually impossible to integrate on any large scale.

Double Jeopardy The guarantee in the Fifth Amendment to the Constitution that one may not be twice put in jeopardy of life or limb for the same offense. Thus, a person who has been tried may not be tried again for the same crime. The guarantee does not, however, apply to trials by both the national government and a state, or by two different states for offenses growing out of a single criminal act. Trial following a mistrial is not double jeopardy unless the prosecution has deliberately forced a mistrial in order to get better evidence or a more favorable jury. In 1969, the Supreme Court held the protection against double jeopardy applicable to the states through the Fourteenth Amendment (*Benton v. Maryland,* 395 U.S. 784). *See also Bartkus v. Illinois,* page 88.

Significance Although considerable confusion exists as to what constitutes double jeopardy in specific instances, this guarantee does afford protection against continual harassment of accused persons. Also, the courts and the accused are spared endless costs and time-consuming litigation.

Due Process of Law Protection against arbitrary deprivation of life, liberty, or property. The Fifth and Fourteenth amendments forbid the national and state governments, respectively, to deny any person his life, liberty, or property without due process of law. While no precise definition of this term has ever been made, it establishes the principle of limited government. Two types of due process—procedural and substantive—have emerged in the course of litigation. Though used sparingly in recent years, substantive due process has been used by the judiciary to strike down legislative and executive acts that are arbitrary or lacking in reasonableness, or that cover subject matter beyond the reach of government. Procedural due process was defined by Daniel Webster as procedure "which hears before it condemns, which proceeds upon inquiry, and renders judgment only after trial." The Supreme Court, in a long series of cases, has marked out the general meaning of the phrase so as to forbid any procedure that is shocking to the conscience or that makes impossible a fair and enlightened system of justice for a civilized people. *See also Moore v. Dempsey,* page 97; *Palko v. Connecticut,* page 99.

Significance Protection against arbitrary treatment is basic to the American system of government. Due process functions both as a limitation on public officials and as a power in the hands of the judiciary, which has wide latitude in applying it. Judges can determine whether a law bears a reasonable relationship to a proper governmental function and whether the procedure used, particularly in criminal cases, is fair and reasonable.

Eminent Domain   The power inherent in all governments to take over private property, provided that it is taken for a public purpose and that just compensation is awarded. Disputes as to purpose or price are generally settled in the courts in suits referred to as condemnation proceedings. *See also* CONFISCATION, page 308.

Significance   The right to own and use private property is high in the American scheme of values. Yet, without the power of eminent domain, projects that benefit many persons, such as slum clearance or highway projects, would be impossible. Individual rights, however, are recognized by the provision for equitable compensation.

Equal Protection of the Law   A requirement of the Fourteenth Amendment that state laws may not arbitrarily discriminate against persons. Identical treatment is not required. Classification of persons is permitted provided that the classification is reasonable and bears some relationship to the end sought. Hence, taxation in accordance with ability to pay has been held to be a reasonable classification, whereas classification according to color, religion, or social class has been held to bear no reasonable relationship to the functions of government. Current interest in the application of equal protection centers on the desegregation of races in public facilities, equal justice for the poor, inequality in state legislative apportionment, and equality for women. Though the Constitution does not contain a similar restriction on the national government, the courts have read the equal protection concept into the meaning of the due process clause of the Fifth Amendment. *See also Baker v. Carr,* page 194; *Bolling v. Sharpe,* page 89; *Brown v. Board of Education of Topeka,* page 89; FINE, page 68.

Significance   Equal protection of the law emanates from the democratic concepts of the equality of men under the law and their right to equality of opportunity. Arbitrary or irrelevant barriers to full enjoyment of rights are forbidden. Although the constitutional prohibition does not extend to private discrimination both the national and many state governments have acted to forbid private discrimination against persons based on color, creed, sex, or national origin.

Equal Rights   The movement to equalize the rights of men and women. Traditionally in American law, women have not enjoyed the same rights as men, and this has manifested itself in many areas of American life including property rights, education, and employment opportunities. State laws vary widely, although many are protective of women rather than directly discriminatory. Women's suffrage led to a gradual narrowing of legal differences, but with increasing intensity since the 1960s, an extensive body of new laws and administrative regulations, as well as court decisions, have provided protection against sex discrimination. In March 1972 Congress proposed to the states a constitutional amendment which provided that "Equality of rights under the law shall not be denied or abridged by the United States or any state on account of sex." This proposed amendment will go into effect two years after ratification. *See also* AFFIRMATIVE ACTION, page 57; WOMEN'S LIBERATION MOVEMENT, page 148.

Significance The concept of equal rights has had a dramatic impact upon American life, equal to, if not greater than, the impact of changing race relations. Many constitutional authorities believe that changes already brought about in behalf of women's rights as well as liberal application of equal protection of the law concepts will diminish the impact of the proposed equal rights amendment. Others note, however, that the amendment will give rise to a host of constitutional problems relating to the traditional roles of men and women. The equal rights movement achieved two major victories in the 1960s—the passage of the Equal Pay Act of 1963, which requires equal pay for men and women doing similar work; and the Civil Rights Act of 1964, which forbids discrimination against women in hiring and other personnel policies.

Ex Post Facto Law A criminal law that is retroactive and that has an adverse effect upon one accused of a crime. Thus, an ex post facto law is one that makes an act a crime that was not a crime when committed, that increases the penalty for a crime after its commission, or that changes the rules of evidence so as to make conviction easier. Neither the state nor the national governments may enact such laws under provisions of Article I, sections 9 and 10 of the Constitution. The prohibition does not extend to civil laws or laws favorable to an accused person.

Significance The ex post facto prohibition emphasizes that each individual is free to o those things not specifically forbidden by existing law without fear of future punishment. This is pertinent to the concept of a government of laws and not of men, for it prevents abuse of power by governmental officials, who might otherwise retrospectively apply new laws for vindictive purposes.

Fair Employment Practices Laws Laws that forbid private and/or public employers, labor unions, or employment agencies to discriminate in hiring or in other personnel policies on the grounds of race, color, creed, or national origin. More than thirty states have enacted such laws. In the Civil Rights Act of 1964, Congress provided for equal employment opportunities in businesses and labor unions engaged in interstate commerce. Equal treatment for women is also required by the Act, *See also* AFFIRMATIVE ACTION, page 57; EQUAL EMPLOYMENT OPPORTUNITY COMMISSION, page 87.

Significance Fair employment laws represent positive governmental action in the field of private rights, in contrast to the traditional concept of civil liberties as a restraint against government. Both the national and state laws stress education and conciliation, although several state laws provide criminal sanctions. The national law encourages state action in this field. For a number of years, presidential executive orders had prohibited racial discrimination in public employment and by government contractors.

Fifth Amendment A part of the Bill of Rights that imposes a number of restrictions on the national government with respect to the rights of persons accused of crime. It provides for indictment by grand jury, protection against double jeopardy and self-incrimination, and forbids denial of life, liberty, or property without due process of law. In addition, the Fifth Amendment prohibits the taking of property without just compensation. *See also* DOUBLE JEOPARDY, **page**

65; DUE PROCESS, page 65; EMINENT DOMAIN, page 66; GRAND JURY, page 250; IMMUNITY, page 71; SELF-INCRIMINATION, page 81.

Significance Together with the Fourth, Sixth, and Eighth amendments, and with provisions in the Constitution relative to habeas corpus, ex post facto laws, and bills of attainder, the Fifth Amendment is a significant source of liberty. The Amendment has come into contemporary prominence because of the self-incrimination clause. Persons refusing to testify before congressional committees or courts have frequently "taken the Fifth," a shorthand phrase for claiming the privilege against self-incrimination.

Fine   A sum of money paid as a penalty for an illegal act. A fine may constitute the total penalty or it may be levied in addition to or as a substitute for imprisonment. The Supreme Court has held it to be a denial of equal protection to either extend a jail sentence for inability to pay a fine (*Williams v. Illinois,* 399 U.S. 925 [1970]) or to put an indigent person in jail for an offense punishable only by a fine (*Tate v. Short,* 401 U.S. 395 [1971]). *See also* EQUAL PROTECTION OF THE LAW, page 66.

Significance Fines are common penalties for minor offenses, such as traffic violations, but are also levied for major offenses, especially when funds have been accumulated as a result of violation of law. Fines serve as both a painful penalty and a source of governmental revenue. Recent decisions of the Supreme Court assure equal justice for the poor who otherwise would be jailed for longer periods than those able to pay fines.

Fourteenth Amendment   A post-Civil War Amendment (1868) that defines citizenship, restricts the power of the states in their relations with their inhabitants, requires reduction of a state's representation in Congress for denials of suffrage, disqualifies former officeholders who participated in the rebellion, and invalidates any war debts of rebellious states. The most important provisions are those that forbid a state to deprive any person of life, liberty, or property without due process of law, or deny to any person the equal protection of the law. *See also Barron v. Baltimore,* page 88; CITIZEN, page 47; DUE PROCESS OF LAW, page 65; EQUAL PROTECTION OF THE LAW, page 66; INCORPORATION DOCTRINE, page 72.

Significance Since its enactment, the Fourteenth Amendment has produced extensive controversy over the intentions of its framers and in its specific applications by the Supreme Court. Whatever the intent of the framers may have been, the uses of the Fourteenth Amendment have altered the federal system. The due process clause and the equal protection clause have been prominent in constitutional disputes for many years. Both have made possible federal intervention against alleged state encroachment on the rights of the people. For a time, the due process clause was used mainly to limit the states in the exercise of their taxing and police powers in business regulation. Since 1925, the due process clause has been interpreted by the courts to forbid state denials of First Amendment freedoms as well as of essential procedural rights found in the Fourth, Fifth, Sixth, and Eighth Amendments. The equal protection clause has been invoked to restrain racial segregation practices, to maintain fair legislative apportionment by state governments, to gain equal justice for the poor, and to gain equal treatment for women.

Freedom of Assembly   The right of the people to congregate for the discussion of public questions and to organize into political parties or pressure groups for the purpose of influencing public policy. The right of assembly does not authorize meetings designed to accomplish an illegal purpose or those that lead to a breach of the peace or resistance to lawful authority. Freedom of assembly is guaranteed by the First Amendment and state constitutions. In addition, the Supreme Court has ruled that the due process clause of the Fourteenth Amendment protects the individual's freedom of assembly against infringement by state governments. *See also Hague v. CIO,* page 92.

Significance   In a democratic society, the people must have the right to meet freely in peaceable assemblage to consider public questions. This right is closely related to freedoms of speech and of petition. All act as a restraint upon legislators and other public officials. Peace and civil rights protest movements have put the right of assembly to severe tests because of the potentials for violence in civil disobedience.

Freedom of Association   The right to organize for political, religious, or other social purposes. The Constitution makes no mention of freedom of association, but it is implicit in guarantees of freedom of speech, assembly, and religion. *See also* GUILT BY ASSOCIATION, page 70; *Keyishian v. Board of Regents,* page 95; *NAACP v. Alabama,* page 97; *Scales v. United States,* page 101.

Significance   The American people are noted for being organization-minded; many Americans belong to several organizations. The right to associate has received much attention because of laws passed to curtail the activities and rights of alleged subversive organizations and their members. Such laws have been attacked in some quarters as imputing guilt by association, since members of a group may not necessarily subscribe to all its beliefs or actions. Persons do not, however, have the right to organize in order to accomplish illegal aims. Some southern states have attempted to impede the activities of civil rights groups promoting desegregation. The courts have not, however, permitted any limitations to be placed upon lawful groups. The right to associate is recognized as essential in a democratic society since, generally, an individual can accomplish more with a group than by acting alone.

Freedom of the Press   The right to publish and disseminate information without prior restraint, subject to penalties for abuse of the right. Abuses include libel, obscenity, incitement to crime, contempt of court, or sedition. Freedom of the press is protected by the First and Fourteenth Amendments to the Constitution and by all state constitutions. Major contemporary problems have involved censorship of books and movies for alleged obscenity, restraints on Communist publications, governmental secrecy, and the difficulty of safeguarding both freedom of the press and a fair trial. *See also Miller v. California,* page 96; *Near v. Minnesota,* page 98; *New York Times v. Sullivan,* page 98; *New York Times v. United States,* page 98; *Roth v. United States,* page 100.

Significance   A free press is essential to a free society, particularly as it relates to the dissemination of political information. The Supreme Court has narrowly restricted any efforts at political censorship and has permitted wide latitude to criticize public officials. In dealing with obscenity, the courts have had difficulty in developing a formula to identify this abuse. The conflict between a free press and a fair trial involves a clash between two essential rights. The problem arises from the difficulty of holding a trial free from bias when press, radio, and television publicize details of the crime and the trial. The Court has held, for example, that television may not be used in notorious trials because of its adverse effect on parties to the trial (*Estes v. Texas,* 381 U.S. 532 [1965]). A major free press issue arose in 1971 when newspapers secured access to government documents classified as top secret. The Court held that the government could not restrain a newspaper from publishing the "Pentagon Papers" on the Vietnam war without showing that this could lead to grave danger to the nation's security (*New York Times v. United States,* 403 U.S. 713 [1971]).

Freedom of Religion   Freedom of worship and religious practice. The national government under the First Amendment, and the states under their constitutions and the Fourteenth Amendment, may not abridge this right of worship. Any religious practice that is contrary to public peace or morality may be outlawed, such as snake-handling or polygamy. *See also Jehovah's Witnesses Cases,* page 94; *Reynolds v. United States,* page 100; SEPARATION OF CHURCH AND STATE, page 82.

  Significance   In a nation with such diversity of religious groups, the free exercise of religion and the separation of church and state are essential. This was foremost in the minds of the Founding Fathers, who provided that there be no religious test for public office. Religious freedom is the first item in the Bill of Rights, reflecting the need for freedom of conscience in a free society. Any interference of state with church or of church with state constitutes a danger to both. The free exercise of religion has not proved to be as controversial a matter in American life as has the concept of the separation of church and state.

Freedom of Speech   The right to speak without prior restraint, subject to penalties for abuse of the right. Abuses include slander, obscenity, incitement to crime, contempt of court, or sedition. By virtue of the First and Fourteenth amendments and state bills of rights, neither the national government nor the states may abridge the right of freedom of speech. *See also* BAD TENDENCY RULE, page 59; CLEAR AND PRESENT DANGER RULE, page 62; FREEDOM OF THE PRESS, page 69.

  Significance   Freedom is impossible without the right to disseminate ideas. Generally, the courts have treated the guarantee liberally. With regard to the advocacy of Communist doctrine, the courts have distinguished between mere advocacy of abstract doctrine and conspiratorial advocacy. Anti-war protests and the civil rights movement have also tested American tolerance for dissent. For the most part, the courts have protected the peaceful expression of unpopular ideas including the right to "symbolic speech" such as picketing or the wearing of protest insignia. In placing limitations on freedom of speech, the courts have attempted to apply such concepts as "clear and present danger" to determine whether a given situation justifies restriction.

Guilt by Association   Attribution of criminal or wrongful behavior or beliefs to a person because of his association with certain people or groups. *See also Elfbrandt v. Russell,* page 91; FREEDOM OF ASSOCIATION, page 69; INTERNAL SECURITY ACT, page 107; *Keyishian v. Board of Regents,* page 95; *Scales v. United States,* page 101.

Significance Guilt by association is a denial of the concept underlying American justice that guilt is personal and that an individual should not suffer any disabilities because of conduct or ideas attributed to his associates. The problem relates to those who lose their jobs or suffer other penalties as a result of membership in an alleged subversive or unpopular group. The issue is whether mere membership or association proves agreement with all the tenets of the group. The Supreme Court has sustained the power of national, state, and local governments to impose disabilities upon members of particular groups or exponents of certain ideas. However, recent decisions have overturned this position, with the Court striking down most laws that penalize people for mere membership in an organization. Guilt by association should not be confused with conviction for conspiracy to commit a crime, which involves actual and deliberate participation in the planning of a wrongful act.

Habeas Corpus A court order directing an official who has a person in custody to bring the prisoner to court and to show cause for his detention. The Constitution guarantees the right to a writ of habeas corpus, but Congress may suspend it in cases of rebellion or invasion (Art. I, sec. 9). Though President Lincoln suspended the writ on his own volition, Congress subsequently affirmed his action. A number of state constitutions absolutely forbid its suspension.

Significance Habeas corpus is generally considered to be the most important guarantee of liberty, in that it prevents arbitrary arrest and imprisonment—the fearful knock at the door, and the disappearance of the seized person. A prisoner must be released unless sufficient cause to detain him can be shown. Habeas corpus may also be used by persons serving sentences in state and federal prisons to reopen their cases on the ground of illegal detention because of rights denied before or during their trials.

Immunity A privilege granted to a person that exempts him from prosecution for any self-incriminating testimony given by him before a court, grand jury, or investigating committee. Immunity involves an enforced waiver of the constitutional right against self-incrimination, so that an individual can be compelled to give testimony or be punished for contempt. No evidence revealed by a witness who has been granted immunity may be used against him in any criminal prosecution, state or federal, or subject him to any penalty by either level of government (*Murphy v. Waterfront Commission,* 378 U.S. 52 [1964]). In the Organized Crime Control Act of 1970, Congress provided that immunity extends to use of a witness's testimony against himself, but not to his freedom from prosecution from any and all acts mentioned by him, provided that any evidence is derived from sources independent of his testimony. The Supreme Court upheld this narrowed immunity in *Kastigar v. United States,* 406 U.S. 411 (1972). *See also* SELF-INCRIMINA-TION, page 81.

Significance A grant of immunity is designed to compel testimony from persons who refuse to answer questions on the ground that their answers would tend to incriminate them and subject them to prosecution. Some legal scholars question the propriety of this procedure because it forces an individual to waive a constitutional right. Immunity will not be granted unless the information likely to be secured is of great public importance. Care must be taken not to make immunity a loophole for notorious criminals to escape punishment.

Incorporation Doctrine   The legal concept under which the Supreme Court has "national-ized" the Bill of Rights by making most of its provisions applicable to the states through the Fourteenth Amendment. The court has interpreted the due process clause of the Fourteenth Amendment to require states to adhere to safeguards and procedures essential to a scheme of ordered liberty. As a consequence of decisions in a series of cases, the Court has made binding upon the states all provisions of the Bill of Rights except for the Second, Third, Seventh, and Tenth amendments and the requirement of indictment by grand jury found in the Fifth Amendment. *See also Barron v. Baltimore,* page 88; FOURTEENTH AMENDMENT, page 68; *Gideon v. Wain-wright,* page 92; *Gitlow v. New York,* page 92; *Hurtado v. California,* page 93; *Palko v. Connecti-cut,* page 99.

Significance   The incorporation doctrine ranks among the most significant developments in American constitutional history. It overcame (but did not overrule) the decision in *Barron v. Baltimore* (7 Peters 243 [1833]), that the Bill of Rights limits only the national government. The incorporation process made possible national involvement in protection of individual rights against state and local officials and has had the effect of equalizing the rights of the people regardless of residence. The concept of national protection of individual rights has now been extended beyond traditional bill of rights concerns of free expression and criminal procedures to protection of minorities, the lower economic classes, and women.

Involuntary Servitude   Slavery, peonage, or the forcing of a person to work to fulfill a contract or work out a debt. The Thirteenth Amendment provides that neither slavery nor involuntary servitude, except in punishment for crime, may exist anywhere in the United States. *See also Pollock v. Williams,* page 99; SELECTIVE SERVICE, page 424; THIRTEENTH AMENDMENT, page 84.

Significance   Though aimed primarily at putting an end to slavery, the Thirteenth Amendment serves as a guarantee of free and voluntary labor, which may be threatened by situations less drastic than outright slavery. Congress has supplemented this Amendment by passage of the Antipeonage Act of 1867, which is still vigorously enforced to protect debtors.

Juvenile Delinquent   A child whose behavior is unlawful and who is subject to governmen-tal custody. The definition of a delinquent child is determined by law and usually applies to persons under sixteen or eighteen years of age. All states have developed special courts to process juvenile cases. Juvenile courts have operated under informal procedures, but recent court decisions have imposed basic constitutional due process requirements upon them. *See also In Re Gault,* page 93.

Significance   Child delinquency status has been viewed as a civil rather than criminal matter on the theory that a child is not fully responsible for his unlawful acts. Juvenile courts are usually closed to the public, cases are handled under flexible procedures, and, theoretically, the emphasis is on redemption rather than punishment. In 1967, however, the Supreme Court held in *In Re Gault,* 387 U.S. 1, that constitutional standards of notice, right to counsel, protection against self-incrimination, and the right to confront witnesses apply to juveniles accused of crime. Further, the Court held that in juvenile cases, as in adult cases, conviction must be based on proof beyond a reasonable doubt (*In Re Winship,* 397 U.S. 358 [1970]). Yet, in order to preserve some flexibility for juvenile courts, the Court refused to require jury trials for juveniles (*McKeiver v. Pennsylvania,* 403 U.S. 528 [1971]). A high proportion of criminal offenses involve juveniles and in the Juvenile Delinquency Prevention and Control Act of 1968 Congress provided for federal grants to the states for delinquency prevention and rehabilitation of offenders.

Libel and Slander Defamation of character, written, in the case of libel, and oral, in the case of slander. Both include statements that expose a person to hatred, contempt, or ridicule, or that injure his reputation by imputing to him a criminal act, or that harm him in his trade or profession. Libel and slander usually involve suits for civil damages, but they may also be punished under criminal laws. Libel is generally considered more serious than slander because the written word is more durable than a passing remark. The reputation of those involved, the nature of the audience, and the conditions under which the words were written or spoken may prove pertinent in a suit for damages. Truth of a statement is generally an absolute defense. *See also New York Times v. Sullivan,* page 98.

Significance Libel and slander are limitations on the freedoms of speech and press, and many state constitutions expressly make this distinction. Libel and slander do not apply to comment made about public officials or newsworthy people unless malicious intent is proved, since such comments are considered to be in the public interest (*New York Times v. Sullivan,* 376 U.S. 255 [1964]). Major recent problems concern: (1) the harm done to private reputations by legislative or executive officials who enjoy immunity from suit for remarks made in the line of duty; (2) whether remarks made on radio and television are libel or slander (for example, do oral remarks made on these mediums have the impact of the printed word?); and (3) "group libel" laws, which make it illegal to impugn the reputation of an entire minority group.

Loyalty Oath An oath that requires an individual to disavow or abjure certain beliefs and associations. Such oaths were exacted during the Revolutionary War, the Civil War, and the "red scare" of the 1920s. Recent loyalty oaths, inspired by the cold war, generally require persons to swear that they do not advocate the violent overthrow of government nor belong to any organization so advocating it. Loyalty oaths are generally required of public employees, teachers, attorneys, defense workers, and recipients of governmental benefits. The courts have struck down most loyalty oath laws after earlier acceptance, usually on the grounds that the oath did not excuse those whose associations were innocent of illegal intent or because the oath was totally unrelated to any governmental purpose. In 1970, the United States Civil Service Commission dropped the loyalty oath requirement for federal employees. Test oaths for students receiving federal aid, for Job Corps members, and for recipients of medicare have also been dropped. *See also Elfbrandt v. Russell,* page 91.

Significance Few people object to taking an ordinary oath of allegiance declaring loyalty to the United States and swearing to uphold the Constitution. However, loyalty or "test" oaths have met numerous objections based largely on the reversal of the presumption of innocence, since an individual may be considered disloyal unless he swears that he is not. It is also charged that such oaths abridge freedoms of speech and assembly by the discretion vested in the imposer of the oath to determine suitable beliefs and associations. Moreover, many doubt the utility of oaths as a weapon against subversives who would undoubtedly swear falsely to the oath. The major utility of loyalty oaths lies in making the oath taker aware of possible illegal activities or associations and in bringing perjury charges against those who swear falsely.

Loyalty-Security Programs   Programs carried on by national and state governments to rid the public service of disloyal persons or persons suspected of being security risks. The national government's loyalty program had its inception in 1947 when President Truman ordered that governmental employees be dismissed if grounds existed to doubt their loyalty. President Eisenhower extended the program to include all "security risks"—disloyal as well as generally untrustworthy people. The programs have also been applied to the armed forces, defense plants, maritime workers, and other government-connected activities. Appeal procedures are provided for discharged persons but do not always permit confrontation with informers. Many persons have been denied jobs without knowing the precise reasons, and the programs have resulted in numerous dismissals. Although the courts have sustained these programs, they have, in recent years, limited their application to persons holding sensitive positions and those whose activities encompass illegal aims. Similar programs have been undertaken in the states, although most states have limited their loyalty requirements to the taking of a loyalty oath. *See also* ATTORNEY GENERAL'S LIST, page 59; *Keyishian v. Board of Regents,* page 95.

    Significance   Few people insist that disloyal persons should work for the government. Many people, however, have protested the procedures used in the loyalty-security programs, preferring normal police work to uncover dangerous persons. The use of unidentified informers raises much criticism. Many persons are concerned with the effects on the morale of governmental employees who are subject to investigation of all their activities and beliefs. Loyalty-security programs will undoubtedly be part of the American scene as long as the international situation continues to be dangerous.

McCarthyism   Unsubstantiated accusations of disloyalty and abuse of legislative investigatory power that engender fear over real or imagined threats to the security of the nation. The term was derived in the early 1950s from the actions of Senator Joseph R. McCarthy of Wisconsin who made repeated charges against public officials and private individuals under the protection of his senatorial immunity.

    Significance   McCarthyism was a post-World War II phenomenon that fed on the fears generated by the cold war between the United States and the Soviet Union. The period was marked by loyalty-security investigations into the lives of public employees, surveillance of scientists and teachers, the imposition of loyalty oaths, and passage of anti-Communist legislation. Many vestiges of the period remain. McCarthyism utilizes the catchwords of "loyalty" and "security" as justification for limitations on civil liberties. Ultraconservative groups use similar tactics to fight social reform. McCarthyism fosters suspicion among neighbors, distrust of public officials, and the idea of "guilt by association."

Magna Carta   The Great Charter of freedom granted in 1215 by King John of England on demands by his barons. The Magna Carta contained such ideas as trial by a jury of one's peers and the guarantee against loss of life, liberty, property, except in accordance with law.

Significance The source for many of the basic freedoms found in American law are traceable to the Magna Carta. While originally limited to privileged classes, the major concepts of the Magna Carta eventually spread to all free people.

Natural Rights An underlying assumption of the American political creed that men are endowed by their Creator with certain rights that may not be abridged by government. *See also* NATURAL LAW, page 13

Significance The Judeo-Christian doctrine, as embodied in the American creed, assumes the inviolability of man's basic rights, as contrasted with the forces of absolutism, which assert that man has only such rights as the government decides to give him. The doctrine of natural rights assumes that man had his rights in a "state of nature" and creates government to protect those rights.

Ninth Amendment A part of the Bill of Rights that reads, "The enumeration in the Constitution, of certain rights, shall not be construed to deny or disparage others retained by the people." This provision reaffirms the tradition of the natural rights philosophy, supported by those who feared that a listing of rights in the Bill of Rights might be interpreted to mean that no other rights were held by the people. *See also* PRIVACY, page 76; *Roe v. Wade,* page 100.

Significance The "other" rights that the people retain have not been extensively defined nor has the Ninth Amendment been prominently used in litigation. In the case of *Mitchell v. United States,* 313 U.S. 80 (1941), the Supreme Court noted that the Amendment protected the right to political activity by the people. In *Griswold v. Connecticut,* 381 U.S. 479 (1965), the Court struck down a law that forbade counseling married couples to use contraceptives as an invasion of the right of privacy protected by the First and Ninth amendments. In striking down state laws regulating abortions (*Roe v. Wade,* 410 U.S. 113 [1973]) as violating the right to privacy guaranteed by the Ninth and Fourteenth amendments, the Court brought the Ninth Amendment to new prominence by making it the cornerstone of the developing right to privacy.

Petition A request to a public official that seeks to correct a wrong or to influence public policy. The First Amendment guarantees to the people the right to "petition the government for a redress of grievances." This provision, like all provisions of the First Amendment, is applicable to the states through the Fourteenth Amendment, although most state constitutions contain a similar provision. The right of petition, closely related to freedoms of speech, press, and assembly, is generally exercised through letter writing to public officials and through pressure-group activity.

Significance It is vital in a free society that persons be able to call the attention of their representatives to their grievances. In this way, government can remain continually responsive to the people and can be made aware of their opinions at times other than at elections. The right of petition is most effectively exercised through the lobbying activities of interest groups and by mass demonstrations and picketing by groups having limited access to the political power structure.

Police Power   The power inherent in state governments to protect the health, safety, morals, and welfare of the people. In the area of civil rights and liberties, a lawful exercise of the police power may justify abridgment of personal or property rights. For example, through use of the police power, a state may destroy property that endangers public health or may limit freedom of speech or assembly when the public safety is jeopardized. *See also* BALANCING DOCTRINE, page 59; POLICE POWER, page 40.

Significance   The police power rests on the assumption that rights are not absolute. The extent of the power is generally determined by the courts when they are faced with concrete situations in which the police power comes into conflict with personal liberties. In a typical civil liberty-police power case, the courts must strike a balance between the needs of society and the rights of the individual.

Political Right   The right to participate in the management of government and to influence public policy. Typical political rights include the right to vote, to form a political party, and to participate in pressure-group activity.

Significance   Political rights are essential for the operations of a free government. Citizens must be given the opportunity not only to speak out on public issues but to take positive action to influence or control the government. So long as these rights remain inviolate, regardless of the party in power, dictatorship cannot take hold. Any group denied these rights is left with the sole recourse of violent revolution to accomplish its goals. In recent years, emphasis has been placed on securing political rights for minority groups who may be denied access to the polls. Limitations, however, have been placed upon the political activities of subversive groups who seek to eliminate such rights.

Political Trial   Prosecution direction against alleged enemies of the government or the political system. Sedition laws and other loyalty-security measures are common legislative acts that define political crimes. Prosecutions resulting from such laws are often referred to as "political trials," designed to expose rather than punish. *See also* MCCARTHYISM, page 74; SEDITION, page 81.

Significance   All nations define political crimes and have experienced political trials. In times of tension or alleged threats to national security, sedition laws are actively enforced against leaders of groups in opposition to the government. Political trials direct national attention to security threats. Conversely, those opposed to the system are often eager to use the forum of a sensational trial to propagate their ideas. The nine-month trial of the Communist leadership for violation of the Smith Act in 1948 is a leading American example of such a trial. Many prosecutions of civil rights leaders and those who led Vietnam War protests during the 1960s had strong overtones of political trials.

Privacy   The right to determine one's personal affairs free of governmental interference and to control dissemination of information about oneself. The Constitution makes no mention of a right of privacy but the Supreme Court has recognized it as falling within the "penumbra" (borderline) of the First, Fourth, Fifth, Ninth, and Fourteenth amendments. In the Privacy Act of 1974 Congress provided, for the first time, that individuals may inspect information about themselves in public agency files and challenge, correct, or amend materials. Agencies may not make their files on an individual available to other agencies without that individual's consent. Exempted from the law, however, are law enforcement agencies, the Central Intelligence Agency, the Secret Service, and certain files pertaining to federal employment. Among the problems which have given rise to privacy concerns are the widespread development of computerized data banks, increased use of electronic listening devices, and cultural changes forcing an end to governmental regulation of contraception, abortion, homosexuality, and pornography. *See also* NINTH AMEND-MENT, page 75; *Roe v. Wade*, page 100; WIRETAPPING page 85.

Significance In a free society, a large measure of personal privacy must be assumed for each individual. At the same time, demands for governmental service create situations which intrude upon privacy. A welfare or medical care system, for example, requires the acquisition of detailed personal information about citizens, which when stored in computers, may be easily retrieved for illegitimate uses. Technological developments, such as eavesdropping devices, may help to curb crime but are dangerously subject to abusive intrusions on privacy. Changes in life style have diminished tolerance for government's traditional role in protecting the morals of the people, requiring governmental officials to balance the need for social order against greater individual liberty.

Privilege An advantage, benefit, or opportunity granted to an individual or group to which it has no right. The range of privileges bestowed by government is very broad and includes government employment, medicare, public housing, tax exemptions, welfare programs, professional licenses, and veterans' benefits. The government may attach qualifications or demands before a privilege is granted, but these must pass the test of reasonableness. Any withdrawal of a privilege from an individual must be done under procedures that afford minimal due process rights, such as notice and hearing. *See also* *Goldberg v. Kelly*, page 374; *Keyishian v. Board of Regents*, page 95.

Significance The distinction between a right and a privilege has narrowed considerably. In the past, an individual could lose a privilege under procedures and circumstances that would not be permissible if a right were abridged. This enabled the government to control behavior by the threat of withholding a benefit. The courts have held, however, that neither the granting nor the withholding of a privilege may be conditioned upon the surrender of constitutional rights. For example, government employment cannot be conditioned on standards of belief or association which violate First Amendment rights, nor may recipients of government aid be subjected to arbitrary treatment.

Procedural Rights Protection against arbitrary actions by public officials. Under American constitutional law, no person may be deprived of his life, liberty, or property or any other guaranteed right, except under well-defined procedures, including a fair hearing before a judicial tribunal. American procedural rights are generally considered to be those listed in the Bill of Rights, particularly in the Fourth through the Eighth Amendments. *Procedural* rights are to be distinguished from *substantive* rights. The latter include those elements that are considered to be of the very essence of freedom, such as freedom of speech, whereas the former are concerned with the methods by which rights are protected. *See also* DUE PROCESS OF LAW, page 65; SUBSTANTIVE RIGHTS, page 84.

Significance A crucial difference between a free society and an authoritarian society lies in the procedures afforded citizens to protect them against arbitrary treatment. Under American law, one may not be tried and condemned except in conformity with due process of law, and any errors in procedure may render a conviction void.

Quartering of Soldiers A prohibition found in the Third Amendment against housing soldiers in private homes during time of peace without consent of the owner. In wartime, quartering of soldiers may be done under conditions prescribed by law.

Significance The Third Amendment was a reaction against the practice of the British, during the colonial era, of quartering soldiers in private homes. This has never been done in the United States, and no cases have arisen concerning this provision. It is one of the elements of civilian control over the military.

Racism A belief that differences among people are rooted in ethnic stock. These differences include color, religion, bloodline, or national origin. Racism usually involves the assumption that one's own race is superior, and that social and political organization should reflect that superiority. Nazi persecution of Jews prior to and during World War II on the theory that German Aryans constituted a superior race is a leading example of racism. In the United States the term, "white racism," is used to describe discrimination against black people in social and political institutions.

Significance "White racism" was cited by the President's National Advisory Commission on Civil Disorders (Kerner Report, so named after the Commission Chairman, Governor Otto Kerner of Illinois) in 1968 as the underlying cause of racial disorder in the United States. "What white Americans have never fully understood—but what the Negro can never forget—," wrote the Commission, "is that white society is deeply implicated in the ghetto. White institutions created it, white institutions maintain it, and white society condones it." The most bitter fruit of white racism, said the Commission, was the exclusion of Negroes from the benefits of economic progress and it called for a massive national commitment to reform. The concept of racism is rejected by many Americans who find the charge to be insulting. Nevertheless, contemporary history makes it difficult to refute the Kerner Report's warning that the nation "is moving toward two societies, one black, one white—separate and unequal." Congressional legislation, executive action, and court decisions in the past twenty years demonstrate American commitment to eradication of racism as official policy in the United States. Nevertheless, the existence of white racism intensifies the race problem in America and, according to reports of the United States Commission on Civil Rights, extends to other nonwhite Americans as well, such as Chicanos and Indians.

Reasonable Doubt The standard for determining the guilt of a person charged with a criminal offense. The prosecution must persuade the judge or jury that the evidence proves guilt beyond a reasonable doubt. Though long accepted as part of the common law tradition, it was not until 1970 that the Supreme Court held "lest there remain any doubt about the constitutional stature of the reasonable doubt standard, we explicitly hold that the Due Process Clause protects the accused against conviction except upon proof beyond a reasonable doubt of every fact necessary to constitute the crime with which he is charged" (*In Re Winship,* 397 U.S. 358 [1970]). The standard applies to both adult and juvenile criminal cases.

Significance The reasonable doubt standard is to be distinguished from the "preponderance of evidence" standard used in civil cases. In criminal cases, it is especially important that the accused be safeguarded against a dubious conviction and that the judge or jury be as certain of the decision as is humanly possible. The high standard of proof beyond a reasonable doubt enhances respect for the law and protects the innocent.

Religious Test A requirement that one profess belief in a particular religious faith or in a Supreme Being as a condition to holding public office. Article VI of the Constitution prohibits such tests. Several state constitutions contain a requirement that public officials profess a belief in God, but in 1961 the Supreme Court held such a Maryland provision unconstitutional (*Torcaso v. Watkins,* 367 U.S. 488). *See also* SEPARATION OF CHURCH AND STATE, page 82.

Significance The prohibition against religious tests for office is a necessary component of the separation of church and state. Until the election of John F. Kennedy, a Catholic, to the presidency in 1960, there appeared to be an "unofficial" religious test for the office of President, since it was widely believed that a non-Protestant could not be elected. Kennedy's victory and the Supreme Court decision in the Maryland case have contributed to the effectiveness of the religious test prohibition.

Restrictive Covenant A clause entered in deeds to protect the value of properties by restricting their uses. Some restrictive covenants prohibit the sale of property to blacks or other minority groups. *See also* CIVIL RIGHTS ACT OF 1968, page 105; *Jones v. Mayer,* page 94.

Significance In one of its early civil rights decisions, the Supreme Court held that racially restrictive covenants could not be enforced in the courts, since such action would constitute governmental support of discrimination contrary to the equal protection clause of the Fourteenth Amendment (*Shelley v. Kramer,* 334 U.S. 1 [1948]). National law now prohibits discrimination based on race, religion, or national origin designed to restrict property rights.

Right to Bear Arms The guarantee in the Second Amendment of the right to keep weapons, recognizing that "A well regulated miltia [is] necessary to the security of a free state." Similar provisions are found in many state constitutions. The right to bear arms is an implicit recognition of the right of revolution, stemming from the idea that a tyrant could not be overthrown if the people were denied the means. In addition, this guarantee was included in the Bill of Rights to assure the states that the national government would not disarm the state militias.

Significance The assassination of prominent political leaders, widespread use of weapons in civil disturbances, and an increasing crime rate have aroused nationwide concern over the ease of securing firearms and produced pressures for national legislation to control their sale and use. Counterpressures from the National Rifle Association, sportsmen, and some fearful citizens have been successful in preventing enactment of effective gun control laws. The keeping and use of arms, however, is extensively regulated. Possession of certain types of weapons, such as machine guns or sawed-off shotguns, is prohibited, and registration of some weapons is required. Nevertheless, effective regulation has proved impossible because firearms regulation remains largely a state and local responsibility.

Right to Counsel   The guarantee in the Sixth Amendment to the Constitution that a defendant in a criminal case have the assistance of an attorney. The Supreme Court has ruled that the national government (*Johnson v. Zerbst,* 304 U.S. 458 [1938]) and state governments (*Gideon v. Wainwright,* 372 U.S. 335 [1963]) must furnish counsel for indigent defendants. An accused must be permitted to confer with counsel prior to interrogation by the police and at any other critical stage in proceedings against him, such as a preliminary hearing, lineup, or appeal. He may waive his right to counsel, but the waiver must be an intelligent one in which the the defendant recognizes the consequences of his action. *See also Gideon v. Wainwright,* page 92; *Miranda v. Arizona,* page 97; PUBLIC DEFENDER, page 260.

Significance Right to counsel is based on the assumption that the average person is unable to understand the intricacies of the law or to know the full extent of his rights. In the *Gideon* case, the Court sought to overcome the advantages of those able to afford counsel by providing "equal justice for the poor." The Supreme Court's insistence that indigent defendants be furnished counsel has led to extensive use of the public defender system.

Search and Seizure   Methods by which police officers gather evidence and make arrests. The Fourth Amendment prohibits "unreasonable" searches and seizures. Under ordinary or "reasonable" circumstances, a search warrant must be secured from a judge or magistrate. This written order, issued under oath, describes the place to be searched and the person or things to be seized. A warrant is not essential if it can be shown that time or circumstances did not reasonably permit securing it. Evidence gathered through illegal or unreasonable means is not admissible in federal trials nor, under the Fourteenth Amendment, in state trials (*Weeks v. United States,* 232 U.S. 383 [1914]; *Mapp v. Ohio,* 367 U.S. 643 [1961]). Such evidence may be used, however, as a basis for questioning a witness before a grand jury (*United States v. Calandra,* 410 U.S. 925 [1974]). *See also* ARREST WARRANT, page 58; *Mapp v. Ohio,* page 96; WIRETAPPING, page 85.

Significance The Fourth Amendment has proved to be one of the more troublesome provisions of the Bill of Rights. What constitutes an "unreasonable" search and seizure? No precise definition can be made and the courts have treated the issue on a case-to-case basis, considering all the circumstances involved. Concern over crime rates and drug addiction has led to Supreme Court approval of laws authorizing police to "stop and frisk" suspicious persons (*Terry v. Ohio,* 392 U.S. 1 [1968]) and congressional endorsement of "no-knock" search warrants in the District of Columbia Crime Control Act of 1970 and the Drug Abuse Prevention and Control Act of 1970. Abuse of "no-knock" procedures, however, led to their repeal in 1974. The most serious contemporary problem is the reasonabless of search through wiretapping and other electronic devices. Evidence that is obtained through an unreasonable search and seizure is inadmissible on the ground that it constitutes self-incrimination—forcing the accused to reveal what he has a right to conceal.

Sedition   Actions that incite rebellion or discontent against duly established government. Espionage, sabotage, or attempts to overthrow the government constitute sedition, as does advocacy by publication or speech to accomplish these goals. The Sedition Acts of 1798 and 1918 put severe limitations on mere criticism of the government. Recent sedition legislation has been aimed at outlawing Communist conspirarcies and advocacy of doctrines aimed at overthrow of government by force. *See also* ALIEN AND SEDITION LAWS, page 103; COMMUNIST CONTROL ACT, page 106; *Dennis v. United States,* page 90; INTERNAL SECURITY ACT, page 107; SMITH ACT, page 103.

Significance   Though closely akin to treason, sedition does not require the precise standard of proof that the Constitution requires for treason convictions. Few people question the legality or wisdom of outlawing and punishing seditious *actions.* Punishment for seditious *speech,* however, resulted in severe restrictions on nonconformists in postrevolutionary America and during World War I. The Supreme Court has sustained convictions of Communists but has drawn a distinction between mere advocacy of abstract doctrine and conspiracy to advocate concrete action (*Yates v. United States,* 354 U.S. 298 [1957]). A law that makes mere criticism of government a crime makes free government impossible, since one may criticize and be loyal at the same time.

Segregation   The separation of the white and black races in public and private facilities. Laws requiring the segregation of the races (Jim Crow laws) have been on the statute books of several states. In 1896, the Supreme Court upheld such laws under the "separate but equal" doctrine whereby the Negro could be segregated if he were provided with equal facilities (*Plessy v. Ferguson,* 163 U.S. 537). Under this doctrine, a wide pattern of segregation developed in schools, transportation, recreation, and housing. Beginning in the 1940s, the Court began to weaken the separate but equal doctrine by insisting that the facilities provided for Negroes, particularly in education, be equal, indeed. Finally, in 1954, the Court struck down the separate but equal formula, holding that segregation based on color denied the equal protection of the laws (*Brown v. Board of Education of Topeka,* 347 U.S. 483). *See also Brown v. Board of Education of Topeka,* page 89; CIVIL RIGHTS ACTS, page 104; *Milliken v. Bradley,* page 96; *Plessy v. Ferguson,* page 99; *Swann v. Charlotte,* page 102.

Significance   Segregation has been part of the pattern of life in the seventeen southern states and the District of Columbia. The Supreme Court's 1954 decision has simultaneously strained and improved the status of the American Negro. Since 1954, integration has proceeded at various speeds and, in some states, little progress has been made. In certain parts of the country integration has precipitated violence. Since 1954, however, with the law no longer permitting separate treatment, the Negro has sought to make the ruling a reality by "sit-ins," political action, marches, and mass demonstrations. Moreover, Congress has passed civil rights measures in 1957, 1960, 1964, 1965, and 1968 to increase black political and civil rights. Southern states have sought to resist integration by various evasive schemes but few have found favor in the courts. Unofficial patterns of segregation still exist on a wide scale in both the North and the South and are likely to continue for many years.

Self-incrimination   Testimony by a person that reveals facts that may result in a criminal prosecution against him. The Fifth Amendment of the Constitution provides that no person "shall be compelled in any criminal case to be a witness against himself." Though originally applied to persons on trial, the concept has been extended to cover testimony before legislative committees or executive agencies. A person may not refuse to testify in order to protect another person, nor because his answers might bring disgrace upon himself. The guarantee extends only to testimony that might involve the person himself in a criminal prosecution. A person who has been given immunity or a pardon, or who has already been convicted of the particular offense (so that he may not be tried again), may not refuse to testify. No unfavorable inferences may legally be drawn from proper use of the Fifth Amendment guarantee against self-incrimination. This applies with equal force to both state and federal proceedings (*Malloy v. Hogan,* 378 U.S. 1 [1964]). *See also* IMMUNITY, page 71; *Malloy v. Hogan,* page 95; *Miranda v. Arizona,* page 97; SEARCH AND SEIZURE, page 80.

Significance In a criminal case, the burden of proof is on the prosecution. The right against self-incrimination is designed to prevent the shifting of the burden to the defendant by forcing him to reveal incriminating facts. It also prevents the use of torture or inquisitorial procedures to coerce confessions, as well as the use of evidence illegally obtained. A major problem involves the question of whether the witness has waived his right by answering questions directly or indirectly related to a matter that might incriminate him. Once the witness begins to answer a line of questions, he may have unknowingly waived the right; for this reason, many witnesses have refused to answer any questions. This has been particularly true in congressional investigations into subversion and racketeering. A person, however, may be found in contempt if he uses the right as a mere dodge and refuses to answer proper questions. While one may not suffer any legal penalty for invoking the Fifth Amendment, loss of reputation or employment may result. The protection against self-incrimination is one of the hallmarks of a free society, but, refusal to testify by "taking the Fifth" in legislative investigations often arouses widespread indignation.

Separation of Church and State A basic principle of American government that prohibits the mingling of church and state. The principle rests on the First Amendment clause forbidding the passage of any law "respecting an establishment of religion." In a series of controversial cases, the Supreme Court has held that the state must be committed to a position of neutrality and may neither advance nor retard religion. No public funds may be expended on behalf of any church nor may the government favor one church over another. Public schools may not be used for sectarian religious observances, and official requirements for Bible reading or prayer recitals are forbidden. Laws that have a predominantly secular effect, such as public bus transportation for parochial schools or Sunday closing laws, have been upheld. The permissible extent of public aid to church-related schools remains, however, unresolved. The national government, under the Elementary and Secondary Education Act of 1965, and many state governments provide for aid to parochial schools. The Supreme Court has struck down state programs that paid the salaries of teachers in church-related schools, for instruction in nonreligious subjects, as "excessive entanglement between government and religion" and, on similar grounds, voided programs of tuition aid through reimbursement or tax relief to families of children attending nonpublic schools. At the same time, however, the Court upheld federal and state construction grants to church-related colleges. The distinction was made by the Court on the grounds that precollege parochial schools are more involved in religious indoctrination, and that the state programs would involve continuing controversy over public support. *See also Committee for Public Education and Religious Liberty v. Nyquist,* page 90; ELEMENTARY AND SECONDARY EDUCATION ACT, page 375; *Everson v. Board of Education of Ewing Township,* page 91; HIGHER EDUCATION ACT, page 376; RELI-

GIOUS TEST, page 79; *School District of Abington Township v. Schempp,* page 101; *Zorach v. Clauson*, page 103.

Significance The principle of the separation of church and state is most controversial when applied to the role of religion in the public schools and to the use of public funds for parochial schools. The Supreme Court has supported Thomas Jefferson's idea that the establishment clause was intended to erect "a wall of separation between church and state" toward the end that official governmental support not be placed behind the tenets of any religious orthodoxy and that public institutions not become embroiled in sectarian controversy.

Seventh Amendment A part of the Bill of Rights that guarantees the preservation of the right to a jury trial in a suit at common law where the value in controversy exceeds $20. It also provides that facts tried by the jury may not be reexamined in any court except in accordance with common law rules. A jury of six persons may be used in such suits.

Significance The Seventh Amendment is a rarely litigated item that applies only to cases in which Congress permits common law rules to be used. It does not apply to cases arising out of statutory law nor in equity proceedings. The Seventh Amendment is an example of a portion of the Bill of Rights that is not made applicable to the states by the Fourteenth Amendment, since it involves no right that is basic to fairness or that is so important as to be ranked as fundamental.

Sixth Amendment A part of the Bill of Rights that stipulates the basic requirements of procedural due process in federal criminal trials. These include a speedy and public trial, an impartial jury, trial in the area where the crime was committed, notice of the charges, the right to confront witnesses and to obtain favorable witnesses, and the right to counsel. All have been made binding on the states through the due process clause of the Fourteenth Amendment. *See also* CONFRONTATION CLAUSE, page 63; JURY, page 253; RIGHT TO COUNSEL, page 80; SPEEDY TRIAL, page 83; TRIAL, page 265; VENUE, page 266; WITNESS, page 86.

Significance The brief but highly important Sixth Amendment sums up the essential procedures of a fair and impartial trial. An improper denial of any of these ingredients may be sufficient to void a conviction.

Speedy Trial A requirement found in the Sixth Amendment that criminal prosecutions must be undertaken without undue delay. In a 1972 decision (*Barker v. Wingo,* 407 U.S. 514) the Supreme Court recognized the difficulty of precise definition of "speedy," but suggested four criteria; the length of the delay, the reasons for the delay, whether the delay was prejudicial to the defendant, and whether the defendant had demanded a speedy trial. In the Speedy Trial Act of 1974, Congress provided that, by 1980, the permissible period between arrest and trial cannot exceed 100 days. The arrested person must be charged within 30 days, arraigned within 10 days of being charged, and tried within 60 days of arraignment. Discretion is vested in judges to determine when delay is essential, as in the case of need for a mental examination, and whether delay is to result in dismissal of charges with or without possibility of reprosecution. *See also* ARRAIGNMENT, page 58.

Significance The speedy trial requirement is designed to protect a suspect against the harsh uncertainties of a criminal prosecution and to assure that testimony of witnesses will be available and reliable. The neglect or avoidance of the constitutional requirement has become a national scandal, though both the defendant and the prosecutor may be at fault. For example, in *Barker v. Wingo* the Court held that a five-year delay in a murder case was not a violation, since in the given circumstances the delay did not prejudice the defendant who had not pressed for trial. Crowded court dockets due to increased crime rates and inadequate court facilities and staffs are also a cause of delay. Congressional adoption of some minimal time requirement after which a suspect must be freed is in keeping with the philosophy of the speedy trial requirement "that justice delayed is justice denied."

State Action An official act by a state or local governmental agency or officer. The term usually refers to any abridgment of individual rights by state or local governmental agencies, laws, or officials, which is forbidden by the Fourteenth Amendment to the Constitution. Invasions of individual rights by private individuals are not within the purview of the Amendment. For example, a law imposing racial segregation is state action, whereas an individual's discriminatory act does not violate the Fourteenth Amendment, although the individual action may be forbidden by statute. *See also* FOURTEENTH AMENDMENT, page 68.

Significance The state action concept has been crucial to the legal assault on racial segregation. Discrimination based on segregation ordinances or on official support by elected officials or police officers has been held by the courts to be state action. Judicial enforcement of racially restrictive real estate convenants has been likewise prohibited as state action. The major contemporary problem is whether private discrimination becomes state action if an individual seeks governmental support to protect his private interests. The present tests of state action appear to be whether the public interest is strong enough to transform private actions into matters of state concern, and the degree of official involvement in the discriminatory act.

Substantive Rights Constitutional guarantees essential for personal liberty. These generally include those rights listed in the First, Thirteenth, and Fourteenth amendments—freedoms of speech, press, religion, assembly, and petition, freedom from involuntary servitude, and the right to equal protection of the law. *Substantive* rights are to be distinguished from *procedural* rights, which are concerned with the manner in which the substantive rights are protected, as by due process and fair trial. *See also* PROCEDURAL RIGHTS, page 77.

Significance No precise listing of substantive rights is possible; they include those personal liberties essential to a free society. No person can be considered free if he does not have liberty to express himself in speech, press, or prayer, or if he is arbitrarily discriminated against. Necessary limitations, however, may be placed on substantive rights. Thus, one may be confined to jail or have his speech limited, but only in accordance with due process of law.

Thirteenth Amendment An amendment to the Constitution, adopted in 1865, forbidding slavery or involuntary servitude anywhere in the United States or any place subject to its jurisdiction. It applies to individuals as well as to government. The Amendment is a guarantee against forced labor and, under recent Supreme Court rulings, gives Congress power to legislate against any acts which impose a "badge of slavery" on anyone. *See also* INVOLUNTARY SERVITUDE, page 72; *Jones v. Mayer*, page 94.

Significance The Thirteenth Amendment closed a sad chapter in American history. With the exception of some post-Civil War leaders, the Amendment has been viewed essentially as outlawing slavery. In 1968 the Supreme Court upheld an 1866 law, passed under authority of the Thirteenth Amendment, which outlawed racial discrimination in the sale or rental of property (*Jones v. Mayer*, 392 U.S. 409). The Court ruled that the Amendment gives Congress authority well beyond that of forbidding slavery. This decision, along with another upholding an 1871 law authorizing private suits against persons who conspire to violate the rights of others (*Griffin v. Breckenridge*, 403 U.S. 88 [1971]), gives new vitality to the Thirteenth Amendment.

Treason A disloyal act, which, as defined by Article III, section 3 of the Constitution, "shall consist only in levying war against [the United States], or in adhering to their enemies, giving them aid and comfort." The Constitution further provides that one may not be convicted of treason "unless on the testimony of two witnesses to the same overt act, or on confession in open court." *See also* SEDITION, page 81.

Significance Treason is the only crime precisely defined in the Constitution as a safeguard against irresponsible charges for this most serious of crimes. Levying war or adhering to enemies of the United States are the only grounds for bringing a prosecution and, unless the suspect confesses, two witnesses must testify that they saw him commit the act. Acts of disloyalty that do not fall within the constitutional definition may be prosecuted under sedition laws. Communist subversive activities are not considered treason since we are not, technically, at war with Communist states. Many state constitutions contain treason provisions, but it is questionable whether one could commit treason against a state and not against the United States. John Brown, hanged in 1859 for his raid on Harpers Ferry, Virginia, is believed to be the only person executed in this country for treason against a state. Treason trials have not been numerous and no one has been executed for treason by the national government.

Wiretapping The use of any electronic device to intercept private conversations. After years of confusion over the permissible bounds for the gathering and use of electronic eavesdropping, the Supreme Court ruled that the requirements of the Fourth Amendment's protection against unreasonable searches and seizures must be met (*Berger v. New York*, 388 U.S. 41, *Katz v. United States*, 389 U.S. 347 [1967]). Congress, in the Omnibus Crime Control and Safe Streets Act of 1968, authorized use of telephone taps and bugging devices if a warrant is secured from a judge. In emergency cases, involving national security or organized crime, warrants are not required for forty-eight hours under the Act. *See also Berger v. New York*, page 89; PRIVACY, page 76; SEARCH AND SEIZURE, page 80.

Significance Technological refinements of electronic listening devices have vastly complicated traditional rules of search and seizure and illustrate the difficulty of keeping the Bill of Rights abreast of modern developments. Electronic eavesdropping presents special problems not generally involved in searches and seizures: a search warrant ordinarily is used at one time only, not for an extended period; innocent people involved in conversations with a suspect lose their privacy;

and the suspect is completely unaware of the intrusion. Wiretapping has and will continue to consume considerable judicial and legislative attention in the years ahead.

Witness   A person who presents information or evidence in a trial or investigation. Under the Sixth Amendment and most state constitutions, a person accused of a crime is entitled to confront the witnesses against him and to compel the attendance of witnesses in his favor. In 1965, the Supreme Court ruled that the right of confrontation of witnesses applies in state trials under the due process clause of the Fourteenth Amendment (*Pointer v. Texas,* 380 U.S. 400). The right to compel the attendance of witnesses was similarly applied to the states in 1967 (*Washington v. Texas,* 388 U.S. 14). *See also* CONFRONTATION CLAUSE, page 63; SUBPOENA, page 262.

Significance   In a criminal case, the government must permit cross-examination of any witness it uses. If it wishes to conceal the identity of an informant, then that person may not be put on the stand, nor may his testimony be introduced. In addition, the defendant is entitled to see any reports made to the police by a witness, unless the judge rules otherwise. The right to compel the attendance of favorable witnesses is an important corollary to the right of confrontation, and the defendant has the right to government aid to subpoena any reluctant witness. Though these rights are fairly well established in criminal trials, attention in recent years has been directed to the lack of these rights in congressional investigations. In hearings on subversion or crime, criticism has been made of the fact that while persons are usually permitted to testify, they are not permitted to confront and cross-examine accusers nor to compel the attendance of favorable witnesses.

IMPORTANT AGENCIES

Civil Rights Commission   Established by the federal Civil Rights Act of 1957 as a bipartisan commission of six members to investigate the broad area of civil rights. The Commission has conducted investigations and published reports on such matters as voting rights, education, housing, employment, and the administration of justice. The Civil Rights Act of 1964 strengthened the Commission's investigatory power and established it as a national clearing house for civil rights information. In 1972, its jurisdiction was expanded to include sex discrimination.

Significance   The Commission has uncovered evidence of abuses of civil rights in all areas of its investigations. Its findings and recommendations played a vital role in the enactment of the Civil Rights Acts of 1960, 1964, 1965, and 1968. The Commission has taken the initiative in issuing extended reports on civil rights, thereby calling attention to the great gap between the promise of the law and the plight of minorities, and it has not hesitated to criticize Congress or specific agencies for inaction.

Community Relations Service   Established by the Civil Rights Act of 1964 to help communities resolve civil rights problems. The Service is part of the Justice Department, headed by a director responsible to the Attorney General. The facilities of the Service are made available either upon request or through its own initiative. It is directed by law to seek the cooperation of state and local agencies and to carry on its work without publicity.

Significance The Community Relations Service is patterned after the human relations or community relations agencies found in numerous state and local governments that make available conciliatory services to temper dangerous community tensions. Though its activities do not receive publicity, indications are that the Service has been involved in a large number of cases.

Department of Justice The Department of Justice has three divisions that are particularly concerned with civil liberty matters. The Federal Bureau of Investigation (FBI), the Department's best-known agency, is responsible for investigation of violations of federal law. The Criminal Division prosecutes violations of federal law and, since 1973, bears responsibility for internal security matters, a function formerly assigned to a special Internal Security Division. The Civil Rights Division is responsible for the enforcement of all statutes affecting civil rights including the Civil Rights Acts, antipeonage laws, election frauds, and obstructions of justice. *See also* COMMUNITY RELATIONS SERVICE, page 86.

Significance The Department of Justice is playing an increasingly large role in the field of civil liberties. The transfer of internal security matters to the criminal division reflects decreasing concern with subversion, but an increasing crime rate and an intensification of racial conflict have expanded the activities of the FBI, Criminal, and Civil Rights Divisions. As the scope of federal law enforcement grows, so does the influence of the Justice Department.

Equal Employment Opportunity Commission (EEOC) Established by the Civil Rights Act of 1964 to investigate and conciliate disputes involving discrimination because of race or sex by employers, unions, and employment agencies. EEOC consists of five members appointed for five-year terms by the President with Senate consent. EEOC stresses confidential persuasion and conciliation to achieve its objectives, but may, if conciliation fails, institute legal action. Action by state fair employment agencies is encouraged by the Act. *See also* FAIR EMPLOYMENT PRACTICES LAWS, page 67.

Significance The EEOC represents a major victory for civil rights proponents who had sought fair employment practice legislation from Congress for many years. For some years, discrimination had already been forbidden by executive order in governmental employment and in private companies filling governmental contracts. While almost thirty states have established fair employment commissions with varying degrees of enforcement power, the EEOC represents a national commitment to equality of opportunity throughout, the nation in both public and private employment. Though given authority in 1972 to institute legal action, the EEOC lacks authority to issue cease and desist orders.

Subversive Activities Control Board An independent agency established in 1950 under the Internal Security Act and abolished in 1973. Its major function was to conduct hearings, upon the request of the Attorney General, to determine whether an organization was a Communist action, front, or infiltrated group subject to the registration requirements of the Internal Security Act. *See also* ATTORNEY GENERAL'S LIST, page 59; INTERNAL SECURITY ACT, page 107.

Significance The Subversive Activities Control Board was established by Congress to gather evidence that would identify subversive groups. The Board ordered a few organizations to register, including the Communist party, and the Supreme Court upheld the order with regard to the party (*Communist Party v. Subversive Activities Control Board*, 367 U.S. 1 [1961]). Since no person registered for the Communist party, however, the Board ordered party leaders to register as individual members, as provided by law. This order was declared invalid by the Supreme Court as an invasion of the right against self-incrimination (*Albertson v. Subversive Activities Control Board*, 382 U.S. 70 [1965]). Congress amended the law in 1967 authorizing the Board itself to register individuals. Judicial rejection of key provisions of the Internal Security Act weakened the Board to the point that it became idle.

IMPORTANT CASES

Ashcraft v. Tennessee, 322 U.S. 143 (1944): Ruled that a confession obtained from a suspect after prolonged interrogation under hot lights by a relay of officers is not admissible in a state trial. Such coercive methods to obtain confessions violate the Fourteenth Amendment. *See also* CONFESSION, page 63.

Significance Earlier, in *Brown v. Mississippi*, 297 U.S. 278 (1936), the Court announced for the first time that a confession extracted through brutality and torture violated the Fourteenth Amendment. In the *Ashcraft* case, the Court extended this rule to confessions acquired as a result of psychological rather than physical maltreatment. The Court has since examined carefully convictions based on confessions in order to ensure that the confessions have been wholly voluntary.

Barron v. Baltimore, 7 Peters 243 (1833): Held that the Bill of Rights limits only the national government and not the state governments. This decision is still operative today although its impact has been greatly modified in practice through interpretations of the Fourteenth Amendment. The Supreme Court has incorporated most of the provisions of the Bill of Rights into the due process clause of the Fourteenth Amendment, thus making them applicable to state governments. *See also* FOURTEENTH AMENDMENT, page 68; *Gitlow v. New York*, page 92; INCORPORATION DOCTRINE, page 72.

Significance *Barron v. Baltimore* illustrates the application of the federal principle to civil liberties—the Bill of Rights was clearly designed to limit the power of the national government and not the states. Subsequent interpretation of the Fourteenth Amendment so as to incorporate most of the Bill of Rights and make it binding on the states has all but eliminated the strong impact that the *Barron* decision had for almost one hundred years.

Bartkus v. Illinois 355 U.S. 281 (1958): Denied a claim of double jeopardy appealed from a conviction in a state court for bank robbery following acquittal by a federal court for the same bank robbery. *See also* DOUBLE JEOPARDY, page 65.

Significance The *Bartkus* case underscores the rule that double jeopardy refers only to repeated trials on the same charge by the same jurisdiction. A person may, therefore, be tried by both the national and state courts for a single offense. He may not, however, be tried by a state and a city within that state for the same offense (*Waller v. Florida*, 397 U.S. 387 [1970]), nor for robbery of one victim after he has been acquitted of robbing another victim in the same incident (*Ashe v. Swenson*, 397 U.S. 436 [1970]).

Berger v. New York, 388 U.S. 41 (1967): A decision in which the Supreme Court brought wiretapping within the protection of the Fourth Amendment search and seizure provisions. The Court declared unconstitutional a New York law which authorized a judge to issue an eavesdrop order but which did not require indication of any specific offense, conversation, or special circumstance. *See also* WIRETAPPING, page 85.

Significance By holding that the use of an electronic device to capture conversations is a search within the meaning of the Fourth Amendment, the Court clarified one of the more puzzling aspects of the permissible use of electronic eavesdropping. Prior to the *Berger* case, the Court had treated the problem as a matter of statutory rather than constitutional law unless an actual physical invasion of property took place. In another important ruling shortly after the *Berger* decision (*Katz v. United States*, 389 U.S. 347 [1967]), the Court held that federal officials conducted an unlawful search and seizure by eavesdropping on conversations in a public telephone booth. Even though there was no physical invasion of property, such an intrusion into privacy without judicial safeguards afforded by the Fourth Amendment could not stand. It can now be said that "words" as well as "things" are protected against unreasonable searches and seizures. Congress has since provided for wiretapping and bugging by state and national officials in the Omnibus Crime Control Act of 1968, requiring warrants under most, but not all, circumstances.

Bolling v. Sharpe, 347 U.S. 497 (1954): Declared, in one of the school segregation cases, that segregation in the public schools of the District of Columbia violated the due process clause of the Fifth Amendment. *See also Brown v. Board of Education of Topeka* page 89; EQUAL PROTECTION, page 66.

Significance The Constitution contains no requirement that the national government afford "equal protection of the laws." The "equal protection" clause is found in the Fourteenth Amendment and is a limitation on the states. Nevertheless, the Court held that segregation of the races by the national government is an arbitrary denial of liberty without due process of law.

Brown v. Board of Education of Topeka, 347 U.S. 483 (1954); 349 U.S. 294 (1955): Established in a major decision that segregation of the races in public schools violates the equal protection clause of the Fourteenth Amendment. The Supreme Court in 1954 overruled the "separate but equal" doctrine that had been in effect since 1896, noting that "Separate educational facilities are inherently unequal." In 1955, the Court ordered desegregation to proceed "with all deliberate speed," leaving it to the federal district courts to determine implementations of the ruling in specific cases brought before them. *See also Bolling v. Sharpe*, page 89; SEGREGATION, page 81.

Significance The *Brown* decision ranks among the most important in American constitutional history. Extensive desegregation of schools has occurred, sometimes with violent results. Other segregation practices have also been declared unconstitutional following this decision. The *Brown* case created a crisis in national-state relations and helped spur the Negro protest movement. The decision initiated a social revolution, since supported by major national Civil Rights Acts and by state and local legislation.

Committee for Public Education and Religious Liberty v. Nyquist, 413 U.S. 756 (1973): Struck down, as a violation of the First Amendment's establishment of religion clause, a New York law providing for maintenance and repair grants to nonpublic schools, tuition reimbursement for low-income families with children in parochial schools, and tax relief for families not qualifying for tuition reimbursement. The Court found the primary effect of these provisions to be an advancement of religious rather than secular interests, and an excessive entanglement between church and state. *See also Everson v. Board of Education,* page 91; SEPARATION OF CHURCH AND STATE, page 82.

Significance Soaring educational costs have put parochial schools under considerable economic pressure, resulting in persistent and increasing demands for public subsidy. Nevertheless, the Supreme Court has taken a dim view of direct or indirect financial aids which are clearly designed to sustain church schools rather than aid the pupil. Earlier the Court had declared unconstitutional state programs that paid salaries of teachers of secular subjects in parochial schools (*Lemon v. Kurtzman,* 403 U.S. 602 [1971]). However, construction aids to church-related colleges and universities have received judicial support on the grounds that colleges are less religiously oriented and the students less impressionable than at lower educational levels (*Tilton v. Richardson,* 403 U.S. 672 [1971]; *Hunt v. McNair,* 410 U.S. 952 [1973]). The degree of political controversy apt to be generated by a given form of aid appears to be crucial to the court in making decisions in the area of aid to nonpublic schools.

Dennis v. United States, 341 U.S. 494 (1951): Sustained, in a major decision, the conviction of eleven top Communist party leaders for conspiring to teach and to advocate the violent overthrow of the government. The decision upheld the Smith Act of 1940. *See also* ALIEN REGISTRATION ACT, page 103.

Significance The *Dennis* case attracted wide notice because of the sharp conflict between freedom of speech guaranteed by the First Amendment and the indictment against the Communist leaders for advocating their doctrine. The Supreme Court narrowed the interpretation of the clear and present danger rule by holding that in the interest of self-preservation it was not essential for the government to wait until the conspiracy ripened into action. This decision led to numerous prosecutions of other Communist leaders. In 1957, however, in *Yates v. United States,* 354 U.S. 298, the Supreme Court modified its ruling in the *Dennis* case by holding that a distinction must be drawn between urging people to *believe* in something and urging people to *do* something. In the *Yates* case, the Court found that the defendants were merely preaching Communist doctrine in the abstract and were neither teaching nor advocating unlawful conduct. The *Yates* case has restored the clear and present danger rule to some extent and has made it more difficult for the government to prosecute Communists without proving some measure of concrete action to overthrow the government by force. The *Yates* ruling was extended to state laws in 1969 in *Brandenburg v. Ohio,* 395 U.S. 444, in which the court reversed the conviction of a Ku Klux Klan leader for advocating violence.

Elfbrandt v. Russell, 384 U.S. 11 (1966): struck down a state loyalty oath requirement which bound state employees not to become members of the Communist party. The Court held that a law that applies to membership without specific intent to further illegal aims rests on the unacceptable doctrine of guilt by association. A statute touching First Amendment rights must be narrowly drawn. *See also* LOYALTY OATH, page 73.

Significance The *Elfbrandt* case was one of several in which the Supreme Court struck down loyalty oaths after having sustained their imposition in 1951 in *Garner v. Board of Public Works,* 341 U.S. 716. In the *Garner* case the Court upheld a non-Communist affidavit as a reasonable requirement for public employment. Thereafter, the Court tended to find some infirmity in test oaths, holding that they must include knowledge of the illegal aims of proscribed organizations (*Wieman v. Updegraff,* 344 U.S. 183 [1952]) and not be unduly vague (*Baggitt v. Bullitt,* 377 U.S. 360 [1964]). The Court has been especially suspicious of the use of test oaths as a condition of securing a public benefit, such as a tax exemption (*Speiser v. Randall,* 357 U.S. 513 [1958]). In 1972 an oath requiring state employees to swear opposition to forceful overthrow of government was upheld (*Cole v. Richardson,* 405 U.S. 676); this was the first such decision in many years.

Everson v. Board of Education of Ewing Township, 330 U.S. 1 (1947): Decided that it is not a violation of the First Amendment's establishment of religion clause for a state to pay for the transportation of children to parochial schools. The Court found this to be a benefit to the children rather than an aid to the church. *See also Committee for Public Education and Religious Liberty v. Nyquist,* page 90; SEPARATION OF CHURCH AND STATE, page 82.

Significance This case was the first major test of the establishment of religion clause. In its decision, the Court emphasized that the First Amendment was designed to "erect a wall of separation between church and state." Nevertheless, it found that in this instance the wall had not been breached. The *Everson* case serves as a precedent supporting a variety of state and federal aids, including textbooks for parochial schools (*Board of Education v. Allen,* 392 U.S. 236 [1968]) and tax exemptions for churches (*Walz v. Tax Commission,* 397 U.S. 664 [1970]).

Freedman v. Maryland, 380 U.S. 51 (1965): Held that motion picture censorship is permissible provided that the procedure followed assures prompt judicial review of the censor's decision. By this decision, the Court affirmed its ruling in *Times Film Corporation v. Chicago,* 365 U.S. 43 (1961) that initial submission of a motion picture to a censoring board may be required, but it held that the board's decision could not be final. *See also* CENSORSHIP, page 60.

Significance The *Freedman* case raised motion pictures to a level more closely approximating the protection from prior restraint that other forms of expression have than was previously the case. In 1952, movies had been brought within the protection of the First and Fourteenth amendments' guarantees of freedom of speech and press (*Burstyn v. Wilson,* 343 U.S. 495). Films still do not enjoy, however, the same degree of freedom as books, since, under the *Times Film* rule, some form of prior submission to a censor is permitted. In the *Freedman* ruling, the Court sought to promote adequate safeguards against undue inhibition of lawful expression, but was not willing to forbid censorship of movies altogether.

Gideon v. Wainwright, 372 U.S. 335 (1963): A landmark ruling that state courts are required by the due process clause of the Fourteenth Amendment to provide counsel to indigent defendants in criminal cases. This had been required in *federal* criminal trials since the 1938 decision in *Johnson v. Zerbst,* 304 U.S. 458, but state courts were required to furnish counsel to needy defendants only in capital cases (*Powell v. Alabama,* 287 U.S. 45 [1932]) or when special circumstances, such as youth, mental incompetence, or inexperience, necessitated the furnishing of counsel to assure a fair trial (*Betts v. Brady,* 316 U.S. 455 [1942]). In *Gideon,* the Court held that defense by counsel is a fundamental right available to all regardless of social position. *See also* RIGHT TO COUNSEL, page 80.

Significance The *Gideon* case was a major step in the nationalization of the Bill of Rights through the Fourteenth Amendment, because it applied to state cases the guarantee of the assistance of counsel found in the Sixth Amendment. The case was also a forerunner of nationwide concern with equal justice for the poor. The *Gideon* decision not only overcame an illogical distinction between federal and state criminal proceedings, but recognized that most defendants lack the knowledge and skill to defend themselves against experienced prosecutors. Since the *Gideon* case the Court has extended the right to counsel from arrest to appeal.

Gitlow v. New York, 268 U.S. 652 (1925): Established, in a landmark case, that the freedoms of speech and press are protected against state impairment by the due process clause of the Fourteenth Amendment. Nevertheless, in this case, the Court upheld a conviction for publishing and circulating materials advocating the overthrow of government by force.

Significance Prior to this decision, the Court had consistently held that the Fourteenth Amendment did not incorporate any part of the Bill of Rights. Since the *Gitlow* decision, the Court has applied the entire First Amendment, as well as most other portions of the Bill of Rights, to the states under the due process clause of the Fourteenth Amendment. The impact of this decision has been an increasing involvement of the national government in the protection of the people against abuse of their liberties by the states.

Hague v. CIO, 307 U.S. 496 (1939): Declared unconstitutional under the Fourteenth Amendment an ordinance of Jersey City, N.J., that required permission to hold a meeting in or upon public streets, parks, or buildings. Under the ordinance, the officials of Jersey City had molested union organizers of the CIO and had denied them permission to hold meetings or to circulate handbills. *See also* FREEDOM OF ASSEMBLY, page 68.

Significance The *Hague* case established that the right to assemble applies not merely to meetings of private groups but to public meetings in public places. The Court has, in other cases, frowned upon any prior restraints by governmental officials upon public meetings unless some reasonable standards are established for the granting of permits to meet. These standards must in some way be related to the health, safety, and welfare of the people. For example, one might legally be required to secure a permit in order to hold a parade (*Cox v. New Hampshire,* 312 U.S. 569 [1941]), and the government is not obliged to permit use of all public property, such as courthouses and jails, for demonstrations of protest (*Adderly v. Florida,* 385 U.S. 39 [1966]).

Heart of Atlanta Motel v. United States, 379 U.S. 241 (1964): Upheld the constitutionality of Title II of the Civil Rights Act of 1964, a provision barring discrimination in restaurants, hotels, and other places of public accommodation, on the ground that it is a valid exercise of the power to regulate interstate commerce. In 1883, the Supreme Court struck down a similar federal law (*Civil Rights Cases,* 109 U.S. 3) on the ground that private acts of discrimination could not be forbidden by the national government. In the *Heart of Atlanta* case and its companion case, *Katzenbach v. McClung,* 379 U.S. 294 (1964), the Court found ample power in the commerce clause for the national government to prohibit discrimination against persons in accommodations that serve substantial numbers of interstate travelers or that rely upon interstate commerce for a substantial part of their supplies and materials. *See also* CIVIL RIGHTS ACT OF 1964, page 105.

Significance The *Heart of Atlanta Motel* case underscored the determination of the Supreme Court to accord Congress the necessary constitutional tools to meet the crisis in racial discrimination. Many scholars believe that Congress has power under the Fourteenth Amendment to deter discrimination in privately owned public accommodations but, because of the 1883 *Civil Rights Cases,* considerable doubt existed. The commerce power has long been used by Congress to enact social welfare legislation and to control individual behavior.

Hurtado v. California, 110 U.S. 516 (1884): Established that a state is not required by the due process clause of the Fourteenth Amendment to provide for indictment by grand jury in felony cases. Indictment by information is consistent with fair procedure. *See also* GRAND JURY, page 250.

Significance This was the first major test of the meaning of the due process clause of the Fourteenth Amendment. In this case, the Court made it clear that the Fourteenth Amendment did not make the Bill of Rights applicable to the states, and that merely because indictment by grand jury is required by the Fifth Amendment, the states are not thereby bound. While the Supreme Court has made most provisions of the Bill of Rights that relate to criminal procedures binding on the states, the *Hurtado* rule still applies. Few states use the grand jury today.

In Re Gault, 387 U.S. 1 (1967): Held that the due process clause of the Fourteenth Amendment requires the essentials of fair treatment in case involving juveniles accused of crime. The Court reversed a decision committing a child to an industrial school for six years, holding, that in juvenile proceedings: (1) adequate notice of a hearing must be given; (2) the child must be informed of his right to counsel and the privilege against self-incrimination; and (3) he must be given an opportunity to confront and cross-examine witnesses. *See also* JUVENILE DELINQUENT, page 72.

Significance Prior to the *Gault* ruling, juvenile court proceedings had been informal and confidential. The Court did not insist that *all* requirements of a criminal trial be observed in juvenile cases. It noted that compassion and benevolence did not always mark juvenile proceedings and that, in fact, juveniles faced severe sentences in "schools" rather than prisons. In 1970 the

Court held that juveniles, like adults, must be proven guilty beyond a reasonable doubt (*In Re Winship*, 397 U.S. 358), but held in 1971 that juries need not be used in juvenile cses (*McKeiver v. Pennsylvania*, 403 U.S. 528). The Court has tried to maintain some of the flexibility necessary in juvenile cases while guarding essential constitutional rights.

Jehovah's Witnesses Cases Involved, in a series of cases, the religious sect known as Jehovah's Witnesses, testing the scope of religious freedom under the First and Fourteenth Amendments. Among the various decisions were those that held unconstitutional: (1) laws requiring prior official approval to solicit funds for religious purposes (*Cantwell v. Connecticut*, 310 U.S. 296 [1940]); (2) laws levying license taxes on peddlers of religious tracts (*Murdock v. Pennsylvania*, 319 U.S. 105 [1943]); (3) laws prohibiting door-to-door distribution of religious handbills (*Martin v. Struthers*, 319 U.S. 141 [1943]); (4) laws requiring official approval to hold public worship meetings in public parks (*Niemotko v. Maryland*, 340 U.S. 268 [1951]); and (5) an official requirement that children be compelled to salute the flag contrary to their religious beliefs (*West Virginia State Board of Education v. Barnette*, 319 U.S. 624 [1943]). On the other hand, the Court has held that the sect may not under the guise of religious freedom: (1) hold a parade without permission (*Cox v. New Hampshire*, 312 U.S. 569 [1941]); (2) have a young child sell magazines on a street corner late at night, contrary to state child welfare laws (*Prince v. Massachusetts*, 321 U.S. 158 [1944]); or (3) create a breach of peace in the course of a public meeting (*Chaplinsky v. New Hampshire*, 315 U.S. 568 [1942]). *See also* FREEDOM OF RELIGION, page 70.

Significance Through these and other cases, Jehovah's Witnesses have forced the courts to consider the constitutional scope of, and limitations on, the practice of religion. For the most part, the Supreme Court has been sympathetic with the proselytizing activities of the sect except when their actions were in conflict with reasonable measures designed to protect the public welfare.

Jones v. Mayer, 392 U.S. 409 (1968): Held that all racial discrimination, private as well as public, in the sale or rental of property, is outlawed by an 1866 act passed under authority of the Thirteenth Amendment. The 1866 law provides that black citizens have the same rights enjoyed by white citizens "to inherit, purchase, lease, sell, hold, and convey real and personal property." The Court held that Congress has authority "to abolish all badges and incidents of slavery." *See also* CIVIL RIGHTS ACT OF 1968, page 105.

Significance *Jones v. Mayer* is noteworthy on two major counts. First, the Court resurrected the antislavery Thirteenth Amendment to renewed importance, thereby giving Congress an important weapon with which to combat racial discrimination. Second, it gave strong underpinning to the Negroes' fight for open and fair housing opportunities, which is probably the most sensitive civil rights issue facing the nation. The decision was rendered just two months after the enactment of the Civil Rights Act of 1968 which bans discrimination in the sale or rental of about 80 percent of the nation's housing. The Court held that its decision did not diminish the significance of the 1968 Act inasmuch as it was a detailed law, applicable to a broad range of discriminatory practices and enforceable by federal authority, whereas the 1866 law was general, applicable only to racial discrimination and enforceable only by private suit. The Supreme Court's strong commitment to open housing is also demonstrated by its decisions which struck down a California constitutional amendment permitting private discrimination in housing (*Reitman v. Mulkey*, 387 U.S. 369

[1967]) and a city charter amendment requiring a referendum on fair housing ordinances (*Hunter v. Erickson,* 393 U.S. 385 [1969]).

Keyishian v. Board of Regents of New York, 385 U.S. 589 (1967): Struck down a state law which disqualified from public employment any person who advocated, or was a member of a group that advocated, the overthrow of government by force, violence, or any unlawful means. The law was held to violate First Amendment rights of speech and association and to be void because of vagueness. The Court emphasized the need for precision in laws touching basic liberties and that public employment could not be conditioned on the surrender of constitutional rights. Specific intent to further illegal aims must be proven. *See also* LOYALTY-SECURITY PROGRAMS, page 74.

Significance The *Keyishian* case capped the Supreme Court's retreat from its earlier defense of state and local loyalty legislation. The decision overruled *Adler v. Board of Education,* 342 U.S. 485 (1952) which had upheld the very same law condemned here. During the 1950s the Court took the view that no one had a right to public employment and that evidence of certain beliefs and associations could be demanded. The Court gradually moved away from that position and completely rejected it in the *Keyishian* decision.

McNabb v. United States, 318 U.S. 332 (1943): Held that the federal courts may not convict a person of a crime on the basis of a confession secured while he was unlawfully detained. The Court ruled that a prisoner must be taken before a judicial officer for arraignment without delay. *See also* ARRAIGNMENT, page 58.

Significance The *McNabb* rule prohibits police officials from unduly detaining a suspect in order to secure a confession. The Court reaffirmed this in *Mallory v. United States,* 354 U.S. 449 (1957), which involved the release of a confessed criminal because of a delay in arraignment. In the Omnibus Crime Control and Safe Streets Act of 1968, Congress provided for modification of the rule by permitting admission of voluntary confessions in federal cases in spite of a delay of up to six hours in arraignment.

Malloy v. Hogan, 378 U.S. 1 (1964): Held that protection against self-incrimination found in the Fifth Amendment to the Constitution applies to the states through the Fourteenth Amendment in the same manner that it limits the national government. *See also* SELF-INCRIMINATION, page 81.

Significance The *Malloy* case overturned a long-standing ruling that states were not bound by the Fifth Amendment's guarantee against self-incrimination (*Twining v. New Jersey,* 211 U.S. 78 [1908], reaffirmed in *Adamson v. California,* 332 U.S. 46 [1947]. The ruling was part of a pattern of the 1960s, in which the Supreme Court largely abolished the double standard between federal and state criminal procedures. Formerly, state procedures were held to violate the Constitution only when they were shockingly unjust.

Mapp v. Ohio, 367 U.S. 643 (1961): Ruled that a state may not use illegally seized evidence in criminal trials. This decision overruled *Wolf v. Colorado,* 338 U.S. 25 (1949), which held that a state could use evidence secured through an illegal search and seizure. *See also* SEARCH AND SEIZURE, page 80.

Significance Prior to the *Mapp* decision, about half the states admitted illegally seized evidence in criminal trials, although in federal criminal trials such evidence is not admissible (*Weeks v. United States,* 232 U.S. 383 [1914]). In *Mapp v. Ohio,* the Court declared that the Wolf rule made the constitutional protection against unlawful search and seizure meaningless. The *Mapp* decision is a major example of national supervision of state criminal procedures through the Fourteenth Amendment, and of the Supreme Court's nationalization of the Bill of Rights so as to equalize the rights of accused persons in state and federal criminal trials.

Miller v. California, 413 U.S. 5 (1973): Established a major reformulation of the legal test for determining obscenity. The Supreme Court reaffirmed its earlier rulings that obscene material was not protected by the First Amendment but limited the scope of regulation to works depicting or describing sexual conduct as specifically defined by state law. The basic test is to be whether the average person, applying contemporary community (local, not national) standards would find that the work, taken as a whole, appeals to prurient interest in sex, portrays sexual conduct in a patently offensive way as defined by law, and which, taken as a whole, does not have serious literary, artistic, political, or scientific value. *See also Roth v. United States,* page 100.

Significance *Miller v. California* was the first case since the 1957 decision in *Roth v. United States* (354 U.S. 476) in which a majority of the Court could agree on guidelines intended to isolate "hard-core" pornography from protected expression. Since 1957 the Court considered numerous cases under the *Roth* test, but its application to concrete issues caused much confusion. Critics fear that the *Miller* formula will not clarify the issue. Most concern is directed at permitting localized determinations of obscenity and of the standards to be applied to determine whether an allegedly obscene film or book has serious literary, artistic, political, or scientific value. In reaching its decision in the *Miller* case, the Court specifically rejected the view formerly held by some justices that a work, to be judged obscene, must be "utterly without redeeming social value" and the position taken by others that the entire problem could be eliminated by limiting access to pornographic materials to consenting adults.

Milliken v. Bradley, 418 U.S. 717 (1974): Ruled that a federal court could not order bussing of school children across school district boundary lines to achieve racial integration unless each school district affected had been found to practice racial discrimination, or the school district lines had been deliberately drawn to provide for racially segregated schools. The decision overturned a major cross-county bussing order involving the city of Detroit, Michigan, and 53 surrounding suburban schools. The Supreme Court gave strong support to the concept of the neighborhood school, even if substantial de facto racial segregation existed. *See also* DE FACTO SEGREGATION, page 64; SEGREGATION, page 81; *Swann v. Charlotte,* page 102.

Significance *Milliken v. Bradley* is a major reversal of a trend established in 1954 to favor all efforts made to integrate schools. In the *Milliken* case, the Court drew a distinction between state imposed (de jure) segregation and segregation existing as a result of residential patterns without legal restraints (de facto). In holding that school district lines could not ordinarily be ignored, the Court effectively put an end to the likelihood of extensive integration of schools in major metropolitan areas where, typically, black students are concentrated in inner city schools and whites are clustered in surrounding suburbs. The *Milliken* decision came at a time when Congress was taking a strong stand against bussing of students to achieve racial integration.

Miranda v. Arizona, 384 U.S. 436 (1966): A major ruling on criminal procedure to secure the privilege against self-incrimination. The Court held that "Prior to any questioning, the person must be warned that he has a right to remain silent, that any statement he does make may be used against him, and that he has a right to the presence of an attorney, either retained or appointed." The defendant may "knowingly" waive these rights. *See also* SELF-INCRIMINATION, page 81.

Significance The *Miranda* case followed the highly controversial 1964 decision of *Escobedo v. Illinois,* 378 U.S. 478, which held that when an investigation begins to focus upon an accused, the police must inform him of his right to remain silent and honor his request to consult counsel. The *Miranda* case extended these rights to all accused persons. Police officials generally opposed the rulings as did many citizens who saw them as stumbling blocks to adequate law enforcement. Support came from those who agreed with the Court that criminal law enforcement is more reliable when based on independently secured evidence rather than confessions secured through prolonged interrogation in the absence of counsel. In the Omnibus Crime Control and Safe Streets Act of 1968, Congress provided that in federal cases a voluntary confession can be used in evidence even if the accused was not warned of his rights.

Moore v. Dempsey, 261 U.S. 86 (1923): Declared that a trial conducted under the influence of a mob, in which public passion dominates the judge, jury, witnesses, and defense counsel, is a denial of due process of law. In this case, the trial of five Negroes was conducted under the duress of a mob, making the outcome a certainty. *See also* DUE PROCESS, page 65.

Significance The *Moore* case emphasizes that it is not enough that the mere forms of a trial be observed. The proceedings must be fair and provide the defendant with the full measure of his rights. While the Court is usually concerned with specific aspects of a case, it will, as it did here, insist that the entire proceedings be conducted in an atmosphere that will assure a fair trial.

National Association for the Advancement of Colored People v. Alabama, 357 U.S. 449 (1958): Established that a state may not compel the disclosure of the membership lists of an organization that is pursuing lawful ends, if members are likely to suffer physical, economic, and other hostile reprisals from such disclosure. *See also* FREEDOM OF ASSOCIATION, page 69.

Significance The racial integration movement in the South led to an effort on the part of some states to harass and impede the activities of the NAACP and other organizations active in behalf of Negro rights. In this case, the Court stressed the importance of the freedom to associate, noting that any interference is subject to close scrutiny.

Near v. Minnesota, 283 U.S. 697 (1931): Defined freedom of the press to mean that the press is to be free from prior restraint or censorship. A state may not, under the due process clause of the Fourteenth Amendment, permanently enjoin a newspaper from being published. If a newspaper abuses its privilege, it may be tried subsequently. The Court held unconstitutional a Minnesota statute that authorized officials to forbid publication of "malicious, scandalous and defamatory" newspapers. *See also* FREEDOM OF THE PRESS, page 69.

Significance The *Near* case was the first important decision of the Supreme Court on censorship. The Court admitted that under exceptional circumstances, such as war, a paper might be prevented from publishing certain information but it stressed that freedom of the press means freedom from governmental censorship or ban. Otherwise, governmental officials would be in a position to suppress news merely, as in the *Near* case, because it was critical of them.

New York Times v. Sullivan, 376 U.S. 254 (1964): Held that a public official could not recover civil libel damages for criticism of his official conduct by a newspaper or other persons. The rule applies even if the criticism is exaggerated or false, unless deliberate malice and reckless disregard for the truth or falsity of the statement can be shown. This principle was extended to suits for criminal libel in *Garrison v. Louisiana,* 379 U.S. 64 (1965). *See also* LIBEL AND SLANDER, page 73.

Significance The *New York Times* case gives the widest latitude to the freedoms of speech and of the press when they are used to criticize public officials. The Court maintained that the limitation on libel suits was necessary to insure free discussion of public affairs, one of the major purposes of the First Amendment guarantees. Later decisions have extended the ruling to newsworthy people engaged in public controversy (*Associated Press v. Walker,* 388 U.S. 130 [1967]) and with some limitations to ordinary private citizens involved in events of general interest (*Rosenbloom v. Metromedia, Inc.,* 403 U.S. 29 [1971]; *Gertz v. Robert Welch, Inc.,* 418 U.S. 323 [1974]).

New York Times v. United States, 403 U.S. 713 (1971): Held that any prior restraint of freedom of expression by the government carries a heavy presumption of unconstitutionality. In this case the Court held that the Nixon Administration could not forbid newspaper publication of classified documents on the Vietnam war since the government had failed to bear the heavy burden of justification for censorship. *See also* FREEDOM OF THE PRESS, page 69.

Significance The *New York Times* case, also known as the "Pentagon Papers" case, involved publication of secret documents on the history of American policy in Vietnam which had been leaked to the press. The case was the first involving an effort by the national government to restrain newspaper publication of material in its possession. While the Court permitted publication in this instance, the opinions of the justices left unclear the question of whether the government could enjoin publication of information which presents a serious threat to national security.

Norris v. Alabama, 294 U.S. 587 (1935): Held, in what is popularly known as the Second Scottsboro case, that Negroes could not be systematically excluded from jury service. *See also* JURY, page 253.

Significance Under the *Norris* rule, a black defendant does not have a right to have members of his race serve on the jury in his trial. Negroes may not, however, deliberately be excluded. In this case, the Court found that no Negroes had ever served on juries in the counties involved and showed that it would look behind the nondiscriminatory wording of the state law to see what the actual practice was with regard to jury selection. Jury discrimination has been a continuing problem leading to reversals of many convictions of black defendants and to national legislation in 1968 requiring random selection from voting lists in federal juror selection.

Palko v. Connecticut, 302 U.S. 319 (1937): Ruled that the double jeopardy provision of the Fifth Amendment does not apply to the states through the Fourteenth Amendment. In the *Palko* case, the Supreme Court permitted the state to appeal a conviction of a defendant to ask for a more severe sentence. The *Palko* case was overruled in 1969 in *Benton v. Maryland,* 395 U.S. 784. *See also* INCORPORATION DOCTRINE page 72.

Significance The *Palko* case is noteworthy because of the Court's opinion, written by Justice Benjamin N. Cardozo, setting forth the criteria by which the Court determines whether a state violates the rights protected by the due process clause of the Fourteenth Amendment. These include those rights "implicit in the concept of ordered liberty," which are "so rooted in the traditions and conscience of our people as to be ranked as fundamental" or "essential to a fair and enlightened system of justice," or those rights whose denial would be "shocking to the sense of justice of the civilized world." Within this framework, Justice Cardozo indicated that the freedoms of speech, press, religion, and assembly were essential for liberty and hence covered by the Fourteenth Amendment, but that variations in criminal procedures were permissible so long as they violated no fundamental principles of justice. On a case-to-case basis, the Court has marked out the limits of the due process clause, permitting the states, for example, to abolish the grand jury. On the other hand, the Court has forbidden states to conduct unreasonable searches and seizures or to permit cruel and unusual punishment. In the 1960s, the Court moved toward an equalization of rights for state and federal defendants through incorporation of most of the Bill of Rights provisions into the due process clause of the Fourteenth Amendment.

Plessy v. Ferguson, 163 U.S. 537 (1896): Upheld, in a famous decision, a state law requiring segregation of the races in public transportation. The Court held that under the equal protection clause of the Fourteenth Amedment, a state could provide "separate but equal" facilities for Negroes. This case was overruled in *Brown v. Board of Education of Topeka,* 347 U.S. 483 (1954).

Significance The *Plessy* case served as justification for the segregation policies of many states until 1954. Although it is no longer effective, the decision demonstrates the great power of the Supreme Court in giving direction to the law. Until the case was overturned, the Court limited itself to considering whether facilities provided for Negroes were indeed equal though separate.

Pollock v. Williams, 322 U.S. 4 (1944): Decided that a state lends support to slavery or peonage, contrary to the Thirteenth Amendment, when it requires that a person must work to discharge a debt or go to jail. The Court held unconstitutional a law that made it a crime to take money in advance and then refuse to perform the required labor. A state may punish fraud but it cannot make failure to work a crime. *See also* INVOLUNTARY SERVITUDE, page 72.

Significance A surprisingly large number of persons appear to be forced into labor because they are ignorant of their rights. The Justice Department gets numerous complaints of involuntary servitude involving persons who are forced to work through indebtedness to their employers. The Court's decision makes clear that it will outlaw practices that are just short of slavery.

Reynolds v. United States, 98 U.S. 145 (1879): Established that religious freedom does not protect a person who commits a crime or an act contrary to accepted public morals. In this case, the Court upheld the enforcement of antipolygamy laws against Mormons who, prior to 1890, practiced polygamy as a religious doctrine. *See also* FREEDOM OF RELIGION, page 70.

Significance The *Reynolds* case established one of the clearest legal principles involving the free exercise of religion. A person is free to believe and worship as he pleases so long as his conduct violates no laws that validly protect the health, safety, or morals of the community.

Roe v. Wade, 410 U.S. 113 (1973): Held that criminal laws which prohibit abortions except to save the life of the mother are unconstitutional violations of the right to privacy embraced within the personal liberty protected by the due process clause of the Fourteenth Amendment. Specifically the Court held that (1) prior to the first trimester, abortion must be left to medical judgment; (2) during the second trimester, the state may, if it chooses, regulate abortion to protect maternal health but may not prohibit abortion; and (3) during the third trimester, the stage subsequent to vitality, the state may regulate or even prohibit abortion except where necessary, in medical judgment, to preserve the life of the mother. *See also* PRIVACY, page 76.

Significance *Roe v. Wade* illustrates the rise of the concept of privacy in American law, particularly as it relates to marriage and procreation. Growing concern for the rights of women is also reflected in the ruling. The case stirred extensive controversy, touching as it does on sensitive and emotional issues, with strong religious undertones. Demands for a constitutional amendment to overcome the decision has been strong and the issue will undoubtedly be a vital one in future electoral campaigns.

Roth v. United States, 354 U.S. 476 (1957): Excluded obscenity from the area of constitutionally protected speech and press. The Court held that the proper standard to determine obscenity is "whether to the average person, applying contemporary community standards, the dominant theme of the material taken as a whole appeals to prurient interest." The Court reformulated this standard in 1973 in *Miller v. California* (413 U.S. 5). *See also* CENSORSHIP, page 60; *Miller v. California;* page 96.

Significance The Roth decision was the first effort by the Supreme Court to define obscenity, a matter that has long puzzled American courts. In denying constitutional protection to obscene publications, the Court expressed the view that obscenity was withut the "redeeming social importance" of the kinds of speech that the First Amendment is designed to protect. In a companion case, *Alberts v. California,* 354 U.S. 476 (1957), the Court applied the same rule to state obscenity laws. Whether or not particular publication is obscene is determined on a case-to-case basis. In 1964, the Court defined the "community standards" rule of the *Roth* case to mean national rather than local standards (*Jacobellis v. Ohio,* 378 U.S. 184). In 1966, the Court held that the intent of the publisher as evidenced by the nature of the advertising for a publication is an additional factor in determining obscenity (*Ginzburg v. United States,* 383 U.S. 463). A law forbidding sale of obscene materials to persons under seventeen was upheld (*Ginsberg v. New York,* 390 U.S. 629 [1968]), but the Court held that private possession of obscene materials in one's home could not be made a crime (*Stanley v. Georgia,* 394 U.S. 557 [1969]). In upholding a national law banning the mailing of obscene materials, the Court did not reconcile how one could possess such materials in his home if it could not be obtained legally (*United States v. Reidel,* 402 U.S. 351 [1971]). In all censorship cases the Court has insisted that prompt judicial review be made available, but continued confusion led to a redefinition which would confine obscenity to offensive sexual conduct as defined by state law within guidelines established by the Court in *Miller v. California.*

Scales v. United States, 367 U.S. 203 (1961): Sustained that portion of the Smith Act of 1940 that makes it a crime to be a member of an organization that advocates overthrow of the government by force if one knows this to be the purpose of the organization. The Court drew a distinction between active membership and mere membership, noting that only active membership in a party that has illegal aims is not constitutionally protected. *See also* ALIEN REGISTRATION ACT, page 103.

Significance In the *Scales* decision, the Court sought to avoid imputing guilty by mere association by insisting that the government must prove that an individual was an active participant in illegal activities. This formulation has been applied to most loyalty legislation, forcing both the national and state governments to use greater restraint in imposing disabilities upon persons for their associations.

Schenck v. United States, 249 U.S. 47 (1919): Upheld a conviction against Schenck, who had circulated materials urging men to resist the call to military service during World War I. The Court held that this was a justified infringement upon the freedoms of speech and press in view of the wartime emergency. *See also* FREEDOM OF SPEECH, page 70.

Significance The *Schenck* case is noteworthy because of the Court's opinion, written by Justice Oliver Wendell Holmes, which established the clear and present danger doctrine. Justice Holmes wrote that "The question in every case is whether the words used are used in such circumstances and are of such a nature as to create a clear and present danger that they will bring about the substantive evils that Congress has a right to prevent." With these words, Justice Holmes provided the formula that has been used in many free speech cases since that time. The *Schenck* case is also noted for the distinction drawn between speech that may be permissible in peacetime but not when the nation is at war.

School District of Abington Township v. Schempp, 374 U.S. 203 (1963): Held devotional Bible reading and/or the recitation of the Lord's Prayer in public schools to be an unconstitutional violation of the establishment clause of the First Amendment as applied to the states through the Fourteenth Amendment. The Court reasoned that while the study of religion could be part of a school curriculum, an organ of government (the public school) could not be used for essentially religious purposes. The Court held that the fact that students could excuse themselves from the devotional exercises was irrelevant, since the exercises in themselves constituted an establishment of religion. "In the relationship between man and religion," said the Court, "the state is firmly committed to a position of neutrality." *See also* SEPARATION OF CHURCH AND STATE, page 82.

Significance The *Schempp* decision ranks among the most controversial rendered by the Supreme Court. In 1962 in *Engel v. Vitale,* 370 U.S. 421, the Court struck down a nondenominational prayer written by the New York Board of Regents for public school recitation on the ground that it was improper for public officials to write or sanction official prayers. The *Schempp* and *Engel* cases led numerous political leaders and citizen groups to demand a constitutional amendment to permit school prayers, although many citizens and church leaders agreed with the Court's interpretation of the establishment clause.

Swann v. Charlotte-Mecklenburg Board of Education, 402 U.S. 1 (1971): Held that all vestiges of state-imposed racial segregation in schools must be eliminated at once, and that federal district courts have wide authority to fashion remedies to accomplish this. Among the remedies approved were bussing, racial quotas, and pairing and grouping of noncontiguous school zones. School boards must eliminate racial distinctions in the assignment and treatment of students and faculty and in school construction decisions. *See also Milliken v. Bradley,* page 96; SEGREGATION, page 81.

Significance Dissatisfaction with the pace of school desegregation since its historic decision in 1954 in *Brown v. Board of Education of Topeka,* 347 U.S. 483, led the Supreme Court to uphold strong positive action on the part of district courts or school boards in the *Swann* decision. In the *Brown* case, the Court had said that desegregation should proceed with "all deliberate speed," but found that this formula did not work. The *Swann* case strongly reaffirmed prior holdings that dual school systems must be replaced with unitary school systems wherein race is not a factor. The decision applies only to state-imposed, not de facto, segregation, and though it appeared to strike a strong blow at the concept of the neighborhood school as the only basis for pupil assignment, the Court supported that concept where de facto segregation exists (*Milliken v. Bradley,* 418 U.S. 717 [1974]).

United States v. Lovett, 328 U.S. 303 (1946): Declared unconstitutional, as a bill of attainder, an act of Congress that named three individuals as ineligible for continued governmental employment, in that the act punished the individuals without judicial trial. *See also* BILL OF ATTAINDER, page 60.

Significance Few cases have arisen in American constitutional history involving bills of attainder. After the Civil War, the Supreme Court found certain laws imposing disabilities upon all persons who participated in the rebellion to be bills of attainder (*Cummings v. Missouri,* 4 Wallace 277, *Ex parte Garland,* 4 Wallace 333 [1867]). Some legislation designed to keep Communists out of public service has been upheld by the Court on the ground that it established general qualifications for employment rather than naming specific individuals (*Garner v. Board of Public Works,*

341 U.S. 716 [1951]). In *United States v. Brown*, 381 U.S. 437 (1965), however, the Court held that the Landrum-Griffin Labor Act section making it a crime for Communists to hold office or employment in a labor union was a bill of attainder.

Zorach v. Clauson, 343 U.S. 306 (1952): Supported New York's released-time program in public schools, under which students are released from classes to attend religious exercises in their respective churches. The Court found no conflict between this practice and the establishment of religion clause in the First Amendment. *See also* SEPARATION OF CHURCH AND STATE, page 82

Significance The teaching of religion in public schools is one of the most controversial questions in public education, going to the heart of the issue of the separation of church and state. The *Zorach* decision attracted wide notice, since it followed the Court's decision in *McCollum v. Board of Education*, 333 U.S. 203 (1948), in which the Court declared unconstitutional a program of released time under which children attended religious classes on school grounds. The *Zorach* ruling rested largely on the fact that the religious classes were not held on school property.

IMPORTANT STATUTES

Alien and Sedition Laws Acts passed in 1798 authorizing the President to deport undesirable aliens and making it a crime to criticize the government or its officials. Through these Acts, the Federalist party sought to silence opposition. About twenty-five persons were jailed or fined for criticizing President John Adams. These Acts were a major reason for the defeat of the Federalist party in the election of 1800. Thomas Jefferson, the winner of that election, pardoned those convicted under the Acts.

Significance With the exception of these laws, Congress did not find it necessary to pass anti-sedition legislation until World War I. The Alien and Sedition Laws were undoubtedly unconstitutional, but they were never tested in the Supreme Court. They serve as a reminder that civil rights are under constant threat unless they are zealously guarded by the people. Free government is not possible unless it is understood that one may be loyal to his nation and, at the same time, be critical of those who make its policies.

Alien Registration Act of 1940(Smith Act) A major sedition law requiring the annual registration of aliens and prohibiting the advocacy of violent overthrow of the government. The major provisions of the Act make it unlawful to teach, advocate, or distribute information advocating the forcible overthrow of government or to knowingly organize or join an organization that so advocates. Other provisions outlaw activities designed to create disloyalty in the armed forces or to encourage participation in a violent revolution or in the assassination of public officials. *See also Dennis v. United States*, page 90; *Scales v. United States*, page 101.

Significance The Smith Act is the first law passed in peacetime since the Alien and Sedition Laws of 1798 that outlaws particular forms of speech and writing. It is also the first act to make it a crime to be a member of an organization; this provision, some critics claim, imputes guilt by association. The advocacy and membership provisions of this Act have been upheld by the Supreme Court (*Dennis v. United States*, 341 U.S. 494 [1951]; *Scales v. United States*, 367 U.S. 203 [1961]). Though the Act does not mention the Communist party by name, and was also intended to apply to Nazi and Fascist groups, it has been applied only against the Communist party leadership.

Civil Rights Acts of 1866, 1870, 1871, and 1875   Laws passed by Congress after the Civil War to guarantee the rights of Negroes. The public-accommodation provisions of the 1875 law were declared unconstitutional by the Supreme Court in the *Civil Rights Cases* (109 U.S. 3 [1883]), as a federal invasion of private rights. Other provisions of these laws were struck down by the courts or repealed by Congress. Today, a few major provisions remain from the Acts of 1866 and 1871. One makes it a federal crime for any person acting under the authority of a state law to deprive another of any rights protected by the Constitution or by laws of the United States. Another authorizes suits for civil damages against state or local officials by persons whose rights are abridged. Others permit actions against persons who conspire to deprive people of their rights. *See also Jones v. Mayer,* page 94.

Significance   The failure of the post-Civil War Acts reflected the general attitude of the time that the national government had a limited role to play in the enforcement of individual rights. The remaining provisions have served occasionally as a weapon in the hands of national officers to restrain state officials who violate the constitutional rights of persons in their charge. Today, as the national government expands its role in the protection of individual rights, particularly in the area of race relations, these laws have taken on new importance. Of particular significance is the Supreme Court's ruling in *Jones v. Mayer,* 392 U.S. 409 (1968), holding that the 1866 law, enacted under authority of the Thirteenth Amendment ban on slavery, bars public and private racial discrimination in the sale or rental of housing.

Civil Rights Act of 1957   The first civil rights law passed by Congress since Reconstruction, designed to secure the right to vote for Negroes. Its major feature empowers the Department of Justice to seek court injunctions against any deprivation of voting rights, and authorizes criminal prosecutions for violations of an injunction. In addition, the Act established a Civil Rights Division, headed by an Assistant Attorney General in the Department of Justice, and created a six-man bipartisan Civil Rights Commission to investigate civil rights violations and to recommend legislation.

Significance   The Civil Rights Act of 1957 marked a major breakthrough in positive federal action in the field of civil rights. The Act is based on the theory that if the Negro is protected in his voting rights, he will be in a better position to seek reform in other areas of discrimination. It is supplemented by voting provisions in the Civil Rights Acts of 1960 and 1964 and by the Voting Rights Act of 1965.

Civil Rights Act of 1960   A law designed to further secure the right to vote for Negroes and to meet problems arising from racial upheavals in the South. The major provision authorizes federal courts to appoint referees who will help blacks to register after a voter-denial conviction is obtained under the 1957 Civil Rights Act, and after a court finding of a "pattern or practice" of discrimination against qualified voters. Other provisions: (1) authorize punishment for persons who obstruct any federal court order, such as a school desegregation order, by threats or force; (2) authorize criminal penalties for transportation of explosives for the purpose of bombing a building; (3) require preservation of voting records for twenty-two months, and authorize the Attorney General to inspect the records; (4) provide for schooling of children of armed forces personnel in the event that a school closes because of an integration dispute.

Significance Continuing the pattern established in the 1957 Civil Rights Act, Congress sought to strengthen the voting rights of citizens and reached out into other problem areas. The Civil Rights Act of 1964 and the Voting Rights Act of 1965 supplement the Acts of 1957 and 1960.

Civil Rights Act of 1964 A major enactment designed to erase racial discrimination in most areas of American life. Major provisions of the Act: (1) outlaw arbitrary discrimination in voter registration and expedite voting rights suits; (2) bar discrimination in public accommodations, such as hotels and restaurants, that have a substantial relation to interstate commerce; (3) authorize the national government to bring suits to desegregate public facilities and schools; (4) extend the life and expand the power of the Civil Rights Commission; (5) provide for the withholding of federal funds from programs administered in a discriminatory manner; (6) establish the right to equality in employment opportunities; (7) establish a Community Relations Service to help resolve civil rights problems. The Act forbids discrimination based on race, color, religion, national origin, and, in the case of employment, sex. Techniques for gaining voluntary compliance are stressed in the Act, and the resolution of civil rights problems through state and local action is encouraged. Discrimination in housing is not covered by the law, but is prohibited by the Civil Rights Act of 1968.

Significance The Civil Rights Act of 1964 is the most far-reaching civil rights legislation since Reconstruction. It was passed after the longest debate in Senate history (eighty-three days) and only after cloture was invoked for the first time to cut off a civil rights filibuster. Compliance with the Act's controversial provisions on public accommodation and equal employment opportunity has been widespread. Title VI of the Act, which authorizes the cutoff of federal funds to state and local programs practicing discrimination proved to be the most effective provision of the Act. For example, a dramatic jump in southern school integration took place when the national government threatened to withhold federal funds from schools failing to comply with desegregation orders. All agencies receiving federal funds are required to submit assurance of compliance with the 1964 Act. Almost 200 grant-in-aid programs are involved, amounting to 15 percent of all state and local revenues. The Supreme Court upheld the public accommodations provisions of the law as a legitimate exercise of the commerce power by Congress (*Heart of Atlanta Motel v. United States,* 379 U.S. 241 [1964]).

Civil Rights Act of 1968 A law which prohibits discrimination in the advertising, financing, sale, or rental of housing, based on race, religion, or national origin. The law covers about 80 percent of all housing. Major exclusions are owner occupied dwellings of up to four units and those selling or renting without services of a broker. Other provisions of the 1968 Act provide criminal penalties for interfering with the exercise of civil rights by others, or for using interstate commerce to incite riots. Administration of the housing provisions is left largely to the Department of Housing and Urban Development which is limited to conciliation and persuasion. Lawsuits may be initiated by the Attorney General or by an individual. *See also Jones v. Mayer,* page 94.

Significance Residential segregation was the last and most sensitive civil rights issue faced by Congress. The 1968 Act was passed in the wake of the assassination of Dr. Martin Luther King, Jr., and after a filibuster was overcome in the Senate. Discrimination in housing isolates minorities, intensifies school segregation problems, and deprives even the economically successful Negro from full enjoyment of housing opportunities. Most housing discrimination results from private acts of bankers, real estate agents, and individual landowners rather than governmental action. Shortly after enactment of the Civil Rights Act of 1968, the Supreme Court ruled in *Jones v. Mayer,* 392 U.S. 409 (1968) that the Civil Rights Act of 1866 outlawed all racial discrimination in housing. The Court reconciled the 1968 law with the 1866 law by noting that the former covers religion and national origin, in addition to race, and provides for enforcement machinery.

Communist Control Act of 1954 An act of Congress that deprives the Communist party of the rights and privileges of other legally organized bodies or political parties and declares it to be a clear and present threat to the security of the United States. The law does not make it a crime to be a Communist.

Significance The full meaning of the law is not clear. It was passed in Congress with little discussion and has not been vigorously enforced. Many authorities question its constitutionality. The main effect has been to keep the Communist party off the ballot. This is the only time in American history that a party has been denied use of the ballot as a means of gaining adherents to its programs. This denial has not received judicial approval when tried under some similar state laws.

District of Columbia Court Reorganization and Criminal Procedure Act of 1970 A "model anti-crime package" for the nation's capital authorizing stringent law enforcement measures. Among these are provisions that: (1) provide for "no-knock" search and arrest warrants, which allow police to enter without notice if they fear destruction of evidence; (2) authorize pre-trial detention of up to sixty days for defendants whose release would endanger the community; (3) revise the juvenile code to lower to fifteen the age at which a juvenile charged with a felony can be tried as an adult and to eliminate jury trials for juveniles; (4) broaden electronic surveillance procedures by police; and (5) increase penalties for crime. In addition, the Act established a modern court system for the District to have jurisdiction over local matters previously handled in the federal courts. Abuse of the controversial "no-knock" provision led to its repeal in 1974 along with a similar provision in the Drug Abuse Prevention and Control Act of 1970.

Significance The Act is considered a "model" by its supporters because if it survives the constitutional challenges likely to be brought against it, and if it succeeds in controlling crime in the District of Columbia, it could be used as a model across the nation. Washington, D.C., has become known as the "crime capital" of the nation with exceptionally high rates of homicides, rapes, and robberies.

Internal Security Act of 1950 (McCarran Act) An act designed to place the Communist party and other totalitarian groups under rigid controls. The Act outlaws any conspiracy, peaceful or violent, that has as its purpose the establishment of a foreign-controlled dictatorship in the United States. A Subversive Activities Control Board had been established to designate Communist "action" groups, "fronts," or Communist "infiltrated" organizations. Once identified, action and front groups must register with the Attorney General, listing their officers and members, financial records, and any printing equipment under their control. Publications of these organizations must be labeled as Communist propaganda. Infiltrated trade unions lose all rights under national labor laws. Individual members of any of these groups may not hold office in a labor union, obtain a passport, or work in any public office; members of action groups are also barred from defense plants. The law also strengthens espionage and sedition laws and immigration requirements and provides for the deportation of Communist aliens. Another provision established procedures for detention of suspected saboteurs in an emergency but was repealed in 1971. *See also* SUBVERSIVE ACTIVITIES CONTROL BOARD, page 87.

Significance Many serious constitutional questions are raised by the McCarran Act and, to date, the Supreme Court has upheld only the organizational registration requirement (*Communist Party v. Subversive Activities Control Board,* 367 U.S. 1 [1961]). An order that individual Communist party leaders register was, however, declared invalid by the Supreme Court as an invasion of the right against self-incrimination (*Albertson v. Subversive Activities Control Board,* 382 U.S. 70 [1965]). The Court also struck down the passport provision as a denial of the right to travel (*Aptheker v. Secretary of State,* 378 U.S. 500 [1964]), and the restriction against defense plant workers as a violation of the right of association (*United States v. Robel,* 389 U.S. 258 [1967]). A 1967 amendment to the Internal Security Act eliminated the self-registration requirement and empowered the Subversive Activities Control Board to register individuals. Finally, the Board itself was abolished in 1973.

Omnibus Crime Control and Safe Streets Act of 1968 The first comprehensive national anticrime legislation. Major provisions of the Act: (1) provide for federal block grants to states to upgrade state and local police forces; (2) authorize wiretapping and bugging by police with and without warrants; and (3) alter federal criminal procedures to modify Supreme Court decisions (*Miranda* and *Mallory* cases) so as to make voluntary confessions admissible irrespective of delay in arraignment or failure to inform a suspect of his rights.

Significance Until 1968 the federal government generally did not participate in local crime control. The concept of a national police force has been abhorrent to most Americans. Extensive violence, rising crime rates, campus unrest, and ghetto riots, along with attacks on Supreme Court rulings led to passage of the Act. It places the national government into a new and expanding role in state and local police activitiy. In 1968, Congress also passed the Juvenile Delinquency Prevention and Control Act which provides grants to states to prevent delinquency and to rehabilitate youthful offenders.

Organized Crime Control Act of 1970 A comprehensive law designed to strengthen the hands of the federal government to combat organized crime. Major provisions: (1) authorize special grand juries to investigate organized criminal activities; (2) standardize witness-immunity laws for legislative, administrative, and judicial bodies; (3) limit challenges to illegally seized evidence; (4) forbid use of income from organized criminal activity to establish a legitimate business; (5) extend federal jurisdiction over gambling and use of explosives; and (6) authorize increased prison terms, up to twenty-five years, for dangerous offenders.

Significance The existence of an organized national network of crime, as well as the extensive corruptive influence of criminals in some state and local governments, appears to be well established. Under the American system of government, police activity is rigidly localized and often unable to cope with widespread organized criminal activity that transcends geographic boundaries. The Organized Crime Control Act is designed to cope with this problem by expanding national jurisdiction over some of the more obvious outlets for organized crime. Some of the Act's provisions are controversial, notably those that involve procedural rights.

6 Parties, Politics, Pressure Groups, and Elections

Absentee Voting Provisions of state laws or constitutions that enable qualified voters to cast their ballots in an election without going to the polls on election day. If a person expects to be unable to vote on election day, he obtains a ballot within a specifield period preceding the election, marks it, has it notarized, and returns it to the proper official. *See also* VOTING QUALIFICATIONS, page 148.

Significance Most states have provisions for absentee voting, although some limit the practice to members of the armed forces. Several million potential voters, because of travel or illness, are unable to vote on election day, but few go to the trouble of securing an absentee ballot. Absentee voters can sometimes affect the outcome of an election, as in 1960, when a late count of absentee ballots in California swung that state's electoral votes from John F. Kennedy to Richard M. Nixon.

Absolute Majority Any number over 50 percent of the total votes cast by *all* the voters participating in a given election. A *simple* majority, in contrast, is any number over 50 percent of the votes cast on any single issue in an election, even though many voters who go to the polls may not vote on the specific issue. A *plurality* consists of sufficient votes to win an election, but not necessarily a majority. *See also* MAJORITY RULE page 12; PLURALITY, page 133.

Significance No federal and only a few state and local elections are conducted with a requirement of an absolute majority. Some states require an absolute majority of all voters participating in any phase of the election to vote "yes" on a question of calling a state constitutional convention or ratifying an amendment to a state constitution. Hence, failure to vote on that issue while otherwise participating in the election is the equivalent of a "no" vote.

Alienation An individual's estrangement from society. Political alienation results when individuals believe they have lost their ability to participate effectively in the political process and to influence its outcome. Individuals tend to suffer political alienation when their government is unresponsive to their needs or hopes, or fails to quiet their fears. Alienation may involve feelings of distrust, scorn, or fear toward a political system that may produce anomie (a collapse of the

109

social structures governing society) and a rejection of the entire political system. *See also* NEW LEFT, page 129.

Significance Various theories have sought to explain the alienation of modern man and have offered, through political and economic ideologies, the means for overcoming it. Marxism, for example, posits that the destruction of capitalism will restore man's societal and cooperative nature. Modern society has produced widespread feelings of anomie and rootlessness through the impersonalizing forces of machine technology and mass culture. Underlying mass movements and protest demonstrations by minorities, for example, is the alienation of such groups from the rest of society. Those alienated often fail to vote or participate in the regular arena for making political decisions.

At Large The election of members of a legislative body by the voters of an entire governmental unit rather than from subdivisions thereof. Congressmen at large are elected by the whole electorate of the state when a state legislature fails to redistrict after a decennial census. United States senators and Electoral College electors are elected at large in each state. On the local level, members of city commissions are, in some cases, elected at large by the voters of the entire city rather than from wards, especially under the commission and city manager forms. *See also* SINGLE-MEMBER DISTRICT, page 143.

Significance Election of representatives at large tends to foster a broader statewide or citywide approach to issues rather than the more restrictive "mirroring" of local interests by those chosen from districts or wards. The case against election at large is that representatives so chosen will not respond to the wishes or interests of the voters because of the size, population, and variety of views of the larger electorate. In contrast with the ward or district system, at large elections also tend to limit or eliminate representation of minority groups in local governments since they cannot usually muster enough citywide or countywide support to win. Proponents of election at large claim that it reduces parochialism in politics and makes fuller use of available political talent by allowing several good candidates living in the same area to be elected simultaneously, which is not possible under the single-member district system.

Australian Ballot A secret ballot prepared, distributed, and tabulated by government officials at public expense. Voting machines are mechanical adaptations of the Australian ballot.

Significance For over a century, many American voters were denied a secret ballot. Oral voting and differently colored ballots, prepared by the parties, were used. Extreme pressures could be exerted upon voters who were forced to cast their ballot publicly. Threats of retaliation frequently coerced voters into voting against their choice of candidates. Since 1888, all states have used the Australian ballot.

Availability The qualifications of a potential candidate which are analyzed by his party in making its selection of a nominee. A candidate whom the party believes has the qualities and background to make him a winner is "available." *See also* BALANCED TICKET, page 111; DARK HORSE, page 118; FAVORITE SON, page 121; STALKING HORSE, page 143.

Significance The question of availability is especially important in the selection of presidential nominees. Millions of members of each party meet the constitutional and legal requirements for the presidency, but few have the qualifications needed to win. Availability depends on whether the potential nominee has ever alienated a large economic, ethnic, or religious voting group, whether he comes from a key state or strategic section, whether he has demonstrated real vote-getting ability, whether he is too closely identified with one wing or faction in the party, whether he is a good family man—in short, whether his background and his personal and political qualities all appear to add up to victory for the party in the presidential election. Increasingly the availability qualifications of potential candidates are shaped by television and measured by public opinion polls.

Balanced Ticket The influence of personal backgrounds and qualifications in the selection of candidates by a political party, with the objective of maximizing voter appeal. A balanced ticket may incorporate ideological, geographic, racial, ethnic, age, sex, or other diversities among the slate of party candidates. *See also* AVAILABILITY, page 110; PLURALISM, page 133.

Significance A balanced ticket strategy typifies party activity in selecting slates of candidates. American pluralism dictates that successful party tickets recognize the extent of heterogeneity in the nation and in the states. The best-known historical example of ticket balancing has been in the selection of vice presidential candidates who have often provided the diversity necessary to supplement the broad-gauged appeal of presidential candidates.

Bandwagon Effect A tendency in politics for some individuals to associate themselves with a cause, party, or candidate they believe will prevail. The bandwagon effect is identified with emotional behavior rather than with rational calculation, that one's interests will be served by joining forces with the expected winner. In elections, for example, polls published prior to election day may change the outcome because some voters affected by the "herd instinct" seek to "climb aboard the bandwagon" of the candidate they expect to win. The *underdog effect* partly offsets the bandwagon effect because it involves the tendency of some voters to feel sorry for a losing candidate or party and, for this reason, to switch their votes. *See also* CAMPAIGN, page 112.

Significance Many campaign and voting studies have disclosed that voters in the United States are often influenced in their decisions by psychological factors, such as the bandwagon or underdog effects. Some states have tried to reduce the impact of such factors on election outcomes, for example, by prohibiting campaigning on election day. Congress recognized the impact that such factors might have on the outcome of federal elections by establishing a uniform poll-closing time for all states so that voters in states with different time zones would be less influenced by announcements of election results. By the time many Californians have gone to the polls in past elections, television commentators have already announced winners-to-be as the result of projections based on voting in the states in the Eastern Time Zone.

Boss A political leader who dominates a highly disciplined state or local party organization that tends to monopolize power in its area. Political bosses retain power through patronage disposition, control over nominations, use of "honest" and dishonest graft, and manipulation of voting and elections. Sometimes the term "boss" is used to discredit the successful leader of an opposing party. *See also* DEMAGOGUE, page 118; POLITICAL MACHINE, page 134; WATERGATE, page 214.

Significance American politics has proved to be a fertile ground for the growth of political machines and party bosses. This growth stems largely from the decentralization of power in the party system and the apathy of large numbers of voters. Some of the leading party bosses in past years have been Edward J. Flynn of New York's Bronx County, Edward "Boss" Crump of Memphis, Ed Kelly of Chicago, Frank Hague of Jersey City, and Carmine DeSapio of the Tammany Hall machine in New York City. Political bosses have been equally successful in the countryside and in the big cities. The heyday of the political boss has waned, and few remain who are bosses in the old tradition. The direct primary, a better-educated electorate, electoral laws aimed at making elections fair and honest, and public welfare programs that have removed welfare aid from politics are among the chief reasons for the demise of "bossism." Many of the activities of high officials of the Nixon Administration involved in the "Watergate" scandals and abuses of power, however, were typical of earlier party bosses and corrupt political machines.

Campaign The competitive effort of rival candidates for public office to win support of the voters in the period preceding an election. Candidates use diverse means for reaching the voters—television, radio, telephone, the mails, door-to-door solicitation, speeches, coffee hours, factory visits—and various kinds of propaganda appeals aimed at influencing the thinking, emotions, and, ultimately, the voting actions of the public. The key problems for conducting a successful campaign are financing and organization. *See also* CORRUPT PRACTICES ACTS, page 116; FEDERAL ELECTION CAMPAIGN ACTS OF 1972 AND 1974, page 151; PROPAGANDA, page 138.

Significance During the 1960s, political campaigns for major offices in the United States increasingly centered around and depended upon the impact of television. As a result, campaign costs soared, and, with rare exceptions, only wealthy individuals or those with the financial support of major interest groups were able to compete effectively for national or state offices or for big city mayoralties. Voter reaction against the decisive role television plays in campaigning occurred in the early 1970s. It took the form of voter rejection of some candidates who depended too heavily on television's "hard-sell" techniques, and passage of the Federal Election Campaign Acts of 1972 and 1974 to limit the amounts that candidates could collect and spend during their campaigns.

Canvassing Board An official body, usually bipartisan, that tabulates the election returns and certifies the election of the winners. When the polls close on election day, the returns from each precinct are forwarded to city and county canvassing boards. These consolidate the returns and forward them to the state canvassing authority, which, usually in a few days, certifies the election of the winners. The local group is the county board of supervisors or county board of election. The state canvassing board consists of several ex officio members of the state government, headed by the secretary of state. Each election winner receives a certificate of election from the county or state board. *See also* CHALLENGE, page 113; POLL WATCHER, page 135.

Significance Extensive coverage of election returns by newspapers, radio, and television makes the results of most elections known to the public before canvassing boards certify them. In exceptionally close elections, however, the final outcome may turn on the official tabulation and certification. Disputed elections are commonly settled in the courts or through an official recount.

Caucus A closed meeting of party leaders to select party candidates. In the early days of the Republic, party members in Congress and in the state legislatures selected their party's candidates for national and state office. Presidential candidates were chosen by party caucuses in Congress. Locally, leading members of each party met behind closed doors to select candidates for various local offices. Some local candidates are still nominated by caucus. The term "to caucus" is also commonly used to describe any private meeting of politicians seeking to reach agreement on a course of political action. *See also* CAUCUS, page 159; NOMINATION, page 130.

Significance Most significant decisions in American politics are officially ratified following agreements reached "in caucus" by political leaders. As a nominating device, "King Caucus" flourished for several decades of early American history. Because Andrew Jackson had been refused nomination for the presidency by the congressional Democratic caucus in 1824, he repudiated the system when he won office in 1828. By 1835, the legislative caucus as a means of making nominations for public office had almost disappeared. On both national and state levels the nominating caucus was largely replaced by the convention method. Reasons for the demise of the caucus included: (1) its unrepresentative character; (2) its violation of the separation of powers theory; (3) use of secret deals and logrolling to manipulate the caucus; and (4) widespread use of the "snap caucus," by which small cliques control the nominating process by not notifying all eligible participants of a caucus meeting. Supporters of the nominating caucus, however, point out that it is less costly than primaries for all concerned, it tends to produce compromise among ideological wings and leaders within each party, and it tends to overcome the more divisive effects of the separation of powers system.

Challenge An allegation by a poll watcher that a potential voter is unqualified or that a vote is invalid. Most states provide for a bipartisan group of election judges in each precinct to help decide disputes. An inspector usually takes charge of each precinct and makes the final decision. In some closed-primary states, a voter's party affiliation may be challenged. If he cannot prove his affiliation to the satisfaction of that party's poll watcher, he can be deprived of his vote in the primary. *See also* POLL WATCHER, page 135.

Significance Bipartisan selection of poll watchers and their right to challenge voters and votes are designed to prevent fraud in elections. This procedure is aimed at building confidence, not always warranted, in the incorruptibility of the ballot. In closed primary states, the objective is to limit participation in the selection of candidates to bonafide party members.

Charisma An attribute of leadership based on personal qualities of the individual. A charismatic leader, typically, has a magnetic personality, a dedication to achieving his objectives, unusual powers of persuasion, and ability to excite and gain the loyalty of supporters. Although a charismatic leader is usually flamboyant, he may have a mystical, withdrawn personality. *See also* AVAILABILITY, page 110.

Significance Every candidate for political office seeks to exude some degree of charisma that will set him apart as a leader of men. Charisma has, however, a potentiality for demagoguery, and excessive charismatic qualities characterize totalitarian leaders. Failure to achieve stated goals may weaken the position of charismatic leaders with their followers.

Closed Primary The selection of a party's candidates in an election limited to avowed party members. Voters must declare their party affiliation, either when they register or at the primary election. In some states, party officials at the polls may challenge their right to vote in the closed primary. *See also* DIRECT PRIMARY, page 119; OPEN PRIMARY, page 131.

Significance The closed-primary system seeks to prevent the "cross-over" of registered voters of one party into the other party's primary for the purpose of trying to nominate its weakest candidate or to affect the ideological direction of the rival party. Party organizations tend to favor the closed primary because it promotes party unity, regularity, and responsibility. Many voters oppose it because it limits their freedom of action to select anew at each primary election the party in which they wish to choose nominees, as in the open primary. Independent voters are altogether excluded from participating in the nominating process in closed-primary states. Most states use the closed primary.

Coalition The fusion of various political elements into a major American party. In multiparty countries, the fusion involves a coalition of a number of individual parties into a working majority. In the United States, however, both major parties combine factions of liberals, moderates, and conservatives. Coalition is also used to describe any alliance among political groups, such as the congressional alliance between conservative Republicans and southern Democrats. *See also* MINOR PARTY, page 126; MULTIPARTY SYSTEM, page 127; TWO-PARTY SYSTEM, page 146.

Significance The coalition character of American major parties avoids black and white extremes of position that might split the American people into two hostile groups. Conversely, the American system has been criticized on the ground that because both parties are so similar in their makeup, satisfactory alternatives are not presented to the voters. Yet a number of active minor parties run candidates and thus permit voters to express their dissatisfactions.

Coattail Effect The tendency for a candidate heading a party ticket to attract votes for other candidates of his or her party on the same ballot. Popular presidential, gubernatorial, and strong-mayor candidates typically offer the greatest pulling power for those running for lesser offices. Negative coattail impact may also exist, with an unpopular candidate for high office likely to prejudice voter sentiment against other candidates of the party on the same ballot. *See also* PARTY-COLUMN BALLOT, page 131; STRAIGHT TICKET, page 144.

Significance The coattail effect is likely to be most pronounced in elections with party-column ballots that encourage straight ticket voting. Examples of exceptional coattail pulling power include President Franklin D. Roosevelt in the 1936 election, and Mayor Richard Daley of Chicago in a number of local elections. Negative coattail effect was demonstrated in the Republican debacle of 1964 when Barry Goldwater headed the ticket, and in 1972 when George McGovern headed the Democratic ticket. An indirect coattail effect may occur in off-year elections as, for example, in 1974 when Independents and Republicans, angered by Watergate revelations of misconduct by the Nixon Administration, helped to produce a major Democratic victory on the national, state, and local levels.

Conflict of Interest　The situation that occurs when an official's public actions are affected by his personal interests. A conflict-of-interest charge usually alleges that an elected or appointed official realized some direct or indirect financial gain from governmental actions he participated in, or that the public decisions he made were motivated by his efforts to protect his personal financial interests or those of close friends or political supporters. *See also* CORRUPT PRACTICES ACTS, page 116.

　Significance　The United States has been particularly plagued with conflict of interest problems throughout its history, dating back to the Yazoo Land Fraud of 1795 which involved almost every member of the Georgia legislature. The extent of American involvement in conflict-of-interest problems may relate to the extremely large number of part-time politicians with predominantly private interests, to the American value system which tends to tolerate similar practices in the private world of business and finance, or to the historical role of party bosses and machines steeped in the pursuit of "honest" graft. In the national government, both the executive and legislative branches have undertaken policies to control conflicts of interest by developing codes of ethics and requiring disclosures of private financial interests. In the House and Senate, members are required to make reports to ethics committees. In the early 1970s, grand jury and congressional investigations divulged numerous cases of conflict of interest behavior among high officials of the Nixon Administration, leading to new efforts to control the problem, especially by financial disclosure and regulatory laws.

Congressional and Senatorial Campaign Committees　House and Senate groups consisting of Republican and Democratic members selected by fellow party members in their respective chambers to organize and to help finance election campaigns. The House Republican Campaign Committee consists of one congressman from each state having Republican representation in the House. House Democrats use this formula also, but supplement it with women members from some states as selected by the committee chairman. Senate committees consist of six or seven members selected from the Senate by each party's caucus chairman. *See also* CAMPAIGN, page 112.

　Significance　In a presidential election year, each committee may integrate its efforts with those of its national committee, depending upon the "coattail" vote-pulling potential of the party's presidential candidate. In off-year contests, the committees operate more independently. Maintaining permanent staffs, the committees raise funds, furnish speakers, distribute literature, and generally take charge of congressional campaigns. Their efforts may also be integrated with those of state and local committees of their parties.

Convention　A meeting of party delegates at the national, state, or local levels to decide upon party policy and strategy and to nominate candidates for elective office. Each party holds a national convention every four years to nominate its presidential candidate and adopt a platform.

In most states, both parties hold county and state conventions annually. Typically, delegates to the county conventions are selected by party voters in precinct elections; delegates to state conventions are selected by county conventions; and delegates to national conventions are selected by state or district conventions, or, in approximately one-half of the states, by voters in presidential primaries. *See also* NATIONAL CONVENTION, page 128; NOMINATION, page 130.

Significance Although state and local conventions have lost most of their nominating power, they continue to serve as the basic policymakers of the American political parties. Decisions made at national, state, and local conventions give direction to party committees and chairmen in the periods between conventions. On state and local levels, nomination for most elective offices has been taken from conventions and placed under direct primary systems. This has been the result, partly, of increasing democratization of elections and, partly, of convention malpractices that allowed small cliques to dominate them through manipulation. An advantage of the convention system in making policy and deciding nominations is that it tends to force conflicting wings of the party to work out compromises that help hold tenuous intraparty coalitions together.

Corrupt Practices Acts Laws that seek to limit and regulate the size and sources of contributions and expenditures in political campaigns. Since 1925, a variety of federal corrupt practices acts were enacted to regulate campaign finance but they proved unrealistic and unenforceable. For example, the Political Activities Act of 1939 (Hatch Act) outlawed political activity by federal employees and forbade a political committee to spend more than $3 million in any campaign and limited individual contributions of a committee to $5000, both of which could be circumvented by the creation of additional committees. The Federal Election Campaign Acts of 1972 and 1974 swept aside many past laws and instituted major reforms that tried to take into account the problems of reaching a large electorate. In a related action, designed to broaden the base of campaign financing, Congress authorized, in the Revenue Act of 1971, a system of voluntary one-dollar checkoffs on federal income tax returns for a general campaign fund to be made available to major party candidates. State and local political campaign finances are regulated by state laws, which vary considerably. *See also* FEDERAL ELECTION CAMPAIGN ACTS OF 1972 AND 1974, page 151.

Significance The underlying purposes of corrupt practices legislation are to free public officials from being beholden to heavy contributors and to restrain the increasing tendency to limit office seeking to people of means. The Federal Elections Campaign Acts of 1972 and 1974 modernize rules governing campaign finance by taking cognizance of the vast costs of mass media advertising, but they leave uncovered many areas of financial strain for candidates, such as direct mail advertising, staff salaries, and travel costs. The new law, like its past counterparts, and similar state and local restrictions, will be difficult to monitor without a considerable amount of bureaucratic oversight. In the wake of Watergate campaign scandals and other disclosures of irregularities in the 1970s, most of the states have followed the national government's lead and have enacted new laws requiring open meetings, lobby controls, campaign reforms, and financial disclosures. In a key decision rendered in 1972, the Supreme Court ruled that the Corrupt Practices Act that bars contributions by labor organizations to any federal election campaign does not prohibit union contributions from funds obtained from voluntary contributions made without deception or threat of reprisal (*Pipefitter Local Union v. United States,* 407 U.S. 385 [1972]).

Countervailing Theory of Pressure Politics   The concept that in American politics the competition among major business, labor, farm, racial, and other interest groups tends to balance their respective power and influence. *See also* PRESSURE GROUP, page 138; PUBLIC POLICY MODELS, page 140.

Significance   The countervailing theory of pressure politics seeks to explain why democratic pluralism can continue to exist in the United States and why no single dominant social group controls the direction of American politics and policies. The theory postulates that from this competition of diverse interests, the public interest tends to emerge. Some investigators challenge the theory and hold that empirical evidence refutes the ideas of "balance" and the emergence of the public interest from group conflict. Many American liberals believe the power scales are overloaded in favor of business and industry, whereas many conservatives believe that labor unions have upset the balance.

Credentials Committee   A committee used by political parties to determine which delegates may participate in their conventions. The credentials committee prepares a roll of all delegates entitled to be seated at the convention. Controversy over contested seats arises when rival groups claim to be the official party organization for a county, district, or state. In such cases, the committee makes recommendations to the convention. *See also* NATIONAL CONVENTION, page 128.

Significance   Recommendations made by the credentials committee to the convention are usually approved without debate or roll call. Conventions have, however, on occasion rejected these recommendations in whole or in part. In national conventions, decisions on seating of delegates from certain states, when two or more rival delegations appear at the convention, may be a decisive factor in the selection of the presidential nominee. As an example, in 1952 at the Republican Convention, rival delegations supporting General Dwight D. Eisenhower and Senator Robert A. Taft arrived from five southern states. The success of the Eisenhower supporters in getting their delegates seated was instrumental in securing the General's nomination. In the 1972 Democratic National Convention, a new delegate-selection process gave greater representation to women, the poor, and to minority groups. In some states, Democratic party regulars also sent delegates, who contested the seating of those selected under the new rules. The Credentials Committee, backed by the Convention majority, gave support to the new delegates, leading to McGovern's nomination.

Cumulative Voting   A method of voting in which the individual casts more than one vote in the simultaneous election of several officials, as a means of securing greater representation for minor parties. Each voter is allowed two or more votes, which he can cast for a single candidate or distribute among several. Candidates of minor parties can usually win seats because their supporters concentrate their additional votes for them, whereas major party supporters tend to distribute their votes among several candidates. Cumulative voting is used in electing members of the lower house of the Illinois legislature, with three representatives elected from each district and with each voter casting three votes. *See also* HARE PLAN, page 123; PROPORTIONAL REPRESENTATION, page 139.

Significance Cumulative voting is an attempt to provide some direct representation for minority groups. Proponents support it as more accurately representative (and, hence, more democratic) than the two-party system. Opponents point out that it may have a tendency to foster a host of splinter parties with the result that, frequently, none is able to gain a majority and unstable coalition government results.

Dark Horse A marginal candidate or noncandidate for public office who has little support and almost no chance to win nomination or election. When a consensus cannot be achieved in support of one of the leading candidates, however, the party or voters may suddenly and dramatically shift their support to a dark horse. The role of the dark horse in American politics relates particularly to the presidential nominating conventions of the two major political parties. *See also* AVAILABILITY, page 110; PRESIDENTIAL ELECTION PROCESS, page 136.

Significance Because the two major American political parties are coalitions of diverse and often antagonistic ideological and sectional wings, convention deadlocks over the selection of presidential candidates have not been uncommon. Historically, a dark horse candidate remained a definite possibility at almost every major party convention, except for those renominating an incumbent president.

Demagogue An unscrupulous politican who seeks to win and hold office through emotional appeals to mass prejudices and passions. Half-truths, outright lies, and various means of card-stacking may be used in attempts to dupe the voters. Typically, a demagogue may try to win support from one group by blaming another for its misfortunes. *See also* BOSS, page 111; CHARISMA, page 113; KNOWNOTHINGISM, page 124; MCCARTHYISM, page 74.

Significance Demagogues may thrive in either a dictatorship or a democracy. In the latter, however, because of free speech and press guarantees and frequent elections, the chances of unseating a demagogue are infinitely greater. Generally, the success of American demagogues has been rather short-lived.

Democratic Party A major American party that evolved from the Democratic-Republican group supporting Thomas Jefferson. Andrew Jackson, regarded by Democrats as cofounder with Jefferson, changed the name to Democratic party in keeping with his ultrademocratic philosophy. Further development of party principles occurred under the more recent leadership of Woodrow Wilson and Franklin D. Roosevelt. Since 1932, the Democratic party has dominated the American political scene, holding the presidency for all but the eight Eisenhower years (1953–1961) and eight Nixon-Ford years (1969–1976); it also held a majority in Congress for all but four years (1947–1954). *See also* JACKSONIAN DEMOCRACY, page 10; JEFFERSONIANISM, page 10; POLITICAL PARTY, page 134; REPUBLICAN PARTY, page 141.

Significance Many studies show strong Democratic party preference by low-income groups, organized labor, young people, and religious and racial minority groups. In recent years, the Democratic party has generally stood for freer trade, more extensive international commitments, a greater measure of governmental regulation of the economy, and expanded civil rights guarantees. On the issue of states' rights, the party has reversed its early position and, in modern times, has consistently favored expanded national responsibilities. Its policies have generally been more liberal than Republican party policies, although both include a coalition of liberals, moderates, and conservatives. Polls indicate that there are considerably more Democrats than Republicans registered to vote in the United States.

Direct Primary An intraparty election in which the voters select the candidates who will run on a party's ticket in the subsequent general election. Primaries are also used to choose convention delegates and party leaders. In a closed primary, used in more than 40 states, the selection process is limited to avowed party adherents; in an open primary, voters participate regardless of party affiliation or the absence of any. In the states of Alaska and Washington, a "blanket primary" permits the voter to split his ticket by voting for candidates of more than one party. Other than these exceptions, voters are limited in both open and closed primaries to selecting candidates of a single party. Some state and local governments use nonpartisan primaries to reduce the number of candidates for the general election. Candidates get their names on a primary ballot, typically, through petitions signed by a required number of registered voters. Other means include caucus, preprimary convention, and self-announcement. *See also* CLOSED PRIMARY, page 114; OPEN PRIMARY, page 131; PRESIDENTIAL PRIMARIES, page 137; RUNOFF PRIMARY, page 142; *Smith v. Allwright*, page 150; *United States v. Classic*, page 150.

Significance Since 1900, the direct primary has gradually superseded the convention as a nominating device. All states today use the direct primary system, in one form or another, for some offices. The primary system gives rank-and-file voters a larger voice in party affairs and enables the voters to get rid of an unpopular, but strongly entrenched, elected official or party leader. Disadvantages include greater expense for the candidate and the taxpayer and, generally, a weakening of party organization and responsibility.

Disfranchise Taking away the privilege of voting. Persons may be disfranchised if they lose their citizenship, if they fail to register when required, or if they are convicted of certain crimes. Many people are disfranchised temporarily when they move, either within the state or from state to state, until they establish new residence. Voters may also be wholly or partially disfranchised indirectly as a result of dishonesty in ballot counts or through political manipulation, such as gerrymandering. *See also* VOTING QUALIFICATIONS, page 148.

Significance Each election finds many Americans denied the privilege of voting despite their previous participation. Disfranchisement for loss of citizenship and conviction for crime is infrequent, but failure to register or reregister is the main cause for disfranchisement in the United States. Much voter disfranchisement would be removed by reducing residence requirements for most elections and eliminating them for presidental contests. Judicial oversight of state redistricting to ensure substantial equality in voting power and increased federal action to prevent disfranchisement because of color or race through the Civil Rights Acts have reduced both indirect and direct disfranchisement.

Electoral College The presidential electors from each state who meet in their respective state capitals, following their popular election, and cast ballots for President and Vice President. The

Electoral College never meets as a national body. The process starts with the nomination of partisan slates of electors by party conventions, primaries, or committees in each state. The number of electors in each state is equal to its number of representatives in both houses of Congress; the Twenty-third Amendment allots three electors for the District of Columbia, making a total electoral vote of 538. In the November presidential election, the slate of electors receiving a plurality of popular votes in each state is elected. The electors usually pledge themselves to vote for their party's candidates for President and Vice President, although the Constitution permits them to use discretion. After casting electoral ballots in their respective state capitals in December, the ballots are counted and certified before a joint session of Congress early in January. The candidates who receive a majority of the electoral votes (270) are certified as President-elect and Vice President-elect. If none receives a majority of the electoral vote, the election of the President is decided by the House of Representatives from among the three highest candidates, with each state having one vote, and that of the Vice President by the Senate from the two highest candidates, with each senator having one vote. Normally, the people of the United States know who has been elected following the popular election in November, and the rest of the process is largely a formality. The rise of political parties that nominate pledged electors has distorted the original intention of the Founding Fathers. They had intended that the electors should be chosen as each state would determine and that they would exercise complete discretion in the selection of the President *See also* ELECTORAL COUNT ACT, page 150; MINORITY PRESIDENT, page 205; PRESIDENTIAL ELECTION PROCESS, page 136; TWELFTH AMENDMENT, page 145.

Significance The Electoral College system has come under severe criticism at times in American history. Several recurring grounds for criticism have been: (1) sometimes candidates with a minority of the popular vote have won election; (2) the machinery has become an anachronism, since the electors no longer actually perform the selecting function envisioned by the Founding Fathers; (3) the unit system under which all of a state's electoral votes go to that party which polls a statewide plurality is unfair to other candidates and their supporters; and (4) the complicated nature of the entire system tends to confuse voters and complicate the selection process. Proposals for reform include: (1) discarding the Electoral College machinery and placing the election on a direct popular vote on the basis of a nationwide constituency; (2) eliminating the electors but retaining a state basis for voting, with a plurality needed in a majority of states to win; (3) eliminating the electors but retaining an electoral vote divided in each state at approximately the same ratio as the popular vote; (4) selection of electors in each state in the same manner as members of the House and Senate are chosen. The Congress has rejected several constitutional amendment proposals that would have provided for the elimination of, or substantial alteration of, the Electoral College. Opposition to direct election of the President, for example, reflects the fears of small states of being overwhelmed by the large urban vote and concern of the major parties that the change would give minor parties a more influential role. Political leaders as well as the general public tend to be wary of changing the basic system for electing the President because they are fearful of how change would affect the outcome of future elections.

Elite Persons who exercise a major influence on, or control the making of, political, economic, and social decisions. Elites achieve their power position through wealth, family status, caste systems, or intellectual superiority. Elites constitute the "power structure" or "establishment" of local and national communities. *See also* OLIGARCHY, page 14; PUBLIC POLICY MODELS, page 140.

Significance An elite group may hold power openly and officially or may exercise control over those in authority. On the national level in the United States, no elite group is dominant; on specific issues, however, business, labor, military, and other elites may exercise a decisive influence. In many cities, a business elite constitutes "the establishment" or power structure. Elitism contravenes democratic theory but in practice pervades most institutions. Much political science literature is concerned with description and analysis of the role of elites in decision making.

Equal Time A fairness rule of the Federal Communications Act of 1934 which provides that all candidates for a public office be given equal access to the free or paid use of television and radio. The equal time provision means, for example, that during a political campaign, if a radio or television station or network provides time for one candidate or party, it must then offer equal time on the same basis for the opposition candidates or parties. The rule is administered by the Federal Communications Commission (FCC) and was upheld by the Supreme Court (*Red Lion Broadcasting Co. v. Federal Communications Commission*, 395 U.S. 367 [1969]). *See also* CAMPAIGN, page 112; FEDERAL COMMUNICATIONS COMMISSION, page 321.

Significance The equal time provision is based on the assumption that democracy requires that the people have the opportunity to hear opposing views on political issues before making up their minds. Unlike newspapers and other published materials which are not governed by an "equal space" provision, radio and television broadcasts utilize public property in beaming their broadcasts over the airwaves, and are subject to control by Congress through regulation by the Federal Communications Commission. In 1960, Congress by special act exempted the Kennedy-Nixon television debates from the equal time provision so that a number of minor parties could not demand equal time. The precedent, however, was not followed in subsequent elections. Most candidate and party radio and television presentations are limited to paid advertising since the stations would have to provide free time to as many as a dozen or more minor parties if they offered it to the two major parties. The public educational media, however, provide free time for candidates of all parties.

Favorite Son A state political leader—often the governor—whose name is placed in nomination for the presidency at a national nominating convention by members of his state's delegation. Usually a favorite son is not a serious candidate and his nomination is merely a means of honoring him or of delaying commitment of the state delegation's votes. *See also* DARK HORSE, page 118; STALKING HORSE, page 143.

Significance A "favorite son" nominee is seldom given serious consideration by the convention. Delegation members generally vote for their favorite son on the first ballot, especially if a real contest between leading candidates is shaping up. In this way, the delegation can remain noncommittal until after the first ballot gives some indication of the relative strength of leading candidates. At this point, the favorite son will probably withdraw his own nomination and throw his delegation's votes to one of the front-runners. If the recipient of these votes should go on to win the presidency, the favorite son will be in a good bargaining position to obtain a high-level political appointment or other favors. In order to broaden grass-roots participation and reduce backroom manipulation, the Democratic party, since 1970, requires that to be placed in nomination, a candidate must have the support of 50 delegates, with no more than 20 from one state.

Federalist Party The first American political party, which evolved during the later phases of George Washington's presidency. Its leaders, Alexander Hamilton and John Adams, gained the support of the financial, industrial, and commercial interests for the new party. Many of its members had strongly supported the adoption of the new Constitution and the creation of the federal Union. *See also* HAMILTONIANISM, page 9; MADISONIANISM, page 12; REPUBLICAN PARTY, page 141.

Significance The Federalist party developed national financial and economic programs, which included a protective tariff, an excise tax, the creation of a National Bank, and the assumption of state debts by the national government. To justify the expansion of national powers, the Federalists insisted on a loose interpretation of the Constitution. As a reaction to these policies, Thomas Jefferson and James Madison rallied the small farmers and artisans and the planters of the South into a coalition of Anti-Federalists. In this manner the two-party political system was born in the United States. After Jefferson's defeat of the Federalists in the election of 1800, the party began to decline in popularity. In 1816, it disappeared completely from the American scene. Its demise resulted from quarrels among its leaders and from its discredit for both its attempt to silence the opposition through the Alien and Sedition Acts and its failure to support the War of 1812. In 1832, the Whig party evolved as a successor to the Federalists, and, in 1860, the Republican party superseded the Whigs.

Fifteenth Amendment An amendment to the Constitution, adopted in 1870, that forbids a state to deny a person the right to vote because of race, color, or previous condition of servitude. *See also* CIVIL RIGHTS ACTS, page 104; *Guinn v. United States,* page 149; *Smith v. Allwright,* page 150.

Significance Although the Fifteenth Amendment does not give anyone the right to vote, it does prohibit any discrimination because of race or color. Not until recent years has the Negro made significant advances in realizing the goals established by the Amendment. In 1960, for example, the Supreme Court ruled that the racial gerrymandering of Tuskegee, Alabama, so as to exclude all black voters from city elections violated the Fifteenth Amendment (*Gomillion v. Lightfoot,* 364 U.S. 339). The Civil Rights Acts of 1957, 1960, 1964, and the Voting Rights Acts of 1965 and 1970 were passed by Congress, and the Twenty-fourth Amendment was adopted to aid the Negro in overcoming the various devices used by some southern states to frustrate the purposes of the Fifteenth Amendment.

Filing The legal act of declaring candidacy for a public elective office. Most states provide that aspirants first circulate candidacy petitions to be signed by a stipulated number of registered voters. The aspirant presents the petitions, and files for candidacy with the appropriate official (secretary of state, county clerk, or city clerk). The candidate may then run against other candidates of his party for the office in a direct primary election to determine which of them will become the party's standard-bearer in the general election. In some states, persons seeking candidacy for local office may file simply by declaring their intentions before an official. In other states, a candidate may file by depositing a sum of money in lieu of petitions, which may be refunded if the candidate polls enough votes. *See also* NOMINATION, page 130; PETITION, page 132.

Significance Filing is a means by which running for office can be limited to "serious" candidates. A balance must be struck: if the requirements are too difficult, competent, public-spirited citizens may be discouraged from seeking candidacy; if too lenient, a horde of candidates may confuse the voters. In Britain, this problem is met by requiring all candidates to deposit a modest filing fee which is forfeited if the candidate fails to secure a minimum percentage of the vote.

General Election A statewide election, usually held shortly after a primary election, to fill state and national offices. States hold national presidential elections every four years, in November, and national congressional elections in the even-numbered years. Typically, states hold state and county general elections every November in the even-numbered years, although some states elect some important state officials and judges in general elections held in odd-numbered years, frequently in the spring. *See also* DIRECT PRIMARY, page 119; PRESIDENTIAL ELECTION PROCESS, page 136.

Significance Voters make their final choice in selecting their public officials in the general election. Such an election is to be distinguished from a primary election, which is a nominating process, and from a special election, which is one called at irregular intervals. General elections are conducted by states and are governed largely by state constitutional and statutory provisions, although the national government has become increasingly involved in expanding and protecting voting rights.

Hare Plan A system of proportional representation, occasionally used in the United States, that is based on a single, transferable vote. Candidates vie in open competition for a number of elective offices. A quota is established and all candidates obtaining sufficient votes to meet it are declared elected. Surplus votes of winning candidates and the votes of candidates eliminated for low-vote totals are distributed according to the second choices expressed by the voters on their ballots. Votes are transferred in this manner until sufficient candidates have been declared elected to fill all elective seats. *See also* CUMULATIVE VOTING, page 117; PROPORTIONAL REPRESENTATION, page 139.

Significance The Hare Plan seeks to record the voters' wishes more accurately than can be achieved through the common American elective system of single-member districts, in which all votes not cast for the winning candidate are discarded. Economic and social minority-interest groups are more likely to gain representation under it, giving a broader consensus to the government. The obvious weakness of the Hare Plan, and a characteristic shortcoming of all proportional representation systems, is the difficulty of building in the government a majority that can make decisions. Diverse interest groups often have conflicting views on matters of public policy, and frequently these cannot be reconciled. Government by compromise tends to replace government by majority rule. Only a dozen or so municipalities have adopted the Hare Plan in the United States, many dropping it after a short trial period.

Incumbent A person who holds an office or an official position. Many states make voters aware that some candidates are incumbents by printing their official titles or offices on the ballot.

Significance An incumbent usually has an advantage in seeking reelection, since he has an established following, is better known to the voters, and has campaign experience. Printing offices or titles on the ballot give an advantage to incumbents because the voter is thus given a choice between a candidate who obviously has had experience in the office and other untried and often unknown persons. Studies have disclosed that incumbents usually win elections whether or not they are identified on the ballot. Disagreement exists as to whether a person who has been appointed to fill an elective office is an incumbent.

Independent A voter who disregards party affiliation of candidates running for elective office and casts his ballot for the "best man" or on the basis of issues. Most independents are not party members, but a few retain membership in a party, enabling them to vote in primaries while exercising their own judgment in general elections. Empirical studies of voting behavior tend to show that most independents are politically apathetic and possess less information about candidates and issues than strong party supporters. *See also* CLOSED PRIMARY, page 114; POLITICAL ACTIVIST, page 133.

Significance Although independents are often critized for not contributing actively to the democratic process through political parties, they are wooed by both major parties. Independent voters may be decisive in determining the outcome of elections, including presidential contests. A large number of independent voters encourages political parties to focus on crucial issues in the campaign. Some political analysts question whether there is such a thing as an independent, holding the view that all voters have a predisposition toward one party or the other.

Indicator Precincts Voting units that tend to serve as election barometers. An indicator precinct typically constitutes a micro cross-section of the entire electoral system because the same factors that affect general voting behavior are present. Indicator preincts may also be used to predict voting behavior by showing how ethnic, racial, or social groups will react to candidates or issues. *See also* PRECINCT, page 136.

Significance Political parties, candidates, campaign managers, political scientists, the news media, and others have devoted much time and effort to discovering indicator precincts. The ability to predict election outcomes is often closely related to the judicious selection of indicator precincts as well as to interviewing and polling techniques. Some indicator precincts, for example, have voted for the winning candidates in every presidential election in the twentieth century. As a result, their role in the selection of presidential nominees for both major parties is substantial.

Knownothingism Political activity on an uninformed, largely emotional level, which exploits the suspicions, hatreds, ignorance, and fears of American voters. The term is derived from the radical right-wing Know-Nothing party of the mid-nineteenth century that functioned in American politics as an antiforeign, anti-Catholic, secret society. The party's name evolved because members professed ignorance when queried about party activities. *See also* DEMAGOGUE, page 118; MCCARTHYISM, page 74.

Significance American politics has always been characterized by a substantial element of knownothingism, but its impact is most serious during times of domestic crises or foreign threats, real or imaginary. The period of McCarthyism in the late 1940s and early 1950s, for example, involved a major revival of knownothingism. Knownothingism can be contrasted with the fundamental concepts of liberal democracy, which assume that man is basically a rational creature who can make intelligent choices on social issues.

Literacy Test   A suffrage qualification used to determine fitness for voting by means of a reading or "understanding" test. Because literacy tests have been used to discriminate against prospective voters in several states, Congress suspended their use for five years in the Voting Rights Act of 1970. *See also* VOTING QUALIFICATIONS, page 148; VOTING RIGHTS ACT OF 1970, page 153.

Significance   Literacy tests offer an effective means of discriminating against voters because examining officials have great discretion, especially when the tests are administered orally. In some southern states, for example, Negro college graduates were once disqualified because they failed to interpret constitutional passages to the satisfaction of a white board of examiners. Evidence of discriminatory use of literacy and related tests in six southern states led to passage of the Voting Rights Act of 1965. This Act suspended the use of such tests and authorized appointment of federal voting examiners to order registration of Negroes in states and voting districts where less than 50 percent of eligible voters were registered. New York's system, generally regarded as nondiscriminatory, consisted of a reading and writing test administered through the state educational department to all persons who had not completed sixth-grade schoolwork. The suspension of all literacy tests by the Voting Rights Act of 1970 was upheld by the Supreme Court in *Oregon v. Mitchell*, 400 U.S. 112· (1970).

Lobbyist   A person, usually acting as an agent for a pressure group, who seeks to bring about the passage or defeat of legislative bills or to influence their contents. Lobbyists, often called the "Third House" of the legislature, are experts who testify before committees and present important facts on legislative proposals to support their clients' interests. They also often use large sums of money in a variety of ways .to influence legislative outcomes. Many states and the national government require the registration of lobbyists and disclosure of information concerning their employers, their salaries, and the amounts spent to influence legislation. Lobbyists are also active in trying to influence decisions made by executive officials, administrators, and the courts. *See also* PRESSURE GROUP, page 138; REGULATION OF LOBBYING ACT, page 198; *United States v. Harriss*, page 195.

Significance   Lobbyists furnish important factual data to legislators and provide effective representation for organized groups. They are criticized because they use selected facts, often distorted for propaganda purposes, and are more concerned with particular interests than with general interests. Except for laws prohibiting bribery and related criminal offenses, governmental action toward lobbyists has not sought to restrict their activities but to publicize them. Attempts by government to restrict lobbyists and lobbying unduly might be regarded by the courts as an infringement of the First Amendment freedom to petition the government.

Long Ballot The typical state and local ballot, sometimes called the "bedsheet ballot" or "jungle ballot," which has a large number of offices to be filled, candidates to be selected, and issues to be decided. *See also* SHORT BALLOT, page 142.

Significance The long ballot emerged during the era of Jacksonian Democracy in the 1830s on the theory that the way to expand democracy is to increase the number of elective officials. Today, political observers question this assumption. They argue that with a smaller number of elective officials, the voter can know the candidates, their qualifications, and the issues of the campaign. The long ballot may enable political machines to retain power because of voter apathy or confusion. The short ballot movement, which started around the turn of the century, has had some success in reducing the length of the ballot in a few states, but the basic problem remains.

Mandate Popular support for a political program. A mandate is assumed to emerge from an election as a result of popular support given to a political party or to elected officials who ran on a set of pledges to the voters. A mandate may be vague or specific, depending upon the clarity with which alternatives are presented to the voters. *See also* RESPONSIBLE PARTY SYSTEM, page 141.

Significance The mandate concept is best implemented where a responsible, well-disciplined party, ready and able to carry out its promised program, exists. The American party system, unlike the British, lacks these qualities, and the mandate concept is consequently weakened. Other factors in the American political milieu that weaken the applicability of the mandate concept include the separation of powers, bicameralism, and gerrymandering. The trend, however, is toward evolving an American political system in which voter action produces political change.

Mass Media The technical means of communication with millions of people, exemplified by television, radio, newspapers, motion pictures, magazines, and periodicals. Television, in particular, is used with increasing impact to build an "image campaign" in which special techniques (contrived situations, spot announcements, editing of videotapes, and the like) are used to achieve short-term perceptual shifts in voter behavior. *See also* CAMPAIGN page 112; PROPAGANDA, page 138.

Significance The mass media of communication have become extremely important to government and politics as a means of informing and influencing millions of citizens. Objectives include the winning of elections, the marshaling of support for or opposition to programs, and the education of the public on major issues. Political scientists, aware of the increasing significance of the mass media in decision making and of their abuse in totalitarian states, have expressed concern for their effect on the democratic process. The trend in the United States is toward concentration of the ownership of the mass media in fewer hands. The problem of seeking corctions for this situation raises many serious issues, including those concerning the constitutional rights of free expression and property.

Minor Party A party movement, often based on a single idea or principle, that usually has little influence on elections because its support is either localized or widely scattered. Some American political observers distinguish a minor party from a third party, a new party based on a protest movement which may influence the outcome of a major election. *See also* THIRD PARTY, page 144.

Significance Minor parties have played a significant role in American political life in initiating and successfully publicizing political, economic, and social reforms over a period of years. When a minor party gains a substantial number of adherents to its basic principles, a major party often incorporates these principles into its own platform so as to gain voter support. The Prohibition party, for example, convinced large numbers of people of the wisdom of prohibition; the Republican party thereupon included a prohibition plank in its platform and, after winning at the polls, instituted Prohibition. Minor parties found on the ballot in many states today include the American Independent, Prohibition, Socialist Labor, and Socialist Workers.

Multiparty System An electoral system, usually based on proportional representation, that requires a coalition of several parties to form a majority to run the government. Multiparty systems are typical of continental European democracies. The system can be distinguished from the Anglo-American two-party system, not by the existence of numerous parties, but rather in that many parties seriously compete for, and actually win, seats in the legislature. *See also* PROPORTIONAL REPRESENTATION, page 139; TWO-PARTY SYSTEM, page 146.

Significance Multiparty systems tend to provide a broader, more diverse representation of the electorate. This strength is, at the same time, a major weakness. Coalition governments, by their very nature, are unstable governments that tend to disintegrate when the parties comprising the coalition have a falling out over a major issue. France, for example, had twenty coalition governments during the period of the Fourth Republic, from 1946 to 1958. In Italy, since World War II, governments have changed with even greater frequency. The American people have shunned a multiparty approach to politics by refusing to give substantial support to any but the two major parties. Moreover, the single-member district system, as distinguished from proportional representation, tends to perpetuate the two-party system because typically only two parties or party coalitions have the voting strength to compete effectively for political power.

National Chairman The chairman of a political party's national committee. The national chairman is generally chosen by the party's presidential candidate, with the national committee ratifying the choice. *See also* NATIONAL COMMITTEE, page 127; POLITICAL PARTY, page 134.

Significance The major responsibility of a national chairman is the management of the national election campaign. Working through the national committee, the chairman may exercise a considerable influence over state and local party organizations, although no formal control mechanism exists. His specific responsibilities include establishing national party headquarters, directing party affairs during and between campaigns, and raising and distributing campaign funds.

National Committee A standing committee of a national political party established to direct and coordinate party activities during the four-year periods between national party conventions. The Democratic National Committee includes two members, a man and a woman, from each state, from the District of Columbia, and from several territories; the Republican National Committee uses the same formula but adds state chairmen from all states carried by the Republican party in the preceding presidential, gubernatorial, or congressional election. National committeemen and committeewomen are chosen every four years by the various delegations to the national convention. Each committee ratifies the presidential nominee's selection of a national chairman who acts as spokesman for his party. *See also* NATIONAL CHAIRMAN, PAGE 127; POLITICAL PARTY, page 134.

Significance Although the national committee appears to top the hierarchical permanent structure of each party, its power and influence are not great. The real locus of power in both party organizations remains at the local and state levels. Each national committee is concerned mainly with the presidential election and points most of its activities toward planning the next campaign. Other important functions include planning the national convention, securing financial contributions, and publicizing the party.

National Convention   A quadrennial meeting held by each major party to select presidential and vice presidential candidates, write a platform, choose a national committee, and conduct party business. Presidential candidates have been nominated by the convention method in every election since 1832. Delegates are apportioned on the basis of state representation with bonuses for states showing voting majorities for the party in preceding elections. Delegates are selected by party conventions or committees in approximately one-half of the states and by presidential primaries in the remaining states. Both parties also accredit delegates from the District of Columbia, Puerto Rico, and the Virgin Islands. The nomination of, and voting on, candidates is conducted by a call of the states in alphabetical order. Democratic party conventions no longer authorize use of the unit rule. Both conventions nominate their candidates by an absolute majority vote. *See also* CREDENTIAS COMMITTEE, page 117; FAVORITE SON, page 121; PLATFORM, page 132; PRESIDENTIAL ELECTION PROCESS, page 136; PRESIDENTIAL PRIMARIES, page 137; UNIT RULE, page 147.

Significance Although national party conventions are typified by excitement, both artificial and natural, their responsibilities are extremely important. Most convention efforts and oratory are pointed toward the imminent fall campaign. Despite extensive television coverage in recent years, the national convention remains a puzzling phenomenon for most Americans. Much criticism has been directed at it for its clownish atmosphere, the use of pressure tactics and secret bargains, and the lack of popular participation in the candidate-selection process. Yet, conventions seldom ignore public opinion and have chosen many distinguished candidates. Conventions generally are free from federal regulation.

Nepotism   Granting of political favors to relatives, often in the form of appointments to office. Civil service merit systems have helped to reduce the incidence of nepotism.

Significance Nepotism has been carried on by various kinds of public officials on all levels of government throughout American history. Although nepotism occasionally may result in the appointment of capable, highly qualified individuals to public office, it is more likely to result in the appointment of less capable persons and therefore is generally frowned upon by the voting public.

New Left A radical-liberal mass movement, particularly of college youth, that emerged during the 1960s. The New Left subscribed to a multifaceted radical ideology, with many uncoordinated campaigns and organizations challenging the established political, social, and economic order. The main unifying themes of the New Left were common opposition to the Vietnam War, the draft, the military-industrial complex, racial discrimination, the machinations of the establishment or power structure, the plundering and pollution of the planet, and economic deprivation of poor people. The New Left also provided the vanguard of the cultural revolution of the 1960s and 1970s which changed the attitudes and social practices of millions concerning hair styles, drugs, sex, rock music, religion, education, and pornography. "Participatory democracy," or direct decision making by interested, active local mass groups became the basic political objective, a means by which the New Left sought to reform what it regarded as the perversion of the democratic process by the rich and powerful. *See also* ALIENATION, page 109; POLITICAL ACTIVIST, page 133; WOMEN'S LIBERATION MOVEMENT, page 148.

Significance The origins of the New Left movement might be traced to the Free Speech campaign at the University of California at Berkeley in the late 1950s. During the 1960s and 1970s, the New Left proved to be one of the most powerful protest movements in American history, radically changing many aspects of individual and social life. Its impact spilled over American borders and it became an almost worldwide phenomenon, although most pronounced in its impact on rich, industrialized countries. The New Left differed from the "Old Left" of Communist and Socialist party members, mainly in its broad heterogeneity, its lack of discipline, its shifting leadership, its lack of clear ideological goals for establishing the "best" society, its emphasis on protest, reform, and change rather than revolution, and its libertarian emphasis on individualism and freedom. Although the New Left began as a pacifist, antiauthoritarian force, repression from the police and the military led to a growing militancy within the movement. The New Left, like other radical movements in American history, was relatively short-lived in generating mass support, but some of its ideas are likely to have lasting impact on the American political and social system.

Nineteenth Amendment An amendment to the Constitution, adopted in 1920, that prohibits any state from denying the right to vote to any citizen because of sex. Wyoming took the initiative, in 1869, in granting suffrage to women, but only a few states followed this lead. Suffragette agitation during the early part of the twentieth century culminated in the Nineteenth Amendment, which was adopted in time for women to vote in the presidential election of 1920. *See also* EQUAL RIGHTS, page 66; WOMEN'S LIBERATION MOVEMENT, page 148.

Significance Like the Fifteenth Amendment, the Nineteenth does not grant the right to vote to anyone, but it does restrict the states from discriminating on the basis of sex. The Amendment resulted in the largest increase in the electorate in American history. Since 1920, there have been no attempts to interfere with the voting rights of women. Because women voters outnumber eligible male voters today, campaigns have acquired more of a feminine touch, and candidate qualifications now include that of "sex appeal." Most political campaigners publicly recognize "equal rights" for women, and the Nineteenth Amendment is often described as the forerunner to the equal rights amendment.

Nomination   The official designation of an individual as a candidate for public office. Methods for selecting candidates in the United States have included the rank-and-file party caucus, legislative and congressional caucuses, the mixed caucus (legislators and party representatives), the party convention, the primary, and petition. Nomination also signifies the first step in the appointment by a chief executive of an executive or judicial official. *See also* APPOINTMENT POWER, page 199; AVAILABILITY, page 110; CAUCUS, page 113; CONVENTION page 115; DIRECT PRIMARY, page 119; NATIONAL CONVENTION, page 128; PETITION, page 132.

Significance   The direct primary is the most widely used nominating device, being mandatory or optional in all fifty states. The convention system, discredited and largely replaced by the direct primary by 1910, is once again gaining acceptance on state and local levels. Some disillusionment with the primary system exists, and the convention method is credited with giving greater emphasis to party responsibility and selection of able candidates. The selection of the candidates for the presidency remains in the hands of each party's quadrennial convention. In the appointments of executive and judicial officials, nomination must be followed by confirmation of the nominee by the legislative branch.

Nonpartisan Election   An election in which candidates have no party designations and political parties are prohibited from running candidates. Nonpartisan elections are typically used to elect state and local judges and municipal officials. They are often preceded by nonpartisan primaries in which the number of candidates for each office is reduced to two. *See also* PLURALITY, page 133.

Significance   A progressive movement active early in the twentieth century proposed to get rid of corruption by eliminating political parties and partisan elections. Many nonpartisan electoral reforms were introduced, especially on the local levels. Most nonpartisan systems, however, have not produced the anticipated results, since candidates often remain identified with parties, and parties may seek to influence the election. On the other hand, nonpartisan elections that succeed in divorcing the party from the election tend to rob the voter of his most effective cue-giving source—the party. Political parties have also been weakened by severance from their grass roots. Nonpartisan elections, however, have the major advantage of reducing the impact of state and national partisan issues on local elections.

Office-block Ballot   A form of general election ballot in which candidates for elective office are grouped together under the title of each office. The "office block" or "Massachusetts ballot" is in contradistinction to the other common type of ballot, the "party column" or "Indiana ballot," in which all candidates of a particular party are arranged in one column. *See also* PARTY-COLUMN BALLOT, page 131; STRAIGHT TICKET, page 144.

Significance   The office-block ballot is now used, in some form, in about twenty states. Politicians dislike it because it places more emphasis on the office than on the party and tends to discourage "straight-ticket" voting. Studies have shown that it definitely encourages voters to "split their ticket" in general elections, compared with straight-ticket voting on party column ballots.

Open Primary   A direct primary voting system that permits the voter to choose the party primary in which he wishes to vote without disclosing his party affiliation or allegiance, if any. In an open primary, the voter makes his choice in the privacy of the voting booth. He is limited, however, to casting votes for candidates of only one party. *See also* CLOSED PRIMARY, page 114; DIRECT PRIMARY, page 119.

Significance   Few states use the open primary system. Unlike the closed primary, it permits independents to vote in primaries and does not require public disclosure of party affiliation, regarded as distasteful by many voters. The open primary is criticized because it reduces party responsibility and permits "raiding" by voters of one party who cross over and seek to influence the nomination of weak candidates of the opposing party.

Participatory Democracy   Maximum direct participation in political, economic, and social decision making by interested, active, and knowledgeable local groups. Participatory democracy became a basic objective of the New Left movement during the 1960s. Radical groups pushed the approach as a cure for the perversion of the democratic process by the rich and the powerful. *See also* DIRECT DEMOCRACY, page 119; NEW LEFT page 129; PUBLIC POLICY MODELS, page 140.

Significance   Participatory democracy establishes the ideal of maximum feasible mass action in public decision making. Historically, the idea of mass participation in the political process was applied in the Greek city-states, the Swiss cantons, and the New England town meeting. More recently, it has been tested in the neighborhood block movement in the inner cities. Critics of participatory democracy cite the lack of interest in politics by the masses, their lack of knowledge, and the "iron law of oligarchy" which postulates the impossibility of mass democratic decision making.

Party-column Ballot   A form of general election ballot in which candidates for various offices are arranged in one column under their respective party names and symbols. The "party column" or "Indiana ballot" can be contrasted with the other common type of ballot, the "office block" or "Massachusetts ballot," in which candidates are grouped under each elective office. *See also* COATTAIL EFFECT, page 114; OFFICE-BLOCK BALLOT, page 130; STRAIGHT TICKET, page 144.

Significance   The party-column ballot permits voting for all of a party's candidates for local, state, and national offices by marking a single "X" or by pulling a single lever. Some variation of this kind of ballot is used today in about thirty states. Politicians generally prefer the party-column ballot because it simplifies and encourages "straight-ticket" voting. This is particularly true when a party has an exceptionally strong presidential or gubernatorial candidate to head the list of party candidates.

Patronage   The power to make partisan appointments to office or to confer contracts, franchises, licenses, honors, or other special favors. Patronage powers are vested primarily in the President, in governors and other state elective officials, in mayors, and in various county officers. Through senatorial courtesy and similar practices, legislators on all levels of government also share in patronage disposition. *See also* MERIT SYSTEM, page 228; SENATORIAL COURTESY, page 186; SPOILS SYSTEM, page 231.

Significance An era of unrestricted patronage was ushered in on the national level, by the Jackson Administration's spoils system in 1829. Presidential patronage reached a high watermark during Abraham Lincoln's first term (1861–1864), but began to lose ground progressively after the enactment of the Civil Service Act of 1883 (Pendleton Act). Patronage is often defended as an essential feature of the party system to provide inducements and rewards for party workers. It also enables a chief executive to surround himself with loyal subordinates who support his views and help him redeem his campaign pledges. Antipatronage forces counter these arguments by pointing to the long, disreputable history of the spoils system. Intelligent and well-trained personnel, it is argued, can work effectively with administrations of either party. The county is the major remaining stronghold of the patronage system in the United States.

Petition A method of placing a candidate's name on a primary or general election ballot by submitting a specified number, or percentage, of signatures of registered voters to an appropriate state or local official for certification. Petitions may also be used to commence the initiative and referendum procedures in several states. *See also* DIRECT LEGISLATION, page 166; FILING, page 122; NOMINATION, page 130.

Significance The petition requirement to get an aspirant's name placed on a primary ballot is intended to help restrict the election to serious candidates. In general elections, the petition method provides a means for political independents to get their names on the ballot. Petitions frequently become matters of political controversy, involving charges of invalid signatures.

Pivotal States Those states with large electoral votes that are crucial in winning a presidential election and in which the outcome is doubtful. The term "pivotal states," is also used to describe the twelve most populous states that have a majority of electoral college votes and potentially could elect a President and Vice President over the opposition of the other 38 states and the District of Columbia. *See also* ELECTORAL COLLEGE, page 119; PRESIDENTIAL ELECTION PROCESS, page 136.

Significance Each major party usually concentrates much of its organization, campaign funds, and candidate appearances on the seven most populous states that together comprise 211 of the 270 electoral votes needed to elect a President: California (45), Illinois (26), Michigan (21), New York (41), Ohio (25), Pennsylvania (27), and Texas (26). In most elections, these states have also been given "doubtful" status, adding to the attention given them during campaigns by both parties and their candidates. Popular leaders from pivotal states are also most likely to be nominated as presidential and vice presidential candidates.

Platform A statement of principles and objectives espoused by a party or a candidate that is used during a campaign to win support from voters. Platforms are typically written by platform committees and adopted by national, state, or county party conventions. *See also* NATIONAL CONVENTION, page 128.

Significance American party platforms consist of party pledges and promises plus many generalities and platitudes. They extol the vast accomplishments of their party while indicting the opposition party for its failures. The language used to elaborate positions on those issues on which the party is united, however, is precise and the commitment clear. Party platforms are variously supplemented and modified by candidates and party leaders, but few consider themselves bound by many of the platform commitments when elected. In the British system of responsible parties, conversely, the platform of the winning party is an excellent guide to future governmental actions.

Pluralism   The concept that modern society is made up of heterogeneous institutions and organizations that have diversified religious, economic, ethnic, and cultural interests and share in the exercise of power. Democratic pluralism is based on the assumption that democracy can exist in a society where a variety of elites compete actively in the decision process for the allocation of values, and that new elites can gain access to power through the same political processes. The countervailing theory of pressure politics posits that competition among major interest groups tends to balance power against power, with the result that none is able to dominate the American political system. Some analysts reject the theory and have described the American political system as one dominated by a power elite of military, business, and governmental groups and organizations. *See also* COUNTERVAILING THEORY OF PRESSURE POLITICS, page 117; PUBLIC POLICY MODELS, page 140; SECTIONALISM, page 142.

Significance   The greater the variety in a population, the greater the degree of pluralism likely to exist. Some react with fear in the presence of differences, whereas others derive satisfaction. While diversity is a potential threat to unity, uniformity is a threat to freedom. In countries like the United States, pluralism has given rise to a tremendous proliferation of organized groups, many with some impact on public policy, representing all manner of interests. It has also resulted in a greater variety of approaches to issues than will be found in homogeneous societies.

Plurality   The winning of an election by a candidate who receives more votes than any other candidate but not necessarily a majority of the total vote. Winning by plurality means that it is possible to win an election with, for example, only 30 or 40 percent of the total vote. *See also* ABSOLUTE MAJORITY, page 109; MAJORITY RULE, page 12; MINORITY PRESIDENT, page 205; NONPARTISAN ELECTION, page 130; RUNOFF PRIMARY, page 142.

Significance   Most American electoral laws for national, state, and local elections provide for winning by a plurality vote. Whenever there are more than two strong candidates running for an office, the winner usually secures a plurality rather than a majority vote. An exception is found in the runoff primary system used in several southern states whereby, if no candidate receives a majority vote, a second, runoff election is held between the two highest vote-getters. Typically, nonpartisan primaries also reduce the number of candidates for each office to two, thereby ensuring that the winner will receive a majority vote.

Political Activist   An individual who is extensively and vigorously involved in political activity, either within or outside the party system. Political activists within the party system typically participate in decision making at various levels, verbalize their ideas, attend party functions, campaign, work at the polls, help collect funds, support party candidates, and carry on other forms of activity within the party framework. Political activists outside the party system typically are protestors who build their interest and activity around a major issue, idea, or ideological point of view. Studies of political participation have produced operational definitions and varied categories of activist behavior. *See also* ALIENATION page 109; NEW LEFT, page 129.

Significance New social movements are born when major issues or ideas tend to create large numbers of political activists with similar views on controversial issues and common demands for change in "the system." The decade of the 1960s saw the emergence in the United States of a vast number of protest movements comprised of individuals who had lost confidence in the party system and other institutions as instruments of peaceful change. They became politically active as a result of their search for fundamental change in the political system. Political or party activism is often regarded as a useful component of a democratic system of government so long as it is directed toward nonviolent change.

Political Machine A well-entrenched party organization headed by a boss or small group of autocratic leaders. Political machines usually operate at the city or county level and occasionally on a statewide basis. They may use ruthlessly efficient methods in maintaining themselves in power through such techniques as bribery, patronage, "honest" and dishonest graft, control over nominations, and the rigging of elections. Any successful political organization may, however, be dubbed a "machine" by its opponents. *See also* BOSS, page 111; WATERGATE, page 214.

Significance Political machines have flourished throughout American history, although their number and effectiveness have been reduced in recent years. The direct primary was instituted in the early twentieth century largely as a reform to clean up politics by wresting power from political machines, but new techniques were developed by the bosses to control primaries. A high level of interest, participation, and civic spirit in an aroused community is the best answer to machine politics, but reform movements which incorporate these attributes are often short-lived in their vigor and interest, resulting in a return to power of the machine. Historically, political machines performed certain useful functions that are sometimes overlooked. These included helping to assimilate new immigrants, improving their social condition, and providing a channel through which many aggrieved groups could express their discontent and seek remedies for it.

Political Party A group of individuals, often having some measure of ideological agreement, who organize to win elections, operate government, and determine public policy. A party differs from a pressure group mainly in its basic objective of winning control of the machinery of government. In the United States, political parties are organized on precinct, county, congressional district, state, and national levels, with most decisions made by conventions, chairmen, and committees at the county, state, and national levels. Unlike parties in most countries, power in American political parties is highly decentralized *See also* DEMOCRATIC PARTY, page 118; MANDATE, page 126; MINOR PARTY, page 126; MULTIPARTY SYSTEM, page 127; REPUBLICAN PARTY, page 141; THIRD PARTY, page 144; TWO PARTY SYSTEM, page 146.

Significance Neither of the two major American parties requires ideological conformity as a requirement for participation. In an authoritarian state, a single party, typically requiring rigid adherence to its ideological dogma, is used to develop policies and run the government through dual-party and governmental leadership positions. In multiparty democratic states, in which each party can compete for a share of political power, individuals join the party that best promotes their economic and social interests. Political parties in the United States: (1) stimulate interest in the political process; (2) publicize political issues; (3) recruit candidates and carry on national, state, and local campaigns; (4) raise finances for political activity; (5) help maintain the honesty of elections; (6) take responsibility for operating the machinery of government or providing an organized opposition; (7) mobilize mass political power to control elite groups; (8) help to manage conflict; and (9) contribute to the building of intersectional and interclass consensuses.

Poll   An attempt to uncover public opinion or to forecast an election. Public opinion polling has developed from the early newspaper straw-vote poll of its subscribers to the personal interview technique, based on scientifically determined quota sampling of the voting population. New polling methods in use today involve probability sampling, in which representative precincts are used as barometers to indicate prevailing opinions. Poll results are checked against the actual voting records of the precincts. *See also* INDICATOR PRECINCT, page 124; PUBLIC OPINION, page 139.

Significance   The best-known polls include those conducted by Dr. George Gallup, Elmo Roper, Lou Harris, A. M. Crossley, the Survey Research Center of the University of Michigan, and the Princeton Research Service. Most polling interest is directed toward presidential elections, in which pollsters have often accurately predicted voting behavior. In the 1948 presidential election, however, polling groups failed to predict the Truman victory, resulting in considerable public skepticism of polling techniques and suspicion of pollsters' objectives. New techniques developed since 1948, including electronic computers, have increased predictive accuracy. Polls have also become increasingly significant as a means of keeping elective officials aware of public opinion on important issues, and in the selection of presidential nominees by the major parties. Supporters of polling regard it as a major democratic advance, whereas opponents fear the rigging of polls to influence elections and the restrictions polls may place on policymakers.

Poll Tax   A special head tax that must be paid as a qualification for voting. The Twenty-fourth Amendment to the Constitution outlawed the poll tax in national, but not state, elections. In 1966, the Supreme Court declared that payment of any poll tax as a condition for voting in *any* election is unconstitutional (*Harper v. Virginia State Board of Elections,* 383 U.S. 663). *See also* TWENTY-FOURTH AMENDMENT, page 145.

Significance   Before the *Harper* decision, a poll-tax requirement in five southern states had reduced the voting participation of both whites and blacks. The tax worked a greater hardship upon Negroes because of their lower income status and because of unequal enforcement. Prior to the Twenty-fourth Amendment, poll-tax states had turnouts in national elections of only one-half the size of those in states not using the poll tax. In some states, the poll tax was used to maintain the political machines in power because political leaders paid the tax for many of their supporters. In the *Harper* case, the Supreme Court held that a financial requirement for voting denies equal protection of the law.

Poll Watcher   An individual appointed by a political party to be present at a polling place on election day to ensure the honesty of the election. In many states, both major parties have poll watchers present at all polling places during partisan elections. In closed primary elections, poll

watchers may also be appointed to prevent "raiding." *See also* CHALLENGE, page   ; CLOSED
PRIMARY, page

Significance Poll watchers can play a significant role in maintaining the honesty of elections,
and, in this way, keep American voters from losing confidence in the democratic process. Poll
watching is essential when a party challenges an entrenched political machine.

Precinct The basic unit in the United States in the election process and for party organization.
Cities and counties are divided into precinct polling districts, each containing from 200 to 1000
voters and a polling place. In political organization, each party usually elects or appoints a precinct
captain or committeeman who functions as a party leader within the precinct. Precinct leaders
in the cities may represent their precincts in party ward committees. The precinct also serves for
the election or appointment of delegates to city or county party conventions. *See also* INDICATOR
PRECINCT, page 124; POLITICAL PARTY, page 134.

Significance The precinct, being a small voting district, provides easy access to the polls for
voters on election days. In politics, the precinct organization of the parties is the key to election
success, especially in the metropolitan areas. An effective precinct leader is expected to work
tirelessly the year around gaining party converts, getting voters registered, carrying on routine
party business, and, most significant for his political future, turning out large majorities for his
party on election days.

Presidential Election Process The procedures by which the American people select their
President. The presidential election process involves two races: the first, in which the aspirants
seek to obtain their party's nomination, and the second, in which the nominees of the two major
parties contest. The climax of the aspirant's race for nomination takes place in the summer of the
presidential election year at his party's national nominating convention. This convention is composed of delegates chosen in about one-half of the states by conventions or committees, and in
one-half by the voters in presidential primaries. Following the conventions, the autumn campaign
between the major party candidates begins in earnest. In the national election, held on the first
Tuesday after the first Monday in November, the voters in the fifty states and the District of
Columbia cast ballots for their choice for President, although in fact they are legally electing only
members of the Electoral College. In early January, a joint session of Congress opens the Electoral
College ballots and certifies the winners, who are subsequently sworn into office on January 20.
    In brief, here is a major party candidate's typical schedule in a presidential election year: *Late
winter:* announce candidacy; *spring:* campaign vigorously in key primary contests, particularly
in New Hampshire (the first primary) and in pivotal states; *early summer:* continue primary races
while striving to win delegates at party convention and committee meetings in nonprimary states;
late summer: marshal all possible party strength for final drive to obtain nomination at party's
national nominating convention; *early autumn:* resume campaigning with increasing tempo and
a broader focus to attract votes from independents and rival party members as well as from
members of candidate's own party; *late fall:* build campaign to a climax, with major speeches and
saturation of television and radio with partisan propaganda; *post-election period:* congratulate
opponent and go into seclusion, or if victorious, prepare to take over the reins of power in January.
See also AVAILABILITY, page 110; DARK HORSE, page 118; ELECTORAL COLLEGE, page 119;

MINORITY PRESIDENT, page 205; NATIONAL CONVENTION, page 128; PIVOTAL STATES, page 132; PRESIDENT, page 206; PRESIDENT-ELECT, page 207; PRESIDENTIAL PRIMARIES, page 137; STALK-ING HORSE, page 143; TWENTIETH AMENDMENT, page 211; VOTING QUALIFICATIONS, page 148.

Significance The presidential election process is basically a peaceful struggle for political power waged by the "outs" in their effort to defeat the "ins" and take over operation of the government. The process, described by some pundits as "that quadrennial madness," is often replete with ballyhoo, appeals to the voters' emotions, and a carnival-like atmosphere. Millions of dollars have been spent by each major presidential candidate on television programming alone. Over the years, the presidential election process has produced several great presidents, but it also has resulted in the election of some inferior presidents. Some critics point out that the process has often resulted in a "Hobson's choice" for the voter—that is, no real choice because both major candidates are undesirable. While most presidential elections merely continue the prevailing partisan political situation (*maintaining* elections), they may, as the result of some unusual event or candidate, lead to the defeat of the majority party (*deviating* elections), as in the case of Dwight D. Eisenhower's and Richard M. Nixon's elections. Such an upset often leads to a recapturing of the presidency by the dominant party after the event or personality that led to the disruption leaves the scene (*reinstating* elections). On the other hand, an event may be so dramatic or catastrophic that large numbers of voters change their party identifications (*realigning* elections), as in the struggle over slavery and in the Great Depression.

Presidential Primaries The process of electing delegates to a party's national presidential nominating convention. Most of the states and the District of Columbia hold some form of presidential primary in the weeks or months preceding the conventions; delegates are selected in the other states by political party conventions or committees. Delegates selected in the primaries may or may not be "pledged" to vote for a presidential aspirant. In a few states, delegates are selected by the party organization but are bound to support the candidate designated by the voters in a so-called popularity contest. *See also* DIRECT PRIMARY, page 119; NATIONAL CONVENTION, page 128; PRESIDENTIAL ELECTION PROCESS, page 136.

Significance The presidential primary was pioneered by Wisconsin in 1905. By 1916, both parties selected a majority of their national convention delegates by this method, then it lost considerable ground, but more recently it has regained much of it. The main controversy sur-rounding the presidential primary concerns the "preferential" problem—that is, should pledged or unpledged delegates be elected. Popular influence is reduced because pledged delegates are under no legal, and little moral, obligation to honor such pledges beyond the first ballot, and because many are elected as unpledged delegates. As a result, the presidential primary has not usually been of great significance in choosing presidential nominees. In 1952, for example, Estes Kefauver won most of the delegates in the preferential primary states but was not selected for the presidential nomination by the Democratic convention; Adlai Stevenson, conversely, did not enter any presidential primaries and yet won the Democratic nomination. Presidential primaries, how-ever, are gaining in significance by eliminating those who lack vote-getting ability and building the stature of those who demonstrate widespread popular support, and by discouraging incumbent presidents from running for reelection. Presidents Harry S. Truman and Lyndon B. Johnson, for example, announced their decisions not to seek reelection in 1952 and 1968, shortly after the New Hampshire primary demonstrated lack of party support. Conversely, when John F. Kennedy won the Democratic primary in heavily Protestant West Virginia, he overcame the long-held belief that Catholicism was an insurmountable barrier to the presidency. The "power of the primaries" was most forcefully demonstrated in 1972, when George McGovern gained the Democratic party's nomination despite heavy opposition from many party regulars. Supporters of preferential primaries argue that they prevent bosses from dominating conventions, build interest for the presidential election, and expand democratic influence. Those who oppose them point out that they are not decisive because voter opinion often is split in many directions, that they prolong the presidential election spectacle until voters get weary, and that only a convention free from voter pledges can reconcile party differences and unite the party behind a candidate. Although popular demands have increased in recent years for a nationwide preferential primary system, most professional politicians regard such a system as too costly in money, energy, and confusion.

Pressure Group An organized interest group in which members share common views and objectives and actively carry on programs to influence government officials and policies. Unlike political parties, which seek to win control of and operate the government, pressure groups are mainly interested in influencing the determination of public policies that directly or indirectly affect their members. Such groups vary considerably in size, wealth, power, and objectives. Their methods, however, are quite similar and include lobbying, electioneering, and propagandizing to influence public opinion. Pressure groups seek to influence decisions in the legislative, executive, and judicial branches. *See also* BUSINESS ORGANIZATIONS, page 305; CIVIL RIGHTS ORGANIZATIONS, page 62; COUNTERVAILING THEORY OF PRESSURE POLITICS, page 117; FARM ORGANIZATIONS, page 347; LABOR UNIONS, page 334; LOBBYIST, page 125; REGULATION OF LOBBYING ACT, page 198; VETERANS ORGANIZATIONS, page 370.

Significance In America's pluralistic society, groups rather than individuals exercise most political influence. The most powerful interest groups are those that have emerged out of the three basic economic areas: agriculture, business, and labor. Other significant groupings that carry on pressure activities include professional societies, women's groups, patriotic and veterans' organizations, and religious and racial groups. Pressure-group efforts are directed toward an identification of their particular interests with the general interest. The countervailing theory of pressure politics holds that the major interest groups, powerful as they may be, tend to counteract and balance each others power, which keeps any one from exercising a dominant influence. Many critics have disputed this theory, with conservatives typically charging labor dominance, and liberals attributing a decisive role to business and industry. Congress in 1946 sought to regulate the lobbying activities of pressure groups through the Federal Regulation of Lobbying Act. The Act is largely concerned with publicizing lobbying groups and their activities, but its vague and confusing language and the absence of an enforcement agency have encouraged much noncompliance. The enactment of stiffer laws involving extensive regulation of pressure groups and their activities might involve serious questions of constitutionality concerning basic rights of assembly and petition.

Propaganda Communication aimed at influencing the thinking, emotions, or actions of a group or public. The use of propaganda assumes that changes in people's thinking will prompt changes in their actions. Propaganda is not necessarily true nor false; it is based on a careful selection and manipulation of data. *See also* MASS MEDIA, page 126; PUBLIC OPINION, page 139; UNITED STATES INFORMATION AGENCY, page 413.

Significance The development of mass media has encouraged the use of propaganda to influence governmental decisions indirectly through public opinion. Government also uses propaganda to cultivate support for its programs and policies and to answer criticisms. Propaganda techniques include the use of simple slogans, the identification of propaganda with local situations, the "straight news" approach, the distortion of facts, appeals to idealism, and the "big lie" technique of Adolf Hitler. As a rule, successful mass propaganda must be simple, interesting, credible, consistent, and supported by actual events or experiences. Democracies are characterized by a variety of competing propagandists and their propaganda; dictatorships are maintained by government monopoly of propaganda.

Proportional Representation (PR) An electoral system that allocates seats in the legislative body to each party or group approximately equal to its popular voting strength. Under a system of proportional representation, for example a number of legislators may be elected from the same district by the same voters. A minority party that receives 5 percent of the total vote in that election will win about 5 percent of the legislative seats. The most commonly used systems of PR are the list system, based on voting by party, and the Hare system, based on voting for individuals using the single transferable vote. *See also* CUMULATIVE VOTING, page 117; HARE PLAN, page 123; MULTIPARTY SYSTEM, page 127.

Significance Several American cities, including New York, have experimented with the Hare system to provide some measure of minority representation. Most democratic countries use the continental European PR list system in preference to the Anglo-American, single-member district system. Proponents of PR point out that it provides representation for minority parties, reduces or eliminates machine politics, and is more democratic. Opponents argue that PR tends to proliferate parties, is too complicated for the average voter, and inevitably results in unstable coalition governments.

Public Opinion An aggregate of individual views, attitudes, or beliefs shared by a portion of a community. No single public opinion in the sense of a general will exists; rather, a number of publics hold various opinions on a host of issues. Public opinion can be made known in a democracy through elections, referendums, lobbying and pressure group activities, polls, and by elected representatives who "sound out" grassroots sentiment. *See also* MASS MEDIA, page 126; POLL, page 135; PRESSURE GROUP, page 138; PROPAGANDA, page 138.

Significance A common problem of democracies involves the question of how responsive to public opinion elected representatives should be. Should they, for example, exercise their own best judgment in voting on issues, or should they follow the public opinion positions of their constituents? If the latter, there remain the difficult problems of how to determine the existence of public opinion and how to measure it. Opinion research reveals the existence of a small "attentive public," with the mass public unaware of most issues. Although public opinion is a vague concept, political leaders recognize its significance in the political process and seek to shape it in support of their major policies. Public opinion functions as a *supportive* factor when the general public tends to bolster governmental policies and programs, in a *directive* capacity when it offers cues to political leaders, and as a *permissive* factor when it establishes toleration limits for policy alternatives.

Public Policy Models   Theoretical efforts to explain how public policy is made—or should be made—in the American system of government. Public policy models include (1) the power elite model, which posits that all important decisions in the American system are made by a small group of upper-class or establishment persons who, along with their lackeys, run the private and public sectors; (2) the pluralist model, which holds that policy is the product of group conflict, and that the public interest tends to emerge out of the welter of competing individual and group claims; and (3) the participatory democracy (or mass mobilization) model, which prescribes a changeover to a system wherein the entire citizenry participates directly in the policy process. *See also* ELITE, page 120; PARTICIPATORY DEMOCRACY, page 131; PLURALISM, page 133.

Significance   Political scientists have disagreed over which of the public policy models most accurately describes the decision processes of the American political system, and which is to be prescribed as the most cogent. Many observers have concluded that no one model describes the many-faceted system, and that all contribute to an understanding of its functioning. Public policy models are aimed at answering basic political questions, such as who governs, who gets what, when, and how, and who pays the bill.

Recall   A procedure enabling voters to remove an elected official from office before his term has expired. The required number of valid signatures on petitions results in the calling of a special election. If the majority of voters favor recall, the official is replaced by a successor who is either chosen on the recall ballot or in a subsequent election. Several states and numerous local units of government provide for the recall of elected officials. *See also* DIRECT DEMOCRACY, page 8; DIRECT LEGISLATION, page 166.

Significance   The recall enables the voters to hold their public officials continuously responsible. It is used infrequently, but the threat of recall is ever-present, and does not go unnoticed by elected officials. No provision is made for the recall of federal officials. The recall, along with the initiative and referendum, constitute the basic instruments of direct democracy.

Registration   Enrolling prospective voters prior to their participation in elections. Under a system of *permanent* registration, the voter, once qualified, remains on the eligible list until he dies, moves, or fails to vote in several consecutive elections. *Periodic* registration requires that he enroll at the appropriate local office annually or at fixed intervals. Almost all states now use some form of permanent registration, although in many there is no statewide application. *See also* VOTING QUALIFICATIONS, page 148.

Significance   Registration permits the orderly enforcement of voting qualifications and helps to maintain the honesty of elections. Permanent registration is more economical and less bothersome to voters than periodic, but it involves the problem of keeping voting lists up-to-date by enrolling new voters and deleting those who die, move, or are otherwise disqualified. Partisan or apathetic administration of these functions can result in fraudulent voting. Under periodic registration, lists are kept relatively up-to-date, and vote frauds are discouraged. Periodic registration is most useful in large cities where the mobility of population is high. Under the Voting Rights

Acts of 1965 and 1970, federal registrars enrolled Negroes in southern communities where racial discrimination had foreclosed their registration for many years.

Republican Party A major American party that emerged in the 1850s as an antislavery party. The Republican party is the successor to two earlier major parties—the Federalist and the Whig. It became firmly established in American politics when its candidate, Abraham Lincoln, won the presidency in 1860 and successfully prosecuted the Civil War. The period from 1860 to 1932 was characterized largely by Republican dominance of the American political scene, but in the years since 1932 the Democrats have dominated the presidency except for the elections of Dwight D. Eisenhower and Richard M. Nixon. *See also* DEMOCRATIC PARTY, page 118; HAMIL-TONIANISM, page 9; MADISONIANISM, page 12; POLITICAL PARTY, page 134.

Significance Studies have shown that Republican support among voters tends to increase as their income, property-owning, and educational levels rise. Traditionally, manufacturing, business, financial, and farming interests have been influential in the party except in the Deep South. The Republican party has historically advocated individual initiative, free enterprise, fiscal responsibility, and sound-money policies. Its policies have generally been more conservative than Democratic party policies, although both include a coalition of conservatives, moderates, and liberals. Historically, Republicans have also favored a high protective tariff and isolationism, although in recent years the party has supported lower tariffs and various American international commitments. It has generally opposed the ideas of the welfare state and big government although it has given support to social welfare programs in recent years. In the 1970s, the Republican party's appeal was threatened by a voter backlash resulting from the involvement of many high officials of the Nixon Administration in the crimes and corruption known collectively as "Watergate"

Residence A qualification for voting based on domicile. Such laws require that a person live in the state for a specified period of time, commonly one year, and within a county and a voting precinct, typically ninety days for the former and thirty days for the latter. In 1972, the Supreme Court declared invalid lengthy state (one year) and local (ninety days) residence requirements and suggested thirty days as sufficient (*Dunn v. Blumstein,* 405 U.S. 330). In the Voting Rights Act of 1970, Congress provided that thirty days residence in any state would qualify citizens to vote in presidential elections. *See also* DISFRANCHISE, page 119; VOTING QUALIFICATIONS, page 148;

Significance Residence requirements are intended to prevent the importing of "floaters" to win elections and to ensure that the individual is acquainted with state and local problems and candidates before he becomes eligible. The qualification, however, disfranchises temporarily several million voters in each major election as a result of increasing mobility of the American people. This mobility led the Supreme Court in 1972 to find lengthy residence requirements for voting an interference with the right to travel and change domicile. Congress has also considered legislation that would eliminate residence requirements in all national elections.

Responsible Party System A democratic political system in which parties accept full accountability to the voters in developing policy and operating the government. A responsible party requires internal discipline, so that its members give support to its objectives and platform promises. Following an election, the real test of responsibility is whether the majority party can redeem its pledges to the voters. *See also* MANDATE, page 126; POLITICAL PARTY, page 134.

Significance American political parties are fundamentally irresponsible in that they are highly decentralized and lack ideological cohesion. Moreover, the separation of powers, federalism, and sectionalism provide a political milieu not conducive to the growth of responsibility. In contrast, British parties are hierarchically structured, are disciplined through the party-whip system, and therefore can turn party promises into government policies. Critics of American parties have suggested a realignment of party wings into a new conservative-liberal two-party system so that both could function more responsibly. Reapportionment of American legislative bodies has helped to overcome the divisive impact of the separation of powers on party responsibility.

Runoff Primary   A nominating system used in a number of southern states, in which a second primary election is held between the top candidates if no candidate in the first primary polls a majority vote. *See also* DIRECT PRIMARY, page 119; PLURALITY, page 133.

Significance The runoff primary is particularly advantageous in one-party states where winning the primary is tantamount to election. It guarantees that the nominee will have the majority support of the voters rather than a mere plurality when three or more candidates are in the running. It also gives supporters of a losing candidate in the first primary a chance to coalesce in support of their choice in the runoff or second primary.

Sectionalism   The influence of local or regional loyalties on state or national elections, issues, or party unity. Sectionalism contributes to the heterogeneity that typifies democratic pluralism. *See also* PLURALISM, page 133.

Significance Traditionally, national unity has been seriously challenged by sectional cleavage on such vital issues as slavery, civil rights, "free silver," and the tariff. Most deep-rooted sectional loyalties of the early American period have given way, in the course of a century and a half, to nationalizing and unifying forces. The position of the South on civil rights' issues, for example, is today not substantially different from other sections of the country.

Short Ballot   A ballot containing relatively few offices to be filled by election. It is differentiated from the long ballot, which contains numerous elective offices, especially in the executive and judicial branches. Several states, such as New Jersey and Alaska, have reduced the number of statewide elected executive officials to governor and lieutenant governor and have considerably cut down the number of judicial elections. The national election ballot is already a "short" one, providing for the casting of a single vote for President and Vice President, the election of a single representative, and in two out of three elections, of a senator. The longest ballots, typically, are found on the local government level, especially in the county. *See also* LONG BALLOT, page 126.

Significance During the era of Jacksonian Democracy, the view that "the more numerous the elective offices, the more democratic the system" gained widespread acceptance. In the twentieth century, the short-ballot movement was established to try to reverse this situation. Advocates of the short ballot have called for patterning the state, county, and municipal ballots after the national, by providing for the election of legislators and one or two executive officials, with other executives and judges to be appointive. Underscoring the short-ballot movement is a belief that not only do shorter ballots simplify elections but they also make them more democratic by securing larger and more intelligent voter participation. Opponents adhere to the older doctrines that democracy thrives on numerous elections and that responsibility of office-holders can only be secured with a long ballot.

Single-member District   An electoral district from which a single legislator is chosen, usually by a plurality vote. The single-member district voting system is used in the United States and Britain, and in many former British colonies. It differs from the multimember districts typical of most continental European electoral systems based on proportional representation. France also uses a single-member district system, but a candidate can win only with a *majority* vote either in the initial election or in a subsequent runoff between the two highest vote-getters. *See also* CUMULATIVE VOTING, page 117; PROPORTIONAL REPRESENTATION, page 139; TWO-PARTY SYSTEM, page 146.

Significance   The single-member district system with a single plurality ballot is one of the factors that contributes to maintaining a two-party system because elections are based on the principle of "winner take all." Minor parties as a result are usually unable to win any share of political power and become parties of principle. Some American states depart from the single-member district system in holding elections for one house of the legislature, and many cities have instituted multimember systems with at large elections. Other than these exceptions, American elections are based on single-member districts. Supporters of the single-member district principle argue that it avoids confusion, helps guarantee a majority party, and avoids the pitfalls of government by coalition. Those who oppose it point out that the votes of defeated parties and candidates are wasted, that the principle distorts the final election results, and that it fosters a false majority that does not democratically reflect voter sentiment.

Split Ticket   Voting for candidates of two or more parties for different offices. Split-ticket voting is not permitted in primaries. *See also* OFFICE-BLOCK BALLOT, page 130; STRAIGHT TICKET, page 144.

Significance   Split-ticket voting is encouraged by the "office-block" ballot, which emphasizes individual choice for each office rather than straight-ticket party voting. Some observers regard split-ticket "voting for the best man, not the party" as the most desirable approach to politics. Others oppose it on the grounds that the voter can too easily be fooled by personality and glibness, that issues rather than individuals are most important, and that it tends to weaken party and government responsibility. A frequent result of split-ticket voting is a government in which different parties control the executive and the legislature and in which deadlocks and stalemates are common, with the voters unable to fix responsibility for action or inaction.

Stalking Horse   A candidate for public office, especially for the presidency, whose only role is to function as a cover or decoy on behalf of a stronger but unannounced candidate. The term *stalking horse* comes from the Great Plains states where hunters once used their horses as cover to move in for a close-range shot at bison or other game. Unlike a favorite son candidate, a stalking horse tries to convey the appearance of being a serious candidate so that his impact on the voters can be accurately assessed, and the base prepared for the subsequent candidacy of the party leader for whom he has fronted. Nevertheless, favorite son candidates may also function in the capacity of stalking horses. *See also* PRESIDENTIAL ELECTION PROCESS, page 136.

Significance The stalking horse technique relates especially to the hectic preconvention period of intraparty rivalry among prospective candidates for the presidential nomination. Candidates often accuse each other of being a stalking horse for another as a means of challenging each other's credibility as a serious contender. The main objectives of a stalking horse are to test voter support or to try to divide the opposition. A stalking horse might, for example, want to test voter reaction to a candidacy from a particular wing of his party, or the extent of grass-roots support for a candidate who takes a stand on a major controversial issue. Widespread public opinion polling has substantially reduced the role of stalking horses in presidential nomination contests.

State Central Committee   The principal committee of a political party within a state. State central committees are composed of members representing congressional districts, state legislative districts, or counties. *See also* POLITICAL PARTY, page 134.

Significance The state central committee has responsibility for carrying out policy decisions of the party's state convention. During political campaigns the committee makes decisions concerning strategy and the use of party campaign funds. It also may give direction to the party's state chairman, but, typically, has little influence with the party's state legislators or executive officials after they are elected.

Straight Ticket   Voting for all candidates of a single party for all offices. *See also* COATTAIL EFFECT, page 114; PARTY-COLUMN BALLOT, page 131; SPLIT TICKET, page 143.

Significance Straight-ticket party voting is encouraged by the use of "party-column" ballots, which require the marking of a single "X;' or the pulling of a single lever to vote for all party candidates for all offices. Straight-ticket voting is also encouraged by the "coattail effect," when a popular presidential or gubernatorial candidate heads the party's ticket. Some observers prefer straight-ticket voting because it reduces the impact of personality, places major emphasis on issues, and promotes party and government responsibility. The case against straight-ticket voting is based on the assumption that intelligent voters should "vote for the man, not the party" and that a split ticket encourages the exercise of judgment by the voter.

Third Party   A new party, usually comprised of independents and dissidents from the major parties in a two-party system that, typically, is based on a protest movement and that may rally sufficient voter support to affect the outcome of a state or national election. Some students of government distinguish a third from a *minor* party, a long-standing ideological party that seldom affects a specific election outcome. The objective of American third parties may be to encourage a large protest vote, or to seek to prevent either major party candidate from winning a majority of electoral votes with the result that the election of the President would be thrown into the House of Representatives. Third parties are also known as *splinter* or *secessionist* parties because they are composed largely of adherents who have broken away from one or both major parties. *See also* MINOR PARTY, page 126.

Significance Third parties have played an important role in American politics by influencing the adoption of reforms and by keeping the major parties from becoming too similar in their approach to issues, or too indifferent. When a political, economic, or social consensus breaks down, third-party movements have their best opportunity to present voters with a new and different approach. For example, in 1856 the Republican party was a third party that took the initiative away from the Whig party with a forthright antislavery program and replaced it as a major party. Another significant third-party movement was Theodore Roosevelt's "Bull Moose" party, which split the Republican vote and enabled Woodrow Wilson to win in 1912. The Dixiecrat party in 1948 was a sectional third party that failed to influence the election outcome because of a lack of sympathy outside the Deep South for its protest position. The most recent third party movement was that of George C. Wallace's American Independent party which polled 13.5 percent of the votes cast in the 1968 presidential race. Wallace's return to the Democratic party in subsequent elections eliminated the American Independent party as an effective third party.

Twelfth Amendment An amendment to the Constitution, adopted in 1804, that provides for separate ballots to be used by the electors in voting for President and Vice President. Previously, the vice presidency went to the runner-up in the Electoral College vote. The Amendment also reduces the range of choice of the House of Representatives from the five highest to the three highest candidates when none has received an electoral vote majority. The Senate's choice of Vice President under these circumstances is limited to the two highest candidates. *See also* ELECTORAL COLLEGE, page 119.

Significance The Twelfth Amendment developed out of the confusion in the election of 1800 in which party-pledged electors were chosen for the first time. Since each elector voted for two candidates, the result found Thomas Jefferson, the presidential candidate, tied with his own vice presidential candidate, Aaron Burr. The election was thrown into the House where the lame-duck Federalist party majority finally elected Jefferson President after toying with the idea of electing Burr to embarrass the Jeffersonian Republican party. To avoid such confusion in subsequent elections, the Twelfth Amendment specified that electors "name in their ballots the person voted for as President, and in distinct ballots the person voted for as Vice President." The Amendment adapted the Electoral College to the new political party system, which had not been anticipated by the Founding Fathers.

Twenty-fourth Amendment An amendment to the Constitution, adopted in 1964, that forbids the levying of a poll tax in primary and general elections for national officials, including the President, Vice President, and members of Congress. Although the Amendment does not apply to elections for state or local officials, the Supreme Court in 1966 declared that the levying of a poll tax for *any* election is unconstitutional (*Harper v. Virginia State Board of Elections,* 383 U.S. 663). *See also* VOTING QUALIFICATIONS, page 148.

Significance At the time of the ratification of the Twenty-fourth Amendment, only five states levied poll taxes and the Amendment was generally viewed as an attempt to placate growing Negro demands for voting rights. Failure to outlaw poll taxes in state and local elections made the Amendment largely ineffective, with the result that Congress, in the 1965 Voting Rights Act, authorized a legal test of all poll taxes, which led to the *Harper* decision.

Twenty-sixth Amendment   An amendment to the Constitution, adopted in 1971, that lowers the legal voting age to eighteen in the United States. Although eighteen-year-olds had already been accorded the vote in national elections by the Voting Rights Act of 1970, the Twenty-sixth Amendment assured them the vote in *all* —national, state, and local—elections. The amendment proposal was ratified by the necessary thirty-eight states legislatures in record time during 1971 so that the measure could take effect for the 1972 presidential election. Voting opportunities were increased by the Amendment at the time of its adoption for an estimated eleven million young people. *See also* VOTING QUALIFICATIONS, page 148.

Significance   The Twenty-sixth Amendment accomplished what Congress had unsuccessfully attempted to do by statute. In the Voting Rights Act of 1970, Congress lowered the legal voting age to eighteen in all elections, but the Supreme Court ruled subsequently in *Oregon v. Mitchell,* 400 U.S. 112 (1970), that Congress had the constitutional power to lower the voting age require- ments for national but not for state and local elections. The Twenty-sixth Amendment resulted from that decision. Two factors that encouraged early ratification of the Amendment were the prospective increases in state expenses for maintaining separate registration systems and ballots for national and state elections, and political backing given to the measure by the Democratic party whose members anticipated substantial support from the younger voters. Opponents of the Amendment pointed out that the voters in many states had earlier rejected referendums aimed at extending the vote to eighteen-year-olds.

Twenty-third Amendment   An amendment to the Constitution, adopted in 1961, that enables the people of the District of Columbia to participate in the election of the President. The Twenty-third Amendment allots the District of Columbia three electoral votes. *See also* DISTRICT OF COLUMBIA, page 33; ELECTORAL COLLEGE, page 119.

Significance   The Twenty-third Amendment increased the size of the Electoral College to 538 electors, beginning with the 1964 presidential election. Although President Kennedy proposed that voting eligibility in the District be established by ninety days' residence and at the age of eighteen, the Congress, in 1961, prescribed a residence of one year and a minimum voting age of twenty-one. Various groups in the District are continuing their agitation for congressional repre- sentation and local self-government.

Two-party System   Division of voter loyalties between two major political parties, resulting in the virtual exclusion of minor parties from seriously competing with the major parties or sharing in political power. A state in which the two major parties compete on fairly equal terms may nevertheless contain many electoral districts that are basically one party in voter support, and some may be dominated by a third party. The two-party system is the traditional British system, which has been adopted in many Commonwealth countries and by the United States. *See also* MULTIPARTY SYSTEM, page 127; SINGLE-MEMBER DISTRICT, page 143; THIRD PARTY, page 144

Significance The two-party system stems from tradition, the tendency to view problems in terms of black-or-white alternatives, and the use of the single-member district system. The two-party monopoly on governmental power has, on several occasions in American history, been seriously challenged by the rise of a third party. Under a single-member district electoral system, however, the third party cannot compete effectively for political power unless it displaces one of the major parties, as when the Republicans took over the major party status of the Whigs in 1860. Americans who support the two-party system point out that it assures the election of legislative majorities, provides an effective and cohesive opposition, simplifies the role of the voter, and generally provides stability in government. Opponents of the two-party system, however, charge that it creates artificial legislative majorities, narrows the voter's choice to two alternatives when there may be many, and makes a fetish of stability while denying minority parties and groups representation in the government.

Unit Rule A rule, applicable prior to 1972 in Democratic national conventions, which provided that state delegations could cast their total votes in a block for a single presidential candidate. The unit rule was not imposed by the national convention; it was merely recognized when properly invoked by state party authorities. In order to broaden grass-roots participation, the Democratic party forbid its use in a major reform of its convention procedure in 1970. *See also* NATIONAL CONVENTION, page 128.

Significance Permission to invoke the unit rule in Democratic national conventions reflected the states' rights tradition of the party. It increased the influence of states using the unit rule over those which split their strength among several candidates. Southern state delegations made effective use of the unit rule in maintaining a significant voice in the selection of Democratic presidential candidates. The Republican party does not recognize the unit rule and permits each delegate to cast his ballot individually. Some state conventions, however, continue to permit the invoking of the unit rule by county or district delegations.

Voter Turnout The number of voters who actually participate in an election compared to the total number who are eligible to vote in that election. Voter turnout tends to be higher in presidential elections than in off-year elections, in national elections more than in state and local contests, and in general over primary or special elections. Other factors that may influence the size of voter turnout include geography (higher in the North than in the South and in small towns than in big cities), the type of election (in one-party states, the primary draws better than the general election), and electoral factors (spirited campaigns and glamorous candidates attract voters whereas elections without them suffer from reduced participation). *See also* DIRECT PRIMARY, page 119; GENERAL ELECTION, page 123; VOTING QUALIFICATIONS, page 148.

Significance Political scientists have discovered that the size of voter turnouts often relates directly to election outcomes. A low turnout, for example, tends to favor Republican candidates. If critical economic issues are at stake in an election, Democratic voters tend to turn out in larger numbers. As a general rule, independents tend to have a poorer turnout record than those who have a party preference. Uncontrollable factors such as the weather on election day may also help to determine the size of the turnout and the election outcome. Some nations have tried to increase voter turnout by systems of compulsory voting in which the eligible voter who fails to go to the polls may be fined or lose certain citizenship privileges.

Voting Qualifications   Legal requirements that prospective voters must fulfill to become eligible to vote. Qualifications imposed in all of the states include citizenship, age (eighteen for all elections since the adoption of the Twenty-sixth Amendment in 1971), and residence (although Congress in the Voting Rights Act of 1970 provided that thirty days' residence would qualify citizens to vote in presidential elections). Special qualifications involving lengthy residence, tax payments, property ownership, and literacy may no longer be imposed under Supreme Court rulings. Most states, however, disqualify mental incompetents, prison inmates, election-law violators, and vagrants. According to the Fifteenth and Nineteenth amendments to the Constitution, no person may be disqualified by a state from voting because of race or sex. *See also* DISFRANCHISE, page 119; LITERACY TEST, page 125; REGISTRATION, page 140; RESIDENCE, page 141; TWENTY-FOURTH AMENDMENT, page 145.

Significance   Fewer than 50 percent of the potential voters actually participate in most elections, and the best turnouts in presidential contests have only slightly exceeded 60 percent. Many potential voters are denied the ballot because of failure to qualify. Suggestions for improving voter participation include: (1) reducing residence requirements for most elections and eliminating them for presidential contests; and (2) enforcing the federal Civil Rights Acts of 1957, 1960, 1964, and the Voting Rights Act of 1970 to prevent disfranchisement because of color or race. Under the Twenty-sixth Amendment, voting opportunities were increased for an estimated eleven million young people. Although much can be accomplishe by such actions, many observers believe that alienation, inertia, and lack of interest by millions of people remain the major difficulties.

Women's Liberation Movement   A contemporary militant feminist movement aimed at achieving status and rights for women in society equal to those of men. Commonly referred to as "Women's Lib," it consists of several national and numerous local organizations and "rap groups." The main goal of the movement is to change society and its culture so that the "dominant-inferior relationship of men to women" can be changed. Particular objectives for the more radical elements of the movement include ending the "power-structured system of patriarchy" by which the father dominates family life, and wiping out "sexism," the conscious or subconscious male chauvinist attitudes that treat women as sex objects. Most liberationists, however, are concerned with less philosophical and more immediate problems, such as ending job and pay discrimination, securing abortion reform, setting up tax-supported child care centers, and securing equal treatment under national, state, and municipal laws. *See also* EQUAL RIGHTS, page 66.

Significance   The origins of the Women's Liberation Movement in the United States can be traced back to the nineteenth-century feminist campaigns to secure the ballot. The assumption of the feminists in those days was that the achievement of other basic rights and a dignified position in society would follow the securing of suffrage. The contemporary movement, which began in the early 1960s and gained momentum over the next decade, recognizes that this assumption has proved false, and that political, economic, and social discrimination against females still permeate American society. Women's Lib has taken on some of the characteristics of a radical mass movement, with protests, marches, invasions of male sanctuaries, condemnation of female sex symbols, and direct and indirect political involvement. Some scholars relate Women's Lib to the general problems of anomie and alienation growing out of the increasing urbanization and deper-sonalization of modern life. Since women constitute a majority of Americans of voting age, major political consequences could result from the movement's growing base of support.

IMPORTANT CASES

Gray v. Sanders, 372 U.S. 368 (1963): Ruled that in a given constituency each person's vote must count equally. The case overturned the Georgia "county unit system" for primary elections for statewide officers whereby the election was decided not by direct popular vote but by a system of county unit votes that discriminated against urban areas. *See also Baker v. Carr,* page 194; REDISTRICTING, page 181.

Significance The *Gray* case marked the first explicit application of the "one man, one vote" principle by the Supreme Court. The Court stressed that the concept of political equality found in the Fifteenth, Seventeenth, and Nineteenth amendments required equality of voting power when all voters are members of the same constituency, as in a statewide election of a governor or senator.

Guinn v. United States, 238 U.S. 347 (1915): Declared "grandfather clauses" to be unconsti-tutional under the Fifteenth Amendment. These clauses had been used by many southern states to bestow the franchise upon white voters who had been disfranchised by state tax and literacy requirements intended to keep the Negroes from voting. The grandfather clauses granted the franchise to persons whose ancestors had voted prior to 1867.

Significance Although the grandfather clause might have appeared to be a means of expanding the electorate, a creditable endeavor, the Court uncovered the subterfuge by recognizing the intent behind it to discriminate against blacks. The decision put the Court on record as regarding any attempt, direct or roundabout, to disfranchise any group because of its color or race as a violation of the Fifteenth Amendment.

Hadley v. Junior College District of Kansas City, 397 U.S. 50 (1970): Ruled that the "one man, one vote" principle applies generally to *all*—national, state, and local—elections of governmental officials. The *Hadley* case declared that the "dilution" of the votes of people living in one of the districts comprising the Junior College District of Metropolitan Kansas City violates the equal protection clause of the Fourteenth Amendment. The unconstitutional dilution involved a state apportionment formula whereby 60 percent of the total electorate of the District could elect only 50 percent of the junior college trustees. *See also* APPORTIONMENT, page 155; *Baker v. Carr,* page 194; REDISTRICTING, page 181.

Significance The *Hadley* decision climaxed a series of apportionment cases that began with *Baker v. Carr* in 1962 by declaring conclusively that equal voting power in all popular elections is a fundamental right enjoyed by every American. This right, according to the Court, is "protect-ed by the United States Constitution against dilution or debasement."

Smith v. Allwright, 321 U.S. 649 (1944): Established, finally and conclusively, that the "white primary" was a violation of the Fifteenth Amendment. The case arose over the denial of a ballot to Smith, a Negro resident of Houston, Texas, in the Democratic primary of 1940 for nominating candidates for congressional and state offices. The Court recognized that its earlier decision, allowing the exclusion of blacks from "private" party primaries, in the case *Grovey v. Townsend,* 295 U.S. 45 (1935), had been "in error." The Court reasoned that the party was actually performing a state function in holding a primary election and was not acting as a private group. Moreover, the Court pointed out that a primary is an integral part of the election process.

Significance In southern states, nomination in the Democratic primary is usually tantamount to winning the election. By being denied a vote in the primary, blacks were prevented from effectively participating in the selection of public officials. By invoking the Fifteenth Amendment against a private group (political party), the Court closed a loophole it had opened with its earlier interpretation. This case stands as an important landmark in the continuing legal battles to ensure voting rights for all. This decision resulted in more vigorous use of other techniques by southern states to keep blacks from the polls, such as literacy tests and difficult registration procedures.

United States v. Classic, 313 U.S. 299 (1941): Upheld the power of Congress to supervise the holding of state primary congressional elections to ensure the right of the people to vote and to have their ballot counted. Classic, a Commissioner of Elections in Louisiana, was convicted for vote fraud under a federal criminal law prohibiting interference with constitutional rights. The Court based its decision on Article I, Section 4, of the Constitution which establishes the regulatory powers of Congress over congressional elections, holding that the primary is an integral part of the election process.

Significance The Court's position, that Congress might validly regulate congressional primary elections in the states, overturned its earlier precedent established in *Newberry v. United States,* 256 U.S. 232 (1921). The Court recognized that the "times, places and manner" clause of the Constitution would be meaningless, especially in the one-party states of the South, if it were applied only to general elections and not to the primaries. In 1880, in *Ex parte Siebold,* 100 U.S. 371, the Court had upheld the power of Congress to regulate the conduct of general elections for national office.

IMPORTANT STATUTES

Electoral Count Act An 1887 act of Congress that provides for settlement of disputes over the election of presidential electors. When more than one set of electors are certified by different authorities of a single state, Congress, voting as two separate houses, decides which to accept. If Congress fails to agree, the electors certified by the governor are accepted. *See also* ELECTORAL COLLEGE, page 119.

Significance The Electoral Count Act resulted from the great confusion in the election of 1876. Hayes finally won the presidency over Tilden, 185 electoral votes to 184, after 20 contested electoral votes were awarded to Hayes on a strictly partisan basis by an Electoral Commission hastily created by Congress. The establishment of regular procedures is important not only because the outcome of such disputes within one or a few states may affect the outcome of a close presidential election, but also because the effectiveness of the democratic process depends upon popular confidence in the honesty of elections.

Federal Election Campaign Act of 1972   An act to control the raising and expenditure of funds for political campaigns. Its major provisions include (1) a limitation on the amount that can be spent for political advertising to 10 cents for every eligible voter—in a congressional district for House contests, statewide for Senate contests, and nationwide for presidental races—with a limit of 60 percent of that sum usable for broadcast advertising; (2) a ceiling on the amount that individual candidates and their immediate families can contribute to their own campaigns—$50,000 for a presidential race, $35,000 for the Senate, $25,000 fr the House; and (3) a requirement of complete disclosure of contributions in excess of $10 and expenditures in excess of $100. Other provisions regulate the activities of political campaign committees, labor unions, and corporations, and establish reporting procedures. *See also* CORRUPT PRACTICES ACTS, page 116; FEDERAL ELECTION CAMPAIGN ACT OF 1974, page 151.

Significance   The Federal Election Campaign Act of 1972 replaces various federal corrupt practices legislation enacted since 1908 and is designed to reduce the influence of heavy campaign funds and personal wealth on elections. The limits on broadcast advertising reflect both the huge costs involved in television exposure for candidates and recognition of the impact of television saturation of the electorate. While not all campaign expenditure pressures on candidates are covered by the Act, such as travel and other nonmass media advertising costs, the extensive reporting and disclosure requirements may temper both the giving and spending of funds. Disclosures of widespread illegal and corrupt actions during the 1972 presidential election led Congress to enact the Campaign Act of 1974.

Federal Election Campaign Act of 1974   A major law that alters and supplements the Federal Election Campaign Act of 1972 in regulating campaign financing in national elections. The Federal Election Campaign Act provides for total public financing for presidential general elections, with $20 million to be provided for each major party candidate, and with minor party candidates receiving a proportion of that amount based on votes received. In the drive to win their party's nomination, qualified aspirants can use a mixture of private and public funds. To qualify for public financing in the party's nomination's campaign, a candidate must first raise $5,000 in each of 20 states in contributions no larger than $250 each. Funds for all public financing will be derived from a one-dollar voluntary checkoff on personal income tax returns. Other provisions of the law limit individual contributions to a maximum of $1,000 for a candidate in a national primary or general election, with a $25,000 limit set on any person's total contributions during an election year. Special interest groups and political committees may contribute no more than $5,000 to any candidate in a national primary or general election. Spending limits start with a base figure of $70,000 for each primary and for each general election for House candidates plus a variable system that could raise the total ceiling for some House candidates to over $100,000. Senate candidates are limited in spending for each primary to a base figure of $100,000 or 8 cents per eligible voter, whichever is greater, and to $150,000 or 12 cents per eligible voter for each general election. Spending by each national party organization is limited to $10,000 per candidate in House general elections, to $20,000 or 2 cents per voter for Senate general elections, and to 2 cents per voter in presidential general elections. Enforcement of the campaign finance laws is placed in the hands of a bipartisan six-member Federal Elections Commission. The Senate, House, and President each nominate two members, one from each party, all of whom must be confirmed by both houses of Congress. The Commission is assigned extensive civil enforcement powers, but criminal actions are handled by the Department of Justice. Finally, the Act repealed provisions of the Hatch Act of 1940 which for 35 years barred state and local employees paid in whole or part with federal funds from engaging in partisan political activity. *See also* CORRUPT PRACTICES ACTS, page 116; FEDERAL ELECTION CAMPAIGN ACT OF 1972, page 151; WATERGATE, page 214.

Significance The Federal Election Campaign Act of 1974 was largely the product of public pressures generated by revelations of big-money financing scandals during the 1972 presidential election involving President Richard M. Nixon's reelection committee and various special interests. It was also partly a result of the effective tactics employed by Common Cause, a powerful citizen's public interest lobby group. Not all provisions for the 1974 Act, however, were aimed at strengthening the 1972 Act; for example, the 1974 law included an amendment shortening the statute of limitations from five to three years for exempting corporations and their officers from prosecution. The main changes in the 1974 amendments to the 1972 law involve public financing of presidential election campaigns and the creation of a special regulatory commission to enforce the provisions of both congressional enactments. Although Congress agreed on public financing for presidential elections, the House refused to support the idea of public financing of congressional campaigns on the ground that it would be mainly advantageous to candidates opposing House members. Whether the new campaign financing law will reduce the influence of special interests on election outcomes and policy making in government, and whether the new Federal Elections Commission can effectively enforce the law, will be tested in future national elections. The 1972 and 1974 Acts were the first major election campaign reform acts passed in a half century.

Voting Rights Act of 1965 An act to eliminate restrictions on voting that have been used to discriminate against Negroes. The major provision of the Act automatically suspended the use of literacy or other tests subject to discriminatory manipulation. It authorized the registration of voters by federal registrars in any state or county where such tests were used in the 1964 election and where less than 50 percent of the eligible voters were registered or voted. The states of Alabama, Georgia, Louisiana, Mississippi, South Carolina, Virginia, and parts of North Carolina were mainly affected. Another provision of the Act authorized the Attorney General to bring suit to test the validity of poll taxes in state elections. In 1966, the Supreme Court declared payment of poll taxes as a condition for voting to be unconstitutional (*Harper v. Virginia State Board of Elections,* 383 U.S. 663). Major provisions of the Voting Rights Act of 1965 were upheld by the Supreme Court as a valid exercise of power under the Fifteenth Amendment (*South Carolina v. Katzenbach,* 383 U.S. 301 [1966]). The Act was extended by the Voting Rights Act of 1970. *See also* VOTING RIGHTS ACT OF 1970, page 153.

Significance The Voting Rights Act was passed in response to dramatic Negro demonstrations during 1965 protesting discrimination in voting registration procedures. The voting provisions in the Civil Rights Acts of 1957, 1960, and 1964 relied upon slow moving judicial procedures to control discriminatory practices and proved ineffective. The Johnson Administration moved swiftly to implement the registration procedures and thousands of black voters were added to the voting rolls. The Act had a significant impact upon southern and national elections, including the election of numerous Negro officeholders.

Voting Rights Act of 1970 An act which continued and expanded upon the efforts of the national government to increase the electorate. The Voting Rights Act of 1970: (1) extended the Voting Rights Act of 1965 for five years; (2) provided for the lowering of the minimum voting age from twenty-one to eighteen in all elections; (3) suspended the use of state literacy tests; (4) prohibited the states from disqualifying voters in presidential elections because of their failure to meet state residence requirements beyond thirty days; and (5) provided for uniform national rules for absentee registration and voting in presidential elections. The Supreme Court in a series of cases in 1970 upheld all provisions of the Act except that which lowered the voting age to eighteen in state and local elections, although the eighteen-year-old provision was upheld for presidential and congressional elections (*Oregon v. Mitchell,* 400 U.S. 112). *See also* TWENTY-SIXTH AMEND-MENT, page 146; VOTING QUALIFICATIONS, page 148; VOTING RIGHTS ACT OF 1965, page 152.

Significance The Voting Rights Act of 1970 climaxed the national government's drive during the 1960s to expand the electorate by overcoming discriminatory and restrictive state and local voting laws and state constitutional provisions. This objective was accomplished by Congress and sustained by the Supreme Court through a broad interpretation of the Fourteenth Amendment and the application of the principle of national supremacy. The Twenty-sixth Amendment, which provides for a minimum voting age of eighteen in *all* —national, state, and local—elections, was proposed by Congress following the *Oregon* decision which limited the lower age minimum to national elections. Ratified by the necessary thirty-eight state legislatures in record time, the new Amendment along with the Voting Rights Act of 1970 provided for the greatest expansion in the American electorate since women's suffrage.

Voting Rights Act of 1975 An act which continues and expands the national government's role in increasing the electorate in those states where discriminatory practices exist. The Voting Rights Act of 1975 extends for seven years federal efforts to eliminate voting restrictions first enacted in the Voting Rights Act of 1965 and renewed and expanded in the Voting Rights Act of 1970. *See also* VOTING RIGHTS ACT OF 1965, page 152; VOTING RIGHTS ACT OF 1970, page 153.

Significance The enactment of the Voting Rights Act of 1975 gave congressional recognition to the impact the earlier acts have had on increasing black voting and the election of black officials in the South. The new act extends federal voting protection to all or parts of ten new states, requires bilingual ballots, and provides for approval of any election law changes in those states by either a United States Attorney or a federal court. Additional provisions extend legal protection to the voting rights of Spanish-Americans, Alaskan natives, American Indians, and Asian-Americans.

7 The Legislative Process:

Congress and the State Legislatures

Adjournment To terminate a session of a legislative body. Adjournment sine die means to end the session without definitely fixing a day for reconvening. It is used to end a congressional session officially. "Adjournment to a day certain" means adopting a motion or resolution that specifies the date and time of the next meeting. Neither house of Congress can adjourn for more than three days without the concurrence of the other. *See also* LEGISLATIVE DAY, page 175; SESSION, page 187.

Significance Under the Legislative Reorganization Act of 1946, Congress adjourns no later than the last day of July, unless Congress specifically provides otherwise. Under the Constitution, if the two houses of Congress cannot agree on an adjournment day, the President can determine it. This has never occurred.

Advice and Consent The power vested in the United States Senate by the Constitution (Art. II, sec. 2) to give its advice and consent to the President in treaty making and appointments. A two-thirds vote of the senators present is required for treaties. Appointments are confirmed by a simple majority vote. The Senate may give its advice through consultations between Senate leaders and the President by resolutions setting out its position, or by delegating some of its members actually to sit in on treaty negotiations. *See also* CONFIRMATION, page 163; RATIFICATION, page 180; RATIFICATION, page 208.

Significance Although the Constitution's phraseology seems to associate the Senate with the President throughout the treaty-making process, President Washington, after several attempts to consult with the entire Senate, found it impractical, and initiated the tradition of consulting with the Senate only after a treaty had been negotiated and signed. Since World War II, however, presidents have increasingly expanded the "advice" role of the Senate by inviting influential senators to participate in the negotiation of the treaty that created the United Nations, several treaties that established military alliances, and other significant treaties. The Senate generally accepts the nominees of the President for high-level positions, but in the case of many presidential appointments to federal positions located within states, the rule of "senatorial courtesy" applies.

Amendment   An action of a legislative body to delete, alter, or revise the language of a bill or an act. Bills in Congres may be amended by either house at any one of a number of stages in the legislative process. Generally, amendments are printed, debated, and voted upon in the same way as a bill. Most laws enacted by Congress are, in fact, amendments to existing laws. *See also* AMENDMENT, page 21.

Significance Through the amending process, a bill may undergo such extreme revision or modification that it loses much of its original character. Often, instead of attempting to kill bills outright, legislators will add amendments to make them innocuous. Legislators may also try to kill bills by attaching amendments that are unacceptable to the majority of their house or the other chamber. Once a bill is enacted into law, it can be amended only through passage of new legislation.

Apportionment   The allocation of legislative seats. The Constitution (Art. I, sec. 2), and the Fourteenth Amendment (sec. 2) provide that representatives shall be apportioned among the several states according to their respective numbers. Under the Apportionment Act of 1929, Congress fixed the number of House seats at 435 and provided that the Census Bureau after each decennial census redistribute the seats among the fifty states, subject to congressional control. Each state is assigned one representative before a population formula is applied. Under the 1970 reapportionment, nine states lost, and five states gained, seats in the House. California led with an increase of five seats. *See also* GERRYMANDERING, page 170; REDISTRICTING, page 181.

Significance With the mobility of the American people, gross under or overrepresentation of states in the House is avoided through the "automatic" reapportionment by the Bureau of the Census that follows each ten-year census. Within the states, however, the responsibility for redistricting is then placed upon the majority party in each state legislature.

Appropriation   A legislative grant of money for a specific purpose. The executive pulls together thousands of individual items for the next fiscal year period and submits them as an omnibus budget for consideration by the legislative branch. In the national government, authorization bills establishing specific programs are first enacted by Congress. Then, an appropriation bill must be passed to provide the money to carry out the program. *Appropriation* bills originate in the House of Representatives *by custom; revenue* bills to provide the income to cover appropriations must originate in the House under the Constitution. A *supplemental* appropriation is when a legislative body authorizes additional money for specific purposes after the regular appropriation bills have been enacted. A *deficiency* appropriation is a special bill providing funds to make up the difference between an agency's appropriation for the fiscal year and the amount needed to enable it to continue its operations for the full fiscal year. Unlike regular appropriations, which are made for the next fiscal year, deficiency appropriations are used to make up shortages in the same fiscal year in which they are passed. *Continuing* appropriations relate to the start of a new fiscal year when the legislative body has failed to adopt the budget and authorizes the continuing of appropriations to government agencies at the level of the previous fiscal year. *See also* AUTHORIZATION, page 156; BUDGET, page 275; BUDGET COMMITTEES, page 158; POWER OF THE PURSE, page 177

Significance In the American system of government—including national, state, and local levels—no expenditure of public money can be made unless authorized by law. Thus, Congress, the state legislatures, and local councils, commissions, and boards exercise "control over the purse strings"—one of the most important powers of legislative bodies. Because money is needed to implement most new laws, the appropriations committees wield great power in the House and Senate of the Congress, and in the state legislatures. Supplemental appropriations are useful in correcting miscalculations in the budget process, in meeting new problems, and in reacting to changes in public opinion. Deficiency bills typically are enacted later in the budget year to provide funds for ongoing projects that are threatened by the lack of financial resources to keep them going. Because federal budgets have become major instruments of fiscal policy for maintaining a healthy economy, supplementary and deficiency appropriations may also be called for when the economy needs some stimulative action. Continuing appropriations resolutions, on the other hand, must be adopted when the legislative process is stalemated to forestall an imminent breakdown in governmental operations for lack of money.

Appropriations Committees Standing committees in each house of Congress that consider budgetary grants to support programs up to the ceiling provided in authorization acts. When the Congress receives the annual budget message from the President that sets forth recommended expenditures for the next fiscal year, the proposals are transmitted to the Appropriations Committees for study. *See also* APPROPRIATION, page 155; AUTHORIZATION, page 156; BUDGET COMMITTEES, page 158.

Significance The Appropriations Committees are among the most powerful in the Congress because of their role in the budgetary decision-making process. The "power of the purse," which gives Congress a considerable measure of control over all policy decisions that need financial implementation, is exercised largely by the Appropriations Committees because the two chambers generally accept their recommendations. Most legislation needs financial support to become operational.

Authorization A legislative action that establishes a substantive program, specifies its general purpose and the means for achieving it, and indicates the approximate amount of money needed to implement the program. An authorization bill is ordinarily enacted before the appropriation bill providing financing for the program is considered by Congress. State legislatures also require authorizations prior to the enactment of appropriation measures. *See also* APPROPRIATION, page 155; APPROPRIATIONS COMMITTEES, page 156.

Significance Because programs must be authorized before public money can be appropriated to support them, legislative bodies typically have two opportunities to consider them. Four different committees of Congress—the House and Senate appropriations committees, and a substantive committee in each house—thus have an opportunity to kill, modify, add to, or otherwise change major programs. Although authorization laws specify ceilings on the amounts that can be spent to support programs, appropriation bills seldom provide the full amount permitted by such authorization bills.

Bicameralism   The principle of a two-house legislature, in contrast to unicameralism, or a legislature based on one house. At the Philadelphia convention of 1787, the Founding Fathers adopted a compromise solution for representation in Congress. This "Connecticut Compromise" established a balanced bicameral legislature with one house (House of Representatives) based on population and the second (Senate) based on equality of states. In the states, the Nebraska legislature is the only unicameral legislature. In a bicameral legislature, all bills must pass both houses before becoming law. *See also* CONNECTICUT COMPROMISE, page 23; *Reynolds v. Sims,* page 195; UNICAMERALISM, page 191.

Significance   A two-house legislature provides opportunity for two different types of representation and response to varying interests, such as population, area, and existing political units. Also, the second house can function in a capacity of revising and correcting mistakes made by the First chamber. Bicameralism is consistent with the principle of checks and balances. Opponents of bicameralism regard a single-house legislature as more economical and efficient. Although the Supreme Court has declared that the electoral districts for both houses of state legislatures must be based on population (*Reynolds v. Sims,* 377 U.S. 533 [1964]), the American people continue to support bicameralism.

Biennial Session   A regular meeting of a legislature held every two years. A majority of state legislatures convene in regular session once every two years, while the rest meet annually. In biennial session states, typically, legislatures hold their sessions in the odd-numbered years. *See also* SESSION, page 187.

Significance   The biennial session was established for the state legislatures by state constitution framers early in our nation's history, partly from a desire to save money, and partly because of suspicions that if the legislature convened too frequently it might engage in mischievous doings. Biennial sessions have proved inadequate to meet the vast number of complex problems facing state governments today, and frequent special sessions are necessary.

Bill   A proposed law. Most legislative proposals before Congress are in the form of bills. Members of the House officially "introduce" bills by dropping them into a "hopper"; in the Senate, bills are introduced by verbal announcement. All bills introduced during a two-year congressional term are designated "HR" in the House and "S" in the Senate, with consecutive numbers assigned in the order in which they are introduced in each chamber. Each bill must have three readings in each house, be approved by a majority vote in each house, and, normally, be signed by the President to become law. A bill passed in one house is called an "engrossed bill," and the final authoritative copy of a bill passed by both houses and signed by their presiding officers is called an "enrolled bill." Public bills deal with matters of general concern and may become public laws. Private bills are concerned with individual matters and become private laws if approved. *See also* BILL DRAFTING, page 158; PRIVATE BILL, page 178; READINGS, page 180.

Significance   Thousands of bills are introduced into every Congress. They are drawn up by pressure groups, interested citizens, congressional committees, individual congressmen, and by members of the executive branch. Only members of Congress, however, can introduce bills in their respective chambers. The great majority of these bills are killed because the committees in each house do not act upon them. Some bills are concerned with new issues, but most public bills enacted into law are amendments to existing laws.

Bill Drafting   The process of formulating legislative proposals. Congress and many state legislatures have staff agencies to aid members in this process. In Congress, members seeking assistance in study and research have access to a Congressional Research Service in the Library of Congress. Aid in drawing up bills is supplied by legislative counsel. Some of the most important bills are often drafted by House and Senate standing committees. Many bills are also drawn up by lawyers representing interest groups that will benefit from the legislation. *See also* BILL, page 157; CONGRESSIONAL RESEARCH SERVICE, page 193.

Significance   Bills must be drafted with precision. If enacted, the courts may refuse to sanction their enforcement if they are drawn in vague language that allows enforcement officers to exercise too much discretion. As a result of pressures from Common Cause, a citizen lobby group, most committee bill-drafting sessions, formerly secret, are now open to public scrutiny.

Bloc   Members of a legislative body, not necessarily of the same party, who have common aims and goals. Some examples include the "farm bloc," "high tariff bloc," "silver bloc," and the "anti-bussing bloc." *See also* FARM BLOC, page 168.

Significance   Bloc voting in Congress and in state legislatures is a means by which the interests of a segment of the population can be effectively represented. It is basically a bipartisan approach. The danger inherent in voting blocs results from their narrow positions on specific issues, for thus rivalry is intensified and the legislative body may be split into warring factions. Bloc voting tends to reduce party responsibility because blocs typically represent interests that cross party lines.

Budget Committees   House and Senate committees that recommend policy guidelines each fiscal year to aid Congress in considering the annual federal budget. Recommended in 1973 by a joint budget-reform study committee, Congress in 1974 created the two committees as the main instruments for implementing legislative budget reform. *See also* APPROPRIATION, page 155; APPROPRIATIONS COMMITTEES, page 156; BUDGET POWER, page 200.

Significance   Budget-reform legislation and the creation of the powerful House and Senate Budget Committees to function as super fiscal agents of the Congress were aimed at restoring a greater measure of control over the budget process. For years, the President's budgetary powers have steadily increased, and the establishment of these new committees was aimed at restoring the "power of the purse" to its constitutional source—the legislative branch. Under the enacting legislation, five members of the House Budget Committee must also serve on the House Appropriations Committee, and five on the tax-writing Ways and Means Committee, to coordinate fiscal policies developed by Congress. In the Senate, Budget Committee membership was similarly linked with the Appropriations and Finance Committees. Whether congressional budget committees can restore weakened budgetary powers to the legislative branch remains problematical.

Calendar   An agenda or list that contains the names of bills or resolutions to be considered before committees or in either chamber of a legislature. When a standing committee of the House of Representatives reports out a bill it is placed on one of the five possible calendars: *Consent* (noncontroversial bills), *Discharge* (discharge petitions), *House* (nonfiscal public bills), *Private* (private bills), and *Union* (appropriation and revenue bills). In the Senate, all bills reported out go on a single calendar, although nonlegislative matters (treaties and confirmations) are placed on the *Executive* calendar. *See also* DISCHARGE RULE, page 167; MAJORITY FLOOR LEADER, page 175; RULES COMMITTEE, page 184.

Significance The placement of a bill on a calendar is no guarantee that the bill will be considered by that chamber or that it will be taken up in the listed order. Decisions as to which bills will be debated and voted on are made in the House by the Rules Committee and by the House party leaders, and in the Senate by the Majority Leader. In the Senate, the Minority Leader is consulted frequently in order to ensure unanimous consent agreement to consider bills. Many bills are killed by failing to have them put on a specific calendar, or because they are still on a calendar at the end of a two-year Congress.

Calendar Wednesday A procedure of the House of Representatives whereby Wednesdays may be used to call the roll of the standing committees for the purpose of bringing up any of their bills for consideration from the House or the Union Calendars. General debate on each bill called up in this way is limited to two hours. Calendar Wednesday is not observed during the last two weeks of a session and, by a two-thirds vote, may be suspended any Wednesday, which usually is the case. *See also* CALENDAR, page 158; DISCHARGE RULE, page 167.

Significance Calendar Wednesday is a device by which the committee chairmen in the House of Representatives can, when the rule is operative, bypass the Rules Committee and place a controversial bill before the House for debate and a vote. The frequent suspension of Calendar Wednesday testifies to the power of the House leadership to control the legislative process.

Caucus A meeting of party members in one of the houses of a legislative body for the purpose of making decisions on selections of party leaders and on legislative business. Republicans in Congress prefer to call their party meeting a "conference." The term "to caucus" is also commonly used to describe any informal meeting of legislators seeking to reach agreement on a course of legislative action. *See also* CAUCUS, page 113; POLICY COMMITTEE, page 177.

Significance The majority caucus in each house makes important decisions regarding the organization of its chamber; these decisions then become official when they are ratified by that house in regular session. In Congress, the Democrats provide for "binding" caucus decisions regarding party stands on bills, with a two-thirds vote of the caucus required. No member is bound, however, if the party position involves a question of constitutional construction or a measure contrary to a pledge given by the member to his constituents. Republicans operate their conference on a majority-vote basis but do not seek to bind their members on voting positions. Some observers have recommended that the role of party caucuses in Congress be strengthened by providing for *binding* decisions on important legislative proposals. This, they suggest, would strengthen the democratic process by making the parties more responsible. Following the congressional elections of 1974, liberal Democrats in the House strengthened the Democratic Caucus and used it to break some of the control over the legislative process exercised by conservatives in several key power positions.

Censure A power vested in each chamber of a legislative body by which the chamber can discipline its own members. Under the Constitution, "Each house may . . . punish its members for disorderly behavior, and, with the concurrence of two-thirds, expel a member." (Art. I, sec. 5). *See also* EXPULSION, page 167.

Significance Cases of either house censuring a member are rare. Recent cases include the Senate's motion to "condemn" Senator Joseph McCarthy of Wisconsin in 1954, and the House's vote in 1967 to exclude New York Congressman Adam Clayton Powell, Jr., remove his seniority, and fine him $25,000 for misconduct. Disciplinary measures can range in severity from adoption of a simple motion of censure to withdrawal of privileges and, in extreme cases, expulsion of a member. A censured legislator suffers the ostracism of his colleagues and loses much of his effectiveness as a legislator.

Census A decennial enumeration of the total population of the United States, conducted by the Bureau of the Census. The Constitution provides that the population count be used for the purposes of apportioning direct taxes and representatives among the several states (Art. I, sec. 3). Since the first census in 1790, new ones have been taken every ten years. Approximately one-half of the states conduct a mid-decade census along the same lines as the federal census. The Census Bureau also collects data on a wide variety of subjects useful to Congress and the general public on such matters as business, housing, and units of government. *See also* APPORTIONMENT, page 155; REDISTRICTING, page 181.

Significance The American people have become extremely mobile, with considerable shifts in population occuring within the ten-year periods. The flow of population today is toward the West and the South, resulting in a shift of political power in the same directions. After each census, the Bureau reapportions the seats in the House of Representatives on the basis of the new population statistics. No direct taxes are now levied by the federal government. States use census figures in apportioning grants and allowances for local governments. Census data have also proved useful for scholarly researchers, especially social scientists.

Cloture (or Closure) A parliamentary technique used by a legislative body to end debate and bring the matter under consideration to a vote. Cloture can be invoked under an amendment to Rule 22 in the Senate which provides the method by which debate can be limited and a filibuster broken. One-sixth of the Senate membership can initiate action under cloture by petitioning the Senate to close debate on a pending measure. If such a petition is approved by three-fifths of the Senate (60 Senators), thereafter no senator may speak for more than one hour on the bill being considered. Hence, in a short time, the measure will come up for a vote and the attempt of the minority to "talk the bill to death" by filibuster will have been defeated. *See also* FILIBUSTER, page 168; FREEDOM OF DEBATE, page 169.

Significance Cloture safeguards majority rule by limiting the power of the Senate minority to kill bills by parliamentary maneuvers. Since Rule 22 was amended in 1917, there have been over 100 cloture votes of which only 20 percent have succeeded, including the following notable votes: Versailles Treaty, 1919; World Court, 1926; Branch Banking, 1927; Prohibition Reorganization, 1927; Communication's Satellite, 1962; Civil Rights, 1964; Voting Rights, 1965; Open Housing, 1968; Draft Extension, [twice] 1971; Equal Job Opportunity, 1972; and Public Campaign Financing, 1974. The reluctance of senators to vote cloture stems from pride in the Senate's tradition of freedom of debate as well as from the practical fear of jeopardizing the minority weapon of filibuster, which each senator may some day want to use. Attempts to invoke cloture have occurred with increased frequency since 1960. In 1975, after many unsuccessful attempts since 1917 to make it easier to limit debate, the Senate changed Rule 22 to make it possible to invoke cloture of debate by three-fifths of the entire Senate rather than by the traditional two-thirds of senators present and voting. The two-thirds rule, however, still applies to debate on Senate rule changes.

Committee Chairman The member of the majority party who heads a standing or select legislative committee. In Congress, the chairman of the twenty-two House and eighteen Senate standing committees have been selected mainly under the rule of seniority, although since 1971 the party caucuses must give approval in the House. In most state legislatures, the committee chairmen are appointed by the Speaker in the lower house and are usually selected by a committee on committees in the upper chamber. *See also* REFER TO COMMITTEE, page 182; STANDING COMMITTEE, page 188.

Significance A committee chairman can exercise an almost decisive control over bills assigned to his committee. He normally determines when and if the committee will meet, which bills it will consider and the order of their consideration, whether public hearings will be held, and the appointment of subcommittees. The Legislative Reorganization Act of 1970, however, permits a committee majority to call a meeting of the committee over the opposition of its chairman. But the chairman may, depending upon his political acumen and personal relationships, push bills through his committee, guide them through floor debate, and serve as a member of a conference committee. Next to the Speaker of the House and the Majority Leader in the Senate, committee chairmen exercise the greatest influence over the legislative process. A committee majority seldom overrules its chairman because of a reluctance to challenge "the establishment." In 1975, several powerful committee chairmen of long seniority in the House were replaced by action of the Democratic Steering Committee and/or by decision of the Democratic Caucus.

Committee of the Whole An informal procedure used by a legislative body to expedite business by resolving the official body into a committee for the consideration of bills and other matters. In Congress, this procedure is used only by the lower house, which becomes "The Committee of the Whole House (of Representatives) on the State of the Union." A temporary chairman is appointed by the Speaker, and the formal rules are suspended; any members of the House may participate, with a minimum of 100 needed instead of the official quorum of 218 needed for the House to conduct business.

Significance Most House business is transacted in the Committee of the Whole. Advantages of this procedure include: (1) only 100 members need be present to constitute a quorum; (2) business is expedited through relaxed procedures; (3) the full House retains control, in that it must act upon all decisions made by the Committee of the Whole to make them official. Since 1970, members' votes in Committee of the Whole may be required to be individually recorded.

Committee on Committees Party committees that determine the assignments of party members to standing committees in the House of Representatives. The Republican Committee on Committees consists of one representative from each state having Republican members in the House. In voting within the Committee on Committees, each member casts the number of votes equal to the number of Republican members his state has in the House. The Democrats have given the power to the House Democratic Steering Committee, subject to oversight by the Speaker and the Caucus. In the Senate, where only one-third of the seats are filled in each biennial election, a majority party Steering Committee makes the necessary adjustments for each standing committee. In the state legislatures, committees in the lower house are appointed by the Speaker of the House. In the upper house, the procedure varies: selections may be made by the presiding officer, by the chamber as a whole, or by a committee on committees. *See also* STANDING COMMITTEE, page 188.

Significance Selections of standing committee personnel made unofficially by committees on committees are, typically, approved by the respective party caucuses and thence by their respective chambers. The power to assign committee members is significant because it will largely determine the role that an individual legislator will play in that chamber, and may affect the consideration of bills by standing committees for many years. In effect, a committee on committees can determine the power structure in a legislative body. In 1975, a dramatic change in the seniority system occurred when the Democratic Steering Committee and the House Democratic Caucus removed several powerful committee chairmen of long seniority from their chairmanships.

Concurrent Resolution A special measure passed by one house of Congress with the other concurring, but not requiring the President's signature. Concurrent resolutions of Congress are used to make or amend joint rules or to express the sentiment of Congress on some issue or event. *See also* JOINT RESOLUTION, page 174; SIMPLE RESOLUTION, page 187.

Significance The most important use of concurrent resolutions is as a legislative veto over the President's exercise of powers delegated to him by Congress. Examples might include congressional disapproval of presidential reorganization plans or congressional opinion regarding fixing the date for adjournment, creating joint committees, and welcoming official foreign visitors to the United States with special greetings.

Conference Committee A special joint committee appointed to reconcile differences when a bill passes the two houses of Congress in different forms. A joint conference committee consists of three to nine "managers" appointed by the Speaker of the House and the President of the Senate. Efforts are directed toward a compromise version of the bill, which must be approved by a majority of the managers for each house voting separately. This compromise version, in the form of a "conference report," then goes for approval to each house where it cannot be amended, and, if rejected by either house, it goes back to conference for further negotiation. *See also* BICAMERALISM, page 157.

Significance The most important bills frequently end up in conference committees; differences over bills of lesser importance are usually ironed out by securing the agreement of each chamber to the other's amendments. Frequently, great power is wielded by conference committees. Many important bills are substantially rewritten in conference or are killed through failure to achieve a compromise agreement. Meetings of the committees are always secret. Their power is reflected in the large number of times that the two houses accept conference reports and enact them into law.

Confirmation   The power of a legislative body to approve nominations made to fill executive and judicial positions. Nominations for such offices made by the President must be confirmed by the Senate with a majority vote. In addition, the Twenty-fifth Amendment gives the President the power to fill a vacancy in the office of Vice President with the approval of a majority of both houses of Congress. Many of the appointments made by the governors in the various states must also be approved by the upper houses of the legislatures. *See also* APPOINTMENT POWER, page 199; SENATORIAL COURTESY, page 186.

Significance   All federal judges are appointed subject to senatorial confirmation. Most important diplomatic and administrative positions not under civil service or other merit systems also come under senatorial scrutiny. Often a President will confer with Senate leaders before nominating an individual for a cabinet position, to determine in advance that he is *persona grata* (acceptable). In the case of appointments to federal positions located in the several states, the senior senator of the President's party from the state in which the appointment is to be made actually selects the appointee and gives the name to the President, thus reversing the constitutional procedure. This is known as "senatorial courtesy."

Congressional Directory   A handbook published annually that contains information regarding the organization of Congress and its committees and brief biographical sketches of the senators and representatives. *See also United States Government Organization Manual,* page 231.

Significance   The *Congressional Directory,* which can be found in most libraries, is a useful reference guide for citizens and students of government. It supplements the *United States Government Organization Manual* which gives pertinent information about the three branches of American government.

Congressional District   A political-geographical division of a state from which one member of the House of Representatives is elected. A congressional district is usually a portion of a state, but if a state's population entitles it to only one representative, as in the case of Alaska and Nevada, the entire state is the congressional district. *See also* GERRYMANDERING, page 170; REDISTRICTING, page 181; *Wesberry v. Sanders,* page 196.

Significance   Districts generally are drawn up by the partisan majorities in state legislatures in such a way as to favor their party's candidates in congressional elections (gerrymandering). For many years, Congress provided that state legislatures draw up congressional districts as "compact and contiguous" areas, substantially equal in population; but since 1929, Congress has not specified criteria for redistricting. The Supreme Court's 1964 decision in *Wesberry v. Sanders,* 376 U.S. 1, holds that congressional districts must be based on substantial equality of population.

Congressional Record   A record of the proceedings (debates, speeches, and votes) in both the House and the Senate, printed daily. Members may edit their remarks and speeches before they are printed, and they also may insert material, called "extension of remarks," that was not actually delivered on the floor of their chamber. *See also* EXTENSION OF REMARKS, page 168.

Significance The *Congressional Record* is a valuable source of data and resource materials for the student of Congress. The inclusion of committee reports enhances its utility. The increasing length, the propagandistic nature of much of the material (excerpts are often used for campaign purposes), and rising costs of the *Record*, however, are matters of concern often voiced by congressional critics. Because many congressmen substantially alter their floor comments by "revising and extending" their remarks, the *Congressional Record* is not a verbatim record of House and Senate proceedings.

Congressman at Large   A member of the House of Representatives who is elected by the voters of an entire state rather than by those of a specific district. If a state gains seats following a decennial reapportionment and fails to redistrict, the new seats will be filled by election at large. If a state loses seats and fails to redistrict, then all of the state's congressmen will be elected at large, an arrangement that may result in one party winning all the seats. States with only one member of the House will, of course, always elect that one at large. Decisions concerning redistricting are made by the majority party in the state legislatures. *See also* AT LARGE, page 110.

Significance Election of congressmen at large in states with more than one congressman usually results from a partisan legislative deadlock or the refusal of a court to accept a redistricting plan. Increasing pressures from the courts to redistrict on a population basis after each decennial census, however, have reduced the likelihood of electing congressmen at large.

Constituent   A resident of a legislator's district. The district itself is sometimes referred to as the member's constituency. *See also* CONGRESSIONAL DISTRICT, page 163.

Significance Legislators must act in the capacity of a go-between in the relationship of the average citizen with his national and state governments. Much of a legislator's day must be spent in answering letters, running errands, showing the sights to visitors, and similar activities on behalf of his constituents. Although this keeps a congressman in close contact with the voters, some constituents regard their representatives as errand boys. As a result, the legislator may be overburdened and unable to devote sufficient time to the lawmaking function.

Constituent Power   Participation in the process of making, amending, or revising a constitution. The constituent power of Congress consists of its authority to propose amendments to the United States Constitution by a two-thirds vote of both houses, or to call a national convention for this purpose on petition of two-thirds of the state legislatures. Amendment proposals must be ratified by three-fourths of the state legislatures or by specially elected conventions in three-fourths of the states. In the states, the legislatures are usually empowered to propose specific amendments to their state constitutions. Extensive revisions of state constitutions are generally done by constitutional conventions established solely for that purpose. Ratification or final approval of state constitutional changes is vested in the voters of that state. *See also* AMENDMENT, page 21; CONSTITUTIONAL CONVENTION, page 438; RATIFICATION, page 180.

Significance Under a system of limited government, the fundamental law found in the constitution provides for the regulated exercise of power by the three branches of government. To the extent that the legislature exercises some considerable powers of a constituent nature, it can affect and change the nature of the limitations placed upon itself as well as those placed upon the other two branches of government. This can be accomplished not only by participating in the formal amendment process, but also by constitutional interpretation through statutory enactments.

Contempt of Congress Willful obstruction of the legislative process. Authority is vested in both houses of Congress and in their investigating committees to cite for contempt of Congress any subpoenaed witness who refuses to appear or to give testimony under oath. The Supreme Court has upheld this power by asserting: "It is unquestionably the duty of all citizens to cooperate with the Congress ... to respond to subpoenas ... and to testify fully with respect to matters within the province of proper investigation." (*Watkins v. United States*, 354 U.S. 178 [1957]). Contempt citations are referred by the presiding officer of the offended chamber to the Department of Justice for criminal prosecution through the federal courts. *See also* INVESTIGATING COMMITTEE, page 173; *McGrain v. Daugherty*, page 194; *Watkins v. United States*, page 195.

Significance The contempt power of Congress, though it might occasionally be misused, is essential if Congress is to have the authority to conduct meaningful investigations to learn facts on which to base legislative decisions. As currently interpreted by the courts, valid contempt citations may not be issued for refusal of a witness to testify when: (1) the subject under examination is beyond the proper scope of authority of the committee; (2) questions directed to a witness are not pertinent to the subject being investigated; (3) answers of the witness might provide evidence that could be used against him in a criminal case. Most contempt citations of the Congress have been issued by its committees investigating "un-American activities" and organized crime.

Contested Election Controversy over seating competing claimants to a legislative seat or the qualifications of an elected member. Article I, section 5 of the Constitution states: "Each house shall be the judge of the elections, returns, and qualifications of its own members. . . ." State constitutions have similar provisions. When the election of a member is contested, the chamber concerned sets up a committee to conduct an investigation. Similarly, if controversy arises over rival claims of election to the Electoral College, the Congress may determine which Electors shall be accredited and have their votes count in election of the President. *See also* ELECTORAL COUNT ACT, page 150; EXPULSION, page 167.

Significance The Constitution makes Congress the exclusive judge of the qualifications of its members. The House and the Senate on occasion have refused to seat elected members for reasons other than those related to constitutional qualifications. Examples include the barring of a polygamist in 1900, of a Socialist in 1919, of two senators in 1926 because they had exceeded lawful campaign expenditures, and of Adam Clayton Powell, Jr., in 1967 because of misuse of public funds. Similar cases have occurred in several state legislatures. The main Electoral College issue arose in 1887 when Hayes won over Tilden after 20 contested electoral votes were awarded to Hayes on a partisan basis.

Delegation of Power   The transfer of authority from one government or branch of government, which has been constitutionally assigned the power, to another branch or specific agency. Generally, delegations of power have involved the transfer of legislative power by Congress to the President, to an executive department or official, or to independent regulatory commissions. *See also Opp Cotton Mills v. Administrator of Wage and Hour Division*, page 233; QUASI-LEGISLATIVE, page 229.

Significance   The tendency of Congress and state legislatures to delegate legislative powers has increased as legislative workloads have become burdensome and highly technical. Involved in all such delegations, however, is the constitutional question of the legality of the transfer. The Supreme Court, for example, struck down the National Industrial Recovery Act of 1933 in two significant cases in 1935, holding that Congress could not constitutionally transfer its legislative power to the President or to an executive agency (*Panama Refining Co. v. Ryan*, 293 U.S. 388 [1935]; *Schecter Poultry Corp. v. U.S.*, 295 U.S. 495 [1935]). In another case, the Supreme Court held that Congress may not delegate its constitutional powers to the states (*Knickerbocker Ice Co. v. Stewart*, 253 U.S. 149 [1920]). In the field of foreign affairs, however, the Supreme Court upheld a sizable delegation of power to the President by Congress on the ground that the President has a special responsibility in foreign affairs (*United States v. Curtiss-Wright*, 299 U.S. 304 [1936]). The Supreme Court has also laid down the general rule that, if delegations of legislative power are to be considered valid, Congress must determine the general policies and establish clear standards to guide the President or agency in making detailed applications of the general law.

Dilatory Motion   An irrelevant or nongermane motion in a legislative body to delay or prevent action on a bill. Dilatory motions are not allowed under the rules of either house of Congress, but considerable discretion is left to the presiding officers in enforcement of these rules. *See also* FILIBUSTER, page 168.

Significance   Dilatory motions are often used by the minority to force concessions by disrupting the time schedule of the majority. In the Senate, their most effective use is by a minority that is trying to kill an important bill by use of the filibuster. Disagreement often exists as to whether a particular action is a dilatory motion or whether it is a relevant and germane motion that should be given careful consideration.

Direct Legislation   Electoral devices that enable voters to participate directly in deciding governmental policies. Direct methods include the initiative and the referendum. The recall, a technique by which the people can remove elected officials before their term of office ends, can also indirectly affect government policies. *See also* RECALL, page 140; REFERENDUM, page 182.

Significance   About twenty states authorize the initiative and/or the referendum. The initiative enables the people of a state to circumvent the inaction of their state legislature. The referendum is a means by which the people can "veto" laws passed by their state legislature before they become effective. In both the initiative and the referendum, the legislature cannot repeal the action of the people. There are no provisions for direct legislation in the national government.

Discharge Rule A procedure by which a bill in the House of Representatives may be forced out of a committee (discharged) that has refused to report it out for consideration by the House. Bills not reported out within thirty days after referral to a committee may be subject to discharge, although the Rules Committee may be discharged of a bill after it has held it for only seven legislative days. The discharge petition must be signed by an absolute majority (218) of the House membership. After a week's delay, any member who has signed the petition may move that the bill be discharged from committee. If the motion is carried by a simple majority vote, consideration of the bill then becomes a matter of high privilege. *See also* CALENDAR WEDNESDAY, page 159; PIGEONHOLE, page 176; STANDING COMMITTEE, page 188.

Significance The discharge rule is one means by which the majority of the House can overcome the "minority" power of legislative committees, which can kill bills by refusing to report them out for consideration. It is used only on rare occasions, since members are reluctant to challenge the prerogatives of committees and their chairmen. Similar to the House discharge rule is the discharge resolution in the Senate, which may be initiated by an ordinary motion. Many state legislatures also vest discharge powers in the majority of each house.

Division A method of voting used in a legislative body. In a division or "standing vote," members voting for or against the motion alternately rise and are counted by the presiding officer. *See also* RECORD VOTE, page 181; TELLER VOTE, page 189; VIVA VOCE VOTE, page 191.

Significance No record is made of how individual members vote in a division. Division has the advantage of enabling an accurate count to be made without delay. Its disadvantage lies in the way members may successfully hide their vote from their constituents, thus weakening democratic responsibility.

Executive Session A meeting of a legislative body, board, commission, or committee that is closed to the public. Executive sessions are used mainly by committees to interrogate witnesses and to discuss controversial bills. Under the Legislative Reorganization Act of 1970, all votes taken in secret committee sessions must be made part of the public record. *See also* LEGISLATIVE REORGANIZATION ACT OF 1970, page 197.

Significance Executive sessions permit greater freedom for members to express themselves, knowing they will not be put on record. The main disadvantage is that they may tend to encourage irresponsible action which can be hidden from public view. Although most committee decisions are made in closed sessions in Congress and in state legislatures, the vote of individual members of Congress must be made available to the public. City commissions and councils and other local policy-determining bodies often make important decisions in executive session prior to the public meeting. Thus, in the formal meeting the group may give the impression of consensus and agreement, when, in reality, major battles had already been fought out at the earlier secret session. State and local governments are moving in the direction of reducing or abolishing the use of executive sessions of public bodies as a result of new statutes and court decisions.

Expulsion The power of a legislative body, usually exercised by each chamber separately, to expel a member as an extreme disciplinary measure. Typical grounds for expulsion include conduct unbecoming a member, disloyalty, and moral turpitude. By Article I, section 5 of the Constitution, each house is empowered to expel a member with the concurrence of two-thirds of the members of that chamber. State constitutions generally vest similar powers in state legislatures. *See also* CENSURE, page 160.

Significance Expulsion is a rarely used power of legislative bodies. Members usually try to reconcile differences and, if absolutely necessary, to mete out punishment only in the form of censure or denial of privileges. In addition to expulsion, each chamber of Congress has the power, subject to judicial review, to refuse to seat an elected member. This power, however, was limited by the Supreme Court in 1969 when it held that a member-elect could be barred from taking his seat only if he failed to meet constitutional qualifications (*Powell v. McCormack,* 395 U.S. 486).

Extension of Remarks Material incorporated into the *Congressional Record* by a member of Congress, although not delivered verbally on the floor of either chamber. Permission to extend remarks is required by the member's house and is ordinarily granted. Material that elaborates on remarks made by the member on the floor follows the text of his speech; other insertions are printed in the appendix. *See also* CONGRESSIONAL RECORD, page 164.

Significance The extension-of-remarks privilege enables a member to record his position on legislative matters even though he was not able, or did not wish, to do so orally on the floor of his chamber. Many such insertions are aimed at influencing a congressman's constituents more than other members. Some students of Congress criticize the tendency of members of Congress to misuse the extension-of-remarks privilege by inserting irrelevant materials and personal propaganda. Excerpts are often mailed to constituents who may view such materials as officially endorsed by Congress.

Farm Bloc A group made up of both Democratic and Republican representatives and senators from the farm states, who put aside party differences to pass legislation favorable to the farmers. The creation of this voting bloc in the early part of the twentieth century followed the attempts of the farmers to achieve their aims through the creation of various farmers' parties that had been unsuccessful in challenging the two major parties. *See also* BLOC, page 158; FARM ORGANIZATIONS, page 347.

Significance The farm bloc was for many years one of the most consistently successful voting alignments in Congress and in most state legislatures, largely because of overrepresentation of rural areas. Increasing urban and suburban representation is modifying the power of the farm bloc. Moreover, the farm bloc has lost some of its effectiveness because of the failure of farmers and farm organization to agree on solutions to farm problems.

Filibuster A parliamentary device used in the United States Senate by which a minority of senators seek to frustrate the will of the majority by literally "talking a bill to death." Senators are proud of their chamber's reputation for being the world's greatest forum for free discussion. Custom and Senate Rule 22 provide for unlimited debate on a motion before it can be brought to a vote. A filibuster is a misuse of this freedom of debate, since full exploration of the merits and demerits of the pending measure is not its objective. Rather, the minority of senators seeks to gain concessions or the withdrawal of the bill by delaying tactics. These include prolonged debate and speeches on relevant and irrelevant topics, parliamentary maneuvers, dilatory motions, and other tricks of the legislative game. The objective of the minority is to delay action on the measure interminably, until the majority is forced by the press of other business to withdraw it from consideration. *See also* CLOTURE, page 160; FREEDOM OF DEBATE, page 169; LEGISLATIVE DAY, page 175.

Significance Over the years, many important bills have been filibustered to death. Many more have been killed by using the threat of a filibuster to force withdrawal of a bill. Until the enactment of the Civil Rights Act of 1957, for example, the filibuster or threat of it had been used successfully for many years by southern senators to forestall civil rights legislation. Senator Strom Thurmond of South Carolina holds the record for the longest individual filibuster, speaking for more than twenty-four hours against enactment of civil rights legislation in 1957. In 1975, the use of the filibuster to kill legislation was weakened by the Senate by making it easier to invoke cloture on debate under Rule 22. Filibusters may also be defeated by extending the legislative day and holding round-the-clock sessions of the Senate.

Franking Privilege A policy that enables members of Congress to send material through the mail free by substituting their facisimile signature (frank) for postage. Free mail privileges have also been accorded by Congress to other officials and agencies of the national government.

Significance The franking privilege provides a means by which members of Congress can keep their constituents informed on issues, voting records, and other business. It is a recognition that the "representative" function of Congress requires that means be provided by which the individual congressman can keep in contact with his constituents. Controversies often arise during election years over the alleged misuse of the franking privilege to distribute campaign propaganda. The Federal Election Campaign Act of 1974 prohibits congressmen from using their franked mail to solicit campaign funds.

Freedom of Debate The right of members of a legislative body in a democratic system of government to freely discuss, deliberate, and act upon matters of policy without fear of legal action. The Constitution (Art I, sec. 6), provides that "for any speech or debate in either House, they [Senators and Representatives] shall not be questioned in any other place." Utterances that might otherwise be unlawful are privileged, therefore, when made in Congress (*U.S. v. Johnson,* 383 U.S. 169 [1966]). Immunity to suit does not ordinarily apply to statements made outside of Congress. In all cases, however, whether such statements are made in or out of Congress, members can be held to account through the disciplinary powers of their own house. State constitutions generally provide similar immunity for legislators. Freedom of debate is sometimes used to describe the right under Senate Rule 22 to speak indefinitely on a pending measure in the United States Senate unless limited by the invoking of cloture or by unanimous consent. *See also* CLOTURE, page 160; FILIBUSTER, page 168; GAG RULE, page 170.

Significance The purpose of ensuring maximum freedom of debate is to guarantee that decisions made by the legislative body will be freely made after thorough debate. Without such a guarantee, members might become too restricted in their deliberations to do a good job of legislating. On occasion, however, a member can abuse this right by unjustly slurring the reputation of a citizen, who has no recourse in the courts, and in the Senate, a small group can delay action and frustrate the majority will by the use of the filibuster.

Gag Rule   A legislative rule that arbitrarily limits the time available for consideration of a measure. The term "gag rule" refers generally to any special rule that limits debate on a pending bill or resolution beyond that provided by the chamber's regular legislative rules. *See also* CLOTURE, page 160; RULES COMMITTEE, page 184.

Significance   The use of gag rules by a legislative body tends to expedite the legislative process but may give excessive influence to minority elements that have the power to impose special rules. By prohibiting or limiting the proposal of amendments or other parliamentary tactics, a gag rule may have a profound effect on the outcome of the voting on a measure and on the substantive product as well. A special rule is provided by the Rules Committee of the House of Representatives for the consideration of each legislative matter, but in the Senate, freedom of debate may be limited only by the invoking of cloture.

Gerrymandering   The drawing of legislative district boundary lines with a view to obtaining partisan or factional advantage. Gerrymandering is engaged in by partisan majorities in state legislatures when they are drawing up congressional and state legislative districts. The objective is to gain partisan electoral advantage by spreading support for one's own party over many districts and concentrating the support for the other party in few districts. Gerrymandering is possible because of the pattern of consistency in voting behavior of most Americans. *See also* REDISTRICTING, page 181; *Reynolds v. Sims,* page 195; *Wesberry v. Sanders,* page 196.

Significance   Most redistricting laws enacted by state legislatures show evidence of varying degrees of boundary manipulation for partisan advantage. Historically, gerrymandering resulted in gross overrepresentation of rural areas in the House of Representatives and in most state legislatures. In 1964, the Supreme Court ruled that congressional and state legislative districts should be drawn on a basis of substantial equality of population. Nevertheless, the boundaries of districts that are substantially equal in population may still be drawn to secure partisan advantage, and gerrymandering persists. Thus, a minority of a state's voters may elect a majority of that state's congressional delegation and a majority in both houses of the state legislature. A liberal or conservative legislative majority can thereby often maintain its power position by influencing elections through its control over district boundaries.

Hearing   A public session of a committee of a legislative body to obtain information on a proposed law or resolution. In Congress, public hearings are commonly functions of subcommittees, which report their findings to the full committees. The theory behind hearings is that out of the "combat" between contestants using every ethical means to convince committee members of the wisdom of their positions will emerge the "true facts." The members can then make their decision, much like a judge and jury in a judicial proceeding. The hearings thus serve as a means by which American citizens can "petition" their elected representative and seek to influence their decision making. *See also* INVESTIGATING COMMITTEE, page 173.

Significance Most hearings involve only professional lobbyists. Commonly, administration officials are pitted against private lobbyists. In recent years, there has been an increasing tendency for committees to use hearings to try to influence public opinion or executive action, as in the areas of communism, foreign policy, and crime. Public hearings are used extensively and are a valuable legislative aid. All state legislatures also provide for public hearings on important measures.

High Crimes and Misdemeanors The Constitution provides in Article II, section 4, that the President, Vice President, and all civil officers of the United States are subject to impeachment and removal from office upon conviction for "treason, bribery, or other high crimes and misdemeanors." No precise definition of what acts might constitute high crimes and misdemeanors has been developed. Discretion is vested completely in Congress. *See also* IMPEACHMENT, page 171.

Significance In practice, probably based on English historical precedent, the grounds on which impeachment action is taken are usually restricted to unethical conduct and criminal offenses. Congress has not regarded incompetence or political disagreement as grounds for invoking its impeachment powers. Yet, because so much discretion is vested in Congress by the Constitution, the threat of its use may sometimes constitute a potent weapon. In 1974, the House wrestled with the problem of defining and applying "high crimes and misdemeanors" to the conduct of President Richard M. Nixon to determine if he should be impeached. The President's resignation occurred, however, before the House could take that action.

House of Representatives The lower house of the bicameral Congress, in which representation is based on population. The upper house, the Senate of the United States, is based on the principle of state equality. The House was intended by the Founding Fathers to be the popular chamber of Congress, and it was made larger and more responsive to the public will than the Senate, which was intended to represent the states and to function as the more deliberative body. Each state is guaranteed at least one representative. Since 1910, the House has had a permanent membership of 435. The ratio of population to representatives has been steadily increasing until now it is more than 475,000 per representative. The Constitution vests certain powers exclusively in the House. Among them are: (1) the impeachment power; (2) the initiation of revenue bills; (3) the election of a President if no candidate obtains a majority in the Electoral College; (4) the determination of its own rules of procedure; and (5) the discipline of its members. *See also* SENATE, page 185.

Significance Some critics reject the assertion that the House is the more representative of the two houses of Congress. They point out that because many representatives tend to stress local interests, the House may be less responsive to national problems than the Senate. Its unwieldy size, and the power vested in the Rules Committee, often make it less able than the Senate to cope with contemporary legislative problems. Nevertheless, the American voter tends to regard his representative as his most direct contact with the national government.

Impeachment A formal accusation, rendered by the lower house of a legislative body, that commits an accused civil official for trial in the upper house. Impeachment is, therefore, merely the first step in a two-stage process. In the national government, constitutional authority to *impeach* is vested in the House and the power to *try* impeachment cases rests with the Senate. All civil officers of the United States are subject to impeachment, excluding military officers and members of Congress. The impeachment process begins with the preferring of charges by a representative, followed by referral to either the Judiciary Committee or to a special investigating committee. A simple majority vote of the House is sufficient to impeach. "Articles of impeachment" are drawn up, setting forth the basis for removal. The House appoints managers who prosecute the case in a trial before the Senate. If a President is on trial, the Chief Justice of the United States presides. The procedure during the trial closely resembles that of a court of law. A two-thirds vote of the Senators present is necessary for conviction. The only punishments that may be meted out are removal from office and disqualification from holding any office in the future. Once removed, however, the individual may be tried in a regular court of law if he has committed a criminal act. The President's pardoning power does not apply to impeachment convictions. *See also* HIGH CRIMES AND MISDEMEANORS, page 171.

Significance In the course of American history the House has instituted impeachment proceedings against fifty individuals, but only thirteen have been impeached, eleven have come to trial before the Senate, and only four—all judges—have been convicted. In one notable case, President Andrew Johnson was acquitted by the margin of a single vote in 1868 of the charge of violating the Tenure of Office Act by removing an appointed official without congressional consent (the Act was later declared unconstitutional by the Supreme Court); in another case, Justice Samuel Chase was acquitted in 1805 of alleged political conduct on the Supreme Court. Few state officials have been convicted and removed by state legislatures. Occasionally, partisan politics may influence the exercise of the power as was true in the Johnson case and in the removal of several state officials by their legislatures. The process is always political in nature, but open partisanship can weaken public support. In 1974, President Richard M. Nixon resigned in the face of House preparations to begin impeachment proceedings.

Initiative An electoral device by which interested citizens can propose legislation or constitutional amendments through initiatory petitions signed by the required number of registered voters. The number of signatures varies from 5 to 15 percent of the voters in the different states. The proposition is then voted on by the people. Constitutional amendment proposals usually require a greater number of signatures on the petitions. The "direct" initiative involves a vote of the people following the filing of petitions. The "indirect" provides that the proposal, after being filed, be sent to the legislature; if not approved, it then goes before the voters. *See also* DIRECT DEMOCRACY, page 8; DIRECT LEGISLATION, page 166; REFERENDUM, page 182.

Significance Fewer than one-half of the states provide for the initiative in either form. About twenty states permit its use for ordinary laws, and thirteen for constitutional amendments. Only one state, Alaska, has adopted the initiative since 1918. The United States Constitution does not provide for a national initiative, but groups have, from time to time, advocated its adoption. In some states, especially California, the ease with which initiatory proposals can be placed on the ballot has contributed to the "long ballot" problem.

Investigating Committee   A legislative committee that exercises a fact-finding role as an aid to the law-making process. Investigating committees may compel witnesses to attend and to produce relevant materials. Investigations are conducted by both the regular standing committees and by special committees created for that purpose. The purposes behind investigations include: (1) finding of facts on which to base legislation; (2) discovering or developing of public opinion; (3) overseeing of administrative agencies; (4) uncovering the questionable activities of public officials and private individuals; and (5) sometimes securing personal or partisan political gain. In terms of time, effort, and publicity, the investigatory activities of Congress and of some state legislatures have in recent years rivaled their legislative functions. A legislative body may investigate any subject that is properly within the scope of its legislative powers. *See also* EXECUTIVE PRIVILEGE, page 203; *McGrain v. Daugherty,* page 194; WATCHDOG COMMITTEE, page 192; *Watkins v. United States,* page 195.

Significance   Many important topics have been investigated in the over 600 congressional investigations in the nation's history. Some have been mere "fishing expeditions" and others were politically motivated by attempts to embarrass the rival party. Increasingly, Congress has relied on investigations as a means of seeking to regain its position of power vis-à-vis the executive branch, which has steadily gained in relative power during this century. Serious questions have been raised concerning the scope of congressional inquiries, the rights of witnesses who appear before committees, the fairness of procedures, and the extraction of testimony from unwilling witnesses. Congress has sought to deal with some of these problems through the study and correction of procedures and the setting up of a "fair play" guarantee for witnesses. Several presidents have invoked executive privilege in refusing to permit executive officials to appear before investigating committees on matters pertaining to national security or executive prerogatives.

Joint Committee   A legislative committee composed of members of both houses. The number appointed to a joint committee is usually divided equally between the two houses, with each member having one vote. On some, such as conference committees, each chamber may determine the size of its membership on the committee, and the two groups vote separately on measures. Joint committees are usually select (special) committees appointed for a specified purpose: typically, to conduct investigations. Congress has created a few standing (permanent) joint committees, such as the Joint Committee on the Economic Report, and the Joint Committee on Atomic Energy. *See also* CONFERENCE COMMITTEE, page 162.

Significance   Joint committees make it possible for the two houses of a legislative body to work out compromises on bills or resolutions. They tend to encourage greater cooperation between the two chambers. Some observers have recommended that all standing committees of Congress be joint committees, so that time-consuming duplication of the existing dual-committee system could be eliminated. Supporters of this proposal believe that it would result in quicker and more effective action on most bills and would eliminate the need for two appearances before separate House and Senate committees by persons wishing to testify for or against a bill. Opponents point out that such a change would eliminate much of the effectiveness of the checks and balances system inherent in a bicameral legislative body, and it would be likely to result in less careful scrutiny of pending legislation.

Joint Resolution   A measure, similar to a bill, that must be approved in both chambers and by the executive. In Congress, joint resolutions are designated "H J Res" and "S J Res" and, if passed by a simple majority in both houses, must be signed by the President to become law. The procedure is identical to that used in passing a bill into law except when the joint resolution is used to propose an amendment to the Constitution. Then the President's signature is unnecessary. About half of the state legislatures also employ the joint resolution in enacting laws and proposing constitutional amendments. *See also* CONCURRENT RESOLUTION, page 162; SIMPLE RESOLUTION, page 187.

Significance   Joint resolutions are employed by Congress to approve of executive actions in foreign affairs or to take the initiative in foreign policy. They have occasionally proved useful in circumventing the two-thirds vote requirement in the Senate on treaty matters, as in the annexation of Texas and of Hawaii. Joint resolutions are also used for such limited matters as the passing of a single appropriation bill for a designated purpose. The Tonkin Gulf Resolution, which was adopted by Congress in 1964 to authorize the President to take whatever military action he deemed necessary to protect American forces in Asia, became one of the most controversial joint resolutions. In 1970, because of congressional disenchantment with the Vietnam war and disclosures of alleged perfidy in reporting the incidents to Congress that led to its adoption, the Resolution was repealed.

Joint Session   A meeting of the members of both chambers of a legislative body. Congress meets in joint session to count the electoral votes and certify the election of the President, and when addressed by the President or a foreign dignitary. A joint session is never used to consider specific bills. Most state legislatures meet in joint session to receive the governor's annual message. *See also* SESSION, page 187.

Significance   Legislative bodies typically use joint sessions to consider noncontroversial matters and to be informed on current issues. Such sessions of the Congress are usually televised since they are auspicious occasions. Most joint sessions are called to receive messages or reports from the chief executive officer.

Legislative Council   An interim committee employed by some legislatures between sessions to study state problems and to plan a legislative program. In some states, legislative councils have pursued extensive fact-finding research programs. The councils range in size from five members to the entire legislature. Usually, membership is selected from the two houses of the legislature, but, in several states, the governor is authorized to include representation from the executive branch.

Significance   Legislative councils are a means by which the legislatures of three-fourths of the states have sought to develop leadership and planning facilities staffed by their own members. In this way, dependence on the executive to formulate a comprehensive program for consideration by the legislature is reduced. Moreover, as the workload becomes heavier and more complex, legislatures are becoming more dependent upon well-prepared programs worked out carefully in advance. The fear that power might become too concentrated in the hands of those legislators making up the councils has not been justified in the experience of the states that have adopted the plan.

Legislative Day The formal meeting of a legislative chamber that begins with a formal call to order and opening of business and ends with adjournment. A legislative day may cover a period of several calendar days, with the chamber merely recessing at the end of each calendar day rather than adjourning. *See also* FILIBUSTER, page 168; MORNING HOUR, page 175.

Significance The objective of continuing a legislative day over a period of several calendar days may be to expedite business, to avoid the introduction of new, controversial issues before current business has been disposed of, or to facilitate bringing a major bill to a vote. In any case, it is a technique used by the leadership of a legislative house to help in the achievement of some partisan or routine goal. In the Senate, for example, one approach to attempting defeat of a filibuster is to permit each member to speak no more than twice during a legislative day, and, by recessing instead of adjourning, the legislative day is continued indefinitely without adjournment until each Senator has had an opportunity to speak. In this way, debate ultimately ends and a vote is taken. By using this procedure and holding night and day sessions, the Senate leadership has been able to defeat a filibuster on several occasions.

Logrolling An arrangement by which two or more members of a legislative body agree in advance to support each other's bills. The technique pertains especially to the trading of votes among legislators in order to gain support for appropriations beneficial to each legislator's home district. *See also* PORK BARREL LEGISLATION, page 177.

Significance To the extent that logrolling exists, it probably results from the American belief that a representative should seek to "deliver the goods" for his home district. This encourages "horse trading" of votes. Logrolling is inevitable in legislative bodies in which strong party discipline does not prevail. No control over logrolling exists except for the adverse publicity that may result and the ultimate action of the voters on election day.

Majority Floor Leader The chief spokesman and strategist of the majority party who directs the party's forces in legislative battles. In the House, only the Speaker is usually considered to be more influential. In the Senate, the majority leader is the undisputed leader of his party. Floor leaders seek to carry out decisions of their party's caucus or conference and are aided by party whips. Their counterparts in the other party are the minority floor leaders. Floor leaders are selected by their respective party caucuses. Similar party leadership positions exist in most state legislatures. *See also* CAUCUS, page 159; POLICY COMMITTEE, page 177; WHIP, page 192.

Significance Much of the success of a majority floor leader depends on his ability. If he is an able organizer and possesses personal leadership characteristics, he can exercise considerable influence on legislation. In the Senate, he must work closely with the minority leader because much business is transacted through unanimous consent. Because floor leaders hold critical positions in the Congress, they are summoned often to the White House for conferences concerning the President's legislative program.

Morning Hour A period reserved in Congress at the start of a legislative day to consider routine business. The Senate sets aside the first two hours of each new legislative day for such matters as committee reports, the introduction of bills and resolutions, and the receipt of presidential messages. In the House, the morning hour is seldom used since most routine business is transacted in the Committee of the Whole. *See also* COMMITTEE OF THE WHOLE, page 161; LEGISLATIVE DAY, page 175.

Significance The morning hour frees the remainder of the Senate's legislative day for consideration of pending legislation. During the morning hour, Senators may speak on a variety of topics not necessarily related to current business. Senate committees often meet during that chamber's morning hour.

Ombudsman A special official or commissioner appointed by a legislative body or governing board to hear and investigate complaints by private individuals against public officials or agencies. The office of ombudsman, which originated in the Scandinavian countries, is utilized currently in many countries by national, state, and local units of government and other public bodies, including some local agencies in the United States. Typically, the ombudsman has no decision-making authority, but is empowered to carry on inquiry and mediation function. *See also* CONSTITUENT, page 164.

Significance Several American congressmen have recommended the creation of the office of ombudsman to function as an agent of the Congress. The objective would be to free up congressmen for legislative business by turning citizen complaints over to a professional who would focus full attention on handling such problems on a nonpartisan, nonpolitical basis. Most members of Congress, however, have been reluctant to turn their constituents over to an ombudsman or administrative agency for relief, since solving citizen problems is regarded as a lucrative source of votes for reelection.

Pair An understanding reached in advance between two legislators, holding opposing views on a bill, to withhold their votes on a "yea and nay" roll call. In this way, each is assured that his absence from the chamber during the vote will not affect the outcome. In effect, each member of the pair cancels out the other's vote, with one "paired for" the measure and the other "paired against" it. A "special" pair applies to one or several votes taken on the same subject. A "general" pair, occasionally used in the Senate, applies to all votes taken over a specified period of time. On a question requiring a two-thirds vote, two members must be "paired for" the measure to balance off one "paired against" it. *See also* RECORD VOTE, page 181.

Significance The advantage of pairing lies in the nature of the "gentlemen's agreement" between the two lawmakers. Neither can show up unexpectedly and vote in the roll call without breaking the agreement. Each, in effect, casts a vote by cancelling out the other's vote, although they are not counted in "yea" and "nay" vote totals. Members of Congress frequently find it necessary to be absent from their chamber, and pairing enables them to put their position on bills on record.

Pigeonhole To kill a bill in committee by putting it aside and not reporting it out for consideration by the chamber. The term relates to the old-time desks in committee rooms of Congress, which had open "pigeonholes" or cubicles for filing papers. To pigeonhole a bill means, figuratively, to file the bill away and forget it. This usually kills the bill. Killing a bill by pigeonholing is typically accomplished by a committee chairman when a majority of the committee members do not object. *See also* COMMITTEE CHAIRMAN, page 161; DISCHARGE RULE, page 167.

Significance More bills die in committee through pigeonholing each congressional session than are rejected outright by the two houses. The same is true in the state legislatures. Chances for a pigeonholed bill to be enacted into law are slight because members of the committee and chamber are reluctant to challenge the authority of the chairman or to use the extraordinary procedures required to discharge bills from committee.

Policy Committee   A party committee in Congress that functions as an agent of the caucus or conference in formulating legislative plans and strategy. Although the reorganization of Congress in 1946 provided for policy committees to replace the old steering committees, only the Senate has formally created such bodies. House Republicans unofficially converted their steering committee into a policy committee in 1949, but the House Democratic Steering Committee remains operational. In the Senate, the Democrats retained their steering committee to function solely as a committee on committees to fill vacancies on Senate standing committees. *See also* CAUCUS, page 159; COMMITTEE ON COMMITTEES, page 162.

Significance In the Senate, and for House Republicans, the policy committees have superseded the steering committees as the basic party strategy organs and agents of the caucus or conference. In the Senate, the majority policy committee along with the floor leader often determine the order in which measures will be considered. Representation on the policy committees is given to all major regions of the nation and to important factions within the party. Their importance in the legislative process varies, depending upon the degree of party unity and the personalities and drive of the individuals on the committees.

Pork Barrel Legislation   Appropriations made by a legislative body providing for expenditures of sums of public money on local projects not critically needed. The term is closely related to logrolling, in that members of the legislative body usually do not question each other's pet project for fear that their own may be voted down. It is frequently a simple matter of *quid pro quo* —that is, "You scratch my back and I'll scratch yours." *See also* LOGROLLING, page 175.

Significance Pork barrel legislation results in the expenditure of large sums of money each year. Basically, the problem relates to the theory of representation. The American representative goes to his legislature or to Congress as the representative of the people of his district rather than of the state or nation. This means that he will be expected by his constituents to perform creditably on their behalf. If he can obtain "pork" (appropriations for local highways, river and harbor construction projects, and so forth) by raiding the pork barrel (the state or national treasury), he is likely to improve his chances for reelection.

Power of the Purse   The historic power of democratic legislative bodies to control the finances of government. The power of the purse extends to both revenue and appropriation functions. In the national government, the Constitution specifies that "No money shall be drawn from the Treasury, but in consequence of appropriations made by law." (Art I, sec. 9). New programs must be twice approved, first, through authorization and, second, through appropriation to finance them. Expenditures by the executive must be validated by the General Accounting Office to ensure that such outlays fall within the limits of appropriations made by Congress. Additional checks are carried on through the "watchdog" oversight committees of Congress. *See also* APPROPRIATION, page 155; APPROPRIATIONS COMMITTEES, page 156; AUTHORIZATION, page 156; WATCHDOG COMMITTEE, page 192.

Significance The power of the purse remains a major power of all legislative bodies. The power can be used in an affirmative manner to force positive action by government as well as in a negative way to stop action. The threat of budget cutting is usually enough to elicit cooperation from executive officials. Historically, legislative bodies first succeeded in limiting executive absolutism through control of the purse. One of the major grievances leading to the American Revolution was the taxation of the colonists without their consent. Some measure of the impact of the power of the purse may be assessed from the fact that Congress appropriates over $300 billion each fiscal year.

President Pro Tempore   The temporary presiding officer of the Senate in the absence of the Vice President. The President pro tempore is elected by the Senate, following his nomination by the majority party caucus. He is eligible for the presidency of the United States following the death or disability of the President, Vice President, and Speaker of the House. State senates also select presidents pro tempore. *See also* PRESIDENTIAL SUCCESSION, page 207; VICE PRESIDENT, page 191.

Significance Like the Speaker of the House, the President pro tempore is a partisan officer who may use his position to aid the program of the majority party. Although the office is usually overshadowed by that of the majority floor leader, it is one of considerable prestige and is usually awarded to the senior member of the majority party in the Senate.

Previous Question   A motion in a legislative body to cease debate and force a vote on a pending measure. In Congress, the rules permit previous question motions in the House but not in the Senate. The motion itself cannot be debated nor laid on the table. If the motion carries before any debate on the bill has occurred, each side is allowed twenty minutes to present its case. State legislatures use similar rules to limit debate. *See also* SUSPENSION OF RULES, page 189; UNANIMOUS CONSENT, page 190.

Significance The previous question rule in the House makes it possible to avoid unlimited discussion such as occurs during a filibuster in the Senate. With 435 members in the House, such a rule is necessary to prevent the chamber from bogging down in endless debate. It is also used as a parliamentary device to prevent amendments which might cripple a bill, or it may be employed by supporters or by opponents of a bill who may regard an extensive debate of its merits as detrimental to their position. Previous question is augmented by other parliamentary devices to speed up the legislative process, such as suspension of rules and unanimous consent.

Private Bill   Bills introduced into a legislative body that deal with specific matters and individuals rather than with general legislative affairs. In Congress, although the number of private bills was considerably reduced by the Reorganization Act of 1946, thousands are still introduced at each session. The main categories include: (1) immigration and naturalization bills applying to specific individuals; (2) claim bills not subject to administrative resolution; and (3) land bills assigning title to individuals. Private bills are introduced by congressmen who are petitioned by their constituents to right a government-inflicted wrong or to deal with a matter not covered by general statute. If enacted, they become private law and apply only to specific individuals named in the act. All state legislatures allow introduction of private bills. *See also* BILL, page 157; OMBUDSMAN, page 176.

Significance Many observers believe that it would add considerably to the efficiency of Congress to reduce further the categories of private bills. Approximately one-third of the laws passed by Congress are private laws despite efforts to reduce or eliminate the need for such actions. Private bills tend to force the legislative body into performing a judicial function in determining the merits of particular claims made by individuals. They are time-consuming and detract from the general lawmaking function of Congress as well as of the legislatures in the states. Further use of administrative agencies to handle these matters could lighten the burden of the legislative body. Yet, many people believe that it is part of the democratic system of government that the legislative body have the power to right governmental wrongs against individuals. In Congress, a private bill is unlikely to become law unless the congressman who introduces it gives his personal attention and strong support.

Quorum The minimum number of members of a legislative chamber who must be present in order to transact business. The Constitution specifies that "a majority of each [house] shall constitute a quorum to do business." (Art. I, sec. 5). This means 218 in the House and 51 in the Senate. In the House, the quorum for the Committee of the Whole is 100. Typically, state legislatures also require a majority of members to be present for the transaction of business. *See also* COMMITTEE OF THE WHOLE, page 161.

Significance The House frequently escapes the quorum requirement of 218 by dissolving into the Committee of the Whole. Decisions reached, however, must be ratified by the duly constituted House. Both chambers often proceed with fewer than a quorum present unless challenged by a point of order. When this occurs, either the chamber must adjourn or the Sergeant at Arms is instructed to round up the absent members. Frequent "quorum calls" or demands that the members present be counted to determine if a quorum is in fact present may be used as a delaying tactic.

Ranking Member That member of the majority party on a legislative committee who ranks first after the chairman in number of years of continuous service (seniority) on the committee. *See also* COMMITTEE CHAIRMAN, page 161; RANKING MINORITY MEMBER, page 180; SENIORITY RULE, page 186.

Significance In Congress, the ranking member automatically succeeds to the chairmanship of a committee if that post is vacated while his party has majority control of that house. The ranking member is often accorded the chairmanship of one of the committee's important subcommittees. Many state legislatures follow the same procedures although factors other than seniority—for example, the political influence of nonsenior members and pressures exerted by powerful interest groups—may be more decisive in making such selections.

Ranking Minority Member   The minority party member of a legislative committee with the longest continuous service (seniority) on the committee. *See also* RANKING MEMBER, page 179; SENIORITY RULE, page 186.

Significance   In Congress, the ranking minority member succeeds to the chairmanship of the committee when his party wins control of that house. Many state legislatures also follow the rule of seniority. The ranking minority member also provides some leadership for the minority members on the committee.

Ratification   A power vested in a legislative body to approve (or reject) agreements entered into with other states, and constitutional amendment proposals. In the states, interstate compacts negotiated by the governors of several states must be ratified or approved by the state legislature of each before becoming effective. Amendments proposed to the United States Constitution must be ratified by legislatures or conventions in three-fourths of the states to become effective. Amendments proposed to state constitutions, however, must be ratified by a vote of the people of that state. The term "ratification" is also popularly used to describe the "consent" function of the United States Senate regarding treaties negotiated by the United States with foreign nations, although here the term more properly applies to the role of the President in accepting or rejecting the Senate approved version of a treaty. *See also* AMENDMENT, page 155; RATIFICATION, page 21; RATIFICATION, page 208.

Significance   Ratification gives the legislative body an effective check over agreements entered into with other states and over changes made in the fundamental law. Often, important agreements and amendment proposals are killed by the failure of legislatures to bring them to a vote or by the failure of proponents to secure the necessary extraordinary majority vote. All amendments to the United States Constitution have been ratified by state legislatures except the Twenty-first, which was ratified by specially elected conventions in the states.

Readings   The three readings of a bill required at different stages of the legislative process. In Congress, the first reading occurs when the bill is introduced and printed by title in the *Congressional Record*. The second, often a reading in full, takes place when the bill is brought out of committee for consideration before the chamber. The third reading, usually by title only, comes after amendments have been voted on and the bill is up for a final vote. State legislative procedure is similar. *See also* BILL, page 157.

Significance   The required three readings of a bill, based on traditional parliamentary law, are expected to ensure careful consideration of all bills and to prevent any from sneaking through almost unnoticed. The procedure is of little significance today in the legislative process of Congress and the state legislatures. On occasion, full reading of a bill may be demanded and used as a delaying tactic. Cases abound wherein legislators have voted for bills without realizing their contents or consequences despite their three readings.

Recommittal   The action of a legislative body of sending a bill back to the committee that had reported it out for consideration. A motion to recommit may instruct the committee to report the bill out again with certain amendments or at a later date. Most motions for recommittal, however, simply call for further study by the committee.

Significance   In most cases, the adoption of a motion to recommit to committee is considered a death blow for a bill. Often legislators prefer not to alienate constituents who support a bill by directly voting it down. Recommittal can accomplish the same purpose without giving the appearance of killing the bill.

Reconsideration   A motion in a legislative body to renew debate and undertake a new vote on a measure that it had already acted on. The motion has the effect of suspending action on the bill until it can be reconsidered. In Congress, both the Senate and the House permit motions for reconsideration from members who have voted with the majority, and the Senate additionally permits them from members who have not voted on the bill. Most State legislatures use similar procedures. *See also*   BILL, page 157.

Significance   Motions to reconsider votes taken on controversial pieces of legislation are quite common in the Senate. Typically, they are defeated by a subsequent motion to table the reconsideration motion, an action which is usually supported by the majority that passed the bill when it was first considered. In the House, motions to reconsider are routinely made after each important bill has been passed. Subsequent tabling removes the passed bill from future reconsideration except by unanimous consent. Reconsideration is, in effect, a last ditch effort to prevent or delay passage of an important piece of legislation.

Record Vote   A "yea" or "nay" roll-call vote in a legislative body in which each member's vote is required to be recorded individually. Those members not voting for or against the measure will either be "paired" or "present." In Congress, the Consitution requires a record vote for overriding a presidential veto, and whenever one-fifth of the members demand it. Record votes are not taken in Committee of the Whole. State constitutions also require record votes on important measures before the state legislatures. *See also*   DIVISION, page 167; TELLER VOTE, page 189; VIVA VOCE VOTE, page 191.

Significance   In Congress, a record vote is demanded on almost all important bills. In a representative system of government it is essential that the voters have an opportunity to examine a legislator's voting record. Prior to the adoption of an electronic voting system in 1973, the House of Representatives frequently used a record roll-call vote as a delaying tactic to allow time for absent members to participate in the vote. Some state legislatures also have installed electronic voting devices so that a complete record of the vote can be made instantaneously. The accountability of the record vote system has been supplemented by a change in the teller vote system. The Legislative Reorganization Act of 1970 permits one-fifth of a House or Committee of the Whole quorum to require that members' teller votes be put on record.

Redistricting   The action of a state legislature or other body in redrawing legislative electoral district lines following a new population census. Redistricting occurs after each decennial federal census when congressional seats are reapportioned among the fifty states. In each state that gains or loses seats, the state legislatures are required by most state constitutions to redraw district boundary lines for electing state representatives and senators to the state legislatures following each federal census. *See also Baker v. Carr,* page 194; GERRYMANDERING, page 170; *Hadley v. Junior College,* page 149; *Reynolds v. Sims,* page 195; *Wesberry v. Sanders,* page 196.

Significance Redistricting decisions, typically, are made by partisan majorities in the legislatures, and the partisan nature of the undertaking is often reflected in the final results, called gerrymandering. In the past, large cities were underrepresented, and rural areas tended to be grossly overrepresented because of state legislative refusals to redistrict or to redistrict on a population basis. Since 1962, federal and state court rulings have required that districts be drawn on a basis of substantial equality of population. This new pattern of redistricting has radically altered the distribution of political power in American legislative bodies in favor of urban and suburban interests.

Referendum An electoral device, available in many states, by which voters can "veto" a bill passed by their legislature. Emergency and financial bills are commonly excluded from referendum action. In states providing for the referendum, bills passed by the legislature do not take effect for a specified period (usually ninety days), during which the bill may be suspended by obtaining the required number of voters' signatures on petitions (usually 5 percent of the total votes cast in a preceding election). A suspended bill is voted on by the electorate and, if disapproved by a majority, it is killed. The *constitutional referendum* gives voters an opportunity to approve or reject amendments or revisions of state constitutions. Many state and local governments may also use the *optional* or *advisory referendum,* by which a legislative body may voluntarily refer a measure to the voters for an expression of popular sentiment. *See also* DIRECT DEMOCRACY, page 8; DIRECT LEGISLATION, page 166.

Significance The referendum was adopted by many states in the early part of the twentieth century as an ultrademocratic weapon to check the objectionable enactments of the legislatures. It is not intended for regular use, but rather remains a "gun behind the door," by means of which the people hold a continuing veto power. The referendum has been used infrequently in most states that provide for it. Supporters of the referendum regard it as a useful check on ill-considered or dangerous actions by the legislature and as an expansion of democracy. Those who oppose it regard it as an unnecessary check on representative government that weakens legislative responsibility, gives great power to organized groups, and provides for the making of decisions on complex or technical issues by the average citizen who may be incapable of voting intelligently on them.

Refer to Committee The sending of a bill that has been introduced into one of the houses of a legislative body to a standing committee. In Congress, public bills are assigned to committees by the parliamentarian under the scrutiny of the presiding officer in each house. Private bills are usually referred to the committee requested by the senator or representative who introduces the bill. *See also* COMMITTEE CHAIRMAN, page 161; STANDING COMMITTEE, page 188.

Significance Referral of bills to the proper committee is generally a routine matter. Some bills may include subject matter pertinent to several committees. In such cases, the presiding officer in each house may exercise some discretion in assigning bills, which may have a significant effect on whether specific bills are killed in committee or reported out. For example, the Speaker of the House would be likely to refer a bill to a committee favoring such legislation if he personally supported it. In each house, in a rarely used procedure, the majority of members can overrule the decision of the presiding officer by removing a bill from one committee's jurisdiction and assigning it to another.

Report   The action of a legislative committee in sending out its findings and recommendations to its chamber following consideration of a bill or investigation of some matter. The report explains the reasons for the committee's actions. Most committee reports are favorable, but on rare occasions a committee will report out a bill with a recommendation that its parent chamber kill the bill. In any case, many reports are not unanimous, and those members of the committee who dissent may file a minority report. If a bill has been amended in committee, the majority report will provide an explanation for this action. *See also* DISCHARGE RULE, page 167; RULES COMMITTEE, page 184; STANDING COMMITTEE, page 188.

Significance   Typically, the great majority of bills introduced each session in most legislative bodies fail to become law because they are not reported out by the various committees to which they have been assigned. Some state legislatures require committees to report out all bills. In the House of Representatives, a committee's refusal to report out a bill for consideration can be overridden only by the rarely used discharge rule, and in the Senate the discharge resolution can be used. Most bills and resolutions reported out with recommendations to the chamber that they be passed are acted on favorably. Recommendations on bills of a controversial political nature are of lesser importance in influencing action in the chamber. In the House, bills reported out by committees are sent first to the Rules Committee, which exercises the power to determine when and how bills will be considered on the floor of the chamber.

Representative   A member of the House of Representatives in Congress or of the lower house of a state legislature. Representatives are elected for two-year terms and, in keeping with the idea that the lower house is to be the more representative of the two chambers, all members' terms end together. The Constitution provides that a representative must be at least twenty-five years of age, a citizen for seven years, and a resident of the state from which he is elected. Vacancies are filled by special election called by the governor. *See also* HOUSE OF REPRESENTATIVES, page 171; REPRESENTATIVE GOVERNMENT, page 16.

Significance   In Congress, representatives, also called "congressmen," serve as the most direct contact between the citizen and his government. The two-year term makes it necessary for the representative to keep in touch with his constituents if he wishes to be reelected. Several presidents have proposed a four-year term coterminous with that of the President to alleviate the pressures of constant campaigning and to provide greater continuity. While neither national nor state representatives enjoy the same prestige accorded members of upper chambers, many who have acquired seniority through long service exercise considerable political power.

Resident Commissioner   A delegate elected by the people of a territory to represent them in the House of Representatives. A resident commissioner may speak in the House and serve on committees, but he may not vote. His salary is the same as that of all congressmen. Guam, Puerto Rico, and the Virgin Islands have resident commissioners. The District of Columbia is also represented in the House of Representatives by a nonvoting delegate. *See also* TERRITORY, page 42.

Significance Permitting a territory to elect a resident commissioner to Congress demonstrates willingness to prepare the territory for self-governance and possible statehood or independence. Since the people of territories are subject to many federal laws, they are entitled to have their interests represented. Nationalistic groups in these areas point out that the nonvoting role of their commissioner is proof of the continuing colonial status of their people.

Rider   A provision, unlikely to pass on its own merits, added to an important bill so that it will "ride" through the legislative process. Riders become law if the bills to which they are attached are passed. What may be considered a rider by one legislator may be regarded by another as an important and germane amendment to the bill. *See also* ITEM VETO, page 204.

Significance In Congress many riders are attached to appropriations bill, although this procedure is technically banned under the rules of the House and Senate. Opponents of the rider and the President are forced to accept the provision if they want the appropriation or other major bill to become law. In several states, the governors have been given the item veto power; this permits them to veto only those sections of a bill with which they disagree, allowing the remainder to become law. Such power vested in the President would go far toward meeting the problem of riders.

Rules Committee   A standing committee of the House of Representatives that can provide special rules under which specific bills will be debated, amended, and considered by the House. The Rules Committee functions as a valve or sifting device to control the flow of bills from House standing committees to the floor for consideration, a power which can be abused by its selective use. *See also* CALENDAR, page 158; DISCHARGE RULE, page 167; GAG RULE, page 170.

Significance Because more bills are reported out of committees than the House has time to consider, the Rules Committee functions as a legislative traffic-control officer. In this role it can exercise a virtual veto power over bills reported out by other committees. It can, conversely, send out bills to be considered under favorable procedures. If a majority of the Committee favors a bill, their approval will most likely be reflected in the rule specified for consideration of that bill. The Committee may also provide a "gag" rule by which amendments to the bill may be forbidden or limited to specified areas. Because of these powers, the Rules Committee can exercise great influence over legislation in the House. Under the House procedure, a bill can be pulled out of the Rules Committee after seven days by means of a discharge petition signed by a majority of House members. This method has not proved satisfactory because of a reluctance of congressmen to challenge committee leadership and prerogatives. In 1961, the membership of the Rules Committee was enlarged by three to a total of fifteen in an attempt to offset the traditional conservative control of the Committee by the addition of liberals. A change in the majority/minority ratio of the committee from 8 to 4 to 10 to 5 was also effected.

Select Committee A legislative committee established for a limited time period and for a special purpose. Select committees may be created by either house or may include members from both houses (joint committee). *See also* INVESTIGATING COMMITTEE, page 173; WATCHDOG COMMITTEE, page 192.

Significance Select committees are given assignments that do not fall within the jurisdiction of any standing committee, or that the latter may prefer not to carry on. Most special committees have been given investigative duties, although others have been assigned supervisory, housekeeping, and coordination responsibilities. The Legislative Reorganization Act of 1946 reduced the need for select committees by placing responsibility for investigations in the standing committees.

Senate The upper house of the United States Congress and of forty-nine state legislatures. Representation in the United States Senate is based on the principle of state equality, and the Constitution specifies that no state may be deprived of its equal representation in the Senate without its consent. The Senate is comprised of one hundred Senators from fifty states. Most state senates have fewer than fifty members. The Vice President is the presiding officer of the Senate; and, in the state legislatures, the lieutenant governor normally presides. In the absence of a presiding officer, a president pro tempore elected from the membership assumes that role. *See also* HOUSE OF REPRESENTATIVES, page 171; SENATOR, page 185.

Significance Many observers regard the Senate as more responsive to national interests than the House because it tends to respond more to the needs of the nation than to local interests. Aside from lawmaking and representational functions, the Senate is also vested with special powers, including the power to try impeachments and to give advice and consent to treaties and appointments. If no candidate for the vice presidency receives a majority of the electoral vote, the Senate then elects the Vice President from the two candidates with the highest electoral votes. State senates, too, exercise special powers, such as confirmation of appointments and trial of impeached officials.

Senator A member of the United States Senate or of the upper house in state legislatures. United States senators have been directly elected by the people of their respective states since the adoption of the Seventeenth Amendment in 1913. The term of office is six years, with one-third of the Senate seats up for election every two years. Vacancies are usually filled by appointment by the state's governor, although the legislature may provide for a special election. The Constitution provides that a senator must be at least thirty years of age, a citizen for nine years, and a resident of the state from which he is elected. In the state legislatures, senators are in all cases elected by the people, usually for four years. *See also* REPRESENTATIVE, page 183; SENATE, page 185; SEVENTEENTH AMENDMENT, page 187.

Significance In Congress, because there are fewer than one-fourth as many senators as congressmen, and because of their longer terms and special powers, senators generally are accorded greater prestige than their colleagues in the lower house. Many representatives aspire to achieve election to the Senate. Most senators represent more constituents than do House members, and the smaller size of the chamber makes possible more thorough deliberation on measures. In state legislatures, the average senator also represents more constituents than does a member of the lower house and usually exercises greater influence in state matters. On the national level, in recent years, most presidential aspirants have been United States senators.

Senatorial Courtesy   Am unwritten agreement among senators that requires the President to confer with the senator or senators of his party from a state before he makes a nomination to fill a federal office located in that state. The Senate will almost invariably reject a presidential nominee when the senator involved raises a personal objection. When neither senator of a state is of the President's party, the President is apt to consult state party leaders. *See also* APPOINT-MENT POWER, page 199; CONFIRMATION, page 163.

Significance   Senatorial courtesy has resulted in the transference of federal patronage within a state from the President to senators of his party. This means that such senators normally choose the appointees and give their names to the President so that he can make the formal appointments. Federal positions affected by senatorial courtesy include judges, district attorneys, customs officials, and field service officials of most important agencies. Presidents may reject senatorial recommendations, but this rarely occurs.

Seniority Rule   A custom nearly always followed in both houses of Congress of awarding chairmanships of committees to the majority party member who has the longest number of years of continuous service on the committee. Each party, majority and minority alike, strictly lists its members on the various committees according to the seniority rule. When a high-ranking member leaves the committee, all members of that party move up one notch on the seniority list. Many state legislatures follow the seniority rule, although other political and personal factors may modify or override seniority. Under public pressure to change the seniority system, both parties in the House agreed in 1973 to permit election of committee chairmen by their respective party caucuses or their agents, but seniority generally continues to be honored in the selection process. *See also* COMMITTEE CHAIRMAN, page 161; RANKING MEMBER, page 179.

Significance   The seniority rule, which emerged in Congress during the latter part of the nineteenth century, has been a source of much controversy. Supporters of seniority argue that it: (1) guarantees chairmen will have had long experience in committee matters; (2) avoids intrigues, conflicts, and deadlocks within the party organizations that would inevitably occur whenever a new chairman is chosen; (3) makes it possible for congressmen from small states to rise to positions of importance; and (4) has produced men of ability and stature in the chairmanships of the important committees. Opponents of seniority argue that it: (1) tends to hold back men of ability while it often moves mediocre men steadily ahead; (2) requires nothing more of a man than that he continue living and getting reelected; (3) tends to favor stagnant, one-party voting areas of the nation over two-party competitive areas that reflect changes in public opinion; and (4) reduces party responsibility by filling most key power positions in both houses with members from the conservative wings of either party. Likelihood of eliminating seniority is remote. Denial of an incumbent's seniority rights may occur, however, in selection of committee chairmen as in 1975, for example, when the House Democratic Caucus denied seniority rights in removing several powerful chairmen from key committees.

Session   The period during which a legislative body assembles and carries on its regular business. Each Congress has two regular sessions based on the requirement in the Constitution that Congress assemble at least once each year. In addition, Congress may be summoned into special session by the President. The first session of a Congress usually begins on January 3 of odd-numbered years, with the start of the terms of all representatives and one-third of the senators. The second session begins on January 3 of even-numbered years. The Congress that assembles in January 1977, for example, is the Ninety-fifth Congress, first session. Adjournment is left up to Congress, although the Constitution provides that if the two houses cannot agree on a date, the President may adjourn them at his discretion. However, no President has exercised this authority. In the states, most legislatures convene in regular session every two years, although many have regular annual sessions. Most state constitutions limit the length of legislative sessions either by specifying the number of days or by cutting off pay and allowances for legislators after a certain date. *See also* SPECIAL SESSION, page 188; TWENTIETH AMENDMENT, page 190.

Significance   To cope with the many complex problems of modern society, a legislative body must be in session regularly and not only at widely separated intervals. Because the Constitution leaves sessions pretty much up to the discretion of Congress, this problem does not exist in the national government. In some of the states, however, sessions continue to be held infrequently and are generally short. Constitutional revision is needed in many states to free the legislatures from restrictions that date back more than a century. Some states have met this problem by calling special sessions of the legislature annually or every other year.

Seventeenth Amendment   An amendment to the Constitution, adopted in 1913, that provides for the direct election of United States senators by the voters of each state. The Amendment changes those sections of Article I that authorized senators to be chosen by the legislatures of the states. It also provides that, when a vacancy occurs, the legislature may authorize the governor to make a temporary appointment until an election can be held. Most legislatures have so authorized their governors. *See also* SENATOR, page 185.

Significance   Prior to the adoption of the Seventeenth Amendment, selection of senators frequently resulted in lengthy distractions from normal state legislative business. Deadlocks in the selection process often kept states unrepresented in the Senate for many months. Although popular election is no guarantee of fitness, most observers believe that senatorial abilities, stature, and responsiveness to the public will, have all tended to increase since 1913. The Seventeenth Amendment signified a shift for senators from representing "sovereign" states to representing the people of their states.

Simple Resolution   A measure adopted by one chamber of a legislative body. It does not require approval either by the other house or by the President. Simple resolutions are designated either "H Res" or "S Res." *See also* CONCURRENT RESOLUTION, page 162; JOINT RESOLUTION, page 174.

Significance   Simple resolutions do not have the force of law. They are usually adopted for the purpose of making or amending rules of procedure. In Congress, one chamber may adopt a resolution to express its sentiment on a current issue or to give advice to the President on foreign policy or other areas of executive responsibility.

Speaker of the House   The presiding officer in the House of Representatives and in the lower chamber of state legislatures. His election by the House is a formality that follows his selection by the majority party caucus. As a member of the House, the Speaker may engage in debate and vote on measures. The Speaker follows the Vice President in the line of succession to the presidency under the Presidential Succession Act of 1947. *See also* PRESIDENTIAL SUCCESSION, page 207; REFER TO COMMITTEE, page 182.

Significance   The Speaker is the most powerful and influential member of the House. As presiding officer, he recognizes members wishing to speak, interprets and applies the rules, and decides questions of order. Although he can be overruled by the House itself, this rarely occurs. He appoints select and conference committees and refers bills to committee. His real influence lies in the fact that, in exercising all of the foregoing powers, the Speaker may use discretion and political acumen. He is thus placed in a strategic position whereby he can influence the passage or rejection of bills at almost every stage in the legislative process in the House. As the leader of the majority party in the House, the Speaker also exercises considerable power in shaping and implementing party decisions on pending legislation. Most Speakers have been men of ability, stature, and tact, able to provide the kind of leadership needed by the majority party. The role and powers of speakers in the various state legislatures are analogous to those of the Speaker in the House of Representatives, and they have the additional power to appoint members of standing committees.

Special Session   An extraordinary session of a legislative body, convoked usually on the initiative of a chief executive. The Constitution grants power to the President to summon Congress or either house into session "on extraordinary occasions" (Art. II, sec. 3). Although the House has never been called into special session, the Senate has been convoked to act upon executive appointments or treaties. In all fifty states, the governors are empowered to call special sessions of the legislatures. In several states, a stipulated number of legislators may petition the governor to call the legislature into session. In a few others, the legislature can call itself into special session. *See also* JOINT SESSION, page 174; SESSION, page 187.

Significance   Congress when called into special session possesses full constitutional power to legislate. In about one-half of the states, legislatures convened in special sessions are similarly free to act, whereas in the other half they are limited to acting upon what the governor specifies in his call. Special sessions may be useful in meeting a sudden crisis or new problem. A chief executive can use the call of a special session as a political weapon to focus public attention on an issue and pressure the legislative body to consider it. Although executive officials may summon legislative bodies into special sessions, they cannot exercise appreciable control over legislative action or inaction once the body convenes.

Standing Committee   A regular committee of a legislative body that considers bills within a subject area. In Congress, there are twenty-two House and eighteen Senate standing committees. House committees range in size from nine to fifty-one members and Senate committees from seven to twenty-four members. Representatives are normally assigned to only one standing committee, senators to two. In the House, the leading standing committees include Rules, Ways and Means, Appropriations, Armed Services, Judiciary, Foreign Affairs, Commerce, and Agriculture. In the

Senate, influential committees include Foreign Relations, Appropriations, Finance, Judiciary, Armed Services, and Banking and Currency. The majority party in each chamber holds a majority vote and the chairmanship on each committee. Positions of importance on the committees are determined under the rule of seniority. Under the Legislative Reorganization Act of 1970, committee votes in executive (secret) sessions must be made public, and committee hearings may for the first time be opened to radio and television coverage if witnesses and a majority of the committee do not object. *See also* COMMITTEE CHAIRMAN, page 161; COMMITTEE ON COMMITTEES, page 162; REFER TO COMMITTEE, page 182; SENIORITY RULE, page 186.

Significance The standing committee system operates on the principle of specialization secured through a division of labor. Most bills receive their most thorough consideration at the committee stage. Members of Congress usually respect the decisions and recommendations made by the standing committees on pending legislation. Thus, the fate of most bills is decided in committee rather than on the floors of the two chambers. This great power led Woodrow Wilson to describe the American political system as "government by the standing committees of Congress."

Statute (Act) A law enacted by Congress or by a state legislature. Simple, concurrent, and joint resolutions adopted by Congress are not considered statutes. Statutes take the form of public and private laws and are numbered consecutively in each session of Congress. *See also* BILL, page 157; CODE, page 242.

Significance All acts of Congress are published first in the form of "slip laws" and are bound after each session in the *Statutes at Large of the United States.* Those applicable today can be found in the *United States Code,* which is revised every six years and supplemented annually. The *Code* is organized on a subject-matter basis. State laws are published but not codified regularly.

Suspension of Rules A time-saving procedure used by a legislative body to bring a measure to a vote. In the House of Representatives, a motion to "suspend the rules and pass the bill" requires a two-thirds vote of members present for passage. Debate on the bill is limited to forty minutes and no amendments are permitted. *See also* PREVIOUS QUESTION, page 178; UNANIMOUS CONSENT, page 190.

Significance The suspension of rules procedure keeps the House from getting bogged down with its complex rules system. Because of the size of the House, a means by which debate can be closed and a measure brought to a vote quickly is necessary to maintain the flow of business. The Senate, with its rules for unlimited debate, can obtain these results only through unanimous consent. Suspension of rules is augmented by other parliamentary devices to speed up the legislative process, such as previous question and unanimous consent, but the former is not used in the Senate.

Teller Vote A vote taken in a legislative body in which members are counted as they file past tellers. In Congress, the House but not the Senate uses teller votes, which can be demanded by one-fifth of a quorum (forty-four in the House, twenty in the Committee of the Whole). When a teller vote is called, two tellers, one for and one against, stand in front of the Speaker's desk and count the votes as the members file past. The Speaker or Chairman presiding over the

Committee of the Whole then announces the results. Although teller votes have traditionally been anonymous under the Legislative Reorganization Act of 1970, one-fifth of a quorum may request that members' individual votes be recorded. *See also* DIVISION, page 167; RECORD VOTE, page 181; VIVA VOCE VOTE, page 191.

Significance In the past, teller votes were often used on important issues when the accuracy of the vote count was essential but House members preferred not to put themselves on record. Because this system encouraged irresponsibility and weakened the members' accountability to their constituents, it was modified to provide for a recorded teller vote by the Legislative Reorganization Act. Although both teller vote and record vote systems may now be used to secure accurate vote counts in the House, the electronic record vote system is typically used.

Twentieth Amendment An amendment to the Constitution, adopted in 1933, that provides that a new Congress elected in November of even-numbered years will convene on January 3 of the following year unless Congress sets a different date. Prior to its adoption, a newly elected Congress did not convene in regular session until December of the following year—a lapse of thirteen months. The old Congress, meanwhile, with many members who had failed to win reelection ("lame ducks"), met in perfunctory session for four months following the election. The Amendment also changed the presidential term to start a month and one-half earlier, on January 20 instead of on March 4. *See also* TWENTIETH AMENDMENT, page 211.

Significance The Twentieth Amendment provides for more democracy and greater efficiency. By reducing the interim period between an election and the assumption of office by newly elected members of Congress, the people's mandate may be more quickly and accurately realized. By changing the President's term to start at an earlier date, a new President has the opportunity to present his legislative and budgetary programs to a new Congress. Some observers, including former presidents, have suggested that the interim period be reduced still further so as to enable a new Congress and President to come to grips with pressing problems of government at an even earlier date. That the problem still exists was indicated by the action of the Ninety-first Congress which held the first lame-duck session since 1954. It met after the election of November, 1970, and before newly elected members took their seats, adjourning finally on January 2, 1971, the day before the Ninety-second Congress convened. The Ninety-third Congress also met in lame-duck session in late 1974 and acted on major legislative issues.

Unanimous Consent A time-saving procedure, also known as "without objection," used by a legislative body to adopt noncontroversial motions, amendments, and bills without submitting them to a vote. Both houses of congress use the procedure to expedite business. In the House, an objection from a single member results in the tabling of the bill or motion for two weeks. *See also* PREVIOUS QUESTION, page 178; SUSPENSION OF RULES, page 189.

Significance Unanimous consent can be a useful parliamentary procedure for rapidly disposing of a host of minor matters cluttering up a legislative chamber's agenda. By expediting noncontroversial measures, additional time may be made available for dealing with more critical and controversial issues. Unanimous consent is augmented by other parliamentary devices to speed up the legislative process, such as previous question and suspension of rules.

Unicameralism   The principle of a one-house legislature, as contrasted with bicameralism, a legislature based on two houses. One state legislature—Nebraska's—is unicameral, as are local governmental policy-determining bodies, such as county boards, city councils, township boards, and school boards. *See also* BICAMERALISM, page 157.

Significance   The merits claimed for unicameralism include: (1) greater economy and efficiency of operation; (2) greater prestige, which attracts outstanding citizens; (3) elimination of deadlocks resulting from rivalry and friction between two houses; (4) elimination of the need for conference committees to iron out differing versions of a bill passed by the two chambers; and (5) more accurate fixing of responsibility of elected representatives by the public. Arguments against unicameralism include: (1) hasty, careless, ill-considered legislation may result; (2) special interest lobbies can concentrate their influence more effectively against one house; (3) one house may be more susceptible to aroused popular passions and other democratic excesses; and (4) control over a one-house legislature may be focused in a single major interest group or in a small geographical area.

Vice President   The second highest executive officer of the United States who is designated the presiding officer of the Senate by the Constitution. Although the Vice President's constitutional duties are primarily legislative, in modern times presidents have tended to assign them executive responsibilities. *See also* TWENTY-FIFTH AMENDMENT, page 211; VICE PRESIDENT, page 213.

Significance   Unlike the Speaker of the House, the Vice President as President of the Senate is not the chosen leader of the majority party in the Senate, nor is he a member of the Senate. He cannot speak from the floor on issues and, as presiding officer, he must not show his partisanship. He can cast a vote only in case of a tie. Although the Vice President's powers are negligible, he may, as some have, exercise considerable influence in the Senate's decision making by reason of his ability and personal powers of persuasion. Also, if he is a leader of high standing in the majority party of the Senate, his potential influence is increased. In recent years, a succession of vice presidents selected from the Congress—John N. Garner, Harry S Truman, Alben W. Barkley, Richard M. Nixon, Lyndon B. Johnson, Hubert H. Humphrey, and Gerald R. Ford—have proved to be valuable liaison agents between the President and the Congress. Spiro T. Agnew and Nelson A. Rockefeller have suffered in their role of legislative liaison agent from their lack of congressional experience and because the Congress was controlled by the opposing major party.

Viva Voce Vote   A voice vote in a legislative chamber in which the presiding officer determines the outcome from the volume of response from those for and against the measure. The viva voce vote procedure is used mainly to make minor, generally noncontroversial, decisions. *See also* DIVISION, page 167; RECORD VOTE, page 181; TELLER VOTE, page 189.

Significance   Viva voce votes on important measures are often challenged because it is difficult to determine voice volume with precision. Much discretion can be exercised by the presiding officer if his decision is left unchallenged. The main advantage of this vote lies in the speed with which it permits great quantities of business to be transacted. A defect of this procedure is that individual votes are not recorded, making it difficult for the voters to hold their elected representatives responsible.

Watchdog Committee A committee established by a legislative body for the purpose of overseeing the administration of the laws. In Congress, prior to 1946, each house created a number of select committees to perform this oversight function. In the legislative Reorganization Act of 1946, Congress vested the "watchdog" responsibility in the standing committees, each responsible for overseeing the execution of laws within its jurisdiction. *See also* INVESTIGATING COMMITTEE, page 173; STANDING COMMITTEE, page 188.

Significance In its report in 1946 that led to the Reorganization Act, the Joint Committee commented on the watchdog committee function: "Without effective legislative oversight of the activities of the vast executive branch, the line of democracy wears thin." The committee recommended "a continuous review of the agencies administering laws originally reported by the committees." The Government Operations Committees of the House and the Senate have been given the special responsibility of "studying the operation of government activities at all levels with a view to determining its economy and efficiency." Congressional oversight can be distinguished from congressional investigations in that the former is more a continuing scrutiny of executive operations, whereas the latter involves a more intense digging for facts within a limited problem area.

Ways and Means Committee A standing committee of the House of Representatives to which all bills for raising revenue are referred. Its members study tax and tariff bills and make recommendations to the full House. Occasionally, the Committee itself writes new tax measures. *See also* COMMITTEE CHAIRMAN, page 161; STANDING COMMITTEE, page 188.

Significance The Ways and Means Committee is usually regarded as second in importance only to the House Rules Committee. Democratic members of the Committee are chosen by the Democratic caucus. Prior to 1974 these members functioned as a committee on committees to assign the Democratic members to all other House committees, subject to caucus approval. In a liberal revolt after the 1974 congressional election, the House Democratic Caucus took this committee assignment power from Committee members and gave it to the House Democratic Steering Committee, subject to Caucus oversight. Republican members of the Committee have never exercised this power. When the Ways and Means Committee holds public hearings on tax and tariff measures, large numbers of citizens and lobbyists testify before the Committee, reflecting the importance of the revenue raising function. The chairman of Ways and Means has often been one of the most powerful individuals in the Congress. In the 1974 post-election Democratic revolt, the Committee was also enlarged from 25 to 37 members in an attempt by the liberals to end conservative control.

Whip An assistant floor leader who aids the majority or minority floor leaders of each party in each house of Congress. Whips are selected in party caucuses, usually on the recommendation of the floor leaders. Each whip in the House appoints several assistants to aid him, whereas the Senate whips are aided by the secretaries to their respective party policy committees. *See also* CAUCUS, page 159; MAJORITY FLOOR LEADER, page 175.

Significance The duties of the whips include: (1) canvassing fellow party members so as to inform party leaders of the number of votes which can be counted on; (2) taking action to bring full voting power of their party to bear on key issues; and (3) acting for the floor leaders when they are absent from the chamber. On crucial issues, when close votes are anticipated, much depends on the party organization and the effectiveness of the whips' operations. Unlike party whips in the British Parliament, congressional whips do not have the power to compel party members to support party policy.

IMPORTANT AGENCIES

Congressional Research Service (CRS) A staff agency of Congress which provides research data to aid committees and members of Congress in their legislative duties. Created as the Legislative Reference Service in the Library of Congress in 1914, it was redesignated Congressional Research Service and given expanded responsibilities by the Legislative Reorganization Act of 1970. Each year, various studies, statistics, charts, and the like are provided for congressmen and committees in response to thousands of inquiries. Many state legislatures have created similar staff facilities. *See also* BILL DRAFTING, page 158; LIBRARY OF CONGRESS, page 193.

Significance The creation of the Legislative Reference Service and its expansion into the Congressional Research Service resulted at least in part from the reluctance of Congress to be dependent upon "experts" in the executive branch for information. The CRS not only performs essential staff functions, but, because of the nature of its work, has a considerable effect on the end product of legislation. The 1970 Act, for example, provides that the CRS, when requested, advise and assist a committee of Congress "in the analysis, appraisal and evaluation of legislative proposals within that committee's jurisdiction or of recommendation submitted to Congress by the President or any Executive agency. . . ." The CRS is also authorized by the Act to function as an agent of a congressional committee and, in this role, may request any executive department or agency to produce its books, records, and documents.

Library of Congress The national library of the United States, which serves the entire national government and state and local governments as well as the public. The Library of Congress was created in 1800 by Congress and is headed by the Librarian of Congress, who is appointed by the President with Senate approval. Two important divisions of the Library are the Copyright Office and the Congressional Research Service. *See also* COPYRIGHT, page 309; CONGRESSIONAL RESEARCH SERVICE, page 193.

Significance The Library of Congress is particularly useful to Congress and the executive branch because it is a vast storehouse of official records and documents. Much legislation involves extensive studies and research, and the role of the Library has grown as governmental activities have increased and grown more complex. Most copyrighted publications are given a Library of Congress catalog card number. Today, the Library has more than 16 million books, 30 million manuscripts, and vast numbers of maps, records, films, and photographs in its collection.

IMPORTANT CASES

Baker v. Carr, 369 U.S. 186 (1962): Ruled in an epic Supreme Court decision that federal courts have jurisdiction over lawsuits challenging the apportionment of legislative districts, on the ground that malapportioned districts may violate the equal protection clause of the Fourteenth Amendment. The case had the effect of overturning *Colegrove v. Green,* 328 U.S. 549 (1946) in which the Court held that the issue of malapportioned legislative districts was a political question and relief should be sought through the political process. The *Baker* case involved a suit to compel the Tennessee legislature to redistrict state legislative districts on a population basis, a provision of the Tennessee Constitution that the legislature had ignored for over sixty years. *See also* REDISTRICTING, page 181.

Significance Before the *Baker* case, many state legislatures had long refused to provide for equitable apportionment for state legislative and congressional election districts. The *Baker* decision reflected the new view of the Court's majority that it is unrealistic to seek to achieve a fair system of representation through the ballot box, since state legislators often maintain themselves in power through gerrymandering and refusals to redistrict. The *Baker* case led to a plethora of challenges to districting patterns in most states. Subsequently, the Supreme Court ruled that in statewide primary elections for United States senators and state executive officers, each person's vote must count equally (*Gray v. Sanders,* 372 U.S. 368 [1963]), that congressional districts must be substantially equal in population (*Wesberry v. Sanders,* 376 U.S. 1 [1964]), and, that both houses of a bicameral state legislature must be apportioned on a population basis (*Reynolds v. Sims,* 377 U.S. 533 [1964]). These and later decisions have affirmed that the basic constitutional principle of voting equality can mean only one thing—"one person, one vote." Many observers regard the *Baker* and subsequent apportionment decisions as the most important precedents established by the Warren Court because of their impact on legislative decision making.

McGrain v. Daugherty, 273 U.S. 135 (1927): Decided that Congress has the right to compel testimony from private individuals as an aid to its power to pass laws. The *McGrain* case concerned the congressional investigation which arose out of the Teapot Dome scandal involving bribery and other illegal acts by public officials. The Court held that Congress could subpoena a private individual as well as a public official when this action is pertinent to a proper legislative function. *See also* INVESTIGATING COMMITTEE, page 173.

Significance The *McGrain* case established the constitutional basis for legislative investigations along with the power to compel testimony and production of papers and other materials. So long as an investigation has a legislative purpose, the courts will not inquire further into the motives of Congress. This includes investigations aimed at gathering information that relates to possible impeachment actions by Congress against executive and judicial officials.

Pacific States Telephone and Telegraph Co. v. Oregon, 223 U.S. 118 (1912): Involved the question of whether the initiative and referendum provisions of the Oregon Constitution destroy the republican form of government guaranteed to all states by the United States Constitution in Article IV, section 4. The Court held it to be a political question not open to judicial inquiry.

See also INITIATIVE, page 172; POLITICAL QUESTION, page 258; REFERENDUM, page 182; REPUBLICAN FORM OF GOVERNMENT, page 41.

Significance Although no provision is made by the Constitution for direct action by the people in the lawmaking process, the Court, in effect, recognized in the *Oregon* case that the states may validly adopt such measures. About one-third of the states and numerous cities have adopted the initiative and referendum, most of them during the first two decades of the twentieth century.

Reynolds v. Sims, 377 U.S. 533 (1964): A landmark decision that under the equal protection clause of the Fourteenth Amendment both houses of a bicameral state legislature must be apportioned on the basis of population. The Court rejected the "federal analogy" that, like Congress, a state legislature could have one house based on a factor other than population. It held that political subdivisions in states are not sovereign entities (on which equal representation of states in the Senate is predicated). Since both houses of a legislature must agree to enact legislation, representation on factors other than population dilutes the votes of citizens living in heavily populated areas. "Legislators represent people, not trees or acres," said the Court, and an apportionment scheme cannot discriminate on the basis of residence any more than it can on the basis of race or economic status. *See also* BICAMERALISM, page 157; REDISTRICTING, page 181.

Significance The *Reynolds v. Sims* case is among the most important decisions in American history, overcoming years of inaction by legislative bodies on the representation problem. It transformed the American political scene by ending dominance of state legislatures by rural minorities in favor of the urban majorities. It also has had a direct impact on national politics, since state legislatures draw congressional district lines. Efforts to overturn the decision by constitutional amendment failed. In the *Reynolds* case and subsequent decisions, the Court has not insisted on absolute equality of representation, permitting "substantial" equality of representation. But the "one person, one vote" principle remains firm as the basic principle governing the American system of representative government.

United States v. Harriss, 347 U.S. 612 (1954): Upheld the constitutionality of the Federal Regulation of Lobbying Act of 1946 against charges that it violates due process, freedom of speech and press, and freedom of petition. *See also* LOBBYIST, page 125; REGULATION OF LOBBYING ACT, page 198.

Significance The Court narrowly construed the application of the Lobbying Act in the *Harriss* case by holding that it applies only to lobbyists who directly seek to influence members of Congress concerning pending or proposed federal legislation. Lobbyists who seek to influence federal legislation indirectly through public opinion do not fall within the scope of "lobbying activities" regulated by the Act. The Court emphasized that the intention of the Lobbying Act was to enable Congress to discover "who is being hired, who is putting up the money, and how much." This is information that Congress is entitled to know.

Watkins v. United States, 354 U.S. 178 (1957): Established that a person may refuse to answer a question put to him by an investigating committee of Congress if the question is not pertinent to the inquiry. The Court upheld Watkins' refusal to answer questions of the House

Committee on Un-American Activities regarding certain persons who had at one time been members of the Communist party. For refusing to answer, Watkins was cited for contempt of Congress. The Court reversed his conviction on the ground that the Committee had failed to demonstrate that the questions were pertinent. *See also* INVESTIGATING COMMITTEE, page 173.

Significance Many rights guaranteed in the Constitution apply to congressional investigations as well as to judicial proceedings. In the same way that an individual is entitled to know the precise charges against him when charged with a crime, he also has the right to know how any particular question asked of him at a legislative investigation pertains to the matter under investigation. Congress may not conduct a "fishing expedition" in the hopes of uncovering information. This case illustrates one of the limitations on the investigatory powers of Congress.

Wesberry v. Sanders, 376 U.S. 1 (1964): Held that congressional districts must be substantially equal in population. The Court based its *Wesberry* ruling on Article I, Section 2, of the Constitution, which provides that the House of Representatives shall be chosen "by the People of the several States." While mathematical precision is impossible, said the Court, the Constitution requires that, as nearly as practicable, each man's vote in a congressional election is to be worth as much as any other man's vote. *See also* REDISTRICTING, page 181.

Significance The *Wesberry* case provided the legal basis for ending overrepresentation of rural areas in the House of Representatives. In a pre-*Wesberry* Congress, for example, a representative from one district represented eight times as many constituents as another congressman. This kind of disparity resulted from redistricting patterns established by state legislatures that were themselves malapportioned in favor of rural minorities. By the 1970s, the gross inequities of representation among House seats had been substantially corrected.

IMPORTANT STATUTES

Budget Reform Act of 1974 A major law that revises old and establishes new procedures by which Congress considers the annual federal budget. Procedures provided by the Budget Reform Act include: (1) adoption of an annual budget resolution that provides target figures for total appropriations and spending, and for needed tax and debt limits; (2) creation of new House and Senate budget committees to study budget data, analyze options, and write budget resolutions; (3) a detailed timetable which sets deadlines for floor action on budget proposals; (4) a change in the national government's fiscal year from the period July 1 to June 30 to the period October 1 to September 30, thus providing an additional three months for congressional action; and (5) limits on "backdoor spending" (that is, spending programs not included in the regular budget) and presidential impoundment powers. To aid the Congress in achieving these and other budget objectives, the Act also created a Congressional Budget Office to provide Congress with the fiscal experts and computers essential to study and analyze the tremendous amount of data found in the President's annual budget message. *See also* BUDGET COMMITTEES, page 158; FISCAL YEAR, page 283; PROGRAM BUDGET, page 290.

Significance The Budget Reform Act of 1974 was an attempt by Congress to regain from the President some of the "powers of the purse" which the Constitution assigns to the Congress, but which the Congress has increasingly delegated to the President. The Act tries to reassert congressional powers over government spending by forcing Congress to undertake a better organized, more careful examination of the annual budget package, and to reduce or refrain from certain related actions that have weakened congressional authority in the past. Previous efforts by Congress, such as in the Legislative Reorganization Act of 1946, to strengthen the congressional power of the purse have met with little success. The effectiveness of the new Budget Act will be tested over a period of years under increasingly difficult budgetary conditions.

Legislative Reorganization Act of 1946   An act to strengthen Congress in its organization and operations. The Act was based on the studies of a bipartisan joint committee that was charged with recommending plans "with a view toward strengthening Congress, simplifying its operations, improving its relations with other branches of the United States Government, and enabling it to meet its responsibilities under the Constitution." The Act provided for structural and procedural changes, including: (1) reducing the number of committees; (2) strengthening the operations of the committees; (3) providing for a legislative budget system; (4) reducing the workload of Congress; (5) increasing the professional assistance available to each member of Congress; (6) increasing congressional salaries and fringe benefits; and (7) regulating lobbying activities. *See also* LEGISLATIVE REORGANIZATION ACT OF 1970, page 197.

Significance Committee functioning was definitely strengthened by the Legislative Reorganization Act of 1946, although the number of subcommittees was increased. Claims legislation was reduced, but many minor matters remained under congressional responsibility. The legislative budget proposal proved unworkable and was discarded. Lobbying was brought under a measure of public and congressional oversight. Congressional salaries were substantially increased and staff assistance was improved both quantitatively and qualitatively. Two persistent problems—the seniority system in committee organization and the filibuster in the Senate—were excluded from any consideration by the joint committee. The 1946 Act was supplemented by the Legislative Reorganization Act of 1970, which was also aimed at making Congress a more representative and responsible institution.

Legislative Reorganization Act of 1970   An act to improve the operations of Congress and make them more responsive to the public will. Provisions of the Act include: (1) modification of the teller vote system (whereby members of the House voted by filing anonymously past a "yes" or "no" recording clerk) so that at the request of one-fifth of a quorum (20 members in Committee of the Whole, 44 in House sessions) each member's vote is now recorded and made public; (2) House committee hearings may be broadcast and televised with the agreement of witnesses and a majority of the committee; (3) votes taken in executive sessions of committees must be made public; (4) a majority of the members of any congressional committee may convene a meeting of the committee over the objection of its chairman; (5) the Legislative Reference Service was renamed the Congressional Research Service and reorganized to provide increased assistance to members of Congress; and (6) installation of an electronic voting device in the House that eliminates the time-consuming roll call of 435 names by the Clerk in all record votes. *See also* LEGISLATIVE REORGANIZATION ACT OF 1946, page 197.

Significance The Legislative Reorganization Act of 1970 constitutes the first substantial legislative reform act in twenty-four years, since the enactment of the Legislative Reorganization Act of 1946. The Act, which took effect in the first session of the Ninety-second Congress beginning in January, 1971, focused most of the changes in the procedures of the House of Representatives. The key congressional problems of seniority and the filibuster were not affected by the Act, however, and in its effort to achieve greater responsiveness to the public will, the Congress failed to find means for developing party responsibility in legislative matters. Following passage of the Act, Congress continued to operate with most of the critical power held by a small group in key power positions, especially committee chairmen.

Regulation of Lobbying Act (Title III, Legislative Reorganization Act of 1946)

The first attempt by Congress to control interest groups, lobbyists, and lobbying activities through legislation. The Act provides for a minimum of *regulation* and a maximum of *publicity*. Specific provisions include: (1) persons or organizations receiving money to be used principally to influence passage or defeat of legislation before Congress must register; (2) persons or groups registering must, under oath, give their name and address, employer, salary, amount and purpose of expenses, and duration of employment; (3) each registered lobbyist must report quarterly full information on his activities, which are then published in the *Congressional Record;* and (4) severe penalties are prescribed, ranging up to a $10,000 fine and a five-year prison term, and including a three-year ban against further lobbying. *See also* FEDERAL ELECTION CAMPAIGN ACT OF 1974, page 151; LOBBYIST, page 125; *United States v. Harriss,* page 195.

Significance The Lobbying Act has been criticized on the ground that its language is confusing and vague, resulting in much noncompliance. No enforcement agency has been created by Congress. The public generally has ignored the publicity given in quarterly reports. It is doubtful whether the Act has had any appreciable effect on lobbyists or their activities. Congress must be careful in enacting lobby-control legislation to avoid regulations that might abridge freedom of speech, press, or petition. Disclosures in the Watergate investigations of the 1970s of widespread corruption and violations of lobby and campaign laws by corporations and their lobbyists led to the enactment of several new laws to tighten federal control, especially in the field of campaign financing.

8 The Executive:
Office and Powers

Amnesty Power exercised by the President to grant a blanket pardon to all members of a group who have violated national law. Amnesties have also been occasionally granted by Congress. Amnesty may be full and complete, or it may be conditional, in that those granted a general pardon must perform certain required acts to qualify. *See also* PARDON, page 205.

Significance Amnesties have been used generally to absolve groups from legal accountability for political offenses. President Thomas Jefferson, for example, granted a general amnesty to all persons convicted under the Alien and Sedition Acts. The best-known amnesties in American history were those granted by Presidents Abraham Lincoln and Andrew Johnson to all Confederates who had participated in rebellion against the United States. An attempt by Congress to limit the effect of Johnson's amnesty proclamation was found by the United States Supreme Court to be an invalid interference with the President's constitutional pardoning powers (*Ex parte Garland*, 4 Wallace 333 [1867]). Whether amnesty should be granted to thousands of draft evaders became a major national issue following the end of American troop involvement in the Vietnam war. In 1974, President Gerald R. Ford offered conditional amnesty to all draft evaders, deserters, and others who had avoided service during the Vietnam war, with each person's case considered individually as to how amnesty could be won. In most cases, amnesty required a period of alternative service in the Peace Corps, VISTA, or some other volunteer service.

Appointment Power The authority vested in a public official to fill a vacancy in a governmental office or position. The appointment power is usually shared by the chief executive, who nominates the candidate, with the legislative body, which confirms the appointee. In the national government, the President possesses the full appointing power for some positions, but must obtain the Senate's "advice and consent" for others. Positions filled by presidential appointment include those in the executive branch, the federal judiciary, commissioned officers in the armed forces, and members of the independent regulatory commissions. Governors and most mayors share a limited appointment power with their state senates and city councils, respectively. The President and governors may make recess appointments between Senate sessions. *See also* CONFIRMATION, page 163; RECESS APPOINTMENT, page 208; REMOVAL POWER, page 209.

Significance The appointment power permits an executive to select persons sympathetic to the politics of his administration. Through patronage appointments, he may control his political party.

The key difference in executive authority between the President and most governors, and between a "strong" and a "weak" mayor, lies in the substantial appointing power of the former in each case. The kinds of individuals appointed—their ideological conviction, political backgrounds, loyalty to the "boss"—can greatly affect the nature and substance of the decisions made on public issues. Gross misconduct by many appointed officials in the Nixon Administration, for example, led to congressional and court actions and to a weakening of the President's leadership. The trend at all levels of government, however, is toward reducing the executive appointing power in favor of merit selection.

Budget Power   The ability to affect political decisions concerning the income and spending of public money. The President's budgetary powers lie in his initiatory role, in his ability to influence Congress during its consideration of the budget, in the threat and use of the veto on appropriations' acts, in the discretion he exercises in spending funds appropriated by Congress, and, in the case of several presidents, in his impoundment powers—that is, his refusal to spend funds provided by Congress. Each year, receipt and expenditure estimates are recommended by the President to the Congress for the next fiscal year. In January of each legislative session, the President sends his annual budget message to Congress as required by the Budget and Accounting Act of 1921. Unlike the State of the Union message, which precedes it, the budget message is not usually delivered in person by the President but is sent to Congress in writing to be read to each chamber by its clerk. Many governors, especially of those states that have undergone recen reorganization, also deliver or send to the legislature annual or biennial budget messages. *See also* BUDGET, page 275; BUDGET AND ACCOUNTING ACT OF 1921, page 301; BUDGET COMMITTEES, page 158; PERFORMANCE BUDGET, PAGE 289; PROGRAM BUDGET, page 290.

Significance   The importance of the President's budget power is that it places responsibility for the initiation of the financial plan for government on the executive. Legislative bodies begin their consideration of financial matters only after the budget message, with its detailed itemization of fiscal recommendations, has been presented to them. Although Congress or a state legislature is free to modify or reject the proposals found in a budget message, its size and specificity tend to reduce legislative discretion. The executive may also use his budget power as a means of arousing public support for certain programs, even though immediate enactment is unlikely, President Richard M. Nixon's broad use of *impoundment* powers—that is, his refusal to spend funds as authorized and appropriated by Congress for specific programs—led to judicial and congressional actions that have reduced but not eliminated the President's impoundment powers. The size and complexity of the national budget has led to the development of a summarized "Budget in Brief" for congressional use. In 1974, Congress passed budget reform legislation under which, for example, the fiscal year was changed from the period July 1 to June 30 to the period October 1 to September 30, and House and Senate Budget Committees were created in an attempt to increase congressional budget powers and restore its "power of the purse."

Cabinet   An advisory group selected by the President to aid him in making decisions. President Washington instituted the Cabinet idea when he began regularly to call together the heads of the four executive departments and the Vice President to consult on matters of policy. The Cabinet remains an informal group, with its membership determined by tradition and presidential discretion. By custom, the heads of the major departments (State; Treasury; Defense; Justice; Interior;

Agriculture; Commerce; Labor; Health, Education, and Welfare; Housing and Urban Development; and Transportation) are members of the Cabinet, and the President may also invite the Vice President and other officials to sit in on Cabinet meetings. *See also* DEPARTMENT page 223.

Significance The Cabinet may be a highly influential or relatively insignificant agency, whichever the President decides to make it. The members of the Cabinet individually are often far more influential in advising the President than is the Cabinet as a body. Some Presidents, such as James Buchanan and Warren G. Harding, placed great reliance on their cabinets; others, such as Woodrow Wilson and both Theodore and Franklin D. Roosevelt, assigned their cabinets an insignificant role. Abraham Lincoln is reported to have summarily rejected a unanimous vote of his Cabinet, an act that illustrates the *advisory* nature of Cabinet decisions. In making Cabinet appointments, presidents, typically, seek to obtain broad geographic and interest-group representation and to give some representation to the different political wings of their party. To promote bipartisanship, especially during periods of national crisis, presidents have appointed members of the opposition party to Cabinet posts. For these reasons, presidents usually prefer to seek advice elsewhere and to confine Cabinet meetings to general discussions of Administration policy. President Richard M. Nixon proposed consolidation of the eleven major departments into three super departments with their heads serving as a "supercabinet," but congressional opposition resulted in failure of the proposal.

Chief Legislator The role of the President in the making of laws. Constitutional powers available to the President to affect legislation include the recommending of legislative programs through messages to the Congress, the veto, and some control over sessions. Informal methods of influencing legislation include the President's personal contacts with congressional leaders, his use of patronage, his ability to arouse public opinion in support of his program, his efforts to influence the election of congressmen sympathetic to his views, and the continuing efforts of executive officials acting as a "presidential lobby" before congressional committees. In addition, the President's legislative powers include the issuing of rules and executive orders having the effect of law under powers delegated to him by the Constitution or by Congress. *See also* EMERGENCY POWERS, page 202; EXECUTIVE ORDER, page 203; PRESIDENT, page 206.

Significance An evaluation of a President's administration is based considerably upon his success or failure in his role as chief legislator. Presidents who have initiated broad legislative programs and successfully pushed them through Congress, using a variety of constitutional and informal political methods and weapons, are generally classified as "strong" presidents; those who have failed to provide effective legislative leadership, through unwillingness or inability, have generally been relegated to the category of "weak" Presidents. Congress, because of its size and diffusion of interests, lacks the means of formulating broad legislative programs and of enacting them into law without the continuing leadership of the President and his aides. Governors and mayors generally play a lesser role than the President in determining legislative outcomes within their political systems.

Chief of State The role of the President as ceremonial head of the government of the United States. Duties of the chief of state include greeting foreign dignitaries, acting as host at state dinners, throwing out the first baseball at the start of the season, and bestowing honors. American chief executives at all governmental levels function in similar ceremonial roles as part of their executive duties.

Significance The President serves in a dual capacity as chief of state and as chief executive. In most countries, these roles are split, as in Britain where the Queen is the ceremonial head of state, and the Prime Minister and Cabinet head the government and formulate policies. Many students of government believe that the role of chief of state detracts from the ability of the President to give sufficient time and energy to his many other significant responsibilities. In addition, his role as chief of state has blended with his political and executive roles, with the result that many Americans reject the President as a symbol of national unity and increasingly involve him in the center of conflict during national crises. Yet, if he plays the chief of state role skillfully, the President may reap considerable advantage in increased public confidence and support for him in his other roles.

Economic Message The annual Economic Report submitted each January by the President to Congress, as required by the Employment Act of 1946. The economic message is concerned with employment levels, production, purchasing power, inflation and deflation, trends of the nation's economy, and recommendations to Congress on maintaining or improving economic activity. The Economic Report is prepared by the President's Council of Economic Advisers, comprised of three leading economists. A joint congressional Committee on the Economic Report, consisting of seven members from each house, studies the message and makes recommendations for implementing it. Ultimately, it is up to the President to initiate specific actions. *See also* COUNCIL OF ECONOMIC ADVISERS, page 298; EMPLOYMENT ACT OF 1946, page 302; KEYNESIAN-ISM, page 287.

Significance The President's annual economic message reflects an acceptance by the national government of responsibility for maintaining stability in the nation's economy through monetary and fiscal policies. This approach, called Keynesianism, substitutes decisions made by the President and his advisers in pursuit of specific social goals for the undirected interplay of market forces. Like other messages, it adds to the President's role as chief legislator by enabling him to initiate and recommend legislative programs and to give them nationwide publicity through the message technique.

Emergency Powers Powers exercised during a period of crisis by the national government, or those powers conferred by Congress upon the President for a limited period of time. The President's exercise of inherent powers in the field of foreign affairs provides an additional source of power during emergencies. *See also* INHERENT POWERS, page 393; WAR POWERS, page 426; *Youngstown Sheet and Tube Co. v. Sawyer,* page 217.

Significance The Constitution does not recognize the need for additional national powers during an emergency. The Supreme Court has made this clear in stating that "emergency does not create power" (*Home Building and Loan Association v. Blaisdell,* 290 U.S. 398 [1934]). Yet, emergencies have helped to develop the use of otherwise dormant powers and the novel application of ordinary powers. Today, presidents exercise vast emergency powers initially delegated to Franklin D. Roosevelt during the 1933 banking crisis and expanded during World War II, the Korean war, the cold war, the Vietnam War, and several domestic crises. Congress is considering repeal of these emergency grants of power so as to restore equilibrium to the separation of powers-checks and balances system.

Executive Agreement An international agreement, reached by the President with foreign heads of state, that does not require senatorial approval. Such agreements are concluded under the President's constitutional power as commander in chief and his general authority in foreign relations, or under power delegated to him by Congress. Executive agreements may be nullified by congressional action and are not binding on future presidents without their consent. *See also* EXECUTIVE AGREEMENT, page 389.

Significance Executive agreements contribute to the President's position of leadership in foreign affairs. Quick, decisive action can be taken during a crisis without having to follow the difficult and time-consuming route of treaty making. Secrecy can be maintained through executive agreements when open debate in the Senate would be dangerous or provocative or doomed to failure. For example, in 1940, before American entry into World War II, President Franklin D. Roosevelt traded 50 overage destroyers to British Prime Minister Winston Churchill for air bases in British Western hemispheric possessions, a critical action but one for which Senate approval was unobtainable. Moreover, by possessing the executive agreement alternative, the President is placed in a better bargaining position with Congress on foreign policy matters.

Executive Order A rule or regulation, issued by the President, a governor, or some administrative authority, that has the effect of law. Executive orders are used to implement and give administrative effect to provisions of the Constitution, to treaties, and to statutes. They may be used to create or modify the organization or procedures of administrative agencies or may have general applicability as law. Under the national Administrative Procedure Act of 1946, all executive orders must be published in the *Federal Register. See also* DELEGATION OF POWER, page 166; FEDERAL REGISTER, page 224; QUASI-LEGISLATIVE, page 229.

Significance The use of executive orders has greatly increased in recent years as a result of the growing tendency of legislative bodies to leave many legislative details to be filled in by the executive branch. The President's power to issue executive orders stems from precedents, custom, and constitutional interpretation, as well as from discretionary powers given to the President by the Congress when enacting legislation. This trend will likely continue as government continues to concern itself with highly complex and technical matters.

Executive Privilege The right of executive officials to refuse to appear before or to withhold information from a legislative committee or a court. Executive privilege is enjoyed by the President and those executive officials accorded the right by the President. No legal means by which executive privilege could be denied to executive officials existed for many years, but in 1974 the Supreme Court established a landmark precedent (*United States v. Nixon,* 418 U.S. 683 [1974]) by unanimously ordering President Richard M. Nixon to release recorded tapes with allegedly criminal information on them that eventually led to his resignation. *See also* CHECKS AND BALANCES, page 23; INVESTIGATING COMMITTEE, page 173; SEPARATION OF POWERS, page 28; *United States v. Nixon,* page 217.

Significance Executive privilege in the American system is claimed as an inherent executive power under the constitutional separation of powers and on time-honored tradition. Although the right of the President to refuse to appear before congressional committees is generally unchallenged, the issue remains as to whether his major advisers should enjoy the same privilege. The right of Congress to obtain information for the lawmaking process and to investigate for possible impeachment actions, and the right of the courts to hear and decide cases involving executive officials, clash with the President's right to function as the head of a coordinate branch of the national government. Critics charge that executive privilege is often invoked to deny the American people information critical of executive policies, as in the case of the disclosures of executive actions revealed in the Pentagon Papers in 1971, which detailed the history of American involvement in the Vietnam War, and in congressional investigations of executive misconduct in the Watergate affairs.

Item Veto   The power exercised by the governor in all but a few states to veto sections or items of an appropriation bill while signing the remainder of the bill into law. Governors in several states can reduce appropriation items and in a few states may veto sections of nonfinancial bills. The legislature may override the vetoed items. The President does not exercise the item veto power. *See also* RIDER, page 184; VETO, page 212.

Significance It is often suggested that the item veto power be given to the President. Many constitutional amendments to this effect have been introduced into the House and Senate, but none has passed. Congress might delegate a limited item veto to the President by inserting such a provision into each appropriation bill. The item veto power is consistent with growing executive responsibility in fiscal affairs. With it, the executive is able to curtail riders, reduce pork barrel legislation, and generally fight legislative extravagance. Those who oppose the item veto regard it as a serious impairment of legislative authority and an unwarranted increase in executive powers. The Nixon Administration used an "item veto" type power at the budget execution stage in impounding money appropriated by Congress for specific programs, but Congress and the courts have reduced the President's impoundment powers.

Kitchen Cabinet   An informal group of close friends and personal advisers to the President. Members of a Kitchen Cabinet may supplement or substantially replace the formal Cabinet as the President's chief source of advice on domestic and foreign policies. The Kitchen Cabinet may, however, include several members of the formal Cabinet. *See also* CABINET, page 200.

Significance The term "Kitchen Cabinet" originated during the presidency of Andrew Jackson. President Jackson was strongly influenced by the advice of a group of close friends who met with him, sometimes in the kitchen of the White House. Often, he preferred their views to those of his formal Cabinet. Most presidents, like Jackson, have placed primary reliance on the advice secured from such relationships, leading frequently to subdued outrage on the part of Cabinet members whose advice is not sought or heeded. President Richard M. Nixon, for example, often undercut his Secretary of State, William Rogers, by seeking his most critical advice on major foreign policy matters from presidential assistant, Henry Kissinger, who later replaced Rogers as Secretary of State.

Minority President   An elected President who has received less than 50 percent of the total *popular* votes cast for all candidates, although obtaining a majority of the *electoral* votes. A winning candidate is most likely to be a minority president when there are several fairly strong minor party candidates in the presidential contest. *See also* ELECTORAL COLLEGE, page 119.

Significance   Although the Constitution does not recognize such a status, many American presidents have been "minority presidents," including Abraham Lincoln, Woodrow Wilson, Harry Truman, John F. Kennedy, and Richard M. Nixon. Two presidents, Rutherford B. Hayes in 1876 and Benjamin Harrison in 1888 won election, even though in each case their major opponent polled more popular votes than they. So long as more than two candidates run for the office and so long as the Electoral College continues to operate, there will always be the possibility of electing a minority president.

Pardon   An executive grant of a release from the punishment or legal consequences of a crime before or after conviction. The President exercises the complete pardoning power for federal offenses except for convictions in impeachment cases. An "absolute pardon" restores the individual to the position he enjoyed prior to his conviction for commission of a crime. A "conditional pardon" requires that certain obligations be met before the pardon becomes effective. Pardons are administered for the President by the Office of the Pardon Attorney in the Department of Justice. Thirty states entrust the governor with the full authority for granting pardons. In the remainder, the governor typically shares the power with a pardon board or with the state senate. Pardons are granted usually to provide a remedy for mistakes made in convictions or to release offenders who have been properly rehabilitated. The President and most state governors also have the power to grant *reprieves,* which postpone the execution of a sentence for humanitarian reasons or to await new evidence. *See also* AMNESTY, page 199; *Ex parte Grossman,* page 216.

Significance   The President's pardoning power extends to all offenses against the United States, including contempt of Congress or of a federal court (*Ex parte Grossman,* 267 U.S. 87 [1925]). Most governors regard the pardoning power as among their most bothersome and distasteful tasks. Relatives and friends of offenders besiege governors with applications and pressures for pardons. The trend in the states is toward vesting greater responsibility in recommending or deciding pardons in full-time boards staffed by correctional experts. One of the most controversial presidential pardons in American history was that extended by President Gerald R. Ford to former President Richard M. Nixon. In that case, President Ford granted a blanket pardon for any crimes that Nixon may have committed during his years in office. The pardon was granted before any specific charges had been made. In a 1974 decision, the Supreme Court held that the President's power to pardon comes directly from the Constitution, and limitations, if any, must also be found in the Constitution (*Schick v. Reed,* 419 U.S. 256 [1974]).

Pocket Veto   A special veto power exercised at the end of a legislative session whereby bills not signed by a chief executive die after a specified time. Under the Constitution, if the President holds a bill for ten days without signing or vetoing it, the bill becomes law if Congress is in session, and it is pocket vetoed if Congress adjourns during the ten days. In about one-third of the states, the governors exercise a similar pocket veto power if they do not approve the measure during a stated period after legislative adjournment. This period varies in these states from three to thirty days. *See also* VETO, page

Significance The pocket veto provides a chief executive with a major legislative power. Unlike the ordinary veto, which is merely suspensive in nature and can be overridden, the Pocket veto is absolute. A bill that is pocket vetoed can, of course, be reintroduced in the next legislative session as a new bill. Whereas the regular veto requires an explanation from the chief executive, the pocket veto does not, although presidents usually defend their position in Memorandums of Disapproval. Most significantly, the pocket veto is available at the crucial period at the end of the legislative session when large numbers of bills are enacted in a last minute legislative rush. In some states, it is the practice of the legislature to recess rather than adjourn when work is completed. It then reassembles briefly to adjourn officially after the pocket veto is no longer effective, thereby preventing its use by the governor.

President The chief executive of the United States and the key official in the American system of government. The Constitution in Article II vests the complete executive power in the President. The President is elected every four years through the Electoral College machinery, and is eligible under the Twenty-second Amendment for one additional term. His chief official advisers are found in the Executive Office of the President and in the Cabinet. Much of his help in reaching decisions comes from an unofficial and informal "Kitchen Cabinet" of close friends and advisers. The President exercises a broad array of powers, some provided by the Constitution, some based on custom and tradition, some delegated to him by Congress, and others that are simply inherent in the nature of his office. Foremost are those broad and largely undefined powers that he exercises in his role as chief of foreign policy. These include the leadership of the armed forces, the recognition of foreign states and governments, the conduct of diplomacy, the making of international agreements and treaties with the Senate's approval, the initiation of new foreign programs, and the providing of leadership for the United States and the free world. In his role of chief administrator, the President exercises broad appointing and removal powers, directs and supervises the operations of the executive branch, directs the formulation of the annual budget, and sees that the laws are faithfully executed. As chief legislator, the President initiates comprehensive legislative programs, delivers regular and special messages to Congress, summons Congress into special sessions, wields a broad veto power, and influences the course of much legislation in his relations with legislative leaders and by arousing public opinion to support his programs. As chief of his party, the President dispenses patronage, influences the direction and nature of party policies, provides leadership to his party's delegation in both houses of Congress, and generally influences and determines party actions and policies. In his role as chief of state, the President maintains relations with other nations and performs numerous ceremonial functions in the United States. The prestige of his office contributes much to the effectiveness of the President in his many roles. His easy access to the mass media of communication aids him in molding public opinion. His many sources of information keep him well-informed on the complex problems facing the nation. *See also* CHIEF LEGISLATOR, page 201; CHIEF OF STATE, page 201; ELECTORAL COLLEGE, page 119; PRESIDENTIAL ELECTION PROCESS, page 136; STEWARDSHIP THEORY, page 210; TAFTIAN OR CONTRACTUAL THEORY, page 211.

Significance The office of President has been shaped by the experiences of the various presidents who have held the office during American history. Much has depended upon the personalities of the individual presidents, their political, economic, and social philosophies, and their conceptions of the office itself. Often, the man and the office have been shaped by the temper of his time, quiet and peaceful or hectic and crisis-filled. Some presidents, such as William H. Taft and Calvin Coolidge, have viewed the presidency largely in terms of administration and law enforcement. Others, like Abraham Lincoln, Woodrow Wilson, and the two Roosevelts, have regarded the presidency as a position that allows and demands strong leadership and the exercise of broad, undefined powers, whenever they are necessary for the security and well-being of the country. The former group has been labeled as "weak," the latter as "strong," presidents. All indications are that the nation is moving in the direction of stronger executive leadership, toward what has often been called "presidential government."

President-Elect   The candidate selected by the Electoral College to be the next President. Following the November popular election, the winning candidate is unofficially called the "President-designate" until the electors are able to ratify the people's choice. Under the Twentieth Amendment, the President-elect is sworn into office at noon on the twentieth day of January, and if the President-elect fails to qualify at that time, the Vice President-elect then acts as President until a President qualifies. If the President-elect dies, the Vice President-elect is then sworn in as President. *See also* TWENTIETH AMENDMENT, page 211; TWENTY-FIFTH AMENDMENT, page 211.

Significance   The status of President-elect is an important one because it enables the new chief executive to prepare for his assumption of the duties and responsibilities of the office. From the November election until the inauguration on January 20, the President-elect may meet periodically with the outgoing President to be briefed on special continuing problems, especially those in the foreign affairs field. The President-elect may also begin unofficially to select his top appointees, prepare some of his legislative messages, study the new budget which he inherits, and make other preparatory efforts.

Presidential Succession   The order of eligibility for filling a vacancy in the office of President, as specified in the Constitution and statutes. The Constitution, in Article II, section 1, stipulates that "In case of the removal of the President from office, or of his death, resignation, or inability to discharge the powers and duties of the said office, the same shall devolve on the Vice-President. . . ." Congress is empowered by the same section of Article II to provide for the officer to act as President in case both the President and Vice President are unable to serve. Congress has from time to time provided by statute for the line of succession, with the present order based on the Presidential Succession Act of 1947. This law provides for succession after the Vice President by the Speaker of the House, President pro tempore of the Senate, and members of the Cabinet, with the Secretary of State first in line. Cabinet members serve only until a Speaker or President pro tempore is available. The Twentieth Amendment provides that the Vice President-elect shall become President if the President-elect is unable to assume office on inauguration day. In addition, the Twenty-fifty Amendment provides for the temporary succession of the Vice President to the presidency in cases of presidential disability and for the President to fill a vacancy in the Vice Presidency with the consent of Congress. *See also* TWENTIETH AMENDMENT, page 211; TWENTY-FIFTH AMENDMENT, page 211; VICE PRESIDENT, page 213.

Significance Nine vice presidents have succeeded to the office of President, eight as a result of the deaths of Presidents in American history, and one—Gerald R. Ford—who succeeded to the office following the resignation of a President. No President, however, has been removed, or been incapacitated to the extent of turning the office over to the Vice President. The question of disability arose on several occasions, but the Constitution made no provision for making such a determination other than for the disabled President to step down voluntarily. As a result of serious illnesses suffered by President Dwight Eisenhower, attempts were made to establish a statutory remedy to this problem, but to no avail. Following his second illness, Eisenhower entered into a pact in 1958 with Vice President Richard Nixon, which provided that the Vice President could determine presidential inability if the President were unable to communicate with the Vice President. Presidents John F. Kennedy and Lyndon B. Johnson entered into similar agreements with their vice presidents. The knotty problem of determining inability led to the adoption of the Twenty-fifth Amendment in 1967 which spells out procedures for determining presidential disability, that permits the Vice President to become acting President under certain conditions, and that provides for filling a vacancy in the office of the Vice President. The latter provision was first invoked in 1973 when Gerald R. Ford was appointed by President Richard M. Nixon to fill the vacancy created when Vice President Spiro T. Agnew resigned. Then, in 1974, when President Nixon resigned as a result of Watergate disclosures, President Ford again invoked the Twenty-fifth Amendment in appointing Nelson A. Rockefeller Vice President.

Ratification The approval by the President of the version of a treaty that has received Senate consent by a two-thirds vote. Ratification may involve the problem of whether a President will accept amendments and reservations to the treaty affixed by the Senate. Amendments would, and reservations might, entail reopening of negotiations with other signatory nations. *See also* ADVICE AND CONSENT, page 154; RATIFICATION, page 403.

Significance Ordinarily, presidential ratification of a treaty requires the exchange of ratification documents with other signatories to the treaty and an official proclamation putting the treaty into effect. When amendments or reservations are made by the Senate, the President must decide whether to try to gain their acceptance by the other parties to the treaty or to drop the matter which kills the treaty as far as the United States is concerned. In a classic case, President Woodrow Wilson refused to accept crippling amendments and reservations to the Versailles Treaty in 1919. The standoff between the President and the Senate resulted in the eventual defeat of the treaty and the refusal of the United States to join the League of Nations. The ratification power serves to enhance the President's role in foreign affairs by leaving the last word with him so far as American approval of treaties is concerned.

Recess Appointment An appointment of a federal official made by the President to fill a vacancy while the Senate is not in session. To prevent the President from postponing appointments until the Senate has adjourned, Congress has by statute prohibited the payment of salary to an officer appointed to fill a vacancy that existed but was not filled while the Senate was still in session. Recess appointments expire at the end of the next congressional session, unless the Senate has confirmed the appointed official by a majority vote. Most state constitutions provide for recess appointments by the governor. *See also* APPOINTMENT POWER, page 199; CONFIRMATION, page 199.

Significance Recess appointments have often been a matter of contention between the President and the Senate. The provision denying salary to an official who was given a recess appointment, although the position became vacant while the Senate was in session, is an obvious attempt to limit the President's use of recess appointments to circumvent the Senate's approval power. Presidents usually refrain from straining relations with the Senate by not giving recess appointments to highly controversial persons or to those previously rejected by the Senate. In the states, recess appointments may be more contentious because of the typical lack of harmony between governors and state senates, and because such appointments are often for long durations, owing to the sizable interims between legislative sessions.

Recognition The power exercised exclusively by the President to establish diplomatic relations with foreign states. Recognition powers are vested in the President by the Constitution, which grants him the power in Article II, section 2 to send and receive ambassadors. The President's recognition power applies to new states as well as new governments. *See also* RECOGNITION, page 403.

Significance The President's recognition power is particularly significant because it involves the ability to refuse to recognize a new state or government as well as to grant recognition. Thus, the act of accrediting foreign diplomats, perhaps intended to be a mere ceremonial function, has become a significant discretionary power in the day-to-day conduct of foreign relations. In deciding whether or not to recognize a new state or government, the President may be influenced by his advisers, by Congress, and by public opinion, but the final decision is his alone. Important recognition controversies in American history have involved the question of whether revolutionary regimes, or states created by conquest, should be recognized. In the case of Communist China, for example, the President has faced a dilemma: should he recognize the Communist regime and thereby strengthen its international standing or should he refuse it and hope thereby to weaken its diplomatic position? In 1974, President Richard M. Nixon straddled the issue by agreeing to a limited form of diplomatic exchange with the People's Republic of China, while continuing to recognize the Nationalist regime on Taiwan (Formosa). Also involved in such recognition controversies has been the question of whether the President considers it advantageous to maintain direct communication with, and observation of, the regime. Presidents have used their discretion in such cases, and no consistent American recognition policy has been developed.

Removal Power The authority of an executive official to dismiss appointed officials from office. Although the Constitution is silent on the subject, the President has always exercised the power to remove executive and administrative officials. As a general rule, all officials appointed by the President serve at his pleasure. Federal judges, however, have life tenure, on good behavior, while members of "independent commissions," and merit system employees can be removed only for cause. The removal power of state governors generally compares unfavorably with that of the President because of the number of elective officials and the sharing of the governor's removal power, in many states, with the state senate. *See also Humphrey's Executor [Rathbun] v. United States,* page 216; *Myers v. United States,* page 216; SEPARATION FROM SERVICE, page 230.

Significance The ability of the President to get the vast national administration to follow his leadership and direction depends to a considerable degree on his authority to dismiss those who disobey his orders, are unsympathetic toward his program, or neglect their duties. Unless the President can surround himself with loyal subordinates who will strive to carry out his program, the system of democratic accountability, focused in the President as the elected national executive official, breaks down. Congress has, on occasion, sought by statute to gain a share of the power to remove executive officials, but the matter was finally decided by the Supreme Court in favor of unrestricted presidential removal power (*Myers v. United States,* 272 U.S. 52 [1926]). This decision, however, was modified by the Supreme Court in holding that members of independent regulatory commissions can be dismissed by the President only for cause as specified by Congress (*Humphrey's Executor [Rathbun] v. United States,* 295 U.S. 602 [1935]). In the states, the recent trend has been toward strengthening and expanding the governors' removal powers, and increased removal authority has also been given to some mayors and city and county managers as well.

State of the Union Message   An annual message to Congress in which the President proposes his legislative program. It is based on the constitutional directive that the President "shall from time to time give to the Congress information of the state of the Union, and recommend to their consideration such measures as he shall judge necessary and expedient. . . ." (Art. II, sec. 3). Although the President may choose his time for the message, it has become customary to transmit it at the beginning of a legislative session. *See also* CHIEF LEGISLATOR, page 201.

Significance   The importance of the State of the Union message lies primarily in its placing the initiative for developing a broad, comprehensive legislative program in the hands of the President. At the opening of a new legislative session, members of Congress busy themselves with routine organizational matters and minor legislative proposals until the President presents them with his legislative program. In his message, the President discusses the major problems facing the nation and recommends statutory solutions. His message is followed up in subsequent months by scores of bills drawn up in the executive departments and introduced in Congress by "administration" congressmen. Presidents usually deliver their State of the Union messages in person. Radio and television have greatly increased the importance of these messages, and the President now speaks not only to Congress but also to the American people and, in a sense, to the world as well. It offers him an opportunity to dramatize his policies and objectives and to gain support for them by arousing public opinion.

Stewardship Theory   A view of presidential powers that holds that the President has not only the right but the duty to do anything needed to safeguard the nation and to protect the American people, unless such action is specifically forbidden by the Constitution. The stewardship theory is usually ascribed to Theodore Roosevelt, although other strong presidents, such as Abraham Lincoln, Woodrow Wilson, and Franklin Roosevelt, followed the basic principle on which the stewardship theory rests. *See also* EMERGENCY POWERS, page   ; TAFTIAN OR CONTRACTUAL THEORY, page 202.

Significance   The stewardship theory is one of several conceptions of the President's powers that has contributed to the shaping of that office. Strong presidents have often acted on the stewardship assumption without theorizing. The theory is closely related to, but is an expansion of, the doctrine of inherent powers. Many presidents have rejected the stewardship view and emphasized the contractual and limiting nature of our constitutional system.

Taftian or Contractual Theory   A view of presidential powers that holds that the President is limited by the specific grants of power authorized in the Constitution and by statute. Supporters of the contractual or Taftian theory, sometimes called "literalists," hold the view that no undefined residuum of power for the office of President exists, and that every executive power must be traced to some specific grant of power or reasonably implied from such a grant. The theory was argued explicitly by President William Howard Taft, who regarded it as the only approach compatible with the separation of powers-checks and balances system of American government. *See also* CONSTITUTIONAL CONSTRUCTION, page 24; MADISONIANISM, page 12; STEWARDSHIP THEORY, page 210.

Significance   The Taftian or contractual theory is one of several conceptions of the President's powers that has contributed to the shaping of that office. In addition to William Howard Taft, Presidents who followed the theory's basic guidelines include Rutherford B. Hayes, Chester A. Arthur, Warren G. Harding, and Calvin Coolidge. Their presidencies were largely periods of legislative dominance of the national government.

Twentieth Amendment   The "lame duck" Amendment to the Constitution, adopted in 1933, which changed the date for beginning the presidential and vice-presidential terms from March 4 to January 20, and that for beginning congressional terms from March 4 to January 3. Other provisions are: (1) if the President-elect dies before taking office, the Vice President-elect shall become President; (2) if a President-elect has not been chosen or fails to qualify by January 20, the Vice President-elect shall act as President until a President is chosen; (3) if neither qualifies, the Congress shall decide who shall act as President until a President or Vice President qualifies; and (4) if the election of the President and Vice President is thrown into the House and the Senate and a candidate dies, Congress shall determine by law what shall be done. *See also* PRESIDENT-ELECT, page 207; TWENTIETH AMENDMENT, page 190.

Significance   The Twentieth Amendment reduced the "lame-duck" period for the outgoing President. The change reflects a disposition to make the office more responsive to democratic influences and enables a newly elected President to proceed to develop his policies and programs with little delay. The provisions in the Amendment regarding the inability of the President-elect and Vice President-elect to serve are designed to close a gap in the original Constitution, which failed to provide for these eventualities.

Twenty-fifth Amendment   An amendment to the Constitution, adopted in 1967, that establishes procedures for filling vacancies in the two top executive offices, and makes provision for situations involving presidential disability. The Twenty-fifth Amendment specifically assigns to the President the power to fill a vacancy in the office of Vice President, with the approval of a majority of both houses of Congress. In case of presidential disability, the Amendment provides: (1) when the President believes that he is incapable of performing the duties of office, he informs the Congress in writing, and the Vice President thereupon serves as acting President until the President can resume his duties; (2) when the President is disabled and unable to communicate, the Vice President and a majority of the Cabinet declare that fact to Congress, and the Vice President then serves as acting President until the President recovers; and (3) when a dispute arises over whether the President is capable of discharging the powers and duties of his office, Congress by a two-thirds vote decides whether the Vice President should continue as acting President or the President should resume his office. *See also* PRESIDENTIAL SUCCESSION, page 207; VICE PRESIDENT, page 213.

Significance The Twenty-fifth Amendment continues the provision incorporated in the original Constitution for the succession of the Vice President to the presidency upon the death of the latter, but it also recognizes that other situations may arise that were not provided for. The problems of succession to the presidency and vice presidency were brought to the attention of the American public by such events as the sudden death of President Franklin D. Roosevelt, the serious illnesses suffered by President Dwight D. Eisenhower, and the assassination of President John F. Kennedy. The Twenty-fifth Amendment replaced the informal agreements that had been worked out between presidents and their vice presidents since President Eisenhower's first major illness. Amazingly, by 1975 the Twenty-fifth Amendment had already been used on three occasions. In the first case, it was used to fill the office of Vice President following the resignation of Spiro T. Agnew in 1973. Agnew's successor, Gerald R. Ford, assumed the presidency in 1974 following the resignation of President Richard M. Nixon. Then, President Ford appointed Nelson A. Rockefeller to be Vice President, and he was confirmed by Congress in 1974.

Twenty-second Amendment   An amendment to the Constitution, adopted in 1951, limiting presidential tenure to two terms for an individual. A Vice President who succeeds to the office may serve as long as ten years as President, provided he has not served more than two years of the uncompleted term of his predecessor. The incumbent President, Harry S Truman, was excluded from the limitations of the Amendment, but he chose not to run for a third term. *See also* PRESIDENT, page 206.

Significance The Twenty-second Amendment was proposed by the Republican-controlled Eightieth Congress in reaction to the four terms of Franklin Roosevelt. Roosevelt had shattered the strong "no-third-term" tradition started by George Washington and followed until 1940. The Amendment was also a reaction to the growth of executive power that had resulted from war and depression crises and reflected a yearning to return to the "normalcy" of congressional domination of weak presidents. Supporters of the Amendment defend it as a useful safeguard against the dangers of executive tyranny and self-perpetuation in power. Opponents argue that it tends to reduce further a second-term President's already weak position as political leader and exhibits a fundamental distrust of the democratic process.

Veto   A legislative power vested in a chief executive to return a bill unsigned to the legislative body with reasons for his objections. The Constitution provides that every bill that passes the House and the Senate must be sent to the President before it becomes law. When the President receives a bill, he may: (1) sign it, whereupon it becomes law; (2) not sign it, whereupon it becomes law after ten congressional working days; (3) veto it, and send it back to the house of its origin; or (4) not sign it, whereupon if Congress adjourns within ten days the bill is killed (pocket veto). The President vetoes a bill by writing "veto" (I forbid) across the face of the bill; he then sends it back to Congress with a message setting forth his objections. Congress may amend the bill according to the President's demands and then repass it, or it may reject the President's objection and override the veto by repassing the bill with a two-thirds roll-call vote in each house. Governors, too, exercise the veto power and, in all but a few states, may item veto individual parts of appropriation bills—a power denied to the President who must either veto or approve each appropriation bill in its entirety. In the states, the number of votes needed to override a gubernatorial veto varies from a simple majority in each house to a two-thirds vote of all members elected to the legislature. *See also* ITEM VETO, page 204; POCKET VETO, page 205.

Significance Presidents employed the veto power infrequently and with great caution until the post-Civil War administration of Andrew Johnson. Since 1865, the veto power has been used with increasing vigor by most presidents; Grover Cleveland with 414 regular and pocket vetoes, and Franklin Roosevelt, with 631, have been its most persistent users. The scope of the veto power has also expanded since 1865. The earlier view that the veto should be used to block unconstitutional or technically imperfect laws has been supplemented by its employment to express disapproval of any kind. Although the veto is merely suspensive in effect, few vetoes are overridden by Congress, since if one-third plus one of the members of *either* house support the President's view, the veto prevails. The *threat* of the veto can also be used effectively by a chief executive to shape and change legislation while it is still in the hands of the legislature.

Vice President The constitutional officer assigned to preside over the Senate and to assume the presidency in case of the death, resignation, removal, or disability of the President. The Vice President is elected on the same ballot with the President and, if no candidate receives a majority of the electoral vote, the Senate chooses the Vice President from the two candidates for that office with the highest number of electoral votes. Although President of the Senate, the Vice President is not considered to be a member, participating only informally, if at all, in its deliberations, and voting only when a tie occurs. *See also* PRESIDENTIAL SUCCESSION, page 207; TWENTY-FIFTH AMENDMENT, page 211; VICE PRESIDENT, page 191.

Significance During most of American history, the vice presidency has been regarded as an insignificant office and as a political graveyard to be avoided by promising politicians. The low repute of this potentially significant office perhaps resulted mainly from the method of selecting vice-presidential candidates—to balance the party ticket or to reward or appease party wings. Recent presidents have sought to make more effective use of their vice presidents as intermediaries between the President and Congress and as roving ambassadors of good will in foreign affairs. Vice Presidents customarily attend Cabinet meetings, and Presidents Eisenhower, Kennedy, Johnson, and Nixon assigned their Vice Presidents additional responsibilities in the executive branch. The trend is toward developing the office into an assistant presidency. Nine vice presidents have succeeded to the office of President, eight upon the death of the President, and one—Gerald R. Ford—when the President resigned, thereby leaving the office of Vice President vacant. In addition, seven vice presidents died in office and two (John C. Calhoun, 1832, and Spiro T. Agnew, 1973) resigned. The Twenty-fifth Amendment, adopted in 1967, permits the President with the consent of Congress to appoint a Vice President when the office is vacant, a process first used in 1973 when President Richard M. Nixon appointed Gerald R. Ford to complete Agnew's term. When President Nixon resigned in 1974, Ford assumed the presidency and appointed Nelson A. Rockefeller to fill the office of Vice President.

Watergate A number and variety of illegal acts perpetrated by high officials in the Nixon Administration, and subsequent "coverup" efforts, that led ultimately to the resignation of President Richard M. Nixon and the succession to the presidency of Vice President Gerald R. Ford. The term, Watergate, relates to the break-in by a group of seven men, under direct orders from the White House, of the Democratic national party headquarters located in the Watergate building complex in Washington, D.C. Other illegal acts included generically within the concept, Watergate, were bribery of high officials, illegal use of the CIA, FBI, and other government agencies for personal and partisan purposes, income tax fraud, establishment and use by the White House staff of an unofficial "plumbers group" for carrying on espionage against private citizens, the use of "dirty tricks" during the 1972 election campaign, illegal campaign contributions, and use of campaign contributions for personal purposes. *See also* CORRUPT PRACTICES ACTS, page 116; EXECUTIVE PRIVILEGE, page 203; FEDERAL ELECTION CAMPAIGN ACT OF 1974, page 151; *United States v. Nixon,* page 217.

Significance The crimes and scandals of the Nixon Administration collectively referred to as "Watergate" constituted the most extensive and serious violations of public trust of any administration in 200 years of American history. Corruption, bribe-taking, and income tax evasion charges led to the resignation of Vice President Spiro T. Agnew in 1973. Charges of coverup of criminal activities by subordinates, obstruction of justice, misuse of the CIA and FBI, and other charges led to the resignation of President Richard M. Nixon. In addition, many cabinet officers, presidential assistants, and other administration officials were convicted for various crimes and misdemeanors. Watergate revelations increased disharmony and disunity among the American people and produced a general suspicion of and distaste for politicians of both major parties. Yet, the American system as a government of laws, not men, along with the system of separation of powers-checks and balances, proved itself by toppling the two highest elective officials and bringing scores of others to justice. Public demands for more effective controls over political activity and corrupt practices in government led to the enactment of a spate of new laws. Watergate also produced a Supreme Court decision which for the first time limited the doctrine of executive privilege by holding that the privilege cannot be used to prohibit disclosure of criminal misconduct (*United States v. Nixon,* 418 U.S. 683 [1974]).

IMPORTANT AGENCIES

Domestic Council An advisory body to the President established in 1970 to formulate and coordinate national domestic policy recommendations. Members of the Domestic Council include the President, Vice President, Cabinet members whose duties are mainly domestic, an Executive Director who heads the Council's staff, and other officials the President requests to participate. The Domestic Council was intended to function in domestic policy development in a manner similar to the role of the National Security Council (NSC) in the foreign policy field. Its mission of recommending policy matters to the President in the formulation stage is balanced off by the role of the Office of Management and Budget (OMB) which gives the President help in the process of executing policy. *See also* EXECUTIVE OFFICE OF THE PRESIDENT, page 215; NATIONAL SECURITY COUNCIL, page 428; OFFICE OF MANAGEMENT AND BUDGET, page 299.

Significance The Domestic Council was created at the initiative of President Richard M. Nixon, who used the National Security Council as a model. Evidence indicates, however, that the Domestic Council has not yet begun to function as the domestic policy equivalent of the NSC. The intent of the 1970 reorganization plan—"to bring together under one roof many of the sources for developing domestic policy and designing specific programs"—implied a growing harmonization of domestic policies that has not yet occurred.

Executive Office of the President The top staff agencies that give the President help and advice in carrying out his major duties. President Franklin D. Roosevelt established the Executive Office by executive order under the Reorganization Act of 1939. The components of the Executive Office have changed over the years, and today the major staff agencies include the Office of Management and Budget, the White House Office, the National Security Council, the Council of Economic Advisers, the National Aeronautics and Space Council, the Office of Economic Opportunity, the Office of Emergency Preparedness, the Office of Science and Technology, the Domestic Council, and the Council on Environmental Quality. Special offices concerned with trade negotiations, telecommunications policy, international economic policy, consumer affairs, intergovernmental relations, and drug abuse prevention have also been established within the Executive Office of the President. *See also* SPECIFIC AGENCIES.

Significance The objective in the creation of the Executive Office was to provide the President with a "general staff" to give him the help needed to direct the far-flung activities of the executive branch. The President has been hampered, however, by the refusal of Congress to place some key agencies within the Executive Office, such as the Civil Service Commission and the General Accounting Office. All indications point to a growth in the importance of the Executive Office as the President's tasks become more extensive and complex and he is forced to place increasing dependence upon his staff. The White House Office, in particular, contains the close confidential advisers whom the President leans on for day-to-day operations of the executive branch.

Secret Service A law-enforcement division of the Treasury Department, which has full responsibility for protecting the life and security of the President and his family. The Secret Service also performs security functions concerned with treasury matters, and in 1970 it was assigned new responsibilities for protecting foreign dignitaries visiting the United States, and for guarding foreign embassies in Washington, D.C. *See also* DEPARTMENT OF THE TREASURY, page 298.

Significance Like the "G-men" of the FBI, the "T-men" of the Treasury Department are carefully selected, rigorously trained, and devoted to duty. Each year, Secret Service agents check out thousands of "crank" and threatening letters sent to the President and investigate numerous threats made against the life of the President or members of his family. Whenever the President travels at home or abroad, all security arrangements are handled by the Secret Service, with the cooperation of the police of the area or country that the President is visiting. Following the assassination of President John F. Kennedy and the Warren Commission Report on the assassination, the Secret Service force was increased, and closer cooperation with the FBI in safeguarding the President was undertaken.

IMPORTANT CASES

Ex parte Grossman, 267 U.S. 87 (1925): Upheld a pardon granted by the President to Grossman, who had been convicted of contempt of Court. It was alleged that the independence of the judiciary depends upon the authority of judges to try without jury individuals who violate court orders, and to sentence them for contempt of court free from interference by other departments of government. The Court rejected this argument and upheld the President, holding that he "can reprieve or pardon all offenses after their commission, either before trial, during trial or after trial, by individuals, or by classes, conditionally or absolutely, and this without modification or regulation by Congress." *See also* PARDON, page 205.

Significance The effect of the *Grossman* case was to extend the President's pardoning power to all federal cases regardless of which branch of government is involved. Only conviction of a public official through impeachment proceedings is beyond the President's pardoning power.

Humphrey's Executor [Rathbun] v. United States, 295 U.S. 602 (1935): Upheld the provisions of the Federal Trade Commission Act providing that members of the Commission may be removed from office only for causes specified in the Act. President Roosevelt had removed Humphrey for political reasons, and in this case, decided after Humphrey's death, the Court held that Congress clearly had the authority to limit the President's removal power to instances of "inefficiency, neglect of duty, or malfeasance in office." The Court pointed out that the broad removal powers accorded to the President in *Myers v. United States,* 272 U.S. 52 (1926), pertained only to purely executive officers, whereas members of the Federal Trade Commission exercise legislative and judicial powers as well. *See also Myers* case, page 216; REMOVAL POWER, page 209.

Significance The *Humphrey* case emphasized the distinction between independent regulatory commissions, such as the FPC, the FTC, the SEC, and the ICC, and agencies of the executive branch. The Court, in recognizing the validity of statutory requirements for tenure of commissioners, cited the character of their work, the need to develop expertness through experience, the legislative intention to keep them free from political domination or control, and the threefold nature of their duties—administrative, quasi-legislative, and quasi-judicial.

Mississippi v. Johnson, 4 Wallace 475 (1867): Rejected an attempt by the State of Mississippi to enjoin President Andrew Johnson from enforcing the Reconstruction Acts of 1867. The Court held that the President cannot be restrained by injunction from carrying out his official duties of a political nature, such as the enforcement of an act of Congress. *See also* INJUNCTION, page 251.

Significance The decision enhanced the position of the President under the separation of powers by freeing him from judicial interference with his law-enforcement duties. Laws alleged to be unconstitutional may be struck down by the courts only after the President has begun to enforce them.

Myers v. United States, 272 U.S. 52 (1926): Upheld the President's removal from office of a postmaster without securing the approval of the Senate to the removal. The Court held that Congress cannot limit the President's power to remove executive officials, and the provisions of the Tenure of Office Act of 1876 requiring the Senate's concurrence in presidential removals was held to be unconstitutional. *See also Humphrey's* case, page 216.

Significance The *Myers* case, with the Court's majority speaking through Chief Justice (former President) William H. Taft, asserted a broad presidential removal power that had been in some doubt during much of American history. In *Humphrey's Executor [Rathbun] v. United States,* 295 U.S. 602 (1935), however, the Court upheld the power of Congress to limit the President's authority to remove members of the independent regulatory commissions.

United States v. Nixon, 418 U.S. 683 (1974): Held that the President's claim of executive privilege to preserve the confidentiality of his conversations with members of his staff or others cannot justify withholding of information bearing on a pending criminal trial. The case grew out of a refusal by President Richard M. Nixon to release tape recordings and documents involving conversations relating to the trials of his former aides for Watergate offenses. The Court rejected claims that either the doctrine of the separation of powers or the need for confidentiality—in the absence of a legitimate claim of national security interests—could sustain an absolute privilege of immunity from judicial process. *See also* EXECUTIVE PRIVILEGE, page 203; *Marbury v. Madison,* page 270; PRIVILEGED COMMUNICATION, page 259; WATERGATE, page 214.

Significance The *Nixon* case was the first court test of the scope of executive privilege. The Supreme Court acknowledged the importance of executive privilege as a means of protecting the public interest in candid expression of opinion in the process of presidential decision making, and as a vital ingredient of the separation of powers doctrine. Nevertheless, the Court insisted that the claim of executive privilege must yield to the nation's commitment to the rule of law so that the integrity of the judicial process and the criminal justice system would be preserved.

Youngstown Sheet and Tube Co. v. Sawyer, 343 U.S. 579 (1952): Struck down the President's Executive Order that had authorized seizure of steel mills and their operation by the national government. President Harry S Truman acted under his inherent power as chief executive and commander in chief to safeguard the nation's security during the Korean war, when a strike in the steel mills threatened the supply of weapons. The Court held that the President has no authority under the Constitution to seize private property unless Congress authorizes the seizure, and that the Constitution does not permit the President to legislate. *See also* EMERGENCY POWERS, page 202; INHERENT POWERS, page 393; WAR POWERS, page 426.

Significance The immediate result of the *Youngstown* case was the return of the steel mills by the government to their private owners and the resumption of the strike by the United Steelworkers Union. More fundamentally, the case established for the first time that limits exist in the exercise of the President's inherent powers in seeking to safeguard the security of the nation. It reaffirmed the inviolability of private property rights under the Fifth Amendment, and that only Congress can exercise legislative powers.

9 Public Administration:
Organization and Personnel

Administration The procedure by which laws are enforced and public policy is carried out. *Public* administration, as distinguished from *private* or *business* administration, is largely the function of the executive branch of government. It carries out the policies established by the legislative branch subject to the oversight and review of both the legislative and judicial branches. Administration is the art or science of managing public affairs with emphasis on such factors as organization, personnel, and finance.

Significance All organizations are faced with the problem of efficient administration. Public administration, however, is increasingly complex because of the tremendous range of responsibilities that modern government has undertaken, the need for organizing and directing millions of employees, and the problem of controlling the expenditure of billions of dollars. The traditional view that administration and policy formation are separate has given way to recognition of the policy-making aspects inherent in administration. This recognition is buttressed by the assignment of rule making and adjudicating functions to many agencies. In recent years, much scholarly attention has been paid to developing sound principles and practices of administration in order to ensure the responsibility and accountability of administrative personnel to the people.

Administrative Order A directive, issued by an administrative agency, that has the force of law. An order is generally distinguished from a "rule" or "regulation" in that an order is specifically directed to an individual or group to correct infractions of a rule. An example would be an order of the National Labor Relations Board to a union or an employer to cease violation of a labor practice that the Board had declared to be unfair. Orders are issued after a hearing conducted by the agency which resembles the procedures of a court of law. Appeals may be brought to the regular courts. Orders of federal agencies are published in the *Federal Register*. *See also* ADMINISTRATIVE PROCEDURE ACT, page 234; CEASE AND DESIST ORDER, page 221; HEARING EXAMINER, page 225; *Opp* case, page 233.

Significance Administrative orders are part of the overall development of the administrative process. Legislative bodies have vested control over complex economic and social problems in various administrative agencies that have been granted broad powers to prescribe rules and regulations and to enforce these rules through orders. In this way, the legislature is saved the impossible job of determining in advance all the aspects of complex matters, and the courts are freed from deciding disputes over technical subjects in which they lack competence. The administrative agency can develop the necessary expertness to handle specialized cases. An increasing number of businesses and individuals are subject to administrative orders.

Administrative Reorganization   The reform of administrative agencies and procedures to improve efficiency, economy, and responsibility. Reorganization movements have generally had as their major purposes the concentration of authority and accountability by: (1) integrating agencies with similar functions to eliminate overlapping and waste; (2) fixing responsibility in some hierarchical arrangement; (3) establishing advisory and centralized housekeeping agencies to aid the chief administrator; (4) eliminating multiheaded boards or commissions and elective officers engaged in purely administrative work; and (5) improving personnel, budget, and auditing procedures. *See also* REORGANIZATION ACT, page 235.

Significance The twentieth century has witnessed increased interest and activity in administrative reorganization at all levels of American government. It has resulted in increased authority for the President, governors, and mayors, the shortening of the ballot, and the adoption of the council-manager plan at the municipal level. Official reorganization studies are continuously carried on, and the President and some governors have been given authority to reshuffle agencies. Budgetary and personnel practices have been improved. Reorganization movements frequently meet resistance from legislatures that fear executive power, from interest groups that seek to protect the position of agencies serving them, and from agency personnel who fear loss of status.

Auxiliary Agency A governmental unit that services other governmental agencies. Typical auxiliary agencies include central purchasing, personnel, and accounting. They perform what is sometimes called housekeeping or technical services. *See also* CIVIL SERVICE COMMISSION, page 232; GENERAL SERVICES ADMINISTRATION, page 233.

Significance Auxiliary agencies not only provide a centralized and less expensive means of dispensing technical services, but they also give the department head or the chief executive an important control mechanism. For example, while it is possible for each agency to do its own hiring or purchasing, improved administration generally results from the assignment of such functions to centralized auxiliary units.

Board A group of persons, usually three or more, who are charged with responsibility for directing a particular governmental function. The term "commission" is frequently used interchangeably with board.

Significance Multiheaded versus singleheaded directorship is one of the most controversial problems of administrative organization. Both forms are found at all levels of government. It is generally agreed that a board is more desirable than one head when the agency has quasi-legislative and quasi-judicial functions, particularly in the area of regulation of the economy. A board permits the use of bipartisan personnel for controversial matters and, where terms of board members overlap, continuity of policy. A board makes it difficult, however, to fix responsibility, and conflict may develop within the board itself. A single head makes for well-defined responsibility and unity of purpose. Administrative experts recommend the single director for purely administrative tasks, but boards or commissions are frequently used for this purpose. A compromise proposal that has found favor is to retain plural bodies for regulatory and adjudicatory functions, but to assign administrative responsibility to the chairman of the board. This has been done, for example, in the Federal Trade Commission and the Civil Service Commission.

Bureau A major working unit of a department or agency. Bureaus are generally assigned specific functions and their heads are responsible to the head of the entire department. Well-known examples include the Federal Bureau of Investigation (FBI) in the Department of Justice and the Census Bureau in the Department of Commerce. Bureaus are usually subdivided into various divisions, branches, or sections, each with responsibility for specialized activities.

Significance While the nomenclature assigned to various parts of an agency is not uniform, it is considered useful for the development of scientific principles of administrative organization. The Hoover Commission, which studied the organization of the federal executive branch, and the "little Hoover commissions" in the states, suggested a standard nomenclature for all administrative units. In this way, responsibility is more clearly fixed within a major department, and persons working within a department better understand their roles.

Bureaucracy Any administrative system, especially of governmental agencies, that carries out policy on a day-to-day basis, that uses standardized procedures, and that is based on a specialization of duties. Bureaucracy also connotes a system wherein excessive growth of administrative agencies is accompanied by concentration of power in administrative officials, excessive red tape, dedication to routine, and resistance to change. The term "the bureaucracy," is often used simply to designate the administrative or executive branch of government.

Significance All modern governments have extensive administrative units. The problem in a democracy is to keep governmental employees responsive to the law and to the elected representatives of the people. Safeguards against the development of irresponsible bureaucracy include congressional oversight of administrative agencies through investigations and the power of the purse, presidential direction of the administration, and judicial review of administrative actions. The increased growth and power of administrative agencies makes imperative strong control over their actions, lest administrative officials obstruct rather than further the policies established by the people's representatives.

Career Service A professionalized civil service wherein employment is based on merit, opportunity is afforded for advancement, and guarantees are provided against arbitrary dismissal. *See also* MERIT SYSTEM, page 228; PROFESSIONAL AND ADMINISTRATIVE CAREER EXAMINATION, page 229; ROGERS ACT, page 415.

Significance Employment by merit has made large inroads on the spoils system, with stress now placed on a career service that emphasizes the opportunity to spend a satisfying lifetime in government service and to reach positions of honor and prestige. In recent years, the national government and some states have attempted to recruit talented college graduates for governmental careers. In the federal civil service, major opportunities are made available to those college graduates who pass the Professional and Administrative Career Examination. The concept of a career service has also been successfully applied in the Foreign Service, which has its own personnel system.

Cease and Desist Order An administrative order directed to an individual, firm, or labor union to refrain from violating the law or the rules and regulations established by an administrative agency. *See also* ADMINISTRATIVE ORDER, page 218.

Significance The cease and desist order has become the major instrument of economic regulation through administrative agencies. The power was first given to the Interstate Commerce Commission and subsequently to most independent regulatory commissions, state and national. Violation of a cease and desist order may result in prosecution or in the loss of benefits that the agency administers, such as a license to do business. Orders are issued after a hearing by the agency, with appeal to the courts possible.

Centralized Purchasing Vesting authority in one agency to purchase and handle supplies and materials for governmental agencies. This is now done for the national government by the General Services Administration, and the practice has been adopted by most states and many local units of government. *See also* GENERAL SERVICES ADMINISTRATION, page 233.

Significance Centralized purchasing has replaced the system whereby each department or agency purchases its own supplies. The advantages include savings through large purchases, standardization of equipment and record keeping, reduction of possibilities of corruption, and centralization of responsibility. The major disadvantage is that standardized purchases may not meet specialized needs of specific agencies, but this problem can be solved by mutual arrangements or by exempting certain items from central purchase.

Certification of Eligibles The practice by which a civil service commission provides a hiring officer of an agency with the names of persons who have qualified for a position. This is usually done in accordance with the ranking of individuals on test scores. The practice in most jurisdictions is to certify the top three names, often called the "rule of three."

Significance Certification is the initial step in the hiring process. The rule of three is designed to give the hiring officer a chance to weigh intangible factors, such as personality, in making a final decision. In some jurisdictions, only the name at the top of the list may be certified, while in others, five or more are required. Personnel experts differ over what constitutes the best practice. Certification rules may be further complicated by limiting certain positions to veterans or by the availability of two or more suitable lists from which a position might be filled. A person whose name is certified but is not selected is returned to the eligible list.

Civil Service A collective term for most persons employed by government who are not members of the military services. It is more generally understood to apply to all those who gain governmental employment through a merit system, more correctly called the "classified civil service." Elective officials and high ranking policy-making officers who are appointed by elected officials, and members of the judiciary are not considered civil servants. *See also* MERIT SYSTEM, page 228.

Significance The civil service has gained prestige in recent years. The merit system in particular has made substantial headway in the national government and in some states and cities. Most county and township governments, however, still retain the spoils system. Marked interest has arisen in professionalizing civil service employment and in applying sound principles of personnel management. In the United States, civil servants are restricted in the scope of their political activities and, though permitted to join labor organizations, may not strike. One of the essential ingredients of modern civil service is the loyalty of the civil servants to whatever administration is in power.

Classified Service Positions of governmental employment that are under the jurisdiction of a civil service commission and that are filled by merit. Congress has permitted some agencies to establish their own personnel systems outside the classified service, such as the Foreign Service, TVA, FBI, and CIA. *See also* GENERAL SCHEDULE, page 224; MERIT SYSTEM, page 228.

Significance It is generally left to the Civil Service Commission to determine which classified positions will be filled by competitive exam and which by noncompetitive exam, or which are exempt from examination. The latter categories include technical or top-ranking positions and positions for which there is no suitable examination procedure, such as laborers or part-time employees. Under federal law, the President may exempt certain positions from the classified service. This includes top-ranking administrators as well as persons holding confidential or highly technical positions. In the states, exemptions may be determined by statute or by a civil service agency. Agencies outside the regular classified service have specialized personnel needs but still use a merit system.

Clientele Agency A governmental unit organized to serve or regulate a social or economic group. While all agencies have some characteristic of this sort, a clientele agency's function is specifically directed toward its client's interests. Examples include the Department of Labor, the Veterans Administration, and the Bureau of Indian Affairs in the Department of the Interior. *See also* ORGANIZATION, page 228.

Significance A clientele agency constitutes recognition by the government of the importance of a group, its need for governmental attention, and assurance that funds will be provided to carry on programs of interest to clients. When the clients approve of the agency, they will resist efforts at reorganization or any other changes that may diminish the power or visibility of the agency. If the clients disapprove, they will act either to abolish the agency or to secure a change in personnel more closely identified with their interests; this can be particularly troublesome when the function of the agency is to regulate the client.

Decentralization An administrative concept applied by large organizations or departments in assigning decision-making responsibility to subunits on a geographical or subject-matter basis. Decentralization usually takes the form of field-service operations or division of tasks through specialization. *See also* FIELD SERVICE, page 224.

Significance It is impossible for the head of a large department to make every decision concerning the operations or services of a particular agency. Decentralization encourages responsible participation by lesser officials and permits adaptation to local needs. Major policy decisions, however, should be made by top officials.

Delegation of Authority The assignment of decision-making responsibility to subordinate officials. The heads of large agencies find it essential to delegate some of their authority to others, but this must be done within clearly defined standards, subject to review by the head. *See also* HIERARCHY, page 226.

Significance In establishing a public agency, Congress often assigns a wide range of power to the agency head. He, in turn, must delegate some of his authority if he is to maintain adequate control over the agency and not have to handle every detail alone. Successful administration requires that delegations of authority be made ungrudgingly and that authority be commensurate with responsibility. Many top officials overburden themselves out of fear of losing power or fear that others will make the wrong decisions. Proper delegation of authority, under standards of policy established at the top, enables the settlement of many matters at lower levels of the administrative hierarchy. Personnel and administrative experts point out that departmental morale is improved by delegation of authority, through giving others a sense of participation.

Department A major administrative unit with responsibility for the conduct of a broad area of government operations. In the national government, the departments are headed by officers who comprise the President's Cabinet. These departments include State; Treasury; Defense; Justice; Commerce; Labor; Agriculture; Interior; Health, Education, and Welfare; Housing and Urban Development; and Transportation. State and local governments also departmentalize major functions. Departments are generally subdivided into bureaus, divisions, sections, and other units. (For specific departments, *see* Index.)

Significance Most of the work of government is conducted through major departments. Departmental status generally indicates a permanent interest on the part of the government to promote a particular function. The Departments of the Army, Navy, and Air Force retain the title but have been incorporated into the Department of Defense. A number of major functions are vested in agencies outside the regular departments, such as independent regulatory commissions and corporations, in order to remove them from direct presidential supervision. Many administrative authorities feel that all functions should be assigned to one of the major departments to prevent diffusion of responsibility.

Ex Officio A Latin term for "by virtue of office." Many persons hold a position on a board or agency by virtue of their holding some other related position. For example, a governor, typically, is a member of numerous state boards and commissions by virtue of his position as governor.

Significance The ex officio principle is designed to involve important officials in the decisions of major agencies. It serves to coordinate the efforts of related agencies and to strengthen responsibility.

Federal Register A United States Government publication initiated by the Federal Register Act of 1935, which requires that presidential proclamations, reorganization plans, and executive orders be published. The Administrative Procedure Act of 1946 requires every public agency to publish a statement of its organization, authority, methods of operation, and statements of general policy in the *Federal Register*. Notice of proposed rules and regulations and administrative orders resulting from the adjudicatory functions of the agency must also be published. The *Federal Register* is published five times each week. The documents are codified in the *Code of Federal Regulations* (CFR). Some states have similar publications.

Significance The increasing growth of executive orders and administrative rules and regulations makes the *Federal Register* one of the most important and widely read government publications. Prior to its publication, the citizen and business interests in particular had no way of knowing what and how new rules applied to them. Publication of proposed rules and regulations assures interested parties an opportunity to be heard prior to their enforcement.

Field Service Decentralized administration typified by local or regional branch offices of a federal or state agency. Operations, personnel, and finance are under the control of the central office in Washington, D.C., or the state capital.

Significance Most governmental work is conducted through field offices. Only about 10 percent of federal employees work in Washington, D.C.; the remaining 90 percent are assigned to field-service offices around the nation and abroad. Field-headquarters relationships pose a continuing problem for sound administration in securing coordination of activity and responsibility. Field offices provide the citizen with close-to-home services and make possible the settlement of most problems where they arise.

Functional Consolidation Combining several administrative units that do related work into one major department. *See also* ADMINISTRATIVE REORGANIZATION, page 219; FUNCTIONAL CONSOLIDATION, page 443.

Significance Functional consolidation is a basic principle of administrative organization. The tendency of legislative bodies to create new agencies to meet new problems results often in diffusion of responsibility and the existence of too many agencies for the chief executive to direct and control effectively. Administrative experts suggest that, on the state level, all agencies should be consolidated into from ten to twenty departments. Both the New Jersey Constitution of 1947 and the Michigan Constitution of 1963 place a limitation of twenty departments in the executive branch. The Hoover Commission suggested, in 1949, that some 1800 federal agencies could logically be consolidated into twenty-two major departments. President Nixon proposed combining seven major departments into four based on general mission, such as natural resources.

General Schedule (GS) The designation of rank and salary in the classified civil service. Ranks range from GS 1 to GS 18 and salaries from about $5,000 to $36,000 per year. Clerical and subprofessional grades are those under GS 5. College graduates usually begin at GS 5 or 7 and those with graduate degrees or extensive experience at GS 7, 9, or 11; salaries for these categories range from $8,000 to $15,000. Agency management personnel ordinarily are at GS 13 to 15 with top-level civil servants at the "supergrades" GS 16 to 18. Each step in the General Schedule has pay rates established by law as well as annual increments. *See also* CLASSIFIED SERVICE, page 222; POSITION CLASSIFICATION, page 228.

Significance The General Schedule is in keeping with the principles of position classification in which jobs are classified according to required skills and duties rather than individuals, and an attempt made to provide equal pay for similar work. Civil service career opportunities and pay scales are competitive with private enterprise and the General Schedule is intended to preserve that situation so that government can recruit and retain competent people.

Government Corporation An agency of government that administers a business enterprise. The corporation form is used when an activity is primarily commercial in nature, produces revenue for its continued existence, and requires greater flexibility than Congress normally permits regular departments. Corporations are used at the national level for such enterprises as electric power distribution (Tennessee Valley Authority), insuring of bank deposits (Federal Deposit Insurance Corporation), and mail service (United States Postal Service). At the state level, corporations (often called "authorities") operate airports, turnpikes, and harbors, the best known being the Port of New York Authority.

Significance The corporation device enables government to operate diverse business services with flexibility similar to private enterprise. Prior to 1945, Congress permitted corporations a great degree of independence, but the Government Corporation Control Act of 1945 subjects them to budgetary and auditing controls and to civil service laws. Corporations are generally run by a board of directors and many are attached to one of the major departments for administrative purposes. The problem of how to balance a corporation's need for flexibility with the democratic requirements of legislative and executive controls remains.

Hearing Adjudication by an administrative or regulatory agency of alleged violations of laws or of rules and regulations administered by it. Hearings are also held to give interested parties an opportunity to be heard prior to the promulgation of a rule. *See also* HEARING, page 250; HEARING EXAMINER, page 225; QUASI-JUDICIAL, page 229.

Significance Hearings may be initiated by the agency itself or by any aggrieved party. They are conducted in a manner similar to, but less formal than, a court of law, under rules established by the Administrative Procedure Act of 1946. Decisions result in the issuance of administrative orders having the force of law. Appeals may be made to the courts, which generally limit themselves to a review of the overall fairness of the hearing and to whether the record substantiates the findings of the agency. The quasi-judicial power of agencies is one of the major administrative developments of the twentieth century. The requirement of a hearing prior to the promulgation of a rule permits parties likely to be affected by a rule to have a part in its formulation.

Hearing Examiner An official who conducts hearings for a regulatory agency and makes recommendations to the heads of the agency on issuance of administrative orders. Under the Administrative Procedure Act of 1946, hearing examiners (recently renamed "administrative law judges") are appointed under civil service rules, and are protected against arbitrary dismissal and loss of salary. *See also* ADMINISTRATIVE PROCEDURE ACT, page 234; QUASI-JUDICIAL, page 229.

Significance Hearing examiners were created in response to the pre-1946 concern that regulatory agencies were both prosecutor and judge of those accused of violating their rules. By giving a degree of independence to hearing examiners, Congress sought to overcome the major weaknesses of administrative adjudication of private rights. Decisions of hearing examiners are presented to the agency heads who may hear appeals from the examiner's recommendations. If no appeal is made from the examiner's recommendations, the decision is final.

Hierarchy A principle of administrative organization in which each person or office is under control of and responsible to the next highest level. In turn, the higher level is responsible to its superior for the conduct of those below. *See also* DECENTRALIZATION, page 222; DELEGATION OF AUTHORITY, page 223; UNITY OF COMMAND, page 231.

Significance All large organizations are arranged according to the principle of hierarchy. The military is the prototype of hierarchical organization. Students of administration recognize, however, that strict hierarchical organization is both inefficient and undesirable, particularly in a free society. Rigid hierarchy demands conformity, impersonality, and centralization of power rather than initiative, flexibility, and decentralization. Informal relations in any organization also tend to weaken strict hierarchical authority. Some contemporary critics of hierarchy urge a collegial or participatory model of organization. Yet, in order for responsibility to be fixed in a democratic society, the huge governmental bureaucracy must adhere to the general principle of hierarchy.

Hoover Commission A commission appointed in 1947 to study the organization of the executive branch. The group of twelve persons (four appointed by the President, four by the President pro tempore of the Senate, and four by the Speaker of the House), known as the Commission on Organization of the Executive Branch, was headed by former President Herbert Hoover. It filed its report in 1949. A second Hoover Commission, similarly appointed in 1953, was charged with the responsibility of suggesting which federal functions might be discontinued. *See also* REORGANIZATION ACT, page 235.

Significance The first Hoover Commission submitted a voluminous but highly regarded series of reports and made almost 300 specific recommendations, approximately 70 percent of which have been adopted. Basically, the Commission proposed greater consolidation of agencies, greater authority and assistance for the President, and improved budget, personnel, and administrative procedures. The Commission inspired the creation of "little Hoover commissions" in about half the states, many of which have met with some success. The second Hoover Commission's concern with policy matters rather than organization has limited the influence of its report.

Independent Agency A federal agency that is not part of the eleven executive departments. The term may include independent regulatory commissions, but is generally used to describe agencies which perform service rather than regulatory functions. Examples of independent agencies are the Civil Service Commission, the Veterans Administration, and the General Services Administration. Many independent agencies are organized like regular departments and are headed by persons responsible to the President.

Significance A large number of agencies have independent status. Some do not fit into any particular major department and others service all departments. In other cases, Congress has wanted to keep a tighter rein on an agency than departmental status would permit or has responded to the pressures of interest groups which seek autonomy for a given function. A few have been given independent status to shield them from partisan politics. Terms of officials frequently overlap to avoid control by any one President, and the removal power of the President may be limited. The existence of large numbers of independent agencies complicates the organizational pattern and lines of responsibility of the executive branch.

Independent Regulatory Commission An agency outside the major executive departments charged with the regulation of important aspects of the economy. The Commissions are the Interstate Commerce Commission, Federal Trade Commission, Federal Power Commission, Securities and Exchange Commission, Federal Communications Commission, National Labor Relations Board, Civil Aeronautics Board, Federal Reserve Board, Federal Maritime Commission, and Consumer Product Safety Commission. All of these agencies are empowered to establish rules for the particular industries they regulate and to prosecute violators. All are multi-headed, with five or seven members, except for the eleven-member Interstate Commerce Commission. (For specific commissions, *see* Index.)

Significance The independent regulatory commissions possess vast authority to determine individual and property rights. They have been established because of the sheer complexity of modern economic problems and the desirability of having agencies that could develop expertness and continuity of policy with regard to these problems. Neither Congress nor the courts have the talent or the time. The agencies are independent of the President in order that their legislative and adjudicatory functions are removed from partisan politics. Members of the commissions are appointed by the President with the Senate's consent, but may be removed only for cause. Terms of office are lengthy and overlapping in order to avoid dominance by the appointees of one President though turnover is quite frequent. No more than a majority of commissioners may be of one party. Problems arise from the tendency of commissions to become captives of the industries they are supposed to regulate, since many officials are necessarily drawn from the regulated industries. Further, the independence of the commissions may result in policies that are contrary to those of the party in power. These commissions have often been called "the headless fourth branch" of government, because of their peculiar place in the organization of the government and lack of continuing supervision from the President or Congress.

Line and Staff An administrative concept that categorizes the work of an agency as an operating or advisory function. The line carries out legislative programs and deals directly with the people. The executive departments such as Agriculture or Labor are typical line departments. The staff serves in an advisory capacity, aiding the chief executive and the line officials through such activities as planning, coordinating, and budgeting. The Office of Management and Budget is a major staff agency of the federal government. *See also* AUXILIARY AGENCY, page 219.

Significance The distinction between line and staff prescribes the division of labor in large organizations. The distinction is, however, by no means a precise one. Line officials may engage in staff or advisory work, as members of the Cabinet generally do, and some staff agencies may engage in operating tasks, as some budgeting or planning offices do.

Merit System   The selection, retention, and promotion of government employees on the basis of demonstrated fitness. Though the term is often used interchangeably with "civil service," the merit system emphasizes positive programs of sound personnel management rather than the mere placing of restraints upon the spoils system. *See also* CERTIFICATION OF ELIGIBLES, page 221; CIVIL SERVICE, page 221; CLASSIFIED SERVICE, page 222; VETERANS' PREFERENCE, page 223.

Significance   The merit system has not been universally adopted in the United States, particularly when viewed as a thoroughgoing personnel program. While much headway has been made at the national level, much remains to be done on the state and local levels, particularly in counties and townships. Originally, the concept of civil service was limited to keeping unfit persons out of government service. The merit system represents a more positive approach looking toward the development of a career service and toward in-service training, position classification, pay standardization, and retirement programs. Obstacles to a complete merit system include the preference given to veterans in recruitment and the practice of permitting recruiting officers to choose from among several qualified people, as in the "rule of three."

Organization   The arrangement of persons for the most effective achievement of a purpose or objective. Public administration experts are concerned with the problem of the best way to organize the government or a particular agency to eliminate friction and to best accomplish the task assigned. This involves decisions as to the nature of line, staff, and auxiliary agencies, the location of responsibility, and the overall coordination of efforts. Activities may be organized according to major purpose (for example, the Department of Agriculture), process or skills (central purchasing), area (fire and police protection), or clientele (Veterans Administration). The use of a single head or a board is another concern of organization. *See also* ADMINISTRATIVE REORGANIZATION, page 219; CLIENTELE AGENCY, page 222; HIERARCHY, page 226.

Significance   Organizational concepts and techniques are mainly the concern of administrative specialists but are also important to all citizens who seek to understand the nature of administrative organization and problems of reorganization. All agencies contain all or some of the organizational patterns, and one is rarely used to the exclusion of others. Much depends on the purposes to be served and, in government in particular, on the desires and influence of legislative bodies and pressure groups.

Position Classification   The grouping of government employment positions on the basis of duties, responsibilities, and qualifications. A position is classified in accordance with the nature of the job rather than the person holding the position. *See also* GENERAL SCHEDULE, page 224; MERIT SYSTEM, page 228.

Significance   Position classification is regarded as an essential ingredient of a sound merit system. The benefits include: (1) simplification of recruitment and selection of personnel through administration of similar tests for similar positions; (2) equal pay for equal work, an important goal of public personnel administration and essential for high morale; (3) well-defined lines of responsibility for the individual worker and top management; and (4) clear avenues of promotion and transfer. The overall objective of position classification is equitable treatment of government employees, which benefits both the employee and the public. It is necessary, however, that classification schemes be reviewed from time to time, lest they act as a straitjacket on effective administration and optimum utilization of employees. Position classification is used in the national government and in several state and local governments.

Professional and Administrative Career Examination (PACE) An examination which serves as the principal means of entry into the federal civil service for college graduates and others with appropriate work experience. PACE includes a battery of written tests designed to measure abilities for a wide variety of jobs and seeks to identify persons with potential for advancement into responsible administrative and professional positions. Ratings are based on test scores and an evaluation of experience and education with extra credit given for outstanding scholarship.

   Significance Most positions filled through the Professional and Administrative Career Examination do not require experience in a specific field. PACE replaces the Federal Service Entrance Examination (FSEE) which had been criticized as being culturally biased against minority groups and unrelated to job performance. PACE measures a wide range of abilities and serves to place candidates according to relative importance of different measured abilities to different job categories. A separate management internship examination, available as an option for greater job opportunities, is also undergoing revision.

Quasi-judicial Powers exercised by administrative agencies that have the characteristics of a judicial act. Independent regulatory commissions, as well as other administrative agencies, exercise quasi-judicial powers when they conduct hearings and make decisions having the force of law. *See also* HEARING, page 225.

   Significance Under the doctrine of the separation of powers, only courts and judges may exercise judicial power. The highly technical nature of modern economic regulation has necessitated the delegation of "quasi-" (Latin for "seemingly" or "resembling") judicial power to expert administrators. For example, Congress has empowered the Federal Trade Commission to determine what constitutes an unfair trade practice. Concern over the inherent violation of the separation of powers led to the passage of the Administrative Procedure Act of 1946, which requires the use of hearing examiners and more judiciallike procedures, and expands the power of judicial review of administrative adjudications.

Quasi-legislative Rule-making powers, exercised by administrative agencies, that have the characteristics of a legislative act. Numerous administrative agencies are authorized to issue rules and regulations having the force of law. These include not only the independent regulatory commissions but a host of other agencies, such as the Department of Agriculture, which issues rules relative to crop quotas and other agricultural practices. *See also* ADMINISTRATIVE ORDER, page 218.

   Significance Under the doctrine of the separation of powers, all legislative power is vested in the legislative body. Congress and the state legislatures, however, cannot legislate in sufficient detail to cover the problems which arise in a complex society. Thus, the legislature delegates power to administrative agencies to "fill in the details" under the standards established by the legislature. The Administrative Procedure Act of 1946 requires administrative agencies to give notice and hold hearings on proposed rules and regulations and to publish all rules and regulations in the *Federal Register*. Congress retains a check on "quasi-" (Latin for "seemingly" or "resembling") legislation by being able to change the basic law of the agency. The courts, too, maintain a check over abuse of powers delegated to agencies. A substantial number of rules that govern the individual originate in administrative agencies rather than in the legislature.

Secretary   The title of most of the heads of the major executive departments in the national government and a few major state officials. *See also* CABINET, page 200; DEPARTMENT, page 223.

Significance   The secretaries of the executive departments are part of the President's Cabinet, and serve at the pleasure of the President. They are the legal and administrative heads of their departments and have broad powers over expenditures and personnel. Several have quasi-legislative and quasi-judicial powers. They set the tone with which a department operates and act as advisers to the President. Generally, they are chosen more for their political acumen and acceptability than for their training in the subject area of the department. State government secretaries may have similar powers and duties but are generally elected. The title is most commonly used in the states for the office of secretary of state.

Separation from Service   Termination of employment in the classified service. Separation may be voluntary, as by resignation, or may be the result of retirement laws, a reduction in force, or disciplinary action for conduct unbecoming a public employee. *See also* TENURE, page 231.

Significance   A public employee may resign at any time without prejudice. Liberal retirement allowances are provided for those who serve twenty years in the federal service. When a reduction in force is ordered because of a cut in appropriations or a lessened need for employees, as after a war or crisis period, due weight is given to such factors as seniority, performance, and veterans' preference. Dismissal from service is permitted "for such causes as will promote the efficiency of said service," and procedures are established by law. Contrary to popular assumption, civil servants may be, and are, dismissed without elaborate procedures. Basically, the head of an agency may hire and fire employees. In order to avoid dismissal for racial, religious, or political reasons, the department head must inform the employee in writing of the causes for his dismissal and give him an opportunity to respond. No hearings are held unless the employee is a veteran and appeals his case to the Civil Service Commission. Those in sensitive positions may also be discharged as "security risks" and all government employees are given security checks. Similar procedures are followed in many states, while, in others, more formal appeal procedures to a commission or court are in effect.

Span of Control   An administrative concept concerned with the number of agencies or subordinates that one person can supervise effectively. Experts have different opinions about what constitutes a manageable span of control, but most agree that no person can direct more than twenty agencies or persons.

Significance The President and almost all governors have too many agencies under their supervision. The same is true for many persons with top-level jobs in government. Most reorganization plans reduce the span of control by drawing many functions into as few departments as possible. In this way, a hierarchy of responsibility can be developed in which no supervisor has more than a few persons reporting directly to him.

Spoils System The award of government jobs to political supporters and friends. The term derives from the expression, "to the victor belongs the spoils." The spoils system is generally associated with President Andrew Jackson. *See also* PATRONAGE, page 131.

Significance The spoils system is usually defended on the grounds that it is essential for the maintenance of a party system, since people are not likely to work for a party without some reward, and that victorious candidates should have as employees those who are loyal to them and to their policies. President Jackson took the view that government work is so simple that anyone could handle it and that rotation in office is necessary and healthy for vigorous administration. Few people today consider government work simple, but many still support the principle of rotation in office, since civil service tenure may result in an administration having unsympathetic employees. Though the merit system has made large inroads on the spoils system, vestiges of the spoils system remain at the local governmental level and many federal jobs are still filled by patronage.

Tenure The right to hold a position or office free from arbitrary dismissal. Public employees in the classified service and teachers achieve tenure after serving a probationary period. *See also* SEPARATION FROM SERVICE, page 230.

Significance Tenure is essential to the operation of a merit system of employment. It encourages freedom of thought and action on the part of the employee and frees him from fear of dismissal for purely personal, political, or arbitrary reasons. Safeguards have been established by law to assure tenure for government employees who are in the classified service and for most public school teachers.

United States Government Organization Manual The official organization handbook of the three branches of the federal government. It lists all federal departments and agencies with detailed descriptions of their powers, duties, and activities. The *Manual* is published annually in July.

Significance The *Manual* is a useful resource for students of government and citizens generally. It includes major agencies of government, various units within the agencies, lists of governmental publications, and charts of the more complex agencies. A list of agencies that have been discontinued in recent years is also provided. Similar information about state agencies can be found in state manuals.

Unity of Command An administrative concept that no person should be subject to the orders of more than one superior. It is related to the idea of "chain of command," which is common to the military services. *See also* HIERARCHY, page 226.

Significance Unity of command is difficult to put into practice in the public service because of the variety of tasks that government undertakes and the large number of persons employed. The problem is most acute in areas of technical specialization, where a clash may occur between general administrators and the specialists. Informal chains of command may develop in an agency when subordinate individuals command more respect than the actual head. Government agencies also may be independent of the chief executive and more responsive to the legislature or a pressure group. To achieve unity of command, agencies with similar functions should be integrated, a hierarchical arrangement of responsibility established, and authority for final decisions vested in one individual to avoid irresponsibility and confusion.

Veterans' Preference Special consideration given to veterans in various aspects of the civil service. These include: (1) the addition of five points to the test scores of veterans, ten points to disabled veterans; (2) the waiver of age, physical, and education requirements in some instances; (3) the limitation of competition for some positions to veterans; (4) the provision for special rights with regard to layoffs and dismissals; and (5) the extension of veterans' preference to wives, widows, and mothers of disabled or deceased veterans. These preferences are provided by almost all civil service jurisdictions in the United States.

Significance Veterans' preference has resulted in filling a majority of civil service positions with veterans. These special considerations are based on the idea that the country owes a debt to the veteran, and veterans' preference is vigorously supported by veterans' interest groups. Yet, personnel experts view veterans' preference as a derogation of the merit principle and an obstacle to qualified nonveterans seeking a government career.

IMPORTANT AGENCIES

Civil Service Commission The central personnel agency of the national government, established in 1883. It is composed of three members appointed to six-year terms by the President with the Senate's consent. Its principal activities include the recruitment, examination, and preparation of eligible lists of prospective governmental employees. The Commission also administers a variety of laws pertaining to governmental employees with regard to veterans' preference, classification, security checks, political activity, retirement, insurance programs, and race and sex discrimination.

Significance The Civil Service Commission is largely concerned with providing leadership in federal personnel administration by establishing standards of good practice and stimulating improvements in personnel methods in the operating agencies. The Commission has ten regional offices in major cities. Day-to-day personnel matters are handled in individual departments and agencies, with the Commission playing policy-making and supervisory roles. Though conflicts often arise between the various governmental agencies and the Commission over personnel policies, the Commission has managed to maintain a strong, independent position in the executive branch. Civil service commissions are also found in most states and in many local units of government.

General Services Administration An independent agency established in 1949 to centralize purchasing and property and records management for the national government. The General Services Administration, headed by an Administrator appointed by the President with Senate approval, is assigned responsibility for the procurement, supply, and transportation of property and services for the executive agencies, the acquisition and management of federally owned or leased property, disposal of surplus property, and records management.

Significance The General Services Administration gathers under one agency a number of functions formerly performed by separate units. The Administration was created upon the suggestion of the Hoover Commission, which noted the need for centralized purchasing and property management in order to avoid waste and duplication in the worldwide operations of the national government. In addition to its service activities, the General Services Administration publishes the *Statutes at Large,* the *Federal Register,* and the *United States Government Organization Manual.*

IMPORTANT CASES

Opp Cotton Mills v. Administrator of Wage and Hour Division, 312 U.S. 126 (1941): Declared that the provisions of the Fair Labor Standards Act of 1938 authorizing an administrative determination of minimum wages in a particular industry do not constitute an unconstitutional delegation of legislative power. *See also* DELEGATION OF POWER, page 166.

Significance The *Opp* case was one of the last in a long series of cases that challenged the right of Congress to vest rule-making power in an administrative agency. The Court pointed out that, in a complex society, Congress could not be expected to fill in the details of all public policies. So long as a standard is established within which the administrative agency must operate, the delegation of authority is permissible. The Court noted further that the Constitution does not demand the impossible and Congress could not be expected to set every wage rate, railroad rate, or every other rule which a business must follow. The *Opp* case put an end to the delegation of power issue in American constitutional law.

Railroad Commission of Texas v. Rowan and Nichols Oil Co., 311 U.S. 570 (1941): Refused to overturn a ruling of the Railroad Commission relating to the amount of oil that could be taken from wells in Texas. The Court noted that the issue was too complex for judges to determine and that the Commission's order must stand in the absence of a showing that it was based on insubstantial evidence.

Significance In this case, as in numerous others challenging specific rulings of state and national administrative agencies, the Court has taken the view that administrative decisions stand if they are supported by "substantial evidence." Otherwise, the Court would be substituting its judgment for that of an expert administrative agency. Congress, in the Administrative Procedure

Act of 1946, has supported the Court's stand by providing that the scope of judicial review of administrative rulings be limited to determining relevant questions of law and by approving the substantial evidence rule. *See also* ADMINISTRATIVE ORDER, page 218.

United Public Workers v. Mitchell, 330 U.S. 75 (1947): Ruled that Congress may prohibit federal employees from participating in political activities. The Court upheld the Hatch Act of 1939, which authorizes the removal of a person from civil service employment for his taking an "active part in political management or political campaigns." The Court reaffirmed it ruling in 1973 in *United States Civil Service Commission v. National Association of Letter Carriers,* 413 U.S. 548.

Significance The Court found no invasion of the constitutional rights of public employees in the Hatch Act. In another case, the Court applied this ruling to state government employees working on projects financed by federal grants-in-aid (*Oklahoma v. United States Civil Service Commission,* 330 U.S. 127 [1947]; reaffirmed in *Broadrick v. Oklahoma,* 413 U.S. 601 [1973]). Critics of these rulings claim that they bar millions of persons from active participation in the democratic process. The Court, however, agreed with Congress that the Hatch Act contributes to the efficiency of the public service and prevents the growth of bureaucratic political machines. In the Federal Election Campaign Act of 1974, Congress removed Hatch Act restrictions on voluntary activities by state and local employees in federal campaigns if not otherwise prohibited by state law.

IMPORTANT STATUTES

Administrative Procedure Act of 1946 A major law governing the procedures of regulatory agencies and providing for standards of judicial review of administrative determinations. The Act requires that every agency publicize its operations, give advance notice of proposed rules, and permit persons to testify, to be accompanied by counsel, and to cross-examine witnesses. The Act provides further that the same official may not act as both prosecutor and judge and that persons may appeal decisions of these agencies to the courts. The courts are authorized to set aside any agency ruling that is arbitrary or unsupported by substantial evidence. *See also* HEARING, page 225.

Significance The Administrative Procedure Act was passed in response to growing criticism of the lack of procedural safeguards in administrative legislation and adjudication. Since so many private rights are now affected by administrative agencies, Congress sought to regulate the internal procedures by which rights are determined and to provide broad standards for judicial review.

Freedom of Information Act of 1966 An act requiring federal agencies to provide citizens access to public records upon request. Exemptions are permitted for national defense materials, confidential personnel and financial data, and law enforcement files. Persons denied access to requested materials may sue for disclosure, and a court may determine whether information is improperly classified and, therefore, improperly withheld.

Significance Public access to public information is essential if public servants are to be held accountable for their actions. While the necessity for confidentiality in some areas is recognized, early experience under the Act showed that too many things were classified as confidential and that requests for material were often met with bureaucratic delay and excessive charges. A 1974 amendment to the Act requires agencies to expedite release of information, facilitates citizen access to courts to compel disclosures, and empowers judges to determine the propriety of any exemptions.

Pendleton Act (Civil Service Act of 1883) This law, as amended over the years, forms the basis for the personnel policies of the national government. The law established the principle of employment on the basis of open, competitive examinations, and created a Civil Service Commission to administer the personnel service. The Pendleton Act extended the merit principle to only 10 percent of national employees, but later laws and executive orders have extended coverage to more than 90 percent of employees.

Significance The Pendleton Act was a direct result of the assassination of President James Garfield by a disappointed office seeker. The Act brought to a close the period of Jacksonian spoils which made governmental employment a reward for political activity. The Pendleton Act turned the tide in favor of employment by merit, which, despite occasional lapses, has spread to all levels of government.

Ramspeck Act (Civil Service Act of 1940) Authorizes the President to place, by executive order, nearly all federal positions under the civil service system. Exemptions include those positions filled by presidential appointment requiring the Senate's approval, and certain special agencies, such as the Tennessee Valley Authority and the Federal Bureau of Investigation, which have merit systems of their own.

Significance The Ramspeck Act is considered to be the culmination of the civil service reforms initiated in 1883 by the Pendleton Act. Presidents since 1940 have used this authority to broaden the coverage of the civil service laws. As a result, most national government positions are covered. At first, this power was used to "freeze" political appointees into their positions, but the net effect has been to strengthen civil service in the United States.

Reorganization Act of 1949 A grant of power to the President to reorganize the executive branch of the government. Plans for reorganization must be submitted to Congress, and either house may veto the proposal within sixty days. The Reorganization Act has been extended several times since 1949.

Significance A vast enterprise needs continuing reorganization to ensure efficiency of operation. The Reorganization Act places the initiative in the hands of the President who bears major responsibility for administration. The veto in the hands of Congress prevents any reshuffling that may threaten the status of any "pet" agencies of members of Congress or major pressure groups.

10 The Judicial Process:
Courts and Law Enforcement

Activism versus Self-restraint Two approaches to judicial decision making in the American political system. Activists hold that a judge should use his position to promote desirable social ends. Proponents of self-restraint counter that in deciding cases a judge should defer to the legislative and executive branches, which are politically responsible to the voters, and not indulge his personal philosophy. Both schools of thought recognize the policy-making nature of judicial decisions on major social questions, but they differ on how that power should be used.

Significance The activism versus self-restraint dichotomy is most clearly evidenced in the United States Supreme Court. This division underscores the policy-making role of the Supreme Court in its decisions on questions of broad policy that are framed in legal terms. Most observers take the view that judges cannot help but inject their personal views into decisions and that one is apt to accept or reject the Court's role, depending upon how it affects the outcome of particular cases. For example, during the New Deal period of the 1930s, liberals opposed the "activism" of the Court in striking down social welfare programs, whereas many of these same liberals today favor Court "activism" on behalf of civil rights.

Administrative Law That branch of law that creates administrative agencies, establishes their methods of procedure, and determines the scope of judicial review of agency practices and actions. The term also describes the rules and regulations made by administrative agencies. Administrative law deals with rate-making, operating rules, the rights of persons and companies regulated by administrative agencies, and the power of the courts to review. *See also* ADMINISTRATIVE PROCEDURE ACT, page 234.

Significance The widespread use of administrative agencies to regulate important aspects of economic and social life results in their producing a great flow of law governing individual conduct. Correspondingly, a body of law controlling operations of administrative agencies to assure fair procedures that protect the rights of persons affected by these operations has evolved. Increasingly, more people are affected by administrative rules than by legislative statutes.

Admiralty Jurisdiction Authority vested in federal courts to hear cases involving shipping and commerce on the high seas and on the navigable waters of the United States. It is a highly technical body of law based on tradition, congressional statutes, and international law. Typical cases involve maritime contracts, collisions, and crimes committed on vessels. *See also* JURISDICTION, page 253; NAVIGABLE WATERS, page 313.

Significance The federal courts have exclusive jurisdiction over admiralty and maritime cases as provided in Article III, section 2, of the Constitution. This assures maintenance of national supremacy over foreign and interstate commerce water routes.

Adversary System A concept underlying judicial procedure in the United States that assumes that from the contest of opposing views justice will emerge. Each side in a civil or criminal trial is expected to press its point of view with vigor and do all it can to refute the opposition's witnesses, evidence, and arguments.

Significance An adversary system of justice assumes that judges will act as passive arbiters of conflict and that the truth will emerge out of genuine controversies. Some critics argue that the result is to make a trial a contest between lawyers, and that judges are restrained from direct participation in resolution of disputes.

Advisory Opinion An opinion given by a court, though no actual case or controversy is before it, on the constitutionality or legal effect of a law. No advisory opinions are rendered by federal judges. A few states, however, do authorize the highest state court to give such opinions upon the request of the legislature or governor. An advisory opinion is not binding except in the state of Colorado.

Significance The advisory opinion avoids the confusion that might result from a declaration of unconstitutionality after a law has been in effect for a long period of time. Such an opinion serves as a guide to the legislature, particularly when a statute appears to break new ground, and to governors in deciding whether to sign or veto legislation. When rendering an advisory opinion, however, a court lacks the benefit of opposing arguments by adverse parties.

Amicus Curiae A legal term meaning "friend of the court." As *amicus curiae,* individuals or groups not parties to a lawsuit may aid or influence the court in reaching its decision. The court may at its discretion give permission to or request persons to appear as *amicus curiae.* Often a party will seek to appear as *amicus curiae* when the decision in the case will affect his rights as well as the rights of those directly involved. In some states, a friend of the court is permanently attached to a court to help it reach decisions in cases involving minors, divorce, or criminal offenders.

Significance Many lawsuits have implications reaching far beyond the interests of the litigants involved in the case. For example, in a case involving civil rights, several interest groups may seek permission to testify or file documents to demonstrate to the court the implications of the case. The federal government, acting through the Solicitor General, frequently exercises its right to appear as *amicus* before the Supreme Court on matters involving federal policies.

Appeal   Taking a case from a lower court to a higher tribunal by the losing party. The term also identifies those types of cases brought to the United States Supreme Court as a matter of right; these include cases from federal courts and highest state courts when state or federal laws are declared in conflict with the Constitution or a treaty. Such cases are brought to the Supreme Court "on appeal." An appeal is generally a complex and costly process. Simplified provisions are made for filing of appeals *in forma pauperis* by indigent appellants in criminal cases. *See also* APPELLATE JURISDICTION, page 238.

Significance   An ordinary appeal is designed to serve as a check upon any errors committed in lower tribunals. When the Supreme Court reviews cases "on appeal," it ensures that controversial questions of constitutionality and national supremacy are decided in the highest court in the land. The Court may, however, decide that the issue lacks significance and simply dismiss it.

Appellate Jurisdiction   Authority of a court to review decisions of an inferior court. In the federal court system, the courts of appeals and the Supreme Court have power to review decisions of district courts and other tribunals. All states have courts of appellate jurisdiction to review decisions of lower state courts. The losing party in a lawsuit generally has the right to appeal the decision to an appellate court. *See also* JURISDICTION, page 253.

Significance   Courts of appellate jurisdiction serve as a check upon errors of law or fact that might arise in the course of trials in lower courts. They also serve to give the losing party a second chance to win his case. The scope of appellate jurisdiction, that is, the types of cases and questions that may be appealed, is determined by rules of procedure established by the courts or by the legislative body.

Arbitration   A method of settling a dispute whereby the parties to the dispute select the arbitrators and agree to accept their decision as binding. A number of states authorize arbitration and make decisions enforceable by the courts. *See also* ARBITRATION, page 330; ARBITRATION, page 381.

Significance   Arbitration provides an informal forum for settlement of disputes, saves the time and expense of court action, and relieves the burden of crowded court dockets. Technical matters can be arbitrated by experts in the field of the dispute. The American Arbitration Association, a private organization, provides a panel of available arbitrators.

Attorney General   The head of the Department of Justice and a member of the President's Cabinet. He serves as legal advisor to the President and to all agencies of the executive branch and is the chief law-enforcement officer of the United States. The Attorney General directs the work of federal district attorneys, United States marshals, and federal penal institutions. Criminal investigations and the conduct of lawsuits involving the United States fall under his charge. An attorney general is also found in each of the states, where he is frequently an elected official. He, too, serves as legal advisor and law-enforcement officer. *See also* ATTORNEY GENERAL, page 238; DEPARTMENT OF JUSTICE, page 267.

Significance The office of Attorney General is one of the most powerful in government. His opinions on legal matters, published as *Opinions of Attorney General,* have the force of law unless overturned by a court. The emphasis given to enforcement of particular laws, such as antitrust or civil rights laws, depends largely on the discretion of the Attorney General. At the national level, broad discretion is vested in the Attorney General in the areas of immigration, citizenship, and subversion.

Bail Funds provided as assurance that a person will appear in court at the proper time. Bail is permitted after arrest and before trial, as well as after conviction pending appeal or sentencing. Bail is usually denied in capital cases. The Eighth Amendment to the Constitution forbids excessive bail; wide discretion is left the courts to determine the amount in relation to the severity of the offense, the record and resources of the defendant, and the likelihood of his reappearing in court. A defendant may appeal a denial of release on bail or the amount of the bail.

Significance Bail rests on the theory that one is innocent until proved guilty and should not have punishment inflicted by unnecessary internment until guilt is established. Bail permits a defendant freedom to prepare his case before trial and to continue his normal work and family life. Since the poor have difficulty raising bail, many jurisdictions now release defendants on their own recognizance when it appears likely that the defendant will not flee to avoid prosecution. This is permitted in federal courts under the Bail Reform Act of 1966.

Brief A document prepared by an attorney for presentation to a court, containing arguments and data in support of a case. The brief will embody points of law, precedents, and, in a case involving major social issues, relevant economic, sociological, and other scientific evidence. Despite its connotation, a brief may be quite lengthy.

Significance A well-prepared brief is often used by judges in preparing their opinions. A brief containing substantial nonlegal data is known as a "Brandeis Brief," named after former Supreme Court Justice Louis D. Brandeis. As an attorney, Brandeis first used such data, in addition to strict reliance on legal precedents, in a case involving regulation of working hours for women (*Muller v. Oregon,* 208 U.S. 412 [1908]).

Capital Punishment The death penalty for conviction of a serious crime, such as murder, rape, kidnapping, or treason. Electrocution is the most commonly used method of execution; lethal gas and hanging are also employed. In 1972, the Supreme Court declared the death penalty, as then applied in the United States, to be cruel and unusual punishment in violation of the Eighth Amendment (*Furman v. Georgia,* 408 U.S. 238). The Court found that capital punishment was assigned in an apparently arbitrary manner, for a variety of crimes, and mainly to blacks and the poor. Though each member of the Court wrote an opinion in the celebrated case, it appeared that a clearly and narrowly drawn death penalty statute would survive constitutional scrutiny. More than half the states have since reinstated the death penalty, as has the Congress (for crimes connected with aircraft hijacking). Two techniques are used in new death penalty laws: one is to make the death penalty mandatory for certain crimes and thereby eliminate arbitrary judgment; the other is to use a two-stage process in which sentence is determined in a second trial after a finding of guilt, wherein specified legislative guidelines are used to determine whether mitigating circumstances justify a sentence other than death. Since 1968 no one may be excluded from a jury because of opposition to capital punishment (*Witherspoon v. Illinois,* 391 U.S. 510).

Significance Capital punishment has long been debated on both moral and legalistic grounds. Many authorities question its utility as a deterrent to crime, while others abhor it for religious or moral reasons. In recent years, legislation had been frequently introduced in Congress and in numerous states to abolish the death penalty. The number of executions had decreased dramatically in recent years, due in part to the reluctance of judges and juries to assign the death penalty and in large measure to pressures from civil rights groups who pointed to the extraordinarily high proportion of blacks sentenced to death compared to whites guilty of similar offenses (53 percent of all persons executed from 1930–1965 were blacks). In the decade of 1930–1939, 1666 persons were executed; 716 in the decade 1950–1959; less than 200 in the decade 1960–1969, with only one execution in 1967, and none since. When the Court decided *Furman v. Georgia* in 1972, more than 600 convicts were awaiting execution, over half of whom were members of minority groups.

Certiorari An order issued by a higher court to a lower court to send up the record of a case for review. Most cases reach the United States Supreme Court through the writ of certiorari, as authorized by the Judiciary Act of 1925. The writ is issued at the discretion of the Court when at least four of the nine justices feel that the case should be reviewed. *See also* JURISPRUDENCE, page 253; SUPREME COURT, page 262.

Significance Though it is commonly assumed that anyone may bring his case to the Supreme Court, only a limited number of cases may be appealed as a matter of right. In all other cases, the party must petition the Court to issue a writ of certiorari. Because of the press of work, fewer than 15 percent of petitions for certiorari are granted, thereby leaving the lower court decision as final. Only cases of importance reaching far beyond the interests of the parties to the suit tend to be heard. Often the Court limits its grant of certiorari to specific questions rather than reviewing all elements of the trial or of lower court decisions.

Challenge Objection to having a prospective juror serve on a jury. A juror may be challenged by either party. A challenge may be either for "cause" or "peremptory." An unlimited number of challenges may be made for cause with approval of the presiding judge. Peremptory challenges, for which no reason need be given, are limited to a specific number, which varies from state to state and depends upon the nature of the offense involved. For crimes punishable by death, as many as forty peremptory challenges may be allowed; as few as five may be permitted for minor offenses. *See also* JURY, page 253.

Significance Both parties to a case are entitled to a trial by an impartial jury. The challenge permits counsel to remove prospective jurors who show bias or who, for any reason, appear unfit to sit in judgment. The limit placed on peremptory challenges prevents unreasonable delay in filling the jury panel.

Charge A statement by the judge to the jury at the conclusion of a trial to aid the jury in reaching its verdict. The judge instructs the jury in the law governing the case and reviews the evidence. The authority of the judge to comment on the facts of a case, as distinguished from the law involved, varies from state to state; federal judges have wide latitude. *See also* JURY, page 253.

Significance The charge to the jury serves to refresh the minds of the jurors, particularly after a lengthy trial. It is for the jury to weigh the truth or falsity of the evidence, but the jury is bound by the law as interpreted by the judge. If the judge is careless in his charge or demonstrates bias, the case may be overturned by a higher court. Nevertheless, the charge to the jury may play a major role in the verdict which the jury eventually reaches.

Chief Justice The highest judicial officer of the United States or of a state. The Chief Justice of the United States is appointed for a life term by the President with the consent of the Senate. He presides over sessions of the United States Supreme Court, assigns the writing of opinions, and performs a variety of administrative duties as head of the federal court system. In the states, the chief justices are chosen in a variety of ways—appointment, election, seniority—usually for a limited term. Their duties are similar to the Chief Justice of the United States, although in many states they lack control over lower court administrative matters.

Significance Aside from administrative duties and a slightly higher salary, chief justices have no more power than other members of highest courts in deciding cases. The position does carry considerable prestige, however, and the chief justice may be in a position to use his post as presiding officer to influence the course of decision making.

Circuit Court A general trial court in the states, sometimes called a district court or a superior court. In many states, the court serves several counties and the judges go on "circuit" from one county to another according to a schedule. In most states, the judges of these courts are elected by the voters of a particular county or circuit, with terms varying from two to six years. These are courts of "original jurisdiction," where important civil and criminal cases begin, trials are held, and juries are frequently used. Cases from minor courts, such as justices of the peace or municipal courts, may be appealed to the circuit court. From circuit courts, cases may be appealed to higher state courts.

Significance For most people, the circuit court represents their main contact with the judicial branch of the government. This includes not only parties to a suit but witnesses and jurors as well. Hence, it is vital that trial courts be efficiently administered in order to maintain respect for the law. Competent judges and juries and simplified procedures, frequently lacking in these courts, are goals of proponents of state judicial reform.

Civil Law The code regulating conduct between private persons. It is to be distinguished from criminal law, which regulates individual conduct and is enforced by the government. Under civil law, the government provides the forum for the settlement of disputes between private parties in such matters as contracts, domestic relations, business relations, and auto accidents. The government may be plaintiff or defendant in a civil suit but, in a criminal case, the government is always the prosecutor. Most civil cases in both state and federal courts are tried without jury. Where juries are used, some states authorize trial by a jury of fewer than twelve persons, and decision by less than unanimous vote. *See also* CRIMINAL LAW, page 246.

Significance Civil law provides stability in private arrangements. Thus, a person who enters into a legal contract can seek the aid of the civil law and the courts to enforce the contract. Civil law provides a substitute for private duels as a means of settling private disputes. The government not only provides an impartial tribunal but will see that any judgment reached (a money award, for example) is enforced.

Code A compilation of laws in force, classified according to subject matter. Federal laws currently in force are collected in the *United States Code,* which is kept up-to-date with annual supplements and is revised every six years. Many states have collected and classified their statutes, including pertinent judicial decisions, under the title *Compiled Laws. See also* STATUTE, page 189.

Significance Without a code, one would have to search through the annual statute books for laws relating to a particular subject. Codes collect all related laws under a subject heading for easy reference use. The failure of some states to keep their codes up-to-date works a hardship on professional legal personnel and laymen alike who want to know "what the law is."

Common Law Judge-made law that originated in England from decisions shaped according to prevailing custom. Decisions were reapplied to similar situations and, thus, gradually became common to the nation. Common law forms the basis of legal procedures in American states, except in Louisiana, where certain French legal traditions are preserved. There is no federal common law, since the national government is one of delegated powers; however, federal judges apply state common law in cases involving citizens of different states, where there is no applicable federal statute. A statute overrides the common law, but many statutes are based upon the common law and are interpreted according to the common law tradition. *See also* EQUITY, page 248; *Erie Railroad v. Tompkins,* page 269; PRECEDENT, page 259; STARE DECISIS, page 261.

Significance Many important matters, such as the idea of a twelve-man jury, are part of the common law. Reliance on precedents (previous judicial decisions) in determining legal rights and duties characterizes the common law tradition. The common law permits judges great flexibility to adjust the law to community needs, thereby enhancing judicial power.

Conciliation A method by which a third party attempts to settle a controversy between disputants outside the courtroom. It is similar to arbitration, except that the decision is not binding upon the parties nor enforceable in court. A number of large cities have established a conciliation branch in their judicial structure.

Significance Conciliation looks toward less formal proceedings for settlement of disputes in the hope of easing the burden on courts and lessening expenses for litigants. Conciliation has proved to be particularly effective in divorce proceedings and labor disputes.

Concurrent Jurisdiction Authority vested in two or more courts to hear cases involving the same subject matter. The term is generally used to indicate those instances in which both federal and state courts may hear the same kind of case. For example, the Congress has conferred concurrent jurisdiction upon state and federal courts in suits between citizens of different states where the amount in controversy exceeds $10,000. The parties to such a suit may choose to have their case heard in either a federal or state court. Suits involving less than $10,000 must be heard in state courts. *See also* DIVERSITY OF CITIZENSHIP, page 247; JURISDICTION, page 253.

Significance Concurrent jurisdiction may serve to ease the burden on a court if a certain type of case tends to crowd the court dockets. For example, auto accidents between citizens of different states have become quite common. By sharing this kind of case with state courts, federal courts have been freed to handle other federal cases.

Concurring Opinion An opinion of one or more judges, usually of an appellate court, that supports the conclusions of a majority of the court but offers different reasons for reaching those conclusions. Concurring opinions are quite common in the United States Supreme Court. *See also* DISSENTING OPINION, page 246.

Significance A concurring opinion is of no legal force or effect. Yet, by offering alternative approaches to the interpretation or application of the law, it frequently serves as a guidepost for future decisions. Thus, a concurring opinion may become the majority view of the court in the future. A concurring opinion signed by a substantial minority of a court or several concurring opinions may reduce the impact of the precedent.

Constitutional Court A federal court established under the provisions of Article III of the Constitution. Constitutional courts are limited to the jurisdiction conferred by Article III and their judges are protected as to tenure and compensation. These are to be distinguished from "legislative courts," which are created by Congress under its delegated powers. The major constitutional courts are the district courts, courts of appeals, and the Supreme Court. Congress has conferred constitutional status upon certain specialized courts, such as the Court of Claims, the Customs Court, and the Court of Customs and Patent Appeals. *See also* LEGISLATIVE COURT, page 255.

Significance Constitutional courts enjoy a greater degree of independence than do legislative courts. Congress has somewhat confused the distinction by conferring constitutional status upon judges of certain specialized or legislative courts while not giving these courts jurisdiction under Article III. In effect, constitutional status today refers mainly to the selection and tenure of judges.

Constitutional Law Law that involves interpretation and application of the Constitution. It is concerned largely with defining the extent and limits of governmental power and the rights of individuals. Final decision as to the meaning of the Constitution is in the hands of the United States Supreme Court. In the case of state constitutions, the highest court of the state renders final decisions, with appeal possible to the United States Supreme Court if conflict with the national Constitution, laws, or treaties can be shown.

Significance Constitutional law represents the highest law, and the Constitution, as interpreted by the Court, is the supreme law of the land, American constitutional law is noted for its flexibility, with the judiciary acting to maintain its vitality to meet changing social and economic conditions.

Typically, constitutional law involves interpretation of such vague phrases as "interstate commerce" or "due process of law." Judges wield their greatest power when they are called upon to interpret the Constitution.

Contempt of Court   Disobedience of a court order, or any action that operates to impair the authority of a court or to interfere with its proper functioning. Contempt may be civil or criminal. Civil contempt involves a refusal to honor a court judgment in a civil case. Criminal contempt involves any interference with court proceedings. Both may be punished by fine or imprisonment or both. Usually, contempt is punished summarily (without trial), when it is committed in the presence of the court, but if a severe sentence is imposed, a separate trial before a different judge may be ordered. A defendant who flagrantly disrupts a trial may be bound and gagged and even removed from the courtroom (*Illinois v. Allen,* 397 U.S. 337 [1970]).

Significance   If a court order is to have any meaning, the court must have power to enforce its order and to punish disobedience. Similarly, judges need authority to maintain order in their courtrooms so that justice may be served. The power to punish criminal contempt may be abused when a judge too hastily censures overemotional lawyers or observers. Equally serious is the conflict with freedom of speech and press that may arise when a judge cites a person for contempt for verbal or published remarks made outside the courtroom that, in his view, obstructs the administration of justice. Increasingly, the Supreme Court has imposed due process hearing requirements upon contempt proceedings involving an extended jail sentence.

Coroner   A county official who investigates deaths that occur by violent means and certifies the cause of deaths unattended by a physician. In the case of violent death, the coroner may conduct an investigation, called an "inquest," to determine if death resulted from a criminal act. A jury of six persons hears evidence presented by the county prosecutor. If the verdict is death by criminal act, the coroner may order the arrest of suspected persons. Most coroners are elected, although a number of states have substituted an appointed medical examiner to perform the duties of the coroner and have transferred his inquest function to the prosecutor.

Significance   Most students of government oppose the election of coroners. The office requires extensive medical knowledge as well as knowledge of criminal investigation and judicial proceedings. Often, the coroner is a layman with no medical or legal training; in some cases, he is an undertaker who may profit personally from his position. The trend is toward the appointment of physicians as medical examiners, the abolishment of the coroner's jury, and the use of the prosecutor for the legal aspects of the office.

Court of Appeals   In the national court system, the appellate court below the Supreme Court. A few states also have an intermediate court of appeals, although in Kentucky, Maryland, and New York, the highest state court is called the Court of Appeals. On the national level, there are eleven courts of appeal. The country is divided into eleven "circuits" including the District of Columbia. Prior to 1948, these courts were known as the Circuit Courts of Appeals. The United States Courts of Appeals have only appellate jurisdiction, being empowered to hear appeals from the district courts in their particular circuit and to hear appeals from decisions of independent regulatory commissions, such as the Federal Trade Commission or Interstate Commerce Commission. Each court normally hears cases in panels of three judges but, on occasion, a full court of nine judges will sit. All judges are appointed for life by the President with the Senate's consent.

Significance In most appeals, decisions of the courts of appeals are final, since few cases reach the Supreme Court. Hence, judges of those courts wield considerable power and influence in American law. Review of decisions of independent regulatory commissions gives the Washington, D.C. circuit, in particular, an important role in development of administrative law.

Court of Claims A court established in 1855 to hear claims of private individuals against the government for breach of contract, for injuries caused by negligent behavior of government employees, or for recovery of other claims, such as back pay. It also determines claims referred by Congress and the executive departments. The Court of Claims has seven judges who sit "en banc" (together) in Washington, D.C. Evidence is gathered by commissioners who travel throughout the United States. Any awards made by the Court cannot be paid unless Congress appropriates the money, which it usually does. Its decisions may be appealed to the Supreme Court by writ of certiorari. Since 1953 it has held the status of a constitutional court, and its judges are appointed for life by the President with the Senate's consent.

Significance The national government may not be sued without its consent, but it would be grossly inefficient if Congress had to consider each claim. The Court of Claims relieves Congress of much of this burden. In most instances, its decisions are final, since the Supreme Court rarely accepts a case from the Court of Claims.

Court of Customs and Patent Appeals A court established by Congress in 1909 which reviews appeals from decisions of the Customs Court, the Patent Office, and the Tariff Commission. The Court has five judges who sit "en banc" (together) in Washington, D.C. They are appointed for life terms by the President with consent of the Senate. Congress designated it a constitutional court in 1958. Decisions may be appealed to the Supreme Court by writ of certiorari.

Significance A large body of specialized law has been developed in the subject areas assigned to the Court of Customs and Patent Appeals. The expertness developed by this court takes an immense burden from the regular federal courts.

Court of Military Appeals A court established by Congress in 1950 to review court-martial decisions. Composed of three civilian judges appointed for fifteen years by the President with consent of the Senate, the court is judicially independent but is part of the Department of Defense for administrative purposes. The court is obligated to review decisions affecting top military personnel, as well as those imposing the death penalty; it has discretion to review certain other cases upon petition, such as bad conduct discharges or those involving lengthy prison terms. The court applies military law, a special body of rules developed by Congress, rather than ordinary federal criminal law. Appeals may be made to the Supreme Court by writ of certiorari. *See also* COURT-MARTIAL, page 418.

Significance Military service for millions of Americans has caused great concern over the standards and procedures of military justice. The Uniform Code of Military Justice, passed by Congress in 1950, attempts to strengthen rights of persons in court-martial proceedings while meeting the needs of military discipline. The Court of Military Appeals is part of this reform effort. By requiring that its judges be civilians and by permitting appeal to the Supreme Court, Congress has assured civilian control over military justice.

Criminal Law   The code that regulates the conduct of individuals, defines crimes, and provides punishment for violations. In criminal cases, the government is always the prosecutor, since all crimes are against public order. The major body of criminal law is enacted by states although the list of federal crimes is growing. Criminal law falls into two categories, felonies and misdemeanors, the former being the more serious. *See also* CIVIL LAW, page 241.

Significance Criminal law reflects the mores of society and protects the public against wrongdoing. Laws that define criminal acts must be clear so that people are put on notice as to what they may or may not do. Violators are prosecuted under procedures established by the Constitution or other law to assure fair treatment. Government prosecution and punishment for crime serves as a civilized substitute for personal vengeance.

Customs Court   A special court established by Congress in 1926 to decide disputes that arise over tariff laws and duties levied on imported goods. The Court consists of nine judges appointed for life terms by the President with the Senate's consent. It sits in divisions at principal ports of entry, with its main office in New York City. In 1956, the Customs Court was given constitutional status by the Congress. Its decisions may be appealed to the Court of Customs and Patent Appeals.

Significance The Customs Court relieves regular courts of the burden of hearing the many disputes arising over classifications and valuations placed by customs officers on imported goods. The court has developed the competence necessary to deal with the problems raised by the increased volume of international trade.

Declaratory Judgment   A court procedure used to declare the rights of parties under a contract, will, or other dispute, before any damage occurs but without ordering any specific action. It is a method of preventive justice contrary to the traditional procedure of suing for damages after the damage results. The national government (since the enactment of the Declaratory Judgments Act of 1934) and most of the states permit the use of this procedure.

Significance Declaratory judgments provide access to the courts to prevent the doing of a wrong as well as to redress a wrong. They differ from advisory opinions in that the parties must have an actual controversy in which loss or injury is likely to occur. Expensive legal entanglements are often forestalled.

Dissenting Opinion   An opinion of one or more judges, usually of an appellate court, that disagrees with the decision reached by a majority of the court. Such opinions are frequently presented on the United States Supreme Court. *See also* CONCURRING OPINION, page 243.

Significance A dissenting opinion has no legal force. Ofttimes, however, a dissenting view has eventually become the law. If a court is sharply divided—for example, a five-four vote on the Supreme Court—a dissenting opinion may weaken the force of the majority view.

District Attorney A county official, elected in all but six states for two or four year terms, who represents the state in prosecutions against violators of criminal laws. In some states, he is called the county attorney, county prosecutor, or, simply, prosecutor. Prosecutions for the national government are handled by United States Attorneys. District attorneys also conduct proceedings before grand juries. In states where grand juries are not used, the district attorney brings charges in the form of an information. In addition, the district attorney acts as legal advisor to the county and represents the county in lawsuits. *See also* PLEA BARGAINING, page 258; UNITED STATES ATTORNEY, page 265.

Significance District attorneys wield great power in local government. Decisions of whether to prosecute alleged violators are within their discretionary powers, often conditioned by their political ambitions. Their recommendations to the court regarding bail or sentences are generally given serious consideration. The office has been used as a political stepping-stone by many young attorneys. The conduct of the office may well depend upon the political climate of a given county, resulting in an uneven application of criminal law within the state.

District Court The federal court of "original jurisdiction," where most federal cases begin. It is the only federal court where trials are held, juries are used, and witnesses are called. Both criminal and civil cases arising under federal law are heard. Each state has at least one district court; a few have as many as four, for a total of 88 in the 50 states. District courts are also found in Washington, D.C., and the territories of Puerto Rico, Guam, the Virgin Islands, and the Panama Canal Zone. Each court has from one to twenty-four judges, depending on the volume of business, but each judge holds court separately. Certain cases are heard by a three-judge panel. All judges are appointed for life terms by the President with the Senate's consent, except those serving in Guam, the Virgin Islands, and the Panama Canal Zone, who have eight-year terms. *See also* FEDERAL MAGISTRATE, page 249.

Significance The bulk of judicial work in federal courts is conducted by the district courts. About 100,000 cases a year are tried, mostly civil cases involving such matters as admiralty law, bankruptcy proceedings, torts, civil rights, and postal laws. A small proportion of cases are appealed to courts of appeals and a few reach the Supreme Court. Thus, for most people, contact with federal justice is limited to district courts.

Diversity of Citizenship Lawsuits involving citizens of different states. The Constitution (Art. III, sec. 2) confers jurisdiction in such cases on the federal courts, which, generally, apply relevant state law. Congress has conferred exclusive jurisdiction on state courts for suits between citizens of different states if the amount in controversy is less than $10,000, and concurrent jurisdiction if more than $10,000 is involved. *See also* CLASS ACTION, page 62; CONCURRENT JURISDICTION, page 242; *Erie Railroad v. Tompkins,* page 269; JURISDICTION, page 253.

Significance A very complicated body of law has developed in diversity of citizenship cases. Originally, the purpose of the constitutional provision was to prevent bias by state courts against out-of-state litigants. Today, federal court dockets are filled with such cases, due to the increasing mobility and interrelationships of the American people. Automobile accidents between citizens of different states, for example, can be cause for a federal case. Congressional action giving state courts jurisdiction over diversity of citizenship cases is aimed at reducing pressures on the federal courts. In turn, the federal courts have tried to cut the number of these cases by applying relevant state law, so that litigants will not "shop around" for more favorable treatment under federal law. Moreover, the Supreme Court has held that a class action suit can be brought to a federal court in a diversity of citizenship case only if each person in the class has a claim of $10,000 or more (*Zahn v. International Paper Co.,* 414 U.S. 291 [1973]).

Docket A record of proceedings in a court of justice. The term is usually used to indicate the list of cases to be tried at a specific term of court and may also be known as the calendar of cases. *See also* ADMINISTRATIVE OFFICE OF THE UNITED STATES COURTS, page 266; JUDICIAL COUNCIL, page 252.

Significance Dockets in criminal cases must be current and cleared with dispatch in order to meet the constitutional guarantee of a speedy trial in criminal prosecutions. Civil case dockets have become a national scandal since one may have to wait several years to have a case heard. More judges and courts are necessary to handle the court business generated by a growing population and increased use of the courts by individuals and groups. Some courts have much more crowded dockets than others. Studies are underway by state judicial councils and the Administrative Office of the United States Courts to improve the handling of dockets. The United States Supreme Court virtually controls its own docket through its discretionary power to determine which cases it will hear.

Eleventh Amendment An amendment to the Constitution, adopted in 1798, that provides that federal courts do not have authority to hear cases brought against a state by an individual citizen of another state or of a foreign state. The Amendment overruled a decision of the Supreme Court in *Chisholm v. Georgia,* 2 Dallas 419 (1793), which had upheld the right of a citizen of one state to sue another state in federal court. *See also Cohens v. Virginia,* page 268.

Significance Although Article III did confer jurisdiction upon federal courts to hear cases between a state and citizens of other states, the states were alarmed by the *Chisholm* decision, which denied the necessity for the state's consent to be sued. The states feared the possibility of many suits against them for defaulting on their debts, as well as the loss of "states' rights." The Eleventh Amendment applies only to suits against the state itself; a suit may be brought against an officer of the state.

Equity A branch of law that provides a remedy where the common law does not apply. The common law is concerned largely with granting of damages after a wrongful action. Equity is designed to provide justice where damages may come too late to be meaningful. In an equity case, the court may order that something be done (specific performance) or forbid certain actions (injunction). In a typical case the court may order a person to fulfill a contract or forbid a union to go on strike under certain conditions. Equity procedures are less formal than regular court procedures, and juries are seldom used. *See also* COMMON LAW, page 242; INJUNCTION, page 251.

Significance Equity is a legal inheritance from England that grew out of petitions to the king to redress wrongs for which the law provided no remedy. It was based largely on abstract principles of justice, but has developed its own body of rules and precedents. A few states have separate courts for equity proceedings, sometimes called chancery. The courts have a wide area of choice in equity cases to provide solutions to impending conflicts. Irreparable damages are thereby avoided.

Ex Parte A judicial proceeding by or for one party without contest by an adverse party. In an ex parte proceeding, there may be no adverse party, or a possible adverse party has had no notice of the case. The term "in re" is sometimes used in place of ex parte.

Significance Individuals frequently bring actions in their own behalf seeking the aid of the court. A typical ex parte proceeding may be one brought by a prisoner seeking a writ of habeas corpus. Such cases are reported under the name of the person bringing the suit preceded by the term "ex parte": *Ex parte Milligan,* for example.

Federal Magistrate A minor judicial officer who holds preliminary hearings in federal criminal cases, issues arrest warrants, sets bail, and holds trial over minor federal offenses where a defendant waives his right to trial in a district court. Under the Federal Magistrates Act of 1968, federal magistrates are attorneys appointed for eight-year terms by federal district judges. They serve in various locations, making it unnecessary to bring federal cases to the district court immediately; this is essential since some district courts serve an entire state or other large area. *See also* MAGISTRATE, page 255.

Significance Federal Magistrates were created in 1968 to replace the United States Commissioner system which had not been reformed for over one hundred years. Commissioners were not necessarily attorneys and were paid by fees, resembling justices of the peace. The Federal Magistrates Act professionalizes and expands the routine but essential functions of federal district courts.

Felony A serious crime punishable by death or by imprisonment in a penitentiary for a year or more. The precise character of a felony varies from state to state and is defined by law. Less serious violations of law are called misdemeanors. Felonies generally include murder, arson, robbery, aggravated assault, and forgery. *See also* JURY, page 253; MISDEMEANOR, page 256.

Significance Persons accused of felonies are accorded the full protection of constitutional guarantees, such as indictment by grand jury or information, and trial by jury. Misdemeanors are generally tried by "summary process," without indictment or trial by jury. Minor state courts rarely have jurisdiction to try felonies, which are usually heard by district or circuit courts. On the national level, felonies are tried in the district courts.

Five-to-Four Decision   A decision of the United States Supreme Court in which the justices divide sharply over the decision or interpretation of the Constitution or law. Such decisions tend to attract wide notice and it is sometimes said that one justice, in effect, decides the case. *See also* DISSENTING OPINION, page 246.

Significance   Many important cases have been decided by a five-four vote. When constitutional questions are involved, a five-four decision emphasizes a philosophical division on the Court over political, social, and economic questions. Since so close a vote casts serious doubt upon the durability of the decision, scholars have suggested that a minimum of six or seven, or even all nine justices must agree when a law is declared unconstitutional.

Grand Jury   A body of from twelve to twenty-three members who hear evidence presented by the prosecuting attorney against persons accused of a serious crime, and decide whether or not to present a "true bill" that "indicts" the accused. If indicted, the accused will be bound over for trial; if not, he goes free. The Fifth Amendment requires that this be done for any capital or infamous crime, generally those for which death or imprisonment may result. Unlike a petit or trial jury, a grand jury does not determine guilt or innocence but only whether the evidence warrants bringing the accused to trial; it meets in secret and decides by a majority rather than a unanimous vote. The grand jury may also conduct investigations on its own when a prosecutor is lax or when official misconduct is suspected. In such cases, any resulting accusation is called a "presentment." The grand jury exercises vast powers under the common law, being empowered to subpoena witnesses and records and to compel testimony under oath. More than half of the states have abolished or limited grand jury indictment to capital cases, replacing it with the "information" that permits the prosecutor alone to bring charges. *See also Hurtado v. California,* page 93; INDICTMENT, page 251; INFORMATION, page 251.

Significance   The grand jury procedure is time-consuming and expensive and the grand jury tends to follow the dictates of the prosecutor. It has been abolished in England, its place of origin, as well as in many states. It does, however, serve as a protection against overzealous prosecutors and as a watchdog against official wrongdoing. It originated with the idea that before an individual could be subjected by capricious prosecutors to the costs and humiliation of a public trial, sufficient evidence to justify such action must be shown and be acceptable to a majority of a grand jury.

Hearing   In an equity case, a hearing is a trial. In a criminal case, a hearing is an examination of the accused to determine if he should be held for trial; this is generally referred to as a "preliminary hearing" or "preliminary examination." If a preliminary hearing is held in an equity case, it is called an interlocutory hearing. *See also* HEARING, page 225.

Significance   The term "hearing" has a technical meaning in law. Whereas in an equity case it is technically the trial of the case, in a criminal proceeding, the hearing is not a trial to determine guilt or innocence but a procedure to protect the accused from unwarranted detention.

Indeterminate Sentence   A sentence of imprisonment with minimum and maximum limits set by the court or by statute. Once the prisoner serves the minimum sentence, he may be released upon approval of a parole board or a special commission. This is the procedure now used in most states in place of the fixed sentence. *See also* PAROLE, page 258.

Significance The indeterminate sentence reflects present policy to reform and rehabilitate criminals rather than to exact revenge for wrongdoing. It provides hope to the prisoner of early release for good behavior and demonstration of fitness to return to society.

Indictment The formal accusation, drawn up by the prosecutor and brought by a grand jury, charging a person with the commission of a crime. *See also* GRAND JURY, page 250.

Significance Indictment is a procedure to avoid arbitrary accusations and to inform the accused of the precise charges against him so that he can prepare his defense. A faulty or vague indictment justifies dismissal of the case. The cumbersome nature of this procedure, however, has resulted in its widespread replacement by the "information."

Information An accusation made under oath by a prosecuting attorney before a court, charging a person with a crime. Though regularly used for minor offenses, more than half the states have substituted the information for indictment by grand jury in serious cases as well. The national government is making increased use of the information for noncapital offenses. *See also* GRAND JURY, page 250.

Significance The trend has definitely been in the direction of substituting the information for the grand jury indictment. Thus, the prosecuting attorney bypasses the grand jury, and final determination of whether the evidence justifies a trial is placed in the hands of the judge. Use of the information instead of the grand jury results from considerations of both efficiency and economy.

Injunction An order issued by a court in an equity proceeding to compel or restrain the performance of an act by an individual or government official. A "mandatory" injunction demands that something be done, although the term "injunction" generally refers to a restraining order. Violation of an injunction constitutes contempt of court, punishable by fine or imprisonment. *See also* EQUITY, page 248; INJUNCTION, page 333; WRIT, page 266.

Significance The injunction prevents irreparable damage to an individual's personal or property rights through the power of courts to issue orders without the necessity of a lawsuit after damages are done. Judges enjoy a great deal of discretion to determine the scope of an injunction.

Intermediate Court A court of appeals below the level of the highest court. It is found in about one-fourth of the states, mainly those with large populations. In about half the states, county courts function as intermediate courts as well as trial courts by hearing cases *de novo* (a new trial) appealed from decisions of municipal and justice of the peace courts. In both cases, "intermediate" refers to the fact that these courts exercise appellate jurisdiction with further appeal possible to a higher court.

Significance The use of the term "intermediate" reflects the great variety in court organization, structure, and jurisdiction, found in the several states. Intermediate courts of appeals serve to lighten the burden on state supreme courts and provide at least one appeal from decisions of minor courts.

Judicial Council An investigative and advisory agency composed of judges, lawyers, and laymen to promote efficient administration in state courts. Councils are used in about three-fourths of the states. Though their composition and authority vary from state to state, they are generally charged with collecting statistics on court operations and recommending changes in court organization, court procedure, assignment of judges, and other matters to improve the handling of court business. *See also* ADMINISTRATIVE OFFICE OF THE UNITED STATES COURTS, page 266.

Significance Little attention has been paid to the efficient administration of court business compared with the amount of concern over the outcome of particular cases. The judicial council is a relatively recent innovation, recognizing the importance of applying sound administrative techniques to the operations of courts. The judicial council acts as a unifying force to counteract the decentralization of most state court systems and the independence of locally elected judges. On the national level, the Administrative Office of the United States Courts performs duties similar to those of a judicial council.

Judicial Review The power of the courts to declare acts of the legislative and executive branches unconstitutional. All courts, both state and national, may exercise this authority, though final decision is usually made by the highest state or federal court. Though the United States Constitution is silent on this matter, the Supreme Court asserted the power of judicial review in the famous case of *Marbury v. Madison,* 1 Cranch 137 (1803). Judicial review is based on the assumptions that the Constitution is the supreme law, that acts contrary to the Constitution are void, and that the judiciary is the guardian of the Constitution. *See also Ashwander v. TVA,* page 267; CONSTITUTIONAL LAW, page 243; *Dred Scott v. Sanford,* page 268; *Eakin v. Raub,* page 269; *Marbury v. Madison,* page 270; SUPREME COURT, page 262.

Significance Judicial review is one of the basic principles of the American system of government. It places in the judiciary, and the Supreme Court in particular, vast power to determine the meaning of the Constitution and to act as final arbiter over questions involving the power of governmental officials at both the state and national levels. Several hundred state laws and about one hundred federal laws have been declared unconstitutional by the Supreme Court. Though this number is small compared with the total number of laws passed, a declaration of unconstitutionality may deter a long line of similar legislation. Courts are reluctant to exercise this vast power, since due respect must be accorded the other branches of government and since the Constitution is susceptible to varying interpretations. A court decision on the Constitution can be changed only by amending the Constitution or by a change of view by the court itself. The exercise of judicial review invariably generates widespread comment from those dissatisfied with the decision, particularly when the court is divided in its decision. Throughout American history, courts have played a major role in the development of public policy by the exercise of this power. Prior to 1937, the

Supreme Court used its authority mainly to protect property rights. Since then, judicial review has been used most often in defense of civil liberties.

Judiciary   A collective term for courts and judges. In the United States, the judiciary is divided into the national and state judiciary. Each is independent of the other with the exception that the United States Supreme Court may, under special circumstances involving federal questions, review a state court decision. Jurisdiction of particular courts or judges is determined by either the national or state constitutions and laws.

Significance   An independent judiciary, coequal with the legislative and executive branches, is one of the cornerstones of the American system of government. The judiciary protects the people against excessive exercise of power by the legislature and executive and provides an impartial forum for the settlement of civil and criminal cases.

Jurisdiction   Authority vested in a court to hear and decide a case. The term literally means power "to say the law." The jurisdiction of national courts is controlled by the Constitution and by Congress. State court jurisdiction is similarly determined by state constitutions and statutes. Jurisdiction may be assigned according to such factors as the amount of money involved or the type of offense. Courts may exercise original or appellate jurisdiction, or both. *See also* ADMIRALTY JURISDICTION, page 236; APPELLATE JURISDICTION, page 238; CONCURRENT JURISDICTION, page 242; DIVERSITY OF CITIZENSHIP, page 247; *Ex parte McCardle,* page 269; ORIGINAL JURISDICTION, page 257.

Significance   Lawsuits must be brought to the court that has authority "to say the law" in such a case. A case brought to the wrong court will either not be heard or be overruled by an appellate court. It is common practice in lawsuits for the attorney to show immediately that the court has authority to hear the case. The separate jurisdiction of state and national courts helps preserve the federal system, since each government maintains control over the application of its law. Within any court system, specialized jurisdiction tends to promote expertness in the courts.

Jurisprudence   The science or philosophy of law. Jurisprudence involves the study of the origins and functions of law, the place of law in society, and the likely consequences of particular courses of legal action. *See also* JUDICIAL REVIEW, page 252; STATUTORY CONSTRUCTION, page 262.

Significance   Jurisprudence would appear to be the province of legal scholars, but no important piece of legislation or lawsuit is free of jurisprudential implications. Judicial opinions, particularly in appellate courts, ordinarily take into account the effect that a given line of reasoning will have beyond the immediate parties to the suit. The United States Supreme Court, in the exercise of its discretion to select the cases it will hear (writ of certiorari), tries to limit itself to those cases and issues apt to have the most far-reaching impact on society. In this way, the Court can either give new direction to the law or bring the law into line with actual practice.

Jury   An impartial body that sits in judgment on charges brought in either criminal or civil cases. A trial jury is also known as a petit jury, to distinguish it from a grand jury. Under the common law, a trial jury must consist of twelve persons, and their decision must be unanimous. The national government and many states authorize trial by less than twelve in certain cases and a decision by less than a unanimous vote. Jury trials may be waived by the accused. Generally, the jury is the judge of the facts, though some states permit the jury to determine the law and the punishment as well as the facts. The jury must be impartial, and no specific class of persons may be deliberately and systematically excluded from jury service. The Supreme Court has ruled that due process requires that persons accused of serious crimes are entitled to a trial by jury (*Duncan v. Louisiana*, 391 U.S. 145 [1968]), defined a serious crime as one for which imprisonment for more than six months is possible (*Baldwin v. New York*, 399 U.S. 66 [1970]), and authorized states to provide juries of less than twelve for the trial of serious offenses (*Williams v. Florida*, 399 U.S. 78 [1970]), and verdict by less than unanimous vote (*Johnson v. Louisiana*, 406 U.S. 356 [1972]). In federal criminal trials, a jury of twelve and a unanimous verdict is still required. Trial by jury is provided for in Article III, section 2, and by the Sixth and Seventh Amendments of the United States Constitution. *See also* CAPITAL PUNISHMENT, page 239; CHALLENGE, page 240; CHARGE, page 240; *Norris v. Alabama*, page 98; PANEL, page 257.

Significance The right to be judged by a jury of one's peers is a long-standing tradition of the common law. The competence of the average jury and the motivations which may lead it to a particular verdict are frequently questioned. Yet, the jury system brings the common sense of the community to bear upon the laws of the state or nation. It permits the citizen to participate in the administration of justice and gives the people more confidence in the application of the law.

Justice of the Peace A judicial officer empowered to try minor civil and criminal cases, such as traffic violations or breaches of peace. In some areas, he conducts preliminary hearings to determine whether a person should be held for trial in a higher court. The justice of the peace is usually elected in rural areas and small towns for a two-year term. He is generally paid through fees. *See also* MAGISTRATE, page 255.

Significance The office of justice of the peace has been under attack in recent years. Not many justices of the peace are learned in the law, although a few states require a law degree. The fee system, it is charged, leads to corruption and biased judgment. Supporters argue that the justice of the peace provides an inexpensive method of dispensing justice in petty cases. In many urban areas, the office of justice of the peace is being replaced by municipal courts.

Justiciable Question A dispute that can be settled through the exercise of judicial power. For a controversy to be justiciable: (1) it must be an actual case, not a trumped-up suit; (2) the person bringing the suit must have a direct interest at stake and have standing to sue; (3) the case must be ripe for adjudication, other remedies having been exhausted; and (4) the court must have jurisdiction over the subject. A question may be ruled "political" rather than justiciable if the court believes that the other branches of the government are better equipped or constitutionally responsible to handle the matter. *See also* CLASS ACTION, page 62; *Frothingham v. Mellon*, page 269; JURISDICTION, page 253; POLITICAL QUESTION, page 258.

Significance The rules regarding justiciable questions help preserve the separation of powers by confining courts to their proper functions. While a court may exercise considerable discretion to determine justiciability, careful adherence to the rules assures that courts will not become embroiled in issues over which they lack competence or that will weaken the judiciary vis-à-vis the other branches. The wide use of "class actions" has somewhat altered the rule of standing to sue by permitting a person not solely liable to sustain a direct injury to bring a suit on behalf of himself and others similarly situated. This has enabled the courts in recent years to entertain several important issues, such as integration and legislative apportionment, involving questions in which litigants did not have an interest beyond that of the general public.

Law A rule of conduct prescribed by or accepted by the governing authority of a state and enforced by courts. The law may derive from a constitution, legislative acts, and administrative rules, or may develop through custom, as have common law and equity. The law controls relations among people and between them and their government. Penalties are imposed for violation of law. *See also* ADMINISTRATIVE LAW, page 236; CIVIL LAW, page 241; COMMON LAW, page 242; CONSTITUTIONAL LAW, page 243; CRIMINAL LAW, page 246; EQUITY, page 248; INTERNATIONAL LAW, page 395; ORDINANCE, page 447.

Significance Democracy is distinguished from totalitarian government largely in terms of the place of law in society. A totalitarian system operates under the whim of the rulers. In a free society, law provides advance notice of what legally is right and wrong. Conflicts are resolved by application of preexisting rules. Law must emanate from and be enforced only by duly constituted authority.

Legislative Court A court established by Congress under its delegated powers rather than under the authority granted in Article III of the Constitution. The judges of legislative courts need not have life tenure, may be assigned nonjudicial functions, and have only that jurisdiction that Congress assigns. For example, the Territorial Courts of Guam, Virgin Islands, and the Panama Canal Zone were created under congressional power to govern the territories. The judges have limited terms, and the courts have regular federal jurisdiction, as well as jurisdiction over matters that ordinarily belong in state courts. Another example is the Court of Military Appeals, created under the power to make rules for the armed forces. *See also* CONSTITUTIONAL COURT, page 243; UNITED STATES TAX COURT, page 300.

Significance By establishing legislative courts, Congress provides flexibility to the court system and relieves the regular courts and Congress, itself, of some burdens. The Court of Claims, the Customs Court, and the Court of Customs and Patent Appeals, originally established as legislative courts, have been granted constitutional status by Congress, and judges of these courts now enjoy life tenure.

Magistrate A minor judicial officer, usually elected in urban areas, with jurisdiction over traffic violations, minor criminal offenses, and civil suits involving small amounts of money. Magistrates may also conduct preliminary hearings in serious criminal cases and commit the offender for trial in a higher court. In some areas, the magistrate court is called a police court, and its authority is similar to that of a justice of the peace serving in a rural area. Juries, though rarely used in magistrate courts, may consist of only six jurors. *See also* FEDERAL MAGISTRATE, page 249; JUSTICE OF THE PEACE, page 254.

Significance Magistrate courts have been established to handle the large number of cases that arise in urban communities. Unlike the justice of the peace, a magistrate is usually paid a salary rather than a fee per case. The magistrate can dispose of large numbers of petty offenses, thereby relieving the burden on higher courts and facilitating matters for offenders. Increasingly, cities are turning to specialized courts, such as traffic courts and domestic relations courts, to handle the large volume of work.

Mandamus An order issued by a court to compel performance of an act. A writ of mandamus may be issued to an individual or corporation as well as to a public official. In the case of public officers, a writ will be issued only to compel performance of a "ministerial" act—one that the officer has a clear legal duty to perform. If he has discretion to determine whether he will perform an act, the court will not order him to do so. *See also* WRIT, page 266.

Significance The authority of the court may be brought to bear upon anyone who fails to perform an act that someone has a legal right to expect. Thus, a contract must be fulfilled as agreed upon, or a court order will be issued. Similarly, a public officer who refuses to issue a license to someone authorized to have one may be ordered to do so by the court. Failure to obey the court order is contempt of court.

Marshal An official of the federal Department of Justice attached to each federal district court. The duties of United States marshals correspond to those of sheriffs in county governments. They make arrests in federal criminal cases, keep accused persons in custody, secure jurors, serve legal papers, keep order in the courtroom, and execute orders and decisions of the court. Marshals are appointed by the President, subject to the Senate's confirmation, for four-year terms.

Significance Marshals are part of the executive, not the judicial, branch and perform federal police duties. Although the job is not quite as glamorous as portrayed on television westerns, modern day United States marshals perform important functions in enforcement of federal law. Deputy marshals are also attached to most district courts. United States marshals have played a prominent role in the enforcement of federal court orders in major desegregation crises.

Misdemeanor A minor criminal offense. The precise nature of a misdemeanor varies from state to state where it is defined by law. It may include such offenses as traffic violations, petty theft, disorderly conduct, and gambling. Punishment is usually limited to light jail terms or fines. Minor courts such as justices of the peace or municipal courts usually hear such cases without a jury. *See also* FELONY, page 249.

Significance Most violations of law are misdemeanors and constitute the bulk of judicial business in the United States. Many such cases are handled by "summary process," without indictment or trial, and are settled by payment of a fine. Misdemeanors are to be distinguished from felonies, which are more serious violations of law, requiring more formalized proceedings in arrests and trials.

Missouri Plan   A method of selecting state judges used in a few states that combines both appointment and election. In Missouri, judges of the Supreme Court, of courts of appeals, and of courts in St. Louis and Kansas City are appointed by the governor from a list of three names prepared by a commission composed of lawyers and laymen. The judge serves one year and then stands for election on the basis of his record. There is no opposition candidate. If the voters approve, he serves for six to twelve years, depending on the court. If he is defeated, the procedure is started anew. Other communities in the state may come under the plan if the voters approve. A similar plan exists in California; here, however, the governor nominates the candidate subject to approval of, rather than from a list prepared by, the commission.

Significance   The issue of appointment versus election of judges is one of the "great debates" of American politics. The Missouri Plan has been hailed as a satisfactory compromise in that it retains power in the electorate while freeing the judges from the necessity of campaigning for office.

Obiter Dictum   A statement in a court opinion on an issue not precisely involved in the case. Since such statements are not relevant to the conclusions reached in the decision, they are not binding as precedents.

Significance   Obiter dicta provide clues to the thinking of the court on issues related to the case at hand and may influence the decisions of the court in similar cases.

Original Jurisdiction   The authority of a court to hear a case in the first instance. Generally, courts of original jurisdiction are minor courts or trial courts. They are to be distinguished from courts of appellate jurisdiction, which hear cases on appeal from courts of original jurisdiction. A court that is primarily appellate may have some original jurisdiction. The United States Supreme Court, for example, has original jurisdiction over suits involving ambassadors and those to which a state is a party. *See also* JURISDICTION, page 253.

Significance   Original jurisdiction is often "final" jurisdiction, since few cases are heard on appeal by higher courts. Even if a case is appealed, the determination of the facts in the case by the judge or jury in the court of original jurisdiction is generally considered to be final, with questions of law heard by the appellate court.

Panel   The list of persons summoned for jury duty. A trial jury is "impaneled" when the parties to the case have agreed to the selection of the jurors from the panel. Panels are selected in a variety of ways in different states by jury commissioners or county or township clerks or other officials. Names are usually selected from voting or taxpayer lists. A 1968 law requires random selection from voter lists for federal juror panels. In 1972 Congress lowered the age requirement for federal jury service to eighteen. *See also* JURY, page 253.

Significance   The major problem in selecting jury panels is to assure fair trials by impaneling representative cross sections of the community. State laws frequently exempt public employees, professional persons, and those who will suffer financial hardship while serving. As a result of these exemptions, it is often difficult to get a representative panel to enable an accused person to be tried by a jury of his peers. No persons may be systematically excluded from jury panels because of sex, race, religion, or color, or, in capital cases, because of attitude toward the death penalty.

Parole   Release from prison prior to the expiration of a sentence. The release is based on the good behavior of the prisoner, who may be returned to prison if he violates the conditions of his parole. In the national government, paroles are administered through the Department of Justice by the Board of Parole, consisting of eight members appointed by the President. In the states, paroles are generally administered by parole boards or by the governors.

Significance   The possibility of parole encourages prisoners to be on their good behavior and to demonstrate fitness to return to a normal life. The parole system illustrates that modern penology emphasizes rehabilitation rather than punishment. A major criticism of parole practice is that parole boards are often composed of political appointees rather than properly qualified persons. Well-qualified parole officers who supervise the parolee while he is out of prison are vital for successful parole administration, as well as adherence to procedural safeguards in parole revocation proceedings.

Plea Bargaining   Negotiations between a prosecutor and an accused person or his counsel to secure a guilty plea from the accused in exchange for a lesser charge or promise of leniency. *See also* DISTRICT ATTORNEY, page 247.

Significance   Plea bargaining takes place in the majority of criminal cases in the United States. The accused is often willing to bargain to avoid a harsher charge and sentence and to avoid the humiliation and cost of a trial. The prosecutor, in turn, is eager to secure a conviction and also to avoid the rigors of a trial. The procedure is criticized because of its obvious potential for abuse, political or otherwise, the extensive discretion it places in the hands of prosecuting attorneys, and the resultant failure to determine the merits of individual cases in open court. Yet, without considerable plea bargaining, chaos would likely result in criminal justice because of the high rate of crime combined with the lack of adequate numbers of law enforcement and judicial personnel. Plea bargaining came to prominent attention during the final year of the Nixon Administration when such bargaining resulted in leniency for Vice President Spiro T. Agnew, accused of taking bribes, and for numerous other prominent defendants involved in the crimes known as the Watergate conspiracy.

Political Question   A doctrine enunciated by the Supreme Court holding that certain constitutional issues cannot be decided by the courts but are to be decided by the executive or legislative branches. The doctrine has generally been invoked when the issue would place the courts in serious conflict with other branches, involve the courts in political controversies, or raise serious enforcement problems. Examples of "political questions" include presidential power to recognize foreign governments, congressional power to determine whether constitutional amendments have been ratified within a reasonable time, and congressional and presidential power to determine whether states have a republican form of government. *See also Baker v. Carr,* page 194; JUSTICIABLE QUESTION, page 254; *Luther v. Borden,* page 44.

Significance The doctrine of the political question is a self-imposed restraint on the Court's power of judicial review. Thus, it is for the Court to decide which issues are "political" and which are "justiciable." Few cases have involved "political questions," and it is impossible to predict with certainty what issues will be considered to be "political." Much depends upon the political climate of the day and the viewpoint of the majority of the Supreme Court.

Precedent A court ruling bearing upon subsequent legal decisions in similar cases. Judges rely upon precedents in deciding cases. The common law is based primarily upon reasoning from precedents. *See also* COMMON LAW, page 242; STARE DECISIS, page 261.

Significance Legal disputes in the United States are fought out largely over the application of precedents to a particular controversy. A lawyer will try to convince the court that the precedents serve to prove his case. Judges, in turn, must decide between competing precedents in reaching a decision. If a precedent appears to be unreasonable or unjust, a court may specifically overrule it and establish a new precedent.

Privileged Communication A discussion between specified individuals which neither can legally be compelled to divulge. This privilege usually extends to communications between husband and wife, attorney and client, priest and penitent, physician and patient.

Significance Privileged communication is one of the major rules for exclusion of evidence in a trial. Though jurisdictions vary on the precise application of what may be excluded as privileged, the general rule is in support of the complete confidentiality of conversations with one's spouse, lawyer, clergyman, or doctor. The protection of the desired relationship between those categories of persons is deemed to be more important than the need to use those particular sources of information in the administration of justice. In the course of the Watergate revelations, President Richard M. Nixon claimed the attorney-client privilege for conversations he held with his White House Counsel, John Dean, but the issue was never precisely tested; in general, President Nixon relied on the more inclusive concept of executive privilege, rather than privileged communication in his abortive attempt to cover up the Watergate scandal.

Probate Court A court, used in about one-half the states, with jurisdiction over wills, estates, guardians, and minors. Probate courts are found at the county level; in states without separate probate courts, such matters are handled by regular county courts. In some areas, probate courts are called surrogate courts. Much of the work connected with probate courts is administrative in nature, concerned largely with proper handling of minors and estates by guardians and administrators. Juries are rarely used. Probate judges are generally elected.

Significance Probating, or proving the authenticity of a will and the subsequent administration of an estate are important elements of American law, reflecting concern with property rights. The rights of minors, too, are zealously protected. Probate courts exist, in the main, to help people, rather than to punish wrongdoers. One major problem is that separate probate courts tend to proliferate an already complicated court system in the states. In a more simplified court system, probate duties would be assigned to regular courts within an integrated system.

Probation   Suspension of the sentence of a person convicted of a crime, permitting him to remain free, subject to good behavior. Persons on probation are subject to supervision by an agent of the court. If the person's conduct justifies it, he will be released from probation after a period of time determined by the court. Failure to observe the terms of probation subjects him to possible imprisonment.

Significance   Imprisonment may do more harm than good to numerous offenders. Probation permits the offender to demonstrate to the court that he can become a good citizen. This technique has been particularly effective with juvenile delinquents. A competent probation office staff is essential for successful administration of probation.

Public Defender   An official whose duty it is to act as attorney for persons accused of crime who are unable to secure their own counsel. Since the Supreme Court ruling in *Gideon v. Wainwright*, 372 U.S. 335 (1963) that indigent defendants must be furnished counsel, many state and local governments have established public defender systems. In 1970, Congress authorized the appointment of federal public defenders by federal courts of appeals or, as an alternative, the establishment of community defender organizations financed by federal grants. *See also* LEGAL SERVICES CORPORATION, page 372; RIGHT TO COUNSEL, page 80.

Significance   The use of a public defender is considered to be superior to the more common practice of assignment of counsel by the court or by a private legal aid association. Assigned counsel not only vary in ability but in willingness to devote attention to the defendant's interests. Moreover, private counsel frequently lack the resources available to the public prosecutor. The public defender tends to equalize the differences between the public prosecutor and the defendant by assuring the latter adequate counsel regardless of his financial resources. In short, the public defender system is designed to assure greater justice for the poor.

Referee   A person, ordinarily an attorney, appointed by the court to conduct a hearing on a particular matter and to report to the court. In federal courts, referees are used often in bankruptcy proceedings to collect information and to present it to the court for final disposition of the case. Under the 1960 Civil Rights Act, the federal courts were authorized to appoint voting referees to help qualified Negroes to register to vote in areas where a pattern or practice of racial discrimination existed.

Significance   The referee relieves the judge of attention to routine matters or matters of detail. Preliminary consideration is given to questions that eventually require judicial decision. This is particularly useful when accounting or administrative detail is involved, as in a bankruptcy case.

Sheriff   The chief law enforcement officer of a county, an elective position in all the states except Rhode Island. His duties pertain to both civil and criminal actions. In addition to general law enforcement, the sheriff, as an officer of the court, serves papers, enforces orders, maintains the jail, and collects taxes, with particular functions varying from state to state. In many jurisdictions, the sheriff is paid through fees for each job performed rather than on a regular salary basis. Law-enforcement activities are generally limited to areas outside cities and to patrol on county highways.

Significance The office of sheriff has had a long history, dating back to ninth-century Anglo-Saxon England. Though the office has declined in power and prestige, it remains strongly entrenched as part of American law enforcement. In many areas, the office has proved to be highly lucrative because of the fee system, but it rarely excels as a police agency. With the growth of population in suburban areas, sheriff's offices are faced with increased responsibilities that untrained sheriffs and appointed deputies are not able to meet. Critics advocate the substitution of a professional, countywide police system.

Small Claims Court A court found in many large cities to expedite minor cases at low cost. Disputes over such issues as fuel or grocery bills or wages are quickly settled by a judge.

Significance Thousands of small claims are settled each year in small claims courts without cluttering the dockets of regular courts and without need for the parties to hire attorneys or go to other great expense. Where small claims courts are not found, such cases are generally heard by justices of the peace who receive a fee for their service.

Solicitor General An important official in the Department of Justice who conducts cases on behalf of the United States before the Supreme Court. In addition, his approval is necessary before any appeal may be taken on behalf of the federal government to any appellate court.

Significance As chief counsel for the national government, the Solicitor General's conduct of cases may decide the fate of many important programs. As supervisor of appeals, he is in a position to affect the administration of federal criminal and civil law by determining which issues or cases are worthy of appeal. His decisions and the general conduct of his office may be important keys to the policies of the administration in power in Washington, as reflected in the types of cases in which appeals are brought and in the arguments made before the Supreme Court.

Stare Decisis A legal term meaning "let the decision stand." It is an important element of the common law whereby a decision applies in similar cases and is binding upon lower courts. Precedents thus established stand until overruled. *See also* PRECEDENT, page 259.

Significance The rule of stare decisis lends stability to the law and to legal arrangements among individuals. Thus lawyers, judges, and the public at large, are bound by what has gone before unless compelling reasons call for establishing new precedents.

Statute of Limitations A state or federal legislative act that establishes a time limit within which lawsuits may be brought, judgments enforced, or crimes prosecuted. The time limit varies among different jurisdictions and with the nature of the case, although for certain major offenses, such as murder, no limits are placed on prosecution.

Significance Statutes of limitations prevent endless harassment of individuals by other persons or by the government. Though certain violations of law may go unchallenged, it is considered desirable that at some point, the threat of prosecution be ended.

Statutory Construction   Judicial interpretation of legislative enactments. The application of a statute is not always clear from the words of the statute. Judges seek "legislative intent" by consulting legislative committee hearings, floor debates, and legislative journals. If these sources do not reveal the legislature's objectives, the court must then discern the meaning of the law. *See also* CONSTITUTIONAL CONSTRUCTION, page 24; JURISPRUDENCE, page 253.

Significance   Statutory construction is one of the most difficult tasks of the judiciary. In a complicated society, most laws can be stated only in the most general terms, with specific application to wide varieties of situations left to judges as disputes arise. While the legislative history of an act may produce needed information, it often fails to reveal how the legislature intended the law to fit a specific situation. It is this lack of clarity that often leads to lawsuits. Legislative bodies may deliberately leave statutes vague so that details can be worked out by judges on a case-by-case basis. The net effect of statutory interpretation is to strengthen greatly the power of the courts.

Subpoena   An order of a court, grand jury, legislative body or committee, or of any duly authorized administrative agency, compelling the attendance of a witness. A *subpoena duces tecum* requires the witness to produce specific documents. Failure to honor a subpoena may subject the person to prosecution for contempt. *See also* WITNESS, page 86.

Significance   Public agencies could not properly perform their functions without the power of subpoena. Persons called may refuse to testify or to reveal certain documents if they validly claim that such action may result in self-incrimination. The power of subpoena is of special importance in judicial proceedings, in which both sides of a case have the right to compel testimony of witnesses.

Summons   A complaint made by an individual or a police officer and signed by a judicial officer requiring a person to appear in court to answer charges made against him.

Significance   The summons is usually the first step in civil suits or minor criminal cases. It gives formal notice to the defendant of the charges made against him. In serious criminal matters, charges are made through indictment by grand jury or through a prosecutor's information. The summons satisfies the requirement that a person not be brought to trial without formal complaint and proper notice of the charges against him.

Supreme Court   The court of last resort in the federal and in most state judicial systems. In a few states, the highest court is called by another title. The Supreme Court of the United States is composed of the Chief Justice of the United States and eight associate justices. The number of justices is established by Congress; it has varied from five to ten, but has been set at nine since 1869. Cases are decided by majority vote. The Supreme Court is the only court specifically provided for in the Constitution, and its original jurisdiction is set therein to include cases affecting ambassadors, public ministers, and consuls, and those to which a state is a party. Its appellate jurisdiction is determined by Congress. Certain cases involving federal questions may be appealed to the Supreme Court from the highest state court. With the exception of certain specified cases involving questions of constitutionality, the Supreme Court determines which cases it will hear through the writ of certiorari. The Court sits from October to June and its decisions are reported in the *United States Reports.* State supreme courts vary in size and jurisdiction in accordance with state constitutions and laws but, except for cases that may be brought to the United States Supreme Court, they are the courts of last resort in each state. Justices of the United States Supreme Court are appointed by the President, with the Senate's consent, for life terms subject to impeachment. Most state supreme court judges are elected. The United States Supreme Court and some state supreme courts oversee their respective court systems in matters of procedure and administration *See also* ACTIVISM VERSUS SELF-RESTRAINT, page 236; *Ashwander v. TVA,* page 267; JUDICIAL REVIEW, page 252; UNITED STATES REPORTS, page 265.

Significance Courts of last resort, particularly the Supreme Court of the United States, wield tremendous power and play a major role in the development of public policy. In the final analysis, these courts determine the meaning of the Constitution and of statutes, the scope of legislative and executive power, and the scope of their own power. Decisions as to the meaning of constitutional phrases have lasting impact, unless overruled by the court itself (as in the segregation cases) or overturned by constitutional amendment (as in the case of the income tax). Decisions are binding upon all lower courts, assuring uniformity of judgments. Because of the importance of the questions that reach it, the United States Supreme Court has often been involved in major economic, political, and social controversies. Appointments to the Court are watched with avid interest to ascertain in which way the new justices may influence the interpretation of the Constitution and laws.

Supreme Court Packing Plan A proposal made in 1937 by President Franklin D. Roosevelt that the President be authorized to appoint an additional justice of the Supreme Court for each justice over the age of seventy who did not retire after ten years of service. The maximum numbers of appointments was to have been six, thereby possibly increasing the size of the Supreme Court from nine to fifteen. The President claimed that this plan would increase the efficiency of the Court, but it was defeated in the Congress on the ground that Roosevelt was trying to "pack" the court to overcome unfavorable decisions on New Deal Programs.

Significance The idea of packing the court so as to affect the nature of decisions is not novel in American history. The size of the Court was altered on six different occasions by Congress, either to prevent appointments by a President or to affect decisions. These instances, plus the Roosevelt plan, point up the significance of the Supreme Court in the formulation of public policy. The plan met with strong resistance from members of the Court and Congress as well as from the public at large, demonstrating general support for the Court as an institution that should not be tampered with. In the course of the debate, the Court reversed its previous position, handing down new interpretations of the Constitution that gave free rein to the New Deal. It is said that President Roosevelt "lost the battle but won the war."

Taxpayer Suit A suit brought by a taxpayer to prevent the expenditure of public funds for a given purpose. Such suits are permissible in most of the states but rarely in federal courts. *See also Frothingham v. Mellon,* page 269.

Significance The taxpayer suit is based on the theory that each taxpayer has an interest in how public funds are spent, regardless of the amount of his contribution. Such suits were not heard in federal courts, because the Supreme Court held that no taxpayer has a sufficient personal interest in the vast expenditures of federal funds (*Frothingham v. Mellon*, 262 U.S. 447 [1923]). However, in 1968, in *Flast v. Cohen*, 389 U.S. 895, the court modified its position to authorize suits which involve a possible breach of a specific constitutional limitation on the power to spend or tax, in this instance a challenge to federal aid to parochial schools.

Territorial Court   A court established by Congress in a territory of the United States. Congress has established district courts in Guam, Puerto Rico, the Virgin Islands, and the Panama Canal Zone, under its power to govern the territories, and has authorized minor courts in some cases. With the exception of Puerto Rico, the federal district courts of the territories also hear cases ordinarily heard in state courts. The two federal judges in Puerto Rico hold life terms, while the one judge in each of the other territorial courts is appointed for an eight-year term. *See also* DISTRICT COURT, page 247; LEGISLATIVE COURT, page 255; TERRITORY, page 42.

Significance   Residents of Guam, Puerto Rico, and the Virgin Islands are citizens of the United States. Though statehood is not in the offing, Congress has provided these areas with regular district courts, thereby establishing the American legal tradition.

Test Case   A lawsuit initiated to assess the constitutionality or application of a legislative or executive act. Since federal courts and most state courts do not give advisory opinions, it is necessary to institute a suit to obtain a judicial ruling on the act. This may require the deliberate violation of the act to compel a prosecution or a suit seeking to restrain enforcement. The term "test case" also refers to any landmark case that is the first test of a major piece of legislation.

Significance   The role of the judiciary in the American system is underscored by the common use of the test case. Interest groups that lose in the legislative or executive arena will turn to the courts for satisfaction. Great care is exercised in the selection of test cases to increase chances for a favorable decision. Often a case will be initiated in several jurisdictions at one time in the hope that varied interpretations will more likely assure Supreme Court review.

Tort   A wrongful act involving injury to persons, property, or reputation, but excluding breach of contract. The injured party may bring suit against the wrongdoer. This is an important and often used branch of law. A major tort problem concerns the responsibility of governmental units for torts committed by government employees against individuals.

Significance   Tort law serves as a substitute for private duels and assures that for most wrongs there will be a remedy. The issue of the tort liability of government has not been definitely resolved. Generally, no one may sue the government without consent. Many states and the national government have authorized suits for certain kinds of torts. At the municipal level, the law varies from state to state, but as a general rule, municipalities are not responsible for torts committed by their employees when they are engaged in purely "governmental" functions. There may, however, be liability for torts committed in the course of "proprietary" functions (such as gas supply, transportation, and other businesslike functions). The Federal Tort Claims Act of 1946 permits claims of $1000 or less against the national government to be settled by administrative officials.

Trial   The examination of a civil or criminal action in accordance with the law of the land before a judge who has jurisdiction. A trial must be public, conducted fairly before an impartial judge, and in the case of criminal trials, started without unreasonable delay. *See also* JURY, page 253; *Moore v. Dempsey,* page 97; SIXTH AMENDMENT, page 83; SPEEDY TRIAL, page 83.

Significance A speedy, impartial, and public trial conducted in conformity with established procedures of the law is one of the major hallmarks of a free and civilized people. Knowledge that disputes will be settled in this manner gives the people confidence in the law and makes unnecessary private feuds for settlement of grievances. American trial procedures give adequate opportunity to each side to present its case for examination by the judge or jury.

Unified Court System   An integrated statewide or areawide court system, organized into divisions for more efficient distribution of case load and judges. A chief judge, aided by a judicial council or business manager, supervises the operations of the courts, shifts judges about to meet case load demands, and, through collection of significant data, promotes the efficient administration of justice. *See also* JUDICIAL COUNCIL, page 252.

Significance Most proponents of judicial reform endorse the unified court plan. Most state and local court systems are organized on a geographic basis, with many types of cases heard in each jurisdiction by the same judge. The unified plan, its proponents claim, will encourage specialization among judges, relieve the situation in which some court dockets are crowded while others are not filled, and promote uniformity in decision making. Overall supervision by a chief judge will result in more efficient use of manpower and money, and expedite the business of the courts.

United States Attorney   A federal official whose principal function is to prosecute violations of federal law. A United States Attorney is assigned to each district in which a federal district court is located. He is appointed for a four-year term by the President with the Senate's consent, and is under general supervision of the Department of Justice and the Attorney General of the United States. *See also* DISTRICT ATTORNEY, page 247.

Significance The functions of the United States Attorney underscore the divided nature of American law enforcement. Though he may cooperate with local law enforcement officials, he is responsible only for violations of federal law. The position is frequently a step toward appointment to the federal judiciary.

United States Reports   The official record of cases heard and disposed of by the United States Supreme Court, including the full opinions of the justices. The volumes are issued at the conclusion of the term of the Court, but opinions are available in "advance sheets" prior to issuance of the volumes. Two or three volumes of the *Reports* may emerge each year, depending on the volume of business and length of opinions. The volumes are numbered consecutively now, but, prior to 1874, at which time the *Reports* totaled ninety volumes, they were identified by the names of the official court reporters. These include: Dallas, Cranch, Wheaton, Peters, Howard, Black, and Wallace. Thus, a case cited as 1 Cranch 137 (1803), means that the case, decided in 1803, can be found on page 137 of the first volume compiled by Cranch. Since 1874, the volumes are simply numbered, beginning with 91. A case cited as 345 U.S. 123 (1953) will be found on page 123 of volume 345 of the *United States Reports,* and was decided in 1953. All recorded legal decisions in any court may be found in similar fashion by locating the title, volume, and page of the *Report* in which it is given. Reports are available from federal courts of appeals (*Federal Reporter*), district courts (*Federal Supplement*), and highest state courts which are identified by the name of the state, for example, 156 Michigan 124. Commercial companies also put out volumes reporting these cases: *The Supreme Court Reporter* (cited as 57 Sup. Ct. 234) and the *Lawyers' Edition* (cited as 57 L. Ed. 234).

Significance The reports of cases are available for use by lawyers, legal scholars, and all persons. The reports of Supreme Court cases, in particular, provide some of the best material available on American political and legal thought and practice. Major social and political issues are apt to find their way to the Supreme Court and the opinions are important social documents.

Venue The county or district in which a prosecution is brought for trial and from which jurors are chosen. Venue refers to a particular area, not to the court that has jurisdiction.

Significance Under American law, trials are held in the area in which the wrong is done. The Sixth Amendment to the Constitution provides that, in federal criminal prosecutions, trials are to be held in the state and district in which the crime was committed. Similar provisions are found in state constitutions. This gives the defendant the benefit of a court and a jury familiar with the problems and people of the area. A defendant may, however, ask for a "change of venue," a transfer of the trial to another locality, on the grounds that the people of the locality are prejudiced against him and that an impartial jury could not be drawn. It is for the judge to determine whether a change of venue is justified.

Writ An order in writing issued by a court ordering the performance of an act or prohibiting some act. A wide variety of writs exists, ranging from orders to appear in court to orders regarding the execution of the court's judgment. *See also* CERTIORARI, page 240; HABEAS CORPUS, page 71; INJUNCTION, page 251; MANDAMUS, page 256.

Significance Courts exercise their power largely through the issuance of writs, which are essential for the orderly progress of judicial functions. The right to enforce a decision is as necessary as the right to hear and decide cases. Failure to honor a writ subjects a person to a fine and/or imprisonment for contempt of court.

IMPORTANT AGENCIES

Administrative Office of the United States Courts An agency that handles administrative matters for all federal and territorial courts except the Supreme Court. The Office, established in 1939, is headed by a director who is appointed by the Supreme Court. Its functions include supervision of administrative personnel of the courts, the fixing of compensation of such personnel, preparation of the budget for the operations of the court system, and care of court funds, books, equipment, and supplies. The Office also gathers statistics on dockets, and supervises administration of bankruptcy and federal probation. *See also* JUDICIAL COUNCIL, page 252.

Significance The Administrative Office of the United States Courts has established centralized control over court administration. In the past, little attention had been paid to the administrative problems involved in maintaining an effective judiciary. A Federal Judicial Center was established in 1967 to conduct research on court management and to develop educational programs for judges and court personnel. A 1970 law authorized court executives to handle administrative duties for each federal judicial circuit. Since 1972, an administrative aide has been appointed by the Chief Justice of the United States to help him in administrative duties pertaining to the operation of the Supreme Court.

Department of Justice A major department of the executive branch concerned with the enforcement of federal laws. The Justice Department is headed by the Attorney General who is a member of the President's Cabinet. The Department furnishes legal counsel in cases involving the national government, interprets laws under which other executive agencies operate, supervises federal penal institutions, directs United States attorneys and marshals, supervises immigration laws, and directs paroles of federal prisoners. The Department includes the Federal Bureau of Investigation (FBI), which is the major police agency for the national government. In 1968 the Law Enforcement Assistance Administration was established within the Department to assist state and local governments to improve their police agencies, courts, corrections and other law enforcement units. *See also* DEPARTMENT OF JUSTICE, page 87.

Significance The Department of Justice maintains a close relationship with all other units of the national government because of its widespread responsibility for law enforcement. Its functions also put it into frequent contact with the judicial branch at all stages of judicial proceedings, from the apprehension of law violators to their imprisonment and parole. The Department is not, however, a part of the judicial branch, as is sometimes erroneously thought; this would constitute a violation of the separation of powers because it would unite prosecutor and judge.

IMPORTANT CASES

Ableman v. Booth, 21 Howard 506 (1859): Established that a state court may not issue a writ of habeas corpus to a prisoner in federal custody.

Significance The *Ableman* case underscores the independence of state and federal courts from each other in their proper spheres of authority. No judicial order can have any effect outside the lawful jurisdiction of the court. Neither the states nor the federal courts can intrude into the domain of the other unless the nature of the case demands the exercise of the supreme federal authority.

Ashwander v. TVA, 297 U.S. 288 (1936): Upheld the right of the TVA to sell surplus electric power. Furthermore, the case is well-known for the concurring opinion by Justice Louis D. Brandeis in which he attempted to sum up the rules that the Court had developed in considering the constitutionality of the acts of the legislative and executive branches. Among these were: (1) the Court will not decide questions of a constitutional nature, unless absolutely essential to dispose of the case; (2) the Court will not pass upon a constitutional question if the case can be disposed of on some other ground; (3) the Court will not formulate a constitutional rule broader than is required by the precise facts of the case; and (4) the Court will try to construe a statute so as to avoid ruling on constitutional questions, even if serious doubts exist as to its constitutionality. *See also Ashwander v. TVA,* page 359; JUDICIAL REVIEW, page 252.

Significance The Court's self-denying rules, as formulated by Justice Brandeis, for handling constitutional issues, have governed its course in recent years. It remains reluctant to rule on the constitutionality of federal legislation, and only a few statutory provisions have been declared unconstitutional since 1937. Through these rules, the Court has sought to avoid controversy with the legislative and executive branches.

Cohens v. Virginia, 6 Wheaton 264 (1821): Ruled that state court decisions are subject to review by the Supreme Court if the case involves a question of federal law, treaties, or the Constitution, even though a state is a party to the suit. An appeal brought to a federal court by a defendant who has been convicted in a state court does not constitute a suit against the state contrary to the Eleventh Amendment.

Significance The question of whether the Supreme Court had appellate jurisdiction over cases appealed from state courts was crucial to the development of federal judicial power. Prior to the *Cohens* decision, the Supreme Court held, in *Martin v. Hunter's Lessee,* 1 Wheaton 304 (1816), that it had the right to review state court decisions involving suits between private individuals when a federal question is involved. The *Cohens* decision extended this principle to cases in which a state is a party. In both cases, the Court pointed out that federal jurisdiction is essential to establish uniformity of decision throughout the United States on the interpretation of the Constitution, federal law, or treaties. Otherwise, each state, rather than the national government, would be supreme.

Dred Scott v. Sanford, 19 Howard 393 (1857): Held, in a famous case, that Negroes could not become citizens of the United States nor were they entitled to the rights and privileges of citizenship. The Court also ruled that the Missouri Compromise, which had banned slavery in the territories, was unconstitutional.

Significance The *Dred Scott* decision is considered to be one of the most disastrous handed down by the Supreme Court. The Court itself was badly divided and muddled in its views. The case failed to resolve the slavery issue and contributed to the inevitability of the Civil War. Both the Civil War and the provisions of the Fourteenth Amendment on citizenship were needed to overcome the *Dred Scott* ruling. The *Dred Scott* case is also noted for being the second in which a federal law was declared unconstitutional, following the Supreme Court's exercise of judicial review in *Marbury v. Madison,* 1 Cranch 137 (1803). The crucial role of the Supreme Court in American life and politics is underscored by the *Dred Scott* case.

Eakin v. Raub, 12 S. & R. 330 (1825): Decided by the Supreme Court of the State of Pennsylvania, this case is famous for an opinion by Judge John B. Gibson against the principle of judicial review. Judge Gibson disagreed with the logic of Chief Justice John Marshall's opinion in *Marbury v. Madison*, 1 Cranch 137 (1803) in which Marshall argued that judges had a special duty to interpret the Constitution and to declare any law in conflict with the Constitution null and void. Judge Gibson argued that the judges had no such duty. Rather, the legislature bore the responsibility for unlawful acts and the people should hold them responsible. *See also Marbury v. Madison*, page 270.

Significance Judge Gibson's opinion is the best-known argument by a judge against the principle of judicial review. Although it never overthrew that principle, the position he took is still held by many persons. The student of government may find the complete opinion of Judge Gibson reproduced in many casebooks or textbooks on constitutional law.

Erie Railroad v. Tompkins, 304 U.S. 64 (1938): Ruled that, in diversity of citizenship cases heard in federal courts, the law to be applied is the state law as declared by the state legislature or courts. There is no federal common law. *See also* DIVERSITY OF CITIZENSHIP, page 247.

Significance The *Erie* case overruled *Swift v. Tyson*, 16 Peters 1 (1842), which had held that in the absence of a state statute controlling a case, the federal courts could apply their own principles of the common law. After almost a century of confusion resulting from several versions of the common law, particularly in commercial cases, the Court declared in the *Erie* case that the *Tyson* rule was not only incorrect but unconstitutional as well, since there is no general federal common law.

Ex parte McCardle, 7 Wallace 506 (1869): Declared that the Supreme Court may not exercise appellate jurisdiction over a case when Congress prohibits such jurisdiction. This case arose when Congress repealed an 1867 law that had authorized appeals to the Supreme Court in certain cases involving enforcement of the post-Civil War Reconstruction Acts.

Significance Congress withdrew jurisdiction from the Supreme Court in this case for fear that the Court would declare the Acts unconstitutional. Nevertheless, the Court dismissed the case on the ground that it lacked jurisdiction. The *McCardle* case demonstrates the veto power of Congress over the appellate jurisdiction of the Supreme Court. The Constitution in Article III, section 2, provides that the Supreme Court has appellate jurisdiction in all cases heard in federal courts "with such exceptions, and under such regulations as the Congress shall make." Congress does not grant appellate power but may make exceptions to its exercise.

Frothingham v. Mellon, 262 U.S. 447 (1923): Held that a taxpayer may not bring suit in a federal court to restrain the expenditure of federal funds. The case involved a protest against a federal grant-in-aid to the states for maternity benefits. The Court has since modified the rule to permit taxpayer suits where a specific breach of constitutional power is alleged (*Flast v. Cohen*, 389 U.S. 895 [1968]). *See also Massachusetts v. Mellon*, page 45.

Significance An important element of judicial procedure is that a party to a suit must have standing to sue. That is, a party must be able to show "some direct injury . . . and not merely that he suffers in some indefinite way in common with people generally." Although taxpayer suits are common in state and local courts, the Supreme Court has taken the view that an individual's interest in federal taxation and expenditures is too minute. In *Flast v. Cohen,* the Court ruled that an exception could be made where a taxpayer could establish a link between himself and the taxing or spending law, and could point to a specific constitutional limitation on the right to tax and spend. Thus the Court authorized a challenge to public expenditures for parochial schools since a violation of the First Amendment was possible. The Court reaffirmed the *Frothingham* rule that a taxpayer suit cannot be brought because the taxpayer believes the tax unwise or an interference with the reserved powers of the states.

Marbury v. Madison, 1 Cranch 137 (1803): Struck down, for the first time in American history, an act of Congress as unconstitutional. The Court, speaking through Chief Justice John Marshall, held unconstitutional a portion of the Judiciary Act of 1789 that had added to the original jurisdiction of the Supreme Court, as specified in Article III of the Constitution. Marshall argued that the Constitution was the supreme law, and that judges were bound by their oath and the nature of their positions to act as guardians of the Constitution. Any law in conflict with the Constitution cannot be enforced by the courts. *See also Eakin v. Raub,* page 269; JUDICIAL REVIEW, page 252.

Significance Few cases have had the impact upon American governmental development as has *Marbury v. Madison,* in which Chief Justice Marshall struck a decisive blow for judicial supremacy. The case was essentially a political controversy between the defeated Federalist party and the incoming Jeffersonian party over last-minute Federalist party appointments to the federal courts. Marshall used the occasion to write a strong, logical defense of the role of the judiciary under the separation of powers doctrine, which is generally assumed to reflect the views of the framers of the Constitution. Although the Constitution fails to mention judicial review, the American people have accepted its exercise by the courts as an integral part of the American constitutional system. In 1974, in rejecting President Richard M. Nixon's claim that the separation of powers doctrine precluded judicial review of his claim of executive privilege, the Supreme Court relied heavily on the statement from *Marbury v. Madison* that "it is emphatically the province and duty of the judicial department to say what the law is." (*United States v. Nixon,* 418 U.S. 683).

IMPORTANT STATUTES

Judiciary Act of 1789 A law passed by the first Congress to establish the federal court system. The Act determined the organization and jurisdiction of the courts. Over the years, the Judiciary Act has undergone numerous changes, adding and deleting courts, changing jurisdiction of courts, establishing rules of procedure, and providing for a variety of court officers and employees.

Significance The Judiciary Act of 1789 and its subsequent amendments demonstrate congressional authority over federal court organization, jurisdiction, and procedure. The only constitutional limit placed on Congress is that a Supreme Court must exist with specified original jurisdiction. A portion of the Judiciary Act of 1789 was declared unconstitutional in the famous case of *Marbury v. Madison,* 1 Cranch 137 (1803), because, in it, the Congress had unconstitutionally added to the original jurisdiction of the Supreme Court. Changes of significance include the Act of 1891, which established the courts of appeals and the Act of 1925, which gave the Supreme Court discretionary authority to issue writs of certiorari.

11   Finance and Taxation

Ability Theory   The belief that taxes should be based upon the individual's ability to pay, as indicated by income, property, consumption, or wealth. *See also* INCOME TAX, page 285; PROGRESSIVE TAX, page 290.

Significance   The ability theory is often challenged, particularly by advocates of the benefit theory, who hold that taxes should be paid by those who derive benefits from them. The graduated income tax most nearly approximates the ideal of the ability theory because of its progressive increases in rates as income (and, hence, ability to pay) rises. The federal individual income tax is based theoretically on the ability theory, although in fact many exemptions and other favored treatments have reduced its progressive nature. "Luxury taxes" in the form of excises on goods purchased by high income groups also tend to be based on the ability theory. Recent studies indicate that most Americans pay approximately the same percentage of their income in taxes, whether rich or poor.

Assessed Valuation   Value assigned to property for tax purposes. The general property tax levied by local governments in the United States is based on the valuation placed upon real estate (land, buildings, and other improvements) and personal property, both tangible (machinery, livestock, merchandise) and intangible (stocks, bonds, bank accounts). The tax paid on property is based on the assessed valuation and the millage or tax rate applied to the assessed value. The assessed valuation is based on a proportion of the actual value of each piece of property assessed within a taxing district, usually 30 to 50 percent of true market value, although some political units currently assess at 100 percent value. Assessments can be changed by reappraisals, adjustment of individual inequities by a board of review, adjustment of unequal valuations for different assessment districts by a county or state board of equalization, or by a general revaluation of all assessments within a district. *See also* ASSESSOR, page 273; PROPERTY TAX, page 291.

Significance   The assessment of property for tax purposes is a complex process that produces much controversy among taxpayers, many of whom believe their property is assessed too high or unequally as compared with their neighbor's, or with those of other taxing districts. The fair assessment of personal property poses the greatest problem because of the difficulty for assessors to find and appraise movable property. When a taxing district crosses assessment boundaries, such as a school district that includes a city and several townships, the danger of disparities in assessed valuation is increased. The key to a fair assessment system may be found in the appointment of professional countywide or statewide assessors.

Assessor A public official who determines the value of real and personal property for purposes of taxation. Assessors are commonly elected in towns, townships, or counties. In some midwestern townships, the supervisor serves as the assessor. About 15 percent of city assessors are still elected and the remainder are political or merit system appointees. Many local units hire private assessing specialists in response to taxpayer criticism of elected or appointed governmental assessors. *See also* ASSESSED VALUATION, page 272; PROPERTY TAX, page 291.

Significance Many students of government challenge the election of assessors. The elective method is unlikely to secure competent assessors, and elected officials may undercrassess so as not to antagonize the voters. Critics also charge the town or township is too small a unit for assessment purposes. Many areas have moved in the direction of appointing assessors on a merit basis and making the county the assessment unit. Whether appointed or elected, the assessor is often an important local political official who, it is sometimes charged, tends to favor business and real estate interests.

Auditor An official, usually an agent of a legislative body, who checks on the expenditure of appropriated funds to determine that they will be or have been spent for the purposes approved by the legislature in its appropriation acts. The federal auditor, the Comptroller General, is appointed by the President with the Senate's approval; state and local auditors are either appointed or elected by the voters. *See also* COMPTROLLER GENERAL, page 276; GENERAL ACCOUNTING OFFICE, page 299.

Significance Proper auditing of disbursed funds is essential to fiscal responsibility. In many state and local governments, only a preaudit in the form of a spending authorization is required, with no proper postaudit after expenditures to check their validity. In other cases, the same officials who authorize the expenditures are later called upon to check on the authenticity of their own work. Effective auditing procedures require careful examination of the validity of accounts and payments by competent, independent auditors *after* the expenditures have been made by the executive branch.

Banking Systems The national and state banking systems, which exist side by side in the United States. Congress was not granted the specific power to charter banks, but the power is implied from granted powers that can best be carried on through banks, such as the borrowing and currency powers. Both national and state chartered banks are privately owned financial institutions, which are regulated and have their accounts audited by the respective chartering government. National banks, chartered by the national government since 1863, are supervised by the Comptroller of the Currency in the Treasury Department, and are required to join the Federal Reserve System. Most state banks accept Federal Reserve membership and thereby come under a measure of national as well as state regulation. The citizen can usually distinguish between a national and state chartered bank by their names, such as First National Bank or Industrial State Bank. *See also* FEDERAL RESERVE SYSTEM, page 282.

Significance Federal and state regulation of banks involves such matters as issuance of stock, stockholder liabilities, assets and investments, organization and management, reserves, loans, and depositor security. The public is protected through periodic inspections and audits by examiners, and by deposit insurance, up to $40,000 for each account, guaranteed by the Federal Deposit Insurance Corporation. The dual national-state banking system provides some measure of financial flexibility, although state banks have lost much of their autonomy through membership in the Federal Reserve System.

Benefit Theory The belief that individuals should be taxed in proportion to the benefits they derive from governmental services. Taxes based on the benefit theory are often earmarked for special purposes, thus reducing the flexibility of government policy makers. *See also* ABILITY THEORY, page 272; EARMARKING, page 280; SPECIAL ASSESSMENT, page 296.

Significance The benefit and cost of services theories have largely been superseded by the ability theory, which is regarded as more equitable and easier to determine in a complex society in which benefits derived from taxes often go unnoticed. The benefit theory is still applied in special areas where the benefits can be directly or easily assessed. The 1956 Federal Highway Act, for example, provides for financing of the vast interstate highway system with federal gasoline excise taxes levied on highway users. On the local level, special assessments on improvements that benefit the property owner are used extensively. The cost of governmental services rendered approach as a means of determining tax liability is a form of benefit theory that has generally proved difficult to implement except for assessing taxpayer liability for governmental improvements that increase the value of private property, such as sidewalks and sewers.

Board of Review Public officials charged with the duty of reviewing individual tax assessments on property. The review function is to be distinguished from "equalization," which is the comparison and adjustment of assessments between entire tax-imposing units. The board of review may be elected or composed of local government officials serving ex officio. *See also* ASSESSED VALUATION, page 272; ASSESSOR, page 273; PROPERTY TAX, page 291.

Significance Citizens dissatisfied with their property tax may appeal to a board of review. The board's objective is to tax all citizens equitably, according to the value of their property. Most citizens fail to take advantage of their right of review, not wanting to take the time or trouble, or out of fear that their assessment may be raised. Many taxpayer complaints result from a lack of understanding of assessment and tax-levying procedures.

Bond A certificate of indebtedness, tendered by a borrower to a lender, that constitutes a written obligation for the borrower to repay to the lender the principal plus accrued interest on the loan. A public bond is issued by the national government or by a state or local government as a means of borrowing money for public needs that cannot be financed out of current revenues. *See also* BOND, page 305; DEBT LIMIT, page 277; INTERGOVERNMENTAL TAX IMMUNITY, page 37.

Significance Various types of bonds, such as savings bonds, are issued by the United States government to finance budget deficits and to carry the public debt. State and local governments commonly make use of either serial bonds or sinking fund issues to finance new projects. Sinking fund bonds are paid from a separate fund set aside from revenues over a period of time until the bonds are due for payment. Serial bonds, which are becoming more popular than the sinking fund type, come due at different dates over a period of years, with each series paid off by the borrowing authority from current revenues. Commercial bond rating concerns evaluate the credit ratings of local governments and thus help to determine the interest rates and marketability of bond issues.

Borrowing Power The authority of a government to finance budget deficits that result when expenditures exceed income. The Constitution (Art. I, sec. 8) provides Congress with full borrowing power, free from restrictions. Most state constitutions, however, severely limit the authority of state governments to incur indebtedness, permitting state borrowing only when authorized by constitutional amendment or by a vote of the people. Local units of government are restricted by state constitutional or statutory limitations on their borrowing power. *See also* DEBT LIMIT, page 277; DEFICIT FINANCING, page 278; PUBLIC DEBT, page 291.

Significance The borrowing power is essential for governments to meet short- and long-term crises and to finance major projects that cannot be paid for out of current income. The national government, for example, used its borrowing power extensively during World War II and the economic crisis of the 1930s. Deficit spending to counteract economic recessions has become a standard weapon in the arsenal of federal fiscal policy. Most state and local borrowing, conversely, is used to finance major building projects. Some citizens support borrowing for capital improvements as an investment in the future, similar to borrowing by a family to purchase a home. Others view extensive use of the borrowing power as fiscal irresponsibility. Although economists generally regard the borrowing power as a necessary tool of governmental fiscal policy, political leaders disagree over the extent, timing, and purpose of specific applications of the policy.

Budget An estimate of the receipts and expenditures needed by government to carry out its program in some future period, usually a fiscal year. The President is responsible for formulating the national budget under the Budget and Accounting Act of 1921, and governors of most states likewise operate under an "executive budget" system. The budget process begins with the lengthy and detailed process of preparing estimates, followed by a central review in which budget officers hold hearings during which agency officials defend their estimates. Next, the budget is approved by the chief executive and submitted to the legislative body in a "budget message." After study and the holding of hearings by appropriations committees, the budget is enacted as an appropriation act. This is followed by budget execution, the actual spending of the money during the fiscal period by executive officials. The final step is a post-audit check on the validity of expenditures. Some states and cities use a separate capital budget for financing major public works projects, which are often paid for on a long-term bonding or self-liquidating basis. In the federal budget of more than $300 billion for Fiscal 1975, each federal budget dollar was divided as follows— *Income:* individual income tax, 42¢; social insurance receipts, 28¢; corporation income tax, 16¢; excise taxes, 6¢; miscellaneous, 5¢; and borrowing, 3¢;—*Expenditures:* health, education, and social security, 37¢; national defense, 29¢; state and local grants, 17¢; interest on debt, 7¢; and miscellaneous, 10¢. To strengthen its fiscal role, Congress in 1974 established budget committees in each house to oversee revenue and spending activities, and a new Congressional Budget Office similar to the President's Office of Management and Budget (OMB). *See also* BUDGET AND

ACCOUNTING ACT OF 1921, page 301; OFFICE OF MANAGEMENT AND BUDGET, page 299; PERFOR-
MANCE BUDGET, page 289; PROGRAM BUDGET, page 290.

Significance A budget is a work plan that gives direction to the execution of government policies. The budget process has undergone a major change in the twentieth century with the adoption of the executive budget to replace the formulation of budgets by legislative committees, and the use of performance and program budgets for more effective evaluation of spending. The executive budget gives the chief executive—President, governor, or mayor—extensive control over fiscal affairs. The executive budget power, however, is often diminished by the influence of pressure groups on the budget process, and by the structure of "built-in" appropriations that are protected by a political linkage involving the administrative agency, its clientele, and the legislative appropriations committees. The trend on all levels of government is toward developing program budgets utilizing automatic data processing systems that permit a continuing evaluation of the effectiveness of specific programs carried on by governmental units. Program budgets, however, may also lack evaluative and controlling force if bureaucratic units develop ideas to meet programmatic rather than operational needs.

Business Cycles   The rhythmic fluctuation of a free economy as changes occur in business activity. Business cycles, typically, involve movements from prosperity to recession or depression, followed by economic recovery and the completion of the cycle by a return to the previous high point of economic activity. A new cycle then begins. *See also* DEPRESSION, page 278; FISCAL POLICY, page 283; KEYNESIANISM, page 287; MONETARY POLICY, page 289.

Significance Business cycles were considered to be natural economic phenomena by classical economists, and their recurrence was regarded as inevitable. Since the 1930s, however, it is no longer considered to be politically feasible or economically necessary to allow the cycles to run their course. Policymakers aim at avoiding the heavy costs in unemployment and economic stagnation at low points in the cycles, and the ever-present dangers of inflation at the high points. The national government accordingly employs fiscal and monetary policies in seeking to control the extremes of business cycle activity and inactivity in an attempt to promote general and continuing stability for the economy. The problem remains, however, of developing sophisticated applications of fiscal and monetary policy and applying them at the right time with the correct amount of forcefulness. Theories to explain business cycles have focused on psychological factors, under- and over-savings, the impact of politics, and the expansion and contraction of bank credit. Radical groups have tended to explain business cycles as a natural and defective consequence of the capitalistic system.

Comptroller General   The federal official responsible for auditing the accounts of all national government agencies. Functioning as the financial adviser to Congress, the Comptroller General heads the General Accounting Office (GAO), and is appointed by the President with the Senate's approval for a fifteen-year term. The Comptroller General also has power to validate all payments to ensure that they fall within the purposes and limits of congressional appropriations acts and to standardize accounting systems of government agencies. He can be removed from office by impeachment or by joint resolution of Congress. *See also* AUDITOR, page 273; GENERAL ACCOUNTING OFFICE, page 299.

Significance The Comptroller General acts as an agent of Congress in controlling and auditing the budget execution process in the executive branch. Without his approval, money cannot validly be withdrawn from the Treasury. Controversy has developed on occasion when the Comptroller General has been charged with letting his personal views influence the validation of expenditures. For example, President Franklin Roosevelt became involved in many controversies with the Comptroller General because the latter's open hostility to the New Deal was regarded as the reason for his holding up many emergency spending programs. Numerous observers, including the first Hoover Commission, have recommended that the Comptroller General's "preaudit" validation of payments be transferred to an executive official, leaving the Comptroller General with responsibility for a "postaudit." In recent years, the Comptroller General has expanded his operations by sending his GAO investigators abroad to check on foreign aid and other types of overseas spending.

Corporation Income Tax A national tax levied on corporations, based on their annual net income. The corporation income tax rate in recent years has been a flat 22 percent for the first $25,000 of net income and 48 percent on all net income over that figure. It is, essentially, a tax on the privilege of doing business as a corporation, and, as such, was first enacted prior to the adoption of the Sixteenth Amendment. *See also* EXCESS PROFITS TAX, page 281; INCOME TAX, page 285.

Significance The federal corporation income tax is probably the most complicated tax levied by the national government, resulting from controversy over what constitutes "net income" and "legitimate" expenses for a corporation. It ranks next to the individual income tax in the amount of its annual yield. In recent years, it has produced about 16 percent of total federal income annually. The tax has been attacked for fostering "double taxation," that is, the taxing of corporation income through the corporation income tax, followed by the taxing of shareholders' dividends through the individual income tax. Others have criticized the corporation income tax for its lenient rates and loopholes. The corporation income tax was substantially reduced on 1975 income to help combat a serious economic recession.

Debt Limit A constitutional or statutory limitation upon the ability of a government to incur indebtedness. In the national government, the debt limit is fixed by Congress and can be changed to meet new debt needs. All but a few states, however, are restricted by constitutional provisions that limit state indebtedness, usually to a specified figure. Debt limitations on local governments generally take the form of restricting total debt to a percentage of assessed valuation or involve state approval of bond issues. *See also* DEFICIT FINANCING, page 278; PUBLIC DEBT, page 291.

Significance Self-imposed statutory debt limits established by legislative bodies, as by Congress, are useful only psychologically, if at all. Over the past three decades, Congress has altered the public debt limit on numerous occasions, raising it to almost $500 billion in 1974, with the national debt at about $475 billion at that time. On the state and local levels, cumbersome constitutional restrictions have produced many new techniques for evasion. Although debt limits can ordinarily be exceeded by favorable referendum votes in the state and local governments, voter apathy or conservatism has made this increasingly difficult. Devices that have been used to incur indebtedness beyond state or local limits include borrowing by state agencies instead of the state, per se, and borrowing on a self-liquidating basis without state certification of bonds. For example, state toll road authorities borrow large sums to construct highways, and repay the debt out of income from tolls. Despite efforts to keep debt limited on the national, state, and local levels, new demands for governmental functions and services beyond the means of current income and the increasing tendency to use federal deficits to stimulate a sluggish economy keep debt rising in the United States.

Deficit Financing   A technique of fiscal policy that utilizes government spending beyond income to combat an economic slump. The use of deficit financing to "prime the pump" of the free enterprise economy was popularized by the British economist, John Maynard Keynes, in the 1930s. It has since become generally accepted and used as a basic tool of federal economic policy. *See also* DEBT LIMIT, page 277; FISCAL POLICY, page 283; KEYNESIANISM, page 287; PUBLIC DEBT, page 291.

Significance   The objective of deficit financing is to inject new purchasing power into the economy to stimulate an upturn in economic activity during a period of stagnation resulting from overproduction or underconsumption. Deficit financing is accepted today by most economists and politicians, on the assumption that deficits incurred during economic slumps will be paid off with budget surpluses during periods of prosperity. Some conservatives still oppose it on the grounds that it involves fiscal irresponsibility and is ineffectual, and they usually demand government cutbacks in spending as the best means of stimulating the free economy. The national government used deficit financing during the depression of the 1930s and has employed it to combat six post-World War II recessions. Deficit federal budgets have become common, with balanced or surplus budgets increasingly rare. Issues tend to involve the magnitude of the deficit, how the deficit will be spent and its inflationary impact, rather than whether a deficit is ideologically justifiable. The federal budget has, in fact, involved deficit financing in 36 of the 54 years from 1921 to 1975.

Deflation   An economic condition in which the price level is decreased and the value of money in terms of purchasing power is consequently increased. Deflation may result from either a decrease in the amount of money and credit available or an oversupply of consumer goods. *See also* INFLATION, page 286; MONETARY POLICY, page 289.

Significance   Proponents of stable monetary policies regard deflation and inflation, its opposite, as twin evils to be equally avoided. Deflation is characteristically associated with economic depressions, just as inflation tends to accompany prosperity. Most economists believe that deflation can be prevented or controlled through stimulative use of monetary policy by the Federal Reserve Board and the Treasury and by the use of fiscal policy, such as deficit financing. A policy of deflation is sometimes adopted by a nation suffering from an adverse balance of payments, with the objective of reducing prices to make exports more attractive to other countries.

Depression   A business cycle period characterized by a serious economic slump, inadequate purchasing power, deflation, and high unemployment. Typically, major depressions have followed peak periods of prosperity when production facilities and credit have been overextended. A recession is an economic slump of lesser proportions and shorter duration. *See also* BUSINESS CYCLES, page 276; KEYNESIANISM, page 287.

Significance The American economy has experienced numerous recessions and several depressions of serious proportions, but all previous ones were dwarfed by the Great Depression of the 1930s. Classical economic theory held that depressions are inevitable in a free enterprise economy and that self-correcting economic forces set in motion by the depression would in time provide adjustments without governmental interference. Today, economic theory and analysis are aimed at preventing a depression, and most economists believe that governmental monetary and fiscal policies can prevent or quickly remedy a serious depression if they are wisely used and properly timed. Six post-World War II economic recessions have been attacked with monetary and fiscal measures, and the serious downturns in the economy have been arrested and reversed before they could assume depression proportions. Economists and political leaders tend to agree on the definition of recession as involving a reduction in total national production of goods and services for two consecutive quarters. No agreements exists, however, as to when a recession turns into a depression, and the specific criteria for defining the latter.

Devaluation A policy undertaken by a nation to reduce the value of its monetary unit in terms of gold, or its exchange ratio with other national currencies. The United States devalued the dollar by about 59 percent in 1934 by increasing the price of gold to $35 an ounce. The price thereafter remained fixed at $35 an ounce until President Richard M. Nixon agreed in late 1971 to devalue the dollar by raising the official price of gold in exchange for agreement by other major nations to realign their currencies by raising their values in relation to the dollar. Subsequently, the United States ended its selling and buying of gold at a fixed price, thereby in effect severing the dollar's tie with gold. In 1974, Congress changed a forty-year policy by permitting American citizens to own gold, with the price determined by market conditions. *See also* BALANCE OF PAYMENTS, page 382; GOLD STANDARD, page 284; INTERNATIONAL MONETARY FUND, page 287.

Significance Although American devaluation of the dollar in 1934 was based largely on domestic reasons, ordinarily the objective of devaluation is to improve a nation's balance of international payments by reducing imports and expanding exports. These results are likely to occur because devaluation increases the cost of foreign products. Devaluations are often matched by equal or greater devaluations by competitor states in an effort to maintain their position in international trade. Although successive rounds of devaluations were carried on by many states during the 1930s, the only major devaluations in the postwar era occurred in 1949 when Britain and most sterling bloc countries depreciated their currencies by about 30 percent. President Nixon's action during the 1970s of divesting the dollar of its gold base resulted from the chronic imbalance in the American balance of payments and the resulting massive outflow of dollars. One of the major responsibilities of the International Monetary Fund (IMF) of the United Nations is to try to eliminate competitive unilateral devaluation as an international trade weapon.

Direct Tax Any tax paid directly to the government by the taxpayer. An indirect tax, such as a sales or excise tax, conversely, is paid to private business persons who then remit it to the government. The Constitution, in Article I, section 9 states: "No capitation, or other direct tax shall be laid, unless in proportion to the census or enumeration herein before directed to be taken."

This provision means that, for example, the people in a state containing 10 percent of the nation's population would pay 10 percent of any direct tax levied by the national government. *See also* *Pollock v. Farmers Loan and Trust Co.,* page 300.

Significance The question of which taxes are direct and therefore to be apportioned according to the population of the states, has been the subject of much legal controversy. In 1796 (*Hylton v. United States,* 3 Dallas 171), the Supreme Court interpreted "direct taxes" to include poll taxes and taxes on land. In 1895 (*Pollock v. Farmers Loan and Trust Co.,* 158 U.S. 601), the Court struck down an income tax as a direct tax that Congress must apportion among the states. This decision was overcome by the Sixteenth Amendment, which granted the Congress the power to tax incomes "without apportionment among the several states, and without regard to any census or enumeration." Congress has generally refused to levy direct taxes, because apportionment involves many administrative complications and because of inequities that would result since tax-paying ability is not divided equally among the people of the fifty states.

Earmarking Allocation of tax revenues for specific purposes. Earmarking gasoline taxes for highway purposes is the most common example, with about half the states doing so by constitutional provision, and the others by statutory requirement. About half of total state revenue is earmarked for specific purposes, such as highways, education, or welfare. Earmarked taxes are often based on the "benefit theory" of taxation. *See also* BENEFIT THEORY, page 274.

Significance Earmarking tax revenues by constitutional provision reduces legislative and executive control over budgeting and finance. Earmarked programs may be adequately financed while other equally or more deserving public needs go unfilled. It is often easier, however, for the legislature to secure public consent to an earmarked tax, since the people can clearly see the object of the tax, and because powerful interest groups which stand to benefit use propaganda and lobbying tactics to "sell" the tax to the public and to members of the legislature. The most commonly earmarked taxes in the states are those for financing highway building programs, and those that set aside percentages of general sales or income taxes for educational purposes. An example of federal earmarking is the use of gasoline taxes for building interstate highways.

Equalization The review and adjustment of tax assessments among taxing districts in the state. The equalization function may be exercised at the county level to adjust assessments among the townships, cities and other units of the county and, at the state level, to equalize assessments among counties. If property in one area is assessed at 50 percent of value and in another at 30 percent, some adjustment is necessary to equalize the burdens borne by taxpayers. Equalization differs from the local review of assessments in which individual rather than area assessments are reviewed. *See also* PROPERTY TAX, page 291.

Significance One of the characteristics of local government in the United States is the multiplicity of taxing units. This, combined with variable assessment by popularly elected nonprofessional assessors, often results in unequal distribution of tax burdens. Equalization reduces inequities among units of government but does not eliminate them and does not resolve inequities in assessment of individual properties within the same unit.

Estate Tax A tax, usually with progressive rates, levied on the property of deceased persons. Estate taxes apply to the total estate, whereas inheritance taxes are levied on the portions of the estate received by the beneficiaries. The national government has regularly levied an estate tax since 1916, and all states except Nevada have an estate or inheritance tax, in most instances, the latter. The gift tax, having rates nearly as high as the estate tax, is used to plug the loophole by which money was given to relatives and friends before death in order to avoid estate taxes. *See also* PROGRESSIVE TAX, page 290.

Significance The federal estate and gift taxes together have averaged over $5 billion annually in recent years. A high percentage of state death taxes may be offset as a credit against payment of the federal estate tax, which has served as an encouragement for the states to enact such levies. State inheritance taxes are also progressive, with rates increasing sharply as the beneficiary's share rises, and as the relationship of the beneficiary to the deceased becomes more distant. Estate and inheritance taxes are aimed at preventing excessive concentrations of wealth in a few families as well as raising revenue. The use of trusts to avoid the payment of estate and inheritance taxes has become a matter of some concern. The gift tax can also be used to avoid estate taxes in that the first $3,000 given by one person to another is exempted from the gift tax. This can involve many gifts to many people over many years.

Excess Profits Tax A special tax levied during wartime to supplement the corporation income tax. The excess profits tax is calculated on the difference between business earnings in normal years and earnings during the war years when profits soar. An excess profits tax was levied by Congress during World Wars I and II, and during the Korean episode from 1951 to 1953. In the last case, the tax was fixed at 30 percent of the excess profits, with the limitation that the combined corporation income tax and excess profits tax should not exceed 70 percent of net income. The failure to levy an excess profits tax during the Vietnam war contributed to the nation's serious inflation and balance of payments problems of the early 1970s. *See also* CORPORATION INCOME TAX, page 277.

Significance The excess profits tax is designed primarily to recapture abnormal profits and to help finance military expenditures. It also is psychologically motivated to quiet public fears of wartime business profiteering. The opposition of businessmen to the tax, usually quiescent during the war period, has always forced an early repealing of the tax at the war's end.

Excise Tax A tax levied upon the manufacture, transportation, sale, or consumption of goods within a country or state. Federal excise taxes are permitted by the Constitution, and such levies have been placed on a variety of consumer goods. The main excise taxes used by the states are sales and use taxes. Heavy excises on what are regarded as socially undesirable commodities, such as liquor and tobacco, are a form of sumptuary tax. *See also* REGULATORY TAX, page 293; SALES TAX, page 295.

Significance Federal income from excise taxes is exceeded only by the individual and corporation income taxes. The excises on liquor and tobacco provide the greatest yields. State excise taxes, unlike the federal, are often criticized for their regressive character in taxing necessities, with the tax burden falling proportionately heavier on low-income families. Many federal excises were first levied during World War II as emergency income measures, but were continued until 1965 when Congress eliminated some and reduced others.

Federal Reserve Notes   Currency issued by Federal Reserve banks, backed by deposits with the government of discounted commercial paper (such as promissory notes or bills of exchange), government bonds, and gold certificates. *See also* FEDERAL RESERVE SYSTEM, page 282.

Significance Federal Reserve notes are the most important kind of currency in circulation in the United States today. A small volume of silver certificates, treasury notes, federal bank notes, and national bank notes still circulate, but are being slowly retired. Since going off the gold standard in 1934, the United States has had a "managed" currency. Elasticity in the supply of Federal Reserve notes is provided by its commercial paper backing; when borrowing is heavy, more currency can be issued, and when demand for loans shrinks, the issue of currency can be reduced. Gold backing of Federal Reserve notes is fixed by statute at 25 percent.

Federal Reserve System The private-public banking regulatory system in the United States, which establishes banking policies and influences the amount of credit available and the currency in circulation. The Federal Reserve System was created by Congress in 1913. It consists of twelve Federal Reserve banks, each located in one of the twelve Federal Reserve districts into which the country is divided, and a central Board of Governors of seven members appointed by the President and confirmed by the Senate. Each of the Federal Reserve banks is headed by a board of nine directors, six of whom are chosen by the member banks in the district and three by the Federal Reserve Board in Washington. In addition, the system includes a Federal Open Market Committee that makes policy in buying and selling securities and through foreign currency operations, and a Federal Advisory Council, composed of one member from each Federal Reserve Bank, that advises the Board of Governors. Membership in district Federal Reserve banks is required of all national banks and permitted for state banks, and most of the latter have joined. The Federal Reserve banks are actually privately owned "bankers' banks," with all member banks required to hold stock in them. *See also* BOARD OF GOVERNORS, page 297; MONETARY POLICY, page 289; OPEN MARKET OPERATIONS, page 289; REDISCOUNT, page 292; RESERVE RATIO, page 293.

Significance The Federal Reserve System determines the nation's general monetary and credit policies through decisions made by the Board in Washington, D.C., and by the regional directors. The policies are carried out through the Reserve banks and by the thousands of member banks across the country. The "Fed" has played an increasingly significant role in attacking the nation's major economic problems of inflation and recession. In trying to control inflation, the Fed has tried to carry out "hard" money policies during economic boom periods when inflationary pressures are greatest. In fighting recessions, the Fed has carried out more liberal monetary and credit policies designed to stimulate investment and purchasing power. When, however, a condition of "stagflation" exists—that is, both the threat of serious recession and serious inflation plague the economy simultaneously—the Fed's role has been reduced in effectiveness. Such a situation existed during the period of the mid-1970s.

Fiscal Policy   The use by government of its financial powers to influence the nation's economy. Decisions on fiscal policy are made largely by the President and Congress, and are concerned with revenue, expenditure, and debt. John Maynard Keynes, the British economist, was one of the first to develop the theoretical basis and sophisticated applications of fiscal policy in combating economic slumps. *See also* EMPLOYMENT ACT, page 302; KEYNESIANISM, page 287; MONETARY POLICY, page 289.

  Significance   Fiscal policy is usually aimed at using governmental financial programs to maintain economic stability by arresting and reversing violent downswings or upswings in the economy. The objective is to maintain a viable economy while steering a middle course between inflation and recession. Fiscal policies available to fight a serious downturn or recession include compensatory (deficit) spending, public works projects, and tax reductions. Reverse policies of reduced government spending, surplus budgets and debt retirement, and increased taxes are needed to combat inflation. Although the application of governmental fiscal policies to effect changes in the nation's economy is generally accepted as a proper function for government, some opposition exists. Most controversy, however, involves conflicts over the choice of specific policies, and arises, particularly, from groups adversely affected. The most serious challenge to the effective use of fiscal policy to stimulate the economy occurs when the economy is simultaneously beset with the problems of stagnation and inflation—a condition called "stagflation." In such a situation, extensive use of fiscal policy to stimulate the economy may result in increased inflationary dangers.

Fiscal Year   The twelve-month financial period used by a government for record keeping, budgeting, appropriating, revenue collecting, and other aspects of fiscal management. The traditional fiscal year of the national government, which ran from July 1 to June 30 was changed by Congress in 1974 to run from October 1 to September 30. Some state and local governments use the calendar year from January 1 to December 31, while a few states use a two-year fiscal period. *See also* APPROPRIATION, page 155.

  Significance   The student of government must differentiate between those statistics and programs that apply to the calendar year and those that apply to the fiscal year. The national government's fiscal year of July 1 to June 30 was originally selected to conform with the flow of governmental actions involved in budgeting and appropriating. The 1974 change to begin the fiscal year on October 1 recognized the new realities in the budgeting and appropriating functions involving huge budgets and complex processes that had tended to reduce the effectiveness of Congress. Near the end of the federal fiscal year, deficiency appropriations are typically required to finance those programs that have exhausted their financial resources.

General Welfare Clause   The clause in Article I, section 8 of the Constitution that authorizes Congress to lay and collect taxes to provide for the common defense and general welfare of the United States. *See also* CONSTITUTIONAL CONSTRUCTION, page 24; SOCIAL SECURITY CASES page 374.

  Significance   The general welfare clause appears to give Congress an unlimited spending power, but it has been a source of constitutional controversy. The issue is whether Congress can spend tax monies only for purposes authorized in other sections of the Constitution, or whether the general welfare clause gives Congress an unlimited power to spend for whatever might contribute to the "common defense and general welfare." The former position has been held by the strict constructionists, the latter by the loose or liberal constructionists. The liberal constructionist view of the interpretation of the general welfare clause has prevailed, and the spending power as such has never been successfully challenged in the courts. The only limitation suggested by the Supreme Court (*United States v. Butler*, 297 U.S. 1 [1936]), was that taxes levied by Congress be spent for *national* welfare and not for the welfare of particular groups. The general welfare clause has enabled the national government to carry on programs in fields not specifically granted to it by the Constitution, as in the social security programs.

Gold Standard A monetary system in which a nation's currency is backed by gold, has a standard of value measured in gold, and can be exchanged for gold. An international gold standard provides for free convertibility of currencies into gold and the unimpeded movement of gold bullion from one nation to another to pay international debts. The gold standard became universally accepted during the nineteenth and early twentieth centuries; the United States adopted it in 1900. In the worldwide depression of the 1930s, the nations of the world discarded it, with the United States going off the gold standard in 1934. After World War II, much of the world functioned under a gold exchange standard system through which central banks bought and sold national currencies backed by gold at a fixed price. Under this system, the American dollar became the major reserve and trading currency since it was freely exchanged into gold at a fixed rate. In the early 1970s, the Nixon Administration ended the gold exchange standard system by ending the system whereby foreign governments could exchange dollars for gold at a fixed price. *See also* DEVALUATION, page 279; INTERNATIONAL MONETARY FUND, page 287.

Significance The gold standard provided stability in domestic monetary systems, and an "international currency" and self-regulating payments system in international trade and finance, for many years. The severe depression of the 1930s, however, forced the major industrial countries, including the United States, to adopt flexible fiscal and employment policies based on "managed" paper currencies that were incompatible with the gold standard. In discarding the gold standard, Congress provided for calling in gold and gold coin in circulation and fixed the price at $35 for a fine ounce. By the late 1960s, the role of the dollar as a substitute for gold as an international medium of exchange was under considerable pressure. The International Monetary Fund tried to meet the crisis by creating "paper gold" in the form of special drawing rights (SDRs), and a two-tier governmental/private gold market was established in which the official American price was maintained in the governmental market, but was permitted to fluctuate freely in the private market. In 1971, as a result of domestic inflation and heavy international pressure on the dollar, President Richard M. Nixon devalued the dollar in terms of gold and ended the free convertibility of dollars into gold at a fixed price in exchange for a revaluation of other major currencies with the dollar. A special Committee of Twenty was thereupon established by the International Monetary Fund to develop a new international monetary "kingpin" to replace the fallen dollar. In 1974, Congress restored the right of American citizens to own gold, denied to them since the monetary crisis of 1934.

Gross National Product (GNP) A measurement of the total annual output of goods and services of a country expressed in terms of its market value. In the United States, the Department of Commerce gathers GNP data on a quarterly basis and publishes it as an annual figure. A nation's Gross National Product is measured in terms of current monetary values and, hence, reflects inflationary and deflationary factors. Because heavy inflation has reduced the utility of GNP as a measuring device, economists generally use inflation-adjusted figures related to a prior base period for analytical purposes. Net National Product (NNP) is computed by deducting capital consumption allowances (*i.e.,* wearing out of machinery, etc.) from GNP during the period.

Significance The Gross National Product has become a major analytical tool for measuring a nation's economic well-being and for comparing progress in different countries and economic systems. A more accurate picture of economic progress, however, requires analysis of GNP in terms of constant dollars to avoid inflation- or deflation-caused price changes, and measurement of GNP on a per capita basis to take population changes into account to determine standards of living. Comparative economic growth rates are based on annual changes of GNP corrected for price changes. GNP in the United States has grown from about $300 billion in 1949 to a figure in excess of $1.3 trillion in 1974.

Income Tax A tax levied on income received from profits, salaries, rents, interest, dividends, and other sources, less deductions permitted by law. The national government's income tax includes a tax on both individual income and corporation income, with different rates applicable to each. Most of the fifty states also levy income taxes, many applicable to both individual and corporate income. Many cities, because of increasing resistance to higher property taxes, have adopted an income tax. *See also* SIXTEENTH AMENDMENT, page 295; WITHHOLDING TAX, page 297.

Significance The individual income tax is based on ability to pay and provides for progressive or graduated tax-rate increases as income increases. The federal tax rate currently starts at 14 percent and increases progressively to a high of 70 percent. The income tax also permits flexibility in providing greater or lesser yields simply by adjusting a few rates. Its major weakness results from its complicated nature and the successful efforts of various pressure groups to riddle it with exemptions and loopholes. Over forty million persons pay some income tax today, the majority through the payroll withholding system. The individual income tax is the major source of revenue for the national government, producing almost three times the receipts of the next most important source, the corporate income tax. The two together have provided about 70 percent of total national tax receipts in recent years. In the states, the income tax, including individual and corporate, is the third largest source of state revenue. Increased use of income taxes by the states or by local governments is hampered by the extensive preemption of the field by the national government and by public opposition to additional taxes on incomes. In fiscal 1975, 42 cents of each federal budget dollar came from the individual income tax, and 16 cents of each was produced by the corporation income tax.

Indexing A contractual system by which the amounts of monetary payments or receipts are adjusted periodically on the basis of changes that have occurred in the nation's cost of living index. Indexing is aimed at avoiding the financial catastrophes or injustices that occur as a result of the impact of heavy inflationary or deflationary factors on the national economy. In a collective bargaining contract, for example, provision may be made that, if the Consumer Price Index (CPI) rises 10 percent annually, all workers covered by the contract will receive an automatic 10 percent increase in their wages in addition to any other benefits owed to them. *See also* DEFLATION, page 278; INFLATION, page 286.

Significance Indexing systems have developed in the United States largely as a response to heavy inflationary pressures. Brazil was the first country to attempt—with some measure of success—a large-scale national indexing system in an effort to bring runaway inflation under control. With the advent of double-digit inflation in the United States in the 1970s, indexing became commonly associated with such monetary contractual relationships as labor-management agreements, insurance policies, business contracts for future delivery, and private pension systems. In 1972, Congress applied indexing to the Social Security retirement system by providing that pensions and survivor's benefits would be increased automatically each year in the same proportion that prices had increased during the prior year. In contrast to inflation, during a period of deflation the benefits of indexing would be reversed and the other party in each contractual arrangement would gain.

Inflation An economic condition in which the price level is increased and the value of money in terms of purchasing power is consequently decreased. Inflation may result from an increase in the amount of money and credit available or a decrease in the supply of consumer goods, with the result that consumers tend to bid up prices ("demand-pull" inflation). A second source of inflation is rapidly increasing costs of production, such as raw materials, wages, and energy ("cost-push" inflation). A third source ("profit-pull" inflation) occurs when lack of competition permits powerful corporations to seek additional profits by raising prices or by maintaining them at artificially high levels when their costs are going down. Mass psychological factors are also a characteristic ingredient of inflation, regardless of causes. Once underway, inflation is difficult to deal with because of reinforcement factors that encourage it to "feed on itself." *See also* DEFLATION, page 278; INDEXING, page 285; MONETARY POLICY, page 289.

Significance Most economists believe that serious inflation—an increase in the price level of more than three percent per year—can be prevented through proper use of monetary policy by the Federal Reserve Board and the Treasury Department, and by fiscal policy, such as providing for balanced federal budgets and increased taxes. The tradeoffs involved in limiting inflation to three percent or less per year, however, may involve such politically undesirable factors as heavy unemployment and economic slowdown. Although the effects of inflation are largely internal, a nation suffering from a serious inflation may jeopardize its foreign markets with a resulting disequilibrium in its balance of international payments and a serious threat to the international exchange value of its currency. Within a nation, although debtors find that inflation may make it easier for them to repay their creditors, persons living on fixed incomes and those with little job-bargaining power typically suffer the most. In the early 1970s, the Nixon Administration first tried to control the serious Vietnam war-caused inflation by orthodox monetary and fiscal measures, then adopted a new economic policy and imposed a wage-price freeze. Wage-price controls were never fully implemented, and the nation suffered its most serious inflation since the Korean war period. By the mid-1970s, skyrocketing world oil prices and a global food and raw materials shortage made inflation ranging between 10 and 25 percent a worldwide phenomenon. In the United States, the ultimate challenge of inflation occurred when the economy suffered simultaneously from a recession (stagnation) and from inflation, an untypical condition dubbed "stagflation" by economists.

International Monetary Fund (IMF) A specialized agency of the United Nations established by the Bretton Woods Monetary and Financial Conference of 1944 to promote international monetary cooperation. The major objectives of the Fund include: (1) promotion of exchange stability; (2) establishment of a worldwide multilateral payments system; and (3) provision of monetary reserves to help member nations overcome short-run disequilibria in their balances of payments. By 1975, 125 members had joined the Fund and had subscribed to quotas totaling over $25 billion. Voting power in the IMF is determined by the size of a member's contribution, with the United States casting more than one-fourth of the total. Major industrial nations function as a caucus (Group of Ten) to reach decisions in the IMF to defend currency values and to promote international liquidity. *See also* DEVALUATION, page 279; GOLD STANDARD, page 284.

Significance Creation of the International Monetary Fund was aimed at preventing a return to the anarchic financial conditions of the 1930s decade, with its wildly fluctuating exchange rates and competitive depreciations. For many years, major exchange depreciations were generally avoided, but during the 1970s, because of deteriorating world economic conditions, exchange stability had been greatly weakened. The main problems facing the Fund have been the persistent deficit in the American balance of payments, the shortage of international reserves at a time when international trade has expanded rapidly, a dangerously high level of inflation in most countries, and a growing international shortage of energy, raw materials, and food.

Keynesianism A philosophy and practice of utilizing the machinery of government, through fiscal and monetary policies, to guide and direct a free enterprise economy. Keynesianism, based on the principles and analyses originally propounded by the British economist, John Maynard Keynes, seeks to improve rather than replace capitalism by providing an orderly, predictable pattern of economic activity based on economic indicators utilized by policy makers. Techniques used by Keynesians to manage a state's economy include government control and direction of such matters as budgeting, spending, tax policy, interest rates, and credit availability. Keynesianism substitutes rational decisions made by state leaders in pursuit of specific social goals for the undirected free interplay of market forces that characterizes a laissez-faire approach. Keynes recognized over-saving as one of the fundamental problems of a capitalistic system, and Keynesian policymakers tend to prescribe governmental programs to alleviate the problem by stimulating the movement of savings into investment and mass consumer purchasing. *See also* CAPITALISM, page 3; ECONOMIC PLANNING, page 309; EMPLOYMENT ACT OF 1946, page 302; FISCAL POLICY, page 283; LAISSEZ-FAIRE, page 11; MONETARY POLICY, page 289.

Significance Keynesianism has been adopted as state policy in most of the advanced, industrial states of the capitalist world. In the United States, the national government began playing a Keynesian role at the end of World War II. Presidents increasingly have made decisions concerning the national economy on the basis of recommendations offered by economic advisers who have been greatly influenced by Keynesian theories. By managing a nation's economy, Keynesians seek to avoid cyclical movements, stagnation, heavy unemployment, and serious inflation, while at the same time encouraging economic growth and general economic well-being. In the United States, fiscal policy with emphasis on deficit spending carried out by the President and Congress, and monetary policy with emphasis on easy credit developed by the Federal Reserve System, have served as the main tools for implementing Keynesian economic policies. During the early 1970s, however, over-stimulation resulting from huge deficits fostered by the Vietnam war, and a substantial increase in world energy prices produced serious two-digit inflation and, simultaneously, a deepening economic recession. This "stagflation" challenged economic policymakers since the Keynesian prescription for stagnation is governmental stimulation of the economy, whereas the "cure" for inflation is substantial destimulation.

Legal Tender   Any medium of exchange that by law must be accepted in payment of a debt. The Constitution gives the national government full control over the nation's money, and it forbids the states to "make anything but gold and silver coin a tender in payment of debts . . ." (Art. I, sec. 10). *See also* LEGAL TENDER CASES, page 300.

Significance   A major legal controversy developed over the first century of American history as to whether the national government could issue fiat notes not backed by the precious metals as legal tender. A series of cases was climaxed in 1884 by *Juilliard v. Greenman,* 110 U.S. 421, in which the Supreme Court declared that Congress has full power to issue notes as legal tender in the payment of debts. The states for many years authorized state chartered banks to issue notes for circulation as currency, but not as legal tender. Although these issuances did not violate the Constitution, Congress regarded them as a danger to monetary uniformity and stability. In 1865, Congress levied a 10 percent tax upon state notes, that was sustained by the Supreme Court (*Veazie Bank v. Fenno,* 8 Wallace 533 [1869]), and that drove all state notes out of circulation.

Matching Funds   A financial agreement between two levels of government by which one level agrees to provide specific amounts of money for a program, activity, or project if the other will provide specific amounts of money for the same purpose. Matching funds are involved in federal-state, federal-local, and state-local arrangements. For example, if a new city sewage disposal plant will cost $5 million, the national government may encourage the city to build it by offering to pay $4 million of the cost if the city will pay the remaining $1 million. Contributions by a participating state or local government may take the form of "in-kind matching"—that is, may consist of personnel, equipment, or facilities valued at the amount required under the agreement. *See also* GRANT-IN-AID, page 35; REVENUE SHARING page 293.

Significance   Most state and local projects and activities are currently undertaken through matching funds financial arrangements. General Revenue Sharing (GRS) funds, however, may not be used directly or indirectly to obtain federal money under any matching funds agreement between the national government and state or local units. That means that state and local governments must raise their share of matching funds from their own tax programs. The matching funds technique has successfully encouraged cooperation among many governmental units in the American federal system, and it has provided a means by which higher levels of governments have been able to stimulate lower levels into undertaking new programs or activities. The receiving unit, however, may be induced to divert funds from other pressing needs to meet "matching" requirements.

Monetary Policy   Government policy that aims at affecting the amount of currency in circulation and the availability of credit. The Federal Reserve Board uses "tight money" monetary policies to restrain and prolong boom periods in the nation's economy and to fight inflation. "Loose money" policies are used to check deflation and to fight recessions by making money and credit more freely available. *See also* FEDERAL RESERVE SYSTEM, page 282; FISCAL POLICY, page 283; KEYNESIANISM, page 287.

Significance   In the post-World War II period, Federal Reserve monetary policies have been employed in fighting recessions and restraining economic booms. The use of such policies must be delicately and expertly handled lest a serious deflationary or inflationary spiral be touched off. In pursuing a tight or hard money policy, the Federal Reserve Board decreases the availability of money and credit by raising member banks' reserve requirements, by raising the rediscount rate, and by selling government securities through its Open Market Committee. The Federal Reserve Board pursues policies exactly the opposite of these when loose or soft money policies are called for. Monetary policy is particularly effective when harmonized with fiscal policies initiated by the President and Congress and aimed at the same objectives.

Open Market Operations   Buying and selling government securities, bills of exchange, and other commercial paper by the Federal Open Market Committee. The Committee is composed of the Board of Governors of the Federal Reserve System and five directors of the Federal Reserve banks chosen annually by the boards of directors. *See also* FEDERAL RESERVE SYSTEM, page 282.

Significance   The Federal Open Market Committee operations facilitate commerce and business and stabilize credit in the United States. Its functions are particularly useful in implementing the monetary policies determined by the Federal Reserve Board. For example, when inflation threatens, the Committee sells government securities and commercial paper in the open market to restrict the availability of credit; when deflation or recession threatens, the Committee buys so as to make credit more easily available through member banks. The Committee's open market operations are supplemented by other instruments of monetary policy, such as the fixing of the rediscount rate and the reserve requirements for member banks.

Performance Budget   The drawing up of a plan for anticipated expenditures based on the activities, services, and functions (that is, *units* of work) performed by government, rather than allotting funds on the basis of items to be purchased and salaries to be paid by each department and agency. *See also* BUDGET, page 275; PROGRAM BUDGET, page 290.

Significance   Based on the recommendations of the Hoover Commission, Congress adopted the principle of the performance budget in the Budget and Accounting Procedures Act of 1950. Since 1951, the Bureau of the Budget has drawn up much of the general budget for the national government on a performance basis. The major advantage of the performance budget is that by detailing how and for what government functions funds are expended, it gives a clearer accounting of performance than did the itemization system. Performance budgeting has increasingly given way to a new emphasis on program budgeting that evaluates expenditures on the basis of their effectiveness in achieving program objectives.

Personal Property Tax A tax levied on things of value other than real property. Personal property is usually classified as tangible or intangible, the former including valuables of substance, such as business inventories, machinery, jewelry, and household goods, and the latter a right, claim, or interest of value, such as found in bonds, stocks, and bank accounts. *See also* ASSESSED VALUATION, page 272; PROPERTY TAX, page 291.

Significance Property is usually classified for tax purposes, with the tax on personal property applied at a different rate than that on real property. Personal property tax collection involves considerable administrative work, particularly that of getting the owners to declare their property for tax purposes or, if they do not, of finding it. This becomes an almost hopeless task when levying the tax on intangible properties that can easily be concealed from the assessor's eyes. Often, the value of such intangibles as stocks and bonds exceeds the value of real estate and tangibles, yet the taxes levied upon them depend almost entirely on the personal honesty of the individual taxpayer. Most personal property taxes are levied by local governments and are paid mainly by business and industry.

Program Budget A plan for anticipated expenditures based on financial requests that reflect output categories or the "end-products" of governmental operations. A program budget differs from a line-item or incremental budget in that, in the former, all estimated expenditures are pulled together into comprehensive program packages, such as social welfare and environmental protection, rather than based, as in the latter, on such categories as salaries, items to be purchased, maintenance, and supplies. In using a program budget, each governmental unit must justify its appropriation requests in terms of its program objectives. A program budget may also go beyond regular budgeting in providing for a systems-analysis approach by which program performance is quantitatively assessed to determine the effectiveness with which budget dollars are used to attain program objectives. *See also* APPROPRIATION, page 155; BUDGET, page 275; PERFORMANCE BUDGET, page 289.

Significance In the early 1960s, a Program, Planning and Budgeting System (PPBS) was instituted in the Department of Defense as a means for bringing defense expenditures under control and enabling the Secretary of Defense to manage the Department's complex, worldwide operations. Some state and local governments have also adopted program budgeting. Supporters of program budgeting point out that it permits control over the quality and purposes of expenditures and, as a result, over the level of spending as well. It is far more effective in terms of managerial control than the more traditional line-item budget, and it facilitates planning and the consideration of priorities by linking political ends to economic means. Critics charge that program budgeting tends to create conflict because of the highly competitive situation that results when programs are compared, evaluated, and used as a basis for future appropriations. Personnel tend to devote much time to "glamorizing" their programs, and compromise—the essential ingredient of all budget processes—is more difficult to achieve. The trend on all levels of government, however, is in the direction of adopting program budgeting, and even the United Nations has adopted a program budget in an attempt to maximize benefits for the world community.

Progressive Tax Any tax in which the tax *rates* increase as the tax *base* (that is, the amount subject to be taxed) increases. A progressive income tax, for example, might provide for a 10 percent rate on the first $5,000 of income, a 25 percent rate on the second $5,000, and so forth, with, characteristically, a maximum rate for all income over a certain level. It is the opposite of a regressive tax in which tax rates remain uniform or decline as the tax base increases. A progressive tax, therefore, is one which is based essentially on ability to pay. A progressive tax *system* is one which, while it may incorporate both progressive and regressive types of taxes, on balance tends to place the major taxpaying burden on those most able to pay. *See also* ABILITY THEORY, page 272; REGRESSIVE TAX, page 292.

Significance Progressive taxes levied by the national and state governments include the individual and corporate income taxes and the estate and gift taxes. Progressive taxes are based on the principle of ability to pay, as reflected, for example, in the federal individual income tax, in which percentage rates range from 14 percent to 70 percent on taxable income. Supporters of progressive taxation regard it as an equitable means of securing necessary government income. Opponents claim that it penalizes initiative and success.

Property Tax An ad valorem (according to value) tax levied on real or personal, tangible or intangible property. The general property tax is levied by local units of government throughout the country, and most states make limited use of some form of the tax. The tax process includes assessment of property valuations, determination of tax rates (millage), tax computation, and tax collection. To correct injustices, boards of review on the local level adjust inequalities in assessments. Where the taxing jurisdiction crosses political boundaries, central assessment or equalization is often provided to avoid geographical inequities. *See also* ASSESSED VALUATION, page 272; ASSESSOR, page 273; BOARD OF REVIEW, page 274; EQUALIZATION, page 280.

Significance The general property tax provides the fiscal foundation for local units of government across the nation. In recent years, it has provided about 85 percent of the tax revenue for cities, counties, school districts, towns, townships, villages, and other local units. For many years, the general property tax was the nation's major source of revenue, exceeding all state and national levies, until the twentieth century's many crises boosted income and sales taxes. The general property tax has come increasingly under attack in recent years because of difficulties and conflicts involved in assessment, equalization, and exemptions. The flexibility of the tax as a source of revenue has nearly reached exhaustion in many localities because of constitutional or statutory limitations, popular rejections of tax increase referendums, and heavy tax loads resulting from failure to find other tax sources. The Supreme Court has held that the fact that some children's education is more adequately financed than that of others does not serve to invalidate the property tax as the chief means of financing schools (*San Antonio Independent School District v. Rodriguez*, 411 U.S. 1 [1973]).

Public Debt The total indebtedness, including accrued interest, of a government or of a country, the latter embracing the indebtedness of all its units of government. The public debt of the United States government is usually referred to as the national debt. Whenever expenditures exceed revenue during a fiscal year, the deficit is added to the public debt; when revenue exceeds expenditures, the public debt is reduced by the amount of the surplus. Part of the United States' national debt is carried by the public through the purchase of short- and long-term treasury bonds;

the remainder is financed through the Federal Reserve Banking System, and by foreign creditors. *See also* DEBT LIMIT, page 277; DEFICIT FINANCING, page 278.

Significance Over a period of four decades of frequently unbalanced budgets, the United States has built up a national public debt of sizable proportions. The national debt rose from about $16 billion ($132 per capita) in 1930 to almost $43 billion ($367 per capita) in 1940, as a result of deficit financing to stimulate the stagnated economy of the Great Depression. By 1950, it had risen to $257 billion ($1697 per capita) through the financing of World War II and part of the Korean war; from that point, it rose to a level of more than $370 billion ($1806 per capita) in 1970 because of financing defense programs and combating five post-World War II recessions. By 1975, the national debt had soared to over $500 billion as a result of massive deficits by which the Nixon and Ford administrations sought to stimulate the sluggish economy. Much controversy has arisen concerning the rapid rise of the national debt in recent years. Some economists view the debt as a useful governmental weapon for stabilizing the economy, adding to it by "pump-priming" (deficit spending) during economic downturns, and retiring portions of it through surpluses during periods of prosperity to reduce the threat of inflation. Some students of finance are relatively unconcerned about the size of the debt, pointing out that "we owe it to ourselves," that much of the debt constitutes an investment for the future of the American people, and that the debt has actually grown smaller in recent years if measured in relation to national income. The concerned, on the other hand, regard the "owe it to ourselves" argument as specious, and contend that future generations of Americans will suffer from excessive spending, and that the size of the debt threatens not only economic solvency but national security as well. In recent years, state and local debt has increased at a more rapid rate than the national debt. Marxists regard the continuing need to stimulate the economy through monetary and fiscal deficit spending as a "crutch" needed to avoid the collapse of capitalism.

Rediscount Credit granted by a Federal Reserve bank to a member bank on negotiable instruments that had already been discounted (a loan with interest subtracted in advance) when the member bank made loans to its customers. *See also* FEDERAL RESERVE SYSTEM, page 282.

Significance The Federal Reserve System uses the rediscount rate as a tool of monetary policy. By lowering the rediscount rate, the Federal Reserve Board can encourage member banks to liquidate their holdings of commercial paper by having the Federal Reserve banks buy them at a discount of their face value. This frees funds of the member banks and enables them to make additional loans to the public, thus stimulating purchasing power and, thereby, the nation's economy. By raising the rediscount rate, the Federal Reserve banks can obtain the opposite result of contracting the availability of credit in the country. Typically, therefore, the rediscount rate is lowered during a recession to stimulate an upturn in the economy (loose money policy), and raised during a boom period when serious inflation threatens (tight money policy).

Regressive Tax Any tax in which the burden falls relatively more heavily upon low-income groups than upon more wealthy taxpayers. It is the opposite of a progressive tax, in which tax rates increase as ability to pay increases. *See also* PROGRESSIVE TAX, page 290; SALES TAX, page 295.

Significance Regressive taxes are used mainly by the state and local governments and include, for example, the sales tax and the uniform or declining rate income tax. Such taxes take a higher percentage of the total income of low-income groups than of the total income of high-income groups, even though the rates are uniform. Sales taxes on the necessities of life are probably the most regressive in nature, since a major portion of the expenditures of low-income families are for such commodities. Graduated income taxes, which are generally regarded as the most progressive type of tax, can also be substantially regressive in their impact as a result of exemptions and deductions favoring high income groups.

Regulatory Tax A tax levied for purposes other than the raising of revenue. A protective tariff is a clear example of a regulatory tax. More subtle uses of taxing power for nonrevenue regulatory purposes include restricting the marketing of a product (the heavy tax on oleomargarine many years ago to maintain the butter market), or adding to the government's arsenal against illegal or undesirable activities (a tax on gamblers), sometimes called a sumptuary tax. *See also Veazie Bank v. Fenno,* page 301.

Significance Most taxes have a regulatory function even when levied primarily for revenue. The income tax, for example, controls the distribution of wealth and is used to promote specific fiscal policies. With rare exceptions, the courts will not question the motives of the legislature in levying a tax. A regulatory tax may be used to reinforce an existing power of government or to reach a problem for which no direct legislative authority exists. For example, a heavy tax on a commodity may effectively keep it off the market though no power exists to do so directly. Also, a tax levied by one level of government may help another to enforce its laws. The federal tax on gambling devices, for example, helps states enforce antigambling laws.

Reserve Ratio The percentage of liquid assets held by a bank as a reserve for its deposits. The *legal* reserve ratio is that percentage set by government to ensure that banks will maintain a safe proportion of ready cash to meet depositors' demands for their money. Under the Federal Reserve System, the legal reserve requirement is set for the member banks within each district by the Federal Reserve Board of Governors. Reserve requirements for state banks are usually set by law in each state. *See also* FEDERAL RESERVE SYSTEM, page 282.

Significance Legal reserve requirements are set by government to protect the accounts of individual depositors. Through the Federal Reserve System, the government additionally obtains a powerful means of carrying out monetary policy and maintaining stability with flexibility in the monetary system. When deflation or economic recessions threaten, the Federal Reserve Board can free money and credit to stimulate business by lowering the reserve requirements of member banks. When inflation threatens, or it is desirable to restrain an economic boom, the Board reduces the availability of money and credit to business and consumers by raising reserve requirements. Along with its open market operations and its rediscount function, the setting of reserve ratio requirements is a major monetary tool that helps the Board set the general direction and tone of the American economy.

Revenue Sharing A system in which one unit of government automatically and regularly turns over a certain portion of its tax yield to another unit of government, according to a formula established by constitution or statute. Revenue sharing differs from a grant-in-aid program in that the transfers of tax monies are completely or largely free from legal and administrative controls by the grantor government, and receiving governments are not required to match the amount. Under general tax sharing, as distinguished from contributions for specific programs, the receiving government determines how, when, and for what purposes the tax monies will be spent, with minimal direction, control, and oversight carried on by the government that collects the taxes. *See also* GRANT-IN-AID, page 35; TAX OFFSET, page 297.

Significance Historically, revenue-sharing programs have involved arrangements between state and local governments. Many state governments, for example, levy and collect sales or income taxes with a constitutional or statutory requirement that a certain percentage of collections be turned over to local governments. Common examples of taxes collected by the states and shared with their local governments are motor fuel, license, income, liquor, cigarette, and sales taxes. In 1972, the State and Local Fiscal Assistance Act was enacted by Congress. Under this sweeping program, the national government funnels billions of dollars into financially pressed state and local units through its General Revenue Sharing program (GRS) on a regular basis. The program provided initially for sharing over $30 billion of federal revenues over a five-year period, with one-third of each state's share for state government and two-thirds for local units. GRS funds may be spent by state governments for any legal purposes, whereas local governments are required to spend GRS funds for such purposes as environmental protection, health, libraries, transportation, recreation, and aid to the poor or aged. Direct citizen participation in determining how local GRS funds are spent is encouraged by the Act. Allocation of revenue-sharing funds among the states is based on a formula that considers each state's population, tax structure, and relative income. For local units, revenue sharing poses the issue of whether such funds should be used to initiate new programs or to reduce taxes. Opposition to federal revenue-sharing programs comes from conservatives who fear the more efficient and progressive taxing programs of the national government, and from liberals who oppose the unconditional nature of the grants. Congressional opposition relates to the loss of influence and control over dollar flows into the states as contrasted with grant-in-aid programs.

Revolving Fund An operational fund established for a governmental agency carrying on proprietary (business-type) functions that make the agency financially self-supporting, or nearly so. Through one form of "backdoor financing", for example, income from the agency's operations is not turned in to the Treasury Department but is spent directly by the agency. The Tennessee Valley Authority (TVA), for example, uses its revenue from electric power sales to finance its continuing operations and its expansion programs. "Backdoor financing" obviously tends to weaken the traditional controls over the purse strings exercised by legislative bodies. *See also* PROPRIETARY FUNCTION, page 314.

Significance A revolving fund gives a public business enterprise the financial flexibility to carry out long-range programs. Agencies ordinarily cannot plan operations beyond those approved by Congress in its annual appropriations, and a revolving fund frees the agency from this kind of dependence. The revolving fund principle has been followed especially in federal lending agencies. Critics object to the lack of control over agencies that use a revolving fund, and some regard competition from such agencies as a threat to private enterprise.

Sales Tax   A tax levied upon the sale of commodities, usually paid by the purchaser. The sales tax may apply generally to all commodities or it may be restricted to certain classifications or specific commodities. Typically, the sales tax is levied on retail sales, but in some cases it is imposed on sales by manufacturers and wholesalers as well. Closely related to the sales tax is the "use" tax, which applies to purchases made outside the taxing jurisdiction and is designed to prevent state residents from avoiding the sales tax through out-of-state purchases. Most of the fifty states levy sales taxes from 2 to 6 percent, and an increasing number of cities also levy sales taxes. A value-added tax is a special type of sales tax in which each stage of production and distribution of the product is taxed, with the consumer paying the ultimate cost of all the value-added taxes. *See also* REGRESSIVE TAX, page 292; TAX INCIDENCE, page 296.

Significance   Most of the states that levy a sales tax adopted it during the depression of the 1930s when they were under heavy obligation to meet rising welfare and general governmental costs. The sales tax has become the single most important source of state revenue. Most opposition to the sales tax centers around its regressive character, which places a heavy tax burden upon the low-income groups. Some states have sought to reduce its regressive impact by exempting food, clothing, medicine, or other necessities. Support for the sales tax is based on the idea that all citizens should contribute to the support of government and that the sales tax makes this possible because all persons are consumers. The national government has studied the possibility of adopting a value-added tax since many trade-competing nations have already imposed such taxes.

Severance Tax   A tax levied upon natural resources at the time they are taken from the land or water. Severance taxes are used by many states for both revenue and conservation purposes. *See also* CONSERVATION, page 344; REGULATORY TAX, page 293.

Significance   Conservation objectives can be achieved through a severance tax by adjusting tax rates to control the "severing" of timber, minerals, and other resources from the soil. Some states accomplish the same purpose without a severance tax per se, by, for example, exempting timberland from the general property tax until the timber has been harvested.

Sixteenth Amendment   An amendment to the Constitution, adopted in 1913, that grants Congress the power to levy taxes on incomes without apportioning them among the states according to population. The individual income tax levied by the national government is based on the power granted by this Amendment. *See also* INCOME TAX, page 285; *Pollock v. Farmers Loan and Trust Co.,* page 300.

Significance   The Sixteenth Amendment resulted from a Supreme Court decision that a federal income tax is a direct tax and, under Article I, section 9, must be apportioned among the states according to population (*Pollock v. Farmers Loan and Trust Co.,* 158 U.S. 601 [1895]). Although a Civil War income tax levy had been upheld by the Supreme Court as an indirect tax, the 1895 decision reversed this view. The controversy, however, continued. The Sixteenth Amendment put aside the question of whether income taxes are direct or indirect by giving Congress blanket power to lay and collect taxes on incomes "from whatever source derived," and without any apportionment or regard to any census. Without this Amendment, income taxes apportioned among the states according to population would have been manifestly unfair and inequitable because of the vast differences in income among the states, and Congress refused to levy such a tax. Since 1913, the individual and corporation income taxes have become the major sources for federal revenue.

Special Assessment   A charge made by a government against a property owner for that part of the cost of public improvements made adjacent to his property that are especially useful or beneficial to his property. Special assessments are different from taxes in that the improvements have been petitioned for by the landowners concerned. *See also* BENEFIT THEORY, page 274.

Significance Special assessments are used mainly by local units of governments in providing facilities for homeowners, such as paved streets, sewers, and sidewalks. A portion of the cost of such public improvements is, typically, borne by the local government out of taxes. This is a recognition that the improvements are generally beneficial to the community as well as to the individual landowner. Such projects are financed through special assessment bonds, which are backed by the government's power to assess for public improvements. The property owner typically makes annual payments over a period of ten to twenty years for interest and to retire the assessment debt.

Tax Exemption   The privilege granted by a government legally freeing certain types of property, sales, or income from general taxpaying obligations. Tax exemptions are government subsidies to special groups. *See also* SUBSIDY, page 317.

Significance Most of the states have established constitutional or statutory exemption of educational and religious properties from the general property tax. Income from certain national, state, or local bonds may be exempted from taxation, and cooperatives from income tax levies. Most state sales taxes exempt certain classes of commodities. Tax exemptions may be used to encourage activities as well as to recognize that exceptions within general taxpaying categories must be acknowledged in the interest of fairness. Often, tax exemptions may merely illustrate the political power of special-interest groups. Exemptions are, in fact, government subsidies to special groups which generally benefit the large taxpayer more than the small. Low-income groups, the aged, and other needy groups may also be aided by tax exemptions on food, drugs, and other necessities.

Tax Incidence   The point at which the actual burden of paying a tax falls, regardless of whom the tax is formally levied upon. Those taxes in which the burden cannot be shifted to someone else by the taxpayer are sometimes classified as *direct* taxes; those in which the burden can be passed on are *indirect* taxes. *See also* PROGRESSIVE TAX, page 290; REGRESSIVE TAX, page 292.

Significance The incidence of almost all taxes that are levied at some point in the production and consumption of goods is ultimately shifted to consumers through higher prices for commodities. The price of a loaf of bread, for example, may include scores of national, state, and local taxes that, having been paid by different farmers, processors, distributors, and retailers, are passed on to the ultimate consumer. Direct taxes for which the burden cannot ordinarily be shifted include income levies, poll taxes, and taxes on land, although when the land is rented the owner can shift the burden of his tax to the renter. The incidence of taxation brings into serious question the fairness of taxes that are indirectly paid by others than those who make the formal tax payments.

Tax Offset   Payment of taxes to one level of government, which reduces the amount of tax liability to another level. The tax offset has been used by the national government to induce states to adopt certain types of taxes or programs by permitting individuals to deduct such state taxes from the amount of federal tax that they would otherwise pay. Some states permit payment of local property taxes to serve as a partial credit against payment of the state income tax. *See also* REVENUE SHARING, page 293.

Significance   The tax offset has been used effectively by the national government to prod the states into adopting such tax programs as unemployment compensation and state inheritance taxes. To induce the states to adopt unemployment compensation programs, for example, the national government levies a payroll tax on employers, but permits them to offset 90 percent of that tax if they contribute to a state unemployment compensation fund. The effect of this tax offset was to secure a nationwide, but state administered, program of unemployment compensation. Some economists regard the tax offset as the best means of inducing all of the states to adopt uniform tax programs to meet growing revenue needs, with none losing ground in the fierce competition among states to attract and hold industry by means of low taxes.

Withholding Tax   Provisions of an income or payroll tax system by which the employer deducts a specified percentage from an employee's wage or salary and remits it to the government's tax bureau. Amounts withheld by employers constitute a credit against the employees' total tax liability. *See also* INCOME TAX, page 285.

Significance   Under the Current Tax Payment Act of 1943, the national government provides for the payment of federal income taxes through employer-withholding of wages and salaries and the payment of an estimated tax in quarterly installments on income derived from other sources. The individual taxpayer must still file a return by April 15 of each year, at which time he must pay any amount owed over his total withholdings or file a refund claim if his tax is less than his withholdings. The withholding system was adopted by Congress during World War II to help finance the military effort. The main advantages of the system are that it makes tax collections more certain and facilitates payment of taxes through relatively "painless" deductions from paychecks. It also provides the Department of the Treasury with sizable funds coming in regularly during the year. Most opposition has come from employers, who dislike the extensive bookkeeping involved, and from other groups who oppose the singling out of wage and salary incomes for withholding. In recent years, Congress has considered extending the withholding principle to other categories of income, such as interest and dividends. Congress also requires quarterly estimated tax payments on nonsalary income not subject to withholding.

IMPORTANT AGENCIES

Board of Governors, Federal Reserve System   A board composed of seven members that determines general monetary and credit policies and oversees the operations of the twelve district Federal Reserve banks and member banks throughout the country. Board members are appointed for fourteen-year terms by the President with the Senate's confirmation, with consideration given to geographical and major business interests in the selection process. The Board is, by statute and practice, independent of the President. *See also* FEDERAL RESERVE SYSTEM, page 282.

Significance The Board of Governors determines monetary policies through its control over the issuance of Federal Reserve notes by Federal Reserve banks, its fixing of the rediscount rate, its Open Market Committee, and the purchase and sale of government and other securities. All of these activities have a profound effect on the amount of money in circulation and the credit available through Federal Reserve member banks, which in turn influences general economic conditions in the country. The Board also sets the margin requirements for purchases of securities and conducts periodic examinations of Federal Reserve and member banks. Some students of government and finance would like to have its activities brought under the direct supervision of the President because of the close, important relationship of its activities to fiscal policies and the stability of the economy. Others consider it essential that the Board retain its independence from presidential control in order that its decisions be free from politics. Because fiscal policy is largely determined by the President whereas monetary policy is dominated by the "Fed," conflicting policies that may tend to nullify the impact of each are sometimes carried on simultaneously.

Council of Economic Advisers (CEA)   A staff agency in the Executive Office of the President. It consists of three leading economists who advise the President on measures to maintain stability in the nation's economy. The Council was established by Congress in the Employment Act of 1946 and was given responsibility by that Act to formulate proposals "to maintain employment, production, and purchasing power." The Council's recommendations are included in the President's annual economic report to Congress, in which he sets forth the economic problems facing the nation and recommends legislative solutions. *See also* EMPLOY-MENT ACT, page 302; KEYNESIANISM, page 287.

Significance The Council of Economic Advisers' role as a leading staff agency reflects the increasing responsibility of the President to provide leadership in keeping the nation's economy healthy. The Council has played a significant role in recommending fiscal policies to help over-come six post-World War II recessions. Its influence depends upon its acceptance as a profession-ally competent body of advisers, but it must avoid detachment from political realities. Sometimes the Council's lack of a direct liaison with the Federal Reserve Board of Governors has resulted in the pursuit of incompatible fiscal and monetary policies by the two agencies. Today the CEA uses a great variety of indices to keep its finger on the pulse of the national economy and engage in constant diagnosis and prognosis.

Department of the Treasury   A major department of the national government, responsible for fiscal management and headed by a Secretary with Cabinet rank. The Department of the Treasury was one of the original departments established in 1789. Important administrative units include the Internal Revenue Service, Bureau of Customs, Bureau of Accounts, Secret Service, Bureau of Public Debt, and Office of the Comptroller of the Currency. *See also* FISCAL POLICY, page 283; PUBLIC DEBT, page 291.

Significance The Department of the Treasury plays a broad and significant role in formulating both monetary and fiscal policies for the national administration. The Secretary of the Treasury is usually regarded as second only to the Secretary of State as a Cabinet adviser to the President.

In addition to its duties to collect taxes and custom duties, administer the public debt, keep accounts for the entire government, and coin money, the Department also registers and licenses ships engaged in foreign and interstate commerce and administers the counterfeiting and narcotics control laws.

General Accounting Office (GAO) An independent agency created by the Budget and Accounting Act of 1921 that controls and audits national government expenditures as an agent of Congress. The GAO is headed by the Comptroller General who is appointed by the President with the Senate's approval for a fifteen-year term and can be removed only through impeachment or a joint resolution of Congress. *See also* COMPTROLLER GENERAL, page 276.

Significance The major functions carried on by the GAO include: (1) prescribing accounting systems for federal agencies; (2) authorizing federal agencies to make specific expenditures (preaudit); and (3) making extensive investigations to determine the validity of the receipt and disbursement of public funds (postaudit). In short, Congress by law determines in general how public money shall be spent, and the GAO acts as an agent of Congress, checking on specific expenditures to ensure that each falls within the intent of Congress. Students of finance object to the system whereby the GAO may make both the preaudit authorization and the postaudit check, holding that the President cannot reasonably be held responsible for executive-spending activities if the GAO can determine the validity and reasonableness of expenditures before they are paid.

Internal Revenue Service (IRS) A unit in the Department of the Treasury that has major responsibility for the collection of federal taxes except for customs duties. The Internal Revenue Service is headed by a Commissioner and operates through district offices, each headed by a director. The IRS collects approximately three-fourths of the total budget receipts of the national government. *See also* INCOME TAX, page 285; WITHHOLDING TAX, page 297.

Significance The Internal Revenue Service collects almost $200 billion each year, mostly in individual and corporation income taxes. Collection costs have averaged less than $.50 for each $100 of tax collected. Because of its discretionary powers in making decisions in specific tax cases, it has become an important agency in the lives of millions of Americans. Taxpayers, however, are entitled to administrative hearings of their cases, and may appeal IRS decisions to the United States Tax Court.

Office of Management and Budget (OMB) An agency in the Executive Office of the President, headed by a Director who has primary responsibility for efficient and economical conduct of government services and for budget preparation and administration. The President appoints the Director with Senate approval. In addition to budget functions, specific activities carried on by the Office include legislative reference, management and organization, statistical standards, and financial management. The Office of Management and Budget was created by Executive Order in 1970 to replace the Bureau of the Budget and perform its statutory functions. *See also* BUDGET, page 275; BUDGET AND ACCOUNTING ACT, page 301.

Significance The Director of the Office Of Management and Budget is empowered, under the Budget and Accounting Act of 1921, to "assemble, correlate, revise, reduce, or increase" the estimates from executive agencies. Broad fiscal powers flow from this grant, both in the planning and estimating stages and, following congressional approval of the budget, in the budget execution stage, when agency heads must obtain approval in financing their programs. In addition to its budgeting function, the Office carries on duties directed toward improving organization and management within the executive branch and acts as a clearinghouse for legislative proposals originating in the executive agencies. Since 1939, when the Bureau of the Budget was transferred from the Department of the Treasury to the Executive Office, it has become the President's major staff agency in fiscal and related matters. The office is one of the best perspectives from which to gain an overview of the operations of the entire national government, since budget and operations are inextricably linked.

United States Tax Court   A special judicial agency that hears controversies between taxpayers and the Commissioner of Internal Revenue and has jurisdiction over excess profits proceedings. Under the Tax Reform Act of 1969, the Tax Court was designated a court of record under Article I of the Constitution. Prior to this designation it had functioned as a quasi-judicial administrative agency. The Court consists of sixteen judges appointed by the President with the Senate's consent, for twelve-year terms. Each judge heads a division and, although the Court and its judges are located in Washington, D.C., trial sessions are held in various places throughout the country.

Significance   The Tax Court provides a relatively easy and inexpensive means (a fee of $10 is prescribed for the filing of a petition) for taxpayers to appeal decisions made by tax officials. It relieves the regular courts of the tremendous burden of suits resulting from the far-reaching effects of federal tax programs. All decisions of the Tax Court, except those involving excess profits, may be appealed to a court of appeals and, by writ of certiorari, to the United States Supreme Court.

IMPORTANT CASES

Legal Tender Cases (Knox v. Lee; Parker v. Davis), 12 Wallace 457 (1871): Recognized the power of Congress to make Treasury notes (paper money) legal tender in place of gold or silver in payment of debt. *See also* FEDERAL RESERVE NOTES, page 282; LEGAL TENDER, page 288.

Significance   The Legal Tender Cases grew out of a wartime debt but, a few years later, the Court also upheld the issuance of paper money as legal tender in time of peace in *Juilliard v. Greenman,* 110 U.S. 421 (1884). In the *Legal Tender Cases* the Court recognized a new category of "resulting powers"—those powers that are not expressly granted nor implied from a single enumerated power but that arise from the aggregate powers of government.

Pollock v. Farmers Loan and Trust Co., 158 U.S. 601 (1895): Held the federal income tax law of 1894 unconstitutional on the ground that it was a direct tax and, therefore, Congress should have apportioned it among the several states according to population as provided in Article

I, section 9 of the Constitution. *See also* INCOME TAX, page 285; SIXTEENTH AMENDMENT, page 295.

Significance The *Pollock* decision was a reversal of earlier decisions by the Court in which the validity of income taxes not apportioned according to the population had been upheld. The inequity of levying income taxes on a population basis restrained Congress from enacting a new income tax law until 1913, when the Sixteenth Amendment was adopted. The Amendment sidestepped the dispute of whether an income tax law is a direct or indirect tax simply by eliminating any legal necessity for apportionment.

South Carolina v. United States, 199 U.S. 437 (1905): Upheld a federal tax levied upon wholesale and retail liquor sales by the state of South Carolina on the ground that exemption of states from federal taxes applies only when a state carries on strictly governmental functions, not when it engages in business of a private nature. The state argued unsuccessfully that because all profits from liquor sales went into the state treasury, it was exercising the sovereign power of the state and should be immune from federal taxes. *See also* INTERGOVERNMENTAL TAX IMMUNITY, page 37; PROPRIETARY FUNCTION, page 314.

Significance The *South Carolina* case laid down the fundamental rule that state immunity from federal taxation does not apply when a state enters a commercial or proprietary field. The case has served to modify substantially the intergovernmental tax immunity rule laid down in *McCulloch v. Maryland,* 4 Wheaton 316 (1819). Generally, the courts will not intervene when Congress decides to tax a state or local proprietary function.

Veazie Bank v. Fenno, 8 Wallace 533 (1869): Upheld the validity of a 10 percent tax on state bank notes levied by Congress in 1866 for the purpose of driving them out of circulation. *See also* LEGAL TENDER, page 288; REGULATORY TAX, page 293.

Significance The *Veazie Bank* decision gave judicial acceptance to the use of a federal tax primarily for a nonrevenue regulatory purpose and it sanctioned the action of Congress in providing a uniform currency for the United States. The objective of the tax sustained in this case has been realized, and state bank notes have been out of circulation for many years.

IMPORTANT STATUTES

Budget and Accounting Act of 1921 A law that established a national budget system and created the Bureau of the Budget (now the Office of Management and Budget), and the General Accounting Office. It provides for the formulation of an annual executive budget by the Bureau under direction of the President, and for the auditing of all government expenditures by the General Accounting Office under the direction of the Comptroller General as an agent of Congress. *See also* GENERAL ACCOUNTING OFFICE, page 299; OFFICE OF MANAGEMENT AND BUDGET, page 299.

Significance Prior to the enactment of the Budget and Accounting Act of 1921, the budget system was a loose and haphazard process in which various executive agencies submitted requests to as many as twenty-four different House and Senate committees. No attempt was made to look at the financial picture from an overall viewpoint, and the President had little or no voice in the entire process. Under the Act, a budget is prepared by fiscal experts under the direction of the President and is submitted as a single-package budget to Congress, where it is assigned to revenue and appropriations committees for study. Congress can now consider the budget as a total picture for the fiscal period of proposed expenditures and anticipated income. Execution of the budget by the spending agencies is done under the watchful eyes of the General Accounting Office, which carries on both preaudit and postaudit functions. The Budget and Accounting Act of 1921 is probably the most significant piece of fiscal control legislation to come out of Congress and, through a process of development and application over a period of fifty years, has served to bring considerable order out of former budgetary chaos.

Employment Act of 1946 An act that establishes responsibility for the national government to maintain stability in the nation's economy. A Council of Economic Advisers (CEA) was created by the Act and placed in the Executive Office to advise the President on economic matters. The Act requires the President to make an annual economic report to Congress setting forth the major economic problems confronting the nation and recommending appropriate legislation. *See also* COUNCIL OF ECONOMIC ADVISERS, page 298; DEFICIT FINANCING, page 278; DEPRESSION, page 278; FISCAL POLICY, page 283; KEYNESIANISM, page 287.

Significance The Employment Act of 1946 was the first legislation to recognize a continuing responsibility of government to use its broad economic powers to promote the nation's economic well-being. Specific goals of the Act include the maintenance of high levels of production, employment, and purchasing power. Since 1946, many demands have been made to include price stability as an additional responsibility of government. Congress has created a Joint Committee on the Economic Report, with seven members from each chamber, to study the President's recommendations and to recommend legislative consideration of specific programs. Although some recommendations and decisions undertaken under the Act have been controversial, the acceptance by government of a responsibility to combat economic downturns has been generally accepted by the American public. The mid-1970s provided a new challenge to the government's role of maintaining stability as the economy reeled from two-digit inflation, growing unemployment, and reduced economic activity.

12   Government and Business

Amtrak   The national semipublic corporation established in 1970 to operate intercity passenger railway traffic. Amtrak is the popular name for the National Railroad Passenger Corporation, which Congress established as a business seeking to earn a profit but which is infused with a public purpose and is under public control. Under Amtrak, the rails remain owned by the private carriers but the rolling stock is managed through joint government-business cooperation. The majority of the Board of Directors is appointed by the President so that government control of policy will be maintained. *See also* BUSINESS AFFECTED WITH A PUBLIC INTEREST, page 305; GOVERNMENT CORPORATION, page 225.

Significance   Amtrak was a product of increasing financial pressures that severely reduced or threatened to eliminate passenger traffic of most railroad systems and contributed to the bankruptcy of others. Amtrak reduced the number of trains by one-half in its campaign to consolidate intercity passenger traffic. Environmental concerns, the energy crisis of the 1970s, and improved service have aided Amtrak in its efforts to expand passenger operations. Yet, extensive federal subsidies have been needed. If Amtrak fails in its mission, nationalization of intercity passenger service may be inevitable. Charges of poor service led to a court test in which the Supreme Court held that the 1970 law establishing Amtrak does not authorize private persons or groups to try to change train routes and service by civil suit action (*National Railroad Passenger Corp. v. National Association of Railroad Passengers,* 414 U.S. 453 [1974]).

Antitrust Laws   Laws intended to regulate or prohibit unfair competition and combinations in restraint of trade, including monopolies, cartels, trusts, and interlocking directorates. The objective of antitrust action by the government is to maintain and strengthen the free enterprise system by ensuring competition in business. Responsibility for the enforcement of antitrust laws is vested in the Antitrust Division of the Department of Justice and in the Federal Trade Commission. *See also* ANTITRUST DIVISION, page 319; CLAYTON ACT, page 328; MONOPOLY, page 312; SHERMAN ANTITRUST ACT, page 328; TRUST, page 318.

Significance   Since the enactment of the Sherman Act in 1890, the national government's antitrust policy has been vigorously enforced at times, while at other times it has been sporadically enforced or ignored. Enforcement has been greatly influenced by Supreme Court decisions limiting or expanding the scope of enforcement authority, by the antitrust philosophy of particular presidents and the "trust busters" of the Antitrust Division, and by the views and pressures of public opinion calling for action or accepting inaction. Much also has depended upon the circumstances of the times, antitrust action having been reduced during periods of war, defense programs, or strenuous foreign competition. During the period 1960–1975, for example, American business went through an unparalleled era of mergers and building of huge conglomerates, with little restraining action by the government.

Bankruptcy   A procedure for discharging unpaid obligations through a court action that frees the individual from further liability for his debts. Bankruptcy proceedings may be initiated either by the insolvent debtor (voluntary bankruptcy) or by a required number of his creditors (involuntary bankruptcy). Such cases are usually handled by federal district courts under equity jurisdiction. The court appoints an officer who sells the bankrupt's assets and pays his creditors on a prorated basis. *See also* EQUITY, page 248; REFEREE, page 260.

Significance   Bankruptcy proceedings enable persons, both human and corporate, to wipe clean a slate of hopeless debt and start anew. Some provisions of this kind are indispensable to protect the credit structure of modern business enterprise. Major federal bankruptcy acts have been passed by Congress in 1898 and 1933, and, although state legislation in this field is possible, the federal law is comprehensive and takes precedence over state enactments. Some critics of bankruptcy proceedings charge that it encourages financial irresponsibility and recommend more restrictive measures concerning voluntary bankruptcy.

Blue Laws   Laws on the books of many states that prohibit certain business operations on Sunday and on religious holidays. Blue laws often make exceptions for amusements or essential activities and for persons who observe a sabbath day other than Sunday. The term, "blue laws," originated in the 17th-century New England colonies where laws regulating public and private behavior were printed on blue paper to indicate that the content of the laws was not proper for general public reading. *See also* FREEDOM OF RELIGION, page 70; POLICE POWER, page 40.

Significance   Blue laws are religious in origin and have been challenged as violations of religious liberty. They are now supported largely as welfare measures to encourage rest and relaxation. In 1961, the Supreme Court upheld a number of such laws on these grounds (*McGowan v. Maryland,* 366 U.S. 420). Blue laws have not been rigorously enforced and permit many exceptions that render them ineffective in practice.

Blue Sky Laws   State laws to protect investors in securities from misrepresentation and outright fraud. Blue sky laws commonly require that companies selling securities be certified by a state agency and furnish detailed information concerning their financial position. *See also* SECURITIES AND EXCHANGE COMMISSION, page 325.

Significance   The term "blue sky" refers to the gullible investor who discovers that the securities he has purchased represent nothing of value but the blue sky above. Blue sky laws have been enacted in almost all states since the early part of the twentieth century. Although most states continue to offer some protection to buyers of securites, most of their functions have been taken over by the Securities and Exchange Commission, created by Congress in 1934.

Bond   A certificate of indebtedness issued by a borrower to a lender as a legal promise to repay the principal of the loan plus accrued interest. Bonds are issued by private corporations, by all levels of government, and by many governmental agencies and corporations. Most bonds have limited negotiability in the security markets. *See also* BOND, page 274; BORROWING POWER, page 275.

Significance   Bonds have generally exceeded new stock issues in their importance in financing business expansion in the United States. Like stocks, the issuance of private corporation bonds is regulated by the Federal Securities and Exchange Commission and by regulatory agencies in most of the states. Unlike stockholders, bondholders are not part owners of the corporation but have merely lent their money to it for investment purposes.

Business Affected with a Public Interest   Any privately owned and operated selling or service activity that, as a matter of public policy, has been brought under the regulatory power of government. Businesses affected with a public interest, such as public utilities, are regulated by government boards and commissions in regard to their services and rates. The doctrine of "business affected with a public interest" was developed by the Supreme Court in *Munn v. Illinois*, 94 U.S. 113 (1876). *See also Munn v. Illinois,* page 327; PUBLIC UTILITY, page 315.

Significance   Many regulatory bodies have been created by national, state, and local governments when policymakers have determined that the free competition of the marketplace has become an insufficient means of protecting the right of the public to obtain satisfactory products or services at reasonable rates. Through such regulation, Americans have decided that such businesses as public carriers and gas and electric companies may operate under conditions of monopoly or near monopoly without danger to the public interest.

Business and Professional Organizations   Groups organized to promote the interests of business and the professions. The leading nationwide organizations of businessmen are the Chamber of Commerce of the United States and the National Association of Manufacturers (NAM). The Chamber is a federation of more than 3000 local chambers of commerce representing almost three million businessmen. The NAM represents about 20,000 large industrial firms. Another powerful business organization, the Business Council, is composed of the chief executives of the largest American corporations and functions as an unofficial adviser to national policymakers. In addition, businessmen are organized according to their trade or industry interests in numerous national and local trade associations. Leading professional associations include the American Medical Association (AMA), the American Bar Association (ABA), and the National Education Association (NEA). *See also* PRESSURE GROUP, page 138.

Significance   Most business and professional organizations reflect conservative attitudes toward taxes, government spending, and welfare programs. The Chamber of Commerce and the NAM spend much effort on public education programs in support of the free enterprise system. The AMA's long battle against Medicare is an outstanding example of pressure group involvement in a major political controversy. While businessmen have traditionally remained aloof from open political involvement, contemporary labor efforts and success on the political scene have encouraged business interests to become directly active in politics. Both business and professional organizations have always been particularly concerned with influencing government policy toward restricting entry and managing competition within their respective fields.

Caveat Venditor   A term meaning literally, "let the seller beware." *Caveat venditor* involves the acceptance by government of a responsibility to regulate business operations for the protection of consumers. It can be contrasted with the philosophy of *caveat emptor* ("let the buyer beware") that typified the free wheeling business practices of the nineteenth-century period of laissez-faire. Both philosophies continue to exist, but *caveat emptor* is on the defensive in today's consumer-based economy. *See also* UNFAIR TRADE PRACTICE, page 318; CONSUMERISM, page 308.

Significance   Under the doctrine of *caveat venditor,* government aloofness has given way, in the twentieth century, to numerous national, state, and local laws and enforcement agencies that operate in the interest of consumer protection. Businesses that sell impure foods or drugs, engage in false advertising, give short measure to buyers, sell dangerous items, or misrepresent their products, may be subject to civil or criminal action. National agencies that are particularly concerned with safeguarding consumer interests include the Food and Drug Administration of the Department of Health, Education, and Welfare, the Consumer Advisory Council, the Consumer Product Safety Commission, and the Federal Trade Commission. Regulation is intended to force business to present certain facts about their products for the information of the public, but sound investments and purchases still require careful buying methods by individual consumers. Ralph Nader and his "Nader's Raiders," a group of young lawyers and students who use legal approaches and lobbying methods to expand consumer rights and protections, have done much to pressure the national government into taking a more forthright stance in protecting the consuming public. New federal laws provide for product safety and require disclosure of finance charges and truth in advertising.

Certificate of Public Convenience, Interest, and Necessity   Permission granted by a regulatory agency to an individual or group to conduct a particular type of business. The standard of "public" convenience, interest, and necessity" has been established by Congress and state legislatures to guide regulatory agencies in issuing licenses and permits to public utilities and communication media. *See also* FRANCHISE, page 310; PUBLIC UTILITY, page 315.

Significance   The public interest is rarely served by the presence of several telephone companies in one community, or by competing railroads or buses. Limited channels for television and radio make regulation essential, lest the airways be jammed. Thus, the determination of which company will be given the right to a television channel or to engage in a public utility enterprise is a major problem facing regulatory agencies. A company granted such a privilege generally receives an asset of considerable financial value and influence, and is subject to continuing regulation of the quality of its service and the rates it may charge. Many agencies, state and national, have been charged with favoritism in the granting of certificates, necessitating constant supervision by the legislature and the public.

Commerce   The buying and selling of commodities, transportation, and commercial intercourse, and the transmission of radio, television, and telephonic and telegraphic messages. The Constitution grants Congress the power to regulate interstate and foreign commerce, and commerce with the Indian tribes. The states retain the power to regulate intrastate commerce. *See also* COMMERCE POWER, page 32; *Cooley v. Board of Wardens,* page 326; *Gibbons v. Ogden,* page 327.

Significance The power of Congress to regulate interstate and foreign commerce has, throughout American history, proved to be one of the key powers of the national government. Through successively broader interpretations by Congress and the Supreme Court, the term "commerce" has come to include almost all forms of business activity, including manufacturing since 1937. Although many legal battles have been fought concerning the extent of the commerce power, the issue since 1937 has become largely a political question rather than a legal one, to be settled by Congress and the people and not, ordinarily, by the Supreme Court. Commerce that is intrastate may come under the regulatory power of Congress if it directly or indirectly affects interstate commerce. States may also regulate interstate commerce if such regulation does not impede the free flow of that commerce and has a reasonable relation to the protection of the public safety, health, morals, or welfare, and if the activity regulated does not require uniform national treatment.

Common Carrier Any company that offers its services to the public for the transportation of goods or persons. Common carriers include airlines, railroads, bus companies, taxicabs, ships, pipelines, and trucking lines. *See also* BUSINESS AFFECTED WITH A PUBLIC INTEREST, page 305; CERTIFICATE OF PUBLIC CONVENIENCE, INTEREST, AND NECESSITY, page 306.

Significance Common carriers have been legally recognized throughout American history as "business affected with a public interest" because of the public's dependence upon their services. They may, therefore, be regulated for the public safety and convenience by the national, state, and local governments, each acting within its sphere of authority. National agencies involved in regulating interstate common carriers include the Civil Aeronautics Board, the Interstate Commerce Commission, the Federal Maritime Commission, and the Federal Power Commission. Regulation of common carriers by governments includes various aspects of their services and the rates they may charge.

COMSAT The joint public-private Communications Satellite Corporation which was created by the Communications Satellite Act of 1962. COMSAT includes several hundred private communications companies as shareholders and a Board of Directors that is composed of public and private officials. In 1963, 18 nations signed agreements to participate in COMSAT operations, leading to the creation of the International Telecommunications Satellite Consortium (INTELSAT) with membership including the United States and more than 50 other nations. INTELSAT provides for international cooperation in operating a global satellite-relay telephonic, telegraphic, radio, and television communications system. *See also* GOVERNMENT CORPORATION, page 225.

Significance COMSAT was created to follow up the spectacular achievement in space technology that occurred when the National Aeronautics and Space Administration (NASA) placed the first communications satellite, Telstar, in orbit. Developed by American Telephone and Telegraph, Telstar revolutionized communications by permitting the transmission of television, radio, telephone, and telegraph programs and messages on a global basis. Spectacular news and other events are regularly beamed thousands of miles via a number of satellites now in orbit, tying the world together with a communications network. COMSAT's public-private ownership and operations arrangement remains a political issue, with opponents of the existing system continuing to favor a more decisive governmental role.

Confiscation   Seizure of private property by a government, usually without compensation. Confiscation on a large scale may be the result of war or revolution; when it is applied selectively against individuals it typically is the result of law violations on their part. *See also* EMINENT DOMAIN, page 66; NATIONALIZATION, page 313.

Significance Major confiscations of properties belonging to enemy aliens occurred during World Wars I and II. Controversy over whether confiscated German and Japanese assets should be returned, or their former owners compensated, continued for many years after the end of World War II. Ordinarily, confiscation of properties used in the commission of a crime is part of the control mechanism utilized routinely by police forces. Typical examples include confiscation of the rifles and other equipment of poachers, and seizure of narcotics and illegal gambling devices.

Consumerism   The popular movement in the United States which aims at achieving effective protection for consumers. Consumerism has sought to achieve increased safety standards, truthful advertising, proper labeling, full compliance with regulatory laws and rules, control over food additives and dangerous herbicides and pesticides, consumer credit and pricing protection, and regulation of certain practices carried on by the legal and medical professions. The leader of the American consumer movement, Ralph Nader, has built an organization of young professionals and students, known as "Nader's Raiders," who use the courts and lobbying techniques to increase consumer protection. *See also* CAVEAT VENDITOR, page 306; CONSUMER PRODUCT SAFETY COMMISSION, page 320; FEDERAL TRADE COMMISSION, page 323; UNFAIR TRADE PRACTICE, page 318.

Significance Although Americans historically have tended to organize along *producer* rather than *consumer* lines, consumer protection movements have appeared from time to time. Some of these movements have sought improvement for the consumer through expanded governmental protection, while others have pursued it through cooperatives and consumer credit organizations of their own making. Consumerism has helped to pressure national, state, and local governments into adopting policies to protect consumer rights, although frequently agencies established to administer such policies have been inefficient or captured by powerful producer groups. Recent protective laws enacted by Congress and state legislatures include "truth in lending," "truth in labeling," and "truth in packaging" laws.

Contract Clause   Article I, section 10 of the Constitution which prohibits any state from passing laws impairing the obligation of contracts. This clause applies to contracts between individuals and to contracts made by the states. The state may neither weaken the effect of a contract nor make it more difficult to enforce. All contracts, however, are subject to the limitation that they may not endanger the health, safety, and welfare of the people—the areas of the states' "police powers."

Significance At one time, the contract clause was a major constitutional defense against state regulation of private property. The framers of the Constitution sought to guard against state practices of relieving private persons (such as debtors) of their contractual obligations. The clause was also used to favor corporations receiving charters from the states by making it impossible for the states to change the charters at a later date (*Dartmouth College v. Woodward,* 4 Wheaton 518 [1819]). State constitutions or statutes now make specific provisions permitting revocation or alteration of corporation charters and other state contracts, subject to the limitations of due process of law. This development, along with police power limitations, has modified the restrictive nature of the contract clause.

Copyright　The exclusive right granted by the Copyright Office in the Library of Congress to the creative products of authors, composers, dramatists, photographers, and others. A copyright is issued to anyone who wants one, following publication of his material and its submission to the Copyright Office. A copyright confers an exclusive privilege for a period of twenty-eight years, with the option of renewal for another twenty-eight year period. Typical copyrighted items include books, newspapers, magazines, musical compositions, translations, cartoons, sermons, motion pictures, photographs, paintings, maps, and charts. The copyright power is based on the constitutional grant to Congress to promote science and the arts by granting authors "the exclusive right to their respective writings. . . ." *See also* PATENT, page 314; TRADEMARK, page 318.

Significance　Copyrights are intended to foster creative efforts and to reward talent. Like patents, they constitute an exception to the laws against monopolies. The Copyright Office makes no effort to enforce the exclusive grant, however, and the individual grantee must take civil suit or injunctive action through the federal courts when he believes his copyright has been infringed. The United States has entered into copyright agreements with most foreign states, but a few have refused to participate in reciprocal protection agreements.

Corporation　A business unit, chartered under state or federal law, owned by stockholders and legally regarded as an artificial person. Private corporations are owned by individual investors and public corporations are partially or wholly owned by government—national, state, or local. The term "public corporation" is also often used to describe a corporation with broad ownership, such as General Motors, whereas one in which the stock is held by a few people or a family is called a "private corporation." *See also* CORPORATION INCOME TAX, page 277; GOVERNMENT CORPORATION, page 225; BOND, page 305.

Significance　The corporation has become the major form of business enterprise in the United States. Individually owned and partnership businesses, although more numerous than corporations, are dwarfed by the corporations in terms of volume of business, numbers of employees, assets, and in the wielding of economic and political power. The corporate form has tended to promote urbanization, industrialization, and increasing impersonality in business life. National defense requirements, corporation mergers, and a high mortality rate for small noncorporative businesses have all tended to accelerate the growth of huge corporations in recent years. National and state legislation extensively regulate the chartering of corporations, their financial and general business operations, and their impact upon competition in the market place.

Economic Planning   The establishment by government of economic goals and the means for reaching them. Economic planning may be concerned with providing some protection against violent swings of the business cycle in a capitalistic economy. At the other extreme, it may involve total governmental control and direction of investment, production, consumption, and other economic forces. *See also* COUNCIL OF ECONOMIC ADVISERS, page 298; KEYNESIANISM, page 287; PLANNING, page 448.

   Significance   The national government, since the depression of the 1930s, has increasingly used economic planning, primarily through the national budget, to fight recessions and to promote full employment. Long-range resources planning was first begun by the National Resources Planning Board, established in 1934, which was charged with studying economic trends and recommending national policies to avoid runaway booms or major slumps in the economy. In the Employment Act of 1946, Congress created a new planning group, the Council of Economic Advisers. The Council is charged with responsibility for short-term planning to recommend governmental policies that will give stability to the nation's economy, promote full employment, and avoid major booms and busts. In Communist and Socialist countries, economic planning is based on setting up national goals for a specific period, such as in a five-year plan, and the marshalling of the nation's work force and resources, often through authoritarian control, to achieve these goals. Some democratic countries, such as France, place much greater emphasis on long-range government planning to achieve economic and social objectives than does the United States.

Franchise   A privilege conferred by government upon a private company to operate a public utility and to use public property for the welfare or convenience of the public. Franchises are granted by the national, state, and local governments to bus companies, railroads, telephone and electric power companies, pipelines, and other private companies performing public services. *See also* CERTIFICATE OF PUBLIC CONVENIENCE, INTEREST, AND NECESSITY, page 306; PUBLIC UTILITY, page 315.

   Significance   A government grants a franchise when a condition of limited competition or natural monopoly exists and unrestricted competition is not practicable. In restricting competition, the government accepts a responsibility to regulate the service and rates of the franchised company to ensure that it operates in the public interest. Most franchises are granted by city governments, and franchise fees constitute a sizable source of municipal funds.

Holding Company   A corporation whose assets consist of stocks in operating companies, usually a controlling share in each of several allegedly competing companies (subsidiaries). Holding companies, although illegal under the common law, have been legalized by statute in many states. The policies and pricing of subsidiary companies are controlled through stock ownership and the membership of holding company officers on the boards of directors of subsidiaries. *See also* PUBLIC UTILITY, page 315.

   Significance   In the late nineteenth and early twentieth centuries, holding companies were used to establish monopoly or near-monopoly pricing conditions in certain industries, especially in electric and gas utilities. By the 1930s, holding companies were recognized as a threat to free enterprise competition and to the welfare of consumers in the gas and electric industries. Congress enacted the Holding Company Act of 1935 to control the operations of such companies engaged in interstate and foreign commerce. One section of this law, the so-called death sentence provision, halted the pyramiding of holding companies by limiting them to the second degree, that is, only two holding companies are permitted beyond the operating level. The effect of the law in dissolving many of the complicated holding company structures, along with increasing regulation of rates and services, have placed the operations of utilities under a greater measure of public control.

Interlocking Directorates   A means by which competing companies reduce or eliminate competition among themselves by having the same individuals as members of the boards of directors of their companies. Through interlocking directorates, companies supposedly in competition with each other establish uniform pricing policies and take other actions of a monopolistic nature. *See also* CLAYTON ACT, page 328.

Significance   The interlocking directory device came into use in the world of big business as a means of evading the provisions of the Sherman Antitrust Act prohibiting combinations in restraint of trade. This loophole was largely closed by the Clayton Act of 1914, which prohibits interlocking directorates in companies if any of them has a capitalization of $1 million and if they are engaged in interstate or foreign commerce and are natural competitors.

Jawboning   The role of the President in applying pressures on businessmen, labor leaders, and other key economic decision makers to make their behavior compatible with national economic goals of full employment and economic growth with price and wage stability. Jawboning has been carried on by most presidents, with its success largely dependent upon the personality of the President and the perception of economic leaders regarding his effectiveness in generating public opinion pressures. *See also* PRESIDENT, page 206.

Significance   The President in his jawboning role acts, as spokesman for the American people and as manager of the nation's prosperity. Some presidents, such as Lyndon B. Johnson, have used jawboning with telling effect to limit the freedom of action of private individuals and groups in the public interest. The threat of more stringent government action vis-à-vis affected companies and groups usually undergirds its effective use. Its most frequent use has been in trying to limit price and wage rises during periods of inflation without resorting to government controls. Both President Richard M. Nixon and Gerald R. Ford used jawboning sporadically but with little success to fight inflationary pressures during the 1970s.

License   A certificate granted under law by administrative officials, permitting private individuals to engage in certain business or professional activities. Licensing power is exercised primarily by the state and local governments, but the national government also uses it to regulate such fields as atomic materials, securities, market exchanges, and radio and television. Licensing is thus a powerful tool in the hands of government officials at all levels. *See also* CERTIFICATE OF PUBLIC CONVENIENCE, INTEREST, AND NECESSITY, page 306.

Significance   Persons seeking a license must meet the requirements established by law. Discretion is exercised by administrative officials when choosing from among many qualified applicants for a limited number of licenses. The power to grant licenses includes the power to suspend, revoke, or refuse to renew licenses for cause. Licensing by government is often demanded by professional or skilled groups, such as physicians and beauty operators, to ensure proper standards and, in some cases, to restrict competition in the field.

Margin   The cash down payment made by a customer who purchases stocks or bonds on credit. The margin or amount of down payment required for the purchase of securities is set by the Board of Governors of the Federal Reserve System. The securities purchased usually constitute the collateral for the loan on the balance owed. Margin decisions by the Federal Reserve Board relate to the level of the stock market, the demand for credit, and the state of the nation's economy. *See also* BOARD OF GOVERNORS, FEDERAL RESERVE SYSTEM, page 297.

Significance   Margin requirements are set by the Federal Reserve because credit purchases of stocks and bonds can have a major impact on inflationary or deflationary monetary policies carried on through the Federal Reserve System. Margin levels are also petinent to the stability of the securities markets. In 1929, for example, margin was not regulated by government, and great overextensions of credit contributed to the collapse of the stock market. For the past twenty-five years, margin requirements have ranged from 40 to 100 percent of the purchase price of securities.

Merger   The pooling of assets of two companies to form a single company. Various kinds of mergers are possible, including those between competing companies (horizontal), those aimed at gaining control of raw material suppliers (vertical-backward), those involving retail outlets (vertical-forward), and those of unrelated businesses (conglomerate). *See also* SHERMAN ANTITRUST ACT, page 328.

Significance   For many years, mergers were regarded as reasonable business combinations not in violation of the antitrust laws. As a result of a rapidly increasing number of business mergers and growing pressure for governmental action, Congress enacted the Celler Antimerger Act in 1950 as an amendment to the Clayton Act. Mergers that reduce competition or that foster the growth of monopoly conditions are prohibited by the law. Many controversies have arisen concerning the application of the Celler amendment because its vague and general language leaves considerable discretion in the hands of enforcement officials. Most such controversies involve the question of whether a specific merger will increase or decrease competition. Companies often seek approval from enforcement officials prior to undertaking a merger. The 1960s and 1970s have been a period of unprecedented merger activity leading to fewer and larger corporations, many operating on a multinational basis.

Monopoly   A market condition characterized by the absence of competition and the artificial fixing of prices for services or commodities, unaffected by the supply-demand forces of the market economy. A monopoly holds exclusive control over a good or service in terms of supply to a particular market. *See also* OLIGOPOLY, page 313.

Significance   Monopolies result when business firms establish conditions in which prices are controlled through mergers, holding companies, interlocking directorates, conspiracies to restrain trade, and collusive bidding. Under the Sherman Act of 1890, the Clayton Act of 1914, and the Federal Trade Commission Act of 1914, the national government seeks to break up monopolies and restrain their price-fixing techniques so as to foster real competition in the free enterprise system. In some cases, however, the national government has permitted and even encouraged monopolies, as, for example, in granting exclusive franchises to public utilities, in conferring patent and copyright privileges, and in fostering the export trade (Webb-Pomerene Act). A natural monopoly is one bestowed by nature on a geographical area, or one that, because of the nature of the enterprise, would make competition wasteful or self-destructive.

Nationalization   The transference of the ownership and operation of private enterprises to a national government. Nationalization may result from purchase or confiscation (expropriation), with or without compensation, and may apply to properties owned by citizens or foreign nationals. *See also* CONFISCATION, page 308; EMINENT DOMAIN, page 66.

Significance Although American nationalization has been limited mainly to the seizure of enemy assets during time of war, other democratic nations, such as Britain, have nationalized some of their basic industries and communications, transportation, banking, and health facilities. Nationalization of private business and industry is a goal of the Socialists and Communists, and in many countries private assets have been confiscated without compensation to the owners. Fear of expropriation has been a significant factor in limiting American private investments abroad, especially in the newly emerging nations of Asia and Africa. American constitutional guarantees limit the nationalization powers of the national government, although private property may be appropriated by law for a public purpose under the power of eminent domain with the payment of just compensation to the private owners.

Navigable Waters   All waters within the boundaries of the United States that are or may be used as highways for interstate or foreign commerce, such as rivers, streams, lakes, and inlets. The Supreme Court in its decision in the *Daniel Ball* case (10 Wallace 557 [1871]), declared that the jurisdiction of Congress extends to all natural waterways that can be used for the transmission of commerce among the states and with foreign nations. *See also* ADMIRALTY JURISDICTION, page 236; *Gibbons v. Ogden,* page 327.

Significance Although the beds of navigable waterways are under state jurisdiction, no state may constitutionally impede or obstruct the flow of commerce on the waters. Approval for construction of bridges over navigable waters by state or local governments must be obtained from the national government through the United States Corps of Engineers.

Oligopoly   A market condition wherein the supply of a commodity is controlled by a few companies, consequently limiting competition. Oligopoly is sometimes referred to as a situation of partial monopoly, because the market price can be fixed through collusion or passive competition. In such a market, a business enjoys *market power* —that is, its pricing policy is set by managerial discretion with little concern for competition rather than by the competitive market forces of supply and demand. *See also* MONOPOLY, page 312.

Significance Oligopoly conditions have tended to increase in many areas of the nation's economy in recent years, especially as a result of business mergers. Oligopoly constitutes an especially difficult enforcement problem in the national government's efforts to maintain effective competition in business, because competition appears to exist when it may not exist in fact.

Original Cost Theory An approach used by government, in fixing rates, to determine a fair return in profits for public utilities. The original cost theory is based on ascertaining the total investment made by the stockholders when the corporation was organized, plus subsequent capital expansions, less depreciation. *See also* RATE-MAKING, page 316; *Smyth v. Ames,* page 327.

Significance The original cost theory is usually favored by utility companies if their major investments have been made during periods of high cost. If made during periods of deflation, "reproduction cost" would be regarded more favorably. Federal regulatory agencies generally follow the original cost less depreciation theory, modified by the "prudent investment theory." Supporters of the original cost thesis argue that it is the only way of accurately computing a company's actual investment and that all other theories are hypothetical and subjective. Those who oppose original cost regard it as inaccurate and unfair because of its failure to take inflationary and deflationary factors into account.

Original Package Doctrine A limitation on the state taxing powers that exempts commodities from state jurisdiction so long as they remain in their original shipping containers. The Supreme Court applied the original package doctrine to products imported from foreign countries (*Brown v. Maryland,* 12 Wheaton 419 [1827]) and to those commodities produced in the United States and shipped in interstate commerce (*Leisy v. Hardin,* 135 U.S. 100 [1890]). *See also Brown v. Maryland,* page 326.

Significance The Supreme Court's original package doctrine was intended to restrain the states from imposing a burden upon the flow of interstate and foreign commerce. Otherwise, commodities could be subjected to a series of crippling taxes levied by each state that the commodities passed through on their way to their final destination.

Patent An exclusive grant to an inventor by which the national government extends to an individual or corporation "the right to exclude others from making, using, or selling the invention throughout the United States" for a period of seventeen years. Patent grants are made only for bona fide "discoveries," and not for improvements upon existing inventions. They apply to any new machine, design, process, composition, substance, or plant variety. The Constitution grants Congress exclusive power to grant patents. Patents are granted by the United States Patent Office in the Department of Commerce. *See also* COPYRIGHT, page 309; TRADEMARK, page 318.

Significance The United States Patent Office has issued almost 4 million patents since it was established by Congress in 1836. In recent years, patent applications have been made at the rate of 1500 each week, and there is a backlog of over 200,000 applications in various stages of processing. As the Founding Fathers intended, the monopoly granted to inventors has served as a major incentive in developing the thousands of useful products that typify the American economy. The United States has entered into patent agreements with most foreign states, although a few have jeopardized inventors' international patent rights by refusing to conclude reciprocal protection agreements.

Proprietary Function A governmental activity involving business-type operations ordinarily carried on by private companies. Proprietary functions include such activities as supplying electricity and gas, recreational facilities, garbage collection, transportation, and operating a liquor business. Proprietary functions carried on by one level of government may be subject to taxes levied by another level. *See also* INTERGOVERNMENTAL TAX IMMUNITY, page 37; REVOLVING FUND, page 294; *South Carolina v. United States,* page 301.

Significance Governments engage in proprietary functions to secure revenue, to provide proper regulation of certain activities, to establish a model operation that private firms can emulate, or to offer services that private companies cannot or will not provide. Neither level of government can tax the other level's purely governmental functions, but the problem of distinguishing between proprietary and ordinary governmental activities has been a troublesome one for the courts. The supplying of water to a city, for example, was held by the courts to be a regular function of government immune from federal taxes, whereas the bottling and selling of mineral waters by a state was held to be a proprietary function.

Prudent Investment Theory An approach used by government in fixing rates to determine a fair return in profits for public utilities. The prudent investment theory is based on ascertaining the original cost of investments in the utility and subtracting from this figure those that have been imprudent or wasteful. *See also* RATE-MAKING, page 316; *Smyth v. Ames,* page 327.

Significance The prudent investment theory is based on the assumption that it would be unrealistic to include imprudent or wasteful investments in calculating the rate base of a utility for determining a fair return on investment. The Supreme Court in recent years has favored the use of the prudent investment theory by federal regulatory agencies, although it has not tried to establish a single formula (*FPC v. Hope Natural Gas Co.,* 320 U.S. 591 [1943]). The prudent investment theory has also been favored by many state courts for use by state regulatory agencies.

Public Service Commission A regulatory agency, found in each of the states, that regulates the rates and services of public utilities operating within the state. Public service commissions vary in size from one to seven members, with most states fixing the number at three. Private utility companies regulated by the commissions include gas and electric suppliers, buses, interurban railway transit systems, taxicabs, oil and gas pipelines, telephone and telegraph services, and in some states, municipal utilities. Some of the larger cities have also established public service commissions, and in many other cities the city council functions in this role. *See also* PUBLIC UTILITY, page 315.

Significance Public service commissions are expected to regulate utilities in the public interest to provide good service and fair rates for consumers. In most states, their efforts are hampered by complicated, court-imposed valuation formulas for determining rates, by inadequate operating funds, and by politically appointed staffs. In some states, the regulated companies are accused of having an inordinate influence over the commissions, which undermines the latter's regulatory role and results in poorer service and higher rates. Organized consumer groups in some states have successfully exerted political pressure to strengthen the regulatory function of commissions. Public service commissions increasingly are required to hold their hearings and make their decisions in public sessions.

Public Utility A privately owned business that performs an essential service for the community and is extensively regulated by government. Congress and the state legislatures establish general criteria for regulation and create government commissions to perform the regulatory function subject to review by the courts. Typical examples of public utilities include transportation facilities, electric and gas suppliers, communication services, and water suppliers. *See also* FRANCHISE, page 310; PUBLIC SERVICE COMMISSION, page 315; RATE-MAKING, page 316.

Significance A public utility is given a license or franchise by government when noncompetitive conditions are desirable. When government grants franchises to private businesses to carry on operations in the public interest free from competition, it has a resulting responsibility to regulate their services and rates. This involves decisions over the types of businesses that can be regulated as public utilities, the respective regulatory spheres of the nation and the states, and the methods of calculating a fair return for the company in fixing rates.

Public Works Improvements in public facilities financed or built by government for the public welfare and convenience. Public works include such projects as parks, bridges, public buildings, roads, sewers, dams, harbors, housing, hospitals, canals, reclamation, irrigation, and navigation. *See also* CORPS OF ENGINEERS, page 354; FISCAL POLICY, page 283; PORK BARREL LEGISLATION, page 177.

Significance Public works projects not only provide facilities for public benefit; they are also useful in carrying out countercyclical fiscal policies to combat economic recessions. Economists suggest that public improvements be carefully planned in advance and, during an economic downturn, be quickly put into effect. Governments on all three levels generally cooperate in carrying out public works programs, with major financing usually provided by the national government. In addition to stimulating the economy by increasing purchasing power and reducing unemployment, public works can greatly strengthen the nation by meeting present and future needs. Critics charge, however, that some public works programs are enacted for political reasons (pork barrel legislation) rather than out of need, such as the annual appropriations for rivers, harbors, and flood control. Some critics of the federal-state welfare system have advocated putting welfare recipients to work on public works projects, while others want private business to handle them on a contractual basis.

Rate-making The determination by governmental regulatory agencies such as the ICC and the FPC, of the charges that privately owned public utilities will be permitted to levy for their services to the publlic. Rate-making agencies usually fix only maximum rates, although minimum rates may be set to avoid rate wars. *See also* ORIGINAL COST THEORY, page 313; PRUDENT INVESTMENT THEORY, page 315; PUBLIC UTILITY, page 315; REPRODUCTION COST THEORY, page 317; *Smyth v. Ames,* page 327.

Significance Rate-making involves the problem of protecting consumer interests while permitting rates high enough for the utility to earn a fair return. Rates are usually fixed to give a return of from 5 to 8 percent, but the difficulty remains of determining the base on which this profit is to be calculated. Utilities often appeal to the courts when they regard their return as too small. Theories of valuation on which rate-making has been based include original cost, reproduction cost, market value, and prudent investment; regulatory agencies generally follow the original cost approach, modified by prudent investment. With the growth of consumer protection, rate-making agencies have come under increasing criticism for their lenient regulation and liberal rate increases. Members of regulatory commissions are often appointed from the industry subject to their regulation and rate-making, resulting often in decisions that favor the industry and penalize consumers.

Reproduction Cost Theory   An approach used by government in fixing rates to determine a fair return in profits for public utilities. The reproduction cost theory is based on ascertaining the cost of reproducing the assets of a utility at current prices less depreciation over the period of their use. *See also* RATE-MAKING, page 316; *Smyth v. Ames,* page 327.

Significance   The reproduction cost theory is favored by utilities during periods of inflation because higher prices tend to increase the size of the rate base on which rates and a fair return are computed. The case for the reproduction cost theory is based on its acceptance of current market conditions as the basis for rate-making, whereas the case against it is based on the view that a fair return can be accurately determined only if based on actual investment figures (original cost theory) and not one established by government rate makers.

Restraint of Trade   The use in the business world of trusts, monopolies, price fixing, collusion, conspiracy, or other practices that hamper or eliminate a market economy based on free competition. The phrase is used in the Sherman Act of 1890 wherein it forbids any "conspiracy in the restraint of trade. . . ." *See also* SHERMAN ANTITRUST ACT, page 328.

Significance   Although the laissez-faire theory of free enterprise calls for economic freedom from governmental controls, some measure of regulation of business and commerce has proved necessary to maintain free competition. Major federal statutes that have sought to prevent private actions in restraint of trade and free competition include the Sherman Act of 1890, the Clayton Act of 1914, and the Federal Trade Commission Act of 1914. Despite the historical emphasis on free enterprise, these acts reflect strong common law precedents for antitrust policy.

Subsidy   Financial or other forms of aid bestowed by government upon private individuals, companies, or groups to improve their economic position and accomplish some public objective. Subsidies may be direct, as in the payment of sums of money to shipbuilders and farmers, or indirect as in the tariff that protects American business, labor, and agriculture from foreign competition. A subsidy may take the form of a grant by one level of government to another level, as in federal revenue sharing. Subsidies may also relate wholly to domestic affairs, or they may be aimed at improving the nation's international performance or achieving some foreign policy objective. *See also* MILITARY-INDUSTRIAL COMPLEX, page 422; PRICE SUPPORT, page 350; REVENUE SHARING, page 293; TAX EXEMPTION, page 296.

Significance   Although subsidies are granted to private individuals by all three levels of American government, the national government has been the most active. The federal income tax, for example, consists of a maze of subsidies aimed at granting favorable treatment to various groups of taxpayers. Since Alexander Hamilton first proposed subsidies in his Financial Program and his famous Report on Manufactures, they have been a continuing and significant function of the national government, amounting to billions of dollars annually in recent years. Major beneficiaries of governmental subsidies are or have been railroads, airlines, farmers, businessmen, home builders, defense contractors, the unemployed, and veterans. In many cases, subsidies to one group may imperil the economic position of another group, as, for example, the effect on railroads of extensive subsidies to airlines.

Trademark   A name, mark, or symbol used by a manufacturer or dealer to identify his product or service to the consuming public. Trademarks are granted by the Patent Office through a procedure similar to that for obtaining patents. Registered trademarks are valid for twenty years, provided registrants file affidavits with the Patent Office every five years attesting to their use, and are renewable for subsequent twenty-year periods. Trademark protection is left up to registrants who can take civil suit action in the courts when infringements occur. *See also* COPYRIGHT, page 309; PATENT, page 314.

Significance   Like patents and copyrights, a trademark bestows a monopoly right upon an individual or company. Trademarks are significant not only to registrants, whose sales of products may be increased through such identification, but also to consumers, who are protected from a welter of confusion of similar marks and symbols when making purchases. In 1946, Congress enacted the Lanham Trademark Act, which revised and codified numerous federal statutes relating to trademarks.

Trust   Two or more corporations linked together by assigning the voting rights of a majority of stockholders in each corporation to a single group of trustees. The term is also commonly used to describe any huge corporation or group of corporations that pursues monopolistic policies in the production or supplying of goods or services. *See also* CLAYTON ACT, page 328; SHERMAN ANTITRUST ACT, page 328.

Significance   The trust as a business combination was used extensively to reduce or eliminate competition among previously competing companies, until it was outlawed by the Sherman Act of 1890. The Supreme Court, however, subsequently modified the antitrust provisions with its "rule of reason," which applied the Sherman Act only to those combinations that are unreasonably restrictive of competition and in which a clear intention of monopoly can be shown. While most trusts fell to renewed competition after the turn of the century, a few continued to flourish until the 1930s when the Department of Justice engaged in a vigorous trust-busting campaign. In recent years, the Department has turned its attention to mergers and collusive practices that, like the trusts of an earlier period, are substantially reducing competition.

Unfair Trade Practice   Any business activity that deceives or misleads the consumer and results in his being sold shoddy, dangerous, or overpriced goods or services. Examples of unfair trade practices include false and misleading advertising, misbranding, improper labeling, conspiracies to fix prices, collusive bidding, discrimination against buyers, price cutting to eliminate competition, and other practices in restraint of trade. *See also* CLAYTON ACT, page 328; CONSUMERISM, page 308; FEDERAL TRADE COMMISSION, page 323.

Significance Unfair trade practices were outlawed by the Congress in two laws enacted in 1914, the Clayton Act and the Federal Trade Commission Act. The former forbids price discrimination, price cutting to restrain trade, and purchases of stock among competitors. The latter seeks to promote fair competition and, through the Wheeler-Lea Act amendments of 1938, outlaws unfair and deceptive practices and false advertising of foods, drugs, cosmetics, and other commodities. Both acts are administered by the Federal Trade Commission. Consumer interests are also protected by the Food and Drug Administration of the Health, Education, and Welfare Department, which safeguards against misbranding, adulteration, and false labeling. Some critics have charged the Federal Trade Commission with using its powers to restrain unfair trade practices to restrict competition in the regulated fields.

Usury The charging of interest in excess of the maximum rate permitted by law. State usury laws provide for civil and criminal actions against persons or lending institutions charging illegal interest rates. During periods of inflation and high interest rates, lending institutions circumvent usury laws by charging maximum rates and adding fees which have the effect of adding to the total cost to the borrower. *See also* CONSUMERISM, page 308.

Significance All states have enacted usury laws, although the legal maximum rates permissible vary considerably. Provisions of usury laws are aimed mainly at holding down interest rates charged by small loan companies and pawnbrokers. Usury laws have gained in importance as the American economy has become increasingly dependent upon consumer credit. When interest rates exceed those permitted by usury laws, either very few loans are made, with a subsequent loss of business activity, or means are found to get around the usury laws.

IMPORTANT AGENCIES

Antitrust Division One of the major divisions of the Department of Justice, which has responsibility for enforcement of the antitrust laws. *See also* ANTITRUST LAWS, page 303.

Significance The forcefulness with which the national government has carried on its antimonopoly programs has depended often on the person chosen by the President and the Attorney General to be in charge of the Antitrust Division. For example, when Thurman W. Arnold, a law professor dedicated to breaking up monopolies, headed the Antitrust Division, almost as many legal proceedings were initiated in the five years of his tenure, from 1938 to 1943, as had been started in the preceding half century since the enactment of the Sherman Act. The Antitrust Division carries on its enforcement duties through both civil and criminal actions.

Civil Aeronautics Board (CAB) A five-member independent regulatory agency that controls the business aspects of private airlines engaged in domestic and foreign transportation. Board members are appointed by the President with the Senate's approval for six-year terms. The CAB was established under the Civil Aeronautics Act of 1938, which gave it responsibility for the "encouragement and development" of civil aviation. Its functions include both the promotion and regulation of the economic aspects of domestic airlines and the operations of both domestic and foreign airlines in the United States. It grants permission to companies to fly specific routes, exercises jurisdiction over rates and fares, and regulates mergers and other business relations in the interest of maintaining competition. The CAB is supplemented in its regulation of the airlines by the Federal Aviation Administration (FAA), which carries out extensive responsibilities related to the safety of air travel. The FAA is in the Department of Transportation and is headed by an Administrator appointed by the President with Senate approval. *See also* INDEPENDENT REGULA-TORY COMMISSION, page 227.

Significance The Civil Aeronautics Board's functions have increased with the growth of the airline industry. CAB decisions are vital to the economic interests of the airlines and to the convenience of the traveling public. Presidential approval is required for CAB decisions affecting foreign air transportation. Additional regulations governing airlines engaged in foreign traffic are provided by the International Civil Aviation Organization (ICAO).

Consumer Product Safety Commission (CPSC) A five-member independent regulatory agency established by Congress in 1972 to reduce the risk of injury to consumers from products sold to them. The Commission has primary responsibility for protecting consumers, superseding the role carried on by a number of other agencies of the national government. The Consumer Product Safety Act of 1972 also authorizes the Commission to carry on research concerning consumer product standards, to engage in various consumer information and education programs, and to establish an Injury Information Clearinghouse. Consumers and consumer organizations are empowered to petition the Commission to secure the issuance, amendment, or revocation of a consumer product safety rule. *See also* CONSUMERISM, page 308.

Significance Congress, by the 1972 Act and by creation of the Consumer Product Safety Commission, reacted to growing political pressures from consumer organizations and from many individuals who have been injured or endangered by consumer products. In addition to the Commission's broad new powers, it also assumed responsibility for enforcing the Flammable Fabrics Act, the Poison Prevention Packaging Act, the Hazardous Substances Act, and the act that requires safety devices on refrigerators. By removing enforcement of consumer product safety from several federal agencies, the Congress sought to achieve both greater effectiveness and political support. However, efforts by Congress to establish a broader, more powerful Consumer Protection Agency during the first half of the 1970s decade met with failure.

Department of Commerce One of the eleven major departments of the national administration headed by a Secretary with Cabinet rank. The Department of Commerce and Labor, founded in 1903, was split in 1913 by Congress into the two separate departments of Commerce and Labor. Major units found in the Department of Commerce, and the main responsibility of each, include: (1) the Bureau of the Census, which conducts the decennial census; (2) the National Oceanic and Atmospheric Administration, which monitors the physical and biological environment including weather forecasting; (3) the Domestic and International Business Administration, which promotes the growth of American exports and develops plans for domestic industrial mobilization; (4) the Maritime Administration, which administers grants to shipbuilders and operators; (5) the National Bureau of Standards, which maintains basic units for testing and measuring in business and industry; (6) the Office of Minority Business Enterprise, which seeks to establish, preserve, and strengthen ownership of business by members of minority groups; (7) the Patent Office, which examines and grants patents and trademarks; (8) the Bureau of Domestic Commerce, which promotes the growth of American industry and commerce; and (9) the Economic Development Administration, which provides aid to areas with substantial and persistent unemployment. *See also* CABINET, page 200.

Significance The Department of Commerce has major responsibility for providing services for the business community. It promotes and protects the interests of businessmen at home and abroad. It is primarily a service, rather than a regulatory, agency. The Secretary of Commerce is, typically, a businessman or a person who has been identified as friendly to the business community.

Department of Transportation One of the eleven major departments of the national administration, headed by a Secretary with Cabinet rank. The Department, established in 1966, brought together more than thirty separate agencies and bureaus dealing with transportation. Its major components now include the Federal Aviation Administration, the Federal Highway Administration, the Federal Railroad Administration, the Urban Mass Transport Administration, the National Highway Traffic Safety Administration, and the Saint Lawrence Seaway Development Corporation. *See also* AMTRAK, page 303; CABINET, page 200.

Significance The Department of Transportation was created to develop national transportation policies and programs to achieve efficient transportation at low cost. Although several important agencies concerned with transportation, such as the Interstate Commerce Commission and Maritime Administration, were not included in the Department, the Secretary of Transportation may suggest policy guidelines to independent agencies. Safety in all forms of transportation is a major concern of the Department.

Export-Import Bank of the United States A government corporation that guarantees private credit and makes direct loans to foreign and domestic businessmen to promote the flow of trade. The Export-Import Bank, originally chartered in 1934, is governed by a five-member bipartisan board appointed by the President with Senate consent.

Significance The Export-Import Bank was originally created to foster trade between the United States and the Soviet Union and with Latin America, but its operations have become almost worldwide in scope. Its loans must be repaid in American dollars, and capital equipment needed by the party receiving the loan must be purchased in the United States. The bank is an important contributor to aid programs for underdeveloped countries, financing the building of steel mills, roads, dams, manufacturing plants, and other projects.

Federal Communications Commission (FCC) A seven-member independent regulatory commission that controls interstate and foreign communication via radio, television, telephone, telegraph, and cable. The FCC was created by and administers the Federal Communications Act of 1934. Under the Act, the FCC grants licenses to broadcasters, enforces regulations prohibiting indecent language and lotteries, and requires equal time for political candidates. The FCC has no power to regulate rates charged sponsors of radio and television programs, but Congress has designated telephone, telegraph, and cable services as "common carriers" and, therefore, subject to extensive regulation of rates and services. The FCC also implements provisions of the Communications Satellite Act of 1962. *See also* COMSAT, page 307; EQUAL TIME, page 121; INDEPENDENT REGULATORY COMMISSION, page 227.

Significance The major responsibility of the FCC in recent years has been that of granting licenses to broadcasters. A limited number of radio frequencies and television channels are available. A television license, for example, is granted free by the FCC but may be worth millions of dollars to the licensee. As a result, the FCC has often had to select from a number of applicants who may bring political pressure to bear on the commissioners. Although its regulation of broadcasting is exercised exclusively, it shares regulation of telephone services with state utility commissions. The latter control rates and services of independent telephone companies and local calls, whereas the FCC controls interstate long-distance calls and all telegraph and cable services. Because all licenses granted by the FCC are for fixed periods and must be renewed, much controversy has centered around renewal hearings on the issue of what constitutes a record of adequate service in the public interest, and whether the licensee has achieved such a record.

Federal Deposit Insurance Corporation (FDIC)   A government corporation established in 1933 that insures depositors' accounts in participating banks up to $40,000 for each account. The FDIC insurance system is financed through annual assessments levied on privately owned banks. Member banks of the Federal Reserve System must participate, and nonmember banks may request to join the program. The FDIC is directed by the Comptroller of the Currency and by two directors appointed by the President with Senate consent. *See also* FEDERAL RESERVE SYSTEM, page 282.

Significance The FDIC program promotes stability in the banking system by maintaining the confidence of depositors that their money is safe. Prior to the establishment of the government's guarantee, "runs" on individual banks and general bank "panics" were quite common. They were difficult to control because banks do not normally keep enough cash on hand to meet widespread demands from depositors for their money. Because such fear is restrained by absolute guarantees of the national government offered through the FDIC, the banking system and, as a consequence, the entire American economy have achieved greater stability. All but a small fraction of the commercial banks in the United States are insured by the FDIC. The Federal Savings and Loan Insurance Corporation (FSLIC) similarly ensures each depositor's account for up to $40,000 in all federally chartered and in most state-chartered savings and loan associations.

Federal Maritime Commission (FMC)   A five-member independent regulatory agency that controls rates and services of water carriers engaged in foreign and domestic off-shore commerce. Members are appointed by the President with the Senate's approval for four-year terms. The FMC's authority includes the approval of routes, the settling of disputes, and the prescribing of working conditions for seamen. The FMC works closely with its international counterpart, the Intergovernmental Maritime Consultative Organization, headquartered in London. *See also* INDEPENDENT REGULATORY COMMISSION, page 227.

Significance The Federal Maritime Commission was established in 1961 as an independent agency to make and enforce regulations relating to the merchant marine. Foreign shippers are freer from governmental controls than are coastal and inland waterway shippers under Interstate Commerce Commission jurisdiction. The Maritime Administration in the Department of Commerce aids shipbuilders and operators through the payment of "construction differentials" and "operating differentials" as subsidies to enable American shippers to compete with foreign companies. The FMC works with the Department of State to eliminate foreign discrimination against American shipping.

Federal Power Commission (FPC) A five-member independent regulatory commission that controls the production and interstate transmission and sale of electrical energy and the interstate transportation and sale of natural gas. Commissioners are appointed by the President with the Senate's approval for five-year terms. The FPC was created as a Cabinet committee in 1920, and given its independent status by the Federal Power Act of 1930. Its functions include granting licenses to private companies to build hydroelectric plants on navigable waters, determining wholesale rates for electric power transmitted across state lines, regulating security issues of private power companies, planning for multipurpose river basin development, developing power resources at government-built dams, and controlling pipeline transmissions and sales of natural gas. *See also* INDEPENDENT REGULATORY COMMISSION, page 227.

Significance National regulation through the FPC of electrical power and natural gas operations of private utility companies stemmed largely from the inability of state utility commissions to protect the public interest in these areas. The FPC undertakes extensive studies and detailed investigations to determine fair prices and reasonable services, rather than relying on information supplied by utility companies at formal hearings—a practice that characterizes much state regulation. The major issues in this area in recent years have been whether the national government or private utility companies should develop some of the few remaining sites for major dams, and the scope of natural gas regulation. The FPC, like most of the regulatory commissions, has often been charged with being dominated by the regulated industries and with making policy more favorable to their interests than to the public interest. During the energy crisis of the 1970s, the natural gas industry mounted a major campaign to obtain substantially higher rates to encourage more exploration and production of gas, a move strongly opposed by numerous consumer protection organizations.

Federal Trade Commission (FTC) A five-member independent regulatory commission established by Congress in 1914 to promote fair competition in business and to restrict unfair business practices in interstate and foreign commerce. Commissioners are appointed by the President with the Senate's approval for seven-year terms. The FTC enforces the Clayton and the Federal Trade Commission Acts of 1914. It seeks to prevent illegal combinations in restraint of trade, deception, price discriminations, price fixing, interlocking directorates, fraudulent advertising of foods, drugs, and cosmetics, and other business activities that reduce competition or endanger or defraud the consumer. The operations of the FTC include making rules and regulations to establish a code of fair competition, holding hearings concerning alleged violations, and enforcing decisions through cease and desist orders and injunctions granted by federal courts. *See also* CAVEAT VENDITOR, page 306; INDEPENDENT REGULATORY COMMISSION, page 227.

Significance Most of the work of the FTC is carried on by persuading businessmen to cease some activity of doubtful legality. The Commission plays a relatively minor role in enforcing antimonopoly legislation and directs most of its efforts to protecting consumer interests by preventing deceptive advertising, fraud, and the sale of dangerous products. Although the duties of the FTC are varied, its underlying purpose is to maintain the free enterprise system by preventing corrupt practices. Yet it has often come under attack from critics who charge it with being probusiness and not energetic enough in protecting the rights of consumers.

Interstate Commerce Commission (ICC)   An eleven-member independent regulatory commission, established in 1887, that regulates the business operations, services, and rates of interstate carriers. Commissioners are appointed by the President and confirmed by the Senate for seven-year terms. The jurisdiction of the ICC extends to railroads, express companies, bus and truck companies, oil pipe lines, intercoastal and inland waterway carriers, and terminal facilities used in transporting goods or persons. The ICC enforces the Interstate Commerce Act of 1887 and six other supplementary statutes, plus numerous amendments. It employs a large staff of attorneys, investigators, economists, examiners, and technicians. Its responsibilities include fixing rates, both maximum and minimum, controlling poolings and consolidations of operating companies, regulating their sales of stocks and bonds, prescribing accounting systems, granting permits and licenses, and providing traffic management. *See also* COMMERCE, page 306; COMMERCE POWER, page 32; INDEPENDENT REGULATORY COMMISSION, page 227.

Significance The ICC was the first of the independent regulatory commissions, all of which have come to play a major role in the national government's regulation of substantial sectors of the nation's economy. The ICC, like the others, performs a threefold function of making rules and regulations (quasi-legislative), administering them, and holding hearings concerning violations and disputes (quasi-judicial). Commissioners work in three-member panels to carry out most of the routine work of the ICC, with appeal to the full Commission possible. The role of the ICC has become increasingly difficult as competition among the various carriers has intensified in recent years. Decisions of the ICC can be appealed to the federal courts for review to ensure protection of property rights from arbitrary actions. The ICC, like other regulatory commissions, has often been charged with making policy rules that favor regulated industries rather than the public interest.

Nuclear Regulatory Commission (NRC)   An independent regulatory body created in 1974 to carry on licensing and regulatory functions in the civil and military fields of nuclear power. The five-member Nuclear Regulatory Commission was established to replace the Atomic Energy Commission (AEC) and to carry on the regulatory functions formerly performed by that agency. The research and development functions in the field of atomic energy assigned to the AEC for many years were transferred at that time to a new Energy Research and Development Administration (ERDA). Responsibility for enforcing the Atomic Energy Acts of 1946 and 1954 is vested in the two agencies. *See also* ATOMIC ENERGY ACTS, page 328; ENERGY RESEARCH AND DEVELOPMENT ADMINISTRATION, page 356.

Significance The Nuclear Regulatory Commission has assumed primary responsibility for maintaining secrecy, security, scientific and engineering safeguards, and environmental control over the development of civilian and military uses of nuclear power. Major production facilities are located at Oak Ridge, Tennessee, and Richland, Washington. The NRC, with its extensive regulatory activities concerning private power companies, is supervised by Congress through a Joint Committee on Atomic Energy.

Securities and Exchange Commission (SEC)   A five-member independent regulatory commission established by the Securities Exchange Act of 1934 to regulate the buying and selling of securities (stocks, bonds, and so forth). Commissioners are appointed by the President, with the Senate's approval, for five-year terms. In addition to the Act of 1934, the SEC enforces the Securities Act of 1933, which compels full disclosure of information concerning new security issues, and the Public Utility Holding Company Act of 1935 under which the SEC tries to limit mergers and combinations of utility companies. *See also* MARGIN, page 312.

Significance   The establishment of the SEC and adoption by Congress of the Acts of 1933 and 1934 grew out of the shocking disclosures of deception, manipulation, fraud, and dishonesty revealed by a Senate investigation of causes of the stock market crash of 1929. The SEC does not guarantee the financial soundness or money-making possibilities of any security; it merely requires disclosure of all pertinent information to prospective buyers and forbids any attempts to manipulate prices. SEC regulatory activities have often been criticized as being more protective of the securities industry than of the nation's economic welfare.

Small Business Administration (SBA)   An independent agency, headed by an administrator, established to make loans to small businesses and to assist them in obtaining government contracts. The SBA was given temporary status by Congress in 1953, and was expanded and made a permanent agency in 1958. Some of its operations since 1961 have been carried on through small-business investment companies around the nation. Principal functions of SBA include financing plant expansion and modernization, aiding disaster victims, helping businessmen to cut through red tape to secure government procurement contracts, and giving managerial advice to small firms. Applicants for loans must show they have been turned down by private banks.

Significance   The SBA was the first agency established for the specific purpose of aiding small business. There are approximately four million small businesses in the United States today with an annual turnover rate of about 10 percent. The SBA utilizes a revolving fund that gives it a measure of freedom from dependence upon annual budget grants from Congress. Although the agency was criticized in its early operations for mainly granting large loans to sizable businesses, it has increased the number of its loans and reduced the average amount of each loan to about $40,000 in recent years.

United States Postal Service   The independent government agency that has the responsibility for operating the United States postal system. The United States Postal Service was created by the Postal Reorganization Act of 1970 to replace the Post Office Department, which had been a major department of the national government, with Cabinet rank, headed by the Postmaster General. Under the Act, the Postal Service Board of Governors appoints postmasters and postal employees, controls rates and classes of mail, and makes general postal operating policy free from political and congressional influence. Civil service status and rights of postal workers were retained under the new Postal Service system. The Postal Service, in addition to carrying the mail, runs a parcel post service, a system of registering, certifying, and insuring mail, sells government bonds, and offers money order, C.O.D., and special delivery services.

Significance The Postal Service operates nearly 32,000 local post offices and is one of the biggest business operations in the world, employing 700,000 persons and handling almost 100 billion pieces of mail annually. The changeover to a new, independent, self-supporting, government-owned postal agency was based on the recommendations of a special Commission on Postal Organization. The change was aimed at correcting some of the major weaknesses of the old system—political influence, senatorial control over all postmasterships, huge subsidies to politically powerful groups, and substantial annual deficits. The effectiveness of the new approach can be assessed accurately only after testing it over a period of years in terms of cost, efficiency, and public support. Critics charge, however, that service has deteriorated and costs have substantially increased since the changeover, and that the announced goals are not being achieved.

IMPORTANT CASES

Brown v. Maryland, 12 Wheaton 419 (1827): Established the "original package" doctrine, which holds that the authority of Congress over foreign commerce does not end until the merchandise arrives at its ultimate destination, the contents of the package are sold or removed for the purpose of selling, and they become mixed together with the general property of a state. The case invalidated a law of Maryland that had required importers of foreign goods to obtain a license before being permitted to sell them. See also COMMERCE, page 306; ORIGINAL PACKAGE DOCTRINE, page 314.

Significance The original package doctrine established in the *Brown* case remains a significant factor in restricting state interference with foreign commerce. In *Leisy v. Hardin,* 135 U.S. 100 (1890), the Court expanded the original package doctrine to include products shipped in interstate as well as foreign commerce. The regulatory power of Congress continues, however, to be more extensive over foreign than over interstate commerce because of the vast powers exercised by the national government in foreign affairs.

Cooley v. Board of Wardens, 12 Howard 299 (1851): Upheld the right of the states to regulate interstate commerce if Congress has not covered the field with its regulations and if the subject regulated by the states is not of a nature to require uniform national regulation. The case involved local regulations for port pilots, which were upheld as a reasonable regulation of interstate commerce by a state since such regulation does not need a uniform national policy. See also COMMERCE, page 306; COMMERCE POWER, page 32.

Significance The *Cooley* case established the precedent on which a vast amount of state regulation of interstate commerce is based today. By permitting states to enter the field, the Court recognized that the national government would be unable to provide all of the regulations needed to control the flow of commerce. Under the *Cooley* rule, the permissible extent of state regulation of interstate commerce in the absence of federal regulation is left to the courts to decide.

Gibbons v. Ogden, 9 Wheaton 1 (1824): Nullified a state grant giving an exclusive right to use navigable waters within the state. The Court held that congressional control over interstate commerce includes navigation. It was the first case involving the commerce clause, and the powers of Congress to regulate interstate commerce were broadly interpreted by Chief Justice Marshall and the Court. They defined interstate commerce to include not only traffic but also all commercial intercourse. *See also* COMMERCE POWER, page 32; NAVIGABLE WATERS, page 313.

Significance The *Gibbons* case opened the door to a vast expansion of national control over commerce through liberal interpretation of the commerce power. The Supreme Court, for example, has held that a farmer could be fined under the commerce power for growing a small amount of wheat for his own consumption in violation of the quota set for him by the Secretary of Agriculture (*Wickard v. Filburn,* 317 U.S. 111 [1942]). Today, the powers of Congress to regulate interstate commerce include the regulation of transportation, communications, buying and selling, and manufacturing. Few areas of economic activity remain outside the regulatory power of Congress.

Munn v. Illinois, 94 U.S. 113 (1876): Held that a state can validly fix maximum rates for a "business affected with a public interest." Regulation of a privately owned grain warehouse by the state of Illinois was upheld on the ground that when a proprietor devotes his property to a public use, he "must submit to be controlled by the public for the common good. . . ." *See also* BUSINESS AFFECTED WITH A PUBLIC INTEREST, page 305.

Significance The *Munn* case was a landmark in establishing the power of government to regulate businesses other than public utilities. Congress and state legislatures have continued to use the flexible criterion of "business affected with a public interest" to regulate many business activities.

Smyth v. Ames, 169 U.S. 466 (1898): Declared, in an historic rate-making case, that government regulatory agencies must consider a number of factors in fixing rates, rather than a single one. The facts in the case involved a dispute over rate-setting for Nebraska railroads, in which the governmental agency based its formula chiefly on "reproduction cost," and the railroads demanded that the rate base be "original cost." The Court held that many factors should be considered in determining fair value, including original cost, cost of improvements, value of securities, reproduction cost, earning capacity, and operating expenses. *See also* RATE-MAKING, page 316.

Significance Because due process requires that rates fixed by government for private businesses be fair and reasonable, the problem of determining the base upon which the fair return will be calculated is a critical one. In recent years, the Court has modified the *Smyth* decision, adopting the "prudent-investment" theory as a guide and using a pragmatic approach to determine whether the rates permit companies to operate successfully (*FPC v. Hope Natural Gas Co.,* 320 U.S. 591 [1943]).

IMPORTANT STATUTES

Atomic Energy Acts of 1946, 1954 The Act of 1946 created the Atomic Energy Commission (AEC) to control and develop the uses of atomic energy. Private mining of fissionable materials was permitted, but all other aspects of atomic energy were kept under strict governmental control. The Act of 1954 modified the public monopoly by permitting private development and operation of atomic power plants and the use of nuclear fuels and the sale of by-products by private firms under government licensing. *See also* ENERGY RESEARCH AND DEVELOPMENT ADMINISTRATION, page 356; NUCLEAR REGULATORY COMMISSION, page 324.

Significance The first Atomic Energy Act placed atomic energy, which had been developed by the military, under civilian control. Growing foreign achievements in the atomic field awakened Congress to the need to stimulate more rapid development of atomic energy for industrial purposes. As a result, the second Act, which sought to unleash private energies within limits of governmental control, was passed. Because of the extremely high cost of producing electricity in atomic power plants, the government contributes a major portion of the cost in building private facilities. Considerable governmental effort is also going into research to try to develop cheaper power. In 1974, Congress abolished the Atomic Energy Commission, transferring its research and development functions to the Energy Research and Development Administration (ERDA), and its licensing and regulatory functions to the Nuclear Regulatory Commission (NRC).

Clayton Act of 1914 A major antitrust act, aimed at increasing competition in business. Provisions of the Clayton Act forbid price cutting and other abuses that tend to weaken competition, restrict corporations from acquiring stock in competing firms or building interlocking directorates, make corporation officers individually liable for violations, and facilitate civil suit procedures by injured parties. Labor unions and agricultural organizations not carrying on business for profit are exempted from the provisions of the Act. *See also* ANTITRUST DIVISION, page 319; ANTITRUST LAWS, page 303.

Significance The Clayton Act was intended to supplement and reinforce the Sherman Act of 1890, which had been weakened by the Supreme Court's interpretation limiting its application to "unreasonable" combinations in restraint of trade. The Act was aimed at reducing the confusion surrounding the Sherman Act by more clearly defining unfair business practices. Enforcement of the Clayton Act, however, has been weakened through administrative unconcern and judicial tolerance, except for a few periods of vigorous enforcement by the Antitrust Division and the Federal Trade Commission.

Sherman Antitrust Act of 1890 The basic federal antimonopoly law that forbids "every contract, combination . . . or conspiracy in the restraint of trade or commerce." Enforcement of the Act is provided through criminal penalties, civil suit action with triple damages to injured parties, injunction, and seizure of property. Responsibility for enforcement is vested in the Antitrust Division of the Department of Justice. *See also* ANTITRUST DIVISION, page 319; ANTITRUST LAWS, page 303.

Significance The Sherman Act was a recognition by Congress that, paradoxical as it might appear to be, governmental intervention in the free economy was essential to preserve competition. Soon after its enactment, the Act was seriously crippled in two major Supreme Court tests. In the first, the Court held that manufacturing trusts were not engaged in commerce and, therefore, could be regulated only by the states (*United States v. E. C. Knight Co.,* 156 U.S. 1 [1895]). In the second, the Court laid down the "rule of reason" by which not *every* combination in restraint of trade (as Congress had explicitly stated in the Act) was illegal, but only those *unreasonably* so (*Standard Oil Co. v. United States,* 221 U.S. 1 [1910]). To supplement and reinforce the Sherman Act, Congress has since adopted the Clayton Act of 1914 and the Federal Trade Commission Act of 1914. The history of the Sherman Act demonstrates the influence of the Supreme Court, the President, the Attorney General, and other high officials in interpreting the language of the Act narrowly or broadly and in vigorously or reluctantly enforcing it.

Webb-Pomerene Act of 1918 An act that exempts business associations engaged in export trade to foreign lands from the provisions of the antitrust laws. Such organizations must register with and submit reports to the Federal Trade Commission. *See also* MONOPOLY, page 312.

Significance The Webb-Pomerene Act was enacted to promote American foreign trade and to put American exporters on a competitive basis with countries that have little or no effective antitrust or anticartel legislation. Although the Act was intended to permit American industries to participate in world monopoly operations but not in domestic activities of a monopolistic nature, critics have charged that such activities tend to have a monopolylike impact on the domestic market.

13 Government and Labor

Arbitration The submission of a labor-management dispute to an impartial board or individual whose decision is binding upon the parties to the dispute. Many collective bargaining agreements provide for arbitration of unresolved grievances. A few states have passed statutes requiring compulsory arbitration of disputes in public utility enterprises, such as electric, gas, and water. *See also* ARBITRATION, page 238; MEDIATION AND CONCILIATION, page 334.

Significance A large number of labor disputes are submitted to private professional arbitrators. Many strikes are thereby avoided. Compulsory arbitration has been used in wartime, but both management and labor fear compulsory arbitration, since both prefer to keep the government out of labor disputes and to pursue their ends through collective bargaining. Compulsory arbitration procedures are provided under the Railway Labor Act to supplement, rather than substitute for, collective bargaining. These procedures have not, however, proved successful, and they have often been bypassed during a railroad labor dispute.

Boycott An economic weapon used by labor to curtail the purchase of products from an employer. Two types of boycotts, primary and secondary, may be distinguished from one another. A primary boycott involves withdrawal of patronage, and the urging of others to withdraw their patronage, from an employer with whom a union is having a labor dispute. A secondary boycott involves a refusal to deal with or patronize anyone who deals with the employer with whom there is a dispute. Secondary boycotts are outlawed by the Taft-Hartley Act of 1947 and, with certain exceptions, by the Landrum-Griffin Act of 1959. Most states also outlaw secondary boycotts.

Significance The primary boycott is lawful but often ineffective for a union. People may continue to cross a picket line to patronize a strikebound store and, in the case of large industrial plants, suppliers may continue to sell to the plant and dealers continue to sell its products. Labor prefers the secondary boycott, which enables it to bring pressure upon others whose continued dealing with the strikebound plant hinders the successful conclusion of the strike. Secondary boycotts are, however, illegal since they interfere with the rights of persons not involved in the dispute, and public policy seeks to confine the dispute to the particular parties involved.

Child Labor The employment of children below the legal age limit. The national government and most states prohibit the employment of children below the age of sixteen and, in certain hazardous occupations, below the age of eighteen. Children are permitted to work outside of school in nonhazardous jobs.

Significance Until about 1910, large numbers of children ten to fifteen years of age were regularly employed. State governments then began to impose restrictions, but states that did not do so were at an advantage over those that did. Agitation for national regulation led to the passage of legislation. The Supreme Court, however, struck down a law aimed at banning products of child labor from interstate commerce (*Hammer v. Dagenhart*, 247 U.S. 251 [1918]), and another law which taxed such products (*Bailey v. Drexel Furniture Co.*, 259 U.S. 20 [1922]). In 1924, Congress submitted to the states a constitutional amendment that would authorize federal regulation of child labor. Strong opposition prevented its ratification, though, by 1937, twenty-eight states, eight short of the required three-fourths, had ratified it. A more liberal view of national power, however, resulted in the passage and Supreme Court approval of the Fair Labor Standards Act of 1938 (*United States v. Darby*, 312 U.S. 100 [1941]), which among other things, prohibited child labor Today child labor poses no major problem, particularly in view of compulsory education laws

Closed Shop An industrial plant that agrees to hire only those persons who are members of a labor union. The closed shop is outlawed by the Taft-Hartley Act of 1947, although later legislation has modified this restriction with regard to the building trades. *See also* RIGHT TO WORK LAW, page 335; UNION SHOP, page 337.

Significance The closed shop is opposed by management because it allegedly places the hiring power in the union rather than in the hands of management. Approximately 30 percent of organized labor, largely in craft industries, were under closed shop agreements prior to 1947. Though forbidden by the Taft-Hartley Act, many establishments continue to operate as closed shops through the mutual agreement of the union and management who are reluctant to upset customary patterns.

Collective Bargaining Negotiation between an employer and a union representing the employees. It is to be distinguished from negotiation between an employer and an individual employee. The right of workers to organize and to bargain collectively through their representatives has been the official policy of the United States since 1935. Collective bargaining imposes upon the employer and labor union an obligation to confer in good faith with respect to working conditions and to execute a written contract embodying the agreements reached. Refusal to bargain by an employer or a duly recognized union may be adjudged an unfair labor practice. *See also NLRB v. Jones and Laughlin Steel Corp.*, page 339; WAGNER ACT, page 343.

Significance Official recognition of the principle of collective bargaining was the culmination of years of industrial strife in which unions sought recognition from employers as legitimate bargaining agents for employees. Both national and state labor-management relations laws were enacted to guarantee the right of collective bargaining in the interest of avoiding continued industrial unrest. The principle of collective bargaining is recognition of the inequality of bargaining power between an employer and an individual employee. National and state laws now extensively regulate the procedures by which agreements are to be reached, the administration of agreements, and the problems attending the breakdown of collective bargaining procedures.

Committee on Political Education (COPE)   The political action organization of the AFL-CIO. COPE combines the political tactics developed over the years by the CIO Political Action Committee (PAC) and the AFL League for Political Education. These were the political action organizations of the two labor federations prior to their merger into the new AFL-CIO in 1955. Funds for COPE's activities are raised through voluntary contributions of trade union members. *See also* LABOR UNIONS, page 334.

Significance   The Taft-Hartley Act of 1947 forbids the use of union dues for partisan political activity. This resulted in the establishment of political "education" committees financed through voluntary contributions. COPE has been active in state and national campaigns since 1956. It educates workers and the general public on candidates and on issues of interest to labor. Its activities have had a considerable effect on elections, especially in the industrial states. Opponents have criticized COPE on the grounds that, allegedly, members are pressured into making contributions and that its education consists, in reality, of partisan political propaganda, usually favorable to the Democratic party.

Cooling-off Period   A period of time, stipulated by the Taft-Hartley Act of 1947, during which parties to a labor-management controversy may not engage in a strike or lockout. Under the Act, an existing collective bargaining contract can be terminated or changed only after sixty days notice to the other party. If no agreement is reached within thirty days, the Federal Mediation and Conciliation Service must be notified. During the sixty-day period no strike or lockout is permitted. In the case of disputes threatening the national welfare, the Taft-Hartley Act authorizes the President to seek an injunction from the courts which maintains the status quo for eighty days. During this time, fact-finding and conciliation efforts are to be made and the workers given a chance to vote on the employer's last offer. If at the end of the eighty-day period no solution is reached, a strike or lockout may take place. Similar procedures are provided for the rail and air transport industries in the Railway Labor Act.

Significance   The sixty-day and eighty-day cooling-off periods are designed to give the parties to the dispute a chance to reach an amicable settlement without resort to disruptive practices. Ofttimes, in practice, the parties "warm up" rather than "cool off" during this period. Both labor and management tend to judge any governmental intrusion into collective bargaining arrangements according to its effect on their respective positions.

Featherbedding   A labor practice requiring an employer to pay for services that are not performed. Featherbedding is considered to be an unfair labor practice and is outlawed by the Taft-Hartley Act. An example of featherbedding is a requirement that a radio station pay musicians who do not play, since phonograph records, rather than "live" musicians, are used. Featherbedding may also take the form of deliberate slowdowns in production or insistence that a job be performed by a particular individual, though others can do it as well.

Significance   The increasing automation of industry has caused concern in labor circles. Featherbedding practices are designed to maintain the employment of persons whose jobs are rendered useless by new techniques. Labor leaders defend the practice by comparing it to the businessman who restricts output to keep prices high, to professions that restrict the licensing of persons seeking to join the profession, and to farmers who are paid not to grow crops. Featherbedding practices are likely to be part of the labor scene except in times of full employment.

General Counsel An official charged with the responsibility for the investigation and prosecution of unfair labor-management practices under the Taft-Hartley Act. His functions include supervision of all regional offices of the National Labor Relations Board and final authority to issue complaints in unfair labor practice cases. These functions were formerly vested in the National Labor Relations Board. The General Counsel is appointed by the President, with the Senate's approval, for a four-year term. *See also* NATIONAL LABOR RELATIONS BOARD, page 338.

Significance The office of General Counsel was created by the Taft-Hartley Act to meet the criticism that the National Labor Relations Board was both prosecutor and judge in unfair labor practice cases. The net effect of this move was to make the Board primarily a quasi-judicial agency to hear appeals from decisions rendered by trial examiners in cases brought by the General Counsel. Basic policy matters remain in the hands of the Board.

Injunction A court order to compel or restrain the performance of an act. In the field of labor, the injunction became a weapon in the hands of management to restrain the activities of labor unions during their formative period. For many years, the injunction was used to enforce the Sherman Antitrust Act against unions. The Norris-LaGuardia Act of 1932 outlawed the use of the labor injunction when labor pursues lawful ends by legitimate means. The Taft-Hartley Act of 1947, however, empowers the President to seek an injunction when a labor dispute threatens the national welfare. *See also* INJUNCTION, page 251.

Significance The labor injunction used prior to 1932 was based on the theory that organized labor was a conspiracy in restraint of trade and that, when a union conducted a strike, it threatened the property rights of the employer. The injunctive power exercised by an unfriendly judiciary made it virtually impossible for labor to pursue its goals. From 1890 to 1932, the major political aim of labor was to eliminate the injunction from labor-management disputes, and success was achieved in the Norris-LaGuardia Act. The return to the injunctive device in the Taft-Hartley Act caused resentment among labor leaders, and presidents have been reluctant to use this power. However, under the Taft-Hartley Act, the injunction can last only eighty days, after which labor is free to strike.

Jurisdictional Strike A strike involving a dispute between unions rather than between a union and an employer. Jurisdictional strikes may occur over the question of which union has the right to represent the workers or over the question of which workers are to do a specific job. For example, both carpenters and metalworkers may claim the right to install metal-framed windows, or one union may try to "raid" another union's territory. The Taft-Hartley Act and many state laws make the jurisdictional strike unlawful. *See also* STRIKE, page 335.

Significance Jurisdictional strikes generally are viewed with little sympathy by the public. The consumer and the employer suffer the consequences of a fight in which they are innocent bystanders. Unions, too, recognize that such strikes harm them in the public eye and have tried to reach voluntary agreements on problems likely to lead to jurisdictional disputes. Nevertheless, workers may be vitally affected by problems arising over which group is to do a specific job. Jurisdictional strikes still erupt from time to time but the number has diminished.

Labor Unions   Organizations of workers that seek to improve the economic status and working conditions of labor through collective bargaining and political action. The largest and most influential labor organization is the American Federation of Labor-Congress of Industrial Organizations (AFL-CIO), a federation of over 130 unions. The AFL-CIO has over 3 million members comprising about 70 percent of organized labor. The remainder of organized labor is in independent unions, such as the Teamsters, Mine Workers, Longshoremen, Railroad Brotherhoods, and a number of smaller unions. *See also* PRESSURE GROUP, page 138.

Significance   Labor unions and the AFL-CIO in particular are major forces on the American scene. The merger of the AFL and CIO strengthened the labor movement and increased its political power. Rivalry among unions and union leaders both within and without the AFL-CIO has, however, reduced its full potential as an economic and political force. Moreover, less than 30 percent of the working force is organized into unions, largely as a result of a decrease in factory-type employment. White-collar workers, teachers, and civil servants, however, are unionizing in increasing numbers. Organized labor's major objectives are improved working conditions, improved wages and hours, and extensive social welfare legislation. For the most part, labor unions have been identified with the Democratic party.

Lockout   Action taken by an employer to close down his plant to keep workers from their jobs in order to force them to accept his position in a labor controversy. Lockouts are lawful unless they violate a collective bargaining agreement or seek a goal that the law declares to be an unfair practice.

Significance   The lockout is to the employer what the strike is to the union—a major weapon to force agreement. Lockouts are not commonly used, but some labor authorities point out that what the public usually considers to be a strike may also be a lockout, since the employer closes his plant by refusing to meet union demands.

Mediation and Conciliation   Terms used interchangeably to refer to the attempt of a third party to settle a labor dispute by bringing the parties together and persuading them to reach a compromise. Unlike arbitration, the mediator or conciliator has no power to make his suggested solutions binding upon the parties. *See also* ARBITRATION, page 330; FEDERAL MEDIATION AND CONCILIATION SERVICE, page 338; NATIONAL MEDIATION BOARD, page 339.

Significance   Elaborate mediation and conciliation machinery has been established by the national government and most state governments. The Federal Mediation and Conciliation Service, an agency established in 1913 in the Department of Labor but given independent status by the Taft-Hartley Act, may be called into a dispute by either party, or it may offer its services. State mediation services operate only on a part-time basis in most states, but the larger industrial states have established full-time agencies. In the railway and air transport industries a federal agency, the National Mediation Board, has been established to mediate disputes in those critical areas of industrial relations.

Picketing   Patrolling the site of a business establishment by workers who are on strike. Peaceful picketing is a form of free speech protected by the First Amendment (*Thornhill v. Alabama*, 310 U.S. 88 [1940]). Under national and state laws, however, picketing may not be used to promote any purpose which is contrary to law or public policy. The Taft-Hartley Act and the Landrum-Griffin Act forbid picketing for such purposes as encouraging secondary boycotts or trying to force employers to recognize a union other than one already lawfully recognized.

Significance   Picketing by a labor group serves both the purposes of informing the public of the controversy and persuading customers and other workers to refrain from dealing with a business establishment. It is a potent labor weapon since many people will not cross a picket line, out of either sympathy for the strike or fear of retaliation. Labor leaders hailed the 1940 Supreme Court decision that made picketing a free speech right, but subsequent legislation and court decisions have placed numerous restrictions upon the practice.

Right to Work Law   A law that prohibits making union membership a qualification for employment. Nineteen states have constitutional or statutory provisions that a person may not be compelled to join a union or to remain a member of a union to hold his job. Right to work laws establish the principle of the "open shop." *See also* CLOSED SHOP, page 331; UNION SHOP, page 337.

Significance   Right to work laws are designed to curtail the closed shop and union shop. Though a union shop is permitted by section 14 (b) of the Taft-Hartley Act, that Act also permits states to pass right to work legislation. These laws are prompted in part by exposures of union corruption and by concern for workers who are penalized by not holding union membership. Some states seek to attract industry by enacting right to work laws that greatly weaken labor unions. Labor leaders strongly oppose these laws. They argue that nonunion members benefit from the union's efforts and that the laws will destroy unions and the principle of collective bargaining. With the exception of the state of Indiana, which repealed it in 1965, no major industrial state has enacted a right to work law.

Strike   A stoppage of work by employees for the purpose of winning concessions from their employer on matters of wages, hours, or working conditions. The right to strike, except for purposes prohibited by law, is considered to be a fundamental right of free workingmen. Government employees are not legally permitted to strike but such strikes, particularly by local government employees and teachers, have increased in recent years. National and state laws contain a variety of limitations on the right to strike. For example, strikes may not be used to promote a secondary boycott or other unfair labor practice. Procedures are also provided by law for "cooling-off" periods, injunctions, fact-finding boards, and mediation services in order to avoid strikes. *See also,* COOLING-OFF PERIOD, page 332; JURISDICTIONAL STRIKE, page 333; LOCKOUT, page 334; PICKETING, page 335.

Significance The strike is labor's most effective weapon but it is often damaging to both sides and to the public. A strike in one industry has an effect on other industries dependent upon the struck plants for supplies. The Taft-Hartley Act of 1947 permits the President to obtain an eighty-day injunction if a strike might cause a national emergency. Workers on strike are not considered to have given up their job, and a lawful dispute may not be interfered with by "strikebreakers" or "scabs" who replace the striking workers. Many unions provide strikers with subsistence allowances during a strike.

Unemployment Insurance A program of insurance under the Social Security Act of 1935 that provides for payment of funds for a limited. period of time to workers who are laid off or discharged for reasons beyond their control. The program is administered by the states under national supervision. Under the plan, Congress imposes a tax on the payroll of employers of four or more workers. Ninety percent of the revenue from this tax is credited to each state that comes under the act (all do), with the remainder used for administrative purposes. All proceeds of the tax are held by the national Department of the Treasury in separate state accounts to be paid out as needed by each state. Each state determines the amount to be paid to each unemployed person, for how long, and under what conditions. Generally, benefits amount to about $65 per week for twenty weeks and are available to unemployed persons who register with the proper state agency and are willing to accept suitable employment. Most states penalize employers with poor employment records by raising their payroll tax. Overall supervision of state plans is in the hands of the Unemployment Insurance Service in the Department of Labor. *See also Social Security Cases,* page 374.

Significance Unemployment insurance is one of the major programs of social insurance in effect today. Unemployment insurance makes public relief unnecessary and puts some purchasing power in the hands of the unemployed. Critics of the plan charge that it encourages laziness, and many oppose the compulsory nature of the plan. Supporters point out that unemployment tends to have a chain effect and that the loss of purchasing power endangers other jobs.

Unfair Labor Practice Activity by a labor union or an employer that is defined by law as constituting a threat to industrial peace. Unfair labor practices are defined in the Taft-Hartley Act of 1947. Employers are forbidden to interfere with the rights of unions to organize, to discriminate against union members, or to refuse to bargain collectively. Unions may not discriminate against or coerce employees who are not union members, or engage in such practices as secondary boycotts, featherbedding, jurisdictional strikes, charging excessive dues or fees, or refusing to bargain collectively. *See also* BOYCOTT, page 330; FEATHERBEDDING, page 332; JURISDICTIONAL STRIKE, page 335; TAFT-HARTLEY ACT, page 342.

Significance By listing unfair labor practices, Congress sought to cope with the more common causes of labor-management unrest. The Taft-Hartley Act represented a departure from previous legislation by listing unfair union tactics as well as unfair employer behavior. The National Labor Relations Board (NLRB) and its General Counsel are charged with the duty of policing unfair activities. Exactly what constitutes an unfair practice is often open to dispute since the law cannot cover every eventuality. Many NLRB decisions on unfair practices are appealed to the federal courts.

Union Shop   An establishment in which all newly hired workers must join the union after a specified period of time, usually thirty days. Unlike the closed shop, now outlawed, the employee need not be a member of the union in order to be hired. *See also* CLOSED SHOP, page 331; RIGHT TO WORK LAW, page 335.

Significance   The union shop is the major form of union security permitted by law. About 75 percent of organized labor works in union shops. The union shop eliminates "free riders" who would benefit from collective bargaining agreements without supporting the union. Many employees object to being forced to join a union, but they must remain members in order to hold their jobs. The Taft-Hartley Act authorizes union shop agreements, but permits states to eliminate them through the right to work laws. In some agreements between management and labor, an "agency shop" is established whereby workers are not required to join a union but must pay a fee to support collective bargaining and help defray the costs of negotiations and administration of the agreement.

Workmen's Compensation   An insurance program, in effect in all states, that provides compensation for workers injured on their jobs and for dependents of workers who are killed in the course of employment. In most states, the program is financed entirely by the employer, who must take out private or public insurance for this purpose. Occupational diseases are also covered in many states. An administrative agency is generally established to settle claims arising under the law with appeal to the courts possible. State laws vary with regard to types of employers and occupations covered.

Significance   Workmen's compensation has replaced the system that required an injured worker to bring a lawsuit against his employer to recover damages. In such lawsuits, the employer could be freed from liability if he could show that the injury was the fault of the worker or of another employee. Workmen's compensation is based on the theory that whatever the cause, workers cannot bear the financial burden of a lawsuit and that insurance is to be carried as a regular cost of production. Workmen's compensation laws have reduced hardship and have sustained families who might otherwise have to seek welfare aid.

IMPORTANT AGENCIES

Department of Labor   A major department of Cabinet status that administers laws designed to promote the welfare of wage earners through improved working conditions and employment opportunities. The Department, established originally in 1903 as Commerce and Labor and separated in 1913, is headed by the Secretary of Labor and is divided into five major operational units: (1) Manpower Administration, which appraises national manpower requirements to deal with unemployment, underemployment, the impact of automation, apprenticeship training, and aspects of the war on poverty including the Job Corps, and administers the unemployment compensation program and the United States Employment Service; (2) Labor-Management Services, which administers laws relating to welfare and pension plans, enforces the Labor-Management Reporting and Disclosure Act relative to internal affairs of labor unions, and provides a wide variety of industrial relations services; (3) International Affairs, which considers the effect of American Labor problems on foreign policy and is responsible for American participation in the International Labor Organization; (4) Employment Standards, which administers the wage and hour laws and seeks to improve working conditions, with special attention to the needs of women, children, and minority groups; and (5) Occupational Safety and Health, which develops and regulates industrial safety and health standards.

Significance The Department of Labor was established to give labor a direct voice at the highest level of government to accord it equal political status with agriculture and business. Increased federal labor legislation and growing American international economic involvement have strengthened the influence and stature of the Department in meeting national and international problems related to labor and the economy in general.

Federal Mediation and Conciliation Service An agency formerly within the Department of Labor but given independent status under the Taft-Hartley Act of 1947. The Service is headed by a director appointed by the President with the Senate's consent. The Service has no law-enforcement authority but relies upon persuasion to prevent strikes that will impede the free flow of interstate commerce. Professional mediators employed by the Service assist in the settlement of labor-management disputes and try to promote good relations between labor and management. The Taft-Hartley Act requires that employers and unions must file notice of any dispute not settled thirty days after either side has expressed an intention to terminate an existing contract. The Mediation and Conciliation Service then tries to conciliate the dispute, but neither side is compelled to accept the solution suggested by the Service. The Service may also offer to enter a dispute on its own motion or at the request of parties. The Service often helps in the selection of arbitrators when both sides accept arbitration. *See also* MEDIATION AND CONCILIATION, page 334.

Significance The Federal Mediation and Conciliation Service reflects government policy to prevent the disruptive influence of strikes whenever possible. The Service has been highly successful in carrying on its functions because of the high prestige of its employees and its independent status in the government organization.

National Labor Relations Board (NLRB) An independent regulatory commission, established in 1935, which administers the Wagner Act and the Taft-Hartley Act relative to unfair labor practices and the designation of appropriate bargaining units. The NLRB consists of five members appointed by the President, with the Senate's consent, for five-year terms, and a General Counsel similarly appointed for a four-year term. The Board is authorized to issue cease-and-desist orders, to hold bargaining representative elections, and to seek court injunctions and other enforcement orders. The General Counsel conducts investigations, issues complaints, and conducts prosecutions before the Board. Actual hearings are held by trial examiners with final orders issuing from the Board. *See also NLRB v. Jones and Laughlin Steel Corp.,* page 339.

Significance The NLRB, like other independent regulatory commissions, reflects the policy of utilizing an independent agency to perform quasi-legislative and quasi-judicial functions in important sectors of the economy. It has played a crucial role in the development of broad policies as well as specific rules to meet the complicated problems posed by the growth of labor unions and the increasing problems of labor-management relations in an industrial society. Whereas all of the independent regulatory commissions have been charged with being captives of the businesses they regulate, many have charged NLRB with being labor dominated.

National Mediation Board An independent agency established in 1934, under an amendment to the Railway Labor Act of 1926, to mediate differences between management and labor in the railroad and airline fields and to determine bargaining representatives. The Board consists of three members appointed by the President with the Senate's consent. For the settlement of disputes growing out of the application of collective bargaining contracts, the National Railroad Adjustment Board, consisting of representatives of the unions and the carriers, is called into action. In the event of deadlocks in the Adjustment Board, the National Mediation Board appoints a referee. Parties may appeal to the courts for enforcement of any settlements reached through this procedure. If the dispute does not involve a collective bargaining agreement, and the National Mediation Board cannot effect a solution, the law authorizes the President to appoint a special fact-finding board and, if this fails, he may place the carrier under government operation. *See also* MEDIATION AND CONCILIATION, page 334.

Significance The National Mediation Board and the related procedures are designed to prevent strikes and lockouts in the crucial areas of rail and air transport. With occasional lapses, these procedures have proved effective and work stoppages in these fields are relatively rare. Every effort is made to avoid government-imposed solutions and to help the parties reach agreement.

IMPORTANT CASES

NLRB v. Jones and Laughlin Steel Corp., 301 U.S. 1 (1937): Upheld the National Labor Relations Act of 1935, which guarantees labor the right to organize and bargain collectively and establishes the National Labor Relations Board to regulate labor-management relations. The Act was upheld as a valid exercise of Congress' power to regulate interstate commerce. *See also* COLLECTIVE BARGAINING, page 331.

Significance The *NLRB* case reflected a major shift in attitude by the Supreme Court toward New Deal regulatory legislation. The Court asserted the right of Congress to regulate activities having "a close and substantial relation to interstate commerce" and to prevent strikes and other industrial disputes that might burden or obstruct the free flow of commerce. In its decision, the Court took a broad view of the power of Congress to meet the challenges of an industrial society. The case was a turning point for the American labor movement, and has been followed by extensive involvement by the national government in labor-management relations.

United States v. Darby Lumber Co., 312 U.S. 100 (1941): Upheld the Fair Labor Standards Act of 1938, which imposes wage-and-hour regulations upon businesses engaged in or producing goods for interstate commerce and places restrictions upon the use of child labor. *See also* FAIR LABOR STANDARDS ACT, page 340.

Significance The *Darby* decision climaxed many years of national efforts to regulate wages, hours, and other conditions of employment in the face of hostile judicial decisions. The *Darby* case specifically overruled *Hammer v. Dagenhart*, 247 U.S. 251 (1918), in which the Supreme Court held unconstitutional a statute which barred goods made by child labor from interstate commerce. In the *Darby* case, the Court repudiated long-held notions that Congress could not regulate production or control wages and hours. The decision virtually put an end to legal challenges to the power of Congress to regulate aspects of business which directly or indirectly affect interstate commerce. The decision also made it unnecessary to secure ratification of the proposed child labor amendment to the Constitution.

West Coast Hotel Co. v. Parrish, 300 U.S. 379 (1937): Supported a minimum wage law of the state of Washington. The Court held that a minimum wage law did not violate freedom of contract under the due process clause of the Fourteenth Amendment.

Significance The *Parrish* case put an end to the use by the Court of the due process clause of the Fourteenth Amendment to restrict state regulation of working conditions. It specifically overruled *Adkins v. Children's Hospital*, 261 U.S. 525 (1923), in which the Court had struck down a federal law establishing minimum wages for women in the District of Columbia. In the *Parrish* case, the Court rejected the notion that wages were beyond legislative control. It also rejected the concept of freedom of contract, which the Court had in earlier decisions injected into the due process clause. Such regulation was upheld as a valid exercise of the police power in the interest of protecting the health, safety, morals, and welfare of the people.

IMPORTANT STATUTES

Fair Labor Standards Act of 1938   An act establishing minimum wages and maximum hours for employees engaged in interstate commerce and outlawing the use of child labor. An eight-hour day and a minimum wage per hour is established ($2.30 in 1976) as the basic requirement, with time and a half for work exceeding forty hours a week. Persons not engaged in interstate commerce are not covered unless state laws make similar provisions. Certain types of work are exempted from coverage, but Congress has progressively increased coverage over the years. *See also United States v. Darby Lumber Co.,* page 339.

Significance The Fair Labor Standards Act was designed to eliminate substandard working conditions and to minimize competition among the states which might be inclined to have lower standards in order to attract industry. The Act has also been successful in eradicating the worst aspects of child labor. Responsibility for enforcement of the Act is lodged in the Department of Labor. Earlier, in 1936, Congress passed the Walsh-Healey Act, which established minimum wages and maximum hours, and outlawed child labor for persons working on federal contracts. The Fair Labor Standards Act was patterned on the Walsh-Healey Act, but has broader coverage. The Equal Pay Act of 1963, an amendment to the Fair Labor Standards Act, requires employers to pay equal wages to men and women doing equal work.

Landrum-Griffin Act (Labor-Management Reporting and Disclosure Act of 1959)   Informally known as the Labor Reform Act of 1959, this law strengthens the Taft-Hartley Act's restrictions upon internal procedures of labor unions and provides a "bill of rights" for members of labor unions. The Act requires detailed reports to the Secretary of Labor on union finances and the operations of union constitutions and bylaws, and it makes misuse of union funds a federal crime. Ex-convicts, Communists, and labor officials with conflicting business interests are barred from holding union office. The "bill of rights" provisions secure the secret ballot in union elections, freedom of speech in union meetings, hearings in disciplinary cases, the right of members to sue the union for unfair practices, and authorize member access to union records. *See also* TAFT-HARTLEY ACT, page 342.

Significance The Landrum-Griffin Act was a direct result of investigations by the Senate Rackets Committee that revealed a variety of corrupt practices by some labor leaders. The Act is designed to protect the integrity of law-abiding labor unions as well as the rights of individual members. The provision barring Communists from union offices was declared unconstitutional as a bill of attainder (*United States v. Brown,* 381 U.S. 437 [1965]). Both the Taft-Hartley Act and the Landrum-Griffin Act reflect a change in governmental policy since the Wagner Act of 1935, from promotion of labor interests to regulation of unions.

Norris-LaGuardia Act of 1932   An act that outlawed "yellow-dog" contracts by which workers agreed not to join unions, and limited the use of the injunction in labor disputes. *See also* INJUNCTION, page 333.

Significance The Norris-LaGuardia Act was one of the first pieces of pro-labor legislation. Its main purpose was to free labor from two major weapons used against it and to enable labor unions to pursue lawful goals. The Act was instrumental in providing the climate in which labor could develop as an economic power. It led to the passage of the Wagner Act in 1935, which guaranteed the right of labor to organize and bargain collectively.

Occupational Safety and Health Act of 1970   A comprehensive industrial safety program which requires employers engaged in interstate commerce to furnish a work place free from hazards to life or health. The Act authorizes the Secretary of Labor to promulgate safety standards, conduct investigations, and to issue citations for noncompliance. An independent agency, the Occupational Safety and Health Review Commission, was established by the Act to adjudicate alleged violations contested by either employers or employees and to assess civil penalties. It is composed of three members appointed by the President with Senate consent, for six-year terms. Appeals from Commission orders may be brought to a federal court of appeals. The Act also authorizes federal grants to states to promote occupational safety.

Significance The Occupational Safety and Health Act climaxed years of effort by organized labor to gain passage of extensive and enforceable industrial safety legislation. In 1969, the year prior to passage of the Act, more than 15,000 persons were killed at work, and estimates of the number suffering disabling injuries exceeded two million. The Act covers environmental as well as mechanical hazards. The division of authority for enforcement between the Secretary of Labor and the independent Review Commission was essential to secure support from business interests who feared centralizing authority over the program in the Department of Labor.

Pension Reform Act of 1974   An act to establish minimum federal standards for private pension plans. The Pension Reform Act does not require businesses to establish a pension plan, but does require certain standards for those that do. Generally, all employees 25 years of age or older, with one year of experience, must be enrolled in any existing plan. After a period of time, part of the worker's pension rights "vest" and is guaranteed to the worker whether he remains with the same employer or not. In some instances, the vested portion may be transferred to another plan if the worker changes jobs. The Act also establishes minimum funding requirements and provides for insurance against failing retirement plans. Special provisions are made for the self-employed to undertake retirement planning by providing for tax incentives to those setting aside funds for retirement.

Significance   The Pension Reform Act is the first effort by the national government to regulate private pension plans. About 30 million workers are covered by private retirement programs, but most required a worker to stay with one employer for many years until retirement. Several pension programs had failed in their investment practices and most lacked adequate safeguards to ensure the worker the retirement security he had envisioned or that he had been promised. The Pension Reform Act adds an important dimension to social welfare programs, notably as a supplement to social security retirement benefits, which have not always proved adequate to support retired persons. The Act is administered by the Department of Labor and the Treasury Department.

Taft-Hartley Act (Labor-Management Relations Act of 1947)   A major revision of the Wagner Act of 1935 that seeks to equalize the power of employers and labor unions. The Act places limitations upon labor union practices, regulates certain internal arrangements of unions, and strengthens the position of the individual worker. Provisions of the Wagner Act relative to unfair practices by employers against unions are retained. Among the major limitations placed upon unions by the Taft-Hartley Act are those outlawing the closed shop (but permitting the union shop), jurisdictional strikes, secondary boycotts, political expenditures, and excessive dues. The Act also permits unions and employers to sue each other for contract violations and provides for the use of the injunction and other "cooling-off" procedures in strikes that threaten the national welfare. Internal affairs of unions are regulated by requiring them to file reports on the use of union funds and organizational procedures. The National Labor Relations Board (NLRB) was increased from three to five members, and the office of General Counsel was established to investigate and prosecute unfair labor charges. See also LANDRUM-GRIFFIN ACT, page 341.

Significance   The Taft-Hartley Act was a reaction to growing union strength, to allegations that the Wagner Act and the NLRB favored unions over employers, and to revelations of communism and corruption in some unions. Since its enactment, it has been criticized concerning the extent to which it involves the government in labor-management relations and restricts the range of free collective bargaining for both labor and management. Many states have passed "little Taft-Hartley" acts. Nineteen states, under section 14 (b) of the Act, have passed "right to work" laws which have further limited the power of unions by curtailing the union shop. Both the national and state laws gave great impetus to the merger of the AFL-CIO in 1955, and have intensified the political activity of organized labor.

Wagner Act (National Labor Relations Act of 1935)   A major enactment of the New Deal period that guarantees the right of labor to organize and bargain collectively through representatives of its own choosing. The Act established the National Labor Relations Board (NLRB) to administer the Act. The Board is authorized to issue cease-and-desist orders to employers who commit unfair labor practices as defined by the law and to certify bargaining representatives for unions. *See also NLRB v. Jones and Laughlin Steel Corp.,* page 339.

Significance The Wagner Act was a boon to the American labor movement. Until the year 1947, when it was amended by the Taft-Hartley Act, union membership grew from four to fifteen million and the overwhelming majority of manufacturing plants were covered by union contracts. This growth was accompanied by increased economic and political power for unions. Criticism of the Act as being too one-sided in favor of organized labor, and discriminatory against employers and individual workers, led to the passage of the Taft-Hartley Act in 1947. Nevertheless, the Wagner Act has significantly altered labor-management relations in the United States. "Little Wagner" acts were also passed in many states to cover workers not engaged in interstate commerce. The underlying purposes of the law—to foster and protect the right of collective bargaining —remains basic to public policy in the labor field.

14   Agriculture, Environment, and Natural Resources

Colorado River Compact   An interstate agreement concluded among seven states concerning their respective rights to the waters of the Colorado River and its tributaries. The Colorado River Compact was concluded in 1922 after years of negotiation and was approved by Congress in 1927. Parties to the compact are Arizona, California, Colorado, Nevada, New Mexico, Utah, and Wyoming. *See also* WATER CONSERVATION, page 353.

Significance   The Colorado River Compact sought to alleviate a long-standing disagreement over the use of the Colorado River waters, permitted Los Angeles to draw an essential water supply from 300 miles to the east, and laid the groundwork for the building of the first huge reclamation dam, the Hoover Dam, by the national government. Droughts and rapidly expanding populations, especially in Arizona and California, have led to greatly increased demands for water, involving compact states in continuing legal disputes over the use of the Colorado River. Water has become a more important commodity than gold, which sparked much of the original westward migration.

Columbia River Compact   An interstate agreement concluded in 1925 among four states—Idaho, Montana, Oregon, and Washington—concerning their respective rights to the waters of the Columbia River and its tributaries. *See also* WATER CONSERVATION, page 353.

Significance   The Columbia River Compact helped lead to the construction of the huge, multipurpose Grand Coulee and Bonneville dams by the national government. Programs of great benefit to the four compact states have been cooperatively developed, including flood control, reclamation, power production, improved navigation, and the conservation of the famed Columbia River salmon.

Conservation   The careful management and wise use of natural resources to prevent depletion and to maximize the production of wealth from their use. Conservation involves the protection, preservation, and replenishment, as well as the planned use of land, forests, wildlife, minerals, and water by private individuals and national, state, and local governments. Conservationists include those who wish to conserve resources for economic reasons, and those who are mainly concerned with ecological and esthetic considerations. *See also* CONSERVATION AND ENVIRONMENTAL

ORGANIZATIONS, page 345; DEPARTMENT OF THE INTERIOR, page 355; ENVIRONMENTAL POLITICS, page 346; SOIL CONSERVATION, page 352; WATER CONSERVATION, page 353.

Significance Conservation was recognized as a new problem area about the turn of the century. Apprehension over the squandering of the nation's natural wealth plus the crusading zeal of President Theodore Roosevelt led to the first conservation programs by the national government in the vast areas of the public domain. These were followed by state efforts, cooperative nation-state programs, and educational and publicly financed efforts in privately owned areas. The major impetus behind the conservation program remains with the national government, although some states have developed extensive programs covering water resources, mineral production, reclamation and irrigation, forest protection and reforestation, and protection of wildlife. Conservation has increasingly come to mean not only the preservation of existing natural wealth, but the planned use of resources to increase wealth and to turn unproductive areas into productive natural assets. This approach, however, has come under increasing attack by environmentalists who regard man's invasion of more and more wild country for productive purposes as destructive of basic ecological balances. Major conservation programs of the national government are carried on by the Departments of Agriculture and the Interior, and conservation, and agricultural departments in state governments have primary responsibility for implementing state programs. In the 1970s, conservationists generally joined forces with the environmental movement to develop a more potent political action program.

Conservation and Environmental Organizations Groups organized to promote conservation and environmental policies and programs on the national, state, local, and international levels. Conservation and environmental organizations most active in the United States today include the Sierra Club, the National Audubon Society, the National Wildlife Federation, the National Parks and Conservation Association, the Scientists' Institute for Public Information, the Wilderness Society, the Conservation Foundation, the International Union for Conservation of Nature and Natural Resources, the Izaak Walton League of America, and Friends of the Earth. Key issues for environmental and conservation organizations include: The preservation of wild country and endangered species; control of pollution of the air, water, and land; limiting population and the encroachments of urban civilization; the wise and careful use of natural resources and energy supplies; protection of the world ocean; and the education of the American public to gain its acceptance of the conservation ethic and the environmental imperative. *See also* ENVIRONMENTAL POLITICS, page 346; PRESSURE GROUP, page 138.

Significance Conservation and environmental organizations have become increasingly active in promoting public awareness of ecological dangers and policy and programmatic approaches to the solution of pollution and other environmental problems. Such groups differ from most American pressure groups in that they are interested mainly in promoting the general interest rather than that of their individual members, and because they are primarily concerned with long-term stabilities rather than with finding solutions to immediate problems. Tactics employed in pursuit of their objectives include litigation in state and federal courts, lobbying and pressure techniques, public education campaigns, and protests, including picketing. The energy crisis of the 1970s placed the conservation and environmental groups on the defensive as political leaders charged them, for example, with responsibility for the oil shortage because of their opposition to the Alaskan pipeline and offshore drilling.

County Agent   The local official charged with promoting agriculture under the federal, state, and county cooperative extension program. The Smith-Lever Act of 1914 created the modern extension service under which the county agent program was developed. *See also* FARM ORGANI-ZATIONS, page 347.

Significance   County agents seek to improve agriculture by encouraging farmers to adopt new methods developed in laboratories and in agricultural research centers. They try to reach the ordinary farmer through advice, demonstrations, and exhibits, and the great increase in farm productivity testifies to their success over the years. The county agent has also been an important factor in many states in the development of the American Farm Bureau Federation, a leading farmers' organization. Although the early integration of the county agent system with the Farm Bureau has been ended, the county agent continues to work closely with the organization in some states.

Environmental Impact Statement   A requirement of the National Environmental Policy Act of 1969 that all federal agencies must consider the effect that any federally sponsored or regulated project or policy may have on environmental stabilities. If a federal or a state or a local agency using federal funds proceeds with a project or policy that threatens substantial environmental damage, the Act provides that private citizens, congressmen, or government officials may undertake legal action to challenge its continuation. Many state and local governments also require environmental impact statements before a government agency or private party can undertake a new project. *See also* NATIONAL ENVIRONMENTAL POLICY ACT OF 1969, page 361.

Significance   The federal requirement of environmental impact statements relates especially to major engineering projects that may threaten an area's biological balance. The Act, however, cannot be invoked retroactively on projects already underway at the time the Act was signed into law. Because of pressure resulting from the energy crisis, Congress set the requirement aside as it applied to the Alaskan Pipeline project. The Act has had the effect of preventing some projects, altering others, and of encouraging long-range planning that includes ecosystem considerations. In many cases, the controversial nature of a national, state, or local project results in public hearings and prolonged debates that may ultimately be resolved by a decision at the ballot box.

Environmental Politics   The social and political movement that seeks to warn the public about ecological dangers and to encourage common action to achieve basic environmental goals. Environmental politics is aimed at pressuring national, state, and local governments to support policies and programs to end pollution of air, water, and land. Environmentalism starts with the assumption that man is rapidly destroying his life-sustaining ecosystems as a result of the triumph in the modern world of the technological and economic growth ethics. The movement is working for the adoption of governmental policies to clean up pollution, to preserve wild areas, to protect living species, to meet the problem of depletion of natural resources, to deal with population and urbanization problems, and generally to move toward restoring ecological balance. *See also* CONSERVATION AND ENVIRONMENTAL ORGANIZATIONS, page 345; COUNCIL ON ENVIRONMEN-TAL QUALITY, page 354; ENVIRONMENTAL PROTECTION AGENCY, page 357; NATIONAL ENVI-RONMENTAL POLICY ACT, page 361.

Significance Environmental politics, long concerned with fighting conservation and esthetic battles, have suddenly assumed a center-stage position in the American political system. Revelations of the extent of pollution of the biosphere by modern industrial societies, the world population explosion, and the dangers of future ecosuicide have enlisted many Americans in the political movement to change the role of government from aiding and abetting environmental degradation to one of seeking to reverse the trend. Earth Day rallies in which many concerned Americans participate in anti-pollution activities are held each spring as a means of building political support for the cause. Congress has reacted to the growing support for environmental policies by enacting a basic National Environmental Policy Act in 1969 and numerous laws dealing with specific forms of pollution. In addition, Congress created a major administering agency, the Environmental Protection Agency (EPA), and a staff agency in the Executive Office, the Council on Environmental Quality. American initiatives have contributed to the establishment of a United Nations Environmental Program (UNEP) and numerous regional programs of cooperation. Securing environmental protection in the United States through court processes was given support by the Supreme Court, when it held that citizens who allege injury by government action affecting the environment, even though that action might also affect large numbers of other people, have standing in court to sue (*United States v. SCRAP,* 412 U.S. 669 [1973]).

Ever-normal Granary   The concept behind the national government's farm programs since 1938 that aimed at securing a stable supply of, and stable prices for, farm products through governmental action. The ever-normal granary system provided for accumulation of reserves of basic farm products by the government during periods of oversupply as a means of maintaining price levels. During droughts or other times of short supply, when prices rose above support levels, the government reversed the process by selling from its granaries to meet market demand and to stabilize price levels. *See also* PRICE SUPPORT, page 350.

Significance The ever-normal granary system sought to maintain some semblance of equilibrium between supply and demand for basic farm products, while maintaining most of the traditional freedom of the farm economy. Since 1938, however, generally good weather, parity price support incentives, and, especially, the scientific revolution in farm technology contributed to surplus production and resulted in huge accumulations of government-owned farm products. In the 1960s, the government sought to dispose of much of its granary holdings through domestic relief programs, the foreign aid Food For Peace (Public Law 480) program, and by fostering an increasing demand in domestic and foreign markets. Acreage controls with direct subsidies to individual farmers also helped by reducing annual surpluses. The main objective of the ever-normal granary system—the fostering by government of an equilibrium condition in supply and demand and pricing of farm products—has never been achieved.

Farm Organizations   Groups organized to promote the interests of the farmer. The oldest and most conservative farmers' organization is the National Grange, which was most effective after the Civil War and now has most of its membership in the New England and Middle Atlantic States. The most powerful and energetic spokesman for the farmers' interest is the American Farm Bureau Federation, which represents all types of farmers throughout the country. The Farm Bureau, now a private organization, grew out of the promotional activities of county agents sponsored by the Department of Agriculture through the agricultural extension services. A third major group is the National Farmer's Union, representing the less prosperous farmers. The newest group is the National Farmer's Organization, which seeks to emulate the strike techniques of labor unions by having farmers withhold products from the marketplace to drive prices up rather than depend upon governmental subsidies. *See also* CONSERVATION AND ENVIRONMENTAL ORGANIZATIONS, page 345; PRESSURE GROUP, page 138.

Significance Farm organizations have long been a political force, strengthened by rural overrepresentation in legislative bodies. The Farm Bureau and the National Farmer's Union represent the major differences among farmers today. While both support governmental research, extension services, and credit facilities for farmers, the Farm Bureau emphasizes free enterprise, while the Farmer's Union supports production controls and subsidies. The declining number of farms and farmers in the United States and the trend toward urban dominance of legislatures pose threats to the continued success of farmers' organizations. The high inflationary period of the 1970s placed farmers under increasing economic pressures and encouraged greater unity among them. In addition to the major farm organizations, most farmers who produce specialized crops or products have also become more politically active as, for example, the Milk Producers Association and the Walnut Growers.

Food and Agriculture Organization (FAO)   A specialized agency of the United Nations established in 1943 to raise levels of nutrition and standards of living by helping member countries to achieve greater efficiency in production and distribution of food. The FAO has also established the goals of improving living conditions for rural populations and helping to create an expanding world economy. In pursuit of these goals, the FAO: (1) collects and distributes information on farming and food products; (2) holds international conferences; (3) recommends national and international actions to improve conservation, production, processing, and marketing; and (4) furnishes technical assistance and organizes agricultural missions. FAO headquarters are located in Rome. *See also* ECONOMIC AND SOCIAL COUNCIL, page 388.

Significance The role of the Food and Agriculture Organization in increasing food production and organizing a global food program has become critical as a result of the world population explosion. In 1974, the FAO held a global food conference in Rome with delegates from 130 countries to develop new food policies. New programs developed by FAO include a world food authority to supervise and coordinate existing organizations, an international food reserve of 500,000 tons of grain to meet the threat of famine, and an early warning system to predict poor harvests. Success of FAO programs depends on the cooperation of the few remaining food-surplus countries, including the United States, Canada, Australia, and several countries of Western Europe.

Food for Peace   A special foreign aid program that provides for the disposal of American surplus food to needy countries. Congress established the Food for Peace program by Public Law 480 in 1954 to reduce American farm surpluses, to increase foreign consumption of American products, and to strengthen United States's foreign policy abroad. Under the program, surplus products—especially wheat—have been sold in huge quantities to many nations for their local currencies, which have often been returned to the aid-receiving state to help preserve domestic stability. In 1973, Congress extended the Food for Peace program at an annual authorization of $2.5 billion for an additional four-year period.

Significance The Food for Peace program has helped to adjust demand for agricultural products to farm production in the United States, and to meet some of the early challenges of the population explosion in the developing world. Local currencies received for food shipments have been used to promote educational and cultural exchanges, to pay for development programs in the aid-receiving state, to build a resistance to internal and external enemies, and to achieve American foreign policy objectives. Under the Act, the President is empowered to provide emergency food aid following natural disasters and during famines. Food aid may be given to friendly governments or to friendly people living under a government that is unfriendly toward the United States. India has been the major recipient of Food for Peace aid, receiving billions of dollars of agricultural products over a period of more than twenty years.

Organization of Petroleum Exporting Countries (OPEC) A group of major oil producing and exporting states that are joined together in an intergovernmental cartel to limit oil supplies on the world market and to maintain prices at agreed levels. OPEC's thirteen members in 1975 included seven Arab states (Abu Dhabi, Algeria, Iraq, Kuwait, Libya, Qatar, and Saudi Arabia), and six Asian, African, and Latin-American states (Indonesia, Iran, Nigeria, Gabon, Ecuador, and Venezuela). Established in 1961, OPEC remained ineffectual during the 1960s. The Middle East war of 1973, however, produced an Arab oil embargo against Western nations that supported Israel, and this new unity along with a vastly increased world demand for oil resulted in an expansion in OPEC membership and a growing militancy among oil producers.

Significance During the first half of the decade of the 1970s, OPEC's price-setting mechanism quadrupled world oil prices. The result was major inflation in most countries, a near-global reduction in economic activity, growing unemployment, and the threat of economic depression in the industrial countries. OPEC oil revenues soared to $70 billion annually by 1975, creating major balance-of-payment difficulties for oil importing countries, and posing the problem of recycling huge accumulations of capital back into the stream of world commerce and investment. The United States sought to counter OPEC's cartel pricing by unifying oil importing countries and developing a common policy approach, by applying diplomatic and economic pressures on OPEC countries, and by threatening military intervention if the West was faced with disaster as a result of OPEC's actions. Other approaches included voluntary cutbacks in oil use, government programs and regulations to reduce oil consumption, and the placing of new emphasis on "Project Independence," the program to free the United States from dependence on imported energy by 1980.

Parity A governmental price policy designed to maintain a level of purchasing power for farmers equal to that of a previous base period that was favorable to agriculture. This means, for example, that if in 1910 a farmer was able to sell ten bushels of wheat and buy a bicycle with the receipts, at full parity today he should be able to work out the same exchange. Parity-support price levels are determined by Congress, and actual parity prices for specific crops are determined each year by the Department of Agriculture. *See also* PRICE SUPPORT, page 350.

Significance The concept of parity has become an integral part of the national government's farm program. It recognizes that the agricultural sector of the economy is basic to the well-being of the rest of the nation's economy, and any serious imbalance might result in a serious slump for the entire economy. Parity does not provide a maximum price, only a minimum, which has often been exceeded on the free market in recent years. Governmental price support programs have generally ranged from 60 to 90 percent of parity, depending upon the supply of each basic crop.

Populist Movement   A radical social and political philosophy and grass-roots action program developed by farmers in the South, West, and Midwest. The movement resulted in the emergence of the Populist party in the late nineteenth century, which favored government ownership of the railroads, free coinage of silver, a vastly expanded supply of paper money, elimination of monopolies, and a graduated income tax. Populism as a continuing American political characteristic describes the role of large numbers of rural and urban poor, who seek by democratic means to use the power of government to cope with the financial giants of business, industry, and commerce. See also FARM BLOC, page 168; PARTICIPATORY DEMOCRACY, page 131.

Significance   The agrarian populist movement has had a radical impact over the years on political, social, and economic policies on both the state and national levels. Although the Populist party failed to displace one of the major parties in the American two-party system, its action program was largely incorporated into the Democratic party's platform in 1896 when William Jennings Bryan won control of that party. The populist movement contributed much to the development of federal regulatory controls over the railroads, support by the national and state governments of economic and social programs to aid farmers, and the enactment by Congress of the Sherman Act and other antitrust legislation. A major resurgence of populist activity occurred during the presidential election campaign of 1972 in support of candidate George McGovern; Governor George Wallace has often been described as the "populist candidate" in the 1976 presidential election.

Price Support   A program of the national government to help stabilize agricultural prices near parity by buying up market surpluses. Price supports, which have been used since 1933, are accompanied by production controls. The Commodity Credit Corporation (CCC) and the Agricultural Stabilization and Conservation Service (ASCS) administer the price support program through outright purchases and, more commonly, by granting loans to farmers, accepting their stored crops as collateral. The individual farmer can, in effect, turn the loan into a government purchase of his crop by simply not paying it off. If, however, the market price of the commodity goes above support level, he may pay off his loan, redeem his stored crop, and sell it on the free market. See also AGRICULTURAL ACT OF 1973, page 359; AGRICULTURAL ADJUSTMENT ACTS, page 360; EVER-NORMAL GRANARY, page 347; Mulford v. Smith, page 359; PARITY, page 349.

Significance   Important commodities that have come under the price support program include corn and other feed grains, cotton, rice, peanuts, tobacco, wheat, wool, and milk. The price support program recognizes the significance of agriculture and demonstrates the extent of agriculture's power in national politics and the farm bloc in Congress. The basic problem of agriculture for many years was to bring the supply of farm products into line with the demand for them. As a result of a technological revolution in farming methods in the 1950s and 1960s, productivity increased to the point where the national government spent about $4 billion annually to manage the surpluses produced, with annual storage costs running into hundreds of millions of dollars. Various domestic and foreign disposal programs helped diminish the size of the government's surpluses in the 1960s, but the problem of overproduction remained. Urban poverty groups increasingly pressured Congress to meet the problem of surpluses by distributing more of them among needy Americans who, studies have shown, are often suffering from inadequate diets. In 1970, Congress modified the price support system by limiting the amount of subsidy any one farmer could receive to no more then $55,000 under each of the three major crop programs— wheat, cotton, and feed grains. In the 1970s, a global food shortage of major proportions led the national government to adopt a policy of "unleashing" agriculture from government controls to encourage greater production.

Public Domain Public lands owned by the United States government. The public domain consists of national parks and forests, grazing districts, Indian reservations, and miscellaneous holdings. The Bureau of Land Management in the Department of the Interior has custody over a large portion of the public domain. *See also* HOMESTEAD ACT, page 361.

Significance Most of the land area of the United States today, with the exception of the thirteen original states and Texas, was once under the proprietorship of the national government. Through many programs, including homesteads, state grants, sales, grants to railroads, aids to education, and grants to soldiers and sailors, the national government has divested itself of most of its public lands. The public domain now comprises approximately 412 million acres, about 20 percent of the nation's total land area. Most of these public lands are found in eleven Western states, in six of which more than half of the state's lands are held by the national government. In the state of Alaska, more than 90 percent of the land remains part of the public domain. Considerable political controversy in recent years has concerned the leasing of vast areas of the public domain for exploitation by private parties, especially mining and petroleum companies, in an effort by the national government to overcome energy shortages.

Public Power The production of electrical energy by government-built and operated dams and power plants. Millions of kilowatts are produced and sold by the national government, especially from generating plants on the Colorado, Columbia, and Tennessee rivers. Public power production has become one of the major functions of the huge governmental dams, along with reclamation, irrigation, navigation, and flood control. Many cities and towns also produce and sell public power. *See also Ashwander v. TVA,* page 359; TENNESSEE VALLEY AUTHORITY, page 358.

Significance Public power development by the national and local governments was negligible until the depression years of the 1930s. The case for public power is based on the multipurpose nature of governmental dams, and on the claims that water power is a public resource and should not be used for private gain, and that public power is necessary to build up underdeveloped regions. The case against public power holds that it is dangerous to free enterprise, that government facilities do not pay taxes or dividends, that the taxpayers of the entire nation subsidize the people of the regions with public power, and that where multipurpose governmental dams are necessary, a partnership should be worked out with private business for buying wholesale power and selling it to the consumers. Over four-fifths of the electricity used in the United States is produced by private companies.

Regional Development Agencies   Federal-state commissions established during the 1960s and 1970s to regulate and develop interstate resources and provide for a unified attack on economic problems that cross state boundaries. Regional development agencies are funded partly by participating state governments and partly by direct federal grants. Federal officials representing the President and state governors from participating states typically share policy control, with each possessing an ultimate veto power. *See also* COOPERATIVE FEDERALISM, page 33; HORIZONTAL FEDERALISM, page 36; INTERSTATE COMPACT, page 38.

Significance   Regional development agencies and commissions constitute a major supplement to the infrequently used interstate compact approach to dealing with problems that cross state boundaries. They emphasize a cooperative vertical- and horizontal-styled federalism in contrast to the limited horizontal nature of cooperation engendered by such compacts. Examples of the new regional agencies include the Delaware River Basin Commission established in 1961, which exercises broad regulatory and developmental powers over water and its products in a four-state area, and the Appalachian Regional Commission established in 1965, which seeks to stimulate economic expansion among the 15 million people living in the thirteen states comprising the depressed area of Appalachia. Federal initiatives, federal standards, and federal funding have combined to make most of the experiments in regional development successful. States, local units of government, and private groups have combined their interests and capabilities in pursuit of common objectives in their regions. Additional regional development agencies are in the process of being organized in five regions under the Public Works and Economic Development Act of 1965: New England, Coastal Plains, Upper Great Lakes, Ozarks, and Four Corners (Colorado, New Mexico, Arizona, and Utah).

Rural Electrification   The governmental program to bring electric service and telephone lines to rural people not serviced by private enterprise. The Roosevelt Administration initiated the electrification program in 1935 with the establishment of the Rural Electrification Administration (REA) by executive order. The telephone program was added by Congress in 1949.

Significance   The REA has encouraged rural electrification by making low-interest loans to farmer cooperatives and local governments to build transmission lines, and to private electrical companies engaged in wiring individual farms. When the program started, only 10 percent of the nation's farms were electrified, whereas today almost all farms have light and power and most have telephone service. Critics of the REA charge that the rural electrification and telephone programs involve a considerable subsidy by the nation's taxpayers because of the low-interest loans, the high administrative costs, and tax exemptions to cooperatives. Supporters of the REA program defend it on the ground that private enterprise has refused to bring electrical services to the farmers because of the lack of profit possibilities, and they note that the improvement of farm conditions benefits the entire nation.

Soil Conservation   A cooperative program of the national government, states, local units, and individual farmers to preserve valuable topsoil from being washed or blown away through erosion and dust storms. Primary responsibility for developing and carrying out a national soil conservation program is vested in the Soil Conservation Service of the Department of Agriculture. *See also* PRICE SUPPORT, page 350.

Significance Although government can spark soil conservation programs and provide some financing, their effectiveness depends almost wholly upon the efforts of individual farmers. Soil-conserving methods include proper drainage, crop rotation, terracing, contour plowing, and strip cropping. The national government provided an incentive for individual farmers to cooperate by requiring all farmers participating in price support subsidy programs to use soil conservation methods. National programs for many years sought to improve soil conservation and reduce agricultural surpluses by paying farmers to retire overworked cropland by planting soil-conserving grasses and trees. Pressure to overcome inflation at home and food shortages abroad have led to abandonment of many such soil conservation programs.

United Nations Environment Program (UNEP) The global program that seeks to preserve ecological stabilities by protecting the land, air, water, and living species from pollution and other forms of environmental degradation. UNEP is headed by a 58-member Governing Council with headquarters in Nairobi, Kenya. The organization was created by the UN General Assembly following the United Nations Conference on the Human Environment in Stockholm in 1972. At that conference, the world community recognized that environmental problems are an international, as well as a regional, national, and local responsibility. *See also* ENVIRONMENTAL POLITICS, page 346.

Significance The United Nations Environment Program has been accorded primary responsibility for developing and implementing an international environmental program. UNEP has responsibility to promote and coordinate diverse programs that involve most nations of the world, numerous international organizations and agencies, private groups and transnational bodies, and much of the United Nations global system of agencies and programs. The decision to locate UNEP's headquarters in Africa—the first major United Nations program to be headquartered in the Third World—represented a political victory for the developing states' bloc in the General Assembly. One of the first programs established by UNEP is "Earthwatch," a global monitoring and information service to provide data on the nature and severity of environmental dangers, so that effective programs and priorities can be created.

Water Conservation The planned use and protection of water resources. Water conservation programs include promoting the navigability of streams, flood control, irrigation, river basin development, pollution control, recreation, reclamation, hydro-electric power, and the use of water for home and industrial consumption. The Bureau of Reclamation of the Department of the Interior, the Soil Conservation Service of the Department of Agriculture, and the United States Army Corps of Engineers play significant and sometimes competing roles in developing the nation's water resources. Since 1970, the Environmental Protection Agency has also participated in programs to protect water purity. *See also* COLORADO RIVER COMPACT, page 344; COLUMBIA RIVER COMPACT, page 344; CORPS OF ENGINEERS, page 354; ENVIRONMENTAL PROTECTION AGENCY, page 357; FEDERAL WATER POLLUTION CONTROL ACT, page 360.

Significance Because the use of water has increased tremendously in the United States, water conservation and pollution control programs have become increasingly critical. Pollution control is carried on through federal and state programs, and through interstate agreements on waterways that flow through several states. The most pressing problem for the future is that of providing adequate supplies of fresh water for human consumption and industrial use. Although President John F. Kennedy initiated a program to develop practical means for converting salt water from the oceans into fresh water, the program has faltered, as other critical problems have diverted attention from it and as budget cuts to fight inflation have reduced the scope of research.

IMPORTANT AGENCIES

Corps of Engineers A branch of the United States Army charged with planning and constructing public works on navigable waterways. The Engineers construct dams and power-generating facilities on many major rivers and develop extensive flood-control projects. In civil projects the Corps has developed a tradition of autonomy from the Army and Department of Defense, functioning as engineering consultants to the Congress. *See also* WATER CONSERVA-TION, page 353.

Significance The construction of governmental dams and other public projects involving multipurpose river development have often produced jurisdictional battles among the Corps of Engineers, the Department of Agriculture, the Department of the Interior, and advocates of valley authorities like the TVA. The Corps of Engineers with strong congressional support has been able to maintain its position as a major agency in the development of river programs. Increasingly, however, the Corps has had to defend its projects from attacks by conservationists and environmentalists who charge it with being concerned only with engineering problems and indifferent toward ecological and social needs.

Council on Environmental Quality A staff agency in the Executive Office that advises the President on measures to control or eliminate air, water, and other forms of pollution, and to promote a high quality of life for the American people. The Council, created by the National Environmental Policy Act of 1969, assists the President in drawing up an annual Environmental Quality Report, which he transmits to the Congress annually with recommendations for appropriate legislative action. Three members appointed by the President with the approval of the Senate comprise the Council, with one of the three selected by the President to serve as chairman. *See also* ENVIRONMENTAL POLITICS, page 346; ENVIRONMENTAL PROTECTION AGENCY, page 357; NATIONAL ENVIRONMENTAL POLICY ACT OF 1969, page 361.

Significance The Council on Environmental Quality's role as an Executive Office staff agency reflects the increasing responsibility of the President to provide leadership in restoring the quality of the nation's environment. The Council also reflects public concern and the outcry against past and present policies that have permitted the degradation of the nation's environment in the interest of private gain. Because the Act creating the Council requires that the individuals appointed to the Council be well-qualified environmentalists, the Council can function as a powerful advocate of effective federal programs. Pressure groups have demanded that Council members be guided by an "environmental ethic," rather than by a "technological ethic" or an "economic growth ethic."

Department of Agriculture A major clientele department of the national government that provides numerous services for farmers and regulates various aspects of agriculture and related fields in the interest of farmers and the general public. The Secretary who heads the Department is appointed by the President with the Senate's approval and serves as a member of the Cabinet. A variety of activities are carried on by the Department's major operational units. They include: (1) Agricultural Research Service which conducts research in crop and livestock production and marketing; (2) Federal Extension Service, which works cooperatively with land-grant colleges and county agents to provide research information to farmers; (3) Forest Service, which protects the national forests from fire and disease; (4) Soil Conservation Service, which conserves soil resources through programs of research, erosion control, reforestation, and flood control; (5) Commodity Exchange Authority, which supervises trading on commodity exchanges where agricultural products are bought and sold; (6) Commodity Credit Corporation and the Agricultural Stabilization and Conservation Service, which are responsible for the stabilization of agricultural prices; (7) Federal Crop Insurance Corporation, which ensures farmers against loss or damage to their crops; (8) Farmers Home Administration, which makes low-interest loans to low-income farmers to improve their crops or facilities; and (9) Rural Electrification Administration, which makes loans to finance the extension of electric power and telephone service to rural areas. *See also* EVER-NORMAL GRANARY, page 347; PRICE SUPPORT, page 350; SOIL CONSERVATION, page 352.

Significance During the 1950s and 1960s, the farm economy underwent a scientific revolution in production, resulting in huge surpluses, low prices for farm products, and an increasing need for governmental assistance. The Department of Agriculture developed various foreign and domestic programs to reduce surpluses and to encourage higher prices. By the mid-1970s, most surpluses were eliminated, and shortages of key crops began to occur as the result of poor growing conditions and unprecedented national and world demand for food. The Department of Agriculture continues to be primarily concerned with maintaining stability in the farm economy, expanding agricultural markets, and helping to achieve supply-demand adjustments in the marketplace. Some critics point out that the Department is largely responsible for market disequilibria as the result of its interference with supply-demand forces. Others have noted that because of the population explosion in the world and a growing dependence for the United States on sales of agricultural products to offset spiraling costs of oil and other necessary imports, an expanded role by government in developing new agricultural technologies and helping secure market adjustments is essential.

Department of the Interior A major department of the national government that has responsibility over a variety of affairs concerning the territories and properties of the United States. The Secretary who heads the Department is appointed by the President with the Senate's approval and serves as a member of the Cabinet. Some of the major operating units found in the Interior Department are the: (1) Fish and Wildlife Service, which improves commercial fishing, and hunting and fishing for sport through research and conservation programs; (2) Bureau of Mines, which promotes health and safety in privately owned mines and compiles statistics on mine operations; (3) Geological Survey, which surveys and classifies public lands and conducts geologic research; (4) Bureau of Indian Affairs, which promotes health, welfare, and educational facilities for Indians; (5) Bureau of Land Management, which supervises the exploitation of natural resources of the public domain by private companies; (6) National Park Service, which develops and administers natural beauty spots and historic sites for the enjoyment of the American people; (7) Bureau of Outdoor Recreation, which maintains a continuing inventory and evaluation of recreational needs and resources; (8) Bureau of Reclamation, which constructs and operates public facilities to generate electric power, promote flood control, and provide irrigation; and (9) Alaska, Bonneville, Southeastern, and Southwestern Power Administrations, which market electric power generated by national dams and power stations in different sections of the country. The Department of the Interior also has responsibility for the economic, social, and political development of the territories of Guam, Samoa, the Virgin Islands, and the Trust Territory of the Pacific Islands. *See also* TERRITORY, page 42; TRUSTEESHIP COUNCIL, page 411.

Significance Most of the agencies in the Department of the Interior are concerned with conservation. Conservation as practiced by the Department means not only the preservation of land, water, forests, natural resources, and wildlife, but their wise and systematic use as well. Not only is the Department the custodian of the nation's natural resources, but its jurisdiction extends to islands in the Caribbean and South Pacific and to lands within the Arctic Circle. Growing interest in environmental, conservational, and ecological problems is helping to move the Department of the Interior into the center of American political activity. Expanding demands for energy and raw materials and a growing interest in environmental, conservational, and ecological problems is helping to thrust the Department into political controversies.

Energy Research and Development Administration (ERDA) The agency with responsibility to manage and coordinate all national energy research and development programs. ERDA was established in 1974 when the Atomic Energy Commission (AEC) was abolished, and its powers and responsibilities were transferred to two new agencies: ERDA, to carry on the research and developmental functions formerly vested in the AEC; and the Nuclear Regulatory Commission (NRC), which was assigned the licensing and regulatory powers formerly exercised by the AEC. *See also* ATOMIC ENERGY ACTS, page 328; FEDERAL ENERGY ADMINISTRATION, page 357; NUCLEAR REGULATORY COMMISSION, page 324.

Significance The creation of the Energy Research and Development Administration was part of a major federal legislative program to cope with the growing problems of energy shortages and environmental dangers. Major research activities are carried on at Argonne National Laboratory near Chicago, and at Brookhaven National Laboratory at Upton, New York. Military, biomedical, and environmental protection research projects are fostered by ERDA. The energy crisis of the 1970s has placed new emphasis on nuclear power for peaceful purposes, although by 1975 only five percent of electrical energy generated in the United States was produced by nuclear power plants. Research emphasis is placed on developing "second-generation" fast-breeder reactors that produce more fuel than they use, and on developing "third-generation" fission-fusion thermonuclear power plants that would use simple, inexhaustible fuels.

Environmental Protection Agency (EPA)   The Agency established by the Presidential Reorganization Plan in 1970 to administer federal programs aimed at controlling pollution and protecting the nation's environment. Headed by an Administrator, the Environmental Protection Agency is concerned with air and water pollution, pesticide research and control, radiation dangers, and basic ecological research. The Agency administers the National Environmental Policy Act of 1969 and those acts that Congress has passed to deal with specific pollution problems. The Clean Air Act of 1970, for example, initially required *inter alia*, that auto-making companies reduce hazardous emissions by 90 percent within five years. The Water Quality Improvement Act of 1970 establishes liability for cleanup costs for ocean spills and provides for extensive control over the Great Lakes and pesticide drainage. Under the Resource Recovery Act of 1970, a major effort is underway to recycle and recover useful materials and energy from solid wastes. The EPA carries on its operations through regional offices located in ten major cities. *See also* COUNCIL ON ENVIRONMENTAL QUALITY, page 354; ENVIRONMENTAL IMPACT STATEMENT, page 346; ENVIRONMENTAL POLITICS, page 346; NATIONAL ENVIRONMENTAL POLICY ACT OF 1969, page 361.

Significance   The Environmental Protection Agency, along with the Council on Environmental Quality that advises the President on ecological matters, represents part of the federal government's response to the American public's growing concern about pollution. The Agency administers programs transferred to its jurisdiction, along with personnel, from the Departments of Agriculture, Interior, and Health, Education, and Welfare, the Atomic Energy Commission, and the Federal Radiation Council. Expanding programs of environmental protection will likely increase substantially the power and influence of the Environmental Protection Agency during the 1970s.

Farm Credit Administration   An independent agency of the national government that supervises and coordinates the operations of the federal land banks and other corporations and cooperatives that provide credit for farmers in each of the twelve federal farm credit districts. The Farm Credit Administration makes decisions through a part-time thirteen-member Farm Credit Board, appointed by the President and Secretary of Agriculture.

Significance   The Farm Credit Administration plays an important role in the agricultural sector of the economy. Farmers are often in dire need of credit because of their heavy investments in land and machinery and their need to purchase seed and fertilizer in the spring following a period of low income. Availability of credit, particularly when agricultural prices slump, may spell the difference between survival or bankruptcy for individual farmers. In recent years, farmers have borrowed annually in excess of $10 billion from banks and cooperatives that operate under the Farm Credit Administration.

Federal Energy Administration (FEA)   A major federal agency established by Congress in 1973 to deal with a multitude of complex problems growing out of the nation's energy crisis. The Federal Energy Administration is headed by an Administrator whose responsibilities and powers under presidential direction have led the media to describe him as the nation's "Energy

Chief." Specifically, the FEA is responsible for ensuring that the supply of energy available to the United States will continue to be sufficient to meet total energy demand. Issues and programs that the FEA must deal with and administer include fuel shortages, energy distribution among sectors of the economy and regions of the country, increasing consumption of energy, control over exorbitant profits of energy companies during crises, relation of energy problems to environmental problems and programs, imports of foreign oil, and the search for new sources of energy. *See also* ENERGY RESEARCH AND DEVELOPMENT ADMINISTRATION, page 356.

Significance The main task of the Federal Energy Administration and its Administrator is to aid the President in developing a comprehensive national energy policy. The FEA is charged with major responsibility in the national drive to achieve energy self-sufficiency by 1980, known as "Project Independence." The impact of the Arab oil embargo in the wake of the Middle East war of 1973, and the increased prices for oil as a result of cartel pricing by the Organization of Petroleum Exporting Countries (OPEC) have helped to raise energy issues to the highest political levels. The FEA is placing increasing emphasis on relieving the nation's heavy dependence on oil by developing alternate sources of energy, including coal, coal gassification, shale, nuclear, solar, geothermal, ocean tides and currents, wind, and other potential power sources.

Tennessee Valley Authority (TVA) A major corporation of the national government established by Congress in 1933 to provide for the development of the Tennessee River and its tributaries. The TVA has responsibility for the generation, transmission, and sale of electric power, flood control, improvement of navigation, production of fertilizers, reforestation, reclamation, and soil conservation. The TVA operates under a board of three directors appointed by the President with the Senate's approval. Its operations cover an area of over 40,000 square miles in the states of Alabama, Georgia, Kentucky, Mississippi, North Carolina, Tennessee, and Virginia. Development projects are financed through the issuance of bonds by the Authority and through the sale of electric power to private companies. *See also Ashwander v. TVA,* page 359.

Significance The TVA is an outstanding example of regional development fostered by a single independent government corporation. Almost thirty major dams have been constructed, and others are planned. The flood-prone Tennessee River has been tamed. Navigation and farming have been improved and the cheap power supplied by the TVA has encouraged the industrial development of the entire region. The TVA is also a principal source of electric power for the national atomic energy and space programs. All essential features of the program have been sustained by the Supreme Court. Yet, in spite of its success, opposition remains. Many businessmen oppose the TVA as unfair subsidized governmental competition with private power companies. It is often charged with being another step toward national planning and socialism. Some critics in other parts of the country oppose the use of government tax money to subsidize the people of a single region with cheap power. Much opposition has resulted from the attraction of industry away from other sections of the country to the Tennessee Valley. Private power companies operating in the area oppose the use of TVA rates as a "yardstick" to measure the fairness of the rates they charge consumers. Despite the political controversy over TVA, several additional valley authorities have been proposed, including a Missouri Valley and a Columbia Valley authority, but none has yet received congressional approval.

IMPORTANT CASES

Ashwander v. TVA, 297 U.S. 288 (1936): Upheld the construction of major dams by an agency of the national government under the war and commerce powers, and upheld the authority of such an agency to build transmission lines and to sell electrical energy generated at the dams. The Court held that Congress could properly build huge dams if needed for national defense and to improve navigation, and that it could, under the Constitution, sell property belonging to the United States, such as electric power. *See also* Ashwander v. TVA, page 267.

Significance The *Ashwander* decision sustained the legal basis for the vast complex of the TVA and its multipurpose program. The case emphasizes the broad application of the commerce clause and the domestic implications resulting from a liberal interpretation of the war power.

Mulford v. Smith, 307 U.S. 38 (1939): Sustained the constitutionality of the Agriculture Act of 1938, holding that Congress may limit the amount of a crop sold in interstate commerce, and that the delegation of powers to the Secretary of Agriculture by Congress was proper, since definite standards were laid down in the Act. It also held that Congress may validly exercise its power to regulate interstate commerce through a regulatory tax. *See also* COMMERCE POWER, page 32; REGULATORY TAX, page 293.

Significance The *Mulford* case sanctioned the attempts by Congress and the Department of Agriculture to provide a more orderly marketing system for the basic crops of cotton, wheat, corn, tobacco, and rice. National government procedures involved under the Act include loans, marketing quotas, storage of crop reserves, and the parity concept aimed at securing fair prices for farmers. This case had the effect of overruling the Supreme Court's earlier decision in *United States v. Butler,* 297 U.S. 1 (1936), in which it held that national regulation of farm prices invaded the reserved powers of the states. Since the *Mulford* decision, the national government's handling of the farm problem has involved primarily political and economic rather than legal problems.

IMPORTANT STATUTES

Agricultural and Consumer Protection Act of 1973   A new farm law that recognizes the changing conditions that prevail in the 1970s in the field of agriculture and in the marketing of farm products. The Agricultural and Consumer Protection Act retains subsidies in the form of a price support program for wheat, feed grains, and cotton if the free market fails to achieve a minimum "target price" set by Congress for each commodity. This guaranteed price can be increased each year to reflect changing costs of production for farmers. The Act also: (1) gives the Department of Agriculture authority to pay farmers for retiring land from production (soil bank program),but only if surpluses exist; (2) limits soil bank subsidies to $20,000 annually for each farmer participating in the program; (3) supports milk prices at 80 percent of parity; (4) extends the Food for Peace program for four additional years at an annual authorization of $2.5 billion; and (5) changes the operations of the Rural Electrification Administration (REA) into a program to provide insured and guaranteed private loans at 2 percent for extending electric and telephone systems to poor rural areas. *See also* PRICE SUPPORT, page 350.

Significance The enactment of the Agricultural and Consumer Protection Act of 1973 reflects the changing conditions in the field of agriculture, including a growing world demand for food stuffs, shortages, and increasingly high consumer prices for food. The Act was intended to "unleash" the American farmer to produce the surpluses needed to meet the growing demands of a hungry world caught up in explosive population growth. It also was aimed at correcting some of the abuses of past federal farm programs that had, for example, permitted a few wealthy farmers to receive huge sums in annual subsidies while millions of poor farmers received little or no help. Opponents, however, point out that the new Act does not adequately remedy those policies of the past decade that helped drive millions of farmers off of the land into the big urban centers.

Agricultural Adjustment Acts of 1933, 1938 Broad agricultural programs sponsored by the Roosevelt Administration and enacted by Congress to maintain farm income through parity price supports and production controls for basic crops. After the first Agricultural Adjustment Act (AAA) had been declared unconstitutional by the Supreme Court in *United States v. Butler,* 297 U.S. 1 (1936), a second AAA, containing much of the first program but eliminating or modifying those sections that had failed the constitutionality test, was adopted in 1938. The 1933 Act was held to be an invalid use of the taxing power, whereas the 1938 Act was upheld as a valid exercise of the commerce power, (*Mulford v. Smith,* 307 U.S. 38 [1939]). *See also Mulford v. Smith,* page 359.

Significance Most of the procedures for aiding agriculture that were initiated in these two AAA programs remain the basic approach used by the national government today. Features continued today include direct governmental payments to individual farmers for reducing acreage for soil conservation purposes, governmental loans on surplus crops when overproduction drives prices down, support of farm crop prices at a parity level, and establishment of acreage allotments and marketing quotas on basic crops when farmers choose them through a two-thirds majority vote in a national referendum.

Federal Water Pollution Control Act of 1972 A major statute administered by the Environmental Protection Agency that mandates a sweeping federal-state campaign to "restore and maintain the chemical, physical, and biological integrity of the Nation's waters." The Water Pollution Control Act establishes two basic goals: (1) By 1983, water in the United States should generally be clean enough for swimming and to support fish, shellfish, and wildlife; and (2) by 1985, all discharges of pollutants in the nation's waters will be ended. Specific actions by national, state, and local governments and by industries are called for, with strict deadlines and enforcement provisions in the Act. Special emphasis is placed on solving the problems of industrial pollution and municipal sewage treatment. *See also* NATIONAL ENVIROMENTAL POLICY ACT, page 361; WATER CONSERVATION, page 353.

Significance The Federal Water Pollution Control Act of 1972 expanded and strengthened earlier water pollution control legislation. Water increasingly has become a major political issue among local and national governmental and private decision makers because of skyrocketing needs for clean water. Conservation and environmental groups have also boosted their pressures on governments on all three levels for positive action. For the first time, the new Act extends national pollution control programs to *all* United States' waters rather than only to those interstate waters covered by earlier programs. Since 1972, great amounts of money and effort have been expended in trying to clean up the nation's waters, but many pollution activities have continued apace.

Homestead Act of 1862   An historic act in which Congress offered 160 acres of the public domain to any person who would pay a $10 registration fee and live on the land for five years.

Significance   The Homestead Act opened up the vast areas of the public domain in the Midwest and West to farming. Millions of acres were parceled out to pioneering "homesteaders," and by 1910 restrictions had to be imposed to keep some governmental lands under public ownership. The Homestead Act contributed greatly to the growing strength of the nation by opening the West and encouraging land and home ownership.

National Environmental Policy Act of 1969   The basic declaration of national policy aimed at encouraging "productive and enjoyable harmony between man and his environment" and promoting efforts that "prevent or eliminate damage to the environment and biosphere and stimulate the health and welfare of man. . . ." The Act established a Council on Environmental Quality in the Executive Office to advise the President. Each year the President is required by the Act to transmit an Environmental Quality Report to the Congress in which he reviews the current situation and makes recommendations for legislative programs. The Act in effect recognizes that modern technology and the "growth ethic" of capitalism must be redirected so that they function more in harmony with the natural environment. *See also* COUNCIL OF ENVIRONMENTAL QUALITY, page 354; ENVIRONMENTAL POLITICS, page 346; ENVIRONMENTAL PROTECTION AGENCY, page 357.

Significance   The National Environmental Policy Act of 1969 was passed by Congress with bipartisan support, strong presidential urgings, and broad public demands. The Act, however, is phrased in hortatory language with few specifics. Yet, the Environmental Act explicitly recognizes a new important role for the national government. Some critics point out, however, that the effort to achieve continuous economic expansion in the interest of full employment and economic stability may produce the kinds and extent of pollution that the Environmental Act will be unable to cope with.

15   Health, Education, and Welfare

Aid to Families with Dependent Children (AFDC)   Financial aid provided under the categorical assistance program of the Social Security Act of 1935 for children who lack adequate support but are living with one parent or relative. Some provision also has been made for support of children in foster homes. The program is administered by the states with the assistance of federal funds and under regulations established by the national government. The program is supervised by the Social and Rehabilitation Service of the Department of Health, Education, and Welfare. *See also* CATEGORICAL ASSISTANCE, page 363.

   Significance   The aid to dependent children program is designed to preserve a private home environment for children who otherwise would have to be put into orphanages, institutions, or foster homes. The program makes it possible for children to remain with a parent, grandparent, or other close relative and to receive the love and attention unavailable in even the best institutions. Considerable controversy has arisen over AFDC because of allegations that liberal allowances in some states have encouraged migration to those states, that the program encourages illegitimacy, and that men are induced to leave their families in order to make their children eligible. Critics charge that AFDC is mainly concerned with rules and enforcement procedures, rather than with improving the living conditions of children and rendering them productive citizens. Congress has attempted to require and encourage mothers of fatherless children to work by providing job training and child care centers, but such programs have been neither sufficient in scope nor realistic approaches to the social and economic dimensions of the problem. The number of recipients of AFDC, including parents and children, has risen dramatically from less than three million in 1955 to more than ten million in 1974.

Aid to the Blind   Financial aid given to the needy blind under the categorical assistance program of the Social Security Act. Originally, payments were made under standards established in each state, with funds provided by both the national and state governments. Under the Supplemental Security Income (SSI) program inaugurated in 1974, the program is funded by the national government and may be supplemented by a state. Aid to the blind is supervised by the Social and Rehabilitation Service of the Department of Health, Education, and Welfare. *See also* CATEGORICAL ASSISTANCE, page 363; SUPPLEMENTAL SECURITY INCOME, page 368.

Significance About one-third of the blind people in the United States (approximately two million) are aided through this categorical aid program. The specific degree of eyesight deficiency necessary to qualify for aid is determined by law. With proper training, many blind people are able to engage in productive work. Congress has provided that blind persons are to have priority to operate vending stands on federal property.

Aid to the Totally and Permanently Disabled A program inaugurated in 1950 as part of the categorical aid program of the Social Security Act, which provides for financial aid to persons over eighteen whose physical condition makes it impossible to engage in gainful employment. The program, originally administered by the states with the assistance of federal funds, is now fully funded by the national government under the Supplemental Security Income (SSI) plan and administered by the Rehabilitation Services Administration in the Department of Health, Education, and Welfare. *See also* CATEGORICAL ASSISTANCE, page 363; SUPPLEMENTAL SECURITY INCOME, page 368.

Significance Aid to the totally and permanently disabled is made available for a wide variety of infirmities as determined by law. Training programs are made available to help restore the handicapped to gainful employment, but many people are unable to take advantage of retraining. SSI provides a basic income for those unfortunate people who cannot earn a living for reasons beyond their control. The number of recipients of such aid has grown consistently over the years, from 240,000 in 1955 to 1,275,000 in 1974.

Categorical Assistance Welfare programs provided under the Social Security Act. These programs include: (1) old-age assistance; (2) aid to the blind; (3) aid to dependent children; and (4) aid to the totally and permanently disabled. Persons who fall within these categories and are in need of financial assistance have received aid from their state from funds supplemented by federal grants. Under the Supplemental Security Income (SSI) program, initiated in 1974, aid to the adult categories—needy aged, blind, and disabled—is assumed by the national government though states may choose to supplement the basic amount provided. Overall responsibility for the categorical aid programs rests with the Department of Health, Education, and Welfare. The programs also extend to the District of Columbia, Puerto Rico, Guam, and the Virgin Islands. *See also Goldberg v. Kelly,* page 374; SOCIAL SECURITY ACT, page 378; SUPPLEMENTAL SECURITY INCOME, page 368.

Significance Categorical assistance establishes a continuing program of aid for major categories of destitute people. Categorical assistance has made it possible for many helpless people to continue living outside of public institutions. In former years, it was common for local governments to provide poorhouses or almshouses for the care of the needy. Congress requires that any state participating in the program must establish a state agency, staffed by the merit system, to conduct the program or to supervise local units which conduct the program. Persons denied aid must be given opportunity to appeal to the state supervisory agency. Under the Supreme Court's decision in *Goldberg v. Kelly* (397 U.S. 254 [1970]) termination of aid can take place only after a due process hearing. The states may establish their own requirements that individuals must meet to receive assistance, but the Supreme Court has outlawed state residence requirements as denying the poor the freedom to travel (*Shapiro v. Thompson,* 394 U.S. 618 [1969]). Support for complete federal assumption of the categorical aid programs has grown in recent years. Critics charge that state-to-state variations encourage movement of needy people to states paying higher benefits, and that the programs encourage deceitfulness and the breakup of families. Supplemental Security Income is designed to guarantee a minimum support level for the needy.

Community Action Program (CAP)   A "war on poverty" program created by the Economic Opportunity Act of 1964 to stimulate communities to mobilize their resources against poverty. Federal aid is given to local public and private agencies to undertake antipoverty programs that involve the poor themselves in operating the programs. Possible projects include literacy instruction, job training, vocational rehabilitation, homemaker services, job development and health services. *See also* COMMUNITY SERVICES ADMINISTRATION, page 371; ECONOMIC OPPORTUNITY ACT, page 374; LEGAL SERVICES CORPORATION, page 372.

Significance   The Community Action Program encourages public and private nonprofit agencies to engage in positive and varied programs to meet and, if possible, conquer the causes of poverty in the community. Many Community Action Programs have stimulated fresh approaches to the poverty problem other than direct handouts to the poor. The Program has been very controversial and has had to withstand numerous efforts to curtail its activities or have it abolished. Most criticism has been directed at the tendency of local public agencies to use the program for political patronage, the lack of sufficient involvement of poor people in the administration of community projects, the use of programs as centers for the promotion of social activist causes, and evidence of corruption and exploitation of target communities in some areas.

Federal Aid to Education   Various programs of federal grants-in-aid to the states for educational purposes. Such aid has taken the form of land grants for schools and colleges; grants for vocational education and vocational rehabilitation; school lunch programs; scholarship funds for science, mathematics, and other programs in the interest of national defense; grants to veterans to attend school; and grants to areas with a heavy influx of students because of the establishment of a military base or other national facility. In recent years, numerous aids to higher education have been enacted by Congress, and in 1965, the first general aid-to-education bill, providing substantial aid to elementary and secondary schools, was passed. *See also* ELEMENTARY AND SECONDARY EDUCATION ACT, page 375; HIGHER EDUCATION ACT, page 376; NATIONAL DEFENSE EDUCATION ACT, page 377.

Significance   Much controversy has been engendered by general federal aid to education. Opponents point out that education has traditionally been a state and local concern, and that federal aid means federal supervision and control of the school system and curriculum. Supporters point to the wide variety of federal aids to education carried on over a long period of American history without undue federal interference. They claim that the states are in no position to finance the increasing need for better educational facilities. Deeply involved in the controversy is the issue of aid for parochial schools. Many persons oppose aid to religious institutions as a violation of the principle of separation of church and state. Others argue that all children should benefit from such aid, and, hence, no restriction should be placed on the type of school affected. Additional controversy has been aroused over the use of federal aid to education in the enforcement of racial integration, particularly where such aid is withheld as a sanction against continuing segregation of the races. The issue of equal rights for women has also emerged as a factor in administration of federal aid to education.

Indoor Relief Care of the needy in public institutions. Indoor relief is usually provided for the aged, the chronically ill, and the mentally incompetent. Prior to 1935 and the passage of the Social Security Act, many poor but healthy persons were cared for in public almshouses, poorhouses, poor farms, asylums, county homes, or institutions of like names. Indoor relief has largely been replaced by "outdoor relief," which provides money, food, and medical care to persons who continue to live in their own homes. *See also* OUTDOOR RELIEF, page 367.

Significance Indoor relief is largely the responsibility of local governments. At one time, it was common practice to put all kinds of helpless people—dependent children, the blind, the aged, the sick—in the same institution. National and state programs now make separate provisions for many of these people under the categorical assistance program. Numerous public institutions are maintained, however, largely for the aged who are unable to care for themselves, and for other persons who cannot be provided for in private homes. Modern institutions now take the form of nursing homes, many of which are supported by local and state governments.

Job Corps A program, authorized by the Economic Opportunity Act of 1964, that enables jobless youths from sixteen to twenty-one to work and study at training centers or in conservation camps. Emphasis is placed upon education, vocational training, and work experiences. The Job Corps is managed by the Department of Labor, which contracts with local public and private agencies to establish training centers. *See also* ECONOMIC OPPORTUNITY ACT, page 374.

Significance The Job Corps was inaugurated as part of the Johnson Administration's "war on poverty." Its aim is to attack the causes rather than the effects of unemployment. Through the Job Corps program, it is hoped that school dropouts and underprivileged youth will become useful and productive citizens. While learning, Corpsmen receive living and travel allowances.

Land-grant College An agricultural and mechanical college, or the agricultural and mechanical school of a state university, established under the provisions of the Morrill Act of 1862. The Morrill Act provided for the granting of land (amounting to nearly 11 million acres) by the national governments to the states for the support of colleges to teach agriculture, engineering, and home economics. Since that time, Congress has continued to make money grants to these institutions, supplementing funds given by state and private agencies. Experimental stations for agriculture, and an extension service that carries education directly to the farmer in the rural areas, have also been established at land-grant colleges.

Significance Most of the great state universities and agricultural colleges in the United States are a direct result of the land-grant policy. Congress did not exclude the teaching of other subjects from these schools and all of them provide education in the humanities and scientific fields. The agricultural and mechanical divisions, however, continue to receive special attention from Congress. The farmer has benefited most from the facilities made available through the land-grant college. Efforts to apply the land-grant concept to the support of urban universities and urban needs have not been successful.

Maternal and Child Welfare Program   A feature of the Social Security Act of 1935 that provides for grants to the states for maternal and child health services, crippled children services, and general child welfare programs. Grants are made to the states not for payments to particular persons, as is true under the categorical aid programs, but for support of state welfare programs. Maternal and child health services include care of mothers before and after childbirth, and immunization of children against communicable diseases. Another program seeks to provide therapy and rehabilitation for crippled children whose parents lack independent means to care for them. Child welfare activities include counseling and care of neglected, mentally retarded, and emotionally disturbed youngsters, and care of delinquent children. *See also* SOCIAL SECURITY ACT, page 378.

Significance   The maternal and child welfare program has had remarkable success in reducing infant and maternal mortality and has benefited thousands of crippled, neglected, and emotionally disturbed children. All states have established agencies to carry out these functions. Overall administration is in the hands of the Office of Child Development of the Department of Health, Education, and Welfare.

Medicare   A health insurance program enacted in 1965 as an amendment to the Social Security Act to provide medical care for the elderly. Two health care programs are involved. One, which is compulsory and financed by increases in the social security payroll tax, covers most hospital and nursing home costs, home health service visits, and diagnostic services for persons aged sixty-five or older. The second is a voluntary supplementary health program for persons over sixty-five, which covers a variety of health services both in and out of medical institutions and pays a substantial part of physician costs. The supplementary plan is financed by a small charge to the person enrolled and by an equal amount paid by the national government out of general revenue. Impoverished persons unable to qualify under Medicare and who are in need of medical services are assisted under a federally supported state program, called Medicaid. The Medicaid program was established by the Kerr-Mills Act of 1960.

Significance   The passage of Medicare in 1965 climaxed a twenty-year fight over what the American Medical Association and other opposition groups called "socialized medicine." The program recognizes that illness can quickly exhaust the resources of most families and that elderly persons, who suffer most health problems, cannot afford private health insurance. The Medicare program represents a major step in social welfare legislation, with social insurance programs now covering most major hazards. In adopting the Medicare program, the United States has followed the lead of most democratic states, some of which instituted public medical care programs in the nineteenth century. The expansion of Medicare to persons of all ages in the form of national health insurance has been one of the major issues of the 1960s and 1970s.

Old-Age, Survivors, and Disability Insurance (OASDI)   An insurance program, commonly called "social security," administered by the national government under the provisions of the Social Security Act of 1935. Its major purposes are to provide a retirement income for elderly persons, income for workers who are totally disabled, income for the spouses and minor children of deceased wage earners, and medical care for the aged (Medicare). Specifically exempted from coverage are federal employees under the civil service retirement system, ministers (optional), state and local employees not authorized coverage by state law, and some persons whose incomes are not sufficient to qualify. All other persons are required to contribute a certain percent of their income that is matched by their employer. The amount paid by the employee appears on his tax-withholding form as FICA (Federal Insurance Contribution Act). Self-employed persons also contribute. These contributions are credited to each worker's account and, upon death, retirement, or disablement, funds are allocated in accordance with the formulas provided by law for each eventuality. Retirement usually takes place at the age of sixty-five, but one may retire at sixty-two with reduced benefits. Retired persons may continue to work but may have their benefits reduced if they earn more than $2,520 a year. After the age of seventy-two, no limitations are placed on earnings. The program is administered directly by the Social Security Administration in the Department of Health, Education, and Welfare. *See also* MEDICARE, page 366; SOCIAL SECURITY CASES, page 374.

Significance OASDI is a compulsory savings plan designed to meet the problems of an increasingly aging population. Modern health programs have contributed to a rapid increase in the number of persons over sixty-five. In addition, OASDI provides for the disabled and the families of deceased workers who would otherwise become public charges. Insurance has taken the place of public and private charity and maintains the dignity of those who receive funds from the program. The program is a direct result of the depression of the 1930s, during which many people became destitute. Some persons object to the compulsory nature of the program and to the amounts spent on its administration. The program has, however, received the endorsement of both major parties and benefits and coverage have been regularly increased, as has the cost to contributors, OASDI and Medicare now represent a significant portion of both private and public expenditures.

Old-age Assistance Financial aid provided under the categorical assistance program of the Social Security Act for the needy aged who are not covered by the Old-Age, Survivors, and Disability Insurance program. Old-age assistance was furnished through the states under grants-in-aid from the national government under supervision of the Social and Rehabilitation Service of the Department of Health, Education, and Welfare. Since 1974, the program is financed and administered by the national government under the Supplemental Security Income (SSI) program with provision for voluntary state supplementary aid. *See also* CATEGORICAL ASSISTANCE, page 363; SUPPLEMENTAL SECURITY INCOME, page 368.

Significance Old-age assistance is designed to provide aid to those needy people who retired prior to the enactment of the Old-Age, Survivors, and Disability Insurance program or whose occupations are not covered by the insurance program. Congress has extended the coverage of social security insurance to many more occupations in recent years. In future years, the need for the old-age assistance program should diminish considerably. Since 1955, the number of recipients has decreased from 2.5 million to 1.8 million in 1974.

Outdoor Relief Financial aid or food and medical care provided needy persons outside of public institutions. Outdoor relief programs are administered by state and local governments under a general relief program or with the aid of the national government under the categorical assistance program. *See also* INDOOR RELIEF, page 365.

Significance Outdoor relief is generally preferred to indoor relief unless the health or mental incompetence of an individual compels that he be placed under constant institutional care. Outdoor relief permits greater flexibility in administration and preserves the dignity of those in need of aid. One drawback of outdoor relief is that it may encourage persons to seek aid who, under the threat of having to go to a poorhouse, would make greater efforts to rehabilitate themselves. Yet, careful administration of the program can assure that only those in need are provided with aid. In this way, the needy can continue to maintain their homes and play a useful part in society.

Public Housing Government construction and maintenance of dwellings for low-income families. Since 1937, and with increasing emphasis after 1949, the national government has given assistance to local governments to clear slum areas and to construct housing. Local governments need state authorization to participate in the program and the local community can reject public housing by referendum. A local housing authority must be established which administers the funds provided by the federal government and floats bonds. Rentals are used to repay the federal loan and private bondholders. Rentals are kept very low and the federal government subsidizes the difference between costs and rental receipts. Only persons with limited incomes are eligible to occupy the housing. Some cities and states have undertaken their own public housing programs without federal aid. In a major revision of housing programs in the Housing and Community Development Act of 1974 Congress continued conventional public housing and increased rental-assistance programs. *See also Goldberg v. Kelly,* page 374; HOUSING ACT OF 1949, page 376; HOUSING AND COMMUNITY DEVELOPMENT ACT OF 1974, page 377; URBAN RENEWAL, page 369.

Significance The depression and World War II contributed to a housing shortage and continuing deterioration of slum areas. Rising costs have made it impossible for many low-income families to secure decent housing. Poor housing and slums increase delinquency, impair family ties, and are costly to the community in welfare services and police and fire protection. Opponents of public housing object to the government competing with private industry. It is argued, too, that the availability of public housing discourages tenants to earn higher incomes, since they may be forced to move if their income rises. Serious controversy has arisen over the role of public housing policy in stimulating or preventing racial and economic integration in city neighborhood patterns. The tendency of much public housing to resemble vertical ghetto prisons has also drawn criticism. The 1974 Housing and Community Development Act attempts to meet some of these objections by encouraging comprehensive community planning and requiring dispersal of low-income rental housing.

Supplemental Security Income (SSI) A program adopted by Congress in 1972 and initiated in 1974 providing for federal assumption of adult categories of public assistance, namely aid to the blind, aid to the totally and permanently disabled, and old-age assistance. A basic amount of money is made available to needy adults falling within the designated categories according to marital and family status, not individually determined need. States with prior existing higher benefits may continue to supplement SSI. *See also* CATEGORICAL ASSISTANCE, page 363; SOCIAL SECURITY ACT, page 378.

Significance The pressures of increased costs and case loads have intensified the drive for reform of the welfare program. Under the Social Security Act of 1935, each state sets its own standards for aid to the needy and receives grants-in-aid from the national government. This has led to wide variations in payments and criteria for aid, resulting, it is charged, with migration of the poor to areas with high welfare payments. Case loads have risen sharply due to unemployment and inflation and to underlying social problems connected with minority groups. State costs have skyrocketed to the point of causing financial crises in urban states. Public assistance payments go to more than 5 percent of the population nationally, but, in urban areas, up to 15 percent of the population may be on welfare. In minority ghetto areas, the figures may reach as high as 50 percent. Administrative costs associated with identifying the needy and checking their eligibility for aid have been criticized. SSI seeks to simplify welfare programs by establishing income levels as the index of need, eliminating the red tape and confusion of present programs, lessening differences in benefit levels, and reducing the burden imposed on the states by the grant-in-aid matching requirements. SSI is a step toward complete federal assumption of all welfare programs, a step favored by many social welfare authorities.

Urban Renewal Programs conducted by cities to prevent the spread of urban blight, to rehabilitate areas that can be restored, and to clear and redevelop slum areas that are beyond repair. The Housing Act of 1949 and subsequent legislation provide for procedures by which cities can submit programs to obtain federal aid. Aid is provided for planning and clearance programs and for public housing. Federal mortgage insurance is made available to private investors in reconstruction and rehabilitation projects. An expansion of the program in 1970 includes "new community development," which can take the form of additions to cities, free-standing new communities, or construction within existing cities. In the Housing and Community Development Act of 1974, Congress undertook a major revision of urban development policy and made urban renewal one aspect of an integrated block grant program for community development. *See also* HOUSING ACT OF 1949, page 376; HOUSING AND COMMUNITY DEVELOPMENT ACT OF 1974, page 377.

Significance Urban renewal is designed to restore rapidly deteriorating cities and to make the city an attractive place in which to live and work. The growth of suburbia has cost cities a good deal in tax resources. Slum areas are a blight on a community and a drain on its financial resources. Suitable housing is needed in most large cities to attract residents and to rehabilitate slum dwellers. Downtown areas need restoring to attract business concerns and customers. Industrial areas need to be developed to provide jobs. The new community development program is designed to accommodate an additional 75 million people by the year 2000. All of these problems, and the need to prevent future blight, are the underlying concerns of the urban renewal program. It represents a major attempt on the part of the national government to gain the cooperation of both local governments and private capital to save the cities. Critics of the urban renewal program charge that it uproots entire neighborhoods and deprives poor people of property in favor of investment capital, and that waste and politics mark the program. The Housing and Community Development Act of 1974 requires cities to demonstrate that they are, in fact, serving the needs of the poor and restoring blighted areas.

Veterans Organizations   Groups organized to promote the interests of former members of the armed forces and their families. The largest and most influential group is the American Legion, with more than 2 million members, followed by the Veterans of Foreign Wars, with over a million members. Both organizations take firm stands on political issues and are basically conservative in outlook. The American Veterans Committee, with less than 30,000 members, supports liberal programs and generally opposes special benefits for veterans. Numerous other veterans organizations are based on religious, ethnic, specific war experiences, or military unit considerations. *See also* PRESSURE GROUP, page 138.

Significance   Veterans organizations have been successful at all levels of government in furthering the economic interests of veterans. Public benefits for veterans include bonuses and pensions, educational aids, civil service preference, loans and insurance, even burial allowances. With the heavy military involvement of the United States in the twentieth century, almost every American family has a veteran. Legislative bodies find it difficult to resist pressure from organized veterans groups. Veterans groups have been particularly active in promoting patriotism and military preparedness.

Vocational Rehabilitation   The training of the physically and mentally handicapped for useful work. The national government provides grants-in-aid to the states for such programs under supervision of the Rehabilitation Services Administration in the Department of Health, Education, and Welfare. Another major program is in the hands of the Veterans Administration which cooperates with various state educational agencies for the training of handicapped veterans.

Significance   Vocational rehabilitation is made available to any handicapped person who can become self-sufficient. If the person can pay for the service, he is required to do so, but those unable to pay are provided free training. The program has been expanded in recent years on the theory that it is better for the individual and for society to rehabilitate the handicapped than to provide a dole. The restored worker is not only able to sustain himself, but also contributes taxes to the community.

Voluntarism   A doctrine that institutions should be supported by voluntary action and contributions, and not by the state. Voluntarism is a major factor in American health, education, and welfare and takes a variety of forms. Examples include health and hospital support (American Cancer Society, Heart Fund, Shriners' Children Hospitals), disaster relief (American Red Cross, volunteer firemen), aid to the destitute (Salvation Army, suicide-prevention centers), aid to the disadvantaged (Big Brothers, settlement houses), church or ethnic groups (Catholic Charities, United Jewish Appeal), and general community charities (United Fund). A large number of persons volunteer their services to aid the disabled, the aged, the mentally ill, and the socially deprived. Many more contribute funds to private charitable causes, supported by generous provisions for tax deductions. Official recognition of voluntary action is also taken by government through the establishment of Action, the independent agency which embraces a number of government-sponsored volunteer programs. *See also* ACTION, page 371.

Significance   Voluntarism is rooted in the belief, strongly held by many Americans, that the private, noncoercive sector of society has a major role to play, particularly in the most sensitive areas of human interaction. It is only recently that government has emerged as a major supporter of the health and welfare of the people. Growth of population, technological developments, urban density and rising costs have led to greater demands for governmental involvement in health programs, educational support services, and welfare programs for the needy. Still, any realistic assessment of health, education, and welfare in the United States must take into account the extraordinary amount of voluntarism and resultant decreases in public costs for many vital services. Many volunteer agencies resemble quasi-public organizations in the sense that the public expects and relies upon their services; this is true, for example, of volunteer firemen and the American Red Cross, and the numerous hospitals supported by private religious or secular groups.

IMPORTANT AGENCIES

Action   An independent agency established in 1971 to bring together a number of voluntary action programs of the national government. Action is headed by a director appointed by the President with Senate consent. Most prominent of the programs brought into Action are the Peace Corps (from the Department of State) and Volunteers in Service to America (from the Office of Economic Opportunity). Other programs include Foster Grandparents and Retired Senior Volunteer Program (from the Department of Health, Education, and Welfare), Office of Volunteer Action (from the Department of Housing and Urban Development), and the Service Corps of Retired Executives and Active Corps of Executives (from the Small Business Administration). *See also* PEACE CORPS, page 412; VOLUNTARISM, page 370; VOLUNTEERS IN SERVICE TO AMERICA, page 373.

Significance   Action seeks to coordinate and exploit the extensive American tradition of voluntary citizen involvement in worthy causes. Action was created through an executive order by President Richard M. Nixon, who argued that a single agency would promote efficiency and encourage freer exchange of ideas and personnel. Opponents claimed that Action would adversely affect domestic poverty projects.

Community Services Administration   An independent agency established by the Economic Opportunity Act of 1964. The Agency, formerly known as the Office of Economic Opportunity in the Executive Office of the President, coordinates federal antipoverty programs and carries on programs of its own. Its stated purpose is to "eliminate the paradox of poverty in the midst of plenty in this Nation by opening to everyone the opportunity for education and training, the opportunity to work, and the opportunity to live in decency and dignity." Among its programs are urban and rural community action, work and training programs, employment and investment incentives, preschool programs, such as Head Start and day care, and provision of health service to the poor. The Office is headed by a director appointed by the President. *See also* COMMUNITY ACTION PROGRAM, page 364; LEGAL SERVICES CORPORATION, page 372.

Significance   The Office of Economic Opportunity and its successor, Community Services Administration, has been controversial from its inception. Basically the controversy centers around the question of the role of government in rooting out the "culture of poverty." Supporters charge that the agency and its programs are poorly funded and do not allow for sufficient participation by the poor. Critics doubt the utility of the agency and its programs in helping the poor, and allege that the programs are dominated by political considerations.

Department of Health, Education, and Welfare (HEW)   A major department of the national government established in 1953 to unify administration of federal activities in the fields of health, education, and social security. The Department is headed by a Secretary who is a member of the Cabinet. Its major operating units include: (1) the Social Security Administration, which administers the Old-Age, Survivors, and Disability Insurance program; (2) the Social and Rehabilitation Service, which administers the categorical aid programs; (3) the Office of Education, which administers grants-in-aid for educational purposes; and (4) The Public Health Service, which carries on far-flung programs in health and hospital care and disease control and research.

Significance   The Department reflects the commitment of the national government to protect the public health and welfare through vast programs of social security, education, and disease prevention. Most of these programs, once highly controversial, are now accepted by both major political parties and by the American people. The Department's budget is second only to the Department of Defense and in numbers of employees it is only behind Defense and the Postal Service.

Department of Housing and Urban Development (HUD)   A major department of Cabinet status, established in 1965, with responsibility for the housing, home finance, and community-development functions of the national government. The Department, headed by a Secretary, has as its major operational units: (1) Housing Production and Mortgage Credit and Federal Housing Commission, which administers programs related to the production and financing of housing both public and private; (2) Federal Insurance Administration, which protects against losses from riots and civil disorders and natural disasters; (3) Community Development, charged with responsibility for urban renewal, model cities, community planning, new communities development, community facilities, and intergovernmental relations; (4) Housing Management, responsible for the social, physical, and financial aspects of housing management; and (5) Equal Opportunity, to promote civil rights in housing and in employment pertaining to housing and urban development.

Significance   Cabinet status for HUD climaxed years of effort to have the problems of metropolitan areas considered at the highest levels of government. It represents a national commitment to meet the growing crises in the highly urbanized areas of housing, urban renewal, and metropolitan planning. With more than 70 percent of the American people living in urban areas, HUD is likely to become an increasingly important center for governmental action programs.

Legal Services Corporation   An independent agency established by Congress in 1974 to make grants and contracts with individuals, law firms, or private organizations to provide legal aid to the poor in noncriminal proceedings. Legal services may be provided in such areas as welfare rights, family problems, and personal finance. Lawsuits involving desegregation of schools, selective service problems, or nontherapeutic abortions are specifically prohibited. The Legal Services Corporation is governed by an eleven-member board appointed by the President and confirmed by the Senate. Advisory councils are established in each state. *See also* COMMUNITY SERVICES ADMINISTRATION, page 371.

Significance The Legal Services Corporation was formerly a program within the Office of Economic Opportunity (OEO). Critics charged that OEO legal services personnel had used their positions to further social activist causes through lawsuits. Consequently, in establishing the Legal Services Corporation as a separate entity, Congress placed strict curbs on political activities of persons associated with the Corporation, forbade funding of independent legal research centers which might become involved in activist political goals, and placed bans on certain kinds of lawsuits. Most bar associations have had "legal aid" services to help poor persons with legal problems, and a number of interest groups provide "pro bono publico" (for the public good) legal services in the interest of social causes. These have not adequately served many persons who are either unaware of their rights or fearful of getting involved with legal processes. The Legal Services Corporation can fill an important need by making services available in poor communities.

Veterans Administration (VA)   An independent agency established in 1930 to coordinate the administration of various laws providing benefits for veterans and their dependents. Included are such programs as compensation for service or nonservice connected disabilities or death, vocational rehabilitation, education, home insurance, life insurance, hospitalization, care of disabled veterans, and burial of veterans. The agency is headed by an administrator appointed by the President with the Senate's consent. *See also* VETERANS ORGANIZATIONS, page 370.

Significance The Veterans Administration's programs represent the aftercost of war. More than 20 million Americans are veterans and, if one includes their families, who are actual or potential beneficiaries, nearly one-half of the American people are concerned with the operations of this agency. Various suggestions to make the VA a part of a major department, such as Health, Education, and Welfare, have met resistance from veterans organizations which prefer the independent status of the VA.

Volunteers in Service to America (VISTA)   A "domestic peace corps" established by the Economic Opportunity Act of 1964 to combat poverty in American communities. VISTA volunteers, paid only a subsistence allowance, work in community action programs, Job Corps and migrant worker camps, Indian reservations, hospitals, and schools. *See also* ECONOMIC OPPORTUNITY ACT, page 374.

Significance VISTA, patterned after the Peace Corps, offers opportunities for Americans to join the "war on poverty." Training programs for volunteers stress field experiences that contribute to program goals. The basic objectives of VISTA are to raise the health and educational levels of poor people and to eradicate the causes of poverty. VISTA is now part of the Action Agency established in 1971 to consolidate a number of government-sponsored volunteer groups.

IMPORTANT CASES

Goldberg v. Kelly, 397 U.S. 254 (1970): Held that welfare benefits may not be terminated without due process. This requires a pretermination hearing with adequate notice, oral presentation, confrontation and cross-examination, right to retain an attorney, an impartial decision maker, and a decision based on rules and evidence adduced in the hearing. The hearing, said the Court, need not have the characteristics of a trial but should have minimal procedural safeguards adapted to the educational and social characteristics of the welfare recipient. *See also* CATEGORICAL ASSISTANCE, page 363; PRIVILEGE, page 77.

Significance The *Goldberg* ruling epitomizes a dramatic new direction in American law that recognizes economic and social benefits as rights rather than privileges. The concept of entitlement to an economic benefit that cannot be arbitrarily withdrawn is common in American law, such as subsidies to businesses and farms or grants of airline routes and television channels; but extension of similar benefits to the poor is a relatively new trend. In 1969, the Court declared that state residence requirements to qualify for welfare violated equal protection by imposing an unreasonable obstacle to the right of the poor to travel freely throughout the land (*Shapiro v. Thompson,* 394 U.S. 618). The Court also held that notice and hearing were essential prior to garnishment of wages (*Sniadach v. Family Finance Corp.,* 395 U.S. 337 [1969]) and prior to eviction from federally assisted housing (*Thorpe v. Housing Authority,* 393 U.S. 268 [1969]).

Social Security Cases: Two cases in which the Supreme Court upheld the Social Security Act of 1935. In *Steward Machine Co. v. Davis,* 301 U.S. 548 (1937), the Court upheld the unemployment insurance feature of the Act. The Court reasoned that the tax for relief of the unemployed was within the power of Congress to provide for the national welfare and that the states were not coerced to join the plan. In *Helvering v. Davis,* 301 U.S. 619 (1937), decided the same day, the Court upheld the Old-Age, Survivors, and Disability Insurance provisions. The Court recognized the broad power of Congress to promote the general welfare and maintained that the scope of the general welfare was for Congress to determine. The Court denied that the tax on payrolls for Old-Age, Survivors, and Disability Insurance benefited only a particular class of persons or invaded the powers of the states. *See also* SOCIAL SECURITY ACT, page 378.

Significance The Social Security Cases involved major interpretations of the general welfare clause of the Constitution. The decisions gave Congress almost unlimited power to tax and spend for whatever purposes it deems necessary to promote the general welfare. These cases established the legal framework for the extensive system of social welfare measures carried on by the national government with the cooperation of state and local governments.

IMPORTANT STATUTES

Economic Opportunity Act of 1964   An act to help the poor become productive citizens through a "war on poverty." The Act places stress on education and training through such programs as the Job Corps, Neighborhood Youth Corps, and work-study programs. Community action programs are encouraged under the Act to stimulate local action to meet the needs of low-income people. Loan programs are made available to farmers and small businessmen. VISTA (Volunteers in Service to America) has been established by the Act to aid in community welfare projects. Programs are administered by the Community Services Administration (formerly the Office of Economic Opportunity), the Department of Labor, the Department of Health, Education, and Welfare, and the Action Agency. *See also* COMMUNITY ACTION PROGRAM, page 364; COMMUNITY SERVICES ADMINISTRATION, page 371; JOB CORPS, page 365; VOLUNTEERS IN SERVICE TO AMERICA, page 373.

Significance The Economic Opportunity Act is aimed at overcoming the causes of poverty by encouraging both community and individual programs of education and training for employment. While the Act provides for aid to older persons, stress is placed on programs for the young, including preschool children and college youth. Opponents of the "war on poverty" have criticized it for not involving sufficient numbers of low-income people and for its potential control by political machines. More basic criticism is aimed at the underlying purposes of the program and the enlarged role of the national government in meeting social and economic problems.

Elementary and Secondary Education Act of 1965 The first general aid-to-education law enacted by Congress. It provides federal aid to most of the nation's school districts. The Act authorizes aid on the basis of the number of children from low-income families in each district. It applies to both public and nonpublic schools. Other major provisions authorize grants for textbooks and library materials for all schools, educational centers to provide programs that individual schools cannot afford, and grants for improvement of educational research and administration. In extending the Act in 1974, Congress revised the aid formula so as to shift aid from wealthier urban states to poorer, rural ones. Federal aid was also extended to programs of emerging importance such as reading, career education, and adult education. The 1974 law also provides for parent and student access to school records so as to protect the student's right to privacy. In its most controversial action, Congress declared the neighborhood school to be the proper basis for pupil assignment and sharply restricted the use of bussing to achieve racial integration. *See also* FEDERAL AID TO EDUCATION, page 364.

Significance The Elementary and Secondary Education Act of 1965 is a landmark in relations between the nation and the states, representing a commitment on the part of both to nationwide equality of educational opportunity. Numerous past efforts to enact such legislation failed because of fear of federal control of education, racial segregation in schools, and controversy over aid to nonpublic, church-related schools. Many opponents of federal aid were defeated in the Democratic landslide of 1964, the school segregation issue was no longer legally relevant, and the church-state issue was overcome by basing the school aid formula on benefiting low-income children rather than the parochial schools. Legal questions on federal aid to nonpublic schools, however, remain to be tested. Extensive de facto racial segregation has given rise to persistent problems in the administration of the Act. Whatever its merits, it is clear that federal aid to education has involved the national government in the education of the nation's children.

Higher Education Act of 1965   An act to broaden higher education opportunities through federal aid. Major programs include scholarships, work-study programs, guaranteed low-interest loans, aid to developing colleges, aid to college and university community service programs with emphasis on urban problems, aid for library resources, a National Teachers Corps to work in slum areas, and aid for fellowships for present and future teachers. In addition, the Act increased aid under the Higher Education Facilities Act of 1963, which authorized grants and loans for construction of public and private academic facilities.

Significance   The Higher Education Act of 1965 is a major extension of existing federal aids to higher education. A notable innovation provides scholarships, grants and loans for general undergraduate education. The Act's major purpose is to overcome rising costs of higher education for low- and middle-income families. Soaring and then declining enrollments in colleges and universities have strained the resources of most institutions of higher learning, while the desire to secure a college education has become common in all classes of the population. The Higher Education Act, together with the Elementary and Secondary Education Act of 1965, commits the national government to extensive involvement in education from the preschool level through graduate education. The Supreme Court upheld construction grants to church-related colleges under the Higher Education Facilities Act, but voided a provision that would authorize use of such buildings for religious purposes after twenty years (*Tilton v. Richardson,* 403 U.S. 672 [1971]).

Housing Act of 1949   An act providing for federal assistance to local governments for low-rent public housing, slum clearance, and urban renewal. The Housing Act of 1949 continued a program, begun under the Housing Act of 1937, that had been interrupted by World War II. The 1949 Act called for the construction of 810,000 housing units over a period of six years, but Congress reduced this figure in subsequent legislation. In amendments to the Act since 1949, additional housing units have been authorized and increased emphasis given to urban renewal and new community development. Various specialized housing programs have been instituted, such as those for college dormitories, housing for the aged, and rent subsidies for the poor. Funds have also been made available for municipal public works, such as sewers and transportation. In 1974, Congress consolidated many of the programs and authorized block grants to local governments. The Department of Housing and Urban Development supervises administration of the Act. *See also* HOUSING AND COMMUNITY DEVELOPMENT ACT OF 1974, page 377; PUBLIC HOUSING, page 368; URBAN RENEWAL, page 369.

Significance   In the Housing Act of 1949, Congress declared its goal to be "a decent home and a suitable living environment for every American family." The national government is now committed to a "total" housing program that takes account of all aspects of community development. These programs result from an acute housing shortage for low-income families, slums and blight, and increasing urbanization which multiplies the service needs of millions of city dwellers and suburbanites. Many persons object to the intrusion of the national government into these areas, but Congress has continued to expand existing programs, encouraging the use of private capital when possible.

Housing and Community Development Act of 1974   A major revision and extension of urban development programs, which consolidates ten categorical programs into block grants for comprehensive community development, and establishes an extensive rental subsidy program for low- and moderate-income families. The Act also continues public housing programs, mortgage credit, and expanded aid for rural housing development. Each eligible community is apportioned funds based on a formula that takes into account the ratio of poverty, population, and housing needs. Cities, in turn, must survey their needs more accurately than in the past, and avoid undue concentrations of low-income housing and people in special neighborhoods. Additionally, the Act puts new emphasis on cash subsidies for rentals in nonpublic housing. Public participation in formulation of development plans is required. Block grants may be used in the discretion of the community for urban renewal, model cities, housing code enforcement, open spaces, neighborhood facilities, water and sewer facilities, planning, and aid to displaced families. *See also* HOUSING ACT OF 1949, page 376; PUBLIC HOUSING, page 368; URBAN RENEWAL, page 369.

Significance The Housing and Community Development Act of 1974 was the first major housing bill passed in many years and gives metropolitan areas, in particular, unprecedented freedom in deciding how to spend federal funds on urban redevelopment. The Act is designed to provide stability to a wide variety of programs which had been characterized by waste, politics, and confusion. Because the Act requires communities to develop comprehensive plans to receive the block grants, and to take into consideration both physical and human factors involved in the rehabilitation of decaying communities, the Act could chart a new course for national-local relations in community development.

National Defense Education Act of 1958   An act to encourage education in science, mathematics, engineering, languages, humanities, social sciences, and teacher education. The Act provides for loans to needy college students, with preference given to those pursuing those courses of study; one-half the loan is forgiven if the student teaches for five years after graduation. In addition, the Act provides funds for graduate fellowships, and for public schools to purchase educational equipment and to improve guidance and testing services.

Significance Congress enacted the National Defense Education Act in response to Soviet achievements in the field of science. This started a trend of greater national involvement in education. The Act is designed to serve national security needs by equalizing educational opportunities throughout the nation in critical subject matter fields. In order to meet the major objections to federal aid to education, the Act specifically provides that no national official may exercise any control over curriculum or personnel in any school system.

National Mental Health Act of 1946   A nationwide program for the care and treatment of the mentally ill. The Act provides for grants-in-aid to the states for psychiatric personnel, community psychiatric services, and research into prevention and care of mental illness. The Act is administered by the Public Health Service in the Department of Health, Education, and Welfare.

Significance Mental health is one of the most pressing health problems in the United States. Though more than half the hospital beds are occupied by the mentally ill, an acute shortage of trained personnel and facilities exists. Much progress has been made since the passage of the

National Mental Health Act. The national government has also taken action to provide grants for medical education, hospital construction and for the control and treatment of other serious diseases such as tuberculosis, cancer, heart diseases, and drug and alcohol abuse.

Social Security Act of 1935   The basic social welfare legislation embodying social insurance, public assistance, and child health and welfare services. Social insurance programs include Old-Age, Survivors, and Disability Insurance, Medicare, and unemployment insurance. Public assistance is provided under the categorical assistance program to the needy aged, blind, permanently and totally disabled, and to dependent children. Child health and welfare services are provided under the Act for maternal care, crippled children, and general child welfare services. With the exception of the Old-Age, Survivors, and Disability Insurance and Medicare programs, which are financed and administered exclusively by the national government, all others are administered in cooperation with the states. Responsibility for overall supervision rests with the Department of Health, Education, and Welfare. In addition, the Social Security Act provides for widespread public health services through grants to the states under supervision of the Department of Health, Education, and Welfare. *See also* SOCIAL SECURITY CASES, page 374; SUPPLEMENTAL SECURITY INCOME, page 368.

Significance   The Social Security Act is the most comprehensive social welfare legislation passed in the United States. The program grew out of the experience of the Great Depression and reflected a basic change in public attitudes toward the needy and the role of the government. The Act, at first highly controversial, is now generally accepted by the American people; both major political parties have expanded the scope of benefits available under the law. The partnership of the national and state governments in the administration of the Act provides a leading example of cooperative federalism in action to meet common national problems. The movement now is toward complete national assumption of welfare programs.

16 Foreign Policy and International Affairs

Aggression The use of armed force by a state against the sovereignty, territorial integrity, or political independence of another state. Much of the literature of international law is concerned with the problem of identifying aggression and differentiating it from self-defense. The cold war has been characterized by nations arming and concluding alliances to protect themselves from aggression. The United Nations collective security system was established to protect states from aggression, or to deal with aggression collectively, if it should occur. *See also* COLLECTIVE SECURITY, page 383; SANCTIONS, page 405.

Significance The community of nations has seldom been able to agree on a definition of what constitutes aggression. On occasion, however, international bodies have identified and fixed responsibility for aggression. For example, individuals were punished for the crimes of waging aggressive war and for committing acts against humanity in the post-World War II Nuremberg and Tokyo trials of Nazi and Japanese war leaders. The United Nations Charter does not define aggression; aggression has occurred when an authorized organ of the world organization makes such a determination through its voting procedure. Such was the case in 1950, when the Security Council branded North Korea an aggressor. The United Nations Special Committee on the Question of Defining Aggression in 1974 submitted its objective criteria to be used in deciding whether acts of aggression have been committed. Extensive Assembly debates have been carried on, but final agreement by the world community has not been reached except for agreement that the Security Council must continue to make the determination of when aggression has been committed.

Alliance A multilateral agreement by states to improve their power position by joining together in defense of their common interests. Most alliances are now characterized by an agreement to regard "an attack upon any member of the alliance as an attack upon all." Hence, an alliance is a way of informing friend and foe that an attack against any individual nation will precipitate a general war. Balance of power systems tend to encourage the growth of alliances. *See also* BALANCE OF POWER, page 382; NORTH ATLANTIC TREATY ORGANIZATION (NATO), page 400.

Significance Throughout most of American history, President George Washington's advice to "steer clear of permanent alliances" was carefully observed. Since the advent of the cold war, however, the United States has assumed a position of leadership in the anti-Communist world, rejecting its time-honored policy of isolationism, and has become the world's leading advocate of security through defensive alliances. Alliances have been concluded with over forty nations to forestall a Communist attack, or to meet it if it should occur. Mutual security alliances include the Rio Treaty, the North Atlantic Treaty (NATO), the Southeast Asia Treaty (SEATO), a trilateral treaty with Australia and New Zealand (ANZUS), and bilateral pacts with Japan, the Philippines, Nationalist China, and South Korea.

Alliance for Progress A program of foreign aid for Latin America developed by the Kennedy Administration. Congress authorized $500 million in 1961 to initiate the program. Latin American countries—all except Cuba—have participated in Alliance programs. Continued aid to these nations is offered if internal economic reforms are instituted and if social progress moves forward with economic development. The Inter-American Development Bank was created in 1961 to play a major role in implementing the program through development loans. Its efforts are supplemented by the Development Loan Fund, the Export-Import Bank, and the Agency for International Development. *See also* ORGANIZATION OF AMERICAN STATES, page 401.

Significance The emphasis in the Alliance for Progress program is on securing economic and social progress in Latin America through close hemispheric cooperation. American help is intended to aid these countries in getting started on the road to self-sustaining growth. Closer economic ties leading to some measure of economic integration have been encouraged by the program. Additional objectives include the strengthening of political relations through the Organization of American States (OAS) and the collective security system under the Rio Treaty. By the 1970s, much of the vitality and early enthusiasm for the Alliance programs had disappeared. The vast amounts of private investment capital anticipated by the program have not been transferred to the Latin American region.

Ambassador The top-ranking diplomat sent by the government of a sovereign state as its official representative to another state. An ambassador is the head of an embassy in the capital city of the foreign state. Official relations between governments are carried on mainly through an exchange of ambassadors. In the United States, an ambassador is the personal representative of the President in his role as chief of state. *See also* DIPLOMATIC IMMUNITY, page 387; PERSONA NON GRATA, page 402.

Significance In the United States, ambassadors are appointed by the President and confirmed by the Senate. Personal and political considerations, such as campaign contributions and party service, may be important in making such appointments. The trend, however, is in the direction of appointing foreign service career diplomats. Because an ambassador is the personal representative of the President, he is charged with implementing the foreign policy of the administration in power in the United States. Consequently some ambassadors, especially those assigned to the more important posts, are replaced after a new President takes office.

ANZUS Pact A tripartite security treaty concluded in 1951 among Australia, New Zealand, and the United States. The ANZUS treaty, which has no terminal date, declares that an attack upon any of the members would constitute a common danger, and each would act to meet it according to its constitutional processes. *See also* ALLIANCE, page 379.

Significance ANZUS is an attempt to provide security against Communist encroachment in a large area of the Pacific. The Pact reflects a growing dependence upon the United States for leadership in providing security in the Pacific. In 1954, the security system of the ANZUS Pact was expanded into the Southeast Asia Treaty Organization (SEATO) defense arrangement, but the ANZUS Pact still remains in force.

Appeasement   A term used to describe concessions made to a warlike potential enemy in the hope that they will satiate his appetite for expansion, and that peace will be secure. Prime Minister Neville Chamberlain's agreement at Munich in 1938 to accept Adolf Hitler's demand for the partition of Czechoslovakia in exchange for a vague guarantee of "peace in our time" is a classic example of appeasement. *See also* DIPLOMACY, page 387.

Significance The fear of appeasement makes diplomatic negotiations extremely difficult. Successful diplomacy requires concessions from both sides. Frequently, the cry of "appeasement" can sabotage a diplomat's position. Concessions are played up, while counterconcessions are overlooked. The problem of appeasement is particularly acute when diplomats are engaged in "open" or "public" negotiations.

Arbitration   A method of settling a dispute between states by judges selected by the parties to the dispute. The judges, who have standing as international jurists, must render a decision or award based on international law, and the parties agree in advance to accept the decision as binding. Arbitration dates back many centuries, but its modern use began with the famous *Alabama Claims* settlement between the United States and Great Britain growing out of Civil War controversies. In arbitration, disputing parties enter into a *compromis* or agreement that specifies the issues to be resolved and procedures to be followed. *See also* PACIFIC SETTLEMENT OF DISPUTES, page 402.

Significance Many conflicts between states involving their secondary interests have been solved through arbitration. Generally, states are reluctant to submit disputes involving their *primary* national interests to an arbitration tribunal. Contrary to popular myth, states that have accepted arbitration have almost always abided by the decision of the tribunal. The main weakness of arbitration is the difficulty of getting states to accept it as a means of settling their dispute.

Attache   A technical specialist who functions as an official with diplomatic rank and who is attached to an embassy or foreign mission. Attachés specialize in political, military, economic, agricultural, informational, labor, aviation, petroleum, and cultural fields. *See also* DIPLOMACY, page 387.

Significance Attachés seek to establish good relations with similar officials in the country to which they are accredited. They also comprise the eyes and ears of the United States in gaining specialized information concerning the conditions that exist in that country.

Balance of Payments   The net balance between total income and expenditures of a nation in its business and trade relations with the rest of the world. A balance of payments includes all debit and credit monetary transactions, such as imports and exports of goods, tourist expenditures, investments, and income from investments. The balance of trade that includes all transactions involving tangible goods is often the key component of the balance of payments. *See also* ECONOMIC NATIONALISM, page 389.

Significance   Nations usually seek to maintain a "favorable" balance of payments. This means that they strive to increase income over expenditure, to the extent that balances of foreign currencies and gold can be built up. Nations with "unfavorable" or deficit balances are like individuals who spend beyond their income. In the short run, this situation may not be serious. If it persists, corrective action must be taken. This may take the form of higher tariffs, exchange controls, export subsidies, austerity programs, currency depreciation, or other kinds of state action. The United States has suffered from a deficit balance of payments for many years, resulting in an outflow of gold and sizable dollar balances into foreign hands. The balance of payments is an excellent analytical tool for determining the relative economic position of nations.

Balance of Power   A system of power alignments in which peace and security may be maintained through an equilibrium of power between rival blocs. States participating in a balance of power system enter into alliances with friendly states in attempts to protect and enhance their power positions. *See also* ALLIANCE, page 379; NORTH ATLANTIC TREATY ORGANIZATION (NATO), page 400.

Significance   If a balance of power works well, peace may be maintained for a period of years. So long as a near equilibrium is thought to exist, neither side will dare to launch an attack upon the other. However, with the military buildup characteristic of a balance of power system, there is always the danger that war will result from border incidents, miscalculations, or causes other than planned attack. Historically, balance of power systems have kept the peace for short and long periods, but have often deteriorated into war. For more than thirty years a worldwide balance of power system has existed between the Communist and capitalist world camps, resulting in the greatest armaments race in the history of the world.

Bipartisanship   Close cooperation between the two major American political parties in dealing with foreign problems. Bipartisanship usually takes the form of frequent consultations between the leaders of both parties in Congress, and between these leaders and the President. During time of war or threat of war, when bipartisanship typically comes into vogue, the President may appoint members of the opposition party to key Cabinet posts.

Significance   Bipartisanship is a means by which a democracy can overcome its divisions and present a solid front to the world. "Partisanship ends at the water's edge" is a frequently repeated description of bipartisanship. Disadvantages resulting from such cooperation include the loss of the function of the "loyal opposition" within the government, and the lack of critical discussion of vital issues. Flexibility is usually reduced, a solid wall of consensus may develop, freezing all options except those put forth by the Administration, and criticism of government policy may be equated with disloyalty.

Central Treaty Organization (CENTO)　A Middle East alliance adhered to by Britain, Iran, Pakistan, and Turkey. Originally known as the Baghdad Pact, the name was changed to CENTO, and headquarters were moved from Baghdad to Ankara when a neutralist government seized power in Iraq in 1958 and withdrew from the alliance. *See also* ALLIANCE, page 379.

Significance　CENTO was established on American initiative to provide a mutual security shield against Communist expansion in the Middle East. The United States participates in CENTO planning, is a member of CENTO committees, and provides military support to CENTO members, but has never joined the alliance. American guarantees of assistance to CENTO members in case of attack, however, are covered by NATO, SEATO, and, in the case of Iran, by a bilateral pact. Growing neutralism among pact members, Britain's withdrawal from the Persian Gulf, and a growing Arab arms race in the Middle East have tended to reduce solidarity within the CENTO arrangement.

Chargé d'Affaires　The Foreign Service official temporarily placed in charge of an embassy or legation in the absence of the ambassador or minister. *See also* DIPLOMACY, page 387.

Significance　When the United States seeks to indicate displeasure with the actions of a foreign government, but does not wish to take the serious step of severing diplomatic relations, it usually withdraws its ambassador. Under such conditions, the chargé d'affaires assumes a position of grave importance. In this way, a "listening post" to the foreign country is kept open, as are diplomatic channels.

Charter of the United Nations　A multilateral treaty that serves as the constitution for the United Nations Organization. The Charter was drawn up and signed at San Francisco on June 26, 1945; it was ratified by fifty-one nations and put into effect on October 24, 1945, since designated United Nations Day. The document consists of a preamble and 111 articles that provide for the creation of six major organs and the powers to be exercised by each. (*See also* Index: United Nations.)

Significance　The Charter represents an effort by the community of nations to establish norms of international conduct by outlawing war, providing for the peaceful settlement of international disputes, and encouraging cooperation among nations in dealing with economic and social problems. Like the United States Constitution, the Charter has proved to be a flexible document, subject to broad interpretations. Without this feature of adaptability, the United Nations would probably have collapsed under the impact of the cold war. For many years, the Charter had to be adapted to deal with East-West cold war problems, and more recently, to deal with North-South conflicts involving Third World states and the industrialized states.

Collective Security　A worldwide security system by which all or most nations agree in advance to take collective action against any state or states that break the peace by committing aggression. Collective security is based on the assumption that, normally, no nation or group of nations would dare to challenge the power of the world community, but, if an attack should occur, all nations would honor their commitments to take collective police action. The United Nations embodies the concept of collective security. Under Chapter VII of its Charter, the organization can take such action, including military, as may be necessary to preserve world peace. Primary responsibility is vested in the five great powers (U.S., USSR, Britain, France, China), each having the veto power in the Security Council. Since 1950, the General Assembly also has been empowered under the Uniting for Peace Resolution to authorize collective security action if the Security Council is stymied with a veto. Collective security is also used sometimes to describe alliances established under a balance of power system. *See also* SANCTIONS, page 405; SECURITY COUNCIL, page 407.

Significance The first universal collective security arrangement, the League of Nations, broke down in the 1930s under the impact of aggressions by the Axis powers, Germany, Italy, and Japan. Collective security military sanctions were invoked by the United Nations in 1950 against North Korea for its attack upon South Korea. Although this police action left much to be resolved, the United Nations was successful in halting the aggression. In 1956, the world organization was faced simultaneously with an attack by the Soviet Union upon Hungary and an attack by Britain, France, and Israel against Egypt. Although the United Nations was able to cope with the latter successfully, in the Hungarian case only moral sanctions were employed because of a fear of general war. The organization refrained from undertaking any form of collective security action during the Vietnam war, and it has preferred to handle Middle East conflicts as international disputes rather than as acts of aggression.

Comity   Courtesies extended between nations in their formal relations with each other. Examples of comity include extradition of fugitives in absence of a treaty, and immunity of diplomats. *See also* INTERNATIONAL LAW, page 395.

Significance Most acts of comity between nations are based on customary international practice. It is important that nations abide by certain principles of conduct so that their relations can be harmonious and fruitful. Comity is not regarded as binding in character or enforceable in court. Before comity became accepted practice, diplomacy was hampered by disputes over matters of prestige, honor, and precedence in negotiations.

Comparative Advantage   A theory, first advanced by David Ricardo in 1817, that explains why each country tends to specialize in the production of those commodities for which its costs are relatively lowest. The concept of comparative advantage or comparative cost modified Adam Smith's theory of an international specialization based on *absolute* national advantage. In rebutting Smith's doctrine, Ricardo noted that few countries have a clear cost superiority in the production of goods for the world market, and that labor, capital, and enterprise are relatively immobile internationally and are unlikely to move to those places where absolute advantage could be maintained. *See also* FREE TRADE, page 391; LAISSEZ-FAIRE, page 11.

Significance The Ricardian comparative advantage doctrine has served as a theoretical base for positing an international division of labor to maximize trade. According to the theory, if each country specializes in the production of those articles of commerce that it can produce most efficiently and trades with other countries to obtain the things it needs, all will be likely to enjoy a higher standard of living. These ideas continue to serve as the basic American rationale for supporting freer international trade.

Consul An official appointed by a government to reside in a foreign country in order to assist citizens of the appointing state and to advance their commercial interests. American consuls are members of the Foreign Service. *See also* DIPLOMACY, page 387.

Significance The United States maintains consulates in most of the important commercial cities of the world. Responsibilities of an American consul include jurisdiction over American vessels (the settling of shipboard disputes, sanitary inspections, sending mutinous and shipwrecked sailors home), granting visas to foreigners seeking entry into the United States, and opening up new business and trade opportunities.

Containment A general policy adopted in 1947 by the Truman Administration to build "situations of strength" around the globe in order to contain Communist power within its existing boundaries. Underlying the containment policy was a belief that, if Soviet expansion could be stopped, communism would collapse of its own internal weaknesses. The policy was first applied in the Truman Doctrine of 1947 in a program of military aid to Greece and Turkey. *See also* TRUMAN DOCTRINE, page 410.

Significance Under general guidelines of containment policy, the Truman Administration embarked on vast new programs that included: (1) rearmament; (2) establishment of military bases around the world; (3) mutual security alliances with friendly powers; (4) an economic aid program to rebuild war-shattered economies in Western Europe (Marshall Plan); and (5) a program of technical and economic aid to underdeveloped countries. Through these and other programs, Communist expansion was slowed down but not completely halted. American actions in Korea and South Vietnam were based on the policy of containing Communist power.

Convergence Theory The view that capitalist and communist systems are evolving in their economic functions and modes of operations in increasingly similar ways. Ultimately, the convergence theory holds, the two systems will become almost indistinguishable in their basic forms, and consequently will no longer constitute a threat to each other. Both systems are being shaped by the same forces of science and technology, cybernetics and automation, industrialization and urbanization, and by cultures shaped by the space age. *See also* CAPITALISM, page 3; COMMUNISM, page 4.

Significance The evidence on which the convergence theory is based includes the growing role of the government in capitalist states in subsidizing, regulating, and promoting the "free" economy, the increasing collective control of private corporations and divorcing of management from ownership, and the growing need for governmental rationing of scarce energy sources and supplies. On the Communist side, changes in recent years include increasing decentralization of economic decision making, more emphasis on production of consumer goods, growing competition among producers, and cash incentives for increased productivity. Some movement toward the creation of a "market economy" governed by supply-demand forces has occurred in several Communist states. Critics of the convergence theory, however, hold that the gulf that exists between the two systems is too large and fundamental to be overcome by a few surface similarities.

De Facto Recognition   The preliminary recognition of a new state or government by another state. De facto recognition is usually followed by *de jure,* or full, legal recognition with exchange of ambassadors. De facto recognition also refers to a theory advanced by some international jurists (sometimes called the declarative theory) that new states and governments should be recognized if, in fact, they do exist, regardless of how they came into being or of their political nature. *See also* RECOGNITION, page 403.

Significance   Premature granting of recognition to a revolutionary regime, or continued withholding of it from a government on ideological grounds, has produced much turmoil in the world. Communist China and East Germany were subjects of recognition controversies for many years. Great Britain maintained de facto recognition of Communist China for more than twenty years without an exchange of ambassadors. The United States withheld recognition from Communist China for many years, communicating with it through other nations and in conversations between the ambassadors of the two countries in Warsaw. In 1973, the Nixon Administration granted de facto recognition by opening a liaison office in Peking, but continued recognition of Taiwan ruled out full *de jure* recognition by the United States.

De Jure Recognition   Full legal recognition of a new state or government by another state, usually accompanied by an exchange of ambassadors or ministers. *De jure* recognition also refers to a theory advanced by some international jurists (sometimes called the constitutive theory) that only those states and governments that have come into existence through peaceful, constitutional means are deserving of recognition. *See also* RECOGNITION, page 403.

Significance   The *de jure* recognition theory is used mainly by those nations that seek to preserve the status quo in the world. In an ideological struggle, such as the present day cold war, rigid theories frequently give way to expediency as each side uses its power to recognize or to withhold recognition as a diplomatic weapon. Many nations, including the United States, refused to extend *de jure* recognition to Communist China for many years. Beginning with the Wilson Administration, the United States has granted or withheld recognition on the basis of national interest considerations as determined by the President, but currently American policy is moving toward recognition of almost all states and governments.

Détente   A French diplomatic term that describes a condition of an easing of confrontations and reduced strain between two or more countries. A period of détente offers an improved environment which may contribute to the resolution of specific issues or reduce the tensions stemming from the political problems that created the hostile relationship. A détente may result from understandings reached between heads of state at a summit meeting, from concluding a major treaty, or from changes in basic strategies and tactics of the states involved. *See also* DIPLOMACY, page 387; STRATEGIC ARMS LIMITATION TALKS, page 408.

Significance   Achievement of a measure of détente between the United States and the Soviet Union, and between the United States and the Peoples Republic of China, constituted the major foreign policy achievements of the Nixon and Ford administrations during the first half of the 1970s decade. American-Soviet détente was initiated through personal summit diplomacy involving President Richard M. Nixon and Communist Party Secretary Leonid Brezhnev. American-Chinese détente began with conversations between President Nixon and Chinese Premier Chou

En-lai and Communist Party Chairman Mao Tse-tung. The Soviet-American and Chinese-American détentes reflect the exploding costs and dangers of the nuclear arms race, the belief that improved relations and increased trade will benefit both sides, general acceptance of peaceful coexistence as a working diplomatic construct, and deteriorating relations between the Soviet Union and Communist China, that have encouraged both to seek improved relations with the United States. The period of détente involves a major shift in foreign policy away from the ideas of containment, the Truman Doctrine, and the cold war. It has resulted in American troop withdrawals from Indochina, in great power consultation over Middle Eastern issues, in scientific exchanges in such fields as cancer research, weather forecasting, and space probes, and in SALT negotiations and agreements to limit nuclear weapons' systems.

Diplomacy   The total process by means of which states carry on political relations with each other. The machinery of diplomacy includes a policy-making foreign office (Department of State in the United States) and diplomatic missions abroad (Foreign Service). Diplomacy may be carried on through open or conference negotiations or in secret. Occasionally diplomacy is undertaken by heads of state, a process commonly called "summit" diplomacy. *See also* APPEASEMENT, page 381; DIPLOMATIC PRIVILEGES AND IMMUNITIES, page 387; DOLLAR DIPLOMACY, page 387; PACIFIC SETTLEMENT OF DISPUTES, page 402; QUID PRO QUO, page 403.

Significance   Diplomacy is an art that can be mastered only by skilled negotiators. A good diplomat knows how, when, and what to compromise and how to achieve maximum benefit from compromise. In critical situations, war may result if diplomacy fails. Diplomacy contributes to an orderly system of international relations and is the key technique used in the peaceful settlement of international disputes.

Diplomatic Privileges and Immunities   Under international law, ambassadors and other diplomatic officials enjoy special rights and are immune from the jurisdiction of the state to which they are accredited. The embassy grounds may not be trespassed upon by local officials unless permission is granted by the diplomat or by his government. The diplomat, his family, and his official staff are immune from arrest and from civil jurisdiction unless his own government waives this immunity. *See also* DIPLOMACY, page 387; PERSONA NON GRATA, page 402.

Significance   The purpose of diplomatic immunity is to ensure that the diplomat will have the freedom to carry on effectively the relations between the two states. Though not subject to the laws of the state to which he is accredited, he nevertheless is expected to abide by them under normal conditions. A diplomat who misuses his immunity may be reported to his superiors for discipline or, in severe cases, his recall may be demanded by the government of the state to which he is accredited, and he may be declared *persona non grata*.

Dollar Diplomacy   A term used historically by Latin Americans to show their disapproval of the role the American government and giant American corporations have played in using economic, diplomatic, and military power to open up foreign markets and to exploit the people of these under-developed countries. Under the Roosevelt Corollary of the Monroe Doctrine, American marines were frequently sent into countries of Central America. Protectorates were established over Cuba, Haiti, Nicaragua, and Santo Domingo in the early part of the twentieth century. The term, dollar diplomacy, may also be used in the contemporary world to describe any use of a state's economic, political, or military power to further the economic interests of its citizens or large business enterprises in foreign lands. *See also* GOOD NEIGHBOR POLICY, page 392.

Significance American relations with Latin America improved with the inauguration of the Good Neighbor policy in the 1930s and the establishment of the Alliance for Progress aid program in 1961. Mutual solving of problems through the Organization of American States has further improved the position of the United States with Latin America. Yet reservoirs of ill-feeling remain and are exploited by political leaders unfriendly to the United States. New contemporary forms of economic imperialism, which use political and economic pressures rather than military interventions and are carried on by large powerful American corporations, have also tended to weaken relations and to recall earlier days of dollar diplomacy for Latin Americans.

Domino Theory   The doctrine which assumes that if some key nation or geographical region falls into Communist control, a string of other nations will subsequently topple "like a row of dominoes." The Domino Theory was applied by President Dwight D. Eisenhower and his top advisers in 1954 to describe the dangers of Communist expansion in Asia if Indochina were to fall. *See also* CONTAINMENT, page 385.

Significance The Domino Theory has been expounded periodically since 1954 by top American leaders who used it as justification for expanding military programs in Southeast Asia. Originally applied to all of Indochina, the doctrine was subsequently linked to South Vietnam as the key state in the region by the Johnson Administration, which intervened in the latter half of the 1960s with over one-half million American troops to keep that "first domino" from falling. President Richard M. Nixon, who as Vice President in the Eisenhower Administration was one of the first to apply the Domino Theory to Indochina, refrained from invoking it during his own tenure in the White House. President Gerald R. Ford, however, reinvoked the theory in 1975 in holding that, if the United States permitted the Communists to win in Indochina, American alliance guarantees for other small nations would no longer be credible, and a series of Communist victories could be expected. Critics of the theory charge that the Indochinese wars have been largely indigenous in nature, that no such monolithic force as "world communism" exists, and that the theory is used as a propaganda scare tactic to try to justify unwarranted intervention policies.

Economic and Social Council (ECOSOC)   A major organ of the United Nations concerned with promoting higher standards of living and social justice throughout the world. The Council includes twenty-seven members elected by the General Assembly, nine chosen each year for three-year terms. Responsibilities include: (1) coordinating the activities of the Specializd Agencies, such as the World Health Organization (WHO) and the Food and Agriculture Organization (FAO); (2) administering United Nations functions in economic, social, educational, cultural, and related areas; (3) promoting worldwide observance of human rights and fundamental freedoms. *See also* CHARTER OF THE UNITED NATIONS, page 383.

Significance The Economic and Social Council has successfully coordinated the operations of diverse agencies in seeking to solve pressing social and economic problems. ECOSOC has established regional Economic Commissions for Asia and the Far East (ECAFE), Europe (ECE),

Africa (ECA), and Latin America (ECLA) to make comprehensive studies and recommendations on how economic conditions can be improved. It has also established various commissions to study international problems, including: Fiscal, Human Rights, Narcotic Drugs, Population, Social, Statistical, Status of Women, and Transport and Communications.

Economic Nationalism   An economic policy by which a nation seeks to attain economic prosperity or to correct a disequilibrium in its balance of payments by protecting the home market and/or opening up foreign markets through unilateral or bilateral governmental action. It is the opposite of a multilateral trading system with free flow of trade and free convertibility of currencies. It is characterized by extensive governmental control of trade and the subjection of economic matters to overriding considerations of political or military policy. Techniques employed by states pursuing policies of economic nationalism include: (1) austerity programs; (2) barter arrangements; (3) currency depreciation; (4) exchange controls; (5) export subsidies; (6) licensing; (7) quota restrictions; and (8) tariffs. *See also* TARIFF, page 409.

Significance   A state cannot normally pursue a policy of economic nationalism without inciting retaliatory action from other states that have suffered harm from such policies. The great danger is that, once started, the process tends to escalate, with action and counteraction building up to the point of stifling most trade. This is what happened in the 1930s, when the Smoot-Hawley Tariff Act raised tariff rates to the highest point in American history in an effort to protect the home market from foreign competition. The action touched off extensive retaliation which precipitated a world trade crisis. Today, bloc trading systems, such as the European Economic Community (Common Market) and the Soviet bloc, tend to reduce restrictive trade practices among member nations but to encourage increasing economic warfare between blocs.

Executive Agreement   An international agreement between the President and foreign heads of state that, unlike a treaty, does not require Senate consent. Most notably, trade agreements are concluded under powers granted to the President by Congress. Others are concluded by the President acting under his constitutional powers over foreign relations. The Constitution makes no explicit provision for executive agreements. *See also* EXECUTIVE AGREEMENT, page 203; TREATY, PAGE 410.

Significance   Legally, an executive agreement is similar to a treaty. In recent years, the trend has been toward more agreements, fewer treaties. For example, in 1930, 11 agreements and 25 treaties were concluded; in 1958, there were 182 agreements and 3 treaties; in 1968, more than 200 agreements and 16 treaties. By 1975, the United States was party to almost 1,000 treaties and to more than 4,000 executive agreements. Advantages of the executive agreement include avoidance of the power of the Senate to cripple or kill a treaty, and the maintenance of secrecy when desirable, as in a wartime agreement. Disadvantages include the frequent need for further implementation of the agreement by *both* houses of Congress through statutes and appropriations. When secrecy is involved, congressional and public suspicions may be aroused. When substantial public support is needed, presidents usually fall back on the treaty procedure. Executive agreements concluded by presidents in recent years, without congressional consent, have committed the nation to military action in Indochina and provided for the sale of wheat to the Soviet Union on terms that cost the American taxpayer $300 million in subsidies and contributed to shortages of food and inflation of food prices. As a result of such agreements, Congress adopted the Case Amendment in 1972 that requires the President to inform Congress of every foreign commitment he makes.

Extradition   Return by one nation to another of a person accused of a crime. The extradition process resembles that of interstate rendition, which occurs within the United States. In the international field, extradition usually depends upon treaty arrangements between the two nations concerned. Some international jurists regard it as a matter of reciprocal interest covered by customary international law in the absence of any treaty. *See also* INTERSTATE RENDITION, page 38.

Significance   Because there is no international criminal law, without extradition a criminal could escape punishment by simply crossing a border. The whole process of law enforcement would become infinitely more difficult under such circumstances. States usually extradite persons sought by other states; however, political offenses are not generally recognized as ground for extradition. In the United States, the President is not legally empowered to extradite in the absence of treaty provisions.

Foreign Aid   The granting of economic or military assistance to foreign countries. American economic aid includes disposal of food surpluses, technical assistance, development loans, capital grants, and investment guarantees. The aid has been offered to over ninety countries bilaterally and to additional nations through United Nations and regional programs. Major programs in which the United States participates include the Alliance for Progress, the Peace Corps, the Colombo Plan, the Organization for Economic Cooperation and Development, the Asian and Inter-American Development Banks, the World Bank Group (IBRD, IDA, and IFC), and the United Nations Development Program. Military aid, taking the form of weapons, training, and defense support, and paying civilian costs to make up for the money the aid-receiving country has spent in its own defense, is given on a selective basis to strengthen resistance to external or internal Communist aggression. Foreign economic aid programs are administered by the Agency for International Development (AID), and military aid by the Defense Department. *See also* AGENCY FOR INTERNATIONAL DEVELOPMENT (AID), page 411; FOOD FOR PEACE, page 348; PEACE CORPS, page 412.

Significance   The United States has provided almost $200 billion in aid to foreign countries in the period 1945-1975. Aid programs started with Lend-Lease assistance to the Allies in World War II and in postwar years included the Marshall Plan to aid European recovery, the Truman Doctrine of military and economic assistance to Greece and Turkey to "contain" communism, and the Mutual Security Program of military aid to bolster NATO defenses in Western Europe. In the 1960s and 1970s, most American aid has gone to developing countries to encourage their "self-help" efforts. Approaches have included the encouragement of internal reforms by the Alliance for Progress, the offering of human resources through the Peace Corps, and the disposing of surplus food to needy peoples through the Food for Peace (Public Law 480) program. Most American foreign aid has gone to a few key countries of great strategic importance or to those policymakers believed to be most critical in the pursuit of American foreign policy objectives. Since 1950, India has been the major beneficiary of American economic and food aid, and South

Vietnam has been the major beneficiary of military aid. Most foreign aid is used to pay for purchases of American products and services, thus constituting a substantial subsidy for American industry and labor. Whereas recipient countries have preferred capital aid to help them industrialize, American programs have focused mainly on technical assistance, infrastructure development, military security, import subsidies, food, health, and educational forms of aid.

Free Trade   The elimination of all governmental regulations and controls so as to allow the free flow of commodities among countries. The theory is associated with Adam Smith, who believed that a free trade system would foster an international specialization that would result in higher productivity and standards of living for all nations. *See also* CAPITALISM, page 3.

   Significance   Desirable as free trade appears in theory, all nations practice varying degrees of protectionism. Many economists still support the idea of free trade, but political considerations tend to override economic theories. Many nations seek a measure of self-sufficiency, particularly in critical sectors of their economy, rather than overspecialization. World peace and security are indispensable conditions to a system of free trade.

General Agreement on Tariffs and Trade (GATT)   An international organization that promotes trade among its members by serving as a center for harmonizing trade policies and reducing tariffs and other barriers. GATT first met at Geneva in 1947 as an *ad hoc* conference to start a multilateral attack on trade barriers, prior to the establishment of the proposed International Trade Organization (ITO) as a specialized agency of the United Nations. When the United States Senate refused to approve the ITO, GATT—which is based on executive agreements rather than on a treaty requiring Senate approval—was developed as the main instrument to encourage freer trade. GATT's membership has increased from its original twenty-three participants to nearly one hundred members and associate members. Its main functions are negotiating reciprocal reductions in tariffs and other trade barriers, developing new trade policies, adjusting trade disputes, and establishing rules to govern the trade policies of members. Because all GATT agreements to lower tariffs include the most-favored-nation clause, concessions apply equally to all members, whether or not they are parties to the agreement. *See also* MOST-FAVORED-NATION STATUS, page 398; TARIFF, page 409.

   Significance   GATT's members have successfully negotiated reductions in tariff and other trade barriers over a period of three decades. Tariffs on industrial goods have been substantially lowered, especially between the United States, Western Europe, and Japan, but many national barriers to imports of primary commodities remain high, and nontariff barriers to trade, such as quotas, continue to impede the flow of commerce. GATT's efforts to liberalize trade also have been weakened by the refusal of many Third World developing countries to join what they refer to as "the rich man's club." Trade between GATT members and Communist states has increased more rapidly in recent years than trade between GATT members. The success of the Organization of Petroleum Exporting Countries (OPEC) in raising oil prices during the 1970s and a spiraling world inflation have also had a negative effect on GATT-member trade.

General Assembly   The major organ of the United Nations in which all members (141 in 1975) are equally represented. The Assembly has evolved into the focus for the multifold activities of the United Nations. In one sense, it is a continuing international conference; in another, it is an international forum in which each member nation can discuss its international problems with all others. It is a "Town Meeting of the World," through which world public opinion can be aroused and brought to bear on a problem. Its functions directly or indirectly relate to almost all of the activities carried on by the world organization. Specific responsibilities include: (1) election of some or all members of the other five major organs; (2) an annual review of the activities of all segments of the organization; (3) control over the budget; and (4) decision making and recommendations to members on all subjects within United Nations jurisdiction. Measures are adopted ordinarily by a simple majority vote, but "important questions," as defined by the Charter or as determined by a majority of the Assembly, require a two-thirds vote of members present and voting. The most important power of the Assembly—to deal with acts of aggression and breaches of the peace when the Security Council is stalemated by a veto—was not vested in the Assembly by the Charter, but was assumed by it in 1950 through the Uniting for Peace Resolution. *See also* CHARTER OF THE UNITED NATIONS, page 383; THIRD WORLD, page 409.

Significance   Through an evolutionary process, the Assembly has become the central organ of the United Nations system. Until the great powers cooperate more fully, the Assembly seems destined to overshadow the Security Council. With the admittance of many new members, mostly African states, the prestige and responsibilities of the Assembly have grown accordingly. Assembly activities of the first thirty years have helped to settle many disputes, to stop several conflicts, and to have adopted numerous resolutions setting forth norms for guiding international conduct. The Assembly has also helped in promotion of freer trade and economic development of many nations, and expansion of the scope of international law; further, it has aided colonial peoples in securing independence and statehood, and has strengthened the concern for human rights in the world. Most of all, it has served as a conference center where representatives of almost every nation in the world can meet and discuss their mutual problems. Although the United States dominated the decision processes in the General Assembly for many years, influence and voting power have moved relentlessly toward the Third World majority, leading to a growing apprehension and, in some cases, open hostility toward the United Nations by the American public.

Good Neighbor Policy   American policy toward Latin America initiated in the early 1930s. President Franklin Roosevelt described the change in policy in his inaugural address in March 1933 as follows: "In the field of world policy, I would dedicate this nation to the policy of the good neighbor—the neighbor who resolutely respects himself and, because he does so, respects the rights of others. . . ." Although the policy was directed toward the world at large, it soon came into general usage as descriptive of the American policy of treating Latin-American nations as friends and equals. *See also* ORGANIZATION OF AMERICAN STATES, page 401.

Significance   From the turn of the century until the adoption of the Good Neighbor policy, the United States played the role of "Big Brother" to Latin America. Unilateral actions, dollar diplomacy, and frequent military intervention characterized that policy. Terms such as "Yankee imperialists" and "Colossus of the North" came into common usage in Latin America to indicate displeasure with American policies. The Good Neighbor policy was an about-face, a repudiation of earlier actions. Since its inception, the policy has resulted in two military pacts of mutual assistance (the Act of Chapultepec of 1945 and the Rio Treaty of 1947), the creation of the Organization of American States (OAS), and a general improvement in relations between the United States and the Latin-American countries. The policy occasionally has been strained over United States relations with dictatorial regimes and over unilateral actions by the United States, such as the military intervention in the Dominican Republic in 1965.

Good Offices A method of peaceful settlement by which a third nation seeks to bring two disputing nations into agreement. The state offering its good offices merely seeks to create favorable conditions under which the states in conflict can talk over their differences. Good offices does not include participation in the negotiations nor the offering of a suggested solution, although the disputing states may request them. When they do, good offices is converted into mediation. *See also* PACIFIC SETTLEMENT OF DISPUTES, page 402.

Significance Good offices can be a useful device in "breaking the ice" between disputing states by getting them to talk things over. Neither disputant may be willing to initiate proposals for such talks for fear of demonstrating weakness in its position. The third state that offers its good offices is playing the role of peacemaker on behalf of the world community. In recent years, the United Nations has generally taken over the role of offering good offices to disputing states, usually through the Security Council, the General Assembly, or the Secretary-General. The United States, through Secretary of State Henry Kissinger, has also tendered its good offices to disputants in the Middle East and other areas.

Ideological Warfare A psychological tactic used by the Communist and free world blocs in the cold war. Each side has sought to achieve ideological conformity among its own people while trying to convert the large masses of mankind outside its borders to its basic values and "way of life." Ideology comprises the ideas and ideals of a political and economic system. The contemporary struggle involves competition between Soviet-style communism with its one-party rule and western-style capitalism and democracy, and between Soviet and Chinese Communist systems. *See also* CONVERGENCE THEORY, page 385; IDEOLOGY, page 10; PROPAGANDA, page 138.

Significance The ideological war has developed an inclination toward good and bad classification of national and international actions as each side tries to convince millions of peoples of the soundness and rightness of its position and the imperialistic, warlike, aggressive nature of the other side. Various psychological techniques have been used in disseminating propaganda. In recent years, however, a detente between the rival camps has encouraged a reduction in propaganda, a lessening of tensions, and an expansion in communication and understanding. The basic ideological competition between rival belief systems, however, has continued.

Inherent Powers Powers exercised by the national government in foreign affairs that are neither expressed nor implied in the Constitution. Inherent powers are derived from the concept that the United States exists in a world of many nations and, therefore, must possess powers to meet its international responsibilities. *See also* INHERENT POWERS, page 37; *United States v. Curtiss-Wright Export Corp.*, page 414.

Significance The inherent powers doctrine enables the national government to act in foreign affairs to protect the security and well-being of the American people. The extent to which such action would be permissible has not been specified, although the Supreme Court has stated (*United States v. Curtiss-Wright Export Corp.*, 299 U.S. 304 [1936]): "As a member of the family of nations, the right and power of the United States in that field are equal to the right and power of the other nations of the international family."

International Bank for Reconstruction and Development (IBRD) A specialized Agency of the United Nations, known informally as the World Bank, that makes loans to member nations for economic rehabilitation or developmental purposes. The Bank was created by the Bretton Woods Agreement of 1944 to promote the growth of world trade and higher standards of living by making loans when private capital is not available. The Bank's chief sources of funds are capital subscriptions from member nations and sales of its own bonds to private investors. By 1975, the subscribed capital of the Bank was more than $24 billion, of which almost one-third was subscribed by the United States. The Bank operates by making loans to governments or to private companies, although the latter loans must be guaranteed by a government or its fiscal agent. By 1975, 125 countries were members of the Bank. To meet criticism of the Bank's conservative lending policies, the International Finance Corporation (IFC) was created in 1956 to invest in private enterprises and, in 1960, the International Development Association (IDA) was created as an affiliate of the Bank to offer long-term, low-interest loans. The IBRD, the IFC, and the IDA are known collectively as the World Bank Group. *See also* FOREIGN AID, page 390.

Significance The World Bank has made several hundred loans totalling over $25 billion to more than eighty countries and territories, mostly in the underdeveloped category. Loans are made only after careful and detailed studies convince the Bank's Governing Board of the soundness of the ventures. Because loan decisions are made by the Board using a system of voting weighted on the basis of contributions to the Bank's capitalization, these decisions are controlled by a small group of Western Capitalist countries, with the United States alone possessing more than 25 percent of the total votes of the Bank's members. Terms of loans have varied, with interest rates running close to those in private capital markets, and with payment periods ranging from ten to thirty-five years. Loans have been granted for projects such as irrigation, mining, agriculture, transport and communication, and general industrial development. The Bank has also undertaken a broad technical assistance program to help prepare the ground for useful loans and to help recipients make effective use of loans received. Efforts are also made in granting loans to finance those projects that are most likely to encourage an inflow of private investment capital. Although the Bank has progressively increased the pace of its lending activities, its ability to help developing states meet their capital needs is very limited.

International Court of Justice (ICJ) An international tribunal, known as the World Court, established as one of the six major organs of the United Nations to adjudicate justiciable disputes among nations and to render advisory opinions to organs of the United Nations. The World Court was established in 1945 under an agreement that was annexed to the United Nations Charter, and to which all United Nations member states are parties. Nonmembers of the United Nations may adhere to the agreement under conditions set by the General Assembly and the Security Council. Other states may use the Court if they accept its jurisdiction. The Court, with its headquarters at the Hague, has fifteen judges elected by the General Assembly and the Security Council, no two of whom may be nationals of the same state. Decisions rendered by the Court are final and, if any party to a case refuses to heed the judgment of the Court, the other party has recourse to the Security Council, which may decide on a course of action. *See also* INTERNATIONAL LAW, page 395.

Significance The usefulness of the Court has been impaired because its jurisdiction extends only to cases in which the states concerned have accepted such jurisdiction. No national court system could function under such a limitation. Attempts to correct this weakness through compulsory jurisdiction under the "optional clause" (Article 36 of the Court's Statute) have largely been unsuccessful because of the reservations attached to the acceptance of compulsory jurisdiction by many nations, including the United States (Connally Amendment). Only about thirty cases have been decided and a number of advisory opinions rendered by the Court. Unless leading members of the United Nations resolve their major political differences, the Court may continue to play a limited role, having little impact on world affairs. World peace and security are unlikely to be achieved without world law and an effective court system.

International Labor Organization (ILO) A Specialized Agency of the United Nations that seeks through research and recommendation to improve working conditions throughout the world. Established in 1919, the ILO was the only major agency associated with the League of Nations in which the United States participated. The ILO is concerned with problems of full employment, labor standards, migration of workers, collective bargaining, social security, and workers' health. Its headquarters are in Geneva, and it functions through a General Conference comprised of delegates representing labor, employers, and government. Between annual conferences, an executive Governing Body supervises the operations of ILO committees and commissions and prepares the agenda for future conferences.

Significance Although the ILO cannot make binding decisions, its recommendations have been adopted by many member countries, resulting in improved working and living conditions for millions of workers. Improvements in labor standards can best be accomplished when they are instituted simultaneously by many nations; otherwise those nations acting alone would place themselves at a competitive disadvantage costwise. In recent years, much of the ILO's activity has been directed toward the underdeveloped areas of the world. Hundreds of ILO experts have provided technical assistance to countries in Asia, Africa, Latin America, and the Middle East. As world economic conditions changed in the mid-1970s, the ILO became concerned with the problems of millions of immigrants who had entered the industrialized countries during the labor-shortage years.

International Law A body of rules and principles that guides the relations among nations and between governments and foreign nationals. Sources of international law include treaties, authority (for example, decisions of international courts), reason, and custom. Treaties and other forms of international agreements are the most important source today, as custom was earlier, in the development of international law. The law has been classified into three categories: peace, war, and neutrality, based on the nature of the law, and into public, private and administrative, based on the different sources of the law. *See also* INTERNATIONAL COURT OF JUSTICE, page 394.

Significance Although international law evolved out of the European nation-state system, it has gained nearly universal acceptance by the world community of states. Some theorists reject the entire concept of international law, holding that law must be handed down by a sovereign authority, enforcement agencies must exist, and courts must provide sanctions against violators. Because none of these conditions exist in the state system, the existence of *law* is denied. Others refute this position by noting the universal acceptance of some elements of international law by the world community (such as diplomacy and commerce), and the general obedience of states to its rules. With the world caught up in revolutionary ferment, international law has depreciated in importance, despite efforts of the United Nations to foster its growth and adherence to its principles.

Internationalism The theory and practice of national involvement in cooperative interstate efforts to solve common security, political, economic, and social problems. Internationalism aims at achieving maximum levels of interstate cooperation, support for regional and global international organizations, participation in alliance systems, multilateral trade and monetary policies, and support for a common attack on major social problems. *See also* ISOLATIONISM, page 396.

Significance The United States has relentlessly pursued a policy of internationalism since the end of World War II, perhaps the result of a collective feeling of guilt about the failure of isolationist policies in the 1930s, or perhaps the result of new situational factors that forced American involvement in the world as a counterforce to Soviet power. Some historians have detected a pattern of alternating cycles of isolationism and internationalism in American history. As a result of the Vietnam War and other frustrations in American foreign policy, some observers have detected rising interest in the 1970s in a return to a more isolationist approach to foreign policy.

Isolationism The theory and practice of noninvolvement in the affairs of other nations. Isolationism as a political ideology is nurtured by geographical, ideological, and cultural separateness. *See also* INTERNATIONALISM, page 396.

Significance The United States pursued a policy of isolation during the nineteenth and part of the twentieth century. It was particularly operative in American intentions to remain aloof from the power struggles of Europe by remaining independent of Europe's system of entangling alliances. The doctrine was instrumental in conditioning the American public's belief that the United States should maintain neutrality during the early stages of World War I and World War II and not join the League of Nations. After World War II, American isolationism gave way to a deep commitment to internationalism. Indications of a national trend back toward isolationism, however, began to appear during the 1970s.

League of Nations The first general international organization established to preserve peace and security and to promote cooperation among nations in economic and social fields. The League was created by the victorious powers of World War I in 1919 under the leadership of President Woodrow Wilson, but the United States did not join. The organization operated under a constitutional system established through its Covenant, a section of the Versailles peace treaty. A Council and Assembly were the major organs (similar to the Security Council and General Assembly of the United Nations) and subsidiary committees and commissions were established to deal with special problems in areas such as mandates, military affairs, and disarmament. A Secretariat, headed by a Secretary-General and staffed with international civil servants, provided continuity and expertness in record keeping and research. A World Court (the Permanent Court of International Justice, forerunner of the present International Court of Justice) and the International Labor Organization were independent of the League but worked closely with it. Sixty-three nations joined the League and its headquarters were at Geneva, Switzerland.

Significance In its first decade, the League resolved many postwar problems and settled numerous disputes that threatened the peace. The Great Depression that swept across the world in 1929-1930 rekindled aggressive nationalism and reduced the League's effectiveness. Failure of the League to deal resolutely with the Japanese conquest of Manchuria in 1931, the Italian conquest of Ethiopia in 1935, and the Nazi aggressions in the late 1930s brought about its collapse. Most observers believe that the League's breakdown resulted not only from internal constitutional weaknesses, but also from the failure of key member states to support its principles and from the refusal of the United States to join. Despite its failure to maintain peace, the League did succeed in promoting extensive international cooperation in economic and social affairs and in developing new ideas and procedures for international organizations which have proved useful to its successor, the United Nations. The League voted itself out of existence in 1946 and transferred its assets to the United Nations.

Marshall Plan A proposal made by Secretary of State George C. Marshall in 1947 for a vast program of American economic aid to reconstruct the war-devastated economies of Western Europe. The United States Congress accepted the Plan and, in 1948, established the European Recovery Program under which sixteen nations of Western Europe (later joined by West Germany) received $15 billion in grants and loans from 1948 to 1952. Under the Marshall program, the participating European nations on American request joined together in the Organization for European Economic Cooperation (OEEC) for the purpose of drawing up a collective inventory of resources and requirements. The USSR and other Communist countries were invited to participate, but rejected the offer. *See also* FOREIGN AID, page 390.

Significance The Marshall Plan was successful in thwarting Communist aims of exploiting the economic collapse and political turmoil of the post-World War II era in Western Europe. By 1951, all participating members had raised their production capacities beyond prewar levels. American attempts to promote the integration of European economies through the program were partially successful, especially on the Continent. The Marshall Plan was the first of a series of economic and military programs through which the United States has provided over $200 billion in grants and loans to over one hundred countries.

Monroe Doctrine A unilateral declaration of American foreign policy made by President Monroe in his annual message to Congress in December 1823, opposing any European intervention in the affairs of the American continents. He also reaffirmed the American intention to refrain from interfering in European affairs. The Doctrine was intended to stop the Holy Alliance from aiding Spain in a reconquest of the newly independent Latin-American republics. *See also* DOL-

LAR DIPLOMACY, page 387; GOOD NEIGHBOR POLICY, page 392; ORGANIZATION OF AMERICAN STATES, page 401; RIO TREATY, page 404.

Significance The Monroe Doctrine at the time of its enunciation was largely meaningless because only the British fleet stood between the Holy Alliance and the reconquest of Latin America. Over the years, however, it developed into one of the basic tenets of American policy through restatements, corollaries, and the growing ability of a powerful United States to intervene actively whenever the Doctrine was challenged. Since the Declaration of Lima in 1942, and particularly the Rio Treaty of 1947, the Doctrine has become a common principle by which the American republics have declared their determination to defend themselves against foreign intervention. In recent years, the Doctrine has been challenged by the existence of a Communist government in Cuba and its efforts to promote revolution throughout Latin America, resulting in a conflict between those portions of the Doctrine ruling out foreign intervention and those guaranteeing that each Latin-American state may choose its own economic and political system.

Most-Favored-Nation Status Participation in a trading system in which all tariff concessions agreed upon by negotiating ("most-favored") states are extended to all other states. Inclusion of the most-favored-nation (MFN) clause in a trade agreement means that discrimination against third states is avoided by granting equal treatment to all. Although the term implies the granting of special treatment, it in fact ensures that all members of the trading system will receive the same advantages granted to the state "most favored." In the United States, Congress has delegated power to the President to withhold the application of most-favored-nation treatment from nations that discriminate against American exports. This power has been used by presidents to withhold or withdraw most-favored-nation status from trade carried on with many Communist states. *See also* GENERAL AGREEMENT ON TARIFFS AND TRADE (GATT), page 391; RECIPROCAL TRADE AGREEMENTS ACT OF 1934, page 415; TARIFF, page 409.

Significance The most-favored-nation system can be used to turn an otherwise discriminatory series of bilateral trade agreements into an outward-looking program aimed at the general reduction of trade barriers. Under American leadership, for example, it has been used since 1934 to rebuild a liberal trading system out of the maze of discriminatory barriers established during the period of the Great Depression. Both the Reciprocal Trade Agreements Program and the General Agreement on Tariffs and Trade (GATT) have applied the most-favored-nation principle in all trade agreements. In the 1970s period of détente, the Soviet Union sought most-favored-nation status from the United States as a major diplomatic concession.

National Interest The concept of the security and well-being of the state, used in making foreign policy. A national interest approach to foreign policy demands "realistic" handling of international problems, based on the use of power divorced from moral principles and values. Conflicts of national interest in the state system are resolved through diplomacy, international law, international institutions, or, ultimately, through war. Historically, national interest evolved as *raison d'état* (reason of state), a doctrine developed in the 16th century by Niccolo Machiavelli, that holds that security and national advantage are paramount considerations in state action.

Significance The concept of national interest is hazy and subjective in its application. Exponents of a realistic approach argue that it reduces utopian expectations, recognizes the existence of power politics, produces a steady and sober involvement in world affairs, and limits a state to attainable objectives. Opponents argue that the strongest foreign policy is one built on a firm moral base, and that reliance on unilateral policies of national interest fails to provide for reconciliation of international interests. The doctrine of national interest dictates that moral principles and commitments and agreements should be disregarded if they conflict with state policies or actions.

Nationalism   Social and psychological forces that spring from unique cultural and historical factors to provide unity and inspiration to a given people through a sense of belonging together and of shared values. Nationalism binds together people who possess common cultural, linguistic, racial, historical, or geographical characteristics or experiences and who give their loyalty to the same political group. Modern nationalism began to make its appearance as a major political and ideological force in the early nineteenth century, particularly in Napoleonic France. Nationalism is strengthened in some states by *ethnocentrism* (the belief in the superiority of one's own group and culture), and by *xenophobia* (an exaggerated fear or distrust of foreigners and of the policies and objectives of other nations). *See also* NATION, page 13.

Significance   The spirit of nationalism subjects people to the intangible forces of group psychology and collective behavior, especially when a crisis confronts them with a real or imaginary enemy. Nationalism tends to emphasize the separateness of and differences between groups, such as, Germans versus French or Arabs versus Jews. Most modern wars have been products of extreme nationalism in which mass emotional enthusiasm has been marshaled for one nation against another. It has played a significant role in the march to independence of numerous peoples. Nationalism is waning in Europe, its seedbed, and waxing strong in the new states of Asia and Africa. Nationalism is also a powerful internal force that helps produce unity, loyalty, and durable political, economic, and social institutions.

Neutralism   A "third force" in the cold war power struggle composed of states that pursue policies of nonalignment toward the Capitalist and Communist blocs. Most of the nations of Asia, Africa, and the Middle East and a few states in Europe and Latin America have refused to join military alliance systems propagated by either the United States or Soviet Russia. Although some of these states profess ideological sympathy toward one side or the other, none has committed itself to any kind of military involvement. *Political* neutralism in the cold war should be distinguished from *legal* neutrality, a status under international law in which certain states, such as Switzerland, Austria, and Sweden, renounce all wars in favor of permanent neutrality. *See also* NEUTRALITY, page 400.

Significance Neutralist leaders have consistently emphasized that neutralism is a positive force that endeavors to prevent another catastrophic global war by encouraging a rapprochement (harmonious relations between formerly hostile states) between the East and West. Both rival power blocs have been seeking to win favor with the neutralists. Most of the legally neutral states, such as Sweden and Ireland, are ideologically identified with the West. Many of the neutralist states, such as Yugoslavia and Egypt, are more sympathetic with the goals or current policies of the Communist bloc. Others, such as India and Burma, have tried to steer a middle course.

Neutrality The legal status of a nation that does not participate in a war between other states. Under international law, such a state is free to defend its territory or neutral waters against attack by belligerents. Although public opinion and even the government of a neutral state may sympathize with one side or the other, to retain its neutral position a state may not engage in action that might favor one side in the war. Some states, such as Switzerland, Sweden, and Ireland, have espoused a doctrine of perpetual neutrality. *See also* NEUTRALISM, page 399.

Significance The concept of neutrality has lost some of its meaning in modern times because of the increasingly ruthless nature of war, its expansion into global struggles, and the tendency of neutrals to show some favoritism based on ideological sympathies. In a future global war, neutrals may be placed in as great a position of danger as belligerents because of the possibilities of radioactive fallout, the spread of poisonous gases, and the employment of biological warfare by belligerents.

Nixon Doctrine An attitude or general philosophy of American restraint enunciated by the Nixon Administration as a guideline for foreign policy programs and decision making. The Nixon Doctrine was aimed at limiting United States' aid for friendly and allied nations to military supplies and economic assistance, while insisting that threatened nations assume "primary responsibility" for their own defense. The Doctrine was first suggested by President Richard M. Nixon in an impromptu press conference on Guam Island in 1969, but was subsequently expanded in statements and actions by President Nixon and his top-level defense and foreign policy advisers. *See also* CONTAINMENT, page 385.

Significance Originally known as the "Guam Doctrine" and limited in its applicability to Asian states, the new policy was later expanded into the Nixon Doctrine with global implications. Although critics held that American military support missions in Cambodia and Laos during the early 1970s violated the basic principles of the Doctrine, President Nixon and his advisers emphasized that it ruled out only "American ground combat troops." The central thesis of the Doctrine is that, although the United States will participate in the development of security for friends and allies, the major effort must be made by the governments and peoples of these states. The doctrine was mainly a product of public reaction against the major but largely unsuccessful military intervention by the United States in Vietnam during the 1960s. As policy, its promulgation was directly related to the efforts of the Nixon Administration to extricate American forces from Indochina. The Ford Administration continued the policy.

North Atlantic Treaty Organization (NATO) An organization established under the North Atlantic Treaty of 1949 to create a single unified defense force to safeguard the security of the North Atlantic area. Members agree under Article V of the Treaty to regard an attack upon any of them as an attack upon all, and, if an armed attack occurs, each will render such assistance as it deems necessary. Parties to the North Atlantic Treaty include fifteen members, the original twelve (Belgium, Britain, Canada, Denmark, France, Iceland, Italy, Luxembourg, the Netherlands, Norway, Portugal, and the United States) and three states that joined NATO in the 1950s (Greece, Turkey, and West Germany). NATO's members seek, in addition to attainment of mutual security, "the further development of peaceful and friendly international relations. . . and to eliminate conflict in their international economic policies." *See also* ALLIANCE, page 379.

Significance NATO provides the basic framework of the political-military structure of the west. Important questions, such as the rearmament of West Germany, the establishment of missile bases in Western Europe, the employment of nuclear weapons, and overall strategic and tactical plans have been worked out through the political and military channels of cooperation established within the NATO framework. NATO's solidarity tended to wax and wane over the years as the cold war grew more intense or cooled off. France, under de Gaulle, strained the alliance through independent actions that led ultimately to its withdrawal from NATO in 1966, although it continued as a party to the North Atlantic Treaty. In 1974, Greece also ceased to participate in the integrated military-political system of NATO, following a Turkish invasion of Cyprus using NATO weapons. Since 1969, any NATO member may renounce the Treaty by giving one year's notice.

Organization for Economic Cooperation and Development (OECD) An international organization created in 1961 to achieve expanded cooperation and joint action between the United States and Western Europe and Canada. The OECD is an outgrowth of the Organization for European Economic Cooperation (OEEC) established in 1948 to decide how American aid granted under the Marshall Plan would be distributed. When the OEEC dissolved in 1960, its membership included eighteen European nations which, with the addition of the United States and three new members, comprise the present membership of OECD. Fifteen of the twenty-two members of OECD are NATO allies—the United States, Canada, Belgium, Britain, Denmark, France, Greece, Iceland, Italy, Luxembourg, Netherlands, Norway, Portugal, Turkey, and West Germany. The other seven are Austria, Finland, Ireland, Japan, Spain, Sweden, and Switzerland. *See also* MARSHALL PLAN, page 397.

Significance The objectives of the OECD are: (1) to encourage economic growth and financial stability for member nations; (2) to expand and improve Western aid to underdeveloped countries; (3) to expand trade among members and with the world through more liberal policies; and (4) to provide a forum in which members can consult on mutual economic problems. The United States was the main force behind the creation of the OECD. American policymakers were particularly concerned with overcoming the balance of payments deficit, penetrating the Common Market and Free Trade Association trading blocs in Europe, and ensuring that all Western nations carried their fair share of the program for aiding underdeveloped countries. In the 1970s, OECD has been used by the United States as a central negotiating forum for working out common policies for dealing with world inflation, the deteriorating economies of the industrialized countries, and the problem of escalating world oil prices.

Organization of American States (OAS) A regional political organization comprised of the United States and twenty Latin-American republics, that was created at the Bogotá Conference in 1948. The OAS consists of: (1) the Inter-American Conference, which meets every five years to decide general policies; (2) the Council, with each member state represented by an ambassador, which oversees the implementation of general policies of OAS; (3) the Consultative Meetings of Ministers of Foreign Affairs, which occur whenever urgent problems confront the OAS; (4) the Pan-American Union, which operates through its headquarters in Washington, D. C., as a general secretariat of the OAS; (5) the Specialized Conferences, which are called periodically to enable the members to cooperate in dealing with technical problems; and (6) the Specialized Agencies, which are responsible for eliciting cooperation in economic, social, education, technical, and humanitarian problem areas. The OAS is a regional organization of the type encouraged by the United Nations Charter. Important provisions of the OAS Charter concern the peaceful settlement of disputes among members and procedures for mediation, arbitration, and adjudication. The OAS also implements the Rio Treaty's provision to safeguard the hemisphere from attack. *See also* ALLIANCE FOR PROGRESS, page 380; GOOD NEIGHBOR POLICY, page 392; MONROE DOCTRINE, page 397; RIO TREATY, page 404.

Significance The OAS regional system has institutionalized the principles embodied in the Monroe Doctrine. All major hemispheric problems have been taken up since 1948 through the machinery of the OAS. Communist infiltration into Latin America has been the major problem facing OAS organs. In 1962, the Castro regime of Cuba was expelled for promoting Communist subversion and revolution in Latin America. American unilateral military intervention in the Dominican Republic in 1965 created new strains in the OAS even though the United States claimed that its role was to prevent a Communist take-over, and an OAS peace force soon assumed control. The major challenge facing OAS in the future will be that of meeting increasing internal threats to the security of Latin-American states as a result of population pressures, urbanization, and mass frustrations growing out of failures to make rapid progress in economic development or to alleviate poverty.

Pacific Settlement of Disputes   The peaceful adjustment of international disputes by one or more of the following techniques: negotiation, inquiry, good offices, mediation, conciliation, arbitration, or adjudication. Pacific settlement may be employed through the traditional diplomatic channels, regional organizations or arrangements, or the organs or agencies of the United Nations. Chapter VI of the United Nations Charter sets out in detail the political procedures available to the Security Council and the General Assembly, Chapter XV delegates peaceful settlement responsibilities to the Secretary-General, and Chapter XIV prescribes the legal processes by which the International Court of Justice may attempt to settle justiciable disputes. *See also* ARBITRATION, page 381; DIPLOMACY, page 387; GOOD OFFICES, page 393; INTERNATIONAL COURT OF JUSTICE, page 394.

Significance War occurs not only as a result of planned aggression but also from failure to keep international disputes within peaceful bounds. The United Nations system has bolstered traditional and regional settlement channels by establishing the principle of member responsibility to settle all disputes peacefully and by providing permanent machinery readily available to take up disputes. Although the United Nations has a good record of securing cease fires, it has failed to settle major disputes, including those between India and Pakistan and between the Arab states and Israel. Conflicts in Cyprus and the Congo, and various cold-war controversies, have also proved to be difficult settlement problems for the United Nations.

Persona non Grata   An unacceptable person. *Persona non grata* relates particularly to the situation in which a nation declares that an ambassador or minister is no longer acceptable and requests his recall by his government. All diplomatic officials are therefore regarded as *persona grata* (acceptable) unless declared *persona non grata* by the receiving state. *See also* DIPLOMATIC PRIVILEGES AND IMMUNITIES, page 387.

Significance Each nation is free to accept or reject any person accredited to it as a diplomatic agent. When a diplomat is declared *persona non grata,* his government may consider it an affront, but the procedure is generally recognized and accepted. Numerous incidents involving the declaring of diplomatic agents *persona non grata* occurred during the cold war. In most such cases, retaliation followed, with a diplomat of equal status declared *persona non grata* following the first dismissal.

Quid pro Quo A diplomatic bargaining concept meaning, literally, something for something. Negotiations are typically conducted on a basis of *quid pro quo* and depend on mutual compromises for success. *See also* DIPLOMACY, page 387.

Significance Any nation unable to demand a *quid pro quo* in exchange for its own concessions is in an inferior bargaining (and power) position. Reciprocal concessions are particularly useful in reducing tariffs and other trade barriers through *quid pro quo* bargaining.

Ratification The formal action of the President in giving effect to a treaty that has been approved by the Senate. The President or his representative meets with representatives of the other signatory parties and exchanges ratifications with them. The treaty then is officially proclaimed and becomes legally enforceable. *See also* RATIFICATION, page 208; TREATY, page 410.

Significance Contrary to popular belief, the Senate does not officially ratify a treaty when it gives its advice and consent. In giving its consent, the Senate may attach amendments or reservations that may influence the decision of the President on ratification. The Senate's amendments or reservations, under which portions of a treaty will not be considered binding on the United States, leave the President with three choices: (1) renegotiation of the treaty; (2) ratification with reservations, if acceptable to other signatories; or (3) refusal to ratify. In American history, over nine hundred treaties have been approved by the Senate and ratified by the President. In approximately one hundred other cases, the Senate has either failed to act or has approved the treaties with reservations or amendments of such a nature that either the President or one of the signatories refused to ratify them. In addition, over sixty treaties have been rejected outright by the Senate, thus eliminating the question of ratification. All amendments to a treaty adopted during the Senate process of giving its advice and consent must be renegotiated with other parties to the treaty, or the President may kill the amended treaty by refusing to ratify it. No state, however, can be bound by changes in the treaty that are made unilaterally.

Recognition The discretionary function exercised by the President of deciding whether or not the United States shall officially carry on relations with a new state or a new political regime in an existing state. *See also* DE FACO RECOGNITION, page 386; DE JURE RECOGNITION, page 386; RECOGNITION, page 209.

Significance Each state in the world must determine for itself if and when new states and governments are to be recognized. Premature recognition of a revolutionary regime may lead to a threat of war by the government fighting the insurgent group. Conversely, continued refusal to recognize an existing state or an established government may engender hostility toward the state that withholds it. American recognition policy has varied with different presidents but, since

World War I, it has generally been one of withholding recognition from regimes distasteful to American citizens and of granting it to friendly governments. The worldwide ideological struggle has influenced presidential recognition policies in recent years. A major recognition controversy, linked also with the question of representation in the United Nations, involved the refusal of the United States for many years to accept Communist China in the family of nations. The United States continues to refuse to recognize North Korea, and North Vietnam.

Regionalism   Limited systems of international organization that enable groupings of states to deal cooperatively with political, economic, social, and military problems. Geographical proximity of states typifies most regional organizations, although a community of common interests alone, such as that found in the Commonwealth of Nations, can be the integrating force behind such movements. Regional organizations include the military alliance systems of both the Western and Soviet blocs, political systems such as the Organization of American States and the Council of Europe, and economic groupings such as the Common Market and the Free Trade Association. (*See also* Index: Regional Organizations)

Significance   Although the United Nations Charter encourages regionalism (Article 52), the prolific growth of regional organizations has had a limiting effect on the fostering of worldwide cooperation through the world organization. Supporters of regionalism point out that it represents a gradual approach toward world unity and is more realistic than either unilateralism or universalism because greater disharmony and conflict exist at the global than at the regional level. Opponents argue most international problems are worldwide in scope and that increasing economic and security interdependence can better be met by a universal system like the United Nations than by a regional group like the European Community or NATO. In the 1970s, new regional groups in Africa, Asia, and Latin American are trying to speed up their national development programs by establishing regional common markets, trading associations, and cartel arrangements of producing countries of such commodities as oil, coffee, and copper.

Rio Treaty   The Inter-American Treaty of Reciprocal Assistance of 1947 by which twenty-one American republics agreed "that an armed attack by any State against an American State shall be considered as an attack against all the American States. . ." The Rio Treaty was the first mutual security pact entered into by the United States and it became a model for all subsequent ones. The treaty establishes a hemispheric security zone stretching from the North Pole to the South Pole. If an attack occurs within the zone, members agree to consult about collective measures to be undertaken, while retaining freedom to act individually. The treaty also includes principles and means by which conflicts between American states can be settled peacefully. Decisions concerning implementation of the treaty are reached through organs of the Organization of American States. *See also* ALLIANCE, page 379; ORGANIZATION OF AMERICAN STATES, page 401.

Significance   The Rio Treaty has gained new importance as a result of increasing economic and political pressures in Latin America that threaten the region's stability. The major challenge to the Rio Treaty has been that posed by the establishment of a Communist regime in Cuba without a direct military attack by a nonhemispheric power. The Organization of American States, under the leadership of the United States, has sought to forestall further Communist take-overs in the hemisphere by including internal threats of subversion and revolution within the mutual guarantees provided by the treaty. In several countries, however, left-wing nationalist governments have come to power through elections or by military coups, thus frustrating Rio Treaty objectives.

Sanctions A collective punitive action involving diplomatic, economic, or military measures against a state. Under the United Nations Charter (Chapter VII), when the Security Council determines that a threat to the peace, breach of the peace, or act of aggression exists, members may be called upon to invoke military or nonmilitary sanctions against the lawbreaking state. Since the adoption of the Uniting for Peace Resolution in 1950, the General Assembly is also empowered to levy sanctions against an aggressor by a two-thirds vote. Sanctions may include such actions as breaking diplomatic relations, embargo or blockade, and the use of force. *See also* COLLECTIVE SECURITY, page 383.

Significance An international law enforcement system, like a nation's, must provide enforcement action to be effective. The *threat* of collective sanctions may be more effective in preventing aggression than the enforcement system in dealing with actual aggressions. The League of Nations attempted only once to employ sanctions (an economic boycott was levied against Italy after its attack upon Ethiopia in 1935) but failed to deter the aggressor. The United Nations levied military and economic sanctions against North Korea in 1950 and applied economic measures against Communist China. Regional organizations may also employ sanctions, such as the diplomatic and economic sanctions undertaken by the Organization of American States against the Castro regime in Cuba. Economic sanctions have also been levied by the United Nations against Rhodesia and South Africa in an attempt to pressure them to change their systems of white-minority rule, but few changes in their internal governmental systems have occurred over a ten-year sanctions' period.

Second Development Decade A program adopted by the United Nations General Assembly for the 1970s to foster progress toward modernization in the developing countries. The Second, like the First Development Decade of the 1960s, is aimed at dramatizing, mobilizing, and sustaining support for the measures required of both developed and developing countries to accelerate progress in the latter towards self-sustaining economic growth and social advancement. Growth targets set by the program include an annual 6 percent GNP rate and a 3.5 percent per capita rate of growth for developing countries. For the developed countries, the program established a goal of contributions of financial aid amounting to 1 percent of each nation's GNP, with 75 percent contributed by governments and the rest by private investors. *See also* FOREIGN AID, page 390.

Significance The Second Development Decade's general objectives include improved commodity trade and pricing policies, greater application of science and technology to development drives, and the mobilization of world opinion to support the strategy of the Second Development Decade. Although the more realistic goal of the First Development Decade (5 percent rate of growth for developing countries) was not achieved, substantial progress was made during the 1960s. Architects of the Second Development Decade's 6 percent growth plan sought to restimulate a common international effort. The most difficult problems standing in the way of realization of Second Development Decade goals are overpopulation, capital scarcity in the developing states, global inflation, heavy accumulations of debt, and food and energy shortages.

Secretariat   An organized body of officials and civil servants who have the responsibility of fulfilling administrative, secretarial, and housekeeping functions for an international organization. The United Nations Secretariat is one of the six major organs of the world organization. Its formal structure includes a Secretary-General and eight assistant secretaries-general, each of the latter heading a major Department (Security, Economic, Social, Trusteeship, Legal, Information, General Services, and Administrative and Financial). *See also* SECRETARY-GENERAL, page 406.

Significance   The success or failure of an international organization often depends on the efficiency of its secretariat and the capabilities and dedication of its staff. The United Nations has fostered the concept of an international civil service whose members serve the United Nations without regard for the views of their own countries. Every international organization utilizes some form of secretariat to perform the necessary routine functions of its day-to-day operations. Secretariat officials also play an important role in the life of an international organization by taking the initiative in solving problems and by providing leadership, continuity, and professionalism.

Secretary-General   The chief administrative officer of the United Nations who heads the Secretariat. The Secretary-General is chosen by the General Assembly, upon recommendation by the Security Council, for five-year terms. The United Nations Charter, in an attempt to strengthen the office of Secretary-General over its League of Nations predecessor, gave him authority to place security questions before the Security Council. *See also* SECRETARIAT, page 406.

Significance   The role of the Secretary-General has greatly expanded with the assignment of various political responsibilities in addition to his administrative duties. In theory, the position of Secretary-General is somewhat analogous to that of a city manager; in practice, however, it has evolved into a position of real leadership. Although he must operate within the framework of Assembly or Security Council resolutions, he has considerable decision-making power in implementing these resolutions. Trygve Lie of Norway, the first Secretary-General of the United Nations, provided effective leadership until a Western-Soviet split over the Korean War reduced his ability to function in that role. Dag Hammarskjöld of Sweden, who replaced Lie in 1953, further expanded the executive role of the office and maintained the support of all United Nations members until the Congo crisis of 1960. At that time, the Soviet Union charged Hammarskjöld with partisanship in his handling of the Congo situation. Following the death of Hammarskjöld in 1961, U Thant of Burma was appointed Secretary-General. U Thant, who served for ten years, saw his role primarily as a conciliator. He was succeeded by Kurt Waldheim of Austria in 1972, who has continued the U Thant conciliation approach.

Secretary of State   The leading Cabinet officer, who heads the Department of State and is charged with responsibility for formulating policies and conducting relations with foreign states. The Secretary of State has been recognized by statute as first of the Cabinet officials in the line of succession to the presidency following the Vice President, Speaker, and President pro tempore. His responsibilities include the direction and supervision of policy-making and administrative functions vested in the State Department in Washington, D.C., the diplomatic and consular services, and special missions and agencies abroad. *See also* DEPARTMENT OF STATE, page 412.

Significance   The decision-making role of the Secretary of State may be great or insignificant depending on the President in office. Some presidents, like Woodrow Wilson and Franklin

Roosevelt, largely ignored their secretaries of state and handled foreign policy matters directly and personally. Other presidents have delegated much responsibility to their secretaries of state in foreign affairs. Some have appointed personal assistants who have played a more important role in making foreign policy decisions than the Secretary of State. Still other presidents have depended mainly on personal friends or a "Kitchen Cabinet" to advise them on critical foreign issues. Regardless of where the President gets most of his advice, the Secretary of State typically becomes a political target for the opposition party and is held responsible by the public for foreign policy failures.

Security Council One of the six major organs of the United Nations, which was given primary responsibility for maintaining peace and security in the world. There are five permanent members—Britain, China, France, Soviet Union, and the United States—and ten nonpermanent members elected by the General Assembly for two-year periods, five chosen each year. Procedural and substantive decisions are made by an affirmative vote of nine members but, in the latter case, a negative vote cast by any permanent member constitutes a veto and stops all action. When considering peaceful settlement measures, a Council member that is a party to the dispute must abstain from voting. Nations that are not members of the Council may be invited to participate without a vote in Council deliberations if they are involved in a dispute being considered. Chapter VII of the Charter gives the Security Council the responsibility to "determine the existence of any threat to the peace, breach of the peace, or act of aggression. . . ." The Council can make recommendations or take enforcement action to restore peace and security. *See also* COLLECTIVE SECURITY, page 383.

Significance The Security Council was given the most important responsibilities by the Charter on the assumption that the great powers would continue to cooperate in the postwar period to maintain peace and security. Instead, the major threats to world peace have involved great power rivalry, and over 100 vetoes have reduced the effectiveness of the Council. Some disputes and problems have been dealt with successfully by the Council, but few involving cold-war questions have been resolved. As the Council's ability to act during crises faded, a new role was thrust upon the General Assembly, which has replaced the Council as the central organ of the United Nations. The importance of the Council today lies mainly in its role of providing the machinery for a continuous forum for great power negotiation.

Southeast Asia Treaty Organization (SEATO) A military-economic arrangement based on the Southeast Asia Collective Defense Treaty of 1954. Members who agree to consult about potential collective action whenever any of their number is threatened by external aggression or internal subversion in southeast Asia are Australia, Britain, France, New Zealand, Pakistan, the Philippines, Thailand, and the United States. SEATO headquarters are in Bangkok and include a council and a secretariat. *See also* ALLIANCE, page 379; ANZUS, page 380.

Significance SEATO was created through the efforts of Secretary of State John Foster Dulles to safeguard vital interests against Communist penetration in the southeast Asia area. The economic cooperation sections of the agreement have been overshadowed by the military and anti-Communist provisions. Internal Communist threats, supported with military equipment provided by Sino-Soviet forces, have challenged the effectiveness of SEATO to maintain the security of the southeast Asia area. Although South Vietnam, Laos, and Cambodia are not members of SEATO, their territory was included by protocol to the treaty in the area protected by the treaty. American efforts to invoke the SEATO Treaty during the Vietnam war were only partially successful, and financial inducements were required to encourage SEATO allies to send token forces to Vietnam.

Sovereignty   A legal concept that, in international affairs, means statehood, political independence, and freedom from external control. The concept of sovereignty is one of the most potent and persistent myths that has helped to shape the nature of the global state system. *See also* SOVEREIGNTY, page 18.

Significance   The importance of sovereignty in the modern state system has come largely from the psychological effect it has had on the decision-making processes of states. It has been a difficult force to overcome in creating political, military, and economic international organizations with decision-making powers. Sovereignty remains one of the major legal and psychological obstacles to the effective operation of the United Nations system.

Status Quo   A descriptive term used by international political analysts to describe the foreign policy of a state that aims at preserving the existing distribution of power in the world. The concept is derived from the diplomatic term, *status quo ante bellum,* which is a clause typically inserted into peace treaties providing for the restoration of prewar conditions.

Significance   The term "status quo" is used as an analytical tool in seeking to understand and describe the motivations and actions of states in the struggle for power that characterizes the state system. States pursuing policies of revision provide the challenge that forces the status quo grouping to develop defensive policies and alliances. Since World War II, the United States has pursued a policy of the status quo, vis-à-vis the revisionistic policies of the Soviet bloc.

Strategic Arms Limitation Talks (SALT)   Negotiations between the Soviet Union and the United States aimed at reaching agreement on the control of strategic nuclear weapons, delivery systems, and related offensive and defensive weapons systems. SALT talks, which began in Helsinki in 1969, were initially directed toward reaching agreement to limit or eliminate the costly Anti-Ballistic Missile (ABM) systems which both countries were developing. Subsequently, discussions covered the range of strategic weapons and related systems, including the ABM issue, multiple independently targeted reentry vehicles (MIRVs), nuclear testing, and limits on the number of delivery systems with nuclear warheads.

Significance   The SALT talks supplement those carried on at Geneva under United Nations aegis through the Conference of the Committee on Disarmament (CCD). The Nixon Administration sought an understanding between the major nuclear powers that will reduce the tensions of the arms race, diminish the military research and development costs in each nation's budget, and permit both to focus more attention on domestic problems. Although both nations indicate a desire to secure an arms control agreement, the SALT talks have once again emphasized the difficulties of securing agreement in the critical nuclear weapons field. Some progress, however, has occurred. In the first series of talks (SALT I, 1969-1972), agreement was reached on limiting missile-delivery systems for five years, but not the number of nuclear warheads in each missile. Agreement was also reached to limit the number of Anti-Ballistic Missile (ABM) defense systems to two in each country. Guidelines for SALT II worked out at the 1973 Brezhnev-Nixon Summit in Washington called for (1) achieving permanent ceilings on offensive strategic forces; (2) controlling qualitative aspects of offensive weapons; and (3) providing for ultimate reduction of strategic forces. In the 1974 Nixon-Brezhnev Summit in Moscow, two nuclear weapons agreements were signed, although neither will become effective until ratified. These agreements provide for only one ABM site for each party, and for limiting the magnitude of underground nuclear tests. In late 1974, the Ford-Brezhnev agreement at the Vladivostok Summit placed a ceiling of 2,400 each on the total number of delivery systems with nuclear warheads, and a limit of 1,320 missiles that can be armed on each side with MIRVs. The objective was to set firm limits on major weapons systems to avoid a runaway arms race. Critics of SALT agreements concluded by both President Nixon and Ford claim that they will not stop nor slow down the arms race but merely direct it into different areas. Other critics claim that the United States has been placed at a great disadvantage vis-à-vis the Soviet Union in terms of national security.

Tariff   A tax levied on imports to help protect a nation's industry, business, labor, and agriculture from foreign competition or to raise revenue. Tariffs are discriminatory if they apply unequally on similar products from different countries, and are retaliatory if motivated by the creation of trade barriers by other countries. *See also* RECIPROCAL TRADE AGREEMENTS ACT, page 415; TRADE REFORM ACT OF 1974, page 416; UNITED STATES TARIFF COMMISSION, page 413.

Significance   Tariffs have been used by the United States since 1789 as the principal means of protecting domestic producers from foreign competition. For many years prior to the adoption of an income tax, the tariff was also a primary source of revenue for the federal government. The United States encouraged mutual reductions in tariffs through the Reciprocal Trade Agreements Act of 1934, the General Agreement on Tariffs and Trade of 1947, the Trade Expansion Act of 1962, and the Trade Reform Act of 1974.

Third World   Those nations, constituting a majority of the international state system, that are—with the exception of the oil-producing countries—relatively poor, "have not," and underdeveloped in contrast with the Capitalist and Communist "worlds." Most Third World states have recently gained their freedom and independence from colonial rule and are now seeking to develop and modernize. The Third World as a powerful force in international relations began to emerge at the first meeting of the United Nations Conference on Trade and Development (UNCTAD), when such nations began to meet as the "Caucus of the Seventy-Seven" to achieve political goals through voting solidarity. Membership (although there is no formal organization or membership role) now exceeds 100 states. *See also* GENERAL ASSEMBLY, page 392.

Significance   The Third World functions as an effective decision-making bloc in the United Nations General Assembly and at large international conferences. Third World nations split on some issues, such as those growing out of the cold war and those related to the law of the sea. On other issues, especially those dealing with economic development, ending colonialism, and human rights, they have a record of almost complete voting solidarity. On key issues, the Third World almost always raises a two-thirds majority vote in the General Assembly. As a result, the United States, the Soviet Union, and Western Europe are often on the losing side of issues, whereas

China has increasingly voted with the Third World and is seeking to achieve a role of leadership in that bloc. Third World countries have also increasingly sought to secure capital for financing their development by joining together into cartel arrangements to control supply and fix world prices for such products as oil, copper, bauxite, sugar, and coffee.

Treaty A formal agreement entered into between two or more sovereign states for the purpose of creating or restricting mutual rights and mutual responsibilities. The treaty process includes negotiation, signing, ratification, exchange of ratifications, publishing and proclamation, and treaty execution. Treaties having only two signatory states are called bilateral, whereas those with more than two parties are multilateral. Treaties may expire at the end of a specified time limit, when certain conditions have been met, or by mutual agreement. Renunciation of a treaty by one of its parties may occur when a state of war exists or when conditions have been substantially altered (*rebus sic stantibus*). In the United States, all treaties are negotiated under the direction of the President, with some members of the Senate occasionally participating under the constitutional provision that treaties be made "by and with the advice and consent of the Senate...." Treaties must be approved by a two-thirds vote in the Senate, followed by presidential ratification if the Senate's version is acceptable. *See also* EXECUTIVE AGREEMENT, page 389; *Missouri v. Holland,* pages 413; RATIFICATION, page 403.

Significance Multilateral treaties have become the major source of international law. In the United States, treaties are part of the supreme law of the land and take precedence over state constitutions and laws. The courts have never declared a treaty to be unconstitutional. The Supreme Court has held that a treaty may increase the powers of Congress beyond the powers prescribed in the Constitution (*Missouri v. Holland,* 252 U.S. 416 [1920]). Increasingly, American presidents have come to depend on executive agreements rather than treaties; the latter are generally used only when strong congressional and public opinion support are essential to the success of the arrangements. Only eleven treaties have been voted down by the Senate in the years since adoption of the Constitution, but many have been killed by Senate inaction.

Truman Doctrine The policy, adopted by President Harry Truman in 1947, that called for American support for all free peoples resisting armed subjugation by internal or outside forces. The policy was aimed expressly at halting Communist expansion in southeastern Europe and was expounded in a speech to Congress, in which President Truman asked for an appropriation of $400 million for military and economic aid to Greece and Turkey. The doctrine was linked with the policy of "containment" that called for the building of "situations of strength" around the periphery of Communist power. *See also* CONTAINMENT, page 385.

Significance The Truman Doctrine marked the first official acceptance of the "containment" philosophy of building up free world strength to halt Communist expansionism. The Truman Administration followed it up with the development of the Marshall Plan (1947), a technical assistance program (1949), the North Atlantic Treaty (1949), and a mutual security program (1951). The Truman Doctrine, as applied to Greece and Turkey, was successful in helping the Greek loyalists win the civil war and in building up Turkey as a bastion of free-world strength with a modern army. The policy of containment of communism embodied in the Truman Doctrine has been continued by succeeding presidents, but the Nixon and Ford administrations sought to moderate the policy by fostering a détente between the United States and the two major Communist states.

Trusteeship Council   One of the six major organs of the United Nations, which helps the General Assembly to supervise the administration of the international trusteeship system. Members of the Council include those nations that administer trust territories, permanent members of the Security Council, and enough elected members to provide for parity between nontrust and trust-administering states on the Council. Trust territories include the: (1) former mandates of the League of Nations; (2) Axis colonies: and (3) colonies voluntarily placed under trusteeship. No colonial power has yet volunteered to place a colony under the system. Council powers include considering reports, accepting petitions, and making periodic visits to trust territories. Administration of "strategic" trust territories is supervised by the Security Council, rather than by the Trusteeship Council, because of their military importance.

Significance   Through its supervisory role, the Trusteeship Council has helped trust territories achieve self-government. Libya, Italian Somaliland, and Tanganyika, for example, have become independent states. South Africa, however, has refused to place its League of Nations mandate, Southwest Africa, under the trusteeship system, and little progress has been made toward the self-government of the three island groups under American strategic trust—the Marshalls, the Carolines, and the Marianas—which are known collectively as the Trust Territory of the Pacific Islands. In total, the Trusteeship Council helped transform ten trust territories into independent states, and contributed to the march to independence of 75 nontrust colonies. Its mission has essentially been completed.

IMPORTANT AGENCIES

Agency for International Development (AID)   A semi-independent agency within the Department of State that directs economic and technical assistance aid programs to foreign nations. AID was created by Congress in the Act for International Development of 1961, replacing the International Cooperation Administration (ICA). AID administers the foreign aid program through developmental loans and grants, investment surveys and guarantees, and developmental research. AID is headed by an administrator who has a dual role as chief of the operating agency and political adviser to the Secretary of State and the President. *See also* FOREIGN AID, page 390.

Significance   The Agency for International Development was created particularly to implement President John F. Kennedy's Alliance for Progress program, but its operations became worldwide. AID became an increasingly important agency as the United States stepped up the pace of its global economic offensive of competing with Russia and other Communist states in helping the less-developed nations to make progress. Although military aid outweighed economic aid during the 1950s, the Kennedy, Johnson, Nixon, and Ford administrations all stressed the expansion of economic programs during the 1960s and 1970s. During the last two administrations, however, there was a switch of priorities from foreign to domestic problems, and public support for foreign aid programs dwindled. AID's role has been considerably reduced in the 1970s, as a result of substantial congressional cuts in annual foreign aid budgets.

Department of State   The agency primarily responsible for making and executing American foreign policy. The Secretary of State, who heads the Department, is the President's official adviser on foreign policy matters. The first responsibility of the Department is to formulate programs and policies for the United States in its relations with other nations. Next in importance are its duties of administering laws relating to foreign affairs and conducting the day-to-day relations with foreign countries. The latter responsibility is carried out primarily by the Foreign Service, which is administratively tied to the Department of State, and has been undergoing a gradual process of integrating its personnel with that of the Department. Specific duties of the Department include: (1) negotiating treaties and agreements with foreign states; (2) carrying on extensive communications with foreign governments and American units abroad; (3) issuing passports and, through consular officials abroad, granting visas; (4) promoting cultural relations between foreign peoples and the American people; (5) carrying on propaganda and information programs overseas; (6) planning and administering economic aid programs. The Department and its Secretary are responsible to the President. Important policy-making and primary contact with field operations and foreign missions are carried on through six regional bureaus. These include the African, Inter-American, European, East Asian and Pacific Affairs, Near Eastern and South Asian Affairs Bureaus, and a Bureau of International Organization Affairs, each headed by an Assistant Secretary. The Agency for International Development is a semiautonomous agency within the State Department. *See also* ROGERS ACT, page 415; SECRETARY OF STATE, page 406.

Significance   The State Department is the major agency for foreign policy decision making. The importance of its role mainly depends on the President and Secretary of State. President Rchard M. Nixon, for example, relied heavily on his own abilities and those of close friends in making foreign policy decisions. The historic conflict over the role of the Department has involved the question of whether it should confine itself to policy making or be charged additionally with administering foreign programs. This problem has never been fully resolved, although its primary responsibility remains that of developing policy. The State Department is the smallest of the eleven major departments in personnel and budget, and it is the only one that has its own personnel merit system, rather than relying on Civil Service, as do the other departments.

Peace Corps   An agency that administers the foreign aid program, adopted in 1961, under which American volunteers are sent to developing countries to teach skills and help improve living standards. By the mid-1970s, thousands of Peace Corps volunteers were in training or in service in many countries of Asia, Africa, and Latin America. The Peace Corps, established within the State Department in 1961, was transferred to the Action Agency in 1971. *See also* FOREIGN AID, page 390.

Significance   The Peace Corps employs a new approach to foreign aid in using human resources to help developing societies help themselves through person-to-person contacts. Many other Western countries have followed the American example by establishing similar volunteer programs. Although most Third World countries have welcomed Peace Corps volunteers and praised their efforts, several have been highly critical of the program and have ordered the Peace Corps removed from their territory.

United States Information Agency (USIA)   An independent agency established in 1953 that has responsibility for administration of foreign information programs of the United States. The USIA operates a global network of communications media that beam propaganda programs all over the world. The agency works closely with the State Department and related agencies to harmonize its information programs with American foreign policy. The best-known USIA operation is that of the Voice of America, that broadcasts a great variety of programs in many areas of the world, often with candor and credibility. *See also* IDEOLOGICAL WARFARE, page 393.

Significance The USIA directs American governmental efforts in the psychological phase of the cold war. Activities include round-the-clock radio broadcasts in about forty languages; television programs; distribution and showings of documentary, feature, and newsreel films; and distribution of millions of leaflets, pamphlets, news bulletins, and related propaganda materials. The USIA has operated on the proposition that "truth is our weapon." Its information centers and libraries have often been damaged or destroyed in anti-American demonstrations abroad. The agency employs over 9,000 Americans and foreign nationals in more than 100 countries.

United States Tariff Commission   An independent agency that gives information to Congress and the President on American and foreign tariff and trade matters. The six members of the Tariff Commission, three from each of the major parties, are appointed by the President, with the Senate's approval, for six-year terms. *See also* TARIFF, page 409.

Significance Congress has used the Tariff Commission as a means of keeping the President's tariff reductions, under the Reciprocal Trade Agreements Act of 1934 and the Trade Reform Act of 1974, within some degree of congressional supervision and control. In the "peril point" provisions, the Tariff Commission indicates a rate for each imported product at which it might enter the American market in a quantity sufficient to threaten or injure domestic producers. Under "escape-clause" provisions, the Commission can recommend to the President that a trade agreement be adjusted when its investigations disclose that low tariff rates are threatening to injure or are injuring American producers. If the President rejects the advice of the Tariff Commission, Congress can override him and restore the higher tariff rate by a two-thirds vote in both houses. The escape clause has been invoked by the President to modify agreements with foreign nations on only a few occasions. The role of the Tariff Commission has been substantially increased as a result of the enactment of the Trade Reform Act of 1974, which greatly expanded American tariff bargaining power.

IMPORTANT CASES

Missouri v. Holland, 252 U.S. 416 (1920): Upheld the validity of a federal statute based on a treaty with Great Britain for the protection of birds and waterfowl migrating between Canada and the United States. The question was whether the national government could acquire, through a treaty, power to legislate on domestic matters otherwise reserved to the states. A similar federal law, antedating the treaty and the law in question in this case, had earlier been declared unconstitutional by the lower federal courts. *See also* TREATY, page 410.

Significance The decision in *Missouri v. Holland* means that the national government can actually add to its powers by concluding treaties with foreign states. Opponents of increasing federal responsibility have argued since 1920 that the case should be overturned because it almost obliterates the distinction between the national government's delegated and the state's reserved powers. This viewpoint crystallized in the 1950s in the Bricker Amendment proposal, which, if adopted, would have allowed treaties to become effective within the United States only through legislation valid in the absence of a treaty. Supporters of the decision point out that the alleged danger has not materialized and that to limit the treaty-making powers would constitute a greater danger to the country.

United States v. Curtiss-Wright Export Corp., 299 U.S. 304 (1936): Upheld the validity of a joint resolution of Congress that delegated broad powers to the President to prohibit arms shipments to foreign belligerents. In question was a presidential proclamation levying an embargo on shipment of war matériel to either side in the Gran Chaco war between Bolivia and Paraguay. In the *Curtiss-Wright* case, the Court distinguished between permissible delegations of congressional lawmaking power in domestic areas and those in foreign affairs. The Court noted: "As a member of the family of nations, the right and power of the United States . . . are equal to the right and power of the other nations of the international family. Otherwise the United States is not completely sovereign." *See also* INHERENT POWERS, page 393.

Significance The Court recognized in the *Curtiss-Wright* case the full responsibility of the national government in foreign affairs and the importance of the President's role in this field. By authorizing congressional and presidential actions in foreign affairs that might not be valid in domestic matters, the Court recognized that, in addition to the enumerated and implied powers, a third category of powers, inherent in nature, may be exercised by the President in foreign affairs. The Court reaffirmed the primacy of the national government in foreign affairs in *United States v. Pink*, 315 U.S. 203 (1942), asserting that power over foreign relations "is not shared by the states; it is vested in the national government exclusively." Federalism, the Court noted, stops at the water's edge.

IMPORTANT STATUTES

Battle Act (Mutual Defense Assistance Control Act of 1951)   An act to prohibit trade with Communist countries in strategic goods and to deny American foreign aid to any nation that carried on such trade. The President is empowered to make exceptions if cutting off foreign aid would be contrary to American interests. *See also* DETENTE, page 386; TRADE REFORM ACT OF 1974, page 416.

Significance The Battle Act has resulted in a major reduction of American trade with the Soviet Union and other Communist countries. Much effort was expended by American negotiators during the cold war period to persuade allies and neutralist countries to cut off their strategic trade with the Communists. The policy was moderately successful for a few years, but most of the non-Communist nations of the world rejected American pressures and increased their trade with the Soviet bloc. The United States, itself, has expanded its trade with some Communist countries, such as Yugoslavia, Poland, the People's Republic of China, and the Soviet Union. Bestowal of most-favored-nation (MFN) status on Communist countries under provisions of the Trade Reform Act of 1974 would be likely to further weaken the impact of the Battle Act.

Reciprocal Trade Agreements Act of 1934 A broad tariff program under which the President negotiates trade agreements with foreign countries that provide for mutual reductions in tariff rates. It incorporates the "most-favored-nation" principle of nondiscrimination under which concessions contained in agreements apply to all other nations with which we have most-favored-nation arrangements. The original enactment in 1934 provided that tariff rates of the United States could be lowered or raised up to 50 percent of the existing rates, but renewals have given the President authority to seek additional cuts. Amendments to the Act include "peril-point" and "escape-clause" provisions. The peril-point amendment provides that the Tariff Commission inform the President and Congress at what level a tariff rate might allow imports to threaten or injure a domestic producer. Escape-clause procedures require that tariff rates be raised if they injure domestic producers. The Trade Reform Act of 1974 expands the President's tariff-cutting powers, and strengthens the American bargaining position, especially with the European Common Market countries. *See also* TARIFF, page 409; MOST-FAVORED-NATION STATUS, page 398; TRADE REFORM ACT OF 1974, page 416.

Significance The Reciprocal Trade Agreements Act sought to increase the two-way flow of trade by transferring rate-setting powers from Congress, in which political considerations and logrolling tactics flourished, to the President, who was empowered to lower rates only on a *quid pro quo* basis. Agreements with forty-three countries are currently in force. Reciprocal bargaining has been facilitated through multilateral negotiations carried on through the General Agreement on Tariffs and Trade (GATT) system with a membership of almost 100 nations. Protectionist sentiment has increased in the Congress in recent years as a result of growing competition from imports, but the threat of shrinking world trade and a global depression led Congress to enact the Trade Reform Act of 1974 that encourages international bargaining for lower rates.

Rogers (Foreign Service) Act of 1924 The basic law that established the organization and functions of the Foreign Service as it exists today. The Rogers Act unified the diplomatic and consular services into an integrated Foreign Service, created a career servce based on merit, and established the Foreign Service Institute. Subsequent amendments added in the Foreign Service Acts of 1946 and 1949 have sought to professionalize the Service. Additional changes based on the report of the Wriston Committee in 1954 have sought to "democratize" the Service and integrate its personnel with that of the State Department. *See also* DEPARTMENT OF STATE, page 412.

Significance The Rogers Act initiated a series of reforms which have reshaped the Foreign Service over the years and developed it into a first-rate organization. Appointment to the Foreign Service today is open to most Americans, yet it involves the most careful selection process developed by any government agency. The Foreign Service organization and the quality of its personnel have a direct bearing on making foreign policy and conducting foreign affairs. In 1975, the Foreign Service of the United States operated 129 embassies and 130 consulate offices, the former in capital cities and the latter in major cities and trading centers around the world.

Trade Reform Act of 1974   A major trade enactment by Congress to increase the President's bargaining power in tariff and trade barrier negotiations in GATT, with the objective of stimulating expanded world trade. The Trade Reform Act also contained a highly controversial provision authorizing the President to extend most-favored-nation (MFN) nondiscriminatory status to the Soviet Union for eighteen months, with the understanding that the Soviets would thereby permit a substantial increase in Jewish emigration. The Act empowers the President: (1) to reduce or raise United States' tariffs sharply as negotiating levers; (2) to reduce or eliminate import quotas, export subsidies, investment restrictions, and other nontariff barriers to trade; (3) to retaliate against unreasonable foreign restrictions on American trade; (4) to aid American industries and workers injured by increased imports, with loans to companies and cash payments to unemployed workers; and (5) to increase trade rather than foreign aid to help poor countries develop by allowing their goods duty-free entry into the United States. An additional punitive section of the Act bars nations belonging to the Organization of Petroleum Exporting Countries (OPEC) from receiving tariff preferences offered to other developing nations. *See also* GENERAL AGREEMENT ON TARIFFS AND TRADE, page 391; MOST-FAVORED-NATION STATUS, page 398; ORGANIZATION OF PETROLEUM EXPORTING COUNTRIES, page 349; RECIPROCAL TRADE AGREEMENTS ACT, page 415; TARIFF, page 409.

Significance   The Trade Reform Act of 1974 continued the forty-year campaign by the United States to reduce trade barriers in the world through a process of reciprocal bargaining agreements. This process began in 1934 with the enactment of the Reciprocal Trade Agreements Act, continued with the creation of the General Agreement on Tariffs and Trade (GATT) by executive agreement in 1947, and was further spurred by the Trade Expansion Act of 1962. Most of the debate and delay in the passage of the new Trade Act was occasioned by the effort of key members of Congress to force the Soviet Union to agree to more lenient emigration policies in exchange for MFN status, a position which the Soviets regarded as an unwarranted intrusion into their domestic affairs. Arab and Latin-American OPEC nations were also incensed at the discriminatory trade treatment accorded them under the Act, in retaliation against their cartel pricing for oil.

17   National Defense

Civil Defense   The protection of civilian populations from enemy attack. Civil defense operations are centered in the Defense Civil Preparedness Agency (DCPA) in the Department of Defense. The DCPA is responsible for developing a shelter program, a defense against chemical, biological, and radiological weapons, a warning system, and measures to be undertaken following an attack. DCPA has designated numerous structures as fallout shelters for protection against radioactivity following a nuclear attack and has stocked many of them with supplies; but the question of whether the United States should adopt a major shelter program in the United States remains a controversial issue. *See also* DEPARTMENT OF DEFENSE, page 427.

Significance   The advent of nuclear and other weapons of mass destruction raises the question of whether civil defense is practicable. Officials have estimated that a nuclear attack could result in 150 million American civilian casualties within a matter of hours. Those who favor a major shelter program believe that it would help to deter an attack because it would save millions of civilian lives and permit a subsequent mobilization of civilians as a second line of defense. Opponents claim that the cost of a national shelter program is prohibitive, that it would be ineffective against a massive attack, and that it might accelerate the arms race or encourage an American or Soviet nuclear strike. Most nuclear strategists believe that the best deterrent against a nuclear attack is the possession of a devastatingly powerful second strike or retaliatory capability.

Civilian Control   The American constitutional principle of civilian supremacy over the military to safeguard republican institutions. Civilian control is maintained through constitutional provisions that make the President commander in chief of the armed forces and grant Congress power to raise and support armies, make military law, declare war, and appropriate money for military expenditures for no more than two-year periods. The Second and Third amendments buttress the principle by forbidding the quartering of troops without consent and by granting the people the right to keep and bear arms. Statutory enactments, such as the legal requirement that the Secretary of Defense and the Secretaries of the Army, Navy, and Air Force departments must all be civilians, also encourage civilian control. *See also Ex Parte Milligan,* page 429; MILITARY-INDUSTRIAL COMPLEX, page 422.

Significance Civilian control is especially significant in a democratic nation that is threatened by potential enemies and has built up a great military power. Many Third World countries appear to be democratic but are controlled by military cliques. Many people in the United States have become fearful of the rising power and influence of the military. Yet national defense considerations have increased the nation's dependence upon the military while at the same time alerting the country to the dangers inherent in a military-industrial complex.

Commander in Chief The role of the President, as provided in Article II, section 2 of the Constitution, as supreme commander of the military forces of the United States and of the state national guard units when they are called into federal service. As commander in chief, the President exercises a vast array of "war powers." During periods of war or threat of war, he exercises both military and civilian powers related to defense. *See also* PRESIDENT, page 206; WAR POWERS, page 426; WAR POWERS ACT, page 431.

Significance Under his war powers, the President can deploy American forces anywhere in the world and, as has happened many times in American history, order them into action against a foreign foe without a declaration of war by Congress. American military interventions—in Korea in 1950, in Indochina during the 1960s, and in the Dominican Republic in 1965—without congressional declarations of war illustrate the extent to which a President can commit the nation to a course of military action under his powers as commander in chief. In a reaction against presidents taking foreign military initiatives, the Senate in 1969 passed a "national commitments" resolution requiring congressional approval for any commitment to use American troops abroad.

Counterinsurgency Military force employed against a revolutionary group trying to overthrow an established regime. Counterinsurgency operations describe the efforts of American and indigenous military forces to prevent a Communist take-over through revolution, guerrilla warfare, subversion, and related techniques.

Significance Counterinsurgency operations have developed as a response to the Communist doctrine of promoting "wars of national liberation" enunciated in the late 1950s. In Vietnam, counterinsurgency operations were carried on by American, South Korean, Australian, New Zealand, and South Vietnamese units against Viet Cong guerrillas and North Vietnamese forces. The development of counterinsurgency during the early 1960s helped contribute to confidence in a military solution that led to an expanding American involvement in southeast Asia during the latter half of the 1960s. The ultimate failure of counterinsurgency operations in Indochina has reopened the question of how can the United States react effectively to national liberation wars.

Court-martial A military tribunal that conducts trials of military personnel accused of violating military law. A *summary* court-martial consists of a single officer who tries enlisted men for minor offenses. A *special* court-martial, which can only be convened by a high-ranking officer, usually consists of three officers who may impose moderately severe penalties, such as six months at hard labor, bad conduct discharges, and reductions in rank. A *general* court-martial may be convened by the President or Secretary of Defense or by a Commanding General or Admiral. It consists of five or more members, one-third of whom may be enlisted men if they are requested by the accused. Severe penalties, such as the death penalty, life imprisonment, or dishonorable discharge, may be imposed. *See also* COURT OF MILITARY APPEALS, page 245; MILITARY LAW, page 423.

Significance The court-martial has become an important part of the American system of justice because of the large numbers of Americans in the armed forces. During World War II, almost one-third of the nation's criminal cases were decided by courts-martial. Charges of unfair procedures and a lack of justice led Congress to establish a new Uniform Code of Military Justice in 1950, to provide for enlisted men to serve on *general* courts-martial, and to create a three-man civilian Court of Military Appeals to which convicted military personnel can appeal. Courts-martial have come under closer public observation as a result of the trials of American soldiers for acts of mass murder of civilians during the Vietnam war. Enlisted men may serve on either a special or a general court-martial if requested by an accused enlisted man. On the question of civil versus military jurisdiction, the Supreme Court held in 1969 that a serviceman is entitled to trial by a civilian court for nonservice connected crimes committed off the post and out of uniform (*O'Callahan v. Parker,* 395 U.S. 258). This rule was tempered by the Court in 1971 when it held that an offense committed by a serviceman on a military post against a civilian is "service-connected" and subject to court-martial (*Redford v. U.S. Disciplinary Commandant,* 401 U.S. 355).

Declaration of War A formal announcement by a nation that a state of hostilities exists with another nation. Constitutionally, only Congress can declare war. Under the usual procedure, the President requests a declaration of war, the Congress adopts it by joint resolution, and the President signs it. In 200 years of American history, Congress has declared war only five times— the War of 1812, the Mexican War, the Spanish-American War, World War I, and World War II. *See also* COMMANDER IN CHIEF, page 418; POLICE ACTION, page 424; WAR POWERS ACT, page 431.

Significance In the conditions of modern war, Congress has lost most of its discretionary power to determine when and if war should be declared. Congress may merely recognize that a state of hostilities already exists, as in its declaration of war against the Axis powers following the attack upon Pearl Harbor in 1941. Moreover, the President, as commander in chief, may commit American forces to action without a congressional declaration of war, as when President Franklin Roosevelt ordered a naval convoy for merchant ships prior to America's actual entry into World War II. In the Korean War, American troops ordered into action by President Harry Truman fought from 1950 to 1953 under the United Nations banner without a formal declaration of war by Congress. In South Vietnam, Presidents Dwight Eisenhower, John Kennedy, Lyndon Johnson, and Richard Nixon committed large numbers of American troops to action, and Presidents Johnson and Nixon ordered bombing of North Vietnam, all without a congressional declaration of war. Today, with missiles and hydrogen bombs poised for attack, the decision to launch or repel an attack may be made by the President or, conceivably in an emergency situation, by a military commander in the field, with Congress having little to do with the decision.

Defense Contract An agreement between the Department of Defense (DOD) and a private business or industry by which the latter agrees to supply hardware, equipment, supplies, or services to the military. The three types of defense contracts used extensively by the Defense Department are: (1) the *competitive bid* contract, which ordinarily would be awarded to that company offering to provide the hardware or service at the lowest cost; (2) the *negotiated* contract, in which Defense officials discuss and reach agreement with a private company concerning materials or services and their costs; and (3) the *cost-plus* contract, in which the DOD guarantees the private company repayment of all costs involved in producing the hardware or service, plus a stipulated amount or percentage of costs as profit. *See also* DEPARTMENT OF DEFENSE, page 427; MILITARY-INDUSTRIAL COMPLEX, page 422.

Significance During peacetime, the Defense Department utilizes mainly competitive bid contracting, but, under the pressures of the Korean and Vietnam wars, negotiated and cost-plus contracts were used extensively. The latter types are used to expedite procurement of hardware and services, typically at much greater cost than under competitive bidding. Under cost-plus contracting, for example, the contracting company is encouraged to boost costs of production since the size of its profit may be determined by the magnitude of its costs in producing the military equipment. Congressional committee investigations into DOD procurement activities have uncovered many cases of defense profiteering resulting from excessively high prices paid to private contractors. Under current competitive bidding practices for developing major new weapons systems, private companies have increasingly given low bids to win the contracts and have later requested the Defense Department and Congress to cover major cost overruns, amounting, in some cases, to billions of dollars.

Deterrence Retaliatory capability of a nation's military forces to discourage a potential enemy from launching an attack. The concept implies that a nation's military defenses are so large, diversified, and well protected that a first-strike by an enemy would not cripple its ability to retaliate decisively. *See also* STRATEGY, page 425.

Significance Nuclear weapons have made deterrence an effective and credible strategy. Even if most of a nuclear power's retaliatory capability were destroyed in an initial strike, the potential for mass destruction of enemy cities would remain. Deterrence implies that the people and industry of rival nuclear powers remain perpetual hostages to deter a planned attack by either. The United States' deterrent power includes MIRVs (multiple independently targeted reentry vehicles), intercontinental missiles protected by underground silos, nuclear-powered submarines with Poseidon multiple-warhead nuclear-tipped missiles, and the strategic nuclear bomber fleet, some of which is constantly airborne. Soviet retaliatory power and capabilities (and, hence, deterrence posture) approximate that of the United States.

Intelligence Gathering information about the capabilities and intentions of foreign governments. Most intelligence is secured by analyzing data found in governmental and private publications, but some requires the use of clandestine cloak-and-dagger methods. American agencies actively engaged in the gathering and/or analysis of intelligence include: (1) the Central Intelligence Agency (CIA), which carries on undercover activities around the globe and serves as a central focus for the receipt and evaluation of intelligence; (2) the National Security Agency (NSA), which engages in coding and decoding operations and electronic surveillance; (3) Army Intelligence (G2), which secures data on ground forces and new weapons; (4) Air Force Intelligence (A2), which covers air and space affairs; (5) the Office of Naval Intelligence (ONI), which ferrets out information on foreign navies and fleet movements; (6) the Bureau of Intelligence and Research (I & R) in the State Department, which obtains economic and political data and forecasts trends; (7) the Defense Intelligence Agency (DIA) of the Department of Defense, which evaluates the capabilities of allies and potential enemies; (8) the Nuclear Regulatory Commission (NRC), which seeks data on nuclear weapons and detects nuclear test explosions; and (9) the Federal Bureau of Investigation (FBI), which obtains information on internal threats to security. The United States Intelligence Board, headed by the Director of the CIA, meets regularly to sift information gathered by intelligence agencies and to give a "national intelligence estimate" to the President. *See also* CENTRAL INTELLIGENCE AGENCY, page 427.

Significance Technological advancements in warfare have increased the need for governments to obtain vital information related to the security of the state. Intelligence objectives relate mainly to the military field, but states also gather data on political, economic, and social factors. Not only potential enemies but friendly and allied nations constitute the subjects of intelligence operations, and congressional investigations in the early 1970s revealed that large numbers of American citizens were also under direct surveillance by various American intelligence agencies. Some critics charge that the multiplicity of American intelligence agencies leads to confusion and duplication. When intelligence failures permit a surprise attack—as at Pearl Harbor in 1941—or provide an erroneous assessment of a foreign situation—as in the abortive Bay of Pigs invasion of Cuba in 1961—the results may endanger a nation's vital security interests. The Vietnam war provided numerous examples of the failures of military intelligence agencies to obtain reliable tactical and strategic information and to provide useful estimates about the enemy's intentions and capabilities. The 1973 "Yom Kippur" war between Israel and several Arab states provides another example of a failure of American intelligence to anticipate an outbreak of fighting.

Limited War Any war that is fought without the employment of all major weapons and for objectives other than the complete defeat of the enemy. Limited war involves the use of conventional military forces rather than of nuclear superweapons. It typically also involves pursuit of specific political objectives by means of conventional warfare. *See also* NIXON DOCTRINE, page 400.

Significance In the Korean conflict of the early 1950s and the Vietnam war of the 1960s, the United States and other nations fought limited wars with conventional military forces. Efforts to contain limited wars from spreading into general worldwide conflagrations make decisive victories impossible to achieve. Many critics opposed American defense policies in the 1950s on the ground that too much emphasis was placed upon weapons of mass destruction at the expense of mobile tactical forces of the type needed to fight limited wars. This opposition was based on the belief that since neither the Soviet Union nor the United States would employ nuclear weapons, the United States found itself in an inferior position to combat localized aggressions because of its overemphasis on atomic forces. The Kennedy and Johnson Administrations sought to achieve a "balanced force" of conventional and nuclear weapons. The Nixon Administration, reacting to the Vietnam war experience, enunciated the Nixon Doctrine by which it sought to avoid direct limited war involvements by insisting that each ally assume primary responsibility for its own defense, rather than depending on intervention by American forces.

Martial Law   Military government established over a civilian population during an emergency in which military decrees supersede civilian laws and military tribunals replace civil courts. Martial law may be accompanied by the suspension of the writ of habeas corpus. Although the Constitution does not delegate specific power to declare martial law, it is implied from military and defense powers and can be invoked by the President when necessary for the security of the nation. In the states, the governor as commander in chief of the state militia may declare martial law during an emergency occasioned by internal disorders or a natural disaster. Vast discretion is vested in military officers in enforcing martial law. *See also Ex parte Milligan,* page 429.

Significance   Martial law is sometimes erroneously used to describe the use of troops to aid civil authorities and civil courts in maintaining order, which is far more common than the suspension of civil authority. Rare occasions on which federal martial law has been invoked by the President include Abraham Lincoln's placing the southern and border states under martial law, and Franklin Roosevelt's placing Hawaii under it following the attack upon Pearl Harbor. Mass violence has occasionally led governors to invoke martial law to restore order in local communities.

Military Government   Temporary government established by conquering military forces over occupied enemy territory. Areas occupied by American forces are governed under statutes enacted by Congress, supplemented by orders issued by the President as commander in chief. The military governor of a territory under military government exercises supreme legislative, executive, and judicial authority. Civil government operates to the extent permitted by the military governor.

Significance   Military government was used extensively by the United States and its allies during and following World War II in the occupation of enemy territory. Special army military government units were trained to perform occupation duties. Efforts were made to teach the enemy populace the principles and practices of democracy as defined and applied by the occupying forces. Sovereignty was later restored and military government units were withdrawn from formerly occupied territories.

Military-Industrial Complex   An informal alliance among key military, governmental, and corporate decision makers involved in the highly profitable weapons-procurement and military-support system. The phrase, military-industrial complex, was coined by President Dwight D. Eisenhower in his presidential farewell address in which he warned the American people to guard against the growing and excessive militarization of society. The evolution of the military-industrial complex can be determined through such indicators as the growth of the national defense budget, the increasingly militaristic posture of the nation in foreign policy, the magnitude of profits for those corporations engaged extensively in defense business, and the size of subsidies paid by the Pentagon to defense contractors. *See also* CIVILIAN CONTROL, page 417; DEFENSE CONTRACT, page 419.

Significance   The military-industrial complex is a legacy of World War II, the cold war, and the Korean and Vietnam wars. It exists not only in the United States, where the phrase is commonly applied to the elites who wield economic, political, and social power as a result of the arms race, but in all societies—communist as well as capitalist—caught up in the military technology race. Increasing militarism fostered by military-industrial complexes within many nations threatens the security of all. Within the United States, critics charge that the power of the military-industrial complex prohibits the nation from diverting funds from military expenditures to the many pressing problems that divide and weaken American society.

Military Law　Law, enacted by Congress, that governs the conduct of enlisted men and officers of the armed forces of the United States. Military law also establishes the procedures for trial by courts-martial for alleged infractions. Military law seeks to accord servicemen accused of violations full due process of law. *See also* COURT-MARTIAL, page 418.

Significance　Prior to 1950, separate Articles of War applied to the Army, Navy, and Coast Guard. To secure uniformity and in response to criticism concerning the lack of military justice, Congress, in 1950, enacted a single uniform code for all of the armed forces. This Uniform Code of Military Justice seeks to resolve the problem of balancing the needs for discipline with justice. It also permits the trial of servicemen by civil courts for off-duty offenses committed in the United States. Military law, however, does not ordinarily apply to civilians who are abroad with the armed forces (*Reid v. Covert,* 354 U.S. 1 [1957]) or to discharged servicemen for offenses committed while in the armed forces (*Toth v. Quarles,* 350 U.S. 11 [1955]). Critics of military law allege that military personnel enjoy less than first-class citizenship, in that full constitutional due process is not accorded to servicemen.

Mobilization　Preparing a nation to meet an attack or to fight a war. Mobilization involves placing the armed forces in readiness, calling up reserves to active duty, putting the nation's economy on a war footing, establishing governmental controls over manpower, production, resources, and prices. Mobilization for modern war involves readying the totality of a nation's manpower and physical resources for military action. The Office of Emergency Preparedness in the Executive Office of the President is responsible for planning the nation's nonmilitary defense effort. *See also* EMERGENCY POWERS, page 202; WAR POWERS, page 426.

Significance　Mobilization is directed by the President whose constitutional authority as commander in chief is buttressed by vast delegations of emergency powers by Congress for the duration of the war or crisis. Under the stress of war or threat of war, the courts have not generally interfered with the President's exercise of mobilization powers. Mobilization by a nation during peacetime may decrease the possibility of war by calling a potential aggressor's bluff; conversely, it may increase the likelihood of war if other nations consider it a threat to their security.

National Guard　The volunteer armed forces of the states, formerly called the militia. The Constitution provides for a cooperative system under which each state is responsible for appointing officers and Congress provides for organizing, arming, and disciplining the Guard. Each governor is commander in chief of his state's national guard and may call it out for emergencies, such as floods, fires, and civil disorders. The Guard may be called into federal service at any time, as occurred during World Wars I and II and during several cold war emergencies, such as the Berlin Crisis of 1961.

Significance　During much of American history, state militias constituted a relatively powerful and autonomous group of armed forces. Since 1916, the militias have been organized as the

National Guard, an auxiliary of the regular army subject to substantial national control. Congress may authorize calling the Guard into federal service at any time, but the President, as commander in chief, decides when units will be called, and all state jurisdiction ceases when the Guard becomes part of the regular army. Racial and campus disorders during the 1960s and early 1970s led to the calling out of National Guard units in many states, sometimes with controversial results.

Police Action A military action undertaken against a foreign foe without a congressional declaration of war. A police action initiated by the President has come to replace a state of war for several reasons: (1) Under the United Nations Charter and earlier agreements, war is of dubious legality under international law; (2) domestic public opinion may not support the nation's involvement in war; and (3) a president may fear that Congress would not vote to give him a requested declaration of war. See also COMMANDER IN CHIEF, page 418; DECLARATION OF WAR, page 419.

Significance The advances of science and technology in the military weapons field have placed new emphasis on "police action" as a substitute for war. The time when the issue of whether or not the nation should go to war could be leisurely debated in the Congress is long past. Presidents have ordered troops into action in foreign lands without a declaration of war by Congress on more than 150 occasions in American history. The seriousness of the problem, however, has greatly increased because the Korean and Vietnam wars, as recent examples of police actions, were major wars in terms of manpower casualties, costs, domestic impact, and dangers involved.

Reserves The Army, Navy, Air Force, Coast Guard, and National Guard units not on active duty but available to supplement the regular military services during emergencies. Reservists are divided into "ready reserves," "standby reserves," and "retired reserves." The ready reserve may be called to active duty by the President or Congress. The standby reserve is a pool of trained military personnel who can be called up only in case of war or an emergency declared by Congress. A third category, the retired reserve, can be recalled to active duty by Congress during a major emergency.

Significance The reserves consist largely of men who have completed their active military duty and take weekly training and attend summer training camps. The role of reserves in modern warfare depends on the nature of the military situation. In a major nuclear war, for example, decisive blows might be struck before reserves could be mustered. In a limited war, conversely, a reservoir of trained manpower would probably be essential. During the Berlin crisis in 1961, President John F. Kennedy called up some units of the ready reserves for one year of active duty to bolster the American military posture.

Selective Service The conscription system under which the national government drafts men for service in the armed forces. Selective service is based on the constitutional provisions which give Congress the powers necessary "to raise" armies and "to provide" a navy. See also AMNESTY, page 199; CONSCIENTIOUS OBJECTOR, page 63; Selective Draft Law Cases, page 429.

Significance The national government has drafted manpower for military service during and since the Civil War for wartime or emergency service. During World Wars I and II, millions of

Americans were conscripted for military service. Peacetime selective service systems were also instituted by Congress in 1940 and again in 1948. Selective service activity increased in the 1960s because of larger draft quotas for the Vietnam war. This often resulted in antiselective service demonstrations. Large numbers of young men refused induction and either served prison terms or evaded the draft, with thousands of the latter fleeing to havens in Canada and Sweden. The Supreme Court established a basic precedent in 1918 when it rejected the assertion that selective service violates the constitutional provision against "involuntary servitude" by holding that compulsory military service is, rather, an "involuntary duty" and that draft law violators may be punished (*Selective Draft Law Cases,* 245 U.S. 366 [1918]). In the early 1970s, the Nixon Administration ended peacetime selective service by creating a professional service for each of the armed forces based on voluntary enlistment.

Stockpiling The accumulation of strategic raw materials for use during a national crisis. The United States has amassed a stockpile of about eighty essential raw materials and metals that must be obtained abroad or that might be needed quickly during an emergency. Stockpiled materials range from steel and aluminum to natural rubber, industrial diamonds, and such rare items as selenium and tantalum. The storehouse of agricultural products acquired by the national government under its price support program buttresses the strategic materials stockpile. This reserve has dwindled, however, from the impact of the Food for Peace foreign aid program and the domestic school lunch and food stamp programs. *See also* MOBILIZATION, page 423.

Significance Stockpiling offers a country rich enough to indulge in the practice not only a hedge against future military demands but a powerful weapon for economic warfare as well. A stockpile has domestic as well as international implications. The Johnson Administration, for example, released quantities of steel and aluminum for domestic consumption to ward off inflationary price increases in the mid-1960s. The American stockpiling program gave impetus to the export earnings of some of the developing countries while the materials were being acquired; but when the buying program ceased, inflated productive capacities in these countries led to oversupply and a depressing of prices. The market value of the United States strategic materials stockpile has varied considerably during the 1970s because of widely fluctuating supply and demand conditions in the world market and heavy inflationary pressures on primary commodity price structures.

Strategy A plan or preparations for the potential use of armed forces to achieve a specific goal or result. Strategy in the military field involves the science and art of planning and directing major military operations against a foe or potential foe. The President, aided by his top-level military and civilian planning agencies, is responsible for developing the nation's basic defense strategies. Because events never transpire exactly as planned in basic strategies, contingency planning is an essential part of any successful strategy. *See also* TACTICS, page 426.

Significance A broad, carefully developed strategy is indispensable in the achievement of most major goals, especially if they involve competitive situations. In the United States, current military strategic thinking provides for the execution, if necessary, of three simultaneous wars: nuclear, conventional, and brushfire. This strategic rationale has been used to justify recent military budgets. Included in current strategic thinking that guides the nation's policymakers are the assumptions that the Soviet-Chinese split will continue, that the United States will not be faced with the threat of military action from a unified Communist world, and that the nation will be able to avoid a major land war in Asia, the Middle East, or Africa.

Tactics   The art and science of making decisions concerning the deployment of troops, the weapons to be used, the timing of operations, and other decisions aimed at achieving a military success in a battle or limited engagement. Tactics, unlike strategy, involves short-term, relatively small-scale planning, usually carried out by commanders in the field or middle-level staffs. A decision to engage in terror bombing of enemy cities, for example, is a matter of strategy decided at the highest political and military levels, but the decision of a military commander to use bombing to support his troops in an offensive against enemy forces is a tactical decision. *See also* STRATEGY, page 425.

Significance   A successful military operation depends on effective overall strategic planning implemented by decisive tactical deployment and uses of military forces. Tactical errors may occasionally alter strategic plans, as in the abortive Bay of Pigs invasion of Cuba in 1961, which led to the American-Soviet missile crisis in 1962, and a pledge by the President that no further invasions would be attempted. In the field of nuclear weapons, many observers believe that, once employed in a tactical situation, it would be impossible to limit their use and a massive strategic nuclear exchange would follow.

Unification   The integration of the military services of the United States. Under the National Security Act of 1947, the Army, Navy, and Air Force were unified under a single Department of Defense. *See also* DEFENSE REORGANIZATION ACT OF 1958. page 430; NATIONAL SECURITY ACTS, page 430.

Significance   Critics of separate military departments charged that the system promoted interservice rivalries, prevented integrated planning, increased military costs, encouraged recruiting competition, promoted budget battles, and resulted in duplication and inefficiency. Supporters of independent departments claimed that a single military chief would be too powerful, that it would lead to charges of favoritism against the single head, and that the separate service approach had proved itself in World Wars I and II. Unification has not, in fact, eliminated interservice rivalries, and serious cleavages among the three branches, concerning such questions as basic strategy, budget allocation, and missile development responsibility, have continued.

War Powers   The authority expressly granted by the Constitution, implied from it, or inherent in the duty of protecting the nation from its enemies. War powers include those granted to Congress to tax and spend for the common defense, to declare war and make rules concerning captures, to raise and support armies and provide a navy, to enact military law, and to oversee the state militias. Moreover, the elastic clause permits Congress to do whatever is necessary and proper in executing these powers. The President, as commander in chief, has the inherent power to do whatever is necessary to protect the nation, subject to judicial scrutiny. In times of crisis, Congress delegates legislative powers to the President as "emergency powers." *See also* COMMANDER IN CHIEF, page 418; EMERGENCY POWERS, page 202; WAR POWERS ACT page 431.

Significance Although defense and war powers are subject to constitutional limitations in the same way as other powers, they have been stretched to their limits during serious crises. Presidents Abraham Lincoln, Franklin Roosevelt, and Harry Truman regarded the war powers as a special and undefined category of powers that can be exercised whenever the security of the nation is threatened. Congress, the public, and the courts have generally accepted the primacy of the President's role and his exercise of vast powers during time of war. Under conditions of modern warfare, the war powers include control over the domestic economy as well as the military phases of the conflict.

IMPORTANT AGENCIES

Central Intelligence Agency (CIA) An agency, headed by a Director appointed by the President with Senate approval, that functions under the National Security Council to coordinate intelligence activities in the interest of national security. The CIA evaluates raw intelligence data supplied by the Army, Navy, Air Force, State Department, and other intelligence-gathering civilian and military agencies. This information is disseminated among various units of the national government to aid in decision making. The CIA also engages in worldwide intelligence gathering activities. Critics have charged it with engaging in such clandestine activities as political assassinations, coups and revolutions, and extensive surveillance of American citizens. Congress has created a watchdog select committee to oversee CIA operations, but its findings are not subject to review by the entire Congress because of security requirements. *See also* INTELLIGENCE, page 420.

Significance The CIA operations are supersecret in nature, and even most congressmen cannot inquire into its activities. Its financial status is also unknown, since many of its appropriations are hidden in the general budget. In its operations, experts estimate that the major portion of intelligence information is secured through foreign publications and other materials of an open nature, with only a small amount of information obtained through clandestine "cloak-and-dagger" methods. In 1975, Congress and a special Commission appointed by President Gerald R. Ford undertook separate investigations concerning allegations that the CIA had carried on extensive surveillance of American citizens in direct violation of the law under which it was established. An effort to challenge the budget secrecy under which the CIA operates has been rejected by the Supreme Court (*United States v. Richardson,* 418 U.S. 166 [1974]).

Department of Defense (DOD) A major department of the national government with responsibility to formulate military policies and to maintain the armed forces of the United States. Since 1961, it has assumed responsibility for civil defense functions. The Secretary who heads the Department of Defense is a civilian appointed by the President with the Senate's approval. He serves as a member of the Cabinet. The three major military departments of the Army, Navy, and Air Force are each headed by a civilian secretary responsible to the Secretary of Defense. The Chiefs of Staff of the Army and the Air Force and the Chief of Naval Operations are the top military officers in each service who advise the civilian secretaries. These three military leaders join with the Chief of Staff to the Secretary of Defense to form the Joint Chiefs of Staff.

Significance The Defense Department has become the most important department in the national government in numbers of employees and amounts of money spent. Defense has over one million civilian employees, almost one-half of all national civil servants. The Secretary of Defense ranks after the Secretaries of State and Treasury as Cabinet adviser to the President and in the line of succession to that office. Major expenditures of the Department fall into four categories: procurement of military items, salaries and benefits to personnel, operations, and research and development. Military bases are maintained around the world, and coordinated programs are worked out with the more than forty nations with which the United States is militarily allied. Increasing emphasis is being placed on research and development as the technological race with the Soviet Union accelerates. Unity of command has been achieved through the National Security Acts of 1947 and 1949 and the Defense Reorganization Act of 1958, but interservice rivalries have not completely given way to unity of purpose, especially during budget making.

National Aeronautics and Space Council (NASC) A staff agency in the Executive Office of the President that advises the President on policies, plans, and programs concerning the American space program. Members include the Vice President of the United States, who serves as Chairman, the Secretaries of State and Defense, the Administrator of the National Aeronautics and Space Administration (NASA), who carries out space program decisions, and the Chairman of the Nuclear Regulatory Commission. The NASC was established under the National Aeronautics and Space Act of 1958.

Significance The Council was created to meet the challenge posed when Soviet scientists placed the first "sputnik" in space in 1957. The American failure to secure a "first" was blamed on many factors, among them the lack of a unified program to eliminate duplication and to achieve a common effort. Rival military space teams were brought into an integrated program directed by the civilian NASC and NASA agencies. The approach was generally pronounced a success when lunar module *Eagle* landed the first men on the moon on July 20, 1969. American space activities peaked in the late 1960s, and programs and budgets have declined drastically in the 1970s.

National Security Council (NSC) A staff agency in the Executive Office of the President, established by the National Security Act of 1947, that advises the President on domestic and foreign matters involving national security. The Council is composed of the President, the Vice President, the Secretaries of State and Defense, and the Director of the Office of Emergency Preparedness. The Central Intelligence Agency (CIA) functions under the direction of the Council. The Council's main role is to assess and appraise the objectives, commitments, and risks of the United States in the interests of national security and to make recommendations to the President on specific policies and decisions. *See also* CENTRAL INTELLIGENCE AGENCY, page 427; DOMESTIC COUNCIL, page 214.

Significance The National Security Council is the highest policy-recommending body in defense and related fields. When a serious crisis erupts anywhere in the world, the President may summon the Council into an immediate session. The President is free to reject the advice of the Council, but this is unlikely because it is composed of the highest leaders of his administration in the defense and foreign policy fields. The continuing role and influence of the NSC have depended on the President, with some presidents using it regularly to consider some of the most important questions of foreign policy, whereas others have rarely called it into session.

United States Arms Control and Disarmament Agency (USACDA)   An independent agency established in 1961 to conduct research and to develop disarmament policies. USACDA is headed by a Director, appointed by the President with Senate consent, who also serves as principal adviser to the President and the Secretary of State on disarmament matters. *See also* STRATEGIC ARMS LIMITATION TALKS (SALT), page 408.

Significance USACDA was established in response to American and foreign demands that greater efforts be expended to reach a disarmament agreement. USACDA has carried on extensive "peace research" and has participated in thermonuclear and conventional disarmament negotiations at Geneva and the United Nations. Many of its studies are carried on by private and public institutions on a contractual basis. Major areas of negotiation and research include a ban on all nuclear testing, an antiproliferation treaty to prevent the spread of nuclear weapons among additional states, technical and political problems concerned with the enforcement of a disarmament agreement, and the development of new approaches to disarmament and arms control. USACDA research studies contributed to the concluding of SALT I and SALT II strategic arms limitation agreements between the United States and the Soviet Union.

IMPORTANT CASES

Ex parte Milligan, 4 Wallace 2 (1866): Held that the suspension of the right of writ of habeas corpus and the trial of a civilian by a military tribunal while the civilian courts are operating violate the Constitution. The Court held that neither the President nor Congress could legally deny the accused a civil trial by jury in an area outside an actual theater of war. *See also* CIVILIAN CONTROL, page 417; COURT-MARTIAL; page 418; MARTIAL LAW, page 422.

Significance The *Milligan* case reaffirmed the principles of civilian control over the military and the maintenance of due process of law free from military interference. There have been no further attempts to suspend the writ of habeas corpus in the continental United States. In 1941, following the attack upon Pearl Harbor, President Franklin Roosevelt placed the Hawaiian Islands under martial law and all civil courts were replaced by military tribunals. In a case after the war (*Duncan v. Kahanamoku*, 327 U.S. 304 [1946]), the Court held this action invalid.

Selective Draft Law Cases, 245 U.S. 366 (1918): Upheld the constitutional authority of Congress to draft men into the military forces. The Supreme Court rejected the argument that conscription is "involuntary servitude" in violation of the Thirteenth Amendment, holding that such service by the citizen was "his supreme and noble duty." *See also* CONSCIENTIOUS OBJECTOR, page 63; SELECTIVE SERVICE, page 424.

Significance Although the *Selective Draft Law Cases* dealt with a wartime conscription measure, the constitutionality of the peacetime draft is also based on this precedent. During war and in peacetime, the Army has depended heavily upon the draft to supply needed manpower, whereas the Navy and Air Force have mainly used volunteers.

IMPORTANT STATUTES

Defense Reorganization Act of 1958   An act that sought to overcome administrative weaknesses in the Defense Department created by the National Security Acts of 1947 and 1949. The Act of 1958 made it clear that the Secretaries of the Army, Navy, and Air Force were under the direct authority of the Secretary of Defense. A direct line of command from the Secretary to operational units in in the field replaced the earlier system whereby the Secretary communicated decisions through the Army, Navy, and Air Force secretaries. *See also* DEPARTMENT OF DEFENSE, page 427; NATIONAL SECURITY ACTS OF 1947 AND 1949, page 430.

Significance   In the wake of Soviet space and missile successes, President Dwight Eisenhower proposed a sweeping reorganization of the defense organization. Congress accepted part of the President's proposals in the Act of 1958, but retained a legislative veto over the Defense Secretary's organizational changes, permitted the civilian and military heads of the three services to communicate directly with Congress, and specifically exempted the National Guard and Marine Corps from alteration, except by Congress. Although the Act of 1958 was designed to eliminate interservice rivalries over budgets and weapon development programs, controversy among the services has continued. The Act of 1958 expressly denied any power to the President to merge any of the military services or to create a military chief of staff system.

National Security Acts of 1947 and 1949   The Act of 1947 provided the nation's most comprehensive reorganization of its defense structure. It established a new National Security Organization and placed the three major military forces—Army, Navy, and Air Force—in a National Military Establishment under a single civilian Secretary of Defense. The National Security Council was established as a top-level advisory body. In the National Security Act of 1949 the National Military Establishment was replaced with a single executive department—the Department of Defense—and the National Security Council was transferred to the Executive Office as a staff agency to the President. *See also* DEFENSE REORGANIZATION ACT OF 1958, page 430; DEPARTMENT OF DEFENSE, page 427.

Significance   The National Security Acts of 1947 and 1949 were aimed at unifying and coordinating the efforts of the nation's armed services. Although the 1947 Act stated that the services were not to be merged, it called for "their integration into an efficient team of land, naval, and air forces." The authority given to the Secretary of Defense in the Act of 1947 proved insufficient to unify in fact three separate military services, each largely autonomous in its operations and protective of its traditional role. The Act of 1949 sought to reduce these interservice rivalries further by strengthening the hand of the Secretary of Defense over the military departments. The National Security Acts provide the most cogent example of a major functional consolidation in the national administration.

War Powers Act of 1973   A declaration of congressional authority to participate with the President in making national decisions to use American armed forces abroad. The War Powers Act provides that the President can commit American troops to action only: (1) following a declaration of war by Congress; (2) by specific statutory authorization; and (3) when an attack upon the United States or its armed forces creates a national emergency. When such an attack occurs, the President must report immediately to Congress; if Congress does not thereupon declare war within sixty days, the President must terminate his commitment of American troops. If, however, the President certifies to Congress that military conditions require their continued use for the safety of American troops, an additional thirty days is permitted under the War Powers Act. After ninety days, the Congress may, by concurrent resolution not subject to a presidential veto, require the President to disengage all troops involved in the hostilities. *See also* COMMANDER IN CHIEF, page 418; DECLARATION OF WAR, page 419; WAR POWERS, page 426.

Significance   The War Powers Act was largely a reaction to the disastrous involvement of American troops in Indochina over a period of years as a result of decisions made by several presidents, with little in the way of congressional controls over their actions. Throughout American history, presidents have committed the nation's armed forces to action abroad without a declaration of war or other form of congressional consent. The supporters of the War Powers Act sought to close this constitutional loophole by providing for a sharing of the powers to decide when, where, and under what circumstances military interventions could occur in the future. The Act also reflected the effort by Congress to redress the balance of decision-making power that has moved relentlessly from the legislative to the executive branch as a result of the President's reacting to a series of domestic and foreign crises over a forty-year period. Critics of the Act have charged that the new congressional role undermines the nation's ability to act decisively during an international crisis. This factor, they assert, encourages potential enemies to take provocative actions and weakens our relations with our allies. Although the War Powers Act assigns Congress the *legal* power to participate in all decisions involving the commitment of American troops abroad, the *political* will to invoke it to restrain a President's actions in the field of national security remains problematical.

18   State and Local Government

Alderman A member of a city council. The term originated in England and was used in the American colonies to designate officials chosen by the common council of the city to exercise judicial power and to share in the governing of the city. In the nineteenth century, when bicameral legislatures were common in cities, one house was designated as the Board of Aldermen, the other, as the Common Council. *See also* WARD, page 454.

Significance The commission and council-manager plans of city government have been accompanied by the use of the terms commissioner or councilman to designate members of the city legislative body. Where used, the term alderman is generally associated with cities in which ward systems of representation for the city council function under a mayor-council plan of government.

Annexation The addition of territory to a unit of government. Annexation usually denotes the addition by a city of land adjacent to it, to meet the problems of metropolitan expansion. Procedures for annexation are established by state law and generally require an affirmative vote of both the central city and of the area concerned. In a few states, as in Virginia and Texas, areas may be annexed by action of the city alone or through judicial procedures. *See also* METROPOLITAN AREA, page 446.

Significance Annexation is viewed as one solution to the problems caused by the urbanization of fringe areas of a city. Through annexation a community seeks to eliminate conflicts of authority and duplication of services, and to protect orderly city growth, which is hampered by the existence of numerous units of government. Fringe area dwellers often fear high city taxes and prefer to retain their identity as a community. Cities that annex residential fringe areas not having the broad tax base provided by business and industry, and with soaring needs for costly services, find the annexed areas to be costly for city taxpayers. Also, many annexed areas lack proper planning and zoning, posing special problems for the city administration.

Attorney General The chief legal officer of the state. The office of attorney general is elective in forty-two states. He serves as legal adviser to the governor and to state agencies, represents the state in legal proceedings, and may have general supervisory powers over local prosecuting attorneys. *See also* ATTORNEY GENERAL, page 238; CORPORATION COUNSEL, page 439; DISTRICT ATTORNEY, page 247

Significance Opinions of the attorney general have the force of law unless they are overturned by a court. Many students of state government argue that the office should be appointive, since the governor should have full confidence in his chief legal adviser, similar to that placed by a client in his attorney. The state attorney general holds an office that frequently leads to the governorship or to a judicial appointment.

Board of Education The state or local governing body for public education. State boards of education establish statewide educational and teacher certification standards, determine curricula, and control state educational funds. Most state boards are appointed by the governor; others are elected. Boards usually include the state superintendent of schools, who is often elected, although the trend is toward his appointment by the board. Local school boards are chosen by popular vote in school districts in most states, with a few appointed by the city council. The local school board determines policy but leaves much responsibility in the hands of a school superintendent whom they appoint. Local school boards determine teacher salaries, curricula, and building needs. *See also* SCHOOL DISTRICT, page 448; SUPERINTENDENT OF PUBLIC INSTRUCTION, page 451.

Significance Boards of education administer the largest share of state and local expenditures. The independent status of most boards of education is in keeping with tradition that schools be "kept out of politics." Schools, however, develop "politics" of their own, and no public agency spending huge sums of money is "out of politics." Typically, school boards are controlled by the same political group that dominates other governmental functions of a community and are subjected to considerable community pressures to have the school reflect the views of the community.

Borough A municipal corporation, generally smaller than a city. Boroughs are found mainly in Pennsylvania, Connecticut, and New Jersey, and resemble villages or towns of other states. Borough is also the named assigned to major local government divisions in Alaska, comparable to counties. The city of New York is divided into five boroughs: Manhattan, Brooklyn, Queens, Bronx, and Richmond. *See also* COUNTY page 440.

Significance The term borough is a holdover from England and colonial America. In New York City, the boroughs represent an attempt to decentralize the operations of that huge metropolis. The use of the term in the constitution of Alaska represents a noteworthy departure from tradition. In order to avoid some of the pitfalls of county government and to adapt local government to their peculiar needs, the people of Alaska provided for the creation of boroughs that would embrace an area and population with common interests and that would have a high degree of home rule.

Charter The basic law of a local governmental unit that defines its powers, responsibilities, and organization. Charters are granted, under state constitutional or statutory provisions, to municipal corporations and, in some states, to counties or townships. Charters may be provided by: (1) special act of the legislature applicable to one city, (2) general laws applicable to all cities within a certain classification, (3) optional charter laws whereby a city may choose a charter from a group provided by law, or (4) home rule whereby the people of a city draw up their own charter. *See also* GENERAL LAWS, page 443; HOME RULE, page 444; OPTIONAL CHARTER, page 447; SPECIAL ACT, page 449.

Significance In one sense, every unit of local government has a "charter" composed of the local government provisions of state constitutions, statutes, and the common law. Many cities or other municipal corporations, such as villages, do not have a charter in the form of a *document,* particularly when they operate under special acts or general laws. A charter document is generally found in cities operating under home rule and, sometimes, under optional charters. All local governments are subject to the state constitution and laws, and all actions taken under a charter must conform to these higher laws and to the charter as well.

City A municipal corporation, chartered by the state, that is usually larger than a village, town, borough, or other incorporated area. The term is a legal concept and exactly what constitutes a city is defined by state law. This is generally based on population but may be based on assessed valuation. The Census Bureau has identified more than 18,500 cities as of 1972, comprising about 25 percent of local governmental units.

Significance Cities are generally accorded more authority over fiscal matters and services than are other incorporated units. Cities, too, are organized differently, with the mayor-council plan, commission plan, and council-manager plan generally made available by state law. Most Americans live in cities and their suburbs, and city culture is replacing the traditions of a rural society. Cities have long fought for greater freedom from state control and the trend is toward giving cities home rule.

City Council The policy-making and, in some instances, administrative board of a city. The structure and powers of city councils vary with the plan of city government. In the weak-mayor and commission plans, the council plays a large role in lawmaking and in the direction and control of administrative departments. In the strong-mayor and council-manager plans, the council's job is largely in the realm of lawmaking, with only general oversight of administration. In all cases, the most important jobs of the council are to pass ordinances that determine public policy, and to exercise control over the purse strings. Other functions, which vary from city to city, may include serving as a board of review for tax assessments, issuing licenses, and making appointments. Members of city councils are elected, on a partisan or nonpartisan basis, from wards or districts, at large, or by a combination of both. *See also* COMMISSION PLAN, page 436; COUNCIL-MANAGER PLAN, page 439; MAYOR-COUNCIL PLAN, page 446.

Significance City councils are typically unicameral bodies, most commonly of five or seven members, but they range up to fifty. The commission and council-manager forms of city government, which replaced the cumbersome and often corrupt bicameral city councils, have raised the prestige and quality of councilmen. Each state determines by law the structure and powers of city councils.

City-County Consolidation   The merger of county government with all other units within the county to form one unit of government. The plan is suggested as one solution to the problems of a metropolitan area, particularly when it coincides with the county boundary. *See also* MET-ROPOLITAN AREA, page 446; URBAN COUNTY PLAN, page 453.

Significance City-county consolidation simplifies the government of a metropolitan county by eliminating duplication of services and allowing for areawide planning and administration of services. In many areas, such as Philadelphia, Boston, and New Orleans, city and county boundaries are actually or substantially the same. Where several units are involved, residents of smaller municipalities and rural parts of the county tend to resist consolidation. They fear increased costs and want to maintain their individual identity. The consolidations of Baton Rouge, Louisiana, Nashville, Tennessee and Indianapolis, Indiana (the last called "Unigov"), with their counties are examples of successful consolidations. As a solution to metropolitan problems, however, the city-county consolidation plan does not meet the problems of areas that overlap counties or extend through many counties or even states.

City-County Separation   Political separation of the city from the county. Cities are generally part of the county in which they lie and the city residents pay county taxes and receive certain county services. More than thirty cities in Virginia, and the cities of St. Louis, Denver, Baltimore, and San Francisco, are separated from their counties and provide their residents with county services. *See also* METROPOLITAN AREA, page 446.

Significance City-county separation is designed to increase the efficiency of the urban area and to eliminate overlapping government. The urban area, however, tends to continue to spread beyond the city limits. Moreover, the rural areas of the county and smaller municipalities are left without the financial help of the city, and the county must continue to provide services. These problems have been met in part in Virginia by permitting the judiciary to adjust boundary lines to meet urban growth. At one time city-county separation was considered a solution to metropolitan problems, but, except for the state of Virginia, it is rarely used today.

Classification of Cities   The grouping of cities by a state legislature according to population for the purpose of enacting laws or city charters. The practice of classification results from the requirement found in most state constitutions, that the legislature must deal with local governments by general law rather than by special act applicable to one unit. Since general laws may result in putting all cities, large and small, into a uniform mold, legislatures have classified cities and passed general laws applicable to each class. *See also* GENERAL LAWS, page 443.

Significance A classification must be reasonable and attainable by others not yet within the group. For example, state legislatures have tried to evade the purposes of general law requirements by creating classes based on location in such a way as to have the effect of a special act applicable only to one community. However, laws applicable to cities with populations exceeding one million, for example, may actually apply to one city, but, theoretically, other cities may reach that population figure. Classification schemes are used to determine forms of government as well as specific powers that a city may exercise. The courts determine whether a scheme of classification is reasonable.

Commission Plan   One of the forms of city government in the United States wherein both legislative and executive powers are exercised by a commission of three to nine members. Variations in structure are found around the country, but the essential ingredients of the commission plan include: (1) the concentration of legislative and executive powers in a small group elected at large on a nonpartisan ballot; (2) the collective responsibility of the commission to pass ordinances and control the purse strings; (3) the individual responsibility of each commissioner to head a city department, such as public works, finance, and public safety; and (4) the selection of the mayor from among the commissioners but reducing the office to that of ceremonial leadership. *See also* CITY COUNCIL, page 434.

Significance   The commission plan enjoyed great popularity from its inception in Galveston, Texas, in 1901 until about 1920. Its simplicity and its resemblance to business corporation organization appealed to reformers who sought an end to the long ballot and the extremes of partisan politics in municipal government. As its defects became apparent, however, its popularity declined. A major defect is the failure to separate legislative and executive authority, with the result that there is little check on spending and administration is in the hands of amateurs. The lack of a chief executive makes it difficult for the voter to fix responsibility, and, in turn, the city suffers from the absence of political leadership. Furthermore, trying to fit the number of city agencies to the number of commissioners leads to rigidity in organization. To meet these defects, many cities followed the lead of Des Moines, Iowa, and added the initiative, referendum, and recall to the plan, as well as a merit system for selection of governmental employees.

Commonwealth   A designation equivalent to the term "state" used in Pennsylvania, Massachusetts, Virginia, and Kentucky. The term "commonwealth" is generally used to indicate a federation of nations or states in which each unit has a large measure of self-government, such as those of the British Commonwealth of Nations. Puerto Rico is officially designated a "free commonwealth" associated with the United States. *See also* CONFEDERATION, page 32; STATE, page 18; STATE SOVEREIGNTY, page 29; TERRITORY, page 42.

Significance   "Commonwealth" is the historically-derived term used as the official name for several American states, but the term has no legal significance. However, its usage in connection with Puerto Rico does indicate special status for that area as an independent territory of the United States.

Congressional Township   A six mile-square area of land established under laws of Congress for the purpose of surveying the land. The system was started by the Confederation Congress in 1785, and was applied to the land in most states. Excluded are the original thirteen states and Maine, Kentucky, Tennessee, Vermont, West Virginia, and Texas. Under the law, land is divided into townships six miles square, and each township is divided into thirty-six mile-square sections. Each section is further subdivided into quarter sections and less. By the assignment of numbered base lines, similar to the longitude and latitude patterns on maps, any parcel of land may be easily identified. *See also* TOWNSHIP, page 452.

Significance   The congressional township system of land survey was instituted to replace the haphazard "metes and bounds" method of identifying tracts of land wherein landmarks were used rather than precise, numerical points of reference. Accurate records, particularly for real-estate transfers, are made possible by the congressional township plan. A congressional township is not a unit of government and, frequently, the township will overlap county and state boundaries. Many township units of government, however, do follow the congressional township line, accounting for the six-mile-square civil township. Congress reserved one section of the township (section 16) for the support of public schools and many states provide that the proceeds from this section constitute a permanent fund for school purposes.

Consolidation   The union of two or more units of government to form a single unit. Consolidation is often recommended as a solution to metropolitan area problems, but it is also recommended in rural areas as a means of reducing the large number of local governments in existence. State constitutions or statutes designate consolidation procedures, generally requiring the separate consent of all units. *See also* METROPOLITAN AREA, page 446; SCHOOL DISTRICT, page 448.

Significance   In the metropolitan areas, consolidation has the same benefits and meets the same opposition as do annexation proposals. It eliminates conflicting authority and duplication of services but meets opposition from suburban communities desiring to retain their identity. In rural areas, consolidation is viewed as a means of strengthening counties and townships that were established many years ago and no longer contain sizable populations or the means to carry on governmental functions efficiently. By joining together, it is expected that services may be improved and much confusion eliminated. Nonetheless, legal intricacies, tradition, and the opposition of vested interests militate against consolidation. Many school districts, established prior to modern means of transportation, however, have found it desirable to consolidate in order to realize the benefits of larger enrollments and school plants, although this, too, meets strong opposition. The major change in the number of governmental units since the 1940s has been the reduction in the number of school districts through consolidation.

Constitution, State   The organic law of a state that defines and limits governmental power and guarantees the rights of the people. Each state has a constitution and its provisions may not conflict with the United States Constitution. Since state governments have all powers not delegated to the national government, state constitutions, typically, are filled with restrictions on legislative and executive power rather than grants of authority. *See also* CONSTITUTION, page 24.

Significance   State constitutions tend to be unduly lengthy and filled with details better left to statutes. The authority of the legislature and executive is typically restricted in taxation, expenditures, and administration. Local governments and major state services, such as education and highways, tend to be frozen into a specific mold. These defects, among others, have led to considerable agitation for state constitutional reform, since the people's representatives often have their hands tied by the constitution in their attempts to meet day-to-day problems. This has resulted in the frequent amendment of many state constitutions and the thorough revision of others. Proponents of constitutional reform seek a document more like the national Constitution, with emphasis on fundamentals rather than details. Strong opposition to change, however, comes from those whose interests are protected by specific provisions as well as from many who tend to view a constitution as a sacred document.

Constitutional Amendments, State   Changes in, or additions to, a state constitution. Amendment procedures are detailed in each state's constitution. Generally, two proposal methods are available—legislative, by an extraordinary majority, and initiative of the people. Ratification by the people is usually accomplished by simple majority vote, but a few states require an extraordinary majority. Under the initiative method, permitted in fourteen states, the voters draw up a petition with a specified number of signatures (8 or 10 percent of the voters) requesting the desired change. If the petition is in order, the proposal goes on the ballot for ratification by the people.

Significance   Most state constitutions have been amended numerous times to meet changing conditions or the desires of strong interest groups. The legislative proposal method has been used most often because it is simple and inexpensive compared to a constitutional convention. The requirement of extraordinary majorities, however, often makes it difficult to propose controversial measures. Unlike the national Constitution, however, state constitutions have required frequent amendment because of their inflexibility. The initiative method serves as an important weapon for the people when the legislature fails to respond to their demands. It tends, however, to be abused by pressure groups, and many such proposals are rejected. Many states with extremely difficult amending procedures suffer from outmoded organization and procedures in the daily workings of government. Often the average citizen fails to realize that his state constitution is a stumbling block to effective government.

Constitutional Commission   A group of citizens selected by the legislature and/or the governor of a state to study the state constitution and to make recommendations for change.

Significance   Constitutional commissions have been used in a number of states when revision of the constitution has been under consideration. The most notable instance took place in Georgia in 1945, where a commission, established by the legislature, had its proposed revision of the entire constitution ratified by the people as a single amendment to replace the old constitution. In other cases, a commission has served as an educational medium, prior to the calling of a constitutional convention. In still others, the legislature submitted to the people specific proposals of a commission as amendments. Through the commission device, a group of leading citizens, making use of expert advice, can contribute to better understanding of constitutional problems.

Constitutional Convention   A body selected by the people to rewrite the constitution. Most state constitutions make provisions for the calling of a constitutional convention (usually called "Con-Con") but, even if no provisions are made, the power to call a convention is considered to be inherent in the people in their sovereign capacity. Eleven states provide for a mandatory, periodic submission to the people of the question of whether they wish to call a convention. The procedures for a constitutional convention generally involve: (1) the placing of the question on the ballot by the legislature, usually by an extraordinary majority unless it be mandatory for that year; (2) the election of delegates, should the people approve the call; (3) the meeting of the convention, which has deliberations similar in method and procedure to legislative bodies; and (4) the submission of the new constitution to the people for ratification.

Significance   A constitutional convention is an historic event; over 200 have been held in the United States. About sixteen states have held just one convention, but some states have held ten or more. Constitutional conventions are expensive and many people fear that vested interests or longstanding practices will be disturbed. Yet, conventions represent the highest voice of the people and have tended to attract able citizen talent. The voter is brought into the picture at several stages, and the entire process has an excellent educational effect. The provision for the mandatory call of a convention is based on the assumption that each generation should have the opportunity to revise its basic law.

Constitutional Officer   A public official, usually in the executive branch, whose office is established and required by the constitution. State constitutions generally name numerous state and local officials and designate their terms of office and duties. For example, most state constitutions provide for the election of such statewide officers as secretary of state, attorney general, state treasurer, and state auditor. On the local level, the constitution may require election of such officers as sheriff, county clerk, township supervisor, and highway commissioner. *See also* SHORT BALLOT, page 142.

Significance   Constitutional officers present one of the troublesome aspects of state government today because they enjoy much immunity from legislative power and may resist direction from the chief executive, particularly when they belong to different political parties. Reform of state and local government is difficult, since these offices cannot be abolished without constitutional change. Supporters of provisions for constitutional officers maintain that they reduce concentration of power in the chief executive and retain greater control in the hands of voters.

Corporation Counsel   The attorney for a municipal corporation. The term, "corporation counsel" is used to distinguish the city, village, or township attorney from the district attorney or county prosecutor, who serves to enforce statewide and criminal law in the local communities. The corporation counsel is appointed by the mayor and/or council and serves mainly to advise on noncriminal matters. Most local governmental units do not have a regular attorney attached to the official staff but hire a law firm to serve as counsel as needed. *See also* ATTORNEY GENERAL, page 432; DISTRICT ATTORNEY, page 247.

Significance   The corporation counsel, like his counterparts at other levels of government, plays a vital role in the community which he serves. Increasing reliance on legal advice by largely amateur and part-time public officials enhances his authority, particularly as local governments become more involved in state and national relations and various aspects of community development. Where no full-time corporation counsel or legal staff exists, the business for the lawyer or firm chosen to represent the municipal corporation can be lucrative.

Council-manager Plan   A form of city government in which the city council appoints a professional administrator, a manager, to act as the chief executive. With variations from city to city, the essentials of this plan are: (1) a small council or commission of five or seven members elected at large on a nonpartisan ballot, with power to make policy and to hire and fire the manager; (2) a professionally trained manager, with authority to hire and fire his subordinates, who is responsible to the council for efficient administration of the city; and (3) a mayor chosen separately or from within the council, but with no executive functions. The council must refrain from bypassing the manager by interfering with his subordinates or in the details of administration, and the manager must follow the policies outlined by the council. A merit system for selection of employees is generally used under this plan. *See also* CITY COUNCIL, page 434; COUNTY-MANAGER PLAN, page 442; MAYOR-ADMINISTRATOR PLAN, page 445.

Significance The council-manager plan is a product of the twentieth century, and about 2,000 cities use the manager system. A small percentage of cities have abandoned the plan after trying it, usually because of lack of citizen understanding of its operations. More than one-third of cities over 5,000 population, and about one-half of those over 25,000, use the manager plan, but only four over 500,000 (Cincinnati, Dallas, San Antonio, San Diego) have adopted it. Advantages of the plan include its simplicity, clarification of responsibility for both policy and administration, and its use of experts to adopt and utilize modern techniques of budgeting, planning, and overall administration. The profession of city manager has gained in status, and many universities train managers. The manager may also be of invaluable aid to the council and the public in suggesting policy alternatives. Opponents of the plan criticize the lack of a strong political leader, particularly essential in large cities where strong mayors play this role, and charge that the manager plan is undemocratic since the executive is appointed. The council is responsible, however, to the people and has full control over the manager. The plan is now well established in the United States and is growing in popularity.

Councils of Government Voluntary organizations of counties and municipalities concerned with areawide problems. About 200 regional councils have been established, mainly since 1966, under incentives furnished by federal grants. Most are located in metropolitan areas, (for example, South East Michigan Council of Governments [SEMCOG]) and under authority granted by participating units, undertake such tasks as regional planning, community development, pollution control, water systems, and airport construction. Congress has encouraged this development by requiring such Councils to determine the regional effects of programs funded by federal grants. In some cases, the Council becomes the "designated agency" through which federal departments, such as the Department of Housing and Urban Development, work in making grants to local communities. *See also* METROPOLITAN AREA, page 446.

Significance The widespread development of Councils of Government results from a combination of massive problems that transcend artificial geographic boundaries and the reluctance of communities to federate or consolidate into metropolitan governments. The Councils also demonstrate the power inherent in the use of federal programs to promote goals that otherwise would not be met. Though voluntary, the Councils actually possess coercive power because of their authority under federal law to review and clear regional programs. Critics charge that the Councils simply add another layer of government to the metropolitan confusion and that they tend to ignore local social and political problems.

County The major unit of local government in the United States, except in Connecticut, Rhode Island, and Alaska. Louisiana has county units but calls them parishes. Alaska has a new major division of local government called a borough. Connecticut abolished counties in 1959. In New England, counties are relatively unimportant for governmental purposes. Otherwise, county governments exist as principal agencies of the state for statewide purposes, and as important units of local government. There are over 3000 counties in the United States ranging from three in Delaware to 254 in Texas. Their powers and functions vary from state to state and within states as well. Generally, counties perform such functions as law enforcement and maintenance of courts, highways, schools, and welfare agencies. In urban areas, counties may perform a variety of services usually handled by cities. Counties are governed by a board that differs in composition from state to state. Counties have a large number of elected officials, such as sheriff, clerk, coroner, attorney, auditor, register of deeds, surveyor, and treasurer. *See also* COUNTY BOARD, page 441.

Significance Counties were originally established as administrative subdivisions of the state and for local governmental purposes. The number of counties and their organizational patterns have undergone almost no change through the years and tradition militates against change. Many are densely populated and integral parts of metropolitan areas. Others have lost population and are thoroughly rural. The metropolitan counties are faced with the need to expand their services; the rural counties find it difficult to support their regular functions. Thus, in one case, the county has achieved new importance while, in the other, means are sought to relieve it of its burdens. Most counties suffer from outmoded administrative organization, the lack of a chief executive, the long ballot, and the spoils system.

County Board The governing body of the county. The official title of this body varies from state to state with as many as twenty-seven different titles used. Most common are "board of commissioners," "board of supervisors," and "county court," but the term county board is the most popular one. Most county boards are composed of three to five commissioners or supervisors who are elected by the voters of the county. In states with township government, the board is composed of township supervisors and representatives of cities within the county, but these are undergoing change to comply with "one man, one vote" rulings of the Supreme Court that have been applied to county boards (*Avery v. Midland County, Texas,* 390 U.S. 474 [1968]). In several states the board is composed of county judges. The board administers state law in the county, levies taxes, appoints numerous officials, and supervises the general affairs of the county. *See also* COUNTY, page 440.

Significance County boards are important strongholds of political power. The growing importance of the county in urban areas has added to the powers and influence of these boards. In some areas, they have not been adequate to meet new responsibilities, and many persons advocate the use of a county manager since no individual has overall responsibility for the county. Boards are also handicapped by the large number of elected county officials over whom they exercise little control.

County Clerk A county official who is popularly elected in more than half the states. His principal duties include acting as secretary to the county board, supervision of elections, issuance of various business certificates and licenses, and handling of birth, marriage, and death records, collectively known as "vital statistics."

Significance The county clerk's office tends to become a central clearing house for county affairs, and the clerk is often an important political figure. The nature of the office has led some observers to consider it the logical place to vest principal administrative supervisory duties in the absence of a regular county executive.

County-manager Plan   A plan patterned after the council-manager plan used in many cities. The county-manager plan envisages a small county board for policy determination and an appointed professional manager to serve as the executive officer of the county. Few of the more than 3,000 counties in the United States have adopted the manager plan. *See also* COUNCIL-MANAGER PLAN, page 439.

Significance   The county-manager plan is designed to overcome the defects common to most counties—the long ballot, the lack of an integrating executive officer, and the spoils system. General public apathy and a tradition-bound attitude toward county government have made for slow adoption of the plan. Constitutional provisions also make it difficult for counties to reorganize. Such reforms as county home rule or optional charters will probably be necessary before the county-manager plan can spread. Supporters of the plan hold that, in both urban and rural counties, it can make the operation of county government more efficient and clearly fix responsibility. Critics argue that, since the county is principally an administrative arm of the state, the manager would obstruct state supervision of county activities.

Dillon's Rule   A rule enunciated by Judge John F. Dillon, an authority on municipal corporations, to the effect that a municipal corporation can exercise only those powers expressly granted to it by state law, those necessarily implied from the granted powers, and those essential for the purposes of the organization. If any doubt exists, it is to be resolved against the local unit, in favor of the state. *See also* FEDERAL ANALOGY, page 442; HOME RULE, page 444; UNITARY STATE, page 43.

Significance   The spread of home rule has weakened the force of Dillon's Rule and some state constitutions overrule Dillon by providing that local governmental powers are to be liberally interpreted. Yet, Dillon's Rule underscores the subordinate relationship of local government to the state. The rule applies to all local units. Local government is a creature of the state and has only those powers permitted by state constitutions and laws.

Federal Analogy   A concept, usually incorrectly applied, that assumes that the relationship of local governments to state governments is the same as that of the states to the national government. The relationship between the national and state governments is "federal"—a division of power defined by the Constitution; the relationship between a state government and its local subdivisions is "unitary"—the local units are subordinate to the state and have only those powers authorized by state law. *See also* CHARTER, page 433; DILLON'S RULE, page 442; FEDERALISM, page 34; HOME RULE, page 444; *Reynolds v. Sims,* page 195; UNITARY STATE, page 43.

Significance   The federal analogy is usually applied by those who seek to have counties or cities treated as independent entities similar to the states themselves. The concept was specifically rejected by the Supreme Court when it held the "one person, one vote" principle of legislative apportionment applicable to both houses of a state legislature (*Reynolds v. Sims,* 377 U.S. 533 [1964]). The Court declined to hold that one house of a state legislature could be treated like the United States Senate, where representation is based on the equality of states in the union. Some modification of the unitary principle takes place when a state adopts home rule for local governments, but such authority may usually be withdrawn or circumscribed by state law.

Functional Consolidation The cooperation of two or more units of government in providing services to their inhabitants. Several counties may cooperate for common administration of health services, or two cities may agree to have a common water supply or sewerage system. *See also* COUNCILS OF GOVERNMENT, page 440; METROPOLITAN AREA, page 446.

Significance Functional consolidation can help metropolitan areas, with their complex of overlapping governments, as well as rural areas, which lack financial resources. It provides a satisfactory alternative to complete consolidation of units which often meets strong opposition. Another form of consolidation of functions takes place when a state takes over a service, such as highways or education, and relieves local units of these burdens. Functional consolidation has made headway in metropolitan areas, since it serves to solve technical problems while permitting units of government to retain their separate political identity.

General Laws Laws applicable to all local government units of a similar type. Most state constitutions now provide that the legislature may pass only laws of general application rather than special acts applicable only to one unit. To allow for variations the legislatures often classify units according to population. *See also* CLASSIFICATION OF CITIES, page 435.

Significance General laws relieve the burden on the legislature by making it unnecessary to deal with each unit individually. More important, it restricts the favoritism and political in-fighting that characterized the special act system and permitted the legislatures to make decisions for individual cities. Often, however, the legislature's classifications are so specific as to apply, in fact, to a single unit of government.

Governor The chief executive officer of a state. In all states, the governor is elected by the people and serves for four years in most and for two years in others. About one-half the states limit the governor to one or two terms in office. A governor's executive powers include the power of appointment and removal (although this is severely restricted in most states), preparation and execution of the budget, the power to issue executive orders, and general law enforcement. In the legislative field governors enjoy considerable power through exercise of the veto power (in all states but North Carolina), and in all but seven states the governor may veto or reduce items in appropriation bills subject, of course, to legislative override. A governor may call the legislature into special session and, in several states, he may limit the special session to specified subjects. Like the President, the governor may exercise influence over the legislature through his party leadership. Most may grant reprieves and pardons to convicted persons. They also serve as commanders in chief of the National Guard of the state except when it is called into national service. Governors may be removed from office by impeachment and, in a few states, by the recall.

Significance The office of governor is one of considerable prestige and political power and has been steadily growing in influence. One of the major difficulties of the office is the requirement in many states that the governor share his executive authority with several other elected officials. In this respect, the governor is a weaker executive than the President since the governor may not have control over many high executive officials. Reorganization movements have sought to strengthen the appointive and removal powers of the governor by reducing the number of elected officers and eliminating the many boards and commissions that characterize state government.

Recent trends also include increasing the governor's term of office, and expanding his budgetary, management, and personnel powers.

Home Rule The power vested in a local unit of government, usually a city, to draft or change its own charter and to manage its affairs. Home rule limits legislative interference in local affairs. Most states permit some degree of freedom for cities and an increasing number are granting it to counties. Home rule may be required or permitted by the state constitution or be granted by the legislature without specific constitutional authorization. Under home rule, the voters choose a commission to draft a charter that may be approved or rejected by the voters. This is in contrast to the granting of charters by the legislature under special acts, general laws, or optional plans. The city under home rule has control over its local problems provided it does not violate the state constitution or general laws of the state. *See also* CHARTER, page 433; DILLON'S RULE, page 442; UNITARY STATE, page 43; FEDERAL ANALOGY page 442.

Significance Home rule introduces a measure of federalism into state-local relations to modify the usual unitary relation. The legislature is relieved of the burden of handling a variety of local problems that are best handled by those most intimately affected by them. Moreover, it strengthens democracy and local self-government and increases citizen interest. The major problem of home rule is the determination of what constitutes a local problem. The attitude of the legislature and of the courts determines the effectiveness of home-rule provisions.

Incorporated and Unincorporated Areas The legal status of a local unit of government. Incorporated units include cities, villages, and, in some states, towns and boroughs. Unincorporated units include counties, townships, New England towns, and school districts. Incorporated areas are also called municipal corporations and unincorporated places are known as quasi-corporations.

Significance Though variations are found in the laws of the states, incorporated units or municipal corporations have a distinct legal entity and are usually created at the request, and for the benefit, of the inhabitants of the area. Incorporated units have a charter granted under special, general, or optional laws, or under home rule. As municipal corporations they usually have a large measure of self-government and provide services needed by the residents. Unincorporated units or quasi-corporations are created by the state constitution or laws without regard to the wishes of the inhabitants of the area and are primarily designed to carry on state services. The distinction between incorporated and unincorporated areas is rapidly disappearing in many states, as unincorporated units are increasingly given powers formerly reserved for incorporated areas.

Lieutenant Governor The elective official in thirty-nine American states who succeeds to the governorship when that office is declared vacant. Typically, the lieutenant governor presides over the state senate and casts the deciding vote in case of a tie. He is elected at the same time and for the same term as the governor. In some states he serves as an ex officio member of the governor's administrative council and several boards and commissions.

Significance The lieutenant governor, like his counterpart the Vice President in the national government, performs his most important function by being available to take over as chief executive. When the governor is temporarily absent from the state, the lieutenant governor usually takes over until the governor's return. In states without a lieutenant governor, the president pro tempore of the senate or the secretary of state succeeds to the office of governor.

Local Option   Authority vested in local units to approve, reject, or select specific or alternative forms of action. Local option often refers to the power of local units to determine by popular vote whether or not liquor will be served in the community. It may also be used to describe the action taken by communities to select a charter from those made available by state law.

Significance   Local option provides a means whereby state governments are prevented from imposing the same controls over all units of local government. This has proved to be popular in the case of liquor sales, since each community may decide for itself whether it will be "wet" or "dry." Local option is in accord with traditional American theories of local self-government.

Mayor   The chief executive and/or the ceremonial leader of a city. The role of the mayor varies with the form of city government. Under the strong mayor-council plan, the mayor has extensive executive power including control over appointments and removals of city officials and the veto power. Under a weak mayor-council plan, the mayor has limited executive powers. The mayor in the commission and manager plans is largely a ceremonial figure. *See also* MAYOR-COUNCIL PLAN, page 446.

Significance   The power and prestige of the mayor varies not only with the structure of city government but with the personal qualities and political influence of the individual. In most cities, the mayor is a part-time official, but in cities like New York and Chicago his responsibilities are greater than those of many governors. In all cities, people look to the mayor for leadership in municipal affairs. Though many mayors of large cities have achieved national prominence and significant influence in national politics, the position has not generally been a steppingstone to national office.

Mayor-administrator Plan   A plan of city government in which an administrative officer is appointed to assist the mayor in managing the affairs of the city. The plan has been adopted in a number of large cities to free the mayor for broader policy-making duties while using expert aid to supervise the routine administration of city government. The administrator, called the chief administrative officer, is appointed by the mayor with or without council approval and may have extensive appointment and removal power over administrative officials. His duties include budget supervision, coordination of city agencies, personnel direction, and the giving of technical advice to the mayor. *See also* COUNCIL-MANAGER PLAN, page 439; STRONG-MAYOR PLAN, page 451.

Significance   The mayor-administrator plan is a recent development used in large cities under a strong mayor plan of government. The plan makes use of some of the features of the city manager form while retaining the political leadership of a strong mayor. It differs from the council-manager plan in retaining the position of strong mayor and in making the administrator responsible to the mayor rather than to the council.

Mayor-council Plan   A plan of city government in which the mayor is elected to serve as the executive officer of the city and an elective council serves as the legislative body. Wide variations exist from city to city but the plan usually takes the form of a weak- or strong-mayor-council plan depending upon the position of the mayor in the system. *See also* CITY COUNCIL, page 434; STRONG-MAYOR PLAN, page 451; WEAK-MAYOR PLAN, page 454.

Significance   The mayor-council plan reflects the traditional separation of powers between the legislative and executive branches. While the role of the mayor is the key to the nature of any specific application of the plan in a city, the council, in all cases, plays a major role as the legislative body. In recent years, the mayor-council plan has lost ground to the council-manager plan, particularly in small and middle-sized cities. In large cities, however, the plan continues to be in use with the strong-mayor plan favored over the weak-mayor plan. More than one-half of American cities still use some form of the mayor-council plan.

Metropolitan Area   A large city and its surrounding suburbs, which are socially and economically integrated although composed of separate units of government. The term "metropolitan" is derived from the Greek terms "meter" (mother) and "polis" (city). In 1974, the Bureau of the Census identified 265 metropolitan areas (including four in Puerto Rico), up from 212 in 1960. These include each county, or group of contiguous counties, containing at least one city having a population of 50,000 or more. The contiguous counties are included if they are densely populated and economically and socially integrated with the central county. The Census Bureau calls these "standard metropolitan statistical areas." New York and Chicago have been identified as "standard consolidated areas" because of the highly complex nature of these regions which combine several contiguous standard metropolitan statistical areas. More than one-sixth of the population lives in a belt from Boston to Washington, D.C. This "megalopolis" is about 450 miles long, 150 miles wide, and contains 34 contiguous standard metropolitan statistical areas. *See also* ANNEXATION, page 432; CITY-COUNTY CONSOLIDATION, page 434; CITY-COUNTY SEPARATION, page 435; CONSOLIDATION, page 437; COUNCILS OF GOVERNMENT, page 440; FUNCTIONAL CONSOLIDATION, page 443; METROPOLITAN FEDERATION, page 447; URBAN COUNTY PLAN, page 453.

Significance   Approximately 70 percent of the American people live in metropolitan areas, although these occupy only about 10 percent of the land area of the United States. This phenomenon of the twentieth century has brought with it a host of political, social, and economic challenges. Metropolitan areas are characterized by numerous governmental units sharing such major problems as transportation, housing, sewage disposal, and water supply. In recent years, the central city has been losing population to the suburbs, creating severe governmental and fiscal problems for both areas. Proposed solutions to the metropolitan problem include annexation, consolidation, federation, and functional consolidation. None of these proposals has, as yet, proved satisfactory, due largely to the reluctance on the part of the people to change established patterns. On the national scene, the metropolitan areas have had a strong political impact resulting in the establishment of the Department of Housing and Urban Development. New representational patterns in state legislatures stemming from court decisions on reapportionment have altered the balance of political power in favor of metropolitan over rural areas. More than three-fourths of the national population growth during the period of 1960–1970 took place in metropolitan areas, with suburbanites now outnumbering central city dwellers. Minority groups comprise only

5 percent of the suburban population but more than 20 percent of the population in central cities.

Metropolitan Federation   A proposed solution to the problems of metropolitan areas that would create a central metropolitan government to handle problems of the entire metropolitan region, reserving to the local units control over local matters. The plan is based on the principle of federalism which is in effect at the national-state level. The plan has been put into effect in Toronto, Canada, and the metropolitan government of Dade County (Miami), Florida, resembles a federation. Under a federated plan, the metropolitan or central unit might handle such common problems as highways, air terminals, water supply, sewerage, and air pollution. The local units could continue to act in the areas of police, schools, and other matters which the people desire to retain as strictly local functions. *See also* METROPOLITAN AREA, page 446.

Significance   Federation is viewed as one of the more practical means of solving metropolitan problems because it does not destroy the identity of local units. At the same time, areawide services can be provided to units unable to finance them alone. The plan is flexible, since functions can be arranged as need demonstrates and new units can be added as they become part of the metropolitan area. It is difficult, however, to determine what constitutes an areawide or local problem. Further, the plan simply adds another unit of government to an already large number. Disagreement is apt to arise over prope representation of local units in the metropolitan government.

Optional Charter   A plan in effect in about one-third of the states that permits a city to choose a charter from among several provided by state law. Typically, cities may choose various forms of the mayor-council plan, the commission plan, or the council-manager plan. *See also* CHARTER, page 433.

Significance   The optional charter plan represents a compromise between complete legislative domination of cities through special acts and home rule. It permits cities to choose their own forms of government by public referendum. The plan is, however, unlike home rule in that the legislature may change the content of the options at any time. Under home rule, the city itself frames and changes its charter.

Ordinance   A legislative enactment of a local governing body. Ordinances have the force of law, but the term is to be distinguished from the statute-making power of national and state legislatures. Ordinances are issued under authority granted by the sovereign power and, in the case of local governments, must comply with state constitutions, charters, and general laws.

Significance   The subordinate position of local government in its relations to the state is underscored by the fact that the former has only ordinance-making rather than statutory power as that term is generally understood. An interesting sidelight of the use of the term ordinance is that Congress under the Articles of Confederation had only ordinance-making power, demonstrating the sovereignty of the member states.

Planning   Preparation and execution of projects for the future economic, social, and physical development of a community. Planning may be nationwide or statewide in situations in which it encompasses all types of governmental problems, but it is more often associated with the physical development of municipal governments. This includes planning street layouts, parks, public utility routes, and the zoning of areas for residential and commercial purposes. In recent years, emphasis has turned from purely physical aspects of city planning and beautification to social and economic concerns such as urban redevelopment and housing. In metropolitan areas, stress is now being put on the need for countywide or regional planning to provide orderly development. Sound planning must take into consideration population and economic trends as well as future fiscal needs. Many cities and states have official planning agencies. *See also* COUNCILS OF GOVERN-MENT, page 440; HOUSING AND COMMUNITY DEVELOPMENT ACT OF 1974, page 377; ZONING, page 454.

Significance   The American people have been slow to accept the concept of planning, perhaps conceiving it to be similar to the planned economies associated with socialism. Lack of planning has, however, resulted in waste of natural resources and the need for expensive corrective action. The failure of most communities to provide for suitable streets and parking facilities to meet the demands of the automotive age is a major example. Today, planning is generally accepted as a necessary aspect of governmental operations although many communities still resist it. A large number of cities now have master plans for future growth and require that new developments fit into the master plan. Planning is now considered to be a professional specialty, with many colleges and universities offering courses of training.

Register of Deeds   A county officer, sometimes called recorder of deeds, who is elected in about half the states. His major duty is to record and preserve legal documents relating mainly to real-estate ownership and transfers. This function is designed to protect landowners and prospective purchasers of land against flaws in titles to property.

Significance   Few students of government support the idea of electing a register or recorder of deeds. The position is an important one but is not of a policy-making nature. Some counties have adopted modern techniques of recording legal papers through microfilm or other technical processes, but many continue to keep records in longhand in bound volumes.

School District   A governmental unit for the maintenance of schools. In about half the states, school districts are administratively and financially independent and do not follow township, city, or county lines. The town or township plan is dominant in New England and the county plan in the South. In Delaware and Hawaii, the entire state comprises one school district. Typically, school districts are governed by elective boards, which choose a superintendent to administer the system. In some areas, the school is part of city government, and the board is selected by the mayor or council. Approximately one-fifth of all local units of government are school districts and they account for almost one-half of all local units of government expenditures. *See also* BOARD OF EDUCATION, page 433; CONSOLIDATION, page 437.

Significance   In 1942, school districts comprised more than two-thirds of all local governments. There has since been a dramatic decrease in the number of districts (from 108,000 to less than 16,000 or 20 percent of local government units), and this trend continues. All over the country, small school distracts are being consolidated to make larger, more efficient schools. The strong tradition of independent school districts is based on the assumption that schools should not be part of the politics of regular governments nor tied financially to other units. Some authorities claim, however, that the independent school district develops a "politics" of its own and tends to detract from the financial needs of other units.

Secretary of State   A state official elected by popular vote in thirty-nine states and appointed by the governor or legislature in others. His major duties include the preservation of official documents, administration of elections, issuance of business licenses and certificates of incorporation, and registration and issuance of motor vehicle licenses. He is also keeper of the state seal.

Significance   The office of secretary of state is not considered by political scientists to be one that justifies popular election. The office has few, if any, policy-making responsibilities, but its elective position reduces the governor's control over state administration. Appointment by the governor is generally recommended. In most states, the secretary of state enjoys political prominence because his name is affixed to numerous documents, such as driving licenses. Many secretaries go on to higher office. Moreover, in states with widespread patronage or political appointments, this office controls numerous jobs that can be spread out to the party faithful.

Special Act   Legislation applicable to one unit of local government. The special act system prevailed from colonial times to the middle of the nineteenth century and is still in use in several states. Through special acts, state legislatures grant charters to municipalities, amend the charters, and pass legislation on a wide variety of purely local problems. *See also* CHARTER, page 433; GENERAL LAWS, page 443.

Significance   Special acts have the virtue of flexibility but are often abused. The net effect of much special legislation is to vest complete authority over a local unit in the legislative representative from that area since other representatives rarely interfere with his desires. Often "ripper" acts are passed in such states; these abolish particular local offices, such as that of city manager, although such action may be contrary to local wishes. Special acts put a great burden on the legislature and, in some states, more than half the legislation is special in nature. Most states now forbid special legislation by requiring general laws or by permitting home rule. In a few states, the people of an affected area may reject special acts by popular vote.

Special District   A unit of local government established to provide a single service. About one-half of the special districts in the United States are for fire protection, soil conservation, water, and drainage. Other common types of special districts provide cemetery, sewer, parks, recreation, housing, and mosquito-abatement services. A school district may be classified as a special district but the Census Bureau and political scientists classify it separately. Special districts are usually created to meet problems that transcend local government boundaries or to bypass taxation and debt restrictions imposed upon local units by state law. The number of special districts has almost tripled since 1942 (8000 to 24,000), and they now comprise about 30 percent of all local units. The special district is created under state law, usually requiring the consent of the people in the district, and is governed by a small board that has taxing and bonding authority, and in some cases, power of eminent domain.

Significance The dramatic increase in the use of the special district device illustrates the inability of existing units of government to meet modern needs. Tax and debt restrictions can be evaded and high costs shared by several units without upsetting traditional governmental boundary lines. Paradoxically, while attempts are underway to decrease the number of local units of government, the special district is adding to the complexity of local government. The device, however, has strong appeal to interest groups that want to keep a function separate. Many people believe that a special district keeps a function "out of politics," when, in fact, it may exercise great power, spend large sums of money, and have an important impact upon community life. Most special districts and their governing officials have very low public visibility.

State Aid   Funds provided to local governments by the state in the form of grants-in-aid or shared taxes. State grants go primarily to school districts for educational purposes and to counties for welfare and highway functions. Shared taxes are administered by the state, which gives a portion of sales or income taxes to local units, including cities. The amount provided to each unit is usually based on a formula keyed to population, use, and need. *See also* REVENUE SHARING, page 293.

Significance Local units must rely heavily upon the general property tax for income. Since this source has proved insufficient, state aid has increased substantially in recent years and accounts for more than 30 percent of local revenues. Grants-in-aid are usually accompanied by state supervision of the expenditure and a requirement that the local unit put up a matching amount or some percentage of the grant. Such grants have improved local government standards while retaining some measure of local control. Shared taxes are usually free of state controls but, since tax collections vary from year to year, local units cannot depend upon specific amounts.

State Auditor   A state official elected in thirty-one states and appointed by the governor or legislature in others. In some states, the title "comptroller" is used. His major duty is to act as a watchdog over expenditures of state agencies by postauditing accounts. In some states, however, he has preauditing and accounting duties as well. *See also* AUDITOR, page 273.

Significance The position of auditor is essential for ensuring accountability of public expenditures. Political scientists, however, doubt the wisdom of electing this official or of having him appointed by the governor. Selection by and responsibility to the legislature is considered the most desirable situation, because the auditor's job is to ensure that expenditures have been made in accordance with the legislature's enactments.

State Treasurer   A state official popularly elected in forty-one states and chosen by the governor or legislature in others. His major duties are the safekeeping of state funds and the payment of bills on proper warrant. In some states, he has tax collection responsibilities as well.

Significance The popular election of a treasurer is viewed as unnecessary by students of government. Financial matters, except for auditing, should be centralized in a finance office headed by an appointee of the governor. This would make the governor clearly responsible for the handling of state funds.

Strong-mayor Plan A plan of city government in which the mayor is given complete executive authority. Its major features include: (1) election of a mayor as chief executive; (2) concentration of administrative power in the hands of the mayor, including powers of appointment and removal; (3) a veto power over the city council; and (4) strong budgetary controls in the hands of the mayor. *See also* MAYOR-COUNCIL PLAN, page 446.

Significance The strong-mayor plan is used in most large cities and is favored by political scientists over the weak-mayor plan. The main advantages of the plan are the centralization of authority and the clear fixing of executive responsibility. The plan permits the mayor to exercise strong political or policy-making leadership, a particularly desirable condition in large cities with their variety of competing interests. In contrast to the weak-mayor plan, the strong-mayor plan encourages the use of modern administrative techniques and the appointment of able subordinates. Few people, however, combine top administrative and political talent. In several large cities, the mayor-administrator plan is in use to free the mayor from attention to administrative detail.

Superintendent of Public Instruction A state official whose function is to supervise the public school system of the state. In some states he is known as superintendent of schools or commissioner of education. He is elected in about twenty states, appointed by the governor in a few, and, in increasing numbers of states, chosen by the state board of education. In most cases, the superintendent serves on the state board of education and acts as its chief administrative officer. His duties generally include the establishment for standards for schools, curriculum development, setting up teacher qualifications, and control of state-administered school funds. In some states, his authority extends to other educational institutions, such as state colleges and community colleges. *See also* BOARD OF EDUCATION, page 433.

Significance The superintendent of public instruction holds a position of major responsibility because of the value placed upon education in the United States. Because of the high professional standards desirable for this office, many educators and political scientists favor the superintendent's appointment by an elected or appointed board of education or by the governor. Increasingly, superintendents of public instruction are embroiled in public controversy over educational policy because of increased demands for state and national aid to education at all levels.

Supervisor The chief elective officer of the township (called trustee in some states). The supervisor has overall responsibility for township government and presides over the township board. He may represent his township on the county board and serve as tax assessor. *See also* TOWNSHIP, page 452.

Significance In states with township government, the supervisor is an important political figure, who exercises considerable influence at the county and state levels. The growing urbanization of many townships and counties has forced new challenges upon township supervisors whose functions were originally designed for a rural society.

Town   The major unit of local government in New England. The term is used in some states to designate a township or a small urban area but is generally used by political scientists to designate the New England town. With the exception of some incorporated cities, all six states of New England are divided into towns; this division includes both the rural and urban portions of each particular area. The town is responsible for most of those governmental services provided in other states by counties and cities. The town is governed by all the inhabitants through the town meeting and, between meetings, by a board of selectmen and other town officers. In many towns, however, representatives are chosen for town meetings, and some utilize a town manager. *See also* TOWN MEETING, page 452.

Significance   The New England town developed in the colonial period and is deeply rooted in tradition. Growing populations and urbanization of many towns has put a strain upon governmental arrangements suitable for a frontier rural society. Representative town meetings, special finance and budget committees, and town managers now characterize many towns.

Town Meeting   The governing authority of a town or township. All qualified voters may participate in the election of officers and in the passage of taxes or other legislation. Town meetings are used in New England towns and in many midwestern townships. *See also* TOWN, page 452.

Significance   The town meeting represents the ideal of direct democracy in action. It is a product of rural society, however, and has lost much of its vitality in recent years. Areas with large populations cannot hold meetings of all qualified voters; no building can accommodate them and the meetings are unwieldy. Often people are apathetic and power falls into the hands of the few who do attend or those who "pack" the meeting. Many midwestern townships have abolished the town meeting. In New England, representative town meetings are held; as is customary for most legislative bodies, these town meetings are comprised of delegates elected by the voters.

Township   A unit of government, usually a subdivision of a county, found in sixteen states, principally in the midwest and in the northeast. The term "midwestern township" is often used to distinguish it from the New England town. Townships vary in shape and size but tend to cover an area of thirty-six square miles as a result of the congressional township system of identifying land. Some townships have an annual town meeting and all are governed by a township board, usually consisting of three members. Municipal areas are usually excluded from the township territory but in some states, villages, or towns remain part of the township. Township functions tend to be rural in nature, such as maintaining roads, cemeteries, and drains, minor law enforcement, and assessment of property. In urban areas, however, townships have taken on numerous urban services, such as police and fire protection and public works. In some states, the township is the unit for school administration. *See also* CONGRESSIONAL TOWNSHIP, page 436; TOWN, page 452.

Significance   With some exceptions, township government has declined in importance. A product of frontier society and the New England town, it is too small for efficient administration. Modern communication makes it unnecessary as a subdivision of easily accessible county offices. Duplication of services in small areas results. Some states, such as Oklahoma and Iowa, have transferred most township functions to the county. Although there are 17,000 township governments comprising about 20 percent of local governmental units, a general lack of interest in them seems to characterize many areas. In some states, the township has gained strength by taking on municipal functions. Most political scientists favor abolition of the township as a unit of government and transfer of its functions to the county or, in some cases, to nearby city governments.

Uniform State Laws   Laws proposed by the National Conference of Commissioners on Uniform State Laws, a few of which have been adopted by all or many states. Among those proposals that have had wide adoption are the Negotiable Instruments Act, the Warehouse Receipts Act, the Stock Transfer Act, others relating to sales, partnerships, bills of lading, and some traffic, criminal, and family matters. The National Conference has proposed over 100 uniform laws since its inception in 1892, but it has met with only minor success. The Conference consists of three Commissioners from each state, usually lawyers, appointed by the governor. The Council of State Governments acts as secretariat for the Conference. *See also* HORIZONTAL FEDERALISM, page 36.

   Significance   The wide diversity of state laws under the federal system has proved vexing to many people. Persons doing business in several states are often inconvenienced and confused. Confusion exists, too, in such matters as marriage and divorce and traffic laws. The increasing mobility of business and private persons has increased the need for more uniformity. The effort has been retarded by apathetic state legislatures and by the desires of many states to gain an advantage over others by having less stringent rules concerning business transactions or divorce, for example, in order to attract more business to the state.

Urban County Plan   A proposed solution to metropolitan area problems that involves the transfer to county governments of functions exercised by several units of government within the county. Several counties in California have taken over the functions of law enforcement, health services, tax assessments and collections, and prisons. Dade County, Florida, has been established as a metropolitan or urban county. Municipalities within that county, including Miami, have transferred to the county power over traffic problems, planning, sewerage, water supply, and other countywide problems. The urban county plan is to be distinguished from city-county consolidation, which contemplates the complete merger of county government with all other units within the county. *See also* CITY-COUNTY CONSOLIDATION, page 434; METROPOLITAN AREA, page 446.

   Significance   Most metropolitan areas lie within a single county. This facilitates the transfer of functions, since the county is an established unit of government. No new government need be created nor need any unit be abolished. Metropolitan areas are, however, rapidly spreading beyond county lines. Most county governments are poorly organized and have made little progress in the use of modern administrative techniques or of the merit system of personnel management. Most are ill-equipped to handle urban services without considerable reform.

Village   A small urban area, called a town or borough in some states, that is a municipal corporation but one with less authority and simpler organization than a city. The term "village" is a legal concept, varying in meaning from state to state in which the designation is used. Village status may be based upon population, but many villages are larger than regular cities. Villages usually are governed by a small council and a village president or mayor. Limitations are placed by the state upon the taxing and borrowing powers of villages as well as upon the types of functions that they may perform.

Significance Village government developed to accommodate the needs of trading centers in rural areas. Since the county or township could not provide needed services, such areas were permitted to incorporate as villages for limited purposes, such as street maintenance or water supply. Villages may attain city status by a vote of the people or by special act, but many people prefer the lesser designation and the informality of village organization. Increased population may, however, compel change to city status in order to get greater taxing and service authority.

Ward   The division of a city for purposes of electing members to the city council. The ward system is favored in the larger cities, but most cities use an at-large system of electing councilmen, particularly those using the commission or council-manager forms of government. A number of cities now use a combination of both methods, selecting some councilmen from wards and others at large. *See also* ALDERMAN, page 432.

Significance The ward system has declined in recent years but still has many adherents. It provides a more representative council, since the voter can know his representative more intimately and, in turn, the councilman will know more about his ward. This system is particularly favored by minority groups and labor interests who seldom gain representation under the at-large system. The main disadvantage of the ward system is the emphasis it tends to place on special interests of neighborhoods rather than on the interest of the community as a whole. Further, it sometimes makes it more difficult to get qualified candidates and leads inevitably to gerrymandering. These factors have led to the growth of the at-large system or a combination of both ward and at-large elections.

Weak-mayor Plan   A plan of city government in which the mayor must share his executive authority with other elected officials and the city council. Most cities under the mayor-council plan use the weak-mayor form rather than the strong-mayor plan. The major features of the weak-mayor plan include: (1) a long ballot in which the people choose numerous department heads, boards, and commissions, as well as the mayor, for administrative purposes; (2) a limited power of appointment and removal in the hands of the mayor; (3) the appointment of numerous officials by the council alone; (4) a weak or complete absence of a veto power for the mayor; and (5) direct participation by the council in administrative matters, including preparation of the budget. *See also* MAYOR-COUNCIL PLAN, page 446.

Significance In spite of its wide use, political scientists frown upon the weak-mayor plan. The long ballot, the difficulty of fixing responsibility because of the lack of a responsible executive, the lack of coordination, and the use of outmoded administrative and personnel techniques that characterize the plan, lead to a poor quality of municipal government. Yet the plan, which is rooted in the traditions of Jacksonian democracy, prevents the concentration of power and establishes an elaborate system of checks and balances.

Zoning   The division of a city or other unit of government into districts and the regulation by law of the uses of the land. Zoning is concerned with the nature of buildings (residential, industrial, or commercial), their height and density, and the uses made of particular tracts of land. Zoning laws are enacted under the police power of communities to protect the health, safety, and welfare of the people, and the United States Supreme Court upheld zoning as a proper exercise of that power in 1926 in *Euclid v. Amber Realty Co.,* (272 U.S. 365). A zoning board of appeals is usually created to grant exceptions and variances to persons who might suffer undue hardships under a zoning regulation. *See also* PLANNING, page 448.

Significance Comprehensive zoning has been in effect only since the 1920s and still meets resistance in many areas in which the people object to legislative and administrative control of their property. Zoning, however, protects property values in residential areas by forbidding industrial or commercial uses of property, and it contributes to the beauty of a community. Zoning makes possible better planning and administration of public services, such as fire protection and traffic supervision, and contributes to the health and well-being of a community by segregating industrial plants from residential areas. Critics note that zoning is often used by suburban communities to control the character and homogeneity of population through requirements for land usage (lot size, placement of dwelling, construction) that result in costs beyond the capacity of all but the well-to-do. Zoning must be carried out with careful regard for constitutionally protected property rights.

IMPORTANT AGENCIES

Council of State Governments An agency maintained by the state governments to serve as a secretariat, research agency, and clearinghouse for the improvement of state legislative, executive, and judicial administration. It has encouraged interstate cooperation and the general improvement of federal-state relations and state-local relations. The Council is composed of Commissions on Interstate Cooperation that are found in each of the states and that include legislative and executive officials. The Council serves as the secretariat for the American Legislators Association, The Governors' Conference, and similar organizations of chief justices, attorneys general, court, budget, purchasing, parole, and juvenile officials. It publishes a monthly magazine, *State Government,* and the biennial *Book of the States.* Its headquarters is in Chicago.

Significance The Council of State Governments has sponsored conferences and research in problems of common state concern from crime control to fisheries. It has promoted better interstate relations and has influence in Washington and in the state capitals. Its journal, *State Government,* carries informative and up-to-date information on state government developments and problems and the *Book of the States* is a major reference work on state and local government.

Index